Michael Twaddle

CORRUPTION AND THE DECLINE OF ROME

CORRUPTION
AND THE
DECLINE OF ROME

Ramsay MacMullen

Yale University Press
New Haven and London

Set in Laserwriter Goudy Old Style type by
Fox Pond Communications. Printed in the United States
of America by Vail-Ballou Press, Binghamton, New York.

Library of Congress Cataloging-in-Publication Data
MacMullen, Ramsay, 1928–
Corruption and the decline of Rome / Ramsay MacMullen.
p. cm.
Bibliography: p.
Includes index.
ISBN 0–300–04313–9 (cloth)
ISBN 0–300–04799–1 (pbk.)
1. Rome — Politics and government — 30 B.C. – 284 A.D.
2. Power (Social sciences) I. Title
DG270.M33 1988   88–96
937".06 — dc19   CIP

The paper in this book meets the guidelines for permanence and durability
of the Committee on Production Guidelines for Book Longevity of the
Council on Library Resources.

3   5   7   9   10   8   6   4   2

CONTENTS

FIGURES

PREFACE

The plan of this book is very simple. It examines what is conventionally called the decline of Rome, beginning (chapter 1) with a review of various phenomena which good scholars have used to explain it. Not finding in them any broad, clear meaning, I follow up certain hints instead that point to a loss of power in the state, a diminishing control over the empire's latent strengths and resources. In what might be called an exercise in historical sociology (chapter 2), I describe what power was and how it worked when it *did* work, and (chapter 3) when and why it didn't, at the end. Rome's ultimate impotence is easily illustrated (chapter 4) through a selection of specific incidents belonging to the fourth and fifth centuries. On the surface they would all be called political or military. They are selected to demonstrate how historical sociology may sometimes be necessary for the understanding of the schoolboy part of history; that is, battles and political parties and who-did-what-to-whom (with perhaps some special scholarly attention to people's exact names, kin, and titles, and to exact dates). I do not regard all this latter part of history as any less deserving of study than the surrounding values and habits which control people's actions; and, in any case, the schoolboy in all of us would insist on battles and plotting and personalities in every description of the past, to give it life. But it is a very primitive and now old-fashioned historiography that would treat habits and values and glimpses of "Daily Life in Ancient Rome" as mere decorative background, to the neglect of their causal connection with the flow of events.

The first chapter is not meant to be a grand appraisal of all that has ever been said about "Rome's Fall." A book by that title has been written already, with wonderful comprehensiveness and much trenchancy, by Alexander Demandt (1980)![1] The subject is there looked at, however, through the eyes of

1. The nearly five hundred densely packed pages of Demandt's second and third chapters review hundreds of authorities up to, or down to, president Nixon; but Rome's decline is only "geistesgeschichtlich betrachtet" (p. 466).

various observers in the last several centuries, not as a thing in itself; so there is still room for another approach. What I try to do is to show how complicated and far from monolithic the empire and its "decline" really were, and, beyond that, how easy to misunderstand. One could, no doubt, write a book as long as Demandt's criticizing all that has been said wrong about the subject in the past. That might have value but it would be a work of destruction. Its author would have to come at it like a Vandal. I rather preferred, and in fact greatly enjoyed, reviewing some quite recent advances and debates by specialists. My selection, though certainly incomplete, and my presentation, though certainly superficial, surely show how fresh, enlightening, and plain intelligent is the work of scholars in various fields over the last generation; and I include in my admiration some with whom I may have some disagreement. In particular, they seem to me to attain knowledge about more and more aspects of Roman imperial history that is truly probative — knowledge that no one can doubt. Thereby they not only provide a clear view of what happened and must therefore be explained, but they displace all those brilliant essays and fat tomes that magisterially explain what never happened at all — including the decline itself (I merely repeat that there was no single, monolithic event of that name).

The second and, in some ways, the central, chapter attempts to describe the earlier-prevailing, functionally successful structure of power in the empire's society. By "power" I mean only the contrary of obedience. The two are the opposite sides of a single coin. Rome, like any other state, could accomplish large goals only so long as its power-patterns permitted. During the better centuries of its history, enormous amounts of psychic and physical energy, the resolve and muscle of its citizens, could be brought to bear mostly on war but also on the spreading of a pattern of effective ties of obedience throughout the Mediterranean world. They made law enforcement possible, and public construction, and so forth. Local or central government was able to transmit its will through an armature of influence and obedience joining urban, provincial, and imperial leaders and their dependents. It functioned effectively because a generally accepted code of obligations pervaded both its public and private relations. Between those two, in fact, there was little distinction. Gradually, however, a competing code made converts among leaders and dependents alike and diminished the capacity to transmit and focus energy. Both public and private power came to be treated as a source of profit, in the spirit of slaves, freedmen, supply sergeants, and petty accountants. The results were seriously dysfunctional.

I sketch out my argument here against the background of a riddle long puzzling to myself as to others:[2] how it was that a given quantity of people inside the Mediterranean world, with a given quantity of raw materials and inhabiting a given terrain that did not much change, somehow could expand successfully against external enemies at one time and collapse before those enemies at another. I was not concerned with any other aspect of decline: just the military (or one could say, just the delivery of force). Of course, the military has often been chosen as the key to "the" decline. I do not believe in any such single event; but I do believe — and who can doubt? — that physical security behind its frontiers has been the precondition for all other accomplishments of which any civilization may boast.

Beginning around the year A.D. 250, as a map will show (fig. 17), the Roman state began to lose substantial bits and pieces of itself to its enemies. In my fourth and final chapter I consider some instances of this, where we can gain any sort of detailed information on how they happened. I also consider contributing series of events and background. These are the only pages which contain any conventional political narrative. I assume a reader will have enough of that to need no more, or will be able to follow lines of argument that explain themselves adequately without further background. My object is to show through these specific illustrations that the changes discovered in the power structure had demonstrable, almost measurable, consequences in the form of loss of territory; and such loss only expressed geopolitically other changes for the worse in the functioning of the government. As I am interested in processes internal to the empire, it is natural for me to end when the outside broke in — call it A.D. 406, or 429, or some date in between.

In 1981 the Collège de France did me the honor to invite a series of lectures on a subject of my choosing. The four that resulted I have here expanded and fitted out with notes. My long delay over the job I blame on the fact that this book, like most others I have done, had to be written in the midst of administrative duties in my department or in the university, on top of a full teaching load and without any special leaves or assistance; and also I was deflected for a time into quite other scholarly projects. In consequence, my reading has been often interrupted and my writing has not kept up with recent publications. But then, there is always recent publication — meaning

2. My interest in the third, fourth, and fifth centuries began in 1949 with the discovery (not through assigned reading) of state socialism over that long, wrong period. I pursued the topic some years later in a dissertation. On a number of other topics related to the decline I have subsequently offered my views in print, sometimes specifically with this book in mind. That explains, and I hope excuses, so much quoting of myself in the footnotes.

new and different interpretations that crowd out the less new. At least on topics that deserve abiding interest, no one is likely to say the last word. One can only hope to influence the next book on the subject, by someone else, which will be better but still not quite right.

Master's House
Calhoun College

1
CHOOSING
A THEME

1. CONTEMPORARY VIEWS

The people who were declining should have known it; therefore I turn to them first for their views. Indeed I do find them characterizing the whole world around them in despairing terms; only they do so too often. They think the rot had set in decisively beginning in 154, 146, or 133 B.C., or in the reign of the first emperor, or toward the mid-first century A.D. (all of these judges standing in the capital and taking a survey from that point of view); or it is recognized by Dio Chrysostom a generation afterwards, and in the later second century by Dio Cassius and fifty years after that in Africa and elsewhere; around the mid-third century again in Africa and Egypt; in northern Italy in 386; and (more reasonably, we feel) in 410 and 429 by observers of the sack of Rome and the Vandal invasion of north Africa. At all but the last two of these junctures we also hear people exclaiming about the happiness of the times. They do so through festival speeches, public resolutions, and poems. The emperors chime in, especially through the medium of coin legends. Knowing what we do, or think we know, about the true state of the empire, we scout all of these statements that fail to fit our own view while solemnly assenting to others that accord with it. We entitle ourselves to make a choice among the opinions of contemporary observers because we suppose that we are better judges than they. No doubt we are. But we should carry our presumption further, and reject *all* their opinions; for all arise from habits of analysis and a base of information quite inadequate to the task.[1]

2. QUANTIFYING DECLINE

Perhaps an exception should be made of views about literature, gloomily evaluated by Tacitus in the opening sentence of his treatise on oratory: "You often ask me, Justus Fabius" — consul of A.D. 102 (and notice the "often") — "why is it that earlier centuries bloomed with the genius and fame of so many outstanding orators while our own age above all, barren and bereft of praise for eloquence, hardly retains even the word 'orator.'"[2] The loss lamented, of artistic prose, lay absolutely at the center of the empire's highest culture; so its decline was a most serious matter. Modern scholars of Roman antiquity who have, from their schooldays, generally approached their subject by the high road of Caesar's *Commentaries* and (above all) Cicero, cannot but agree. For example Frank Walbank, writing: "Roman literature too provides a faithful reflection of the general process of decline; and by its early demise shows conclusively (if proof is still required) that the decay of the Empire was not due to something which happened a little before A.D. 250, but that some of the operative factors were already active centuries before. The sensitive plant of literature was one of the first to succumb.... After Juvenal and Tacitus, Latin literature has little to show."[3] Were the cause for that explained, as he implies, we would hold the key to understanding all that follows in subsequent centuries.

We here confront a seemingly insoluble problem: how to estimate scientifically a change for the worse, where esthetic considerations are paramount. If any two judges disagreed about just what was "worse," how could the difference be settled? It can only be shown that some opinions are more common than others. Let us attempt it visually. The ancient authors canonized in the Teubner, Oxford, and Loeb Classical Library editions can be projected on a graph (fig. 1).

The results of course do not prove, they merely illustrate; and their apparent exactness may seem too much like science misplaced (as if one were to dust for fingerprints on the pyramids to identify their builders, or interrogate the jawbone of Australopithecus polygraphically, to discover his true date). But the rise and fall of approved literature remains a very large fact to be explained. It presents us with the final yield of a long process of screening. Whatever the original quantity of production to choose from in different periods, choice was somehow made of the more-to-be-preferred against the less. The standards of judgment appear to be, within tolerable limits and within our western culture, absolute, since the writers esteemed by the Romans are also esteemed by ourselves, and writers little valued in antiquity are judged by us, from their fragments, not so deserving of preservation.[4] "Better" and "worse" being defined in Darwinian fashion by their rate of survival, we may then say that Tacitus and Pliny were right. Literature declined.

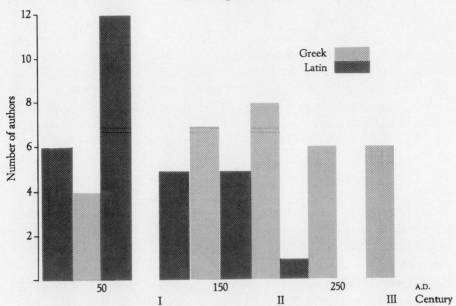

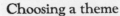

Fig. 1. Authors in Loeb, Oxford and Teubner Libraries (assigned to period by date of death minus ten years)

We notice, however, that the two literatures Greek and Latin exhibit different profiles of abundance. Speaking always within the boundaries just determined, we can say that Greek literature declined far less than Latin; that is, a considerable amount of what was good continued to be produced right through antiquity and into Byzantine times. Deterioration of the whole of Roman civilization, "the decline of Rome," proceeded differently according to different regions.

Why did literature, like a canary in a coal-mine (as Walbank sees it), die first? I pause over this question, to me quite beyond answer, only long enough to raise another and obviously related one. Did the total pool of literacy perhaps diminish? To that question likewise no answer can be found; or, in any case, none has been offered.[5] The nearest statistical approach, however, lies through that hardy form of expression, inscriptions on stone. In the Latin-speaking world, a representative sample of just under two thousand exactly datable texts from among more than a quarter of a million of all sorts distribute themselves chronologically (fig. 2).[6]

The profile of activity here shown could no doubt be extended beyond the mid-third century, since scattered though statistically insignificant texts survive thereafter and could be counted and since their number picks up to a significant level at some point in the reign of Constantine. The extended

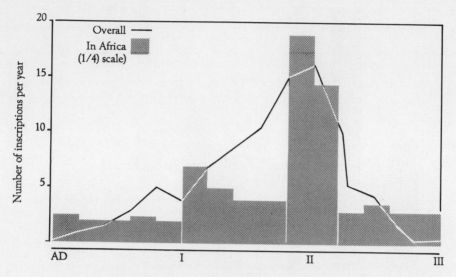

Fig. 2. The frequency-curve of Latin inscriptions

curve from the beginning of the era all the way into the fourth century and
beyond can be sensed also in the corpus of Greek inscriptions. Their number,
however, is relatively very small: less than a tenth of the Latin. Worse: an
adequate sample of the datable ones has yet to be laid out for study. Yet the
mid-third century marks an obvious low point and extends, let us say, to A.D.
325.[7] In one not very large area of the province Asia, where it happened to
be usual to date inscriptions of every sort most faithfully, their distribution
over time assumes the curve shown in fig. 3.[8]

In its rise and fall, the epigraphic habit in the eastern provinces, so far as
it can be measured, quite closely resembles the same habit in the west. How
to explain small differences between the two regions is not clear, however,
nor can we easily explain the broadly pervading ups and downs. That they had
something to do with money is an obvious possibility. To the extent that both
the literacy of the composer of a text and the skill and labor of the mason
involved some cost, there must have been economic factors at work. None
known, however, comes close to fitting the curves in either half of the empire.

The custom of cutting texts on stone thus resembles that of drafting
elaborate speeches, treasured by Tacitus: both had a lifeline. Surely every
civilization is made up of many such. They do not, all at once and together,
begin or terminate, or flourish or the reverse. The line of major Latin poets
ends before the prose-writers are done; that of philosophers in the favored,
Stoic line does not extend past Marcus Aurelius; the line of physicians rises

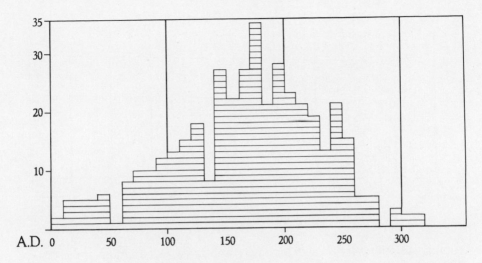

Fig. 3. Numbers of inscriptions in Roman Lydia

to Galen (d. 199), no further; that of jurisconsults does not run past the second decade of the third century, after which the lights of jurisprudence, that quintessentially Roman power of illumination, are abruptly dimmed and mere compilers take over.[9] Relief sculpture attains its acme perhaps under Augustus, perhaps later, but by no means so late as Constantine's Arch (so observed Bernard Berenson, in a well-known explosion of disgust).[10] In these and other expressions of its nature, the "Rome" that "declines" is thus not one single thing but many things, and the search for any one cause across the board is futile. So, too, is the search for any one period in which all aspects of Roman civilization were much changed. No such crucial period exists.

Nevertheless, among causes of change, some were obviously more significant than others and operated on particularly important or characteristic activities. In assessing them, the frequency of inscriptions has a value that goes beyond itself. By way of illustration, consider one such cause of change: the enriching of society around them by the urban elite through more or less spontaneous generosity. For example, they set up endowments. From these derived the annual interest used to pay for public banquets, orphan-care, or municipal building. Our knowledge here derives almost entirely from inscriptions. Distributed across time, those that tell about Italian foundations assume the following curve, according to a study published many years ago (fig. 4).[11]

Subsequently, however, the basis of facts was increased by a half as many

Choosing a theme

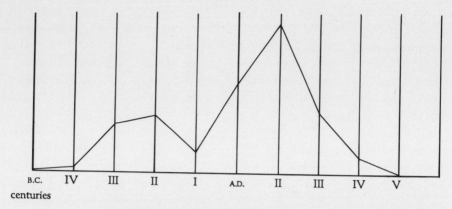

Fig. 4. Italian charitable foundations (as seen in 1914)

more inscriptions. If the fuller picture is presented as a bar graph, it then looks like the graph in fig. 5.[12] The socioeconomic phenomenon made manifest through epigraphic evidence — "the cessation of munificence" — has had to be redated by seventy-five years.

But was it the munificence or the inscriptions that ceased? A crucial distinction. In returning to the frequency curve shown in fig. 3, we discover that an *apparent* falling off in epigraphic testimony to foundations is quite inevitable; for, indeed, texts for the latter constitute a part, though a

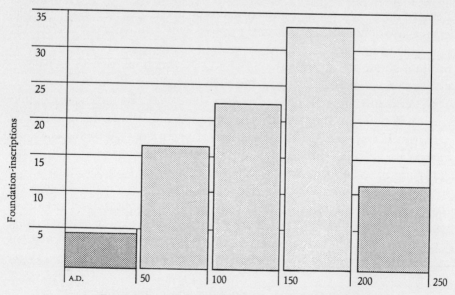

Fig. 5. Italian charitable foundations (as seen in 1965)

small part, of the data base underlying that very curve. We are therefore not entitled to conclude that "the most obvious index of urban decline is the widespread drop during the third century A.D. in the number of datable inscribed stones commemorating the erection of new buildings, charitable foundations," and so on.[13] Such reasoning would require us to suppose that all life in a house had ended when the blinds were drawn and we could no longer look in.

Not that epigraphy cannot be made to yield any conclusions at all; only, its evidence must be handled carefully. As by Stanislaw Mrozek. He notices the profile over time of datable texts commemorating gifts of public buildings and food or cash handouts in Italian cities. While the number of the first peaks sharply a little after the mid-second century, the second peaks and continues a generation or more later. Buildings make a strong showing throughout the first century; distributions, almost none at all.[14] It is not to be supposed that magnificent gifts were not recorded while smaller ones were; so we are entitled to say that building really diminished. To be more specific: donation of such large structures as baths and amphitheaters appears to have ended in the reign of Antoninus Pius. By then, we would naturally suppose that cities had been equipped with what their populations needed, and generosity therefore gradually shifted to other expressions.

The apogee of major gifts comes about where we would nowadays expect it, in the golden age of the Antonines. We would expect it because we are taught to do so by Gibbon and a parade of other historians up to Rostovtzeff, and so on to general works by Vogt, Rémondon, and still more recent scholars.[15] They all agree. Within that Antonine period they tend to focus on the 160s in the search for that moment when everything was as good as it could be, and thereafter only got worse; and they most often concentrate on the ease, good humor, evenness, and abundance of life rather than on brilliance to be found in the Roman world; for brilliance lay some generations back, at least in letters. Statements, however, that prosperity in that golden age was "general," trade "brisk," commerce "intense," and "good profits available" in this or that activity arouse some little disquiet. The terminology is pretty loose. At least in general works, it is not supported by more than an illustration or two. "E. g.," "for example," is or at least may be the most deceitful little signal serving scientific discourse — lineal descendant from "q.v.c.," *quibusdam veteribus codicibus*, that may be sometimes found in the footnotes to seventeenth-century argumentation. To rise above this, to attain a properly modern level of statement in the describing of decline, we need a quantified data base. And just in the last generation of scholarship we begin to have some.

It should not be approached in a spirit of reverence or surrender. Considerable heaps of evidence may prove unhelpful; or trivial. They may actually diminish our knowledge by making us think we know something that really is not true. For example, fig. 6 is a graph recently published.[16] In it, the different bars show the distribution across time of 545 shipwrecks. In drawing the graph, Keith Hopkins also draws the conclusion that "in the High Empire (220 B.C.–A.D. 200), there was more sea-borne trade in the Mediterranean than ever before, and more than there was for the next thousand years." A somewhat suprising apogee, then, for Rome: not the A.D. 160s, more likely some date around the birth of Cicero. How entirely fitting Cicero would have felt that date to be! But Hopkins is uncomfortable with it. He argues away the difference between the third and fourth bars. One could, perhaps, almost equally well argue away the difference between the fourth and fifth — at least between the fourth and the earlier half (the third century) within the fifth bar. That would suit the more conventional picture of Roman imperial history. Indeed, the conventional picture does seem to emerge not too badly when the data are regrouped, in the lighter bars (fig. 7), over the same grand period. Confirmation thus presented through a new type and volume of evidence is very welcome. But we are still left with the unexpected highpoint in the late centuries B.C. Does that really tell us the truth about "sea-borne trade in theMediterranean" and therefore about the probable curve of the empire's

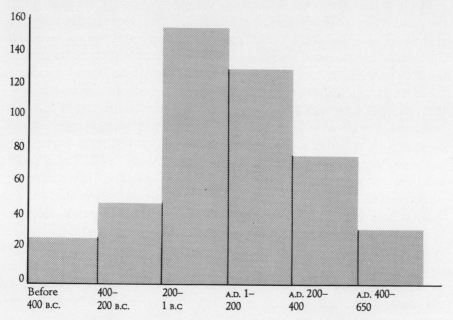

Fig. 6. Shipwrecks in the western Mediterranean (Hopkins)

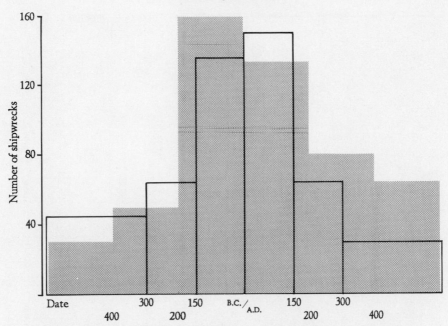

Fig. 7. Shipwrecks in the Western Mediterranean (composite — see n. 16)

general prosperity? No, because when these late-B.C. wrecks are shown on a map (fig. 8), they appear to lie at points dictated by ease of recent exploration and the delights of the summer beaches.[17] A. J. Parker has noted that fact and goes on to suggest, no doubt correctly, that the particular density of wrecks off southern France is to be explained by Italian wine export in the later Republic (he adds, that the wreck-density in the Adriatic of A.D. 1–150 may reflect the growth and pull of Aquileia and the Danube legions). As to wine export, the bulk of it westward from Italy is shown to be at its greatest through quite a different form of evidence, namely, the datable amphorae not only in the wrecks (by which those wrecks themselves must be placed chronologically) but also inland in southern France, up the Rhone, to the Rhine, and, of course, to northern Italy itself.[18] The chief areas of production lay to the south of Rome: Terracina, Sinuessa, Naples and thereabouts, with an apogee at or a little after the date of Cicero's birth in 106 B.C. By a date around A.D. 100, it was all over.

Through the study of shipwrecks we have thus by coincidence bound ourselves to discover the evidence of that particular trade world in which Italy for a time predominated. And we are bound coincidentally to discover many wrecks in which the passengers went armed, especially over the period we know, from literary sources, to have been plagued by piracy. Had we given

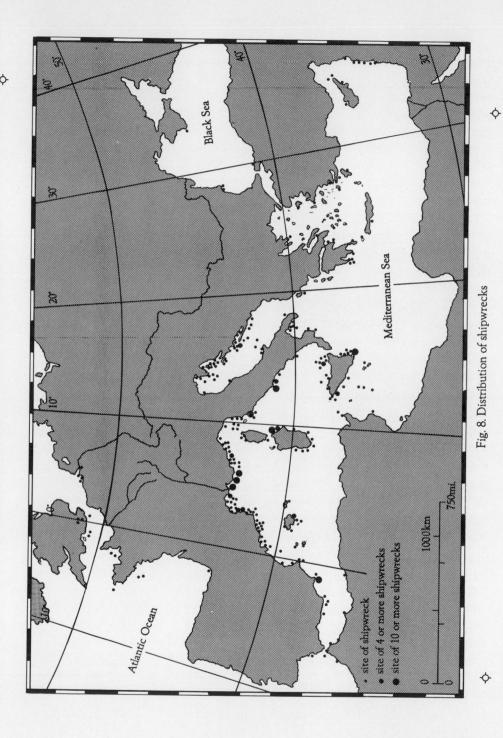

Fig. 8. Distribution of shipwrecks

equal attention to the empire's eastern shores, surely "sea-borne trade in the Mediterranean" would show different ups and downs. Piracy would be at its worst a little later, and so forth.[19] Each region had its own history, whether cultural or economic. As to the eastern, present evidence indicates the highs of commerce before 150 B.C., followed by a great falling off until the turn of the era; thereafter, other peaks of activity especially marked after A.D. 300.

Export from Italy, though not of wine alone, can be quantified in one other area, to the south. It is in Africa, along the coastal areas near Benghazi = Berenice. Finds of coarse pottery there, when dated and distributed over time, are found to constitute a totally insignificant part of any Hellenistic sampling, while under Augustus they more than double their share of the whole; increase that share by five times in the next forty years, and increase it again in the second half of the first century. Thereafter follows a sudden slide in the second to mid-third centuries.[20] The patterns differ intelligibly from those seen among Spanish and French markets.

Finally, two graphs drawn by Andrea Carandini and Clementina Panella. They show the approximate date and point of origin of a tremendous mass of amphorae found at Ostia in recent excavation. These in turn indicate where Rome got her fruit and sauces, wine and olive oil. The first graph (fig. 9) treats the products separately, thereby allowing a more accurate assessment of the role of different climates, some, like north Africa, being more suited to one product than another.[21]

But we can also see that each region had its own history, to be displayed a little more strikingly and of course aligned with much other material from excavations at Pompeii or on Monte Testaccio outside Rome, as well as in the home provinces where the amphorae originated.[22] We may note, among other features, how the agricultural production of Italy, appearing in the upper left of the graph (fig. 10), diminishes almost as dramatically as that of Africa increases, on the right, representing a later period, and how, in the relief (fig. 9), we can see the rapid decline in consumption of Italian oil after the reign of Augustus, and the still more rapid rise of the Spanish condiment, *garum*.

Among several conclusions to be drawn from these and other points in the last two figures, the most immediately useful suggests, or rather statistically demonstrates, in an area of large economic significance, that the Roman empire never was a block. The same point was made a few pages above. Therefore we should never speak of the rise or decline of prosperity in the empire *tout court*; or we might say, better, that we should never venture on causal explanations without first taking account of regional variations. Most particularly and emphatically, we should never allow the accident of evidence — the bulk of tens of thousands of legal decisions in the collections of law, nearly half of all the hundreds of thousands of Latin inscriptions, and the focus of most works of Silver Latin literature such as Columella, Pliny, Tacitus, and many other writers — we should never allow all this that tells us about Italy to dictate to us the history of the empire as a whole.

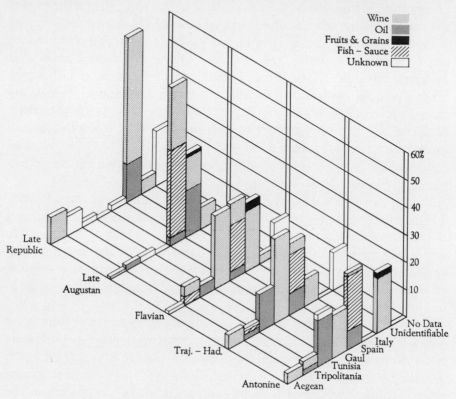

Fig. 9. Import-patterns to Ostia and Rome (a)

Coarse-ware sherds, inscriptions, and shipwrecks are infinitely laborious to evaluate in numbers deserving of quantified treatment; and besides, students of antiquity trained in other specialities than history — classicists, archeologists, epigraphers — have not always had the eye to see the possibilities latent in such evidence. In consequence, it has been only rather recently that the systematic inspection of wide areas, not of individual sites, has been attempted in Syria by Georges Tchalenko, in France by Roger Agache, and in Algeria by Philippe Leveau (I return to these later). Field surveys in Italy, some by American but most by British students, had to wait till the 1960s. It is a part of this methodological story that the history hidden in the materials of study for the figures above was not drawn out, by the likes of Hopkins, Mrozek, Panella, or Parker, until yesterday. And much work remains to be done.

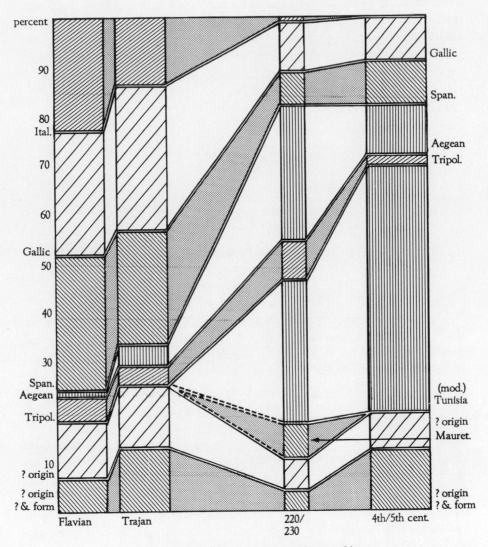

percent

90

80
Ital.

70

60

Gallic
50

40

30

Span.
Aegean

Tripol.

10
? origin

? origin
? & form

Gallic

Span.

Aegean
Tripol.

(mod.)
Tunisia

? origin
Mauret.

? origin
? & form

Flavian   Trajan   220/   4th/5th cent.
                                                  230

Fig. 10. Import patterns to Ostia and Rome (b)

Monte Testaccio is one of those items of unfinished business which has long teased curiosity. There in that hill of scores of millions of discarded food-containers outside the capital lies evidence by the shipload, holding the answer to all sorts of questions about interchange and productivity in the western Mediterranean. Alas, an embarrassment of riches, it has never been assessed. But soundings have been made.[23]

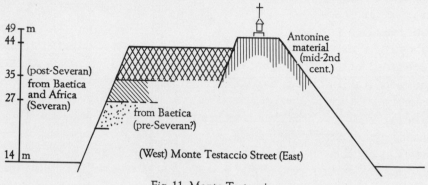

Fig. 11. Monte Testaccio

They indicate one certain development. From a date a few years after the death of Septimius Severus in A.D. 211, the marks on the amphorae reveal that under his rule the fiscus had assumed control of the supplying of oil and wine from Spain to Rome. "I venture the opinion," says Tenney Frank, "that if we had a reliable history of the third century, we should arrive at the conclusion that Septimius Severus dealt the fatal blow to the Empire by his confiscations and by his centralization of vast estates under imperial owner-ship." The emperor thus pointed the way to others who came after him. "The third century was a period of anarchy which ended in a totalitarian government with an economic system centering about the emperor and his army."[24] Or more briefly in the words of Jose-Maria Blazquez, "The amphorae of Monte Testaccio offer knowledge of an important phase in the struggle between private initiative and state dictatorship, which in the fourth century ended in the assassination of Roman civilization."[25]

In these statements can be sensed some little intrusion of sympathies that arise out of modern history, not ancient. They can hardly be excluded — call them sympathies or call them ideologies.[26] For there is nothing more difficult to see clearly and on its own terms than the why of Rome's decline. Still, the attempt at objectivity must be made, using the best approaches one can think of. At the least, it is safe to emphasize once more the need to pick apart the various strands in the problem, which is not one single thing; and it has been emphasized also that analysis should and (thanks to recent scholarship) now can proceed in terms of substantial samplings of evidence, not scattered bits and pieces.

3. A REGIONAL SURVEY

But to return to Italy and her western Mediterranean markets: they appear to have dried up so far as the most obvious and valuable articles are concerned. Fine pottery production had largely gone from Arretium by Tiberius' reign (A.D. 14–37), replaced by production in such famous Gallic centers as La Graufesenque and Lezoux. Terracotta lamp production on an enormous scale in the north of Italy lasted longer, only to wane away in the second quarter of the third century.[27] As we have seen, wine and oil ceased to be exported at an early date and the effects were sooner or later felt in the producing areas of Tuscany and Campania. The best signs are not literary mentions of this or that town shrunken or deserted, though such testimonies obviously have their value. What is more trustworthy is the archeological record, if that in itself is not ambiguous. It is fullest a little above Rome. Surface finds over a broad expanse around both Falerii and Ansedonia (Cosa) show the late Republican drop in numbers of occupied sites carried down yet further in the first half of the second century A.D., with continued decline thereafter, too.[28] At the present moment, in central and southern Italy, only the lower Liris valley can be shown to have enjoyed an actual improvement in its fortunes in the second and third centuries.[29] The fortunes of Ostia are very hard to measure in this period because diminishing show of prosperity in inscriptions is suspect (given the curve of frequency of Latin epigraphy overall) and because the amount and quality of building activity cannot be well evaluated.[30] To the north, we know that Verona by the first century, Luni in the second, and the richest coastal parts of the Istrian peninsula, densely covered with villas, in the third century were all exhibiting clear signs of diminishing wealth or population, or both; and Cisalpine Gaul in general over the course of the second and third centuries was measurably worse off than it had been, due to a decline in the demand for its exports: marble (Luni) but mostly wine.[31]

But for the period of decline conventionally dated after, and perhaps as a result of, the crisis of the third century, we are not well served by the evidence from Italy. Indeed, the conventions themselves plainly do not fit. Political stability was for a while lost in a whirl of civil wars and foreign invasions. But the third century saw no abrupt collapse in the peninsula as a whole; and the fourth, no further, gentler deterioration — so far as we can tell. North of

Rome, in an area thirty or forty kilometers across just referred to, the number of occupied sites continued to diminish. They were the smaller ones: property was being gathered into fewer hands. But the population was evidently shrinking absolutely in every succeeding generation. On the other hand, around modern San Giovanni di Ruoti on the edge of Lucania, the land was abandoned in the third century but reoccupied in the fourth (the survey to date is only a third the size of that in southern Etruria, about thirteen kilometers across). Puteoli under Constantine (A.D. 306–37) began a veritable "renascence."[32] From the Italian south in general we hear very little, but it is of good times (and Sicily's towns and countryside yield far more signs of wealth in the form of artifacts and gold coins, rural church building, and above all the villa of Piazza Armerina, than can be found in earlier centuries).[33] Ostia's richer houses in the fourth century grew more luxurious than ever, though here and there in the town the reuse of architectural fragments and the shoddy repair of mosaics or frescoes tell another story.[34] About Rome's size and prosperity there is little except controversy, from which all that emerges with striking clarity is the series of new, magnificent basilicas which Constantine initiated and to which others were still being added well past the city's sack in A.D. 410.[35] Certainly the wealth of senatorial multimillionaires like Symmachus in the later empire compares very favorably with figures in the Principate; and their handling and use of it involves not only great numbers of tenants, *vilici, actores, procuratores,* and so forth, but implies also a complex, busy structure of wholesalers, retailers, rural and urban markets, roads, shipping, and concentrations of consumers. General mentions of agriculture by Symmachus and Ambrose indicate its healthy condition, and the picture presented by Palladius is painted in neutral colors: neither gloomier nor sunnier than that of his agronomist-predecessors.[36]

Ambrose, of course, is our best witness for conditions of his day. Yet he must be cross-examined carefully. When he describes scenes of urban and rural poverty, he can be shown to draw heavily on Saint Basil's recent homilies dealing with that subject; so there is literary contamination to some unknown degree — not that we need doubt the existence of the poor in any period of antiquity.[37] And when in one of his letters he describes "so many half-destroyed carcasses of cities" along the Via Aemilia, like Claterna, Bononia, Modena, Regium and Placentia, he must not be taken to mean more than he says: the urban centers south of the Po (correctly, Aemilia) were in decline. But precisely here, around Bononia, for example, lie the only villas known to the most recent survey. The coins in one of them run up to Constantine; in another, to the fifth century. They suggest, though a mere dozen are too few to prove, that farming in the region continued into the late empire, though steadily tapering off; and the burials and rare excavated houses are certainly poorer than they had been in earlier centuries.[38] What of the regions Ambrose knew better, to the north of the river? Here, except for Vercelli, we have no mention of urban decay; rather, scattered indications of renewal and investment and, from the time of Diocletian, when Milan began its long history as a government center, many proofs of wealth and growing population in that splendid city.[39] The later empire was also a period of repeated settlements of barbarians throughout the Po valley. They could only be lodged where there was no need to displace active farmers. The conclusion, however, that such settlements must therefore indicate previous or recurring depopulation, rather than the raising of the rural economy to new levels, cannot fairly be drawn.[40] Perhaps the nearest to the truth is Santo Mazzarino's view, that the larger and more successful cities in Transpadana, notably Milan and Ravenna, were drawing off some of the wealth and population of the smaller ones.

In summary, the history of the whole peninsula and Sicily confirms the necessity underlined above, to respect the individual ups and downs of different regions. If, in the obviously deficient evidence, we can find the material for any broad statement about decline, we must date its commencement, for those parts where it can be asserted at all, in the first century.

And what cause for this shall we assert? Rostovtzeff two generations ago first made familiar the only answer it is possible to substantiate: "the economic emancipation of the provinces."[41] In the various trade patterns that can be seen in the figures above, the most recent proofs seem adequate. Other and contributing factors besides provincial competition could of course be suggested with more or less plausibility, short of demonstration. It is best to pretend they do not exist lest, being slipped in as hypotheses on one page, they insolently present themselves as certainties on the next.

One such hypothesis, a decline in the productive role of slavery, has been urged with particular insistence. It is here that I must insert a page or two on that general topic, since only in this particular region, Italy, was slavery in any sense a determinant of prosperity. It seems to me highly probable that its role did diminish over the years from, let us say, Cicero's consulship in 63 B.C. to the death of Nero in A.D. 68. This is my guess, considering the frequency of wars in which captives were taken to be sold and the history of the concentration of purchasing power in Italy. However, I am not aware of any evidence to show that in fact either the supply of slaves really did fall off during this century and a quarter or that those available were put to work in any different ways at the end compared with the beginning. Trustworthy information of broad import is not available. After this period, there is no obvious change in the possible sources of supply until the effects of the barbarian invasions have become settled over the west. There are ups and downs and occasional gluts on the market that are remarked on. It might be possible to make the case for somewhat easier access to supplies of slaves for Italy (as also for other regions) in the period after A.D. 350; but that case is not compelling. One may read the Theodosian Code as well as most of the Justinian without sensing a transition from one world to another, so far at least as the institution or economics of slavery are concerned. And the almost unique glimpse we have of a late landowner's use and number of slaves, in service to Melania the Younger, could just as well fit in Latium or Sicily of 100 B.C. as in A.D. 400.[42] In sum, without denying the significance of servile labor in the setting of Italy's chief resource, agriculture, I cannot detect anything over the last three or four centuries of the empire deserving of the term 'decline.'

In other parts of the empire, though slaves are universally attested and very commonly owned by urban elites in all centuries, their duties lay ordinarily in the house; and, even where they are encountered in rural settings, they can be shown or presumed to have been in domestic service more than field work — therefore not of much significance in economic terms.[43]

Whether servile labor had a negative impact on the development of efficiency in free labor, through discouraging technological advance, is likewise a question often discussed. New methods and devices in agriculture and manufacture can in fact be detected emerging continually in the Roman world. It is the labor-saving ones that might be relevant. Unluckily for the logic of the argument, however, a labor-intensive process in the one industry that engaged slaves at all periods — that is, in spinning and weaving which could be carried on in the slaveowners' houses — appears at just the wrong time, during the supposed decline of slavery.[44] In the eastern provinces, where this latter advance was made, the water mill came into use on about the same scale and developed along much the same lines as in Gaul and Italy, even though the two areas exhibited many differences in the type of labor force characteristic of each; so this important labor-saving device did not develop in a way that the history of slavery can help to explain.[45] When such and many similar points of illogic are fairly considered, it is natural to wonder whether the employer class, and particularly those within it who controlled the most wealth and could best make their views prevail, really appreciated the economic possibilities in industrial technology or whether, in agriculture, they attached as much value to invention as to management.[46] The causal connections between the availability of labor and attempts to conserve it thus come apart when they are carefully considered, very much like the causal connections sought between the slave force in Italy and the level of late Roman prosperity.

Now to resume my survey of the conditions prevailing in the various regions of the late empire: in and just behind the frontier provinces of the Danube and Rhine it would be natural to expect, and there can be found, sure signs of decline. But they do not lend themselves to simple summary. Besides, there is as yet too little exact information about many districts to allow general conclusions. It is only within the last decade, for example, that an entirely new major city has been detected at Slava Rusa (?Libida, some thousand kilometers north of Constantinople) in the late Roman province of Scythia, whose walls most likely belong to the early fourth century and whose peak of size and prosperity was attained a little later.[47] Such significant archeological discoveries, welcome though they certainly are, serve also as reminders of the limits to our knowledge. At Novae on the Danube, excavation is only now beginning to reveal enough of the city to characterize the whole as flourishing in the fourth century. The remains of a number of imposing late Roman buildings have been uncovered.[48] There may have been some benefit to the city from the presence of troops which, at a point perhaps as late as this date, built an aqueduct.[49] Throughout the north Balkans and lower Danube provinces, after a term of relative peace and perhaps prosperity, large-scale admission of the Goths in A.D. 376 brought severe trials. The countryside had to arm itself, or submit to barbarian settlement;[50] and the mentions in written sources of cities like Marcianopolis, Philippopolis, and Hadrianople most often occur within a military context. On the other hand, where the troops were, there too were the later Roman emperors and big payrolls. Between the logic of barbarian destruction and the opposing logic of government expenditures in the region, only more digging can one day adjudicate. Elsewhere in the region we can only list the imperial palaces and villas, Tetrarchic or later, near Gamzigrad in Dacia Ripensis, near Naissus and Constantinople and Sirmium.[51] Among these cities as well the evidence is somewhat ambiguous. When Ammianus refers to new fortifications going up in Sirmium in 374, they are made of pillage from an uncompleted theater; and when a grand residence is discovered there, it has risen on the ruins of smaller houses, perhaps indicating districts laid bare by underpopulation. The mint ceased activity in 388. The best-known and grandest late Roman palace, at Split (Spalato in Dalmatia), seems unrepresentative of a province where most villa sites were beginning to be abandoned.[52]

By contrast, several riverine cities of Upper Moesia and Pannonia are relatively well known, in addition to a great many villas. Of 167 in a published catalogue of the latter sites, 53 were new-built or still in operation in the fourth century.[53] At the moment, the richest region appears to have lain around and south of Lake Balaton in modern Hungary (that is, the older province Pannonia, later Pannonia Prima and Valeria). In the 290s the connecting of it with the Danube had been taken on as an imperial project, still detectable today in the course followed by the modern Sio canal, and great expanses of forest had been cleared. The frontier was well defended. Behind it then flourished those many rural estates just enumerated, of a size generally larger than earlier ones. The trend in this direction is noticeable archeologically in Moesia as well from the late third century, but its most impressive development is to the north and west, in Pannonia, in the form sometimes of quite enormous villas equipped with protective walls, large-scale grain storage facilities, and corner towers. A famous one was built at Valcum (? — Fenekpuszta), the fortified center of an imperial estate at the lower end of Lake Balaton. It amounts almost to a walled town.[54] The concentrations of wealth implied in these structures are something new (no doubt based on grain production). The countryside rose to a higher level of good times than ever before, to a point best set around A.D. 375, and continued to enjoy a slowly diminishing prosperity for another two decades or more. From the fact of these villas being not infrequently fortified, however, it is clear that conditions were troubled. In the neighborhood of one have been found late-fourth-century Hunnish artifacts, from settler populations.

The uncertainty of the frontier, causing that trouble, accounts for the quite different fortunes of Pannonia's cities in the later empire. A few that lay toward the interior did well in the first half of the fourth century. By then, however, the population of most was getting smaller even despite the crowding in of their suburbs under the protection of the cities' walls. At Gorsium, two villas had been built inside on vacant land. Elsewhere, mosaics end around 350; the date of coins from the sites carries up no further than the 370s. The content of burials rises in apparent wealth to mid-century only. At Sopianae, when it became the capital of the new province Valeria, some renovation was achieved, new rich villas sprang up in the suburbs to accommodate (presumably) the administrative elite, and supplies of currency grew in volume noticeably under Constantine and again under Constantius II (A.D. 337–61); but thereafter coins become fewer, and none minted after 378 are found on the site.[55]

Further to the west, the third century brought severe invasions and eventual abandonment of the reentrant formed between the upper Danube and the upper Rhine. In the interior, a city like Virunum enjoyed special protection at the center of Noricum's most populous district; yet even here there was heavy destruction in the 270s, restored under Diocletian. Restoration extending in some sense to the end of the fourth century could not extend also to the security of trade routes, at least for Virunum. Augusta Vindelicum in Raetia for a while managed its commerce better, but the whole province gradually slips out of knowledge.[56]

To what extent, when, and in what parts Gaul and Germany suffered a decline is best determined from the archeological record. For their condition, literary sources are not only rare witnesses but difficult to understand. They neither quantify nor compare; and, without a sense of the state of things at one time relative to some other, we can gain no appreciation of change. Excavation, on the other hand, is likely to provide the comparative materials within a meter or two of each other. From properly cut building blocks in a city wall, for example, next to a piece of sculpture robbed for the use of defense, at the very least we learn that a time of peace and the arts has been succeeded by one of war and confusion. The arming of the Gallic provinces in the third century with city walls is well known, a process in which whole city circuits were greatly reduced and important public buildings or areas of housing were apparently abandoned.[57] From this fact it was first inferred that the subsequent urban population could all fit inside the walls and was therefore permanently reduced by a quarter, a half, or three-quarters at different sites; but the inference, having been tested as much as possible, is now generally doubted and the existence of very substantial suburbs is sometimes demonstrable.[58] On the extent of urban decline therefore a little less is known than used to be thought. Besides, the automatic scholarly reflex, to assign every trace of burning or damage in ancient ruins to the second half of the third century or to enemy action, is manifestly wrong in some instances; for even in the best of times the physical fabric of cities burns, collapses, or naturally deteriorates. The natural should be distinguished from the unnatural and violent; but no survey of the destruction wrought by the crisis has ever been attempted.[59] Yet the severity of the crisis, or at least the duration of its effects, is gradually becoming better known, site by site.

Not that urban life thereafter generally attained the same level as before. A few centers grew larger and richer but many, many more failed to regain the prosperity they had enjoyed in Antonine times. Among the lucky, none could compete with Trier, the capital that served Constantine. It remained an imperial town for another century. Its splendid basilica is well known and still in use, its palace equally imposing. Having great personages in its midst was good for Trier. For the same reason — promotion to the rank of provincial capital and imperial residence — Arles flourished as never before, beginning in, say, A.D. 350 and for a hundred years thereafter.[60] For, as an anonymous writer of the mid-fourth century explains: "The Gallic province abounds in everything, thanks to the ruler's presence — though everything also costs a lot. Trier is, they say, the largest city they have, where the Lord Emperor is said to reside. It is in the midst of that land; but there is likewise a second city to support it in everything, which they call Arles." On a small scale, Tours also enjoyed some new building as a result of becoming the capital of a new, subdivided province in the later fourth century.[61] Toulouse grew vastly greater from the third century on, quadrupling its size, as Ausonius tells us, and occupying no less than ninety hectares,[62] while Autun revived too, thanks to imperial building. Vesontio revived, Vincum revived. A few smaller centers even began their existence in the fourth century, generally as the lodging of troops.[63]

But against the one Gallic city in ten whose fortunes demonstrably improved, beyond mere repair of the worst damage in the wake of the third-century violence, there is a much larger percentage of places that play no further part in history, seeming to have vanished off the map or clearly to have remained within the shrunken circuits of their hastily constructed walls: Aventicum now "deserted but formerly by no means inconsiderable," says Ammianus, recollecting the 350s; Autun also, "its walls indeed far-reaching in their extent but weakened through the decay of old age."[64] Both had plainly declined over the course of recent decades. As to Lyon, it had begun its downward course even in the later second century when its western sector was abandoned.[65] Its territory, too, suffered. From the moment of Albinus' defeat, perhaps, in A.D. 197, the number of occupied sites began a long, steady decline. But, supposing that civil war and confiscations of property worked harm, why no recovery? Lyon's loss of primacy, considering how extremely large, rich, and important it had been, cannot be well explained save by considerations that should apply equally to all of Gaul. I will return to these later. As a parting comment on the condition of the Gallic cities, there is the warning, delivered by the prefect Florentius in 367, that penalties requiring execution of three decurions in each center might in some places prove unenforceable through the lack of even that small number.[66] We have, then, heterogeneous bits and pieces of evidence such as these items, pointing nevertheless to greatly reduced wealth and population in most cities of late Roman Gaul.

Nine out of ten people, however, lived on the land in villages and villas. Their condition is quite as important as that of their urban compatriots. In recent decades sufficiently broad and careful surveys have been made to justify cautious statements about the lot of these rural folk, at least in Brittany and the north, where much more clearly marked changes took place in, and as a result of, the third-century wars and invasions. Some of this surveying has been done through air photographs which, with pollen analysis, opens up new, valuable windows on the past.

Easiest to describe is the fate of Brittany. It simply entered the Dark Ages ahead of all the rest of Gaul by a few hundred years. To judge from its villas, perhaps 1 per cent of which are now known through archeology, the region enjoyed a sharp upswing and Romanization beginning around the mid-first century, in a pattern detectable elsewhere in the province; then leveled off; resumed growth and expansion with Marcus Aurelius' reign (A.D. 161–80) until the end of the Severan dynasty (A.D. 193–235); and soon thereafter began a rapid fall into silence and desolation. Along the coasts, pirates gained control. Attempts at defense by barbarian troops stationed in largely maritime forts in roughly A.D. 280–320 proved quite inadequate. Inland, forests and wild growth advanced across the fields. By the end of the fourth century the whole of the peninsula was scantily populated and primitively farmed. Working villas, though larger, were very few — some taken over in the 300s by squatters, virtually all deserted by 350. The use of money ended a decade or so later.[67]

In the broad northern region lying between Seine and Rhine, Boulogne and Strasbourg, a most interesting and meaning change took place, no doubt in the second half of the third century. Earlier, widely scattered rural sites of habitation and rural cemeteries were abandoned and in due course their successors were planted in a different location, though generally pretty close. The change can only have taken place as a result of the local population fleeing and so being absent for some little time; for a mere summer's absence would hardly suffice to break the ties to one's home or to the tombs of one's ancestors. When resettling their lands, fugitives were less likely to commence in isolated farmsteads. They preferred clusters either on big private estates or in villages; often they established themselves along rivers and highways where they would be less isolated; and the total number of cemeteries and villas in active use in the fourth century and later is much reduced from the third, indicating the more compact clustering of the population. The phenomenon is best explained as a security measure.[68] The general deprivation of this broad northern zone is partly relieved to the east in the neighborhood of Trier. From that capital city radiated the warmth of gold, and around it industry was stimulated, an imperial rural palace (Contionacum = Konz) was built, and other rich, big villas, no doubt for government grandees.[69] But the area benevolently irradiated was not great; safety from attack was not assured. So the fourth century saw the continuing abandonment of their country places by even the rich and powerful in the Cologne-Mainz parts and lower Moselle.[70]

In this broad and manifestly penetrable northern zone below both the Rhine and Danube, raids by barbarians gave rise to a peculiar response: the building of hilltop refuges or the reoccupation of such sites not used since the

Iron Age. One on a cliff some fifteen miles from Trier, in its revival, had only a short life of a few decades. It was given up at the end of the third century. Another in the Moselle valley went on being used into the fifth century.[71] It is surmised that some sites in Germany, even well back from the frontier and in Raetia also, were walled and prepared by nearby rich landowners for their people and livestock in case of emergency.[72] Hilltop or cave refuges appear in southern France here and there; in Liguria and Tuscany too, after 400; and in the third century and later in Macedonia.[73] Fortified villas (a subject I return to in another chapter) appear also in almost all these regions, though especially in Pannonia.[74] Yet they are not very common even there. The Rhine and Danube provinces of the later empire are not to be thought of as a jungle, a no-man's land; only they had lost a good deal of their wealth, luster, and complexity of institutions.

From the initial shock of major disasters that set in toward mid-third century, recovery had been by no means complete. As signs of the patterns of civilized life being radically disturbed, notice peasants in the 280s spreading revolt and pillage in Gaul (and their movement returned in the fifth century).[75] Their roaming violence amounted to whole armies. In that later third century and on into the fourth, notice also how northern roads were equipped with fortlets to safeguard their travelers, evidently against endemic disorder.[76]

The "complexity of institutions" just referred to naturally could not withstand the physical danger and disruption to which there is certain testimony in armed villas, embattled highways, "Fliehbürgen," and recurrent bandit movements. Regions most recently conquered for the empire by Caesar, Augustus, and Tiberius simply reverted to their simpler preconquest condition. No doubt the most serious consequence was a deterioration in commerce. No one would care to entrust himself to travel or carry valuable goods across a threatened countryside. In the resulting constriction of markets within tighter and tighter little circles, we have the most likely explanation for the reduced size and wealth of most cities. They had earlier grown to their maximum in symbiotic relation with the agricultural territory around them. Now the *pax Romana* on which that relation depended had been shaken. It was every man for himself, every villa for itself.

Reversion to more primitive conditions was of course not exact and utter; far from that. But it is sufficiently intelligible and sufficiently supported by archeological fact to be accepted in explanation of the worst regions of decline. Of course refinements and qualifications will continue to emerge. We should recall that, in the Somme basin, which only a generation ago Albert Grenier called poor in villas, a thousand now are known; elsewhere in Gaul where he knew of only two, ninety-one are known. The abundance of data available for more exact descriptions of *what* happened, before anyone tries further to say *why*, is very striking.[77] And we should recall as well that, only recently, the distribution of a certain type of pottery was mapped, showing how widely it was sold over the southwest of France, the south of England, and all around Brittany in the period from about A.D. 280 to a peak of export in the first half of the fourth century. Its center of production was near Bordeaux.[78] Was trade possible, then — even where piracy was prevalent? Obviously there are many obscurities and alternatives in the picture of decline so far sketched which need much fuller examination.

That the main lines are nevertheless clear may be a little better confirmed from the history of the rural areas in Gaul, looking this time at the interior, not the north. We would like to find them differing somewhat from those in the north because they were less exposed to the ravages of the later third century. But no even spread of evidence exists from which to generalize. A number of villas were destroyed at the height of the crisis around A.D. 275, some a bit earlier, and some later.[79] Some were rebuilt; most, not. The southwest in the Aquitaine basin and the "old province" Narbonensis had once been home to a specially large, prosperous number of sites. So much we would predict. But anomalies appear in the evidence. There is some detectable late-second century abandonment of villas in the south; the same in the Auvergne region, where the majority of sites were then deserted, and again, near Limoges, for example, in the "Villa d'Antone" or at Champ de Pois at Berry in the north.[80] What was it about Marcus Aurelius' and Septimius Severus' reigns that caused these various points of blight on the otherwise undisturbed Gallic provinces? For the moment there is no answer.

Fortunately such questions are not enough seriously to disturb the usual picture we have of Gaul in the second, third, fourth, and earlier fifth centuries: traversing a time of growth followed by severe difficulties, with reconstruction thereafter on a new basis and along new lines. To this sequence, mention should be added of autarky. Just as rural residences occasionally showed provision for self-defense in the period after A.D. 300, so also they sometimes aimed at economic self-sufficiency.[81] This fact, which needs much more detailed examination, sheds light on economic conditions quite broadly. To the extent the rural population could satisfy most of its needs by itself, it had no need of cities. We know that most of them declined in size and wealth, since only by providing what was necessary to the surrounding countryside could they maintain their position. Thus (to repeat) physical security was the key; political weakness — the failure adequately to maintain the *pax Romana* — underlay both social and economic regression.

No doubt the changes can be understood in too stark and simple a vision, with the aristocracy of the northern and western provinces ensconced in and never leaving their great rural retreats — a Petit Trianon, even a Versailles, for each and every one of them. It is not hard to discover that vision here and there in modern reconstructions of the period from (let us say) A.D. 350 to 450. It depends in large part on literary evidence, that of Ausonius and Sidonius in particular. But there are dissentient views and facts that don't fit.[82] Many great structures of the late Roman sort rose in the countryside in the first century, even under Augustus. Indeed, while the average size of villas may well have been larger later than under the Principate, it is my impression that, in absolute numbers, there were actually more of these grand rural mansions under the Antonines. Surely their owners were proud of their riches and lineage (most of them descended from a native nobility); surely their literary tastes matched the refinement of their mosaics and frescoes, so as to place them among the likes of Terentius Junior of Italy. About this Terentius, never a visitor to Rome, Pliny exclaims with metropolitan condescension, "Oh how many learned men are hidden and lost to fame either by their own modesty or their love of tranquillity!" And he goes on to describe a person indeed very cultivated who nevertheless lived year-round in the country.[83] It may be no more than an accident of our sources, then, that makes us suppose such a life and such a person much more characteristic of the fifth century in Gaul than of the first century in Italy.

Britain's fortunes traced a different course. Here, too, my interest focuses on signs of disposable wealth and the quality of life measured in the quantity and abundance of building, abundance of coins in circulation, elegance of surviving artifacts, apparent access to distant, even overseas, markets, and numbers of people able to enjoy such things — therefore, population in absolute numbers so far as those numbers can be reasonably surmised. By these quite conventional indices it is pretty clear what happened, but not why. First, cities lost or retained or increased their wealth and prosperity in no one pattern over the late third up to the later fourth century. After A.D. 375, however, all but London show clear deterioration in the form of squatters in half-empty buildings, clogged ditches, and farming introduced into deserted lots or other open spaces.[84] Mosaics in the province are rare before 300, rare again after 370. They are a good test of prosperity. But many, of course, are found in villas, and there we discover decidedly greater wealth and ease of life than ever before, so that the first half of the fourth century can be called by Sheppard Frere "the Golden Age of Roman Britain"; and good times, or at least no sudden deterioration, can be detected for another decade or two.[85] Ammianus' description of the wonderful administration of Count Theodosius in 369, through which he "restored cities and forts" and left the British "provinces dancing for joy,"[86] may thus be taken as marking the edge of the decline rather than the beginning of yet better times.

Britain had experienced no third-century crisis. Indeed, signs of prosperity in the course of the third century slowly multiply both for cities and the countryside, just as signs of the reverse only slowly reveal themselves over the last generation of the fourth century.[87] About both towns and villas, little can be found in the archeological data to explain their history. The growing autarky of villas is neither marked nor different from the phenomenon on the continent, where it is ascribed to increasing disorders and decreasing commerce; yet those two latter phenomena are not known to have existed in later Roman Britain. There is some indication that villa construction then was largely undertaken by imperial officials to be near the towns where they were stationed, not by persons interested in working the land.[88] If rightly interpreted, that evidence fits with the appearance of rich rural residences around the fourth century western capital at Trier. But the interpretation says more about prosperity than decline; and it is decline that I am interested in. So the fortunes of Roman Britain in its last days, aside from brief notices about political events in written sources, cannot be followed through sequences of cause and effect.

Spain's end came, though less abruptly, near the same date as Britain's: to be more specific, in A.D. 409. It was then that barbarians entered the land to stay.[89] In justification of the term *end* is the series we have of imported Roman sarcophagi, of which none can be dated post-400; also, the evidence for mining, which ceases; further, the fact that little more than a third of villas known from before the turn of the fifth century were occupied, or more than drastically contracted, thereafter; and last, that coins ceased to circulate in the north.[90] That is known from the hoards: in those laid down in the early fifth century, only issues of the second third, not the last (adjoining) third, of the fourth century are found. Therefore, in that period ca. 365–400 not only were people, in alarm, hiding their money in the ground as never before, but new issues of coins were not forthcoming to be used or hidden later. We discover a decline anticipating the more dramatic turning point of 409 and directing our attention to earlier developments.

Mention has already been made of the taking over of Spanish oil export to Rome by the emperor Septimius Severus. The scale of that export had been diminishing for some decades anyway and continued to do so in the decades following, until it fell to nothing in the late 250s.[91] It was just then, and again in 275/6, that the Franks and other Germans burst over the Pyrenees and spread destruction far and wide. The signs have been found in the burnt layers of villas and in the use in city walls of salvaged sculpture and architectural

stones from wrecked buildings. Many centers are known to have suffered:
Tarraco, Ilerda, Baetulo, Neapolis of Emporiae, Caesaraugusta, Iruña, Pallan-
tia, and others as well.[92] It is natural to see the latter, the urban part of
civilization in the peninsula, as more vulnerable in the long term than the rural
parts. Walled circuits could do nothing to protect the patterns of exchange
by which the cities met their daily needs. Yet it is not easy to test for a
connection between ease of trade and the economy of cities. At the moment
there seem to be very few though suggestive bits of evidence that concern
maritime commerce in Spain post-275: the absence of any Spanish ports in the
account of the anonymous geographer of the mid-fourth century, in his
Expositio; the description by Avienus, a little later, of Cadiz as impoverished,
deserted, a mere heap of ruins, as well as similar passages about other sites in
Ausonius and Paulinus (though, being post-409/11, they are perhaps not
relevant); and, finally, the total absence of late Roman amphorae along the
coasts.[93] The sum total of these items indicates the increasing economic
isolation of the peninsula and the attendant deterioration of the cities, entirely
in the absence of any cause so obvious as foreign invasions.

While oil was no longer a large export, apparently the famous Spanish fish
sauce, *garum*, continued to be sold all over the empire. By chance we find
good evidence for a special tie also (in the form of very abundant imported
sculpture) between Africa and Tarraco in the late period. That city and a few
others flourished. They are mentioned with admiration in late literary
sources.[94] Italica was rich, necessarily from its chief resource, olives; Emerita's
circus was twice repaired in the later fourth century. In all, Baetica as a whole
remained rich throughout that time.[95] Much that was familiar about the
Spanish urban scene and grand commerce in their best days could still be
found in and even after A.D. 409.

But it was the achievement of the countryside that was most striking in the
wake of the invasions of A.D. 260 and 275. Among villa patterns, which had
by then begun to sort themselves out into the smaller, plainer work centers
and the more sumptuous large ones in which their rich owners were
personally resident, the latter now emerged as favored. Evidently a period of
troubles could be more successfully supported by the substantial landholder
who bought up his neighbors's struggling farms and perhaps physically
defended his home against raiders. So the later third and all of the fourth, even
into the fifth, centuries saw a steady process of consolidation of land into
larger units. At the same time, new villas were built in all regions more or less
evenly rather than in selected districts, whereas in the first century building
had been unevenly active (concentrated around Tarraco and Hispalis-
Italica). All of the peninsula proclaimed the acme of villa life as the mid-fourth

century approached; and the style of that life was quite baronial, to judge from gigantic private bathhouses (Altafulla), sprawling gardens, stone and bronze sculpture, mosaics (as at the Casa de Hylas or Arroniz), frescoes (as at Centcelles or the Villajoyosa), and more basic evidence of wealth in the form of huge storage facilities and housing for troops of laborers.[96] Why all this structure of ease and prosperity began slowly to deteriorate well before the barbarians entered the land in 409 is quite unclear.

A few features match what has been noticed in other provinces: provisions for economic self-sufficiency and perhaps for defense (Liedena) and, close around the diocese capital Emerita, a thick cluster of fourth-century villas, one of which may well have been built by the *vicarius* himself as his palace.[97] It is of notable proportions and luxuriousness.

Across the straits of Gibraltar lay another part of that vicar's domain; for southern Spain and Mauretania Tingitana were combined into one diocese by Diocletian. At the same time, Diocletian withdrew Roman dominion entirely from a portion of the latter province. Just how much is a little uncertain; nor is the history of neighboring Sitifensis or Caesariensis in those times quite clear. By the test of inscriptions which record new building or repairs, the two provinces maintained the fabric of their civilization over the fourth and fifth centuries very much as they had in the third.[98]

That same test, however, augmented by excavation of the ruins, tells a far more detailed and well substantiated story over the rest of Roman north Africa. From the revolt of A.D. 238 until the accession of Diocletian in 284, Proconsularis, Numidia, and Tripolitania all seem to have endured a kind of stagnation.[99] Under his rule there was evidently a great upsurge in urban renewal and, though the next half-century was less happy, a second period of recovery developed in the 350s, lasting far into the 370s.[100] The testimony is drawn from Ammaedara, Middidi, Thibilis, Sitifis, Thuburbo Maius, Thugga, Cuicul, Thubursicu Numidarum, Ad Maiores, and other scattered sites for Diocletian's reign; from Cuicul, Sitifis, and Thugga again for the second of the two good periods, with Djemila, Sufetula, Timgad, and Carthage counted as well. Extravagant bombast about "the splendor of Our Noble Majesties' times" in dedicatory inscriptions must be suitably discounted; only hard evidence of edifices actually erected or actually repaired, whether they be private or more often public, is to be given weight. And certain reservations and details should be noted: for example, one text describing "ruins piled up as high as the tops of buildings in the city" of Cuicul, and the same phrase in another text of Sfax of the same date, have been taken as evidence of accumulated deterioration over prior decades followed by some abrupt improvement. More likely both testify to the earthquake of July 21, 365. But they nevertheless show marked economic strength in the speed and ambition of recovery, which not only undertook repairs but added a brand-new public swimming pool with adjoining solarium and decorative statuary around it.[101] Note is duly taken of Lepcis not sharing the good times because, as Ammianus reports very fully, it fell victim to a combination of beduin raids from the desert and a greedy and inert Roman army commandant. Hadrumetum on the coast likewise seems to show mixed fortunes: its inhabited area shrank in the late third century, the inland roads to it went unrepaired, its ports later silted up in the course of the fourth century. The oil riches on which it had drawn had been perhaps redirected through other towns; but its stagnation fell short of poverty — in fact, produced only a sort of leveling of fortunes, in which signs of comfort and taste appear to have been more widely spread among its citizens' housing and burials than before. As to Carthage, both city and dependent territory enjoyed a prosperity essentially unbroken from the second to the seventh century, to judge from the archeological evidence of their commerce and production.[102]

It is noticed also that a great deal of growth and construction in African cities was ecclesiastical: martyria, baptisteries, chapels, basilicas, storage buildings, and episcopal residences. The scale of these can be appreciated in Optatus' new cathedral overlooking Timgad: 63 x 22m in a compound 200 x 125m filled with other edifices. They contain many mosaics.[103] Date: late fourth century. To Carthage in 411 a conference drew 650 bishops, indicating the huge number of towns in the whole region. Optatus' achievement suggests also that the upturn noted especially in the 360s and 370s really had a very broad reach chronologically, and extending well into the fifth century. It is certainly fair to speak of the whole of late antiquity, the "Bas-Empire" in north Africa to the edge of the Vandal invasion, as a time of marked prosperity, even if it fell short of the best days of the second century.[104] As Eugène Albertini back in the 1930s had already begun to depict the history of the region in these terms, and as his learning qualified him as a good judge, it may seem surprising that broader discussions of the empire's decline overall continued for decades to treat of their subject without any qualification, as one universal collapse. The readjustment of ideas is a slow business.

Better data about Africa that have been assembled recently allow some discussion even of specific ups and downs within the long stretch of time from Diocletian to Gaiseric. In brief, archeology is to be brought into alignment with literary or at least written sources. So the falling-off of public construction under Constantine is attributed to the wars and their demands, in which Maxentius became involved; thereafter, the hard times continued because the emperor had taken to sequestering the cities' income from rental of their corporately owned lands. Not until Julian restored that flow did construction start up again. Valentinian resumed the harsher policy but modified it in 374. And there were also laws that affected the cities' right to enjoy the wealth of their elite in semicompulsory public services. Between these many items of political/administrative history and actual economic behavior, there seem to be incontestable links. They do not quite fit, however, with the particularly high points in the decade after Julian's death. There must have been other important influences at work of which there is at present no adequate knowledge.

Knowledge in great heaps is certainly available about the province of Egypt. In comparative terms, thanks to the survival of papyri, it is familiar to us in great detail. Too much, perhaps — or human history is beyond human comprehension. At Oxyrhynchus, best known of all sites in the province, the metropolites during the troubled decades of the mid-third century actually increased their outlays through ever more expensive inventions of patriotic enthusiasm; and the city's evident prosperity continued on the rise during the very worst moments of the crisis — witness the institution of a corn dole, public works, and ephebic games even in the 250s, 260s, and 270s.[105] Throughout the Roman period, bad moments are detectable in particular districts through depopulation. On close inspection their significance melts away just like the missing citizens reported in tax lists. Where have those citizens gone? They aren't all dead, they have only gone, poor creatures, where conditions are not quite so desperate, and they will return when the local results of a bad year are no longer being so keenly felt.[106] What the great secular changes may have been in Egypt overall cannot be said — unless they were for the better.[107] As to the capital, it is a good guess, though not much better than a guess, that its great size remained more or less unchanged throughout the centuries I am concerned with.[108] If Egypt experienced any decline, then, the means of demonstrating its operation have yet to be discovered.

My counterclockwise circling round the empire continues past the delta of the Nile and into Palestine. The first specific site allowing evaluation is Gerasa in the Decapolis between the Dead Sea and the Sea of Galilee. After sharing to some extent in the third-century hardships that more seriously afflicted Dura and Palmyra, Gerasa shows recovery under Diocletian (A.D. 284–304) and a good level of civic pride and activity in the succeeding years up to A.D. 440. There was plenty of public construction and some growth in population.[109] Palestine as a whole emerged by Diocletian's time in an almost fully municipalized or Hellenized form — that is, small centers or villages and farming territory were assigned to larger centers for administration, as was generally the arrangement throughout the empire. Even in the third century, agriculture appears from the archeological records to have continued prosperous in most areas and in the fourth century the appraisal by Ammianus can be confirmed through other written sources as well as excavation: "Palestine abounds in tilled and rich-looking fields."[110] Prosperity in villages, at least in the frontier zones, is attributable to the military payroll and military construction of the late empire. The fact is most clearly seen in the south, but not only there.[111] Inland, wine and olive production attracts more favorable notice in written sources of all sorts over the course of the fourth to sixth centuries, reflecting a prosperity that can be measured also at most of the 3,000 sites that dot the archeological map of modern Israel. The whole land enjoyed an "economic boom"[112] quantifiable in one very striking statistic: sites where mosaic pavements have been discovered by excavation and which represent a random sampling of an art that served expendable wealth (not to mention high taste) number under a dozen in the whole Principate but 335 in the fourth to sixth centuries.

To the north, Constantius II, in preparation for his eastern campaigns, "cut through a great mountain to let in the sea" to Seleuceia "and there made a large, good port to which ships might come in safety and the fiscal cargoes would not be lost."[113] There we have one city whose fortunes improved. Evidently there were others. To the extent that absolute numbers of inscriptions show command of extra money and a healthy sense of one's community, their rise should be noticed at Apamea over the second, third, fourth, and fifth centuries: in the four periods, respectively, 11, 11, 25, and 62. At Laodicea in the same long span they diminish from the small total of seven to zero, while at Chalcis they rise from zero to four — these latter statistics perhaps being too insignificant to tell us anything.[114] At Antioch the four figures are 22, 11, 43, and 54; and the impression they convey is strengthened by some rise in the number of mosaic floors found in the neighborhood of the city belonging to the later period, as compared with the earlier.

Antioch is known to us through a very unusual abundance of information covering a time from the mid-fourth to the early fifth century. All the information is concordant and overwhelmingly confirms the truth of Julian's panegyrical picture, or John Chrysostom's references to prevailing riches, luxury, and self-indulgence. The anonymous geographer who has been quoted before adds his own comment, too. There is to be found there "an abundance of amenities, especially the circus. Why all these? For the reason that the emperor resides there and all these are necessary on his account."[115] Constantius II, Gallus, Julian, and Valens indeed spent decades in Antioch, also spending a lot of money there. Even after Valens's death, however, there was a kind of construction surge in the 380s quite independent of any imperial presence — unless what Libanius then reports was more or less normal over an extended period. In addition to wealth at work in construction, the population grew, no doubt attracted by jobs and an expanding economy.[116] Public distribution of food began most likely in the 370s and public entertainments and civic services were well maintained.[117]

The riches and buying power of a great urban center are bound to be felt by its rural neighbors. By that logic are best understood the villas and villages which lie one or two hundred kilometers east of Antioch in the hills, and which steadily raised themselves in their degree of comfort, size, and internal organization over the second to seventh centuries. It was Georges Tchalenko who patiently studied the area and all its remains some decades ago, and who uncovered the ruins, measured the size of typical rooms in houses, counted the inscriptions, and connected the olive presses with the farmsteads they served, so as to make the whole eastern plateau of Syria more intelligible. A thin scattering of large estate-centers in the earlier empire gave way to a sort of levelling proliferation of middle-sized farms whose wealth lay principally in oleiculture.[118] The process continued over hundreds of years and extended the essence of late Roman prosperity far beyond the shores of the Mediterranean. With the exception of a very few towns — Gindarus, Hierapolis, Cyrrhus, Emesa[119] — Syria as a whole was clearly for centuries enjoying a very flourishing 'decline.'

Where one would hardly expect prosperity, over a region that had been rather backward heretofore, it is nevertheless to be found: at third-century Side in Pamphylia and Mopsuestia in Cilicia. But that evidence is episodic, and the southeast coastal parts of Asia Minor were often disturbed by passing armies, raiders, and pirates.[120] After A.D. 300, fortunes improved very widely and very noticeably — specifically, after 330, the date chosen by Seton Williams. At about the same time that Georges Tchalenko was concluding his remarkably detailed and instructive survey of the highlands between Syrian Antioch and Chalcis, Seton Williams was walking over the equally forgotten hills, plains, and small valleys of eastern Cilicia, counting and dating a hundred and fifty sites. They revealed to him a great increase in population over districts previously uninhabited; and, in much of the same region but extended around the curve of the coast into Syria, a similar survey many years later confirmed those findings through more counting of sites and specific attention to churches and mosaic pavements, of which the former had obviously to be post-Constantinian and the latter, the mosaics, allow evaluation of "economic and artistic factors."[121]

While there have been no other such broad views taken of Asia Minor, something close to a substitute can be found in a catalogue of scattered site reports regarding some dozen cities. They lie in the western portion or on the western coast. At Ephesus and Sardis there has been excavation amply sufficient to allow a general appraisal of their health in the late empire. It was excellent. From Sardis, George Hanfmann could report a strong upswing in wealth and vitality over the course of the fourth and fifth centuries, evident in the "unified replanning of the major avenue, . . . rebuilding of the gymnasium, . . . the fact that the area was turned from cemeteries to residential large structures in the House of Bronzes region, the building of the city wall, and, finally, the large addition of the Byzantine (fifth century) part to the thermal establishment."[122] Ephesus flourished in the same centuries, up to 614, thanks to its connections with a well-maintained road system, to say nothing of maritime trade; and the vitality of exchange that shows in the recently revealed commercial section paid for the gilded ceiling of the new baths, the main avenue's lighting by lanterns at night, the elaborate renovation of the chief synagogue around A.D. 400, and the triumphal arch of the mid-fifth century. Services like hospitals, water supply, or public entertainments were generously funded. Of other cities we know considerably less: Antioch in Pisidia, Miletus, Smyrna, Pergamon, and others too.[123] In sum and on balance, however, they must be pronounced prosperous: if little Priene had become even smaller, the substantial Nicomedia had been dramatically embellished and enlarged and, when it suffered from an earthquake in Julian's reign, was munificently relieved by him. In 363 he addressed to the Count of the East an announcement suggesting there was a generally high level of economic energy to be found in that official's realm: "Since the desire for marble has enormously increased the price of such stone, in order that this expensive wish may be alleviated by an abundant supply, We permit that all men who wish to quarry shall have the license granted to them. For We consider that the result will be that very many veins of glistening stone will also come to light and into use." [124]

My survey finally returns me to my starting point across the Bosporus, in the Balkan peninsula. Greece was of course by no means a rich land under the Romans and suffered severely from barbarian invasion in the 260s. Recovery came only very late to Athens, which remained badly damaged and reduced in size until after the mid-fourth century. Then began a clear and noteworthy upsurge in population and construction.[125] Corinth must have shared in that phenomenon, since the general area around it has been shown by ongoing field surveys to have experienced pronounced prosperity beginning at about the same point in time — elsewhere in the peninsula and islands, even somewhat earlier.[126]

But of course the greatest achievement in the east was that almost new city, at least called "New Rome," Constantine's capital on the straits. About this magnificent, perfectly enormous, and continually expanding and fattening center of imperial and ecclesiastical ambitions, contemporaries had much to say. Its founder "has sought citizens for it from everywhere and lavished great riches on it to the point of virtually exhausting all the imperial resources on it"; and neither the united abundance of goods from Egypt and Asia nor "grain from Syria and Phoenicia and other nations as the payment of tribute can suffice to satisfy the intoxicated multitude which Constantine transported to Byzantium by emptying other cities."[127] What better than Constantinople could demonstrate the irrepressible life of one whole half of the ancient world, much of it even attaining new heights, while the other half gradually reverted to a lower plane? The decline of the Roman empire was a decline of only its younger part. So Gibbon discovered, struggling along year after year, volume after volume, until his pen finally rested at the date of 1453.

4. SOME GENERAL EXPLANATIONS

Gibbon's discovery invites the recall of fig. 1 above. Comparison there between Latin and Greek literature showed a diversity of fortunes over the long term; and, over the long term, a diversity shows in other arts — of mosaics, frescoes, design of buildings, elaboration of public entertainments — between east and west. Evident wealth in the former was maintained while in the latter it diminished. There might then be a causal connection between wealth and the arts. In fact no one doubts that the heights attained by any civilization in the past required the concentration of its riches in the hands of a leisured patron class supporting a dependent body of creators, performers, architects, painters, and so forth. However, as everyone knows equally well, there is no synchrony to be detected between the high point of the Roman art most valued by the wealthy and cultivated, namely oratory, and the Roman economy. Its decline, judged by its own standards (which remain largely our own), came too early. The decline of jurisprudence, which was likewise a quintessential part of Roman civilization, came too late. And that is true whether we accept Gibbon's dating of the best times, under the Antonines, or set them in the first century. In either case, as in the case also of the medical sciences and various other aspects of higher culture, the history of the ancient economy is of little help in explaining quality. I raised the same point earlier (above, p. 4f.), when discussing the separate histories of the many strands that make up a civilization.

But quality is one thing, quantity another; and similarly, within any civilization, the choosing of characteristic ways in which to express general human impulses is one thing, quantity another. Whether a fresco will be beautifully painted or why a people practices public benefactions, perhaps no one can say; but it is certain that a beautiful fresco and a foundation for orphan relief both cost a lot of money. There will be more of both in a flourishing economy. Therefore, as everyone well knows, we can and do learn a great deal about decline, no matter how broadly defined, from economic history.

For that reason the survey attempted in the preceding section focused on quantity as much as possible. My object was to discover, in significant activities like the laying down of a mosaic floor in one's house or the exporting of olive oil to some distant market, information that indisputably reveals change over time. Such information, so patiently gathered by researchers especially of the last generation, makes possible a number of important generalizations, of which the foremost has already been often underlined: regions differed in their stories. Within regions even of no enormous size, agriculture improved or deteriorated in one district but not in another (as can be seen in Italy, southern Spain, southern and southwestern Gaul). Cities like Lyon and Hadrumetum lost importance, we really are not sure why, and their neighbors got bigger and fatter (I return to this subject a little later). Surely such changes can be observed in any large country over centuries, regardless of its being about to confront its final fall. It is this fact which accounts for a good deal of scholarly disagreement over the timing and severity of decline. Some bad signs can and have been found in every period, simply proofs of man-made things wearing out.[128] The soil of a district may become exhausted. But it will revive.

Granted the importance of prosperity, most people in the empire surely could not have felt they were inhabiting a world in decline during the period that would be proposed today for that description — say, from A.D. 300 to 450 — since the economy surrounding them was demonstrably healthy. That would be true of the more densely populated areas of the east and in a sizeable part of the west as well, in north Africa, until some point in the earlier fifth century. Norman Baynes in 1943 was by no means the first person to understand the plain fact that only the European provinces of the empire collapsed, and, as he explains very modestly, his perception was clarified by his approaching the problem as a Byzantinist.[129] He went on to stress the need to recognize that great fact in choosing any explanatory cause or hypothesis. Whatever was at work in the east but brought on no collapse could not fairly be used to explain what happened in the north and west. He asked rather for the identification of *differentia* between the more and the less fortunate regions as necessary for any good interpretation.

One obvious point of difference lies in degree of urbanization. It looks like a useful point to examine because, as is well known and has been reiterated in the paragraphs above on late Roman Pannonia westward into Gaul, Britain, and Spain, the cities went downhill while the civilization of the countryside retained its prosperity a generation or two longer, or even more, or actually grew more obviously prosperous than it had ever been before. The explanation I offered was a political one (see above p.25): government lacked the strength to insure the peace and security on which commercial inter-course depends, and on which cities depend, too. But large villas proved less vulnerable.

Of alternative explanations there are several to be considered. One is inflation. In terms of the dominant coin, the silver denarius, it proceeded gradually over the first two and a half centuries of the Principate, producing, so far as we can judge, something a little over a doubling of prices. It then rose somewhat steeply for a decade or so to the 260s, near the end of which further increases can be better measured, at least in Egypt, and were gigantic. The story thereafter involves a famous imperial edict regulating prices, a deflation-ary edict, a readjustment under Constantine, and the continuing very steep rise in prices as expressed in bronze currency. It is natural to suppose that all of these events had some serious effect on people's lives. Considering the various possibilities, "it seems likely that the small creditor class and urban pro-fessional (a teacher, for instance), but neither the peasant nor the magnate, suffered as the result of inflation."[130] Beyond such conjectures, Gunnar Mickwitz's good instinct led him to examine people's actual conduct of their affairs. While he could detect certain changes to protect themselves against abrupt price-changes, he could find no sign of major disruption. "Since the direct consequences of steep inflation in Egypt exerted no strong influence on the patterns of economic life, we may conclude that the contemporane-ously-indicated inflation elsewhere in the empire had still less consequence in these regards."[131] More recently, the careful reading of Libanius, Chrysos-tom, and other fourth-century authors has revealed a world in which the use of money, not exchange in kind, was entirely taken for granted.[132] As the evidence that is used comes from provinces with advanced economies, it is safe to guess that others of less complexity and sophistication were corre-spondingly less disturbed by inflation — which, then, cannot have contrib-uted very much to the deterioration of western cities.

Inflation, of course, arose principally from the government's minting more and more coins. There were other contributing factors but that was chief. Since those coins represented some value, inflated or not, it is natural to wonder if the value was being badly distributed in the empire and thus hurt certain parts of it. A quite tiny sample (estimated at 0.1 percent) of issues over

four centuries as they have been recovered from the soil of four regions —
northern Italy, southern France, northern France, and Britain — indeed
indicates pronounced differences in distribution. Compared to the other
three, "Britain shows a remarkably low proportion of coins before 259 and a
remarkably high proportion of coins after 330." In the course of a century and
more, A.D. 294–402, its bronze coins attained a first peak in numbers in
330–348 and an even more pronounced peak in 364–378.[133] Surely such
abundant coinage served and stimulated abundant commerce (that assumption has been generally made by scholars who report on currency levels in a
province or city they are studying). But in actual fact the natural centers of
exchange, the cities throughout the island, did not especially flourish during
the two periods of peak in question. Similarly puzzling, northern Italy's cities
certainly cannot have enjoyed a high of prosperity during the time of tension
between Constantine and Maxentius and the violent sieges of Susa, Torino,
Milano, and Verona, followed by more military engagements around Brescia
and elsewhere; but the region's volume of currency comes to a peak just in
the years 294–317. The curves and statistics thus contain serious anomalies.

We do not really know how coins moved around the empire in large
patterns. Cracco Ruggini draws attention to the wide representation of coins
from all over Europe circulating in north Italy even in the late empire. The
same signs of quite large webs of commerce and exchange can be seen
elsewhere.[134] It is usually assumed, however, that the principal agency by far
in currency distribution was the imperial government, through its collection
of taxes and payment of troops. In fact, the assumption involves several
processes. One is recycling. The rapidity and thoroughness with which the
government drew back the coins it had minted before it paid them out again
varied much from period to period. The reign of Valentinian, for illustration,
was in this respect very vigorous, most likely (though we cannot be sure)
because of his heavy program of frontier fortification. The nearest mint, at
Siscia, was certainly working overtime. In gold coinage alone, the rates of
issue and recall rose in every province to an entirely new and different level
from the beginning of the fourth century onward, whereas in bronze the pace
was far slower and varied from one province to another.[135] No doubt the
explanation lies in the need for donatives in gold to be given regularly to the
army. The emperors had continually to use and reuse a finite supply of the
precious metal for this purpose. But how this was changed into silver and
bronze, in which the great bulk of buying and selling was done, nobody can
really say. The weight as well as the direction of effect produced by the
government on the economy remain to that extent mysterious.

This introduces a second assumption commonly made about the distribution of money: that the army's size and the stationing of its units largely explain the initial placing of coins of *all* metals into circulation — indeed, explain the whole imperial budget, or most of it. But this is certainly far too simple a view and needs further refinement through a method recently much exploited: the quantification of coin issues across time.[136] The money supply ought to rise and fall according to the number of soldiers, the various pay raises across the history of the Roman legions, and special expenses associated with their active service. Those last could be very large indeed, far larger tnan anyone would offhandedly predict of a standing, salaried army.[137] When we look for the manifestation of such matters, however, in the rise and fall of mint activity, we do not always find what we would expect. We do not, for example, find any mints-and-military correlation during the last century and more of the Republic.[138] The year of the Four Emperors (A.D. 69), too, with their newly raised legions and all those legions' campaign and special bonuses to ensure their fidelity, lies along a rise on the graph that had begun several years earlier; and that rise is maintained without change for another several years (fig. 12).

When Domitian in A.D. 83 increased army pay by a third, the line already starts a steep decline — which simply continues! And when Caracalla (A.D. 211–217) added some 70 million denarii to his annual expenditures by still another increase in military pay, the line shows no reaction at all.[139] I assume, despite these and other evident anomalies, that the emperors' army costs did exercise a powerful effect on the imperial overall budget and that the pouring forth of larger quantities of debased silver in the third century, so striking in the graph, was somehow connected with armies and wars.[140] I assume so because there is no other apparent category of imperial debit or outflow that approaches the proportions of the military. Even if the latter can be estimated within certain broad limits, however,[141] it is at present impossible to attain the same rough degree of reliability in estimating the sum total of resources that the emperors commanded each year. The most recent attempt looks rather odd but is hard to control.[142] So we cannot be sure of the size of the nonmilitary part, nor of just where it was spent. If, for instance, the pay, perquisites, and maintenance of palatine personnel and construction in capital cities equalled the military budget for several provinces put together, that would make a difference in our calculations.

From this discussion, having gained only doubts and uncertainties, I return to my starting point a few pages back. The common assumption was there presented, that the empire's economy might have suffered because its yield was dysfunctionally distributed. Granted, the manner and agencies of distribution are not easy to understand; perhaps military expenditures did not after all so nearly monopolize the debit side of the ledger as one might at first

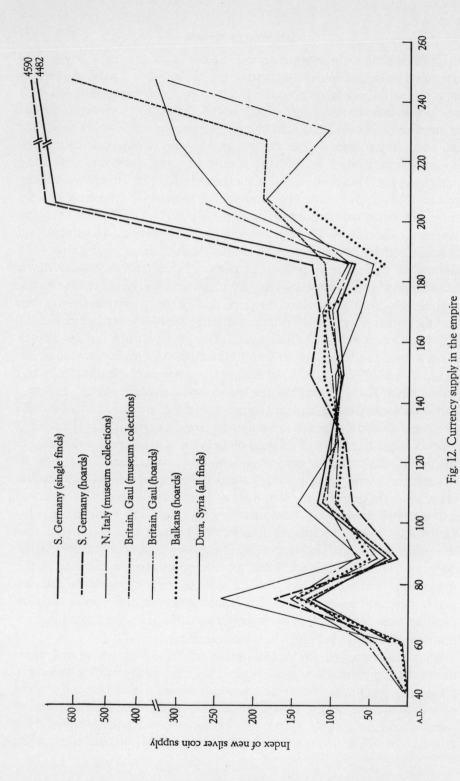

Fig. 12. Currency supply in the empire

S. Germany (single finds)

S. Germany (hoards)

N. Italy (museum collections)

Britain, Gaul (museum colections)

Britain, Gaul (hoards)

Balkans (hoards)

Dura, Syria (all finds)

Index of new silver coin supply

A.D.

4590
4482

suppose. Nevertheless, a great deal of importance attaches to that army payroll. Its stimulating effect upon the frontier zones and more backward provinces in the earlier empire is well known. Urban development, for example, of Lyon or Budapest (Aquincum), is credited to its operation. Since the cities later declined in just these same regions, the reason should then lie in the reversing of this process of development through the withdrawal of the troops and their payroll. But no correspondence appears between the level of prosperity in the provinces once they had developed and the number of troops stationed inside their borders.[143] As a means of explaining how the empire's economy, especially the urban economy, deteriorated where and when it did, the army's history seems to be of little help except insofar as the army failed in its chief function — security. That failure still remains the most likely means of explanation.

Finally, the relation between army size and weight of taxation. If we could trust literary sources, the later empire was one vast armed camp. Its forces of defense were quadrupled around the turn of the fourth century — that would mean well over a million men — and still numbered 645,000 "under the emperors of yore." So say Lactantius, a contemporary of that first statistic in the early fourth century, and Agathias, looking back from a date near the mid-sixth century. A. H. M. Jones, of great and deserved authority, accepts the latter; but Agathias' statement seems to me as ridiculous as Lactantius'.[144] I would set the army total at or under 400,000 throughout the period covered by our two ancient authors. For other purposes, with other arguments and in another context, I return to the matter later (pp. 173f., 185). Here, the point rather lies in the relation between army size and taxes. Whatever that size, did it strain the economy and thus contribute to or even principally account for the decline of Rome?

In answering the question we should not assume at the outset that all taxation in and of itself was automatically dysfunctional. That Roman rule brought with it the collection of tribute and strict, sometimes brutal, exploitation, was not wholly bad; for "fields, some for the first time in their history, must be made to yield not only sustenance for the families that worked them, but a bit extra for a tax, and extra beyond that, for sale to their neighbors," the occupying forces.[145] The point is a little paradoxical, but important. Heightened productivity and a greater need to accumulate cash, with attendant stimulation of commerce at the most natural points of exchange — namely cities — all followed from conquest. These benefits were only what one saw at first glance. Beneath them were others: a variety of new demands introduced by the conquerors, including demand for strange things to eat and drink and strange shapes and designs of vessels from which to eat them; new and more efficient devices and methods of production, including agricultural production; and, after a little while, a market for such novelties that reached beyond the Romans to the Romanized. So the economy, at least in the European provinces and in the early centuries of occupation, clearly improved.

For taxes to have been an agent in the destruction of the empire's economy requires then that they be increased beyond the levels prevalent in "good" times, let us say under the Antonines. They must rise above all capacity to respond, above all beneficially stimulating levels, to the tyrannous and oppressive. How is such a rise to be shown? In default of statistics or statistical hypothesizing that can be trusted, there seems to be no better evidence than the intensity of protest — the government's, in legislation, and the citizens', in cries of outrage — and the accumulation of arrears. Arrears testify to an inability to pay or an inability to collect. In either case, they may fairly be called a bad sign. In the rare settings in which those under the Principate can be measured, they seem to be very considerable: 15 million denarii a year apparently in Italy alone (which had no land tax to worry about), in the early second century; over 12 percent in central Greece in the early first century; 50 percent or more in Egypt in the first and second centuries in certain years and places.[146] These levels remain about as high after A.D. 300 as before.[147] The government then threatens force, it rewards delators.[148] In spite of all, quite uncollectable *reliqua* in the 430s stretching back forty years had to be graciously remitted; just as at other times, in the later empire rulers still burnt the accumulated records of delinquency in the same manner initiated by Trajan.

And why such remissions during the 'decline'? Explanation lies not in the soft heart and easy-going nature of government in those times, which was in fact most savage; but rather, in the realities of enforcement. Influential people could wangle immunity either as individuals or as a class: "the registrars of the municipalities through collusion are transferring the burden of the taxes of *potentiores* to *inferiores*," Constantine angrily declares in 313; or again, in 384, the entire body of senators in Thrace and Macedonia are excused from paying anything at all on their lands.[149] It is the corrupting of the whole process of distribution and collection, not absolute weight, that distinguishes taxation in the decline from taxation during the Principate; for the change appears to date to about the turn of the fourth century.[150] It affects the yield ultimately delivered to the emperors, it affects the development and exercise of rural patronage (*patrocinium*), as well as real and fraudulent landownership; it affects many things, and will need emphasis again, later.

For the moment, there is only one further aspect of collection that needs to be noticed: the wild swings in the quantity of taxes actually raised. Julian, in the most extreme instance known, discovered the prefect in Gaul routinely inflating his demands three and a half times above the authorized. Three hundred and fifty percent is a lot. Rates real or proclaimed appear to have varied pretty generally according to the decision of each governor or prefect.[151] The looseness of such a system facilitated as well as reflected that corruption just emphasized.

So, then: how was late imperial taxation harmful? How, if at all, did it account for any general decline? The question would have provoked some very angry expostulation from the various petitioners for relief, the fugitives from their own debts, merchant and peasant alike, whose voices sound through our surviving documents. A papyrus of Constantine's reign tells of Pamonthius the wine dealer in Egypt who, "being long importuned by the magistrates of his native place with exactions beyond his means, and having for this reason borrowed a great sum of money, and being asked for this and not being able to meet his liabilities, he was compelled by his creditors to sell all that he had, even to the garments that cover his shame; and when these were sold, scarcely could he get together the half of the money for his creditors, who, those pitiless and godless men, carried off all his children."[152]

A moving story; certainly a true one, too. But it could be matched by Philo's eyewitness account nearly three centuries before, and many other similar scenes. It is easy to believe that, as the Haves of the later empire wiggled out of their tax obligations and, for a price, protected those beneath them who had a little land to transfer to their ownership without giving up residence, in the end the more modest and perhaps less aggressive property owners alone were left to bear the whole burden of government demands. Easy to believe but not easy to prove.

I do not dismiss the general reduction of inhabited sites in large regions of Europe and the clustering of the rural population around more ample estates; but that is most easily explained through fear of brigandage or barbarians, not fear of the tax collector (and notice that the reverse happened in parts of the Syrian countryside, though under the same emperors and laws). I do not dismiss the appearance of patronage in rural settings opposing the intrusion of government, whether local or imperial. That is a new phenomenon. But it may actually have worked! — that is, the peasants sheltering under it may have successfully avoided their obligations toward the legitimate authorities. If we can trust the Forty-seventh Oration of Libanius, the villagers serving his family for generations were as well-off in the 300s as at any other time. So we can say also of those same small landholders to the east that I just referred to. As Tchalenko showed, their fortunes were not only improving in this period but went on improving in the centuries that followed. And to the south, corresponding populations of Palestine and Egypt prospered (above, section 3). The countryside of certain European provinces prospered, though more in villas than in villages. It is true that considerable acreage of once-cultivated land was being reported as unworked, from time to time in the later empire. Its totals, however, except in north Africa after A.D. 420, amount to about what one would expect, given the continual temptation among the poor and landless to try their luck on marginal hillsides or semidesert. Then whatever they tried would be registered in the tax lists, and in a few years would be again deserted — and so listed. Under the more careful adding up of taxable resources that characterized the administration after Diocletian, the total of *agri deserti* would thus fast accumulate; but it would tell us more about the habits of late Roman government than about agriculture.[153]

In sum, the inequity and unlawful distortion of taxes does not seem to have had the demonstrable effects that might be expected. A puzzle. But perhaps the distortion affected some group not yet properly considered; and, if taxes are really to be "the root cause of the economic decline of the empire," as A. H. M. Jones believed,[154] there should be no problem in finding such a group. It is the town councillors, the decurions, *curiales*.

The absolutely crucial role played by this small body in the development of everything we admire, and contemporaries valued, in the civilization of the ancient world over the course of its latter four or five centuries is very familiar. On their wealth and spirit everything depended: political leadership, religious leadership, most tasks of urban and district administration, the representing of the city to the imperial authorities, the covering of costs for spectacles and celebrations, and the care, upkeep, and amplifying of all physical facilities, from street-paving to the painting of frescoes on the walls of their own meeting-hall. At Antioch, however, Libanius again and again deplores the reduced honor and dwindling numbers of decurions around him. They are beaten, terrorized, humiliated — and bankrupted. So they flee their status. The vivid picture he paints can be aligned with material in the Theodosian Code, where nearly two hundred constitutions in the title *de decurionibus* testify to the preoccupying importance of the subject. So much consideration given to it shows also how continual was the need for repair and correction. Libanius is confirmed. All the empire was suffering from a universal deterioration in its most crucial part. The root cause: taxation. For this, decurions were responsible even with their own capital, should their efforts at collection fall short of the required totals.

The line of argument here sketched is long established and its various parts amplified by much discussion. It seems to me essentially correct. I would only wish to suggest a few modifications.

Even at the height of its brilliance, the civilization of the cities could not count on the patriotism and generosity of absolutely all its qualified citizens. They tried to avoid enrollment in the curia, to say nothing of avoiding the consequent duties that might come their way.[155] Where such behavior is found after the second century, of course, it can be interpreted as the onset of later fatal tendencies. The falling off of civic spirit in the third century, however, is not easily read nor universal;[156] and there is decidedly too much of that civic spirit still attested in the fourth and fifth — too much, that is, for the usual argument. Claude Lepelley has called attention to its many proofs in north Africa: the citizen of Macomades in Numidia constructing an arch "for the honor of being priest of the imperial cult" in 364–67, illustrative of habits of generosity and ambition still able to endow the cities with those public amenities reviewed above. The honorific listing of the ranks of Timgad's elite in the 360s bears exactly the character of the second century. Piganiol would dismiss it: "In truth, all this beautiful structure is unreal; the magistracies are no more than costly liturgies, *munera*" — "in other words," as Lepelley comments caustically, "since the description has made the mistake of contradicting the historical perspective of modern writers, it can be said without hesitation that it was wrong and its testimony valueless."[157] But even near the very end of the fourth century, Augustine can speak in general terms of "people who even want to ruin themselves by funding actors, theatrical performers, performers in wild beast spectacles, and chariot drivers. How much do they give! How much do they spend! They pour forth their resources, not only their ancestral property but their very souls.... Most who fund spectacles must lament the sale of their villas." No better proof could be asked of the vitality of civic ambition in Augustine's day.

Public entertainment, all sex and violence, of which Augustine had so low an opinion, remained very much the same in Italy as it had been earlier; and, whether Augustine was right or wrong in his estimate of it, at least there is no disputing its great cost, which fell on decurions or their equivalent in Rome (the senators) and provided a good indication of the sense of pride and responsibility among the urban elite. There was plenty of that sense in Italy.[158] In Antioch likewise, John Chrysostom noted and deplored quite similar exhibitions only too lavishly provided by the wealthy[159] and, in an extended description, evokes the magic that moved the urban aristocracy to their efforts:[160]

The theater fills, and the whole citizenry is seated up there, presenting the most brilliant spectacle made up of so many faces, that the very topmost gallery and its covering is blocked out by men's bodies.... Upon the entrance of that benefactor who brought them together, they leap to their feet, uttering a salute as from a single mouth, with one voice calling him guardian and leader of their common city. They stretch forth their arms; then at intervals they compare him to the greatest of all rivers; they liken the grandeur and flow of his civic generosity, in its abundance, to the waters of the Nile, and they call him a very Nile of gifts, himself; and some who flatter still more, declaring the comparison with the Nile too mean, set aside rivers and seas and bring in Ocean, and they say that is what he is, as Ocean among waters, so he in his gifts. They omit no possible term of praise. . . . He himself bows to them, and by this pays his respects, and so he seats himself among the blessings of all, who, every one of them, pray to be such as he— and then to die. . . . And while he revels in his heart's desire like a person drunk with vainglory, to the point that he would spend his very self, he can take in no least sensation of his losses. But when he is at home, . . . then at that moment he understands they were no dream but a reality in hard cash.

This vivid scene no doubt repeated itself across the generations of the decline throughout the east. We need not rely on guesswork. Sermons survive, inscriptions also.[161] We have witnessed such scenes in Carthage and Beneventum. To our astonishment, we learn of a certain "Masclinius Maternus, decurion, ex-aedile, ex-duumvir, ex-curator, priest of the imperial cult, ex-Count of Colonia Agrippinensis" (Cologne) in A.D. 352.[162] Exactly the same sort of person gaining only slightly different titles by just about the same long effort of expenditure and ambition had animated the city centuries earlier. No one can doubt that much had changed over the interval; and yet, in the presence of Masclinius, it is not easy to dogmatize about the extent of the change. He existed. Lacking any density of documentation for his region and period, we are hard put to say whether he was one of very few or one of many. Only the archeological record helps a little in trying to quantify the deterioration of cities in the northwest, just as it more amply confirms the testimony of Augustine, Symmachus, Chrysostom, and others in the more prosperous parts of the empire.

There is one other piece of quantifiable information: of ten laws promul- gated from Constantine's death to mid-century attempting to prevent decurions from deserting their status and its obligations, no less than eight deal with the west, only two with the east.[163] The proportion of decline in the curiae indicated in this way, if it can be trusted, fits with other portions of the picture. It also recalls once-conventional views about the history of late Roman cities: that the life — their elite —was being crushed out of them by the weight of demands laid on them. Nothing else explains the insistent urge of decurions to get out of their curiae. So we return to the older consensus, having presented the modifications that seem necessary in the light of more recent studies.

How insistent that urge to escape really was among decurions can be sensed in their success. It has often been discussed, and illustrations are easy to find. There is, from A.D. 299, the very matter-of-fact statement in the course of official correspondence, that a certain Plutarchus from Egypt, "endeavoring to find for himself a release from municipal offices, some time ago besought the divine fortune of Our Masters the Augusti and Caesars to grant him the rank of 'Excellency,' and the divine fortune consented and granted it" — that is, he was elevated to equestrian rank, which brought with it exemption from the post of decemprimus. The whole process sounds no more complicated than applying for a driver's license, though no doubt there would be some charges to pay. A long generation later, the emperor declares, in a law issued in the east, "Since there is no doubt that curiae have been emptied of decurions who offer as defense the titles they have bought," let all such unmerited exemptions be withdrawn. In spite of which, as Libanius saw it another generation afterwards, in 363, the curiae suffered a drastic decline under Constantius: "They were nothing at all, since nearly the whole of their membership had slipped away to be soldiers or senators." Finally, he says of decurions in Antioch in his own day, one more generation later, "We used to be six hundred — nay, twice that number, by Zeus! But now we are sixty."[164]

The sense of progressive decay conveyed by this series of documents can be enhanced by more detail from Libanius' literary corpus. He mentions a large number of people of his class over the span of his life. From these it can be seen that nearly half of the decurions got out of their rank, or tried to.[165] For dozens of his own friends who wished to escape he assiduously pulled strings and wrote letters. He himself was free through his post as professor of rhetoric; his brother Panolbus left the curia by taking a state job, and his children were likewise lost, one of them (Spectatus) becoming a *notarius* under Constantius while his sister married a praetorian prefect. Their children in turn went into government jobs and connections. Typical.

But to judge from the facts presented a page or two earlier, traditions of attachment to curiae died hard. Many families, or parts of families, could not give them up at all. They retained all the incentive to service that they had had in the Principate, and no doubt the dominant ethos during most of late antiquity, to which city nobles would subscribe even while violating it, required the continuing of noblesse oblige toward one's own fellow citizenry. At the same time, the avenues of exit were many and obviously inviting. Plutarchus from Egypt seems to have gained an individual release without the least difficulty. The contrast with Aelius Aristides' struggles a century and a half earlier (I will return to those briefly, below p. 134) is stark. Slightly later laws suggest how Plutarchus did it: by purchase. Many whole categories of persons were excused: Jews, clerics, guild members (e.g. *centonarii* and *navicularii*), physicians, schoolteachers and professors, soldiers and civil servants (*scriniarii* and *cohortales*). Some of these categories were extremely large.[166] Where it was so simple a matter, or at least quite open to money and effort, to escape, escapes there would be. As most cities had never had a very numerous elite beyond the hundred or so required for decurions, the continued draining away of even a few dozens every decade would have serious consequences for those that remained. Every decade would therefore increase the inducement among the remnant to buy themselves out.

This was well know to the emperors, but not in time. After a while they tried to withdraw privileges and exemptions that they had offered earlier, for example, to clerics. The history of the subject is quite active and complicated. But a chief difficulty defeated them: they were really not in control of their own government, from which a great deal that was never intended by the laws nor by the makers of those laws could be at any time obtained. That large subject remains for the third chapter, as does also the question why "government lacked the strength to insure peace and security."

I repeat these words from a point (p. 37) some pages earlier to show a developing line of argument. In the course of the present review of the causes of 'decline,' I certainly do not intend to suggest that the empire really enjoyed perfect health in all its functions nor that all the 'causes' together added up to nothing but confusion. In fact, the two aspects of weakness already before us — hemorrhaging of the curias and lack of physical security — seem to me adequate to explain the differences between the faltering cities of the north and west, and those of the empire's more prosperous regions. As to the faltering cities, it was insecurity destroying their commerce and depletion of their curiae that operated in combination to bring them down. In this conclusion, however, there is really nothing new, and its level of explanation is rather close to the surface. It is still to be discovered why such a stream of refugees from municipal leadership was ever allowed to flow away, generation after generation, and why safe travel for commercial intercourse could not be insured by so very large an army.

While they appear victims, decurions from another point of view also earned the reputation of oppressors. They, or at least some of them, were both great landowners and in charge of apportioning the city's tax burden. Hence, a double opportunity to intimidate, brutalize, and extort. They are accused of all this in certain passages of the late fourth and fifth centuries. Of one such, Salvian is the author, often quoted: "every decurion a tyrant," he says;[167] and Augustine, for another, describes how poor people around Hippo were turning to the church "against the wickedness of powerful persons, *potentiores*, by whom they are being ground down." The right is no doubt on their side, but only the church "may protect them and avail to assert the laws passed in their defense." Why so? Why could the government not do its job? The answer may wait till my third chapter. With the situation before us, a law of a century earlier may be compared, clearly pointing to the cause of the trouble: "The assessment of extraordinary public services shall not be entrusted to chief decurions, *principales*, and therefore the governors of the provinces shall be admonished that they duly perform this assessment, and with their own hand they shall write out and in ink annex the names of the taxpayers." The insistence on autograph copies is repeated. It is of course an almost unique provision, required by the need strictly to control just who, in what amounts, appeared on those fateful lists.[168] And only the topmost official in his own person would be strong enough to see the law impartially administered.

The contradiction between the two views of decurions, as sufferers or inflictors of suffering, is easily resolved. Most were victims, a few were *potentiores*. Over the course of the third century a sort of elite or executive committee of ten (occasionally of twenty) persons took shape within curiae. These were the *principales* of the law; also, they were or included "the more powerful" of the city.[169] As the fourth century progressed they received increasing prominence in legal, literary, and epigraphic sources — the latter, most clearly in north Africa. Their vast wealth placed them among the foremost public benefactors. They lorded it over the local *defensor* and *curator*, officials intended to introduce an imperial presence inside the cities and thereby to reduce the exploitation of the weak by the strong. In Antioch they had become so many chairmen of specific municipal operations,[170] and many of them did not disdain the chair of honor in which were seated the benefactors Chrysostom describes at the center of the civic theater (above, p. 46).

They had to compete, however, with an even more distinguished group of high officials resident in cities: officials who represented the emperor in a province, as governors or dukes or counts; in a diocese, as *vicarii*; in either one, as fiscal agents; or as close advisers in the palace itself, wherever the emperor made his capital. Besides Rome and Constantinople, many other centers received the court for longer or shorter intervals, from the mid-third century on: Milan, Trier, Arles, Aquileia, Ravenna, Carnuntum, Naissus, Sirmium, Serdica, Thessalonica, Nicomedia, Antioch.[171] It is noticeable how often the late Roman cities which are characterized by their excavators as rich are explained in terms of resident emperors or great officials, through having enjoyed the status of provincial capital: Sirmium, Sopianae, Arles, Trier, London, and other towns in Britain distinguished by rich villas built in their suburbs; also Emerita, for the same reason; at Cuicul and elsewhere in north

Africa; and Antioch in Syria and smaller cities in Asia Minor. The converse is described for us, too, by Basil *(Epp.* 74 and 76): when a thriving town is demoted from being the capital of a big province to being the center only of a small one, it suffers a terrible loss in both wealth and population. Not only rulers and officials but the troops that served as guard to such centers also brought in money, as they did to towns in which they were posted for strategic purposes.[172] Given both the excavators' comments and the logic of the situation, it is safe to say that the anomalous examples of urban prosperity in the northern and western provinces are without exception due to their governmental status. Trier is merely the clearest case; and the anonymous *Expositio totius mundi* (chap. 58) chimes in from the point of view of a contemporary: Antioch enjoys an abundance of everything enjoyable. "And why everything? Because that is where the emperor resides and everything is needed on his account."

That the emperors were generous builders in the cities where they stayed is well known. They built not only palaces for themselves but every other kind of edifice worthy of their efforts. Instances are mentioned in section 3, above: Nicomedia, Seleuceia. But their officials, especially governors, almost matched them in generosity and zeal. To discover how closely, in the Principate, we have ample evidence among inscriptions. Inscriptions become rare after the mid-third century. Combined with literary sources, however, these later texts tell of construction performed by governors throughout Italy in dozens of cities; in Byzacena, Numidia, and Proconsularis in north Africa, in Egypt (a canal), in Achaea at Athens, in Asia Minor at Sardis, Aphrodisias, and Anemurium, all in a pattern of activity that stimulated governors even to rob architectural elements from small towns in order to beautify the large ones.[173] The only city known about in any detail, Antioch, fully confirms this random sampling. After listing all the construction up to a date around 390, Paul Petit concludes that "the greater part of edifices and facilities of the century are owing to imperial office-holders."[174] Whether they were spending municipal money as is sometimes made explicit, specifically but not only for city walls, or whether they were simply the agents for their sovereign's ambitions, is not always clear. Of course it was traditional to the role of emperor that he should foster urban growth,[175] and there are many examples of his doing that — more, it would seem, than in earlier centuries. The economy of cities in that direct fashion, as well as indirectly through the money brought into and spent in the neighborhood of the court by prefects, vicars, and governors, thus depended heavily on the government. Why there was quite so much money in the hands of high officials is a question to be addressed later (chap. 3).

Of all late imperial building, the most complete and glowing picture is found in Eusebius' biography of Constantine, filling most of the third book. It is all ecclesiastical. Since the history of the church tends to be encapsulated among its own readers and experts, just as the history of the ancient world (non-Christian) is likewise encapsulated, discussions of the 'decline' sometimes omit to mention the prodigious amount of construction needed to accommodate the new faith. The evidence invites but has never received broad, synthetic treatment. A good idea of the dimensions of the phenomenon can be gained from city plans of Sitifis, Timgad, or Djemila in north Africa. They show how much activity there must have been in the century before the Vandal invasion, to produce new churches.[176] Milan and, marginally, Tours can also be evaluated for intensity of ecclesiastical construction in the period after 375. Glimpses of certain times and places in the eastern provinces are much clearer.[177] "Many are building walls and setting columns for the church. The marbles glisten, the ceilings shine with gold, the altar is picked out with precious stones." In Syria a small number of inscriptions suggest that fourth- and fifth-century public construction was largely paid for by church officials from the funds at their disposal privately or ex officio. And of course secular funding also built churches there, too.[178] When assessment is made of the level of energy in the late Roman economy, all of this must be remembered.

It must be recalled also how this subject came up in the first place: as a test of a theory. Did excessive demands made by the state on the city elites depress their condition, so that those who had not escaped their civic obligations went bankrupt, and along with them urban civilization? That was the theory. From a review of the condition of decurions, it does appear that they suffered over the course of the two centuries, let us say, after A.D. 250. A pretty considerable shakeout took place; the weaker or slipperier members disappeared from the curia. The stronger remained, however — and with them remained the spirit of civic ambition, of *philotimia*, first developed among the old Greek cities and infused into the Roman by Cicero's lifetime. It had made temples; in due course, cathedrals — for it is this spirit and nothing else that can be found in primitive Christianity to account for the fourth-century glories of ecclesiastical construction. Public games, *venationes*, *ludi*, parades, and banquets continued also to be funded. Even the water supply to countless street-corner fountains was successfully maintained.

So the theory doesn't work, and the simpler and older alternatives remain: the cities declined in some areas, such as Italy, because of changing patterns of production and commerce, and in other areas, such as Germany, Moesia, or Gaul, because there was too frequent, too serious risk on the roads or along the rivers and coasts. Urban ties with the surrounding countryside, still more

across whole provinces or overseas, unravelled. Not that all wealth whatsoever disappeared. Its basis had always been agriculture. Close to that source,
the same great villas that had dotted the richer rural areas of all these lands
still stood, or new ones to replace the old arose, in Ausonius' time, even in the
time of Rutilius (1.25). He mourns the recent destruction of his own by
barbarian invaders. The property of many other Gallic nobles endured
undisturbed. But the archeology of late Roman urban centers in the west, as
opposed to the countryside, is of course decisive.

Failure to keep out raiders or to control rural unrest as a military task in late
Roman Gaul and Spain, where it is attested, and in other provinces such as
Pannonia where it may be inferred from the fortifying of villas, is not easily
explained. Collapse before the big raids of A.D. 405, 407, and later is still more
puzzling. I offer some thoughts about this in the fourth chapter. Explanation
may of course simply acknowledge force majeure.[179] Thus, "ultimately Rome
fell because it was conquered. German tribes took over the Western part of
the empire. If we want a cause," continues Arnaldo Momigliano, "this is the
cause; and we may dignify it by calling it the military superiority of the
conquerors. The truth is that we do not want that cause because we rightly
feel that it does not make the situation meaningful: it is too obvious or too
trivial really to explain what happened."

But something better is sometimes sought in two linked considerations:
that the mass of the population cannot have had any spirit, courage, or love
of country, and that they handed over their fate to barbarian defenders.
Leaders there were, and "in the elite of that period an enlightened, sincere
patriotism. But," continues Camille Jullian in 1926, offering an example of this
interpretation, "it is highly probable that the common folk, the proletariat and
slaves, had little interest in Rome and the empire: the brilliance of the Latin
light did not reach down to them nor was it able to warm them; they knew
the State only by the recruiting sergeant who sent them off to the armies or
the fiscal agent who took from their trifling wealth."[180] True enough, I would
guess. It is perhaps idle to speculate at any length. There were looters and
traitors from among the civilian populace in the mid-third century when the
Goths attacked Pontus. It is likely they were the poorer folk from the villages;
but the peasants of Syria opposed the raiders Sapor led in the same years.[181]
Similarly, Ammianus and other scattered sources of the later fourth and
earlier fifth centuries mention occasional instances of supine surrender, even
of collaboration, but also instances of something quite different. In Thrace,
Phrygia, Pamphylia, Cyrenaica, and Spain we happen to hear of civilian self-
help against raids and invasions during these same fifty years or so. The
balance does not seem to prove very much except the obvious truth: Rome's

empire was no city-state, it was too big to stimulate devotion, and the central government was of little or no help in time of need.[182] To that last fact I will return for more discussion in my last chapter.

What might rather have been expected and did appear in the later empire can be sensed in a graph showing where the real soldiers, not mere local volunteers or militia, were recruited (fig. 13). The dotted lines emphasize how primacy as a recruitment area passed from Italy to the lower Danube. The data compiled by Giovanni Forni[183] are subject to various criticisms and corrections. To make them tell the truth, they would first need to be set against the frequency-curve of both Greek and Latin inscriptions — though there is something to be learned from papyri and other types of sources as a means of control. Then the varying likelihood of information surviving from individual civilian or military sites in one or another of the four periods would have to be weighed. Italy in particular provides us with an immensely disproportionate number of all Latin inscriptions. And so forth. Beyond all such qualification, however, the statistics, being used not absolutely but relatively, seem quite reliably to demonstrate one fact: that the liking for a military career steadily diminished over time according to length of experience of the *pax Romana*. The longer a population had enjoyed security and some degree of membership in the empire, the less likely its youth would be enrolled in the legions.

The explanation is not sinister. It can be read in the words of Joseph Chamberlain addressed to Parliament in 1893. He says:[184] "In the old days we had to fight with the Punjabees, and when we had conquered them they supplied us with our best soldiers in India. But now that we have established peace, and the country is more prosperous than ever before, and people, who were once the most warlike race in India, are settling down, or I should say rising up, into agriculturalists and peasants, we cannot get from them an adequate number of recruits for our Army. We have to go farther afield."

By the same inevitability the Romans first went mostly to Cisalpine and southern Gaul for their soldiers, while at the end they were drawing on the Danube frontier provinces to a degree very notable indeed; and if inscriptions on which we chiefly depend for our information existed in unchanging bulk up to the decades of the barbarian thrust into the empire, in A.D. 407, let us say, or to the A.D. 420s, we could expect to see in them the northward drift of the recruitment process simply continuing, until it lapped over the frontiers and began to draw on populations to whom fighting was, for young males, still a natural part of life. For the Roman as for the British empire, the habituating of subject peoples to a condition of enforced peace made it hard to fill up the draft.

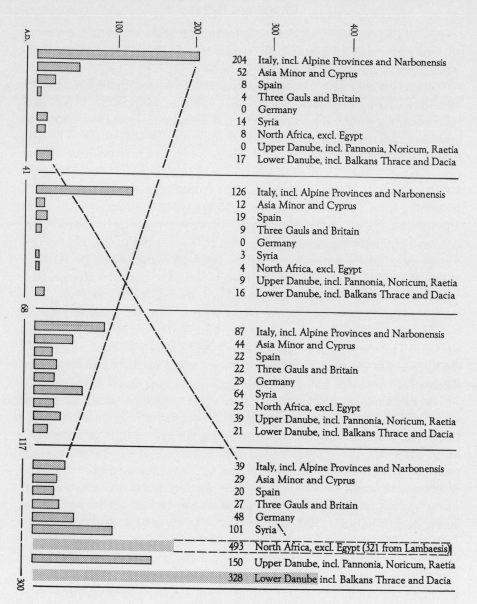

204	Italy, incl. Alpine Provinces and Narbonensis			
52	Asia Minor and Cyprus			
8	Spain			
4	Three Gauls and Britain			
0	Germany			
14	Syria			
8	North Africa, excl. Egypt			
0	Upper Danube, incl. Pannonia, Noricum, Raetia			
17	Lower Danube, incl. Balkans Thrace and Dacia			
126	Italy, incl. Alpine Provinces and Narbonensis			
12	Asia Minor and Cyprus			
19	Spain			
9	Three Gauls and Britain			
0	Germany			
3	Syria			
4	North Africa, excl. Egypt			
9	Upper Danube, incl. Pannonia, Noricum, Raetia			
16	Lower Danube, incl. Balkans Thrace and Dacia			
87	Italy, incl. Alpine Provinces and Narbonensis			
44	Asia Minor and Cyprus			
22	Spain			
22	Three Gauls and Britain			
29	Germany			
64	Syria			
25	North Africa, excl. Egypt			
39	Upper Danube, incl. Pannonia, Noricum, Raetia			
21	Lower Danube, incl. Balkans Thrace and Dacia			
39	Italy, incl. Alpine Provinces and Narbonensis			
29	Asia Minor and Cyprus			
20	Spain			
27	Three Gauls and Britain			
48	Germany			
101	Syria			
493	North Africa, excl. Egypt (321 from Lambaesis)			
150	Upper Danube, incl. Pannonia, Noricum, Raetia			
328	Lower Danube incl. Balkans Thrace and Dacia			

Fig 13. Origins of legionary recruits

In a later chapter the matter of barbarians in the Romans' service will recur for discussion. Here, it appears only among the items of general indictment laid against the later empire. On the cultural level and in the European provinces, there can be no doubt that the influx of strangers across the borders, ordinarily as captives or refugees in the wake of Rome's victorious wars, gradually exceeded her powers of assimilation. Then the manner of burial and the content of graves begins to show a way of life which is quite alien, discoverable in isolated locations in upper Germany, even in the earliest Principate. Generally, however, it is not until the third century that such archeological evidence turns up, and only in the fourth that it abounds. Its occurrences extend west from the Black Sea clear to the mouth of the Rhine and beyond, into Britain, and can be aligned with scores of mentions of barbarian settlements in written sources.[185]

The visible effect on the way of life as it was lived over considerable tracts extending deep into the empire — to the Thames and Garonne, for example, or to northwestern Spain before A.D. 400 — and the resulting impression the observer must form, that the political frontier no longer represented very much of importance to the long developments of history, both find confirmation in our other sources. They are literary, showing the same penetration by north-barbarian images: into military slang-terms and into the habits or procedures that went with them, such as *drungus* in Latin or Greek and the derived *droungarii* of Byzantium, or the war chant, *barritus*.[186] The sources may be the decorative arts, showing us in a fourth-century fresco or mosaic the novel items of clothing introduced into the court by barbarians. From Panticapaeum comes a well-known silver dish displaying in relief a diademed ruler, Constantius II perhaps, in Sarmatian fashion astride his horse in riding trousers and a riding coat — the later Byzantine skaramangion. As is well known, too, the emperors' coronation ceremonies were in various essential respects barbarian, not Roman, from the days of Julian onwards. Still earlier, Eusebius recollects how "I myself have sometimes stood near the entrance of the imperial palace and observed a noticeable array of barbarians in attendance, differing from each other in costume and decoration. . . . All of them in turn would present to the emperor those gifts which their own nation held most in esteem, some offering . . . barbaric garments embroidered with gold flowers." It was in exactly those garments, down to the very words Eusebius chooses, "embroidered with gold and flowers," that he elsewhere describes Constantine himself; but Caracalla far earlier had been the first to make respectable, nay regal, the wearing of such exotic finery. So the development being traced here had a long history.

Whether it belongs to the 'decline' or not may be debated. With other items of cultural change, such as the very portrayal of its subjects, stiff and full-faced, in the Panticapaeum dish as in the Ravenna mosaics, these 'barbarisms' in language, dress, and ceremony represent deterioration only if it can be proved that older Roman ways were good absolutely. *De gustibus non est disputandum!* Indeed, the Roman success from earliest times surely owed much to its capacity to absorb quite alien elements. It is, however, a more serious question whether cultural change weakened other, political, loyalties. The answer appears to be, not in any destructive or significant ways. The aliens themselves, at least the more prominent ones that are much talked about, generally receive a pretty good report for their loyalty from modern historians. Witness Stilicho (died A.D. 408) — but there are hundreds of others whose careers could have been traced just as well by a person of interempire origins.[187] Both of Stilicho's daughters (not at once!) married Honorius, after Stilicho himself had married Theodosius' niece; while Bauto's daughter married Arcadius and Athaulf married Theodosius' daughter. Surely those links testify to the fidelity assumed in the great commanders.

Yet Philostorgius sees in Athaulf's union the kingdom of iron and clay which can end only in the Kingdom of God.[188] And was it a sign of trust or a bribe that the royal house offered so generously? The test should not be whether the barbarians were unwilling to betray the empire to their brothers across the frontier, where there could hardly be much profit for them, but whether they refused to betray their masters to their own schemes and ambitions. Arbogast is one answer; Allobichus the Count of the Imperial Horseguard in 409 is another, who plotted the overthrow of Honorius and the transfer of his realm to Constantine III. But with these tergiversations we have entered a time of barbarian kingdoms and no less than six Augusti. Allobichus could not be blamed for all of them.[189]

Now to conclude this circuit of what seem to be the likelier causes of the empire's weakness: I cannot review them all once again, and I certainly cannot claim to have presented them all in the best and most convincing manner possible. Yet two points, sufficient for my purpose, I think I can discern. First, when the condition of each of the various regions of the empire is considered separately, in the light of recent studies, we can see that they did not all share one and the same experience, but some measurably deteriorated while others flourished. No account of the 'decline,' nor so much as the word itself, can claim validity if it does not apply to and assist in explaining the empire as a whole. As to the parts that did deteriorate in their urban civilization and subsequently dissolved into barbarian kingdoms, the common view — that the curial class and *pax Romana* were not adequately defended — seems to me still true. Yet it needs explanation.

For, second, any discussion should not only make the political narrative of the fourth and fifth centuries easier to understand, but understandable at a level of some depth. Momigliano was right: no one wants simply to be told that the invaders were too strong. To say that is to say too little. *Why* were they too strong, and the Romans to the same degree weak?

In reviewing the historical phenomena of the previous pages, the occasional hints of something helpful to be further considered seem to me to center in the capacities of government. Those hints appeared in connection with the security problem itself, in the European provinces, as also in connection with the deterioration of the curiae; and here and there elsewhere. It will be the task of the pages that follow to develop these hints and see if they open up a view that is neither superficial nor confined to some but not all of the empire.

2
POWER
EFFECTIVE

1. THE OBJECTIVE IN OUTLINE

Roman government has been much studied — from the top down. What the emperors did as emperors is amply reported; also, what proconsuls did; how the great jurisconsults worked and thought; the manner of command over the legions; all that sort of thing. It all deserves study; for government concentrates in the hands of a few people claims on the compliance of many. Thus its structure and operations help to explain how events developed.

However, even in the most heavily bureaucratic or tyrannous modern states, everybody is conscious of obeying private individuals as well: employers most of all, and every day; elder members of the family; teachers, for a time; perhaps also an instructor in one's religious beliefs; purveyors of services, like a headwaiter or the bus driver who asks everyone to move to the rear, please; not to mention some angry drunk at a subway station. Compliance claimed for the demands of all these categories of persons has its own importance, its own history.

In the ancient world, however, claims on compliance, public and private, were asserted in utterly different proportions. Officialdom occupied only a very minor place in life. Its agents were a mere handful; its means of reaching people, few and primitive. Police were virtually nonexistent. There were no social workers or public defenders. Nor were the needs for services that were not addressed by the state adequately addressed by commercial enterprise. Quite to the contrary: there were no bail-bondsmen, no detective agencies, no nursing or real estate or insurance agencies, no lending agencies or banks, no professional advisors about the handling of money, no messenger services. In all sorts of real emergencies, as in a great variety of less pressing, quite predictable affairs, people could find no help either for hire or publicly provided.

In consequence, they turned to each other. Patterns of dependence — that is, of latent compliance on the one hand and of power in the conventional sense on the other — assumed vastly more significance. So, while public power was eagerly pursued then as now, and the title "proconsul" or "duovir" indeed increased one's influence and standing, yet to a far greater degree such ranks merely recognized those attributes already attained. On leaving office, their titleholders did not vanish into obscurity. They only returned to the positions they had formerly enjoyed, now a little enhanced. They had been and continued to be "first man" or "number one" in their village, even in an entire province. Some small part of the evidence for that looser terminology, indicative of larger realities, is gathered in Appendix B, below. As to those larger realities, that greater part of life: to neglect it all and so to seek an understanding of the past only through the titles of public power, proconsul or duovir, would be most hopelessly anachronistic.

Here, then, is a subject for the present chapter, and quite large enough. But beyond the mere description of it (whatever interest that may hold), I shall try to indicate how smoothly private power joined to public. The one was an extension of the other. That was essential. Given the tiny numbers and insignificant presence of imperial or municipal agents to insure compliance with the aims of the state, obviously millionaires and magnates and local leaders of every sort had to cooperate, and willingly. Coercion was out of the question. They had to help in the maintaining of a large army without inviting constant civil wars; in the mediating of disputes among cities or citizens; in the raising of money and other things of value for the needs of the state. They had to help with their special skills, knowledge, and ties to other people.

We see them moving in and out of titled government continually; in and out of retirement. They brought with them their own slaves and intimates to assist them unsalaried and did favors in or out of office, indifferently, for friends and dependents. They protested, and most of them really felt, a warm loyalty toward the throne, whether or not they were at the moment procurators, or delegates to some provincial council. In describing power, one can in fact almost ignore the distinction between public and private, so great was the overlap between the two.

Particularly important were the social norms that helped to define their use of power. Without those, how to prevent endless, constant tests of strength? How to keep down the jungle? Questions of that sort, directed at the thoughts and feelings that underlie broad patterns of behavior and their historical consequences, have been discussed by Max Weber in 1920, Norbert Elias in 1939, Paul Veyne in 1976 — who may at least justify my own attempts.[1] What

I discover are practices and expectations pretty much the same throughout all the provinces, at least among the upper strata of society; and the armature of influence, acquaintance, and kinship by which those strata were connected, and from which depended their clients, tenants, and weaker neighbors, likewise extended over all the empire. Those persons who enjoyed power not only insured civil peace, which was quite beyond the capacities of government to enforce; they also provided the latter with an ethic, a moral code. Imperfect though we may judge it, nevertheless it worked. It worked at that most necessary juncture where government and the upper strata of the private sector touched, just where the demands of the state must be transmitted. If we are rarely able to trace the flow of power from its very origin, perhaps in the palace, to the most remote points of compliance, we should not thereby infer that nothing in fact was transmitted; rather, the reverse. Silence is proof — that, and results. Later, the great noise produced by government proves its malfunctioning.

Not that the norms of better times were always observed, of course. In every period, Rome had its embezzlers, its extortionists, its murderers. In the army and civil service, certain practices were at odds with those of the rest of society, especially of the Haves, the magnates, the *Tonangebenden*. In time, this competing ethic spread more widely. I describe it in my third chapter. Its effects proved baneful to the empire as a whole — baneful or, if one prefers a more scientific-sounding word, dysfunctional. They provide the focus for my fourth chapter.

2. THE APPEARANCE OF POWER

With mention of magnates and Haves, all that might be left would be Have-nots, persons of no substance; hence, a two-class society. That degree of simplification seriously distorts the truth. Among persons near the top, there were some who dared not so much as to address certain others; among those near the bottom, very important perceived differences separated one slave from another, one poor freeborn from another. There was, however, no middle class in any modern sense, defined in terms of place within the economy; nor did contemporaries think of such a thing. They thought instead of dependence or independence, of being among the suppliants or among those who could give. And, naturally, almost all whose opinions we hear belonged to the class of Haves.[2] It is particularly instructive to listen to a Cynic preacher, in whose kind the modern observer is sometimes tempted to find the conscience of the oppressors, spokesman for the masses. But even the Cynic turns out to be aggressively scornful of *hoi polloi*, mocking their money difficulties, dismissive of the popular assemblies. Small wonder such public speakers were heard, and provoked their audience, but attracted little sympathy or following.

Another well-known orator, addressing the council of Prusa in Bithynia toward the turn of the second century, apologizes for any past appearance of sympathy toward the city commoners: it would be resented by men of his own class and held against him. Better "to preserve the distinction between classes and ranks," says Pliny about the same period; "for when they are jumbled up in a confused mass, nothing is more unfair than that egality."[3] Three centuries later, Symmachus offers exactly the same view. In the full range of Latin and Greek authors of the Principate, with hardly a dissentient passage, the *vulgus* as a whole is routinely characterized in critical and contemptuous terms, and specific types within it, whether laborers or artisans or merchants of one sort or another, are still more sharply denigrated.

The habit of hauteur by which the upper class maintained its elevation above everyone else produced in the later empire no kinder tone of address. A law of Constantius, for example, declared, "Let no one aspire to enjoy any standing or rank who is of the lowest merchants, the money-changers, lowly offices or foul agents of some service, all offscourings of offices and supported on assorted disgraceful profits." Cicero had said just that, long before, though in fewer words[4]. It is natural for Jerome, too, to think in terms of stark contrast between "the ignoble masses, and magnates and governors," who make up a crowd visiting Saint Hilarion; and it is evidently natural to see the *vulgus* as the inevitable victims of *potentes viri*.[5] For not only do lowlier folk seem to live in a separate world, but it is one from which their betters, in their own struggles to rise and grow still richer, expect to draw their profits.

As for those higher beings, they are never satisfied. Consider one of the elite of Gaza. I might say to him, " 'Sir Topman, could you tell me, please, how you see yourself within your own town?' And he replies, 'I hold myself to be a pretty grand citizen, quite Number One.' And I say to him, 'If you go off to Caesarea, how do you see yourself there?' He answers, "I see myself better off than the magistrates there.' 'And at Antioch?' 'As a hick' [or rustic outsider, *paganos*]. 'And at Constantinople, before the emperor?' 'As an utter beggar.' "[6] The conversation, though imaginary, brings out the pressing sense of stratification which must have been felt even by a person very important — in his own small town. And it recalls, too, the paradoxical reality noted a little earlier, that even within the elite who thought of themselves as such there were many important distinctions, many steps upward that must be climbed.

Accordingly, the world outdoors, the world of correct manners, was ruled by forms very strictly enforced (we have many glimpses of this, though few of interior scenes). A governor upon coming to town ought to be met well beyond its gates by a parade of "the priestly clans, the active political organizations, and the people," and most particularly by the councillors. They would be punished for any neglect in this respect. In the street, a person riding but of lower status should dismount. Otherwise the senator whom he passed might remember and take revenge. If two men in litters should pass, the lowlier descended first to greet the other, or recalled for years the compliment paid him if the order had been reversed.[7] Ignorance of rank was no excuse. Senators could be easily known from certain items of their dress, to say nothing of its general quality and brilliance; an occasional honored citizen might be awarded the right to wear red around town; officials of any sort later wore the belt of office, *cingulum* or *zone*; and there was some sort of hierarchy expressed by the size of the decorative panels sewn on one's cloak and tunic — even by the cloak itself (fig. 14)[8].

Then, too, important people normally went about in public with a conspicuous retinue; so they could be spotted moving down the street; and you moved aside if they were on foot, or gave way to the coach and pair (and torches, at night). Most of their following or guard would be slaves, but personal friends and dependents clustered about. Anything less than twenty was demeaning, at least by Antioch standards.[9]

Honorific titles of address like "Father of our City," "Son," "Founder,"

Fig. 14. A scene at court (Luxor temple fresco from the camp chapel).

"Nourisher," "Salvation of our City" are common in municipal decrees from the eastern provinces[10]. There is a whole lexicon of yet more imaginative terms of praise in use, too, but not only in the east. In the west, styles favored a vaguer, vaster vocabulary: *perfectissimus, splendidissimus, eminentissimus,* which settled down into one particular term reserved for equestrians, another for senators, a third for certain very high officials. In the fourth century the more exalted of the senate were marked off in additional subdivisions each under its own reserved adjective, originally Latin but with Greek equivalents.[11] One may learn something useful and interesting about Roman society by speculating — merely speculating — on the processes through which certain levels of persons were first accorded certain terms of praise and then successfully asserted prescriptive rights over those terms, until in the fourth century those terms became a matter for legislative statements. Rank was extremely important, by no means the possession of silly conceit.

To continue: it was proper to offer a kiss of greeting, to the hem of the emperor's robe, to a knee, to a hand. Equals kissed on the level.[12] Among officials from decurions on up and from 385 forward, this right too was hedged around with legal definition and privilege. Late Romans, apparently of all provinces (since the legislation is general) and both within and without the church, expected, even demanded, to be listed neither higher nor lower than they knew was their right in official documents or line-ups at receptions or other public occasions; or they only guiltily usurped a higher place and were knocked down ("persons who have presumed to appropriate the insignia of an undue honor shall stand" while others in a curial meeting are seated).[13] While such a concern for place, visibly displayed and asserted, had a long history in the empire, there is a sense of even sharper attention in a description of a certain Valerian, decurion of Emesa in the 440s, who:

> assumed for himself unjustly and surreptitiously the cincture of office of an Illustrious honor, in order that he might rely on the insignia of such high rank and might be able to fulfill his insolent design. For, accompanied by a great horde of barbarians, he rushed into the private council chamber of the governor of the province, he dared to vindicate a front place for himself, he seated himself on the right of the man to whom We have committed the laws, to whom We considered that the fate of the provincials should be entrusted, and thus when he had put to flight all the office staff of the governor, he left everything devastated and deserted. He was not richer in resources than he was full of crimes, he also received decurions at home, in order that the public accounts might be defrauded. He placed a garrison of slaves in opposition to the tax collectors, contrary to public discipline, and thereby the treasury of Our Serenity suffered a great loss through his madness.

For a villain of such a cast, it was not too harsh a punishment to return him to decurion rank and there to require him to work through the routine obligations of that status.[14]

The interest here lies of course not so much in the little story itself as in the horror and outrage that moved the empire's central authorities. They expressed and inculcated their feelings among all the citizen population. Quite true, the criminal had cut off the flow of money to the Treasury and kept it for himself. Bad enough. He had defied lawful authority with force. But he had also sat in the wrong place, worn the wrong clothes, received guests at home in a wrong, magisterial fashion — usurpations all more than symbolic. They were in fact entitlements to certain good things in life.

You should instead wait to be summoned by edict or herald to the governor's presence.[15] Access was a thing granted by the great only after due thought, since it implied their listening, their acquiescence, their favor promised, and therefore their conferring of power of some sort. Thank you, thank you, say the grateful dependents of a mere freedman, "for many acts of grace toward us, *beneficia*, and access granted to you for our whole household on a basis of intimacy"; and "thank you" no doubt would say the weighty members of some magnate's retinue who stood with him on the platform before a crowded meeting, and so drew from his strength while at the same time adding to it.[16] At a trial, the *honorati* from the curia might sit with the governor, who should not assert his superiority by hitching himself up on a higher cushion; the senior clerks likewise enjoyed *consessus*; and the privilege arrogated to themselves by the governor's visitors and cronies, against whose unfair intimacy Libanius protests so often in Antioch, was claimed at the emperor's court by those who visited him privately (but it got to be known), or again in Carthage by those who saw a litigant calling on the prefect through the back door.[17] It was assumed that any contact with a person in power would be used by his lucky intimates to discuss and promote their own affairs. In fact, the very rumor, whether or not there was anything behind it, must enhance their influence in other quarters.

Best of all, you might actually dine with the great man. That implied a special compliment to you, offered prepense, since everyone knew what it meant: so Tiberius soothed the fractious Libo by asking him to his dinner parties, just as the bailiff of his or any broad estate in Italy would condescend to recline at table with the lower workers — though only occasionally during the year, on festivals. You had to be a decurion to dine publicly with others of the group. Their table expressed and defined the *ordo*, just as a higher, imperial table defined membership in the House Guard.[18] Access to it was controlled by law. That sharpened delight in the privilege, which even the almighty Petronius Probus boasted about in his epitaph: Probus "formerly rejoicing in the distinction of dining with the emperor, in conversation with him and in his friendship."[19]

Particular privileges followed. The story can be picked up in Italy of the Republic, where persons of senatorial rank demanded exclusive use of any town's baths whenever they passed through.[20] Then the privilege came to be claimed anywhere in the empire by army officers, and eventually had to be once more cut back by law to the highest ranks. Important ranks and personages also claimed reserved seating in the theaters and amphitheaters: a Greek invention, asserted by the Roman senators in the capital, then by the equestrians, then by voting precincts at Lambaesis, Rusicade, Ephesus, Athens, Stobi; also for certain trade associations at Nimes, and imperial cult officials at Sarmizegethusa in Dacia. No doubt the list of examples could be greatly extended.[21] Local grandees had not only their own statues set up all over town in the most public, much-seen locations — and this by the thousands upon thousands in cities throughout the empire — but they had their painted portraits similarly displayed.[22] In the end, if you counted for enough, you might enjoy a public funeral (if enjoy is the right word).[23]

We have in one inscribed epitaph the protestations of grief uttered by the citizenry at the funeral of a local notable; in another, the acclamations of thanks and rejoicing rendered to a living notable for a great favor done to the city: "The shout went up, 'Long life!' " and so forth, at Mylasa; other unison phrases from Greek or Syrian cities of the second and third centuries, of which one text is drawn from the minutes of the council meeting; a mosaic with a text on it that records the rhythmic shouts of the citizens in anticipation of enjoying a wild-beast hunt, and congratulating the man who must pay for it all: "From you as an example may future benefactors (*munerarii*) learn! May those of the past listen! Whence came such a thing, when, ever? You will furnish the spectacle on the model of the quaestors and at your own expense, on that day. Magerius is paying! That is what wealth is, and resources — that is *it!*"[24] And at the end we have no less than three hundred and six chanted phrases welcoming Augustine's nomination of his successor (" 'Christ hear us, save Heraclius,' eighty times . . . , 'Christ hear us, life to Augustine!' thirty-six times," etc.), nearly matching — but what could match? — the more than fifty phrases and eight hundred and fifty repetitions that greeted the promulgation of the Theodosian Code.[25]

A fascinating glimpse of power on display, which elicits from numbers of important people hours upon hours of cheering. The conventions surrounding high position and, with them, the capacity to exact compliance from others were manifestly of the utmost seriousness, a very part of the reality of power. To see in this nothing but empty adulation is quite wrong. From the audience emerge individuals with individual thoughts to express. Some thoughts are taken up and repeated thirteen times, not eighty (for Heraclius); some ten times, not fifty, at Theodosius' announcement. He notes and listens. The shorthand clerk records all the numbers and whatever is seen as popular and important. The crowds of the African city, quoted above, actually extracted a great gift from their compatriot, through the insistence of their chanting. And we have a similar instance at festival time in an Egyptian city around A.D. 300:[26]

> When the assembly had met, the people cried, "The Roman power forever! Lords Augusti! Prosperous Prefect, prosperity to our ruler! O Ocean, our President, the glory of our city! O Ocean, our Dioscorus, First Citizen! Under you our blessings increase ever more, source of our blessings. . . . Prosperity to the patriot, prosperity to the lover of right! Source of our blessings, founder of the city! . . . Let the president receive the vote on this great day! Many votes do you deserve, for many are the blessings which we enjoy through you, O President. This petition we make to our ruler [the Prefect] about the President, with good wishes to our ruler, asking for the city's President, beneficent ruler, for the city's honest man's governor, the equitable governor, the city's governor, the city's patron, the city's benefactor, the city's founder, the prosperous Prefect, prosperous ruler, beneficent ruler, beneficent Prefect! We beseech you, ruler, concerning the President. Let the President receive the vote, let the President receive the vote on this great day! This is the first necessity." The President said, "I acknowledge with great pleasure the honor which you do me, but I beg that these demonstrations be reserved for a legitimate occasion when you may make them with safety and I shall be justified in accepting them." The people cried, "Many votes do you deserve! . . . The Roman people forever! Prosperous Prefect, prefect of honest men, our ruler! We ask, ruler, for the President, the city's benefactor, the city's founder! We beseech you, ruler, preserve the city for our Lords [the emperors]. Beneficent ruler, we beseech you for the city's well-wisher, the city's patriot!" Aristion the advocate said, "We will refer this matter to the most high council." The people: "We ask, ruler, for the city's patron, the city's founder, upright general, peace of the city! O Ocean, Dioscorides, First Citizen! O Ocean, Seuthes, chief of the citizens, equitable governor, equitable citizen. True and upright advocates, true and upright assessors! Hurrah for all who love the city! Long live the Lords Augusti!"

Not chaos, not adulation, but a species of democracy in action — only not in a guise familiar to our more recent traditions. Therefore it may be misunderstood. In fact, what most people wanted could, by the procedures here on view, emerge tentatively and be shaped and become consensus, and at last become truly imperative; for no one would find it easy to resist expressions in their final form from his own fellows and community.

The forces at work in these moments can be tested by an instance that turned sour. It happened in the Roman Circus in A.D. 217 on the political anniversary of the ruling, now unpopular, imperial family.[27]

> The crowds, since they could find concealment at the races through their great numbers, took increasing courage and made a tremendous hubbub on the contest honoring [Prince] Diadoumenianus' birthday . . . , lamenting and declaring themselves of all men the only ones without a leader or ruler. . . . And they paid no attention at first either to the equestrian bloc or the senatorial [which led] cheers for the emperor and the Prince, . . . 'Hail the wonderful day today! Hail our wonderful rulers!' hoping that the crowds would join in.

The latter, however, raised other chants and naturally won out, being many times more numerous. As a result, a terrible loss of face was suffered by the emperor, that is, loss of power — for the two were the same. "So great," continues our reporter, "so great is the respect somehow inbred among men for sheer power, *to kreitton*, and contempt for the weaker; and from that, [the crowd] conceived Macrinus and Diadoumenianus to be perfect non-beings, and walked all over them as if they no longer existed. Hence, too, as no small cause, the soldiers also held him [Macrinus] in contempt, attaching no value to what he did to cultivate them."

Our same source, Dio (58.5.1–4), himself a senator of much experience, reflects earlier on the rise of Sejanus. Sejanus served as prefect to Tiberius while being also secret aspirant to the throne itself in his final days: "so great a man in the pride of his preeminence and magnitude of his authority as to seem, in plain words, himself the emperor." In political life one could observe persons "who stood out in their own basic worth" compared to those "enjoying only recently acquired decorations." The latter insisted on deference and "assurances of allegiance, *dexiomata*, as being necessary to the fulfilling of their eminence" (that is, here in Dio's words, a loss of face would be a loss of power), and "if they fail to receive such, they take it ill, as a slight, and are angry at the affront. So people are more careful toward such men than to the emperors, we might say. In the latter, it is a virtue to forgive an offense, while in the former that would be taken as a sign of weakness, and attacks and vengeance are thought to provide the validation of their great power."

In public it was important to spare everyone the loss of face and thus to avoid needless provocation, perhaps retaliation as well. How might this be done? Acclamations permitted people to test opinion without committing or even identifying themselves. The device can be seen employed at a certain Roman senate meeting of the late first century in which, as had always been traditional, the upper members stated their opinions in order by seniority; but the moment that counted, the actual division, was a fluid, look-over-your-shoulder process. As Pliny tells us (*Ep.* 2.11.22), on this occasion there did emerge a manifest loser, and a bad one. To be seen to be so weak, so isolated, infuriated him. Far better was the ordinary procedure in which "the senate's perfectly clear agreement was reached, which usually proceeds decrees" (ibid. 3.4.4 — and notice the "usually").

It should not therefore be taken as a sign of sycophantic conformity (to which, however, the Roman senate under early emperors certainly descended) when a vote, a decree, an honorific resolution turned out to be unanimous; instances have been cited (above, note 25). Procedures were no different in the provinces: witness many attestations to this or that action taken "by the universal consent of the decurions," many variations on that phrase, and even a telltale abbreviation for so common a phenomenon, as if today we were to write 'AA' for "all agree" in our council minutes.[28] It was perhaps to avoid the competition that might arise over at least the higher elective positions there that Pompeii's city fathers preferred "political arrangements and political maneuvering,"[29] so as to leave no wounded losers before the populace. Only two candidates for the two annual duumvirates came forward. For even more obvious reasons, the election of an emperor, when one ever came to a vote, was a unanimous affair. Who, after all, would want to have preferred the wrong man?[30] Finally, the church in its councils followed the same procedure, as can be seen from the mid-third century still on into the mid-fifth, through the offering of opinions in order and the reaching of an ultimate result by acclamation: *omnes episcopi dixerunt*.[31] Thus many of the most important decisions throughout the empire's centuries and various provinces could be reached with hardly a voice raised save in unison.

Such might be our first impression, which needs, however, a good deal of qualification. In fact, as we have seen, public displays of disagreement had to be very carefully controlled precisely because public defeat was so very serious for the individual who lost. Just why that was so must be explored a little further; but the key to the matter certainly lies in the fate of the emperor Macrinus, who put his power on display for all to see, in a great theater and with his supporters all about him, and yet was challenged successfully.

A century and more earlier, in the 90s, "a consular by name Rufus was serving as city manager, *curator*, in Smyrna, in a harsh and surly fashion. [The famous sophist there resident], Nicetes, crossing his path in some way, said no more than 'Hail' to him and afterwards would come no more to his court. And for all the time he was in charge of a single city, Rufus thought he had suffered no great affront; but when he took over the Gallic armies he recalled his wrath." He wrote to the emperor reviewing these and many similar charges against Nicetes, which the emperor bade him hear as judge himself. The accused, being summoned, responded; but he defended himself with a beauty of language so perfect that it reduced the judge to tears (that was how connoisseurs of rhetoric were expected to react to a great performance); and the quarrel was then over. All because of a loss of face.[32]

In much the same way, but this time more than a century *after* Macrinus, a new prefect Domitian was sent to the east, to make his headquarters in Antioch. There resided also the Caesar Gallus. Domitian refused to see him, walked right past his palace, and otherwise insulted him. Gallus' own quaestor told him to his face he now lacked the authority to retaliate against the "author of the outrage," the *hybristes*. Whereupon Gallus set his troops on both men, and both were lynched.[33] Deliberate ignoring of a person who should be courted, or at least visited, lay at the heart of a deadly struggle between Theophilus and John, the one of Alexandria and the other of Antioch, both bent on having the bishopric of Constantinople. And it would be easy to multiply illustrations of public slights employed as the means of destroying a rival's influence and position.

Much light can be shed on the nature of power in this world through considering the usages of the word *dignitas*. It might well be applied to those various moments and attributes, displaying high position, which were reviewed a few pages back: the parade of wealth, the shouting herald who went first in the street, the showy costume and large retinue, the holding of oneself apart, and the limitation of familiar address. All this might be called the substance of *dignitas*. But the term had a darker side, too. As used by Cicero, Caesar, or Pliny, it meant the ability to defend one's display by force if need be; to strike back at anyone who offended one or hurt or offended one's dependents; to avenge oneself and others, and to be perceived as capable of all such baneful, alarming conduct.[34] In both Greek and Latin authors, though the Greek have no equivalent for the two-sided Latin word, revenge was approved and a man was called good who could deliver a hard blow as well as extend a kindly gesture.

It was approved also to give fair warning of one's *dignitas* through some of that hauteur already described in public settings, which served to arouse respect too. Most obviously, officeholders gloried in their access of power, even when only designated and before actually entering on their duties.[35] Once a man was wrapped in the full uniform of office, "he was terrifying in his progress: so no one addressed him; but those whom he came across turned aside, and his advance-men announced that no one was to stand by nor stare at him. They should step aside and cast down their eyes." Such, at least, was the extreme of arrogance noted in the praetorian prefect of Severus Alexander.

Even lowlier officials sometimes behaved in very much the same way.

Philostratus, for example, was witness to the experience of a pair of envoys from a certain eastern city sent to plead a case before Caracalla. One of the two envoys took sick. The other, Heliodorus by name, panicked, went to the imperial headquarters half prepared, and, "being called sooner than he had expected, offered in excuse his ailing colleague. The man who called the cases, an insolent ruffian, would not agree to that, but instead brought him into court against his will, hauling him along by his beard."[36] Humiliating, terrifying, extraordinary! Very long remembered, too.

And "there was your brother Dmitry," recalls one of Dostoyevsky's characters, "dragging me by my beard. Dragged me into the square, sir, and just then the schoolboys were coming out of school and Ilyusha [my son] with them. As soon as he saw me in such a state he rushed up to me . . . trying to free me and shouting to my assailant, 'Let him go, let him go! It's my Daddy! Forgive him, sir!' Yes, indeed! 'Forgive him,' he cried. He clutched at him with his hand. He kissed his hand. That same hand — yes, sir, he kissed it. . . . And this is how children — I don't mean yours but ours, sir, the children of the despised but honorable poor, sir — learn about justice on earth even when they are nine years old. . . . My Ilyusha, sir, grasped the whole meaning of the truth at the very moment. That truth entered into him and crushed him forever."[37]

An interesting view into how things might happen! — how a society made up in some sense of only two classes, Haves and Have-nots, managed to teach each rising member his place, through confronting him with both realities and possibilities. There were clear enough lessons offered in any street of the empire. While one person was discovering that "poverty takes away frank speech," *parrhesia*, quite another sort could be learning to "insult abusively just like great folk"; "for from the rich toward those around them there is abuse, insult, mockery, often a blow."[38] Indeed, a great deal of the arrogant behavior that I have been describing thus far had the more or less conscious intent of instructing other people, even casual observers, in the responses that would be expected of them. Those who enjoyed wealth, esteem, and influence secured these things ever more completely by asserting them; those who lacked them understood how they must conduct themselves; and their education of the one or the other sort was no doubt well begun while they were still children, like Ilyusha.

There were advanced lessons, of course, and surprises. To repeat, the Haves in particular arranged themselves on many levels. The two envoys to the emperor's traveling headquarters in Gaul, described by Philostratus, had certainly counted for something in their native town. At court, it meant nothing. After their experience they would have the wisdom of the man from

Gaza (above, at n. 6), and would better know their place. Or perhaps try to improve it.

The impulse to advance oneself and the steady, painful effort ordinarily required to do so are attested in a thousand scenes from the empire. Although its society and standards cannot well be treated anthropologically, nevertheless they give the impression of having been highly competitive. Certainly there was competition at and for the center. As examples, take the tenures of Sejanus and Plautianus in the praetorian prefecture.[39] Epictetus evokes the feelings that attended the attaining of even quite lowly rungs in a career. For a young nobleman, it is a triumph: "'He has been thought worthy of a tribuneship,'" all the world exclaims at the good news, "and everyone who who meets him embraces him, kissing his eyes, another his neck, and his slaves his hands. He comes home, he finds lamps lit, he goes up to the Capitoline and offers sacrifices." As for the senator, farther up the ladder, we have Martial's description of him tirelessly running "all over the city from earliest dawn," exchanging "a thousand kisses. . . . But you do this that you may add a new name to the purple records, or be sent to govern Numidian or Cappadocian tribes."[40] And in the later empire the striving for office, though of a different sort, continued unabated, and the whole new field of ecclesiastical politics opened up, too, within which the rewards, efforts, and campaigns were on the same scale as the secular.[41] Sources for this last field are particularly rich in detail. They also allow a view into the nature of court intrigue and thus into the role of the emperor, which I will return to at the end of this section; but, outside the walls of the palace, the bloody violence of competition in the fourth and fifth centuries is well illustrated too. The bodyguard of many hundreds that accompanied the bishop of Alexandria in 412 betokens the changes in power that emerged from the later empire.[42]

Violence of course was the ultimate support of 'face.' Without a willingness to resort to physical force if need be, all the scowling, swaggering, retinue, riches, and braggart abuse which the Have-nots had to endure from the Haves must someday be challenged. The challenge would have to be met. Though it is true that the later empire saw more common resort to physical attack than in earlier, better times, it is also true that the Haves of all periods numbered quite murderous members among them and a fair degree of willingness to use muscle, through their slaves or other agents, as an instrument of their power.

In trying to understand why the majority of people heeded what they were told by some small minority, I am bound to consider what sights and experiences they were exposed to. Some of these were decidedly intimidating. Great men's houses in Rome could be compared to castles and had, among their troops of slaves, some assigned to armed guard.[43] This was in the first century — no need to bring forward the abundant evidence for private armies and battles in the streets of the late Republic. In Athens in the second century — vital intellectual center or sleepy university town, however one wants to describe it — certain graduate students of rhetoric set their slaves to beat a citizen they disliked and he died of the attack (of course, after the mid-fourth century such stories became more common). The lord of the city, the rhetorician and incidentally billionaire, Herodes Atticus, lived in several mansions of which one in the suburbs was equipped with towers and turrets.[44] There must have been quite a number of suburban or rural residences for the great, similarly strong if not actually designed to withstand a siege, since by the second quarter of the second century we hear of people being kidnapped into them and held in private jails, as slaves,[45] and in the fourth century rural dwellings built for war, though very comfortable within, are well known if not everywhere a very common sight. They particularly distinguished the coun-tryside of Pannonia; they were often seen in Moesia; rare in Gaul but known in all regions, central, west, northern; and rare in Spain.[46] The best-known instances, from both excavation and portrayal in mosaics, are north African; the fewest, in Syria, only along the edges of the province; and the only one described for us in its true capacity is the villa of John Chrysostom's friend five miles outside of Caesarea in Cappadocia.[47] His rich defender, owner of various villas in various places, put him up in this one, giving instructions to her bailiff to provide full service to John if any monks offered him insult or assault; also, "to assemble the peasants from all of her estates and to range them thus against [the monks]"; and finally, "bade myself too to take refuge in a house she owned with a keep, *kastellon*, quite impregnable." Such, then, were the formidable homes in which the great of the land and of the cities, too, maintained their *dignitas*.

In the later empire such structures might be explained as responses to brigandage. Brigandage may very well be the best part of the answer. Not the whole of it, however; for not far from John Chrysostom's safe house, much earlier, a sort of private war is reported between two rich brothers each in command of an army of his dependents;[48] in Egypt we have an unbroken train of complaints about everyday armed violence in the villages and countryside extending from pre-Roman times into the fourth century and beyond; and in Augustine's part of the world a large-scale tenant of land, not some little peasant lad, "for some reason was afraid of the owner of the estate and fled to the Hippo church" — from which, a few days later, just outside its doors, he was kidnapped by a friend of the local count with some borrowed soldiers. How, now, to get him free?[49] Considering how thin the documentation is in which the actors and actions of the empire must be dressed and seen in motion, perhaps these few stories are enough to make a simple point: behind the imposing front of manner and appearance, the Haves, especially in the least-policed settings possessed and were prepared to use physical force to back up their words. Naturally, the necessity arose very, very rarely. Just these few tales would teach prudence to any little challenger. Even near-equals would measure an opponent with care. We may picture them, like other species of competitor, noting the height of the marks on a tree against which another elk has rubbed off the velvet on his horns, another bear has arched up and clawed, or another boar, after an agreeable wallow in the the clay along some river bank, has scratched his back. Reckless rivalry with those simply too great was to be avoided.

The patron who offered safety to John Chrysostom represents a class of landholders with many estates and scores, it might be thousands, of dependents beneath them. The patterns of dependence varied. By very little more than inference from the archeology of the northwest European provinces, but elsewhere through better sources, the outright ownership of entire villages by individual magnates may be traced and taken as a general feature of the empire. Cicero speaks of the rich possessing *vici et prata*, a little later Strabo refers to a number of villages in Italy as "now . . . the property of private individuals"; we have occasional attestation of such in the Danubian provinces and ample proof in north Africa; they were apparently quite common in Syria and Asia Minor, and, above all, were found on imperial estates as "crown villages" in Egypt and elsewhere. They constitute only the most striking, blatant form of control and government by the Haves over the Have-nots — control or government which it is my general purpose in this section to explain. Compared to this, Government with a capital letter was obviously rather unimportant.[50]

But the more natural form of control was exercised as titleholder to scattered acres wherever they could be picked up cheap, and so accumulated, and if possible united for ease of management into largish units. The drive toward the simplifying of one's holdings in this manner is often remarked on by all sorts of writers of all periods;[51] but of course small holdings continued and are attested archeologically in southern Tuscany, southern Numidia, and eastern Syria and, from written sources, in Numidia, Italy, Egypt, Cappadocia, and elsewhere.[52] Scholars have always assumed a steady, cumulatively significant narrowing of land ownership over the centuries of the empire, and I believe they are right, because that can be more often shown than the reverse, in the handful of cases or districts where the picture is clear; but for my purposes the matter makes little difference. What does count and can be

easily sensed — often demonstrated — is the hold over many people enjoyed
by investors in scattered holdings. Wherever they had land, they had tenants
who depended on them: in the better farmlands near Rome, lorded over by
the bigger nobles in the second century; in the better lands near Athens in the
same period, by the towering Herodes Atticus; and around Ormela in Phrygia,
by the well-connected Faustina Ummidia Cornificia.[53] It is naturally unusual
to learn so much about just where people had their investments, but the few
cases mentioned fit very comfortably with broad statements by contemporaries about the influence of the more substantial families. I will turn to them in
a moment.

As might be expected, the leading members of the small urban centers
bought what they could in the neighborhood. That solidified their leadership.
By luck and work, but most of all by marriage, their wealth might be increased.
Then they could look farther afield for investments, and, in the next
generation, for a wife or husband whose property would introduce them to
some other town or district entirely. So property and leadership spread out.
The head of the family or a son might move to the metropolis: Rome,
Carthage, Alexandria. From Alexandria, for example, the tendrils of ownership extended over the length of the Nile valley.[54] Such were the patterns
through property.

The grander the family, the better the chance of knowledge about it
surviving. In the later empire, Symmachus owned estates in both Italy and
Mauretania, and his son married into a family owning in Sicily and southern
Italy. The Mauretanian holdings drew him inevitably into the defense of the
troubled city of Caesarea in 380. Others of his fellow senators owned lands
in north Africa, too: at Thagaste and elsewhere. His friend Marcellus owned
in Gaul but also in Spain. Meropius Pontius Paulinus, great owner in
Aquitania, also had lands at Fundi (and could attend to them while governor
of Campania in 381); Petronius Probus, "the crown of the Anician clan,"
owned in Etruria but on a grand scale also in Asia, through his wife; Basil's
family, through his mother, owned in at least three eastern provinces (no
doubt Cappadocia and adjoining); and Iamblichus of Antioch owned in Syria
but also in Palestine, and other Antiochenes in other, distant Syrian districts.
The popes' lands were of the same magnitude and reach. We may assume the
same of the heads of other churches in major cities.[55] Even a quite random
assortment of famous names and offices thus suggests the scale of diversifica-
tion resulting from a long process of investment, by which the imperial and
even the provincial aristocracy could claim to have a finger in every pie.

While individuals might each represent the center of a nexus of power, big
or small, its still wider extent was implied by their whole kinship. In

combination with wealth, that brought office. It is possible to illustrate this combination by specific instances of fathers getting their sons started in public careers, locally or in service to the emperor; of brothers helping brothers, uncles helping nephews, and so forth. The material is both too abundant and too familiar for anything but a bare mention.[56] It is also perhaps pointless to say that kin were expected to serve each others' interests loyally — but didn't always do so. You could promise no more zealous support of anyone than to say, as Pliny did, "I count his kin as my own"; and, in readying an appeal for help to a person, you needed only to mention that he was "related to the Most Noble Theodore," who can for that reason be presumed to prove well disposed also.[57] There are certain irreducibles in human history deriving from neither culture nor events but rather from the species itself; and historians must not forget what is merely obvious. Anthropologists have it right: "Men care passionately about their prestige, the prestige of their families, and of their kinsmen. Indeed, all these reputations are parts of a single complex. . . . The mere numerical size of a man's kindred is a matter of prestige, because, other things being equal, it means that he is a man who will be taken notice of, assisted, and well-informed wherever he goes."[58]

"A man" or perhaps "a woman." I show here a stemma reconstructed largely thanks to the long genealogical inscription on the tomb of Licinnia Flavilla[59] (fig. 15).[59] It can be supplemented by many other texts. The total of names of assigned place in it could be easily doubled. However, I select only those about which we know more than the spelling, or which serve as links to such other names. For some, the information amounts to no more than a priesthood in the imperial cult; yet the position constituted one of the pinnacles of provincial status and political ambition. To attain equestrian rank, too, let alone senatorial, was a great thing, especially from a part of the empire that might be dismissed as rather a backwater. Toward the center of the stemma is Opramoas, showing how it was most easily done: by calling attention to oneself through extraordinary expenditure on public projects and benefactions. Still, his campaign of advertisement never brought its full reward. Somehow Julius Antonius was luckier — equestrian as well as Lyciarch; and the sister of another Lyciarch, Mettia Ptolemais, had married a consul under Antoninus Pius. To the left, one can see the even grander names of second-century Asiarchs, consuls, pretenders (Avidius Cassius); in the third century, an emperor. Joined to relatives of such extraordinary position, Licinnia, even in little Oenoanada, could have her way across the length and breadth of Lycia, or farther yet.

I know of no other web of relations in the empire which can be so widely and surely reconstructed. However, one or two others come close, thanks to

families as an important, proud part of their heritage.[64] Elsewhere, the servants of the gods, as distinct from their magnanimous patrons, were generally people of no special eminence, sometimes people literally of the servant class.

On the other hand, the hereditary nature of eminence and influence is very widely demonstrable. In an economy and society such as that of the empire, no doubt it was universal. You were born to the top far, far more often than attaining it. So people described in public documents as belonging to "a Gymnasiarch clan," a "Magistrate clan," a "Councillors'" or "First Citizens' clan," and so forth, can easily be found in Asia Minor or Greece; but also in Beneventum, a *patronus* of an association (*collegium*) "from his father, grandfather, great-grandfather and ancestors."[65] In the rivalry for respect, one category of self-praise after another was of course invoked, so as to elevate the not-so-rich but once-rich above mere *nouveaux riches*, or the equally-rich over their like in wealth, by the boast of having had *their* money for a longer time. Still, it was a fact that powerful families retained their character for generation after generation, and in the very familiarity of their presence in a town or region lay a part of their strength. Someone whom your grandfather had bowed to and for whom your sons must work you would not challenge lightly.

It is delightful if surprising to report at least one instance of irreverence for the family pride of the mighty. It happened at Sena in northern Italy in A.D. 70. A Roman senator of the town provoked a crowd of townspeople, or rather the local magistrates, by whose orders he was roughed up and, "as he stood there, he was set about with wailing, lamenting, and parading of ancestral images," as in a nobleman's funeral. Tacitus, humorless where he cannot be savage, is not amused (*Hist.* 4.45); and, for additional insults to the Senate in general, the malefactors were haled to Rome and punished.

In the later empire perhaps society became a little looser; or perhaps there were simply new paths for advancement. Family connections remained, however, a common, important means of securing one's position. There is the family of the praetorian prefect Anthemius sprawling across the later fourth and fifth centuries, a tissue of nepotism; or the remarkable ascendancy of Ausonius, which immediately brought his nonagenarian father, other kin, various in-laws, and even Symmachus's brother into office; for Symmachus, thanks to a carefully cultivated correspondence with two literary friends, friends also of Ausonius, wangled the vicariate of Africa for his brother. Very useful:[66] in Africa the family had large landholdings. Ammianus Marcellinus mentions in passing a great many similar instances of fathers and sons simultaneously in office, or brothers, or various other relatives helping each other. At the very top, among towering military commanders and the imperial house itself, from the fourth into the sixth century, the traceable connections form a truly remarkable stemma, something like that of the Hapsburgs.[67] Since ecclesiastical careers now drew on very much the same social classes as secular careers — that is, decurions and higher — they reveal very much the same patterns of cooperation along lines of kinship. Bishops of the major cities, for which records are more complete, seem to have succeeded their relatives on the throne as often as praetorian prefects or *vicarii*. The subject invites more study than I know how to give it.

Every web of connections of course had some natural center. That may be sensed for some of the individuals in fig. 15, most notably for Licinnia. Her base was Lycia; likewise Opramoas'. There are other sorts of information from which to build up a picture. From Bellunum, the minimum: a local notable named in one inscription, his wife as patron saluted by "the city populace." Of such little glimpses there are a thousand. Next, the inscriptions of the Pullaienus clan of a north African city, some of them miles away in the countryside where the Pullaieni had lands and freedmen; and there even survives one indication of the size of the main estate, in the monumental gateway opening on the estate driveway. Third, the Antistii from elsewhere in the same province, whose presence is known through their clients in a little town, and also in their very large estate twenty kilometers away, and in Rome too, where they attained consulships. Tacitus outlines the position of a family like this but in Istria, "where the Crassi of yore still retained their dependents, lands, and popularity."[68] Then, at Poetovio in Pannonia, the Valerii can be tracked through a number of city magistracies, of which they enjoyed a virtual monopoly — aediles, censors (*quinquennales*), pontifices — while rising also to equestrian rank. Their activity in commerce can be shown; but in the third century their generations of wealth and prominence came to an end. The Titiani of Lilybaeum in Sicily lasted longer and were still spending large sums on their hometown in A.D. 250, while the Nonii of Brescia, besides senatorial rank and consular marriages, left their name not only in the region (Bergamo, Verona, and elsewhere) but in Ephesus as well. They were patrons of a *collegium*, of the whole city too, in Brescia.[69] So far as inscriptions tell, they held no municipal offices. Perhaps they had grown too big.[70] But more often, real success opened up larger horizons without ending the dependence and cordiality that joined such names of places and people as these.

The Nonii, just mentioned, had succeeded in that often attested effort to gain a position in more than one's own home city. Two names already cited also serve as examples: Herodes Atticus of Athens and Opramoas of Rhodiapolis in Lycia. Of the former, Philostratus recalls a moment of challenge when an accuser of Herodes in his presence boasted of a benefaction he had bestowed on an Italian city; whereupon the Athenian said he could boast of the same in every province of the empire. The claim is almost credible. By chance quite a number of cities on his list happen to be known. In one can still be seen parts of the aqueduct he built at a cost of four million drachmae. As to Opramoas, his gifts of money to literally dozens of cities can be easily documented; and, if his exact match is not known, there are others of nearly his sort whose similar wealth, ambition, and regional dominance may be fairly assumed, from much less evidence.[71] Service as a decurion or *bouleutes* in more than one city was quite often taken on, too. In return for the invitation, the honorands were expected to make some substantial contribution. It was a fair bargain. They gained wider prestige and influence by the expense.[72] As the impulses natural to society at large were at work in these ambitious relationships, they are demonstrable wherever the sources cast the least light, and have often been noted.

Since my interest lies in affairs outside of government, I need not here pursue the aspirations of the Haves into offices higher than the municipal. Still, the dividing line is to some degree artificial. Many men (not women) sought the rewards that came only to a career of service under the emperor himself, whether military or civilian, and combined it with something more local. Indeed, the local benefited from the imperial; for, aside from any question of venality, the ethics of officeholding permitted a very considerable amount of active or passive partiality. It was simply expected that a man would do favors for his friends and dependents. Much from earlier, Republican times remained, when "the *dignitas* of the oligarchs made them think of their functions as a personal honor more than as a public 'mission' or responsibility."[73] Accordingly, by very reasonable calculations which spoke for themselves but which there was no harm in emphasizing — "for his outstanding love toward his native place," "benefactor to his *patria*," etc — a city or village might ask an official to be its patron. There are hundreds of examples in epigraphy.[74] In particular, communities hoped to exploit their relations with a native son assigned his duties in the same province. From his point of view it was entirely natural and proper to oblige them.

Thanks to a great increase in the size of the bureaucracy from Diocletian on, the empire's cities contained a much, much larger body of imperial officials in their midst. With these residents their hosts could form mutually desirable ties, especially where the residents were themselves local people simply serving on the staff of some major office. In late Roman Antioch, to give a striking illustration, at least fifteen hundred staff-members regularly resided and worked for the governor, Count of the East, and Master of the

Soldiers; in Carthage, four hundred worked for the governor and three hundred for the *vicarius*, with still more employed by other imperial bureaus like the Sacred Largesses; and even from a city of no great size, Timgad, though most of them were not resident, a total of at least seventy were drawn off to several offices.[75] In the mid-fourth century tax lists of Hermopolis in Egypt, only a tiny fraction of the names were thought to deserve specification of what they are or what they do; but among the local elite of goldsmiths, temple priests, church officials, and so forth, former or serving soldiers and imperial officials vastly preponderate. They appear under quite odd titles: *abaktes = ab actis, abrebis = a breviis, oph = officialis, apo bph = ex beneficiarius,* and so on.[76] From the operation of a relatively well-reported place like Antioch in the fourth century, it can be seen how much such official types were talked about, built houses, appeared grand, spent money, and generally had things their own way.

Rome presents a similar picture, though seen through the window only of patronage over trade associations. Yet that glimpse may be comparative, which is very useful. Up to the fourth century, a *collegium* was likely to choose as its patron its own most successful member or an outsider from as high up as it could reach in surrounding society — meaning decurions, retired army officers, an equestrian, or even a senator. Later, however, its patrons are far more likely to be officials connected administratively with its particular trade.[77] The obvious reason for the change is the vastly more interfering nature of late imperial government, which offered the same person officially in charge, but in a purely private capacity, vastly more opportunity to do favors. The patron was in fact two people combined. Like the Lord High Chancellor in *Iolanthe*, if one of the pair should disagree with the other, he might talk him around and report the results of the colloquy to his dependents: "Victory! Victory! Success has crowned my efforts." But it was really no joke, as we shall see later. Indeed, we have a contemporary speaking in broad terms and telling us of "men great, powerful, formidable, vigorous, who master the largest cities by virtue of some authority [*licentia*]"; and not only cities but entire regions and peoples lie subject to the arbitrage of *potentes, magni, maximi viri,* and imperial officials blending into each other without distinction: "commanders and tribunes of soldiers, but terrifying and raised up on tyrannous powers, or defenders or chiefs of cities, who however never remain within the bounds of those powers and who in various ways always offend."[78] Government unintended by government had thus taken on new, alarming, larger dimensions.

The Haves of the older sort by no means disappeared. Among the elite of Timgad in the 360s more than a quarter could still trace their high rank back at least a century and a half. Very interesting. The great families of Rome naturally claimed pedigrees even longer and much more distinguished — and at least partly credible. In the east, in proof of the antiquity of their name, aristocrats spoke in disgust of *nouveaux arrivés.*[79] They ascribed the wrong sort of eminence to sudden promotion, not steady growth of fame. And they were right. It is indeed the imperial bureaucracy and higher appointment or the favor of great officials that can elevate someone overnight; if not overnight, then by no more than a decade or so of service; if not by that, then in the next generation.[80] "Fathers," says a contemporary, "when they urge on their sons to study zealously, always say, 'Look at that low fellow, born of lowly parents, who achieved power from oratory, held great positions in government, gained great wealth, won a rich wife, built a splendid house, and so is feared and thought glorious by everyone.' " In Spain, in Gaul, ascent lay more often through military service — but not exclusively; in the east, more often through a civilian or ecclesiastical career.[81] For lack of evidence it cannot be said that society in the later empire was more open and fluid; but the point, repeated from an earlier page, is that the upward paths were certainly different. And whether the Haves, the powerful, the rich and esteemed were retired army officers or whether they were the Top Ten of their city, or bishops or prefects, or had no office at all but only friends in the necessary places, their manner of exerting their power was new and different, too.

In the earlier empire the continuum of power, from the little and local to the great, is best traced through epigraphic evidence. That fact is easily sensed. In itself, too, it has some interest. Power is known about because anyone who possessed it trumpeted it to the world. Thereby it was increased. The available media of advertisement included actual heralds for magistrates, to shout and announce; various visible signs and symbols such as priority in seating or the parade of ancestral images at a funeral; but also the unrolling of written statements across the walls of public buildings, stelae, statue bases, and private tombs along the main roads coming into town, on which one could assert oneself through one's father's honors won, through one's grandfather, and so on. It is these latter statements that survive. An example or two have been cited above. However, *self*-assertion could never be so effective as someone else's good opinion offered on one's own behalf. The more important that other person or persons, the more valuable their words, to which the recipient would want to give maximum publicity. Hence the abundance of inscribed texts that detail and praise the character and actions of prominent people.

How seriously these texts were taken can be sensed from the great attention given them. A familiar category illustrates this: the patron plaque, *tabula patronatus*. Made of bronze to be mounted on the most-seen wall inside one's house, it read as a contract between two parties, generally between an individual and a provincial community: date specified, relationship specified, titles and authority of both given in full, and perhaps the occasion of ratification, for instance, through the visit of the agents of one party to the other. A person of real importance would have an impressive display of many such plaques in his atrium, some earned by his forebears but still in force through inheritance. What they declared to anyone who saw them was the owner's ability to protect and help, a certification of power. One senator and governor in an African province had at least five in his house on the Caelian hill in Rome, belonging to the time of Constantine.[82] No doubt he would have had other tablets, too, certifying the devotion of the signatories to his name and house, from the members of various trade or crafts associations. As clients they would rank second after an entire city but deserved attention for the deference they offered; and their place in urban life was likely to be prominent, sometimes semiofficial. In a house in Etruria, dated to A.D. 224, a tablet 70 x 48 cm was on exhibit in one of the grander rooms, declaring the mistress of the house to be the elected patron of the Builders' Association (normally the largest in any Italian town). Her ancestry is praised, her high character, her deeds of favor; a bronze statue of her is commissioned "so that her faithful friendship, *pietas*, toward ourselves and our warm respect, *voluntas*, toward her may be obvious through public display." Precisely the point: everyone should know.[83]

All this evidence is western and Latin and in some particular sense Roman, too. When patrons are encountered in eastern, Greek epigraphy, the Latin term is transliterated as if there were something a little odd about the relation involved. At any rate, there is no exact Greek equivalent (not that protection and dependence in themselves were alien to that world).[84] In contrast, Greek epigraphy preserves much fuller texts and quotations than Latin, allowing a good deal more than a glimpse of another form of certification: letters and resolutions of praise. These, too, were not peculiar to a region, only the evidence for them must be found largely in Greece and Asia Minor; and, like tablets and plaques of clientage, they survive in some abundance because they were given so much publicity.

How else other than by the gratified recipient's special effort would a letter from the very emperor himself find its way into the hands of local officials, and then onto stone? The always worthy Opramoas illustrates the process in the mid-second century; likewise, Herodes Atticus, a little later than Opramoas; while, a little earlier, the magic of such correspondence appears in the defense offered by a certain Flavius Archippus. Being in danger of indictment, Archippus produced "a petition he had presented to Domitian, letters written

by Domitian testifying to his character, a decree voted by the people of
Prusa . . . , a letter written by him to [Trajan] and an edict and letter of
[Trajan's] father, all confirming the benefits granted to him by Domitian"; and
these sufficed to establish his good name and case.[85] Aelius Aristides, roughly
contemporary with Opramoas and of course vastly famous for his oratory, was
at one point nominated for the honorific but very burdensome rank of Top
Ten in his native Smyrna. Like Archippus, he had letters from emperors, by
good luck recently received, and, in appealing against his nomination, he
enclosed copies of them with a covering document to the governor. At the
same time the governor was receiving letters in Aristides' behalf both from
his own and the latter's friends. At Aristides' request, the powerful figure of
Rufinus of Pergamon, ex-consul *ordinarius* of A.D. 142, was roused to write in
Latin (the language of authority), "in which, after a review of other matters,
with some recommendations and some advice, he hinted, concerning the
future, what would happen if [the governor] should not willingly exempt me."
This thoroughly intimidating convergence of weight and favor did the trick,
and the appointment was cancelled.[86]

So that was how letters worked. Their effect is easily imagined, for letters
of the same sort have never ceased to be solicited, written, received, and
considered in deciding on one's own behavior. As today. But the obvious
differences between our own and those of the ancient world should perhaps
be brought out a little more clearly.

"In the very least and slightest signs of deference and good-will on the part
of the one and true Prince are shown, I think," says a beloved courtier, "the
things everyone most values and desires, *amor* and *honor*." The writer is
Fronto. And Julian much later writes, "Perhaps there is something to brag or
show off about, for private citizens to get a letter from the emperor to display;
for they take them to other people who have no experience of such things,
the way tasteless folk wear rings."[87] If you could boast no acquaintance so high,
you showed around the letters from a consul *ordinarius*; if not from a consul,
then from a governor. The governor communicated the emperor's letters, or
himself wrote to your city council in praise of you, because he had heard of
you; and that happened because, most commonly, you had earned his
attention by civic benefactions. Your city council might write him on your
behalf, saying how wonderful you were. It would be answered; the answer,
inscribed on stone.[88] In Spain, a council set up testimony that a member of
the local elite had been recommended by his uncle, a consular; nor should the
recommendation be discounted in any way as a piece of avuncular piety,
because it came from a *severissimus vir*, a rigorous judge "who is earnestly
petitioned, even importuned, for his support" by everyone.[89] If actual letters
were not advertised, it might still be of value to declare in an inscription that

a person was not unknown to the high and mighty. Perhaps he had dined them at his house.[90] That was a privilege even more precious than being dined (above, p. 64f.).

3. HOW POWER WORKED: THROUGH FEAR

I have so far been discussing what powerful people looked like, what their public demeanor was, where and how they lived, and how well known they were and wanted to be. I have yet to set them in motion and show what they could do. It was a mix of good and bad, help and hurt. The one reinforced the other. *Dignitas* properly embodied both; for both were seen as necessary aspects of power, equally valued if not equally advertised. In any case, some actions advertised themselves: as an example, the total destruction of a neighbor's house and then its rebuilding, only so that the gigantic bully responsible could say, "I both know how, and am able, thus to fend off attack and repay a favor."[91]

I begin with the ability to hurt as seen in the most mismatched of all relationships, that between the rural poor, whether landless or nearly so, and some big landowner. Because the countryside was less observed by the cities' population and therefore itself was less observant of the latter's values, it permitted less civilized behavior. Perhaps most familiar may be the warning in James's letter (5.1 and 4): "Next, a word to you who have great possessions. . . . The wages you never paid to the men who mowed your fields are loud against you, and the outcry of the reapers has reached the ears of the Lord." The date lies close to the turn of the second century, when also Pliny was writing about a neighbor to one of his estates whose tenants had fallen behind in their rent; whereupon he sold off their securities and in so doing "spent their strength for the future." They would have no seed or draught animals for the next year's planting. From Italy, though not necessarily from a rural scene, comes the plaint of a poor man whose daughter has been raped by the son of a rich one. "Where would we get such high courage to exact satisfaction from that man? How could poverty bear up against the resentment, if my daughter had wanted to kill a youth numbered among the leaders of the city?"[92] Similarly not specified as rural but more likely to be that than urban violence are the references in the jurisconsults to the sale of one's land for a song, out of plain fear of the bidder — who very likely had his own private lockup to threaten you with.[93] Such practices of extortion and intimidation, which were still an object of legislation into the later empire, serve to introduce certain fourth-century descriptions.

When some magnate is on the rise (Basil reports), being the creation of aggressive avarice:

> then such a person recks not of time or space, will not wait his turn, but resembles the violence of a conflagration that seizes on everything and devours it. . . . Thus men who have arrived at some high degree of power derive from those they have already mastered the capacity for yet further injustice, reducing to slavery under their first victims those that remain. The superabundance of their wickedness serves to increase their power; for those who have suffered earlier supply aid to them under constraint, helping to work harm and injustice upon others. What neighbor, what abutter, what colleague is not swept off his feet? None can withstand the force of the rich man, everything bows to his sway and trembles at his rule. Anyone who has been hurt thinks more about how to avoid something worse than about how to protest in court against past ills. The rich man drives in his yokes of oxen, he plows and sows and harvests what is not his, and, if you protest, there are blows, if you complain, there are writs for assault, you are arrested, you will take up your lodging in jail. False accusers are a clever lot, able to bring your very life into danger.[94]

Basil's picture of how a sufficiently ruthless aggressor operates must reflect what he had sometimes witnessed in Cappadocia. After all, he is directing his sermon to the audience before him. They must see themselves, or at least their own world, in what he tells them. It fits, however, with what John Chrysostom reveals about the region around Antioch.

John's most emphatic description occurs in one of his sermons on Saint Matthew's Gospel:

> Who could be more oppressive than landlords? If you look at the way in which they treat their miserable tenants, you will find them more savage than barbarians. They lay intolerable and continual imposts upon men who are weakened with hunger and toil throughout their lives and they put upon them the burdens of oppressive services. They use their bodies like asses and mules, or rather like stones, hardly letting them breathe, and they strain them equally in good years and bad, never giving the slightest relief. They make them work all through the winter in cold and rain, they deprive them of sleep, and send them home with empty hands, indeed with debts still to pay. Moreover, the tortures and beatings, the exactions and ruthless demands for services which such men suffer from the agents are worse than hunger. Who could recount the ways in which these agents use them for profit and then cheat them? Their labor turns the agent's wine-press; but they receive not a scrap of the produce which they are compelled illegally to bottle for the agent, receiving only a tiny sum for this work. Moreover, the agent extorts more oppressive interest than even pagan law allows, not twelve but fifty per cent from a man with a wife and children, who is filling the agent's barn and wine-store by his own labor.[95]

While this description, unlike Basil's, is spread broadly across all landowners by definition, they cannot have been so universally monstrous. By the same reasoning, the earlier, less full and dramatic indications of avaricious violence in landlord-tenant relations must leave a great deal of room for moderate men like Pliny the Younger. The argument is from human nature, in part; in part, from reasons of convenience and practicality. Outrageous treatment of dependents would in the end defeat its own purposes. But in any case my object here is not to quantify such treatment; rather, to make clear that it existed and that, in consequence, every rural laborer or tenant must, out of prudence, protect himself against the worst by seeking the patronage of the best district magnates known to him. By the same sort of calculation, anyone today buys insurance not because he supposes there is much chance of some particular catastrophe striking, but because he could hardly survive it from his own resources if it did.

The dependency of peasants on big landowners was not complete, nor was justice always on their side in a dispute. They might beat up or even kill the man sent to collect the rents.[96] They might be clumsy, improvident, or lazy, and therefore well deserve eviction. Pliny's difficulties on his estates suggest as much. And it might actually be the owner who supported them in their hardships or in other ways improved their lives. But that only confirmed their dependency. They expressed it by a continual flow of such tiny gifts as their fields or woods afforded: a honeycomb, a rabbit.[97] Such gifts came to be looked on by the recipient as a right . "I saw a poor man in the course of being forced to pay what he could not pay, and dragged off to jail because some great man's table lacked wine," says Ambrose.[98]

Whether for a gift, then, or for their rents, the Haves in the later empire often bore down very hard on the Have-nots, and the latter in that case could only survive by entrusting their defense to some powerful friend. Libanius describes that resort in his often-cited forty-seventh oration, in which the protector is the commander of troops stationed in the district; and Peter Brown has revealed the role of the holy man in likewise mediating between the peasantry and their oppressors, including imperial tax collectors. Such mediation by an abbot, hermit, or wonder-working bishop appears not only in the eastern provinces but in the western as well.[99]

Libanius, in the oration just mentioned (47.2), acknowledges that his words will arouse the hostility of "those who possess power. I expect they are angry and will seek vengeance on me." In the light of what has been pointed out above, concerning the ethic of retaliation, to say nothing of the logic of the situation, the orator surely had reason to fear some act from his opponents. They were, after all, the military. Because of their particular license to bring physical force to bear, they were indeed highly valuable protectors to civilians, whether peasants or aristocrats. They were supposed to make themselves available as guards where criminal violence could be anticipated. In the later empire they were much more often posted in or near cities (see Appendix C). Their availability correspondingly increased. But they were called on earlier, for instance, to help and defend a master seeking runaway slaves.[100]

Two other mentions from Libanius shed light on power relations. In one, a private feud is pursued through some invented charges. From it develop harassing visits by the imperial authorities to the victim's estates, until in the end he is obliged to devote his full strength to their defense. The second mention concerns litigation also. It is, says Libanius, common for people to fake evidence of a fright or attack and then to run to the governor with their complaints. "This is the normal treatment of the weaker at the hands of the more powerful. . . . Brutal masters make use of this technique." Peasants could put up little resistance. "If they do not acquiesce in the extortions that are practised upon them, just a word or two is needed, and a soldier goes down to the farm, ready with fetters; they are arrested, and the jail takes them in."[101] Thus to borrow force from the courts, from their presidents and their agents who were friends, or bribed, or perhaps only dupes, was in fact the most common means by which the Haves asserted their own power to hurt. I have referred to several instances already (nn. 93, 94, and 98).

Admirers of the empire may take pleasure in the fact that power outside of government nevertheless behaved in a civilized fashion in the pursuit of revenge or intimidation — that it petitioned the courts, "played the game," acknowledged authority, and restrained itself from violent, primitive self-help. Or contrariwise: if the courts could be made the instrument of private ends, what had become of the majesty of the law? In comparing that marvelous structure called Roman jurisprudence — marvelous in all its joints and height, in all its niceties and its deliberations — with the justice actually delivered, differences between them emerge all too plainly. The judge was bribed (I deal with that possibility in the next chapter); worse, the judge was honest but brought to the definition of his duty his own ideas of both justice and propriety. He enjoyed great latitude in arriving at his decisions, as litigants did likewise in presenting their case before him. He could not refuse to admit any evidence offered. He himself felt accountable not so much to a system or a discipline as to the general values of the social strata which he served; and jurors drawn from those same strata, or very nearly so, approached *their* duties as he did his. The moral code of judge and jury together tolerated various forms of gentlemen's agreements, the exchange of favors, the expression of one's own *dignitas* from the tribunal; they did not tolerate insolence, meaning the claim to justice as a right by persons too low to deserve it. No, indeed. Right and wrong had to yield to realities — that is, to rank (above, note 3). All this was more bluntly expressed in the question which so often opened the testimony of a witness. He would be asked, What is your place in society, *cuius condicionis?* The quality of his very advocates would be weighed — their *dignitas.*[102] As the case developed, as the crucial points appeared at which it was just one man's word against another's, so long as one knew what sort (what rank) of person one was dealing with, one could be confident of making no really serious errors in judgment.

Our two most reliable records of hearings show how things worked for an accused of fairly high position compared with the judge's. One was the second-century trial of Apuleius, in which he clearly tried to establish himself as someone of wealth and cultivation. Obviously he supposed this would weigh in his favor. The other, the trial of Phileas at Alexandria, belongs to a time of persecutions. Phileas, though a magistrate of the city, was a bishop; so he was at first cruelly handled by the prison guards. Thereafter, however, he was questioned by the provincial prefect with much patience and some show of concern to spare him: "Can you not act rationally? . . . I am doing a favor, a *beneficium* [he uses the Latin word], for your brother. Just do me a favor in return. . . . If you were one of the peasants, the fellahin, who had surrendered from necessity, I would have no mercy on you. But since you have wealth enough to take care not only of your own wants but the whole city's, for the sake of that, be nice to yourself and perform the sacrifice." Whereupon the lawyers that his brother had brought to the hearing break in with their thoughts, and "the jurors and the whole staff of the city-manager begged the prefect to allow him [Phileas] some reflection."[103] So great was the consideration to be shown to a rich magistrate. It was not thus for ordinary accused Christians, as can be easily seen in the rest of the dossier of their trials.

Aelius Aristides, in his panegyric addressed to Rome, does indeed discover in the procedure of appeal to the emperor "a fair and ample equality of the little man as against the great, of the unknown as against the famous, of the poor as against the rich, and of the man with no pedigree against the noble."[104] But there is no difficulty in reconciling that perception of the legal process with what has been presented up to now. For the emperor was, after all, the emperor. He played a particular, well-defined, often expounded, uniquely exalted role as the dispenser of justice to every one of his subjects. *Every* one: so Antoninus Pius whom Aristides was addressing responded to the appeal even of slaves against their masters. They needed only to flee to his statue to gain that attention. When an obscure Jew was arrested as a troublemaker, he,

Saint Paul, could obtain a change of venue to — Nero. Appellants went over the heads of provincial and other judges routinely, still under Diocletian, sometimes under Constantine. At the height of its refinement the judicial process required of judges as an obligation that they report on capital cases to the throne. To the extent of his goodwill, energy, and ease of access, Antoninus Pius therefore answered to Aristides' panegyric. He did so in no unusual degree. As the tenth book of Pliny's correspondence shows for the few years of his appointment, and as Fergus Millar has shown from a great mass of material for both earlier and later centuries, most emperors did indeed work very hard at their role as judges.[105]

But the empire they presided over was vast; communication was slow and difficult, and their working day had only so many hours. Thus in his own difficulties, as we have seen, Aristides never thought of appealing to Antoninus Pius. Instead he brought to bear all the great but lesser names he could command and supposed they would prevail with the judge. He was right (and his views of the judge's venality we shall come to later). Direct or indirect imperial adjudication never touched more than a tiny fraction of the empire's caseload.

We have been able to make a good guess why Aristides won. The judge had been threatened, not obscurely, by a person of gigantic influence. He had been scared. That extra pressure had been required because the other party had appealed against the first verdict — a verdict favorable to Aristides. Initial letters of support had gained Aristides that much, but it was about to be lost. Then arrived another letter from a kinsman and a dear friend of the judge. To top it all, Aristides personally visited the ex-consul Rufinus to solicit the pressure already referred to.[106] Could so substantial a person as the judge be intimidated? Of course. In the same part of the world and at a date not too far removed, another literary man, Lucian, discussed the possibilities of a suit against an attempt to murder him; "but the then governor of Bithynia and Pontus, Avitus [A.D. 165], checked me, all but beseeching and imploring me to leave off, because out of good will to [the ex-consul] Rutilianus he could not, he said, punish [Lucian's enemy] even if he should find him clearly guilty of crime."[107]

In one of Cicero's earliest defenses he refers openly to bystanders present on the persecution's side, "men of the highest nobility and greatest power, whose numbers and attendance would thoroughly alarm anyone, litigant or not." These are the types against whom someone of a much lower rank, even though victim of a rape, could hardly summon the courage to lodge a suit. The realities of such a mismatch were revealed in an oration referred to a few pages above.[108] Centuries later, the likelihood of intimidation in similar circumstances still troubled the imperial government: no one, so its edicts declared, must be deprived of access to justice through the canvassing conducted by his opponent or his own fear of the man's powerful supporters; no one should "dread with good reason a trial to which, according to the menaces of a powerful adversary, he advanced as if already in chains."[109] While some of this evidence concerns Rome and the praetor's edict, other parts touch the provincial scene — not further specified. Of similar broad reach is the comment offered by Tacitus about a prominent Cretan "accused under various charges, as the most powerful of the provincials usually are accused, since they are borne up on their excessive wealth to the hurt of lesser folk." That is, they are bound to make enemies in their rise who would gladly serve as the means of their downfall. Plutarch, too, speaks of "the powerful," "the Top Men" engaged in feuding in their cities, the law courts being one of the theaters or instruments for that. He seems to have in mind more than the cities of his own Greece. Finally, Pliny in the same period discusses a number of trials he had heard about or had to preside over when he was in Bithynia and Pontus, in which the motive of personal vengeance or some other extraneous purpose had evidently produced the charges in the first place.[110] One of them concerned a local notable called Flavius Archippus of Prusa who, through his agent, accused no less an opponent than Dio Chrysostom of malversation of public funds and high treason to boot. The former charge chimes with the orator's own speeches, which betray a certain nervousness about his attempts at urban renewal. It must not be forgotten that criminal cases coming before a judge began with someone laying information before him, that is, with informers. In the absence of public prosecutors, the government could hardly forbid them to operate; so the way lay open to abuse of the law.

A charge of treason was quite chilling even under one of the so-called good emperors. A civil case in which your opponent was serious, whether or not he really had a leg to stand on, could stretch on and on for years and consume endless time and money: for example, a certain Drusilla's suit that was instituted before the appropriate Egyptian court in the early 130s. It concerned an unpaid loan made in 118. After many objections and motions and deaths of legatees and litigants, it was settled only in A.D. 147/8. Delays of just that sort made law a bitter joke in all periods, and Eunapius in the later empire was right to say "they give strength to the unjust cause."[111] Win or lose, then, litigation could be a most effective weapon with which to punish enemies, protect friends, and intimidate the victims of avarice or fraud.

Only in the later period, however, were the possibilities fully realized. For this, the greater harshness of judges was chiefly to blame or to credit. The subject must be reserved for a later page, but I should offer at this point an illustration of it to make vivid how the mere threat of the courts, when their severity was so frightening, could break down opposition. Our account belongs to the first quarter of the fifth century.[112]

> There was, then, a municipal treasurer (*dispensator*) of Carthage city, a man by the name of Florentius; and, in such a position of responsibility for fiscal suits, as is likely to happen to the persons litigating, they run counter to the concerns of the powers for whom they are acting and whose authority they serve. This man had committed an offense to arouse the governor's displeasure, to the hazard of his own head. In this matter, by some order of the governor, he was abruptly commanded to be seized and presented before him. So then, without any delay, the office he worked for obeyed and produced the said treasurer, having been publicly arrested, before the governor, in his chambers. An awful fear straightway overspread the bystanders in their hearts at the spectacle before them, and with fellow-feeling they grieved for the fellow and feared for his danger. Meantime, seeing before him the man whom he sought in his wrath, that person in power arose, showing his anger in a terrifying, threatening tone, and his questioning induced panic in the treasurer. His wits departed from the terror-stricken man, so he could not find the words for his answers. . . . While the treasurer stood there, in doubt of his very life, surrounded by the Interrogators (torturers) and gripped by his fear of the frightening person in power . . . [and so forth].

What needs to be emphasized in this scene is, first, the effect produced upon chance witnesses, "the bystanders," by all they saw and heard. Litigation or the threat of litigation becomes a far heavier weapon in a society exposed to such frightening displays of wrath and strength. In the second place, I should emphasize the initiative here taken not by a private citizen but by an official, a phenomenon far more often reported in the later empire; and, whether for himself or for another person who stands behind him, the increase in authority means correspondingly increased ability to hurt. My focus is still on that negative aspect.

A second, briefer illustration comes from Ravenna a decade or two earlier, where anyone passing through the center of the city could not fail to see and notice "the jail crowded with people awaiting torture and death . . . a crowd condemned to that by various great powers in the Palace."[113] Again, the emphasis is on officials who are applying their authority on a scale and with a harshness unknown in earlier centuries. All of their victims must be supposed to have passed through trial and condemnation.

With these highly charged pictures in their minds, "sycophants" in the ancient sense of the word, that is, false accusers, could go about their business most effectively. Constantine near the outset of his reign fulminated in vain against them, calling them "the one greatest evil to human life" on account of "the accursed ruin" they caused. His own laws against them, of exceptional severity, were renewed or reinforced often thereafter, with more strong language: *delatores* were "the enemies of the human race," and so forth.[114] They remained, however, an essential device of government, in the virtual absence of official prosecutors. Their activities were even encouraged by the promise of a share of property confiscated from persons convicted through their efforts. Julian in Antioch made special efforts at least to contain them, no doubt in vain. Anyway, Libanius recounts to Theodosius how his lowlier fellow-citizens would counterfeit injuries and torn clothing and then run to the governor to lay charges of criminal assault; and he adds that "this is the normal treatment of the weaker at the hands of the powerful, of the penniless at the hands of the wealthy, of the masses at the hands of the elite who expect any charge they make to count for more than proof. This is their experience at the hands of Senators and decurions. . . . This is the treatment accorded to the manufacturing class by organizers of loyal addresses to you and by the lackeys of the governors, toward such as do not gratify their every whim."[115] The courts and jails, through "sycophants," thus served officials as a means of controlling, of bullying, and of extorting obedience and more than obedience; for governors and other officials who enjoyed rights of jurisdiction grew rich from it.[116]

They might also pursue feuds and private ends of other sorts. Ammianus relates how, when an emperor by rare chance was passing through Galatia, the people there "exerted themselves to the point of madness to involve their rivals in charges of high treason." Off in a quite different sector of the empire, Augustine's letter to a prefect of Italy retails the general belief that the prefect had directed Count Marinus to proceed against two of his private enemies on false charges of complicity in a recent rebellion. The count's "power then was great. Hence sprang the ease of lodging false accusations. It was no great business to find someone willing to declare (through a promise of immunity) what he was ordered to say. Those were all recommended practices at that time, with the result that anybody might be snatched to his death on the testimony of a single witness, as if for some hateful yet believable crime, and without risk to the person in charge."[117] We hear of other feuds on the testimony of two bishops from their respective provinces: Synesius in Cyrene, where "informers proliferate evilly" and attack his friends and kin, in one case in a campaign of extortion, and Theodoret in northeastern Syria, where people, he says, find that the things really to fear are "the judge, tribunal, court clerks, attendants and tax exactions; and if a person is poor the fear is doubled." Theodoret's assessment conveys a bleak impression of late Roman justice. Of course the rich could put up a better defense, partly through their influence, partly by hiring some effective lawyer. Libanius congratulates himself that "I have taught the youths," his students in oratory, "how they may be avenged on anyone who has done them an injury." Obviously he is thinking of litigation, not chance name-calling in the agora.[118]

That general belief in the Italian prefect's guilt, which Augustine recounts and evidently shares, was based only on circumstantial evidence. It was known that the prefect had some score to settle with the man arrested. Therefore, the world being what it was, he would certainly seek to be avenged. Besides, he visited the locale, appeared very cozy with the count, "and conferred with him in confidence; . . . rumor grew stronger from the close company [he] kept and such continual private conversations with him." That was in Carthage in 414. Libanius aims exactly similar complaints at the intimates of the governor in Antioch twenty-five years earlier: they crowd his courtroom, hang about his bench, whisper in his ear, and even interrupt his postprandial nap.[119] Such intimacy, or even its appearance, was well worth seeking out because of the rumors it gave rise to. The reputation for being able to influence decisions was a species of power in itself; nor was it necessarily fictional.

Libanius, like Fronto or Aristides (above, n. 86), wrote letter after letter to judges in favor of litigants or to get someone out of jail. He thought his efforts would work. No doubt they did, sometimes. Synesius wrote, so did Augustine, Basil, Symmachus, everyone.[120] It was an obligation of one's power to the degree one had any. Clear proofs of the realities they had to deal with may be read in the laws of the later empire, even more often than in the Principate, denouncing "the powerful" by whose association with a case the verdict was as good as settled. Hence an emperor saying: "Many people, We notice, being without hope for their mis-matched cases, oppose to the persons who are suing them the high titles of the powerful and special rights of senatorial rank. In order that terror inspired by their adversaries may not lead to the usurpation of these names and titles," the practice is forbidden. In vain: the law had to be repeated.[121]

The judge who gave way to the pressures put on him was sometimes very well rewarded. Thanks for his cooperation might be expressed in a material form or in an understanding that a debt had been incurred and must be repaid in the future. Sometimes, of course, the pressures were nothing but threats; but sometimes he had good reason to fear force and influence that could prevail even against his authority. In surveying the various forms of the power to hurt, I thus come finally to those that were aimed against government itself. As a large problem, they belong to the later period and constitute an interesting commentary on the relationship between the state and the private citizen. In illustration, there is the account by the urban prefect of Rome,

Symmachus, who in 384 was hearing a case of unlawful distraint. Despite a court's order, a certain Scirtius had been forcibly locked out of his own land by Olybrius — consular, former praetorian prefect, whose mere agent is a senator. The tenants on the estate had been kidnapped to prevent their giving evidence and hustled off to Olybrius' villa, while a countersuit attempts to prove that the land was given by Scirtius to his children (and, if it were in their hands, it would be easier to get hold of).[122] Against a criminal of this rank and energy Symmachus by himself is really helpless.

The defiance of lawful authority is striking — no more so, however, than Theodosius' need to remind *potentes* in his eastern provinces of their obligation to obey court summonses, or Gratian's protest to the vicar of Rome a decade earlier (A.D. 378/9) that judges' decisions must be vigorously supported; for, he says, "no one should fear that their modest authority will be weakened and uprooted by the powerful and insolent."[123] The confession of weakness offered here is heard again, and at just the same period, in another of Symmachus' reports, stating that "Valerianus of senatorial rank, whose home is said to be in Epirus, is not moved by reverence for rescripts or severity of laws or good faith in agreements or respect of judges. Being first ordered to answer a summons to examination before the praetor, on the petition of Junior of senatorial rank, he evaded the pressure of that order and the decision of high authority. Next, summoned by proconsular command, he baffled the laws with the same cleverness; and now, although under pressure of both civil complaint and criminal charges, he resists commands like a rebel," accounting for the death of one Special Agent (*agens in rebus*) and the wounding of another. In despair of his own resources, Symmachus refers the matter to the emperor, "for Yourself alone duly punishes the misdoings of the most powerful ranks."[124] For so great a nobleman in so high a position to confess defeat, a defeat in which imperial authority is involved and reduced to nothing, the *potentiores* must have indeed deserved their title.

The phenomenon was by no means peculiar to Symmachus' century. Consider the legist Gaius, none more famous. He is discussing the special difficulties entailed in bringing suit "against a man of another province or a *potentior*." Most networks of personal influence had geographical limits, just as they had a geographical center in a person's hometown and landholdings around it. There, he could best defend himself, he was "more powerful"; and *potentiores* (or *potentes*) commanded strength of just that sort. But they were always at the center of some web of influence regardless of where one found them; and, Gaius goes on, "we cannot be a match for *potentior*," a person of greater wealth and influence (which is what the term means). His statement only sounds like a tautology. In fact it goes beyond that: law itself, Gaius is confessing, constitutes no match for a certain type of person well known to us — us ordinary litigants. The type has even gained a sort of title by which he is routinely referred to among the legists.[125] Another of them, Julianus, of almost equal fame, takes up a case where "a man whose troop of slaves prevented a neighbor from drawing water would allow no access to himself, so he could not be sued." *Could not be!*[126] The setting is rural, like that with which Gaius deals; and *potestas* was more easily exerted away from the city, as I pointed out above (pp. 84–86). No matter: it is conceded that in certain parts of the empire law and government did not exist. Or rather, government of another sort existed and enforced its will on the very springs of power, landed estates, by which a senator, equestrian, decurion, or any other person "of wealth and influence" was nourished. To defy the state, only a determination that would not flinch from violence was required. "Like a man who says to his neighbor," runs a quotation from a rabbi, " 'That man will not undergo sentence, for So-and-So is his patron and is protecting him.' " The evidence from Palestine is matched by more of the same from Egypt. Julianus and Gaius have not been speaking in terms of theory alone.[127]

With this quotation we are moving about in the latter part of the third century and now encounter a variant: *potestas* deriving from imperial office. A woman of Theadelphia in Egypt complains that, when her husband died and she was left defenseless, the shepherds of a certain Syrion seized a flock of her sheep. The district judge orders their return. "But look at what Syrion is up to," protests the woman's lawyer. "He resists your commands and the prefects's too, and for this reason we speak out, that you should order him produced." A familiar problem, noncompliance with a summons, here with a new twist: "The lawyer [of Syrion] said, 'Syrion has been sent off on urgent affairs concerning the Treasury, but as soon as he returns he will respond.' "[128] Maybe.

A few papyri, a fragment of Talmud, an anonymous collection of ecclesiastical correspondence, Symmachus, the *Corpus Iuris*, and three lines of ecclesiastical law which I soon come to: the assortment of sources declares the role of chance in our knowledge about the routines, the taken-for-granted realities, of life. It is, for example, almost inevitable that more detail should be forthcoming from the eastern provinces than from anywhere else. Still, the third-century jurists do not localize their discussion of ungovernable power. Neither does Constantine in the 320s, when he instructs *vicarii* to take over cases where some *potentior* "is able to overwhelm a weaker, lowlier judge"; and, he says, "provincial governors, if some *potentior* appears too impudent and they themselves can't punish or examine or denounce him," should refer the problem to Himself.[129] A good deal of subsequent legislation reveals that the powerful expected to defy tax collectors, rural or urban, as well as imperial officials bent on reclaiming the urban services of fugitive decurions. With these laws we have returned to the later fourth century and the decades of Symmachus from which this discussion of violent defiance began. In 384, quite of a piece with Symmachus' complaints, Theodosius promulgated a constitution dealing with government requisition of products in kind throughout the provinces. "Only the houses of the *potentiores*, that is, of the great landholders, have been assigned to this duty [of supply]. However, they are subject to exhortation only, and no necessity is enjoined upon them." A confession of inadequacy, surely.[130] In the face of the *potentes* and their misdeeds, the church, too, at its Toledo council of A.D. 400 confessed its bishops unequal; and a fugitive from the general impossibility of life in the Danube provinces in the second quarter of the fifth century recalls, "if a wealthy, powerful man exerted himself against the law, he need pay no penalty."[131] Exactly as the rabbi had said! — many generations earlier.

What distinguished the whole development here traced was the gradual emergence of particular types among the Haves who belonged because of their wealth and could be explicitly defined as *possessores*, great landowners. Yet they were different. Beyond the leverage that money put in their hands, they asserted independence of a special quality which raised them above the law. Municipal authorities, district judges, governors, prefects of the capital, the emperor himself could not command them. Not that they ever put an army into the field, or ever could have; nor did they ever have to withstand a serious siege. Any company of fifty soldiers could have brought one of them to heel. But it was never attempted. The rules of life would not permit it. They for their part could reach out with their strength to rob or hurt some neighbor and, in the face of officialdom, retreat to safety behind their mere intransigence. There is no sign of them within the empire of Trajan's day, hardly any for a century after that. To explain their triumphant challenge, only broad changes in the empire's types and structure of power will suffice. But that is a matter I reserve for the next chapter.

4. HOW POWER WORKED: THROUGH FAVOR

I now turn to *positive* inducements to obedience that gave the Haves their hold over people around them. This, their more attractive side, is very familiar to anyone who knows the ancient world. At least its outlines, too, could easily be sketched from common sense.

No doubt wealth is the point to start with. Everyone wanted money and the Haves by definition had a lot. Landed property of course was something separate, on which a dependent was not likely to count much, except perhaps through bequest. Cash, on the other hand, or the chance to make, save, or collect it, or excuse from paying it, the Haves could certainly provide. In the later empire their interventions produced savings in taxes for their clients. Though direct evidence for each of these applications of power is very rare,[132] there seems to be no special reason to doubt their operation or really to expect much more. Our sources, however grudging, simply confirm the obvious. However, it is worth noting how little gold and silver has been found in the rich houses of Pompeii, not because the owners managed to escape with it but because they kept their liquid capital constantly at work for them in the form of loans. By that means and the others that anyone can imagine, they laid their needier or greedier fellow-citizens under obligation to them.

It is very well known and obvious, too, that the economic dependence of an individual was matched by that of groups of citizens (trade associations in particular, but cult- and other groups as well) and whole cities themselves. Their dependence extended through both their good times — banquets, entertainments, and so forth — and their bad. Relief of food shortages or gifts specified "in times of high prices" or the like were expected from the rich. The rich covered much of the cost of religious life, and most of the cost of public buildings and major single items of urban improvement like paving and drainage. All this is well known. Points in the relationship can be illustrated, perhaps illuminated. It is the usually bland Antoninus Pius who sets the donor of useful construction in his native city above "most public figures," who are content merely to "gain instant popularity through expenditure on shows and gratis distributions and prizes for contests."[133] "Popularity": that makes explicit what one would have assumed. There is meaning, too, in the fact that "richly" is a term often applied in praise of the activity of leading citizens, who, as we have seen, were fairly shouted into expenditures they had not intended.[134] Thanked, they were not always loved. Not all deserved to be, though that was no impediment to their power. More likely it helped.[135]

Beyond their own money, the great citizens of great cities could bring in the emperor's. Ordinarily they succeeded in this only by seeking him out and asking him for a remission of tribute, exemption of city-owned property, permission to raise their own city's taxes, or an outright grant of some sort. Nonmonetary honors were sought, too, with equal eagerness: the right to some certain title for the city, some certain privilege. Missions to the imperial court were major affairs requiring wealth and eloquence in generous amounts. Many great names of envoys are known to us: Herodes Atticus, for one; orators like Favorinus or Polemo; a saint (Germanus); but also Quintus Cornelius Zosimus, a mere freedman because he was representing the needs of a mere village (near Arles). In the reign of Antoninus Pius he "remained at Rome through many years, following up our complaint also before governors of the province at his own expense, and in this cause made a gift to us of his expenses." From Ephesus, an envoy and benefactor pursued the emperor Septimius Severus all the way to Britain![136] Great effort was needed to maintain the ties of government with the communities for which it was responsible, and most of that effort was expended by the Haves, the powerful, unremunerated. Imperial legates existed and proconsuls, procurators, and other agents sent out from Rome. The emperor kept in touch with them. It was not enough. To so infinitely rich and beneficent a patron as he was perceived to be, direct communication could not fail to reward the right envoys, who waited their turn, spoke their piece, and prayed to the goddess of Safekeeping.

As obviously useful as the money the Haves commanded were their connections. They could count on people to oblige them everywhere, clearly because their name and kin and possessions were everywhere. The Treasury officer Vitalis in Alexandria in 323 scribbled two identical documents, nothing more than a word of introduction to a couple of his acquaintances. The one to the governor of Phoenicia tells him that he, the recipient, who is always so nice to everybody, should please be nice to the bearer, another government servant. So the bearer starts off on his journey assured of receiving help and more letters and probably a good meal and a bed, once he gets to Phoenicia.[137] The arrangement had nothing to do with the people concerned being officials, and it signified nothing that the letters were produced quite mechanically. The needs of life repeat themselves. For that reason Basil wrote letters not yet specifying either bearer or recipient, to deal with the day's most common requests: Please lower taxes on such-and-such a piece of church property, please welcome So-and-So, who is a capital fellow of outstanding character. The names would be filled in as needed.

But if you had to go farther than Phoenicia, you would need other homes to take you in on the way. Commercial people from all over Asia who gathered at the great fair of Cyzicus knew where they would receive hospitality and assistance, and corporately they voted their thanks to the mistress of the house.[138] At Corinth, if you arrived from distant Lycia, whether engaged in your own affairs or as a representative of your native place on *legatio* to the emperor, Junia Theodora would provide welcome and money in generous amounts; better, she was able to "secure the friendship of most of the governors for the province" and make them well disposed. The cities of Myra, Patara, and Telmessos offered her grateful testimonials. Other similar inscriptions express gratitude to a friend in Pergamon, "benefactor of the city in many and great matters, enjoying respect among governors"; at Delphi, to a person "possessing the greatest weight with governors"; at Miletus, to another "employing his friendships and guest-relationships with governors for the good of his native place"; and more of the same sort of praise for Gaius Licinnius Thoantianus, "guest-relation (xenos) and friend of governors and proconsuls and procurators." He takes us back to Oenoanda in Lycia; also, to the great web of kin in fig. 15, above.[139]

In understanding how Roman government worked, it is of the first importance to note and weigh the power relationships existing outside of it yet at many points joined to it. The quite minute numbers of imperial agents in the Principate so assiduously cultivated by Gaius Licinnius Thoantianus — "governors and proconsuls and procurators" — with the best will in the world could handle only a tiny, tiny portion of what we today would call "government's problems"; for they numbered a few hundred at most. Even counting their lictors and full-time scribes, they were quite lost in a sea of humanity (sixty millions, let us say). How different the western world of recent generations! But historians of everything but modern times hardly need to be reminded of that. The reach of formally constituted authority, directly through a spoken word, a physical presence, or indirectly through a written directive or law, is nowadays almost everywhere and was once almost nowhere. Hence, in the civilized administration of less "civilized" peoples, government and the powers outside had to work together; but the latter did the most, by far. They did so through such networks of kin and correspondence, debts and favors, as Gaius Licinnius Thoantianus belonged to.

To the Intendant of Languedoc from the Intendant of Roussillon, April 25, 1676:[140]
    Dear Sir:
I have learned that you would like to know who the sieurs Bazin and Laisné were, whom I stationed last winter in Narbonne to oversee the constructions for the artillery. Since these are men who depend to a certain extent on me [i.e., "are under my patronage"], I am more qualified than anyone else to answer for them before you. Therefore let me inform you that the sieur Bazin is an artillery commissioner who has been connected with my family for a very long time, and that sieur Laisné is an agent of the artillery bureau whose commission is completely controlled by my brother. From this you can clearly see that these two persons are entirely dependent on me and that if they have done anything of which you do not approve, I will compel them to give complete satisfaction. . . . I do not know whether I dare take the liberty of making a very humble plea before you on behalf of messieurs Claviers and de St. Privat. They are brothers-in-law of a gentleman who is one of my particular friends. I haven't the least idea what the affair is about,

but I hope that in your justice and goodness you will do everything you can for them, on my behalf. You will be doing me a great favor if you would let them know that I spoke to you in favor of their interests.

Just such communications joined the two structures of power in the ancient world. Anyone reading Pliny's letters will attest to that. Service under the emperor was a great thing in itself, and respected for what it was. It also extended and enhanced the capacities and connections through which appointment had been won in the first place. So the senate of Aquileia says of a notable son, "whatever influence or power might be gained through the highest equestrian appointments he directed toward the strengthening and beautifying of his native place, thinking himself happiest in his exertions to bestow favors on it."[141] By means of office you could win more benefits, you could control more decisions and careers, visit in grander houses. Through the master or mistress, Junia Theodora or Thoantianus, you could 'govern' the lives of as distant a place as Lycia. When your term of office ended you still had what you started with, the network, by which your control could continue to be exerted through letters to other people of power.

Junia Theodora chose even to be buried with the testimonials she had earned. They were of immense significance to her. Opramoas kept his in a neat chronological file stretching over twenty-five years and, when he published them on stone, stretching over many meters as well. Flavius Archippus had his own handy to brandish in the face of his attackers. Many a dog-eared collection must have been carried around for years and years by worried, humbler people. In the world's estimation such correspondence defined their proportions, their *dignitas*.

To gain more, you must ask. "As soon as it was known that a friend of his had obtained a post, Libanius was overwhelmed by demands for letters of recommendation. Help was not sought by private travellers only; even a newly appointed governor might seek letters of commendation to leading men of his province."[142] The reason for the latter requests lay in considerations of administrative effectiveness, perhaps of personal aggrandizement as well. A term of duty provided ideal opportunities to extend one's presence into new areas, for instance, by accepting invitations to become the patron of some town or of some commercial or craft association. Besides the equestrian official whose relations with his home, Aquileia, were just described, other explicit testimonies indicate what neighbors, kin, friends, and fellow-citizens expected when one of their number attained some new position of influence: he should share it.[143] A good deal of material in further illustration of this was gathered in notes 73–78 above.

Helpful above all else was some position close to the very emperor — even at his feet: his chiropractor. Or as servant to other unspecified parts of his august self: his personal physician.[144] Marcus Aurelius' tutor, Fronto from Cirta, was naturally asked to be its patron by that substantial city. He declined, but gave the names of other commendable persons, all, as he says, "occupying the foremost place at the bar these days." Evidently much of a provincial city's problems would have to be argued out in one or another court at the capital.[145]

At the capital, too, many decisions were made about promotion to the higher ranks of the civil service, and about the traditional magistracies up to the consulships. In the second century perhaps two or three dozen candidacies had to be approved by the emperor every month. I am not at all sure about the number, except that it grew as time went on. In making his choice the emperor had naturally to rely on other people's advice — whose names and importance would be known (and certainly not concealed by themselves, either). They, in turn, must choose among the many names thrust at them by recommenders at the next remove from the locus of decision. And so on. Whatever weight of pressure may have been brought to bear in this process viva voce, surviving evidence is inevitably in writing. There are Pliny's letters in particular; but the rhetor Alexander, we are told, "was the cause of many of them [his pupils] gaining every other honor . . . he passed his whole life doing good for his kin, friends, country and city"; and Libanius did the same for his students at Antioch.[146] Pliny reveals some unexpected casualness and complexity, both, in the award of army commissions. You took care of your own dependents first; then you opened up other slots to be filled by selected friends; they for their part might pass on to *their* friends the right to a slot or two; and ultimately the person who must approve the appointment need know nothing of the finalists but their names. Never mind, he had built up credit on which he could draw at some future time, as had also the other, initial patrons.[147] If any of the appointees should fail signally, then you could hold their patron responsible, like the Intendant of Roussillon.

Important acts of intervention on one's behalf by someone more powerful were called *beneficia*. That was the word Pliny used to describe the business about army tribunates. The same term explains an army rank specially familiar to civilians because specially common in rural police duties and at toll-stations: *beneficiarius consularis*. Greek '*charis*' came close to *beneficium* but had too wide a range of other meanings to be a good synonym — for which reason, perhaps, the Latin after a while came to be transliterated into Greek (e.g., in the Nicene Council canons) as into Hebrew, too. The eastern provinces like the western, from their early contacts with the Romans, were obliged to learn both the vocabulary and the reality of a set of values different from their own, according to which a favor must be borne in mind and returned with the utmost punctuality. The difference of course did not lie in exchanging favors, which everybody did and does all the time; rather, in the seriousness with which the exchange was treated. It was a matter of honor, of worth and integrity, of good faith, *fides*. No doubt Caesar, through the servant assigned to keep his *beneficia*–books, taught strictness to the Gallic chieftains he dealt with, as Acilius Glabrio had once to teach the Aetolians the meaning of *fides*. Centuries later, Plutarch still draws attention to the special ways of the dominant culture.[148] By his day the lessons had been learned, just as Roman citizenship had been acquired by all the local elites whom Romans dealt with. At that level at least it was one world, one ethical system.

The letter of Pliny's concerning army commissions (*Ep.* 2.13), referred to a paragraph earlier, reveals much about proper practices. It begins, "Just as you would eagerly embrace any chance to oblige me, so there is no one above yourself to whom I would be more willingly indebted." The words chosen have a certain Caesarian, bookkeeping quality about them. Cicero, Pliny elsewhere, and Marcus Aurelius see and accept the analogy with legal money debts; Augustine in his *Confessions* (6.10.16) uses the rather strong word *obstricti* to describe the position of people who have received *beneficia*; and Libanius (*Or.* 63.8 and 17) indicates a reaction of surprise and outrage among those who have done favors for someone, *charites*, without receiving any return. Only a philosopher, Seneca, would try self-consciously to raise the whole matter to a higher, purer moral plane. That of course merely underlined the seriousness of the obligations created by *beneficia*. In recommending a person for a favor, like the Intendant of Roussillon, you were in fact conscious of staking your own *dignitas* on his proper sense of duty (so, Pliny again); and you therefore emphasized first and above all else his utter reliability, his *fides*, his record and strength of affection toward yourself. So, Cicero, Seneca, Fronto — and Pliny (*Ep.* 2.13.9): "Those *beneficia* of mine can be in no way better safeguarded than by my adding to them, especially since [the client] reveals himself as worthy of more through being so keenly appreciative of earlier ones." The network of obligations owing to you, *officia*, could thus be expanded to embrace new persons in new areas of life. They would do what you asked at some future time. In Latin, you enjoyed *gratia* with them, a sort of latent right to command. In any language that meant power.

Scholars debate a question especially (but not solely) relevant to promotions in the imperial administration. Were they awarded on the basis of merit and length of service or on the basis of favor? There is evidence on both sides. Candidates and their friends speak in terms that indicate an expectation based on a routine of advancement, and those who recommend or appoint them speak of their particular skills. On the other hand, beyond all the abundant evidence of recommendations, contemporaries sometimes say explicitly that no one can rise without their help.[149] To reconcile these contradictions, it might be better not to ask, merit or favor? — but rather, merit how defined? The first question makes sense only if we imagine government back then to resemble government now. But it didn't; or at least the mix of considerations was quite different, looking far more to the enhancement of one's personal power than to the delivery of essential administrative and judicial services. The fact has just been underlined in discussion of *beneficia/officia, gratia/fides*. Therefore merit in any applicant for a post must include a delicacy of honor and a sense of place ever mindful of obligation.

In confirmation, notice the prominence given to declarations of indebtedness even by persons of very high position, like Pliny himself, to say nothing of younger or lowlier persons on their way up. They positively glory in the "influence," *suffragium*, through which they were accorded a procuratorship. They praise their *patronus* to the skies, often in the most public way and not necessarily where it is relevant.[150] Meanwhile the patron is busy scribbling those notes to his friends and acquaintances, telling them of the bearer's *bona fides* in general, deserving of aid unspecified,[151] or more narrowly describing a dependent's problems with his rank, with his home, his liturgies, burdensome payments and taxes and contracts, his lack of employment, or the like. It is as easy to find such interventions in the fourth and fifth centuries as in the second — indeed easier, because our sources become a little more generous. There are many more collections of letters which of course will contain the correspondence of powerful people; and the church historians are useful, too. From one of them comes the account of Gerontius, first a deacon under Ambrose, later bishop (from A.D. 399 on) in a major city and former capital, Nicomedia, thanks to his getting to know all the right people at Constantinople. Most important (and the dignitary who ordained him) was the bishop of Caesarea, "who did him this service because he [Gerontius] had served as patron, *proxenos*, at the palace to his son, to win him splendid promotions." Such exchanges of service were of the essence of power, constituting a chief motive for seeking it. There was nothing shameful about that, either. Therefore, in a letter which he certainly would have shown to anyone, noble Symmachus in 398/9 wrote to a certain Longinianus congratulating him on his high office at court (perhaps as Count of the Crown Accounts) and going on to say, "The distinction of your official position shines forth through the bestowing of special favors, *beneficia*; and since the estimate of your merit makes you the intimate of most eminent people, may you seek the glory of fame and influence by your gracious acts." Which is a flowery way of saying that the very purpose of one's official position is to increase one's personal fame as a great *private* patron.[152] What Symmachus takes for granted is no different from the ethic of power prevailing in Pliny's day (above, at nn. 80f. and 141).

I set out, some pages past, to describe both the negative and positive, maleficent and beneficent, aspects of power. I now conclude that description with a juncture where the two are on display together. It concerns two people roughly equal in the social stratum they belong to; but the one who tells the story, Apuleius, is somewhat older and happens to know the governor Avitus in nearby Carthage, while the other, his stepson Pontianus, still has his way to make in life. They have clashed in a family lawsuit. Apuleius exerts his power, and Pontianus throws himself at his feet and kisses his hands, partly to gain his mother's forgiveness, partly his stepfather's. "In the humblest manner he begged me to clear him with Senator Lollianus Avitus to whom, not long before, I had recommended him at the beginning of his rhetorical training — for he had found out a few days ago that I had written Lollianus the details of what had happened [meaning, the stepson's bad behavior in the lawsuit]. This too I granted him. So off he went to Carthage with my letter in his hand, where Lollianus Avitus, his term as proconsul nearly over, was awaiting [his successor]. He read my letter and, in character with his great good nature, congratulated Pontianus on having promptly mended his ways; and he wrote back to me through him," Pontianus. Thus a word in the right place, and the news of that word let out on purpose, somehow, could bring a young man literally to his knees. Thus, too, it could be the necessary start to his career.[153]

5. POTENTIORES AND THE GOVERNMENT

If the Haves, *potentiores*, *possessores* — in short, the people who counted — were able to do so much good and ill to the great mass of the people beneath them, then those weaker ones were well advised to seek help from above. A most dramatic reminder is outlined by a rabbi in the second half of the third century. He imagines "a person who has a patron, and his enemies come upon him to seize him" and will do so even "at the gateway of the patron's court, and, while he is yet crying to be let in, the sword is drawn across his neck and he is killed."[154] That was Palestine. But the credibility of the scene is reinforced by many other chance bits of information scattered among the notes above (43–49 and 93–99). They recall scenes or indications of armed violence. There happens to be a specially rich selection for first-century Italy, confirming what

Epictetus supposes are the thoughts of the wise man in this world: "He says to himself, 'There are many robber-bands, tyrants, storms, difficulties, losses of what is most dear. Where shall a man flee for refuge? How shall he travel secure against robbery? What company shall he wait for that he may pass through in safety? To whom shall he attach himself? To So-and-So, the rich man, or the proconsul?' "

There was physical danger, then, at least on occasion and frightening. There was financial loss to be concerned about, perhaps loss of property to a bullying neighbor who pulled up your boundary posts and lied in court. That is attested. He could hire the witnesses he needed. Then, further, there was this or that positive good to be sought from the Haves, already mentioned. The range of such goods was infinite. A poet could gain access to the best audiences and receive fat gifts from them: Horace, a farm; Martial likewise. Martial numbered the Senecas, Quintilian, Annaeus Mela, Calpurnius Piso, Parthenius (Domitian's chamberlain), and others among his patrons. You could hardly have too many of them — unless, of course, they quarreled. Then all you could do was pray.[155] And you could not help it if they themselves were destroyed; but you could get out of the way of their fall.[156]

The Haves used each other to smoothe the not very stony paths of their lives. If they were ambitious to rise and grow greater, they had to rely on that same support, although in more strenuous circumstances. Aelius Aristides has been seen in action of that sort. Of unimportant people pulling such strings as they could reach from below, very little is known in detail. The efforts of a certain Lollianus may serve as example. A public school teacher in an Egyptian town, he felt underpaid in the job. He determined on a petition to the joint rulers Valerian and Gallienus (A.D. 253–60) to obtain the gift of an orchard, the rents from which would supplement his income. He prepared a number of documents, some attesting precedent for the request; some, drafts of the petition itself; some, letters to a nameless but evidently valued acquaintance in another province "who will know the consuls and generally give a lead in the best way of doing things" (though he had so far ignored two previous appeals). "You, Brother," writes Lollianus, "will easily avail yourself of those who come in to Alexandria from the Court, if you send [your letters for me] to Ammonianus the optio. . . . So it will be in your power, you who have so much influence." The *optio* is to bring the reply back just as another low-ranking army figure, a *caniclarius*, will carry Lollianus' packet out of Egypt.[157] The whole process would cost money and, over the course of at least some months of correspondence, had so far produced no results. But the petitioner had thought it all out and persists.

The operation of patronage in favor of one other person of an intermediate rank is known: Titus Sennius Sollemnis, "Superintendent of the Iron-Mines Account, the first such to whom the Three Provinces [of Gaul] ever raised a monument in his own city. The council of the free city of Viducasses provided the location." That much can be seen on the front of a stone (a marble statue-base) which is inscribed on its right and left sides also.[158] The front declares that Sollemnis "was the client of the governor of Gallia Lugdunensis, Claudius Paulinus, who sent him his salary for armed service in gold, with other presents of far greater value; and he was the most trusted client of Aedinius Julianus, governor of the same province, who was praetorian prefect, as is shown in the letter inscribed on the side." That letter is addressed by Julianus to a procurator and vice-governor, recalling how:

> when I was serving as *quinquefascalis* in Gallia Lugdunensis, I observed a number of worthy men, among whom was that Sollemnis, native of Viducasses and priest, whom I began to esteem for his sobriety of life and honorable ways. In addition, when certain persons who thought they had suffered at the hands of my predecessor Claudius Paulinus (according to their deserts) attempted to instigate an attack on him in the Council of the Gauls, as if by a consensus of the provinces, that Sollemnis of mine resisted their motion. He demanded return to the previous business, on the grounds that his own state, when making him delegate with the others, had given him no instructions for a motion and had rather offered its praises; and at this argument, everyone abandoned the accusation. I began more and more to esteem and value the man. Confident of my respect for him, he came to the city [Rome] to see me and, on his setting forth again, asked me to recommend him. You have thus done well if you favored his requests.

On the other side of the stone is another letter, this from Paulinus, explaining the rich presents he has sent along with the salary of Sollemnis. It is advanced even before formal receipt of Sollemnis' army commission. His hometown council had evidently requested these letters, and he himself must have been glad to share what reflected so much credit on him. The reason for the attention given to them here, however, is rather to show how such files of honorific correspondence, already discussed, could be initiated, indeed earned, by the right man at the right time. He had emerged suddenly from the tiniest of towns at the Gallic council meeting of August 220; like the mouse in the fable, he had freed the lion caught in a net by his enemies; he had placed an imperial official in his debt; and three years later he was on his way to that man, their joint patron, now risen to the highest possible office. From praetorian prefects, any recommendation was worth its weight in gold.

Chances for a little mouse to help a lion of course did not appear very frequently. Mice must simply accept their place in the great scheme of things. Accordingly, when poor people or people from obscure communities or obscure families appear active in the support of some magnate, it might be predicted that their role would most often be quite humble: they cheered. They cheered for hire at public readings of literary works; they cheered in favor of some candidate for imperial appointment or honorific endorsement by the council of the province where he had been serving. To that last scene I return very shortly.[159] Cheering in rhythmic phrases has been described, in which a decurion, bishop, or emperor is acclaimed; and theater scenes or moments before a crowd have been described in which a magnate, a *potentior*, a benefactor, is hailed as savior, founder, son or father or mother of the community, *hyios* or *pater* or *meter* (above, n. 10).

"Service and protection," wrote J. C. Baroja, "are the reciprocal links which hold a system of patronage together. At the same time the patron increases his prestige through the possession of clients, while the client participates in the glory of his patron. . . . The system is reinforced through the institution of ritual kinship and expressed in its idiom. The terms *padrino, apadrinar, compadre* (godfather, to sponsor, co-parent) have extensions far beyond the literal sense. *El que tiene padrinos se bautize*, the saying goes. (He who has godparents gets baptized). In the struggle for life, success depends in reality upon the ability, much less to defend one's rights against equals, than to attract the favour of the powerful."[160]

What emerges from modern comparative description is thus no different from the relations discovered in third-century Gaul or second-century Asia Minor; and, just as in certain dependency-structures with which Baroja is concerned, so in antiquity two principal conditions can be distinguished that gave shape to the whole: first, the steepness of socioeconomic stratification in the empire, which translated into the vulnerability and dependence of the many vis-à-vis the few; and second, the limited reach of the government. Rome's empire was not the "stateless society" known to anthropologists — not quite.[161] If the army's strength were turned inward against the civilian population, as can be seen being done on a few occasions by angry tyrants like Caracalla or Theodosius, that was decisive. At all times, too, the prestige of the emperor's authority was overwhelming. Yet army and emperor intervened in real life too rarely to affect its local and day-to-day workings. The Haves with an interest in *pax* of any kind — call it *Romana* if you wish — were thus left to secure themselves and their property within a web of alliances. Kin and clients, friends below or above provided what government could not, the necessary service and protection.

That resources and resorts of this kind belonged to the basic nature of the ancient world, that they were 'structural' in the anthropological sense of the word, appears in their undisturbed continuation straight across the long period I deal with. As illustration, consider two Spanish scenes separated by more than four centuries. In the first, Caesar at Cartagena finds "many assembled there, some to get disputes settled in which they were involved with others, some to arrange affairs of their cities, still others to claim rewards for bravery." They were gathered before him in consequence of his being already great. But his greatness touched his kin, of whom one was present in his retinue. It was the boy Octavius. "The Saguntines also sought asylum with him, having major charges against them and needing help. He represented them and, speaking very ably to Caesar at an open hearing, cleared them of the accusations and sent them home rejoicing, singing his praises to everyone and calling him their savior. From then on, many people flooded in on him to ask for his advocacy. He generally was of value to them, freeing some from charges, for others gaining gifts, and for some winning promotions."[162] The second scene belongs to Galicia in the 360s, home to the young Theodosius. There, as a later panegyrist reminds him, "you used to win over men of every rank and age in the cities by favors, *beneficia*, of one sort or another. You were of help to the interests of your friends and to the affairs of the absent by your close attention, advice, and financial support."[163] What can be seen in Spain at every period could also be seen in every province.

It is to be noticed that government in the conventional sense is not absent even from these pictures of extragovernmental power at work. Reference in them to cities no doubt has to do with the gift of civic status, tax status, and the like; reference to charges implies some system of law; reference to promotions indicates a career ladder. Litigation, business, and property likewise oblige us to think of some prevalent, civilizing authority. So the argument to minimize the role of the state within society must not be pressed too far.

Still, these matters need to be tested a little further. When we read of Sejanus' wish not to alarm Tiberius too early with his own excessive prominence, balanced against the consideration "that he might destroy his own power by fending off the crowds that besieged his residence,"[164] it is natural to wonder whether those crowds sought him out as a praetorian prefect or as a patron. Surely the answer is, as both at once: a better patron (like Aedinius Julianus, above) *because* a prefect. Then government was to some extent a servant, not master. Praetorian prefect not once but several times, Petronius Probus in the 360s and 370s held or had held many other offices as well and "certainly enjoyed great power to the end of his days, through the gaining of gifts and the stringing out of continual official positions, . . . which he was made to seek," continues Ammianus, because of his greedy kinsmen "immersing their patron in public business, so as to carry out their own many crimes in security." His endless public service made Probus a regular cornucopia. Claudian says his name was talked about everywhere: "he did not hide his riches in gloomy cellars or darkness but was rather wont with copious floods to enrich innumerable throngs of men."[165] Was government in his hands a thing in itself, as an instrument of society taken all together, or was its authority rather an extension of his personal power? It was (and at all periods of history has always been) the two together; but the proportions of the mix vary in different times and places.

Some people who could never hold office were nevertheless credited with the shaping of government; and, though they worked behind the scenes where their role is, for us, difficult to evaluate, their support was sought by good judges of reality. The chief category was of course women, at all times; then churchmen, from the third century on; and, depending on one's definition of the word *office*, perhaps one should add slaves and ex-slaves (in the later empire, especially eunuchs). The extent of their power had something to do with that of the person through whom they were able to express it; but many influential women gained access to the emperor or his high officials not through any marital attachment but through sheer ambition and force of character. Most notorious is the reign of Claudius I, marked by many, many policy measures and important decisions that were "less his own than his wives' and freedmen's."[166] Early, bad emperors like Caligula, Claudius, and Nero, through inattention to government, allowed their power to be directed by persons close to them. An old friend, a sister, a sexual favorite, simply asked for and got a favor. Thereafter, sources reflect no great concern about such misdirection of imperial decision-making until the reign of Constantius. From then on, so far as any detailed information survives about affairs in the palace, it is more likely to reveal, not simple requests, but complex linkages of persuasiveness: "intrigues" in the conventional sense of the word. The bringing down of Prince Gallus in 354 would serve as one example, but there are many others in the same and subsequent reigns.[167] Court life brought together many, many more imperial officials in his day than in the Principate. It is specially clear in Constantius' reign that they and their high ladies all defined their pride and power in their titles rather than in their lineage, their great wealth, or their membership in the Senate. Ambition which had brought them to the palace in the first place had thus to play itself out among more numerous rivals, in a more crowded setting, and for a more limited range of rewards — essentially, the ability to get what one wanted from the emperor.

Control over the emperor's knowledge of his empire was quite crucial, involving him in endless struggles. So often as he tried to break through the silence and lying that screened him from his subjects, his courtiers tried to enforce his isolation. They achieved very considerable success, which will receive more discussion in the next chapter. Here I call attention to only one fact and one moment's glimpse of the subject. The fact concerns rescripts (rather, subscripts) to individual petitioners — that is, minimal memoranda written by the emperor at the foot of requests submitted to him. They had the force of law, could cut through layers of delegation and bureaucracy, and put the emperor in absolutely direct touch with his subjects. The most humble person, the kind who could be bullied into a panic over his cottage, could and did avail himself of their wonderful efficacy. By the first half of the second century, after many generations in which they had gradually become familiar, rescripts had established themselves in regular, frequent use. Then under Diocletian they tapered off very abruptly and soon ceased. No similar form of access replaced them. The natural consequences followed.[168]

One little glimpse of those consequences is supplied by Ammianus from the reign of Constantius. An official was charged with high crimes, summoned to the capital, relieved of his duties, and "prevented by the courtiers from approaching the emperor." Only by main force could he burst past them into the consistory and establish the truth before the throne itself.[169] It was of course only one desperate man in ten thousand who would resort to such outrageous behavior. Normally, *potentes*, as Ammianus terms the people who stood in the way, were able to interpret situations to the emperor in ways that suited them and thus guide his unchallenged authority, beneficence, or wrath in whatever direction they wished.

It is the *potentes*, however, who are my subject, not the monarchy. I touch on the monarchy only in the course of trying to estimate its real weight against the likes of the great Petronius Probus or eunuch-chamberlains like Eusebius and Eutropius. I am not even interested in prefects and *cubicularii* on their own account, as lawful agents of the imperial will — only in the extent to which they came to control power stolen from the emperor in his very palace.

Inevitably at all periods, it was from the ranks of the elite that the emperor recruited his more important deputies. In that fact should have lain a contradiction, a potential for conflict. The potential was rarely realized, for reasons about which no one can generalize with much force. It is easy, however, to distinguish two points deserving emphasis. In the first place, the emperor controlled the flow of good things in life on a scale no one else in his realm even approached, and that truth was naturally known to everybody in the abstract and predisposed them to serve him out of purely material self-interest; and the expectation of appointment and promotion and the gift of money, lands, or houses was in fact fulfilled among those who could be most useful — in case of emergency, out of property confiscated from those who were least useful. The evidence for imperial openhandedness is exceptionally full, and from many reigns, telling of settled practises. In short, loyalty paid.[170]

In the second place, it was not difficult to find and confidently identify honorable men to occupy positions of trust. Obviously it was a Roman honor that was sought: *fides* and the implications of that word — in particular, a due sense of the *officia* owing to the giver of *beneficia*. When Fronto was appointed governor of Africa, he turned to those he knew best to help him, just as Antoninus Pius had chosen *him*: "my kinsmen and friends whose *fides* and *integritas* I had sure knowledge of." He goes on to instance a few names, including Julius Senex summoned from Mauretania, "from whom I could expect not only *fides* and diligence but energy in the military line, too." Notice: loyalty first, special skills second.[171] Which is not to say that Fronto was always right in his judgment of people, nor the emperors either. Still, the screening of candidates to discover a certain morality must have worked, since the results, tested in the remarkable duration of some of the worst reigns as well as the still longer good ones, seem to have been so successful over the span of 31 B.C.–A.D. 235. For a half-century thereafter the empire was wrenched this way and that by successive emergencies, in which many emperors were betrayed by persons they had trusted and appointed. The sources are too thin to permit an explanation of what went wrong (plausible guesses, of course, are easy to venture). When the Tetrarchy restored stability, and later in the founding of Constantine's fortunes, the old ways can be seen once more in operation, successfully.

Augustus' autobiography concludes with the word *innumerabilis* to describe — without exaggeration, one may say — the gifts of money he had made to cities in distress, to senators needing his help to attain the financial minimum of the rank, and "singly to his friends, *amici*." *Amici* is again the term used in describing the targets of the wonderful (or excessive and scandalous) largesse dispensed by Nero, Galba, Vespasian, Septimius Severus, Constantine. Well, why should there not have been something genuine in such imperial friendships? Pliny and Tacitus could name individuals who needed no increase in wealth and gave up the pursuit of the Roman magistracies in order to join the circle of Vespasian's or Trajan's *amicitia*.[172] But there were far, far wider circles of supporters rewarded precisely because they were supporters, "on account of [their] merits and services," as Constantine says.[173] Then, being rewarded and being men of honor, they would continue to serve their benefactor loyally.

Honor and interest, picked out for emphasis in explaining the emperor's relations with *potentes*, fit very easily into my discussion of the latter on their own account. Indeed, the emperor as such attached them to himself in exactly the same way and according to exactly the same ethic as that by which they created their own structures of dependency and support. The result was not one single imperial *clientela* of the old Roman type. To understand how Augustus made an empire out of a republic, Anton von Premerstein long ago proposed that model; and it was rejected. "In despite of Premerstein," as Paul Veyne has put it neatly, "the empire could not be a gigantic network of clientship, because it was gigantic."[174] But it was not necessary that all sixty millions should feel themselves the emperor's clients. Sufficient if he could command the allegiance of his more significant appointees (legionary legates, governors, praetorian prefects, and the like) and a preponderant number and variety of senators and provincial magnates as well — such persons as Aelius Aristides had in mind in his address *To Rome* (§4): "everywhere, the greatest, most powerful men defend their own individual mother-states for you." Let them command as large a following beneath them as they wished. Nothing prevented such figures from being at the same time indebted to others of their kind or to those older eminences who had helped them forward in their own early careers. Lines of connection, lines of credit — every great man or woman had them by definition. The more the better. The emperor's alone, however, were *innumerabiles*.

This alternative to Premerstein's model can be tested by studying how to revolt in the empire. A most useful question. It reveals reigns in the moment of formation, where their constituent elements can be seen coming together. Army loyalty must be won over by gifts; if possible, by appeals to ties formed during some earlier command. That much was obvious. More interesting and informative is the systematic, sometimes long-drawn-out, very dangerous but necessary canvass of the Haves and *potentiores* out of office. It can be known that the canvass was necessary because it was undertaken regardless of its risk. Avidius Cassius sounded out Herodes Atticus; in every great city or, for that matter, a city of whatsoever size, discreet appeal must be directed to its Top Men.[175] No matter that they had no troops under them. A reign was not constructed merely out of force. It required far broader, deeper allegiance reaching even to the urban masses.[176] That allegiance, however, must be mediated through local notables. They would be known to everyone in their native settings; they would be patrons to large, confident, semiofficial, and organized associations formed out of some one craft, cult, immigrant enclave, or subscribers to burial insurance. They would have claims on kinsmen, financial dependents, neighbors of their circumjacent estates. No need here to review all the many sorts of power that gave a name to the *potentiores*. Being drawn in to a revolt, they were quite able, in turn, to sway Palmyra, Lyon, Nicomedia, Capua, or half a province.[177]

Once a reign was safely begun, it was time to diminish such great influence. In A.D. 176 "a law was passed then that no one should be governor in his native province." Imperial bureaucrats much later were forbidden duty in their home province.[178] Such bans only underline the strength of extragovernmental authority.

The stability of imperial rule was not wholly dependent on the mediation of municipal and provincial elites. As is very well known, its base was far broader. Besides that ready access to the throne already referred to (above, at n. 168), there was the imperial cult which reached out to every corner of the empire. In connection with it or independently, imperial portraits had an equally wide distribution.[179] The coming of a new emperor was loudly announced in the marketplace of every city and greeted by compulsory parades. Imperial victories were publicized, for example, in the wake of Severus' Persian wars, by letters to eastern cities, and endlessly by coins.[180] Didactic and propagandizing elements could be found, apropos or not, in the promulgation of laws and other statements, and, again endlessly, in announcements of imperial *beneficia*. All of this press of ideas and images on the public must have produced an attachment directly to the individual on the throne independent of mediation by the *potentiores* — in short, stability, acceptance, legitimacy, an infinite power to command. Perhaps.

But the picture needs to be examined critically. Once the orations on kingship are set aside (bismillah! — they are so tedious), once the almost equally jejune panegyrical addresses are discounted, it is surprising how little attention was paid to the emperors by their subjects. There are exceptions. Nero loved the limelight. The contract murder of his mother and his scandalous life produced pasquinades posted in Rome and chilling mention in new Sibylline oracles, whereas the accession of Gaius Caligula had been attended by affectionate crowds in Italy and his illness, not long afterwards, by a corresponding anxiety. It touched even the populace of distant Alexandria. So Philo tells us, ascribing that anxiety to everybody everywhere and heightening the contrast between this early perception of the worst of rulers and the later grim reality.[181] In Rome itself the emperors were seen in the amphitheater, sometimes in the streets, and thus emerged as personalities. The crowds cheered them or, later in their eastern capital, kneeled as their images were borne past.[182] "The Roman populace" or some such phrase describes a more or less active participant in many moments when an emperor is overthrown or raised up, is loved or hated. The many purveyors of goods and services to the palace, or to the mansions of the great who knew and visited the court as guests or on business, would hear news of the imperial family and pass it around. It is predictable that there should have been a

unique degree of political awareness among the population of the capital —
which constituted 1 percent of the empire.

Elsewhere, occasionally someone is heard making a comment about the
emperors; they are said to be on a visit to the vicinity or to be of such-and-
such a general character. The concord of joint rulers may be heard praised in
a provincial city.[183] Hadrian's beard was noticed, at least by the Haves, and
imitated; also, his short hair, or Vespasian's simple diet, or Marcus' food-fads.

On the other hand, those Haves are just the mediators whom I would
expect to discover and whose role, supplementing government, seems to me
so tremendously important. Some were indeed great fans of royalty. True —
but others found imperial pomp and propaganda laughable (above, n. 10).
When we drop down among the masses whom government must reach,
whether directly or indirectly (and that is the question here), we find them in
the city streets and plazas "gossiping with any chance passer-by, listening to
idle talk and concerning themselves 'with the emperor's doings, or So-and-
So's,' as someone put it." The speaker is Dio Chrysostom, in contempt. And
"do people ever tire of abusing Caesar?" asks Epictetus. Again: "They sit
around in the fora and wine shops, men who haven't a shirt to their backs nor
the wherewithal for the next day's needs, and they pass judgment on emperors
and great officials, *potestates*, imagining, forsooth, that they are ruling and
commanding armies" (that scene from Milan in Ambrose's day). Finally: "most
people, *hoi polloi*, don't even know the names of the emperors and army
commanders."[184] And against all the great art that shows the emperors as they
wished to be seen should be set their portrait drawn by a more common hand
(figure 16).[185] It comes from a frontier-province center to the north and
celebrates a pair of them presiding over a wild-boar hunt. The style is
deflating.

With the throne as the principal institution of government were connected
three others in series: provincial council, *curia* or *boule*, and *demos* or *populus*.
All of these have been extensively studied. My interest lies only in the extent
to which they allowed undisturbed communication up and down, so that
what the emperors really wanted got through to their subjects and what the
latter really wanted was likewise expressed and heard without distortion or
interruption.

As to the first institution of government, weightiest of the three, the
provincial councils have already been encountered (above, at n. 158). The
meeting of A.D. 220 in Gallia Lugdunensis took up the evaluation of one of
the emperor's servants. That seems to have been a prominent item of business
for all council meetings. On this occasion, it was very nearly run away with
by a clique of representatives who had arranged their joint action in advance
in order to bring down an enemy. Tacitus reports further that one of the

Fig. 16. The Tetrarchs in a graffito

barons of Crete "was accustomed to declare it within his gift whether thanks should be expressed to the governor," as a result of which, that prerogative of councils in general was for a while withdrawn. On the other hand, governors themselves put great pressure on councils to honor them with laudatory decrees. For that reason, still earlier, under Augustus, such decrees had been forbidden to be passed until sixty days after the governor had left the province. His direct though not his indirect manipulation of the vote was thus prevented.[186] By the early third century the jurisconsults had recognized that a governor might nevertheless gain the alliance of magnates and, through them, also gain protestations of gratitude from the provincial council, no matter how cruel or corrupt he had been. One city could always be played off against another. So, in a matter of the first importance to them — public commendation — the influential people both within and without government were managing to control affairs in their private interests. If worse came to worst and complaint actually reached the Senate, there too, notoriously, were strings one could pull. The case of a north Italian town suggests how. Its counsel, arriving in the capital to begin legal proceedings, backed off once he had talked to more knowledgeable friends and learned how things worked: he should not expect success against an opponent, a senator defending himself within the Senate "on a matter of his influence, fame, and *dignitas*." Better luck might attend a plaintiff if he went directly to the emperor. But he must get there first. Beyond the predictable delays, Severus Alexander discovered that his subjects in Bithynia were being forcibly prevented by his governors and procurators from making the trip to court.

Complaints from provincial councils continued to be submitted to the capital through embassies. Theodosius II, for example, was still encouraging them in A.D. 433. Ammianus indicates that councils met according to a set calendar, at least in Tripolis, and petitions were promised a ready hearing if they were not "impudent" or "unneeded." (It would be important to know exactly what the emperors intended by those terms).[187] Most of the evidence tells us about provincial council meetings in Carthage. There in the forum, before a general assembly of the populace, the names of governors would be read out aloud, to be received by shouts for or against them (no doubt in unison phrases — see above, at nn. 24f.); and "if the shouts are sincere, not lightly emitted through obligation to a patron, We [Constantine] will carefully follow them up."[188] The procedure was meant to discover the honest truth about what sort of administration was being delivered in the emperor's name; but the reference to *clientelae* suggests there was no certainty of success.

The shouting populace in the empire's cities quite drowned out decurions. It is an odd fact that almost nothing at all is known about the *curiae* as a working structure; almost nothing about their internal procedures (no doubt varying in different cities), manner of voting, arrangement of authority (by seniority?), or typical agenda for the members sitting as a group. Only Dio Chrysostom of Prusa indicates any possibility of dissensions and factions among them; and it is a rare chance that gives us the official minutes of a *boule* (of Petra), recording its disposition of a request to appoint legal guardians.[189] The routine of assigning liturgies must have taken up much time. It was of tremendous importance, of course, both to individuals and the community. And there is frequent reference in the epigraphic record to the voting of honors and assigning of public space to memorials. How frequent, can be sensed in the attendant vote being abbreviated to four letters, *l. d. d. d.*, "location assigned, council's decree." But it is hard to gain any idea of politics from this — an idea of the realities of power, with which I am chiefly concerned.

Much of their business they handled jointly with the *demos/populus*. They arrived at their decisions by themselves, concerning lists of candidates for magistracies or public honors to be paid, festival arrangements or embassies; then they presented them to a crowd gathered in front of the *curia* building. Voting there was rare and became rarer as time went on. Acclamation did the job.[190] In emergencies, the imperial government dealt with the *curia* and magistrates as if they were the whole city, not only demanding their help but executing them, for example, or otherwise punishing them for disloyalty.[191] A good case thus can be made for oligarchy or timocracy as the dominant form of local government throughout the empire. Yet it was disturbed and challenged by individuals of salient strength and ambition, and by the urban masses, sometimes in response to those individuals.

As Rabbi Abbahu illustrated in Caesarea in Palestine, a citizen even without office might stand out above all others. In effect, he was its president. In the same sense, Herodes Atticus may be said to have presided over Athens for a time. Appendix B gathers a number of other illustrations attesting to the same sort of authority exercised outside the municipal constitution, yet nevertheless exercised in fact — even officially — in the sense of being invited to participate in some community action. Cities might, for instance, include certain of their most respected citizens on an embassy without bothering to give them any title. They were simply *protoi* or *principes*. Plutarch, in the sector of the Greek-speaking part of the world he knew best, had encountered "the rich, famous man [who] ridicules and shows contempt for the city magistrate, as a common, poor man, and by his own high standing insults that of the municipality and reduces it to nothing." What he says fits with the frequent references in Firmicus Maternus, two centuries later, to "leaders, *principes*, men great, powerful, formidable, energetic, who master the largest cities by virtue of some authority." That is, they had gained some imperial appointment. By his date, he may be referring to city curators, a large proportion of whom were appointed from among the local nobility. Constantine, in whose reign Firmicus writes, in his legislation draws attention to decurions who, in their weakness, turn to some *potentior* for protection.[192] All of these various mentions and examples taken together seem to indicate the weakness of decurions as a corporation in the face of the arrogance of persons whose power-base lay outside the city entirely.

The weakness of *curiae* seems to have increased gradually as their enrollments began to shrink. That phenomenon of the later empire has been referred to above, and is well known.[193] To say, then, that the emperors even from a great remove could claim governance over the cities beneath them through the urban magistracies and councils is a considerable oversimplification; and it becomes a good deal less true after the turn of the third to the fourth century.

I continue discussion of the series of institutions joining the central government to the masses: provincial councils, city senates, "democracy." Unlike the *curiae*, assemblies of the citizen body did permit some view of their operations. While it was a rhetorical convention to make mention of enthusiastic or hostile reactions evinced by one's real or imaginary audience, plainly many meetings of Prusa in Dio Chrysostom's day did have their vociferous moments; and there are not only frequent epigraphic indications of the populace joining the *curia* in some action, but occasional choices of words to show that approval rose a good many decibels above the genteel.[194] Noisiness suggests real feelings really expressed. Sensing that, benefactors could sometimes be induced to be more generous; speakers changed what they were going to say or do, or were in some other way overpowered. Examples come from Tira in the province of Asia, from Sicily, from Africa.[195]

The municipal elite constituting the *curia* and magistracies were no doubt often arrogant, bullying, and thoroughly used to having their own way; and the populace as individuals just as surely could not stand against them; but en masse, it was sometimes a different matter. The spur to revolt was that very arrogance of the Haves, made more intolerable by their greed;[196] and they might have enemies among their peers, too, to take advantage of popular hostility, to organize demonstrations, stir up protests, and so bring about their overthrow.[197] Considerable evidence has been presented above, on the competitive ethic that seems to have prevailed among the Haves or *potentes*. As to hostility that might divide the Haves and the Have-nots, its presence may be felt in the exchange between a crowd gathered one day in the imperial audience chamber and the emperors Diocletian and Maximian: "The emperors in the consistory said, 'Decurions' sons must not be thrown to the wild beasts.' And when shouts arose from the people they repeated their words. 'The idle voice of the people should not be listened to, for their voice does not deserve belief when they have demanded amnesty for the guilty or condemnation for the innocent.' "[198] Though the exchange has no context to explain it, the tone of hauteur is typical of that used by the upper classes to the lower (above, nn. 2f.); and the emperors were evidently confronting a crowd thirsting for the blood of the ranks that ruled them.

6. WHY PRIVATE POWER WORKED

In the previous three sections my interest focused on the command of obedience enjoyed by a few people over many without need of any formally bestowed authority. They did not hold office, or, if they did, they nevertheless needed none to be listened to. More decisions were made every day throughout the empire in obedience to them than to the law, to the emperor, or to his deputies. Those decisions, moreover, were the important ones that concerned property, travel, choice of career, success in farming or commerce or banking; sometimes, even one's physical safety. They intruded frequently into decisions taken by the imperial or municipal government, where one might expect pressure to be exerted entirely in the opposite direction. But the empire at the best of times — "best" in the truest sense, under the so-called good emperors — had a quite tiny civil service and bureaucracy, parsimoniously supported by soldiers seconded to civilian duties; so the force and follow-through that the emperors of the Principate could apply to their task as they saw it never amounted to much. All the more scope for the rich and influential, pedigreed and prestigious, Haves and *potentes*.

In characterizing these folk, I have tried not to make them appear more pacific, unselfish, live-and-let-live than they really were. They present a profile in fact very much resembling that of San Gimignano, bristling with individual declarations of pride, ambitious and intimidating. They constituted only a few percent of the urban or rural population in whose midst they lived, while all around them were the rest that had very much less land, less clothing, respect, food, cash, leisure, and security, and wanted more. In the competitive character of the Haves as in the contrast they presented to the Have-nots lay the potential for conflict that had to be controlled. Every society must confront both such inequalities and such aggression in order to survive. The Roman solution ritualized and moralized dependence, and so fixed people in stable relations with each other.

The ritual most familiar was the entering of a weaker person into the *fides* of a stronger. Its history belongs to the Republic; but its continuation through the approach to a possible *patronus*, and the resulting contract, followed by the display of that contract as a plaque on the patron's atrium wall, were a part of the life of all the western empire. Its benefits were known, if not through *tabulae patronatus*, then through well-understood requirements; and this was so in the eastern provinces as well, where Plutarch speaks generally about them in his essay on municipal politics and where a term like *beneficium* is taken over through transliteration.[199] Dependents needed the strength they received from above. There was no doubt about that. They looked to it for security and much else, and in so doing they looked upward, rarely to their peers. So loyalty to others of their own condition and a sense of class never developed.[200] Singly, they were easy enough to keep in line, and their patrons gloried in their responsibility.

The higher one was in this society, the more one was owed and the less one owed to others. But ties which the most lofty ranks preferred to call friendship, not dependence, united even these in mutual obligation. The very variety of their connections discouraged the formation of blocs of Guelphs and Ghibellines, Liberals and Conservatives. Scattered estates, scattered marital connections, scattered *clientelae* crossed all the more logical lines of alliance. The result was a web of relations very hard to break. It worked like a safety-net. Anyone reading Pliny the Younger's letters about corruption trials in the centumviral court or before the senate must, I think, sense the "mutual connivance" which prevented convictions and which, among senators, he himself notices.[201] The governor of Africa, Pertinax, offers one illustration when first he did condemn a lower official for corruption in office, only later, as emperor, to promote him at the request of a countryman of the victim. It has often been noticed, too, that the close advisers of emperors hung on from reign to reign, no matter what disturbance might mark the transitions, maintaining even their semiofficial title of "friend" to each successive occupant of the throne.[202] They were able to do so not because they were professionals serving like modern bureaucrats beneath the roiled seas of cabinet appointments. It was rather *their* friends who rose to speak for them out of the midst of the new regime. Let it be a transition even after bitter civil strife, still, prominent supporters on the losing side soon turned up among the winners to continue their careers. All their hard work to oblige, all the letters of testimonial they had earned or solicited, all the prospects of service they could promise upon their honor, upon their *fides*, won them security.[203] Still in the later empire, the web of mutual obligation woven by everyone for himself, yet by everyone for everyone, all-inclusive in its entanglements, worked to procure the safety of that great scoundrel Count Romanus. It was only a matter of finding the right court with the right judge.[204] Nevertheless, by his time a different ethic had very much changed the character of the web of connections. I shall return to that in the next chapter.

Ties of dependence, up and down or more or less on a level between peers, provided a stable, resilient power structure well suited to expansion, in the early empire. Bad rulers could be borne for years and years; really awful ones in their overthrow left most of the structure intact. The merry-go-round of pretenders that Maximinus the Thracian set in motion in 235 was kept turning by the army, in which the leadership (witness Maximinus himself) was very different from that of Trajan's day. Meanwhile the rest of government continued about its work undisturbed, so far as the sources indicate.

Its workings can be seen in a thousand junctures, known to us, if very sketchily, through literary texts, inscriptions, papyri, and even some of the city coinage of the east. A few illustrations may suffice. A City Father led in the arrest of Christians in a Pamphylian town, not because the bearer of such a title had orders to do so but because he chose to, and because government in the functional sense was as much the job of local elites with no office at all as it was of imperial legates and prefects. Similarly, it was an official act that instituted orphan relief in Italy, but private persons did so, too, in Italy and the provinces.[205] The provincial donor was the tireless Opramoas (above, fig. 14), of whom the governor Voconius Saxa writes, "Opramoas I praise not only for the things you [the people of Myra in Pamphylia] say he has contributed to your town, your birthplace, but even more for much oversight and forethought he has provided." In short, he had been doing just about what Voconius Saxa would have done ex officio if he had had time. There was no distinguishing between titular and actual government.

Witness further the imperial armies fed and hosted on their way to and from the frontier, any number of times. It was a grand gesture of which we happen to hear largely through inscriptions.[206] Their scale in terms of money astonishes. Help of a very material sort was afforded to the forces of one side or the other in civil wars. It was not disinterested; rather, given for anticipated rewards after victory. But it demonstrated the organizing capabilities of the local *principes*.[207] Perhaps of the greatest significance, because day in, day out, was the labor of arbitrage and adjudication performed by local magnates. Pliny mentions the duty several times, and it is generally attested in rural settings; also, however, in towns and even in the capital, where the mansions of the mighty required rooms of grand dimensions "because these men's homes are so often the setting for meetings on public affairs and also private suits and arbitrations."[208]

With the activities of arbiters, some of whom were in fact court-appointed, we pass from the private to the public sphere. The passage is imperceptible. Under which of the two headings should a vast variety of services and gifts be listed, which the *potentiores, dynatoi, protoi,* or *possessores* offered to their communities? The distinctions among them are likewise imperceptible. Where is the line that divides these services and gifts from municipal liturgies? And liturgies from magistracies? And it is the same people who are to be found in the one sphere or the other, the same people on both sides of the dividing line. Government worked through the sense of dependence that animated the emperors' most selfless servants — while at the same time, of course, they were using their offices to dispense *beneficia* and thus increase the numbers of dependents on themselves. Out of government, that sense insured the obligingness of local leaders to the emperor's deputy among them, in whom they hoped to secure for future needs a useful patron. It is the web of favors given or owed that enables an imperial administration of only a few hundred really to rule an empire.

3
POWER FOR SALE

1. INTRODUCTION

For centuries, interest in Rome has found no more magical figure to focus on than Cicero, no corpus of writings more lovingly to read than his. A hero to his readers, he has supplied them also with a remarkable gallery of antiheroes. First to rise out of those floods of courtroom eloquence, and in some sense the beginning of the orator's career, is the governor of Sicily, Gaius Verres. To the detailed description of his three years in office and the practices of his administration Cicero gave art and energy without measure. Verres had put on a truly comprehensive display of cruelty and greed, never tiring, never at a loss. Therefore, schoolboys, to say nothing of scholars, since the Renaissance have had an intimate knowledge of a Roman scoundrel to match as such the grandeur of a dozen Roman patriots.

Verres' dramatic quality, thanks to Cicero, cannot be questioned. Of his place in history there is much less to say; and it has less to do with provincial government than with life and law in the capital itself.[1] For greater impact, he would have needed a longer run, a wider reach; in short, far larger dimensions. And even so, one is bound to wonder whether Rome's empire could not by any adjustment have grown great under an administration broadly Verrine. That reflection must rule over any discussion of abuse of power as a ponderable subject, not merely as a lurid or scandalous one. After all, what difference could it make? Are there not always criminals in office, threatening dire penalties unless they are paid off, bending their decisions in exchange for gifts, or predictably forgetting important papers which they were never tipped to expedite through the labyrinths of governmental action?

Back in the 1880s, a certain Paul Louis-Lucas published his *Etude sur la vénalité des charges* in two volumes. A monstrous, eccentric piece of scholarship, it offered in one characteristic run of its pages more than three thousand lines of footnotes to support a mere sixty lines of text. The text — clear and consecutive thought — resembled in its tiny proportions the eye of a whale which must illuminate the whole ponderous bulk on which it sits. Needless to say, no one read the book. The subject of venality among the Romans languished unconsidered except in a learned article or two until nearly a hundred years had passed. Now interest has picked up.[2] There would be no novelty, today, in saying that the subject deserves serious study; for we have learned that, on a certain scale, the diverting of force by the servants of government from the directions in which that force was meant to be expended — meant by the society that authorized the force in the first place — can change history. So it deserves serious study.

Scale, however, is the essential consideration in this as in other topics of historical sociology treated by Weber, Elias, or Veyne (above, chap. 2, n. 1). At a level below the raging rulers, battling of dynasts, promulgation of whole codes of law, and all such other great events, the little acts of unimportant people hardly merit study unless they are so frequent as to shape the setting in which great events become impossible, or inevitable. Convention, custom, routine, norms require to be identified and drawn out of the mass of mere anecdotes; or anecdotes must be chosen that clearly tell of routines and norms. All of which means much detail, and might almost excuse the proportions of Louis-Lucas' book.

For my subject in this chapter I have already offered a definition: I mean to focus on the diverting of governmental force, its *mis*direction. The prefix points to two views: the one, of persons who control that force; the other, of persons observing and disapproving. Naturally the observers must be contemporaries, not ourselves. We do not understand the past best when we sit in judgment on it. However, where we detect disagreement among the actors in it, we may fairly follow out the consequences of the different preferences expressed, and compare them, and perhaps conclude at the end that one or the other was destructive or dysfunctional. Cicero (by way of illustration) disapproved of provincial administration so cruel and frightening that all its subjects yielded to it and so greedy that they were stripped bare by it. He assumed that his audience agreed, and he could point to the expression of their agreement in the laws. The laws expressed contemporary norms. They also required the provincials' obedience, which constituted Verres' force. It is not anachronistic, then, to say that Verres was *mis*directing authority held *ex officio*; but there is no good evidence that the state suffered harm in consequence.

2. PRIVATIZING OF PUBLIC OFFICE IN THE PRINCIPATE

In Cicero's and Verres' day there existed several corporations of bureaucrats. They were called *decuriae* because they once numbered ten members each. They performed menial duties for magistrates, running errands, carrying messages, making announcements, disbursing money and keeping accounts. These were ordinarily the duties of slaves, and the *decuriae* for centuries received such, or rather ex-slaves, into their ranks along with the freeborn. In addition to their tiny stipend from the state (paid through the magistrate they served), they could count on perquisites, *commoda*. In the new cities that Rome planted for her veterans according to a model charter of 44 B.C., the stipend amounted to between 300 and 1,200 sesterces per year for lictors, heralds, summoners, and clerks, at a time when a laborer might expect around 3 sesterces per day. The median for the four ranks assisting municipal magistrates therefore only matched a ditchdigger's pay. Nevertheless, candidates were willing to scrimp and save to buy one of these posts whenever its occupant wished to retire, or when his heirs put it up for sale. It was a valuable piece of property. In the empire, as the epigraphic evidence for Italy swells to a great bulk, information about the *decuriae* increases correspondingly, and their members then appear as recipients of municipal honors in return for their civic benefactions. Some attain equestrian rank, which required property worth 400,000 sesterces. Needless to say, wealth of that order could never be attained by no matter how many years of further scrimping and saving on one's salary alone. How, then? The answer can only lie in the *commoda*. For Verres' clerk, 4 percent withholding from a single account under his oversight produced 1,300,000 sesterces. Scandalous, to be sure. Scandal in fact distinguished the whole history, or what very little is known of the history, of the *decuriae*. But the rake-off in Sicily had the governor's approval.[3] That suggests other governors may have given theirs too. In fact, to explain the desirability of a position on the *decuriae* and the substantial wealth of their members in later centuries, we must assume that they were given a pretty free rein to profit from their duties.

In the general repute of the magistrates' staff, certain ambiguities can be sensed. They were disreputable folk, some of them, for their habits of graft and lowly origins. They had come from strata with no money at all, only by much effort buying their way in; or they were former slaves, absolute dirt beneath the feet of the magistrates whom they served. On the other hand, they could become confidential assistants, indeed collaborators, as with Verres; and they could grow rich, which conferred respect if not respectability in the Roman world, never mind where the money came from. They gradually took on the rules and organization of a club; they had their own meeting places, reserved seating in the amphitheater. Particularly to be noticed is the ownership of the positions occupied by these lowly assistants: a monopoly, how limited in number cannot be determined (but scores, not hundreds). They were bought and sold like taxi-medallions in New York City, entitling the owner to offer certain services to the public at a fixed price. Jurisconsults by the early second century are already mentioning litigation over them quite as a matter of course, while defending the rights of lawful purchasers and legatees. What the wealth and standing of the *decuriae* ultimately rested on was public authority exercised for private profit.

To illustrate how that might be acceptable, consider the jurisconsult Paul confronting a delicate problem of administrative rights: "A certain litigant was in charge of the affairs of a municipality and put out the public monies on loan at the usual rate of interest. It was also the custom, however, to exact a higher rate for failure to pay within a given time.... The question arises, should the extra collected as a penalty according to custom accrue as profit to the litigant or to the public account? My answer was that if it was the litigant who stipulated the interest rate for the debtor, only that rate should go to the municipality which was usually exacted by the rule." Rake-offs, tips, or 4 percent belonged to their inventors as of right where they had settled into custom, *consuetudo*.[4]

Originally, ideas about how to conduct the business of governance developed in the most natural ways one can imagine. Officials in the latter decades of the Republic had not made a career of it. They might hold a quaestorship, and put it down, and never hold another thereafter; or they held a praetorship after a few years, possibly a consulship, or went out additionally to a province for a year as governor. From their household in the capital they took what slaves they thought would be useful. That assistance provided the type for what the state was eventually willing to hire and pay for, in the form of two or three salaried persons drawn from a pool, the *decuriae*. Between master and man the relation might then resemble that existing between Cicero and his affectionately regarded Marcus Tullius Tiro.

Tiro could buy his freedom. It is well known that a significant proportion of Roman slaves actually did so. They could somehow afford to despite the fact that they never enjoyed a salary and never could have accumulated the sums necessary from gifts made to them by the family on festival days. Instead, they had held out their hand to all the tradesmen, clients, petitioners of any sort, and no doubt simply to rich friends of the house that came to the door. As we would say, they took tips.[5] Buying into the *decuriae*, ex-slaves went on taking tips. They had no reason to be ashamed of that. The ethic of slavery was simply continued among the heralds, summoners, lictors, and clerks that more officially served Roman noblemen during their terms as governors or the like. In the households of the greatest nobleman of all, Octavian who became Augustus, and his successors, tipping continued, sometimes scandalously. Galba, for example, like Verres, "permitted his intimates and freedmen to give out freely or for a price absolutely everything."[6] It was a matter of choice with him. Another master, another emperor, wouldn't have allowed it. Vespasian in an amusing story interviewed a candidate recommended to him for the job of financial accountant and extracted from him not only how much he had promised to the recommender if the appointment was gained, but the actual sum of money itself. So he, too, "permitted" taking tips (4 percent?), like Verres, and held nothing against a candidate willing to offer them.

It was a genial, oily, present-giving world. "Thank you for those fieldfares," writes Pliny to a friend, "but being at Laurentum I can't match them with anything from town, nor can I send you any fish as long as the weather is bad."[7] And "a wreath of roses or rich spikenard may suit your taste," writes Martial to one of his friends, "but for mine, one of fieldfares." The couplet is one of a hundred and more among his epigrams written to accompany or acknowledge such little gifts. They were continually in circulation, and continued to be so among intimates and peers without ever a thought to the purchasing of favor, right into the fifth century. We have seen them as a feature of country life (above, chap. 2, n. 98), offered by tenants to a landlord. Offered, but also expected.

In fact, it was hard to draw the line between wishing to gain and express some measure of liking, and the wish to influence specific decisions; and the difficulty was compounded when the two parties were not on a level. The landlord had no place in his life for the friendship of his peasants. They both knew that. He had, however, the power to make decisions that profoundly affected their lives. Whatever tokens they brought to his house were bound to be given and received in that knowledge.

Referring to a new assistant appointed in the office of one of the district managers (*strategi*) in Egypt, Gemellus writes to his son, "send him an artaba of olives and some fish, *as we want to make use of him*." The truth is out. No doubt it explains instructions in another letter of Gemellus: "Go to Dionysias to Psiathas the sower . . . and buy us some presents for the Isis festival for the persons we are accustomed to send them to, especially the *strategi*." There is a similar pair of statements, one ambiguous but explained by the other, which Epictetus addresses to an audience of Rome's elite. He imagines how "one man rises at dawn and looks around for some member of the imperial household to salute, someone to say something nice to, someone to send a gift to." This could be a practice of disinterested cordiality. But then he asks, "How did you come to be a judge, whose hand did you kiss . . . , whom did you send presents to?"[8] The presents had a purpose after all. Finally, there is the dictum quoted in general remarks by Ulpian:[9]

> A proconsul need not entirely refrain from "guest-gifts," xenia, but only set some limit, not to refrain entirely in surly fashion nor to exceed the limit in grasping fashion. The deified [Septimius] Severus and the emperor Antoninus [Caracalla] in a letter most elegantly offered guidelines on the matter, a letter reading, "As to xenia, hear Our opinion: it is an old saying, 'oute panta, oute pantote, oute para panton' [not all, nor always, nor from all]." For it is too uncivil to accept from nobody, but contemptible to take from every quarter, and grasping, to accept everything. What is meant by the proconsul's instructions, that neither he himself nor any other official should accept or buy anything beyond the day's subsistence, does not apply to little guest-gifts but to what exceeds the need for food; but not even xenia are to be carried to the point of a sizeable donation.

Like the tips hoped for and more or less exacted by domestic or staff underlings, xenia lay along a boundary separating the two close countries of good feeling and good business. The one was approved, polite; the other, disapproved to the point of legislative prohibition. Yet nothing was easier than to pass from the one to the other almost unawares. The most natural occasions and tendencies induced that passage almost as a part of one person's power and another's dependence. Even a man of honor could thus make an honest mistake.

Pliny found such a man in one of his clients. Julius Bassus, after a term as governor, was charged before the Senate with having, in the words of his own attorney, "naively and unguardedly accepted things from the provincials as a friend of theirs (for he had once been quaestor in the same province). These his accusers called thefts and plunder, but he called them gifts," munuscula. The term is the Latin for xenia, though the latter itself had been taken over as a loan word.[10] Bassus made no secret of the crime, if crime it was. He had mentioned the presents to the emperor himself and sometimes reciprocated to the givers. But it may be guessed that what he called by an exculpating diminutive were really numerous and valuable. Whole days of exquisite oratory were needed to get him off, and the senators did nothing thereafter to define the ambiguous boundaries which he had transgressed.

The same Pliny received a letter from one of his friends accompanying a gift of dates.[11] Please, asks his correspondent, do not take on the people of southern Spain as your clients in their suit for reparations. The case sounds exactly like the one against Bassus. Pliny responds with thanks for the little present and reference to his own good faith and his correspondent's good judgment. The phrasing is self-conscious, as one might expect of a writer who had chosen to occupy high moral ground. He can only promise not to take on the accused as his own client. As to the dates, they were "most excellent." Yet in accompanying a request to a lawyer for a favor that he finds slightly unethical, they do appear to represent more than an overflow of friendliness.

So much for background, intended to show the existence of everyday practices woven into the way of life of the empire, easily discovered because not hidden, indeed defended in the courts, if it came to that. Standards are also discoverable by which some practices were frowned on; but they were not frowned on by everyone. Some people were more strict; others wouldn't bother to hide certain shameful or illegal actions because they didn't think they were shameful. The governor Bassus is a case in point; Verres, another, when he enters into his official accounts the 4 percent reserved by his clerk for his own pocket. There were many circles in society, each with its own slightly different, or very different, ideas of right and wrong, and their differences became known only by the traveler who passed from one to the other, in his innocence like any tourist or businessman abroad asking if one tips in this country, and how much, and for what. In New York state, one judge in ten can be counted on to "fix" a traffic violation for a friend or the friend of a friend; and the carting away and selling of salvageable construction elements when buildings are torn down is "theft" in some places but "mungo" in New York, and so long entrenched there that it cannot be prosecuted. *Consuetudo* prevails.[12]

Consider the young tribune in Rome who investigated the conduct of a mighty lawyer acting for a corporation (the north Italian town of Vicetia). The lawyer had billed his clients double. The tribune "complained that legal advice was sold, appeals were sold, counsels acted in collusion, and large regular profits from the pillage of Roman citizens were considered something to boast about." Yes, at the banquets of the bar association. Pliny, reporting the debate in the senate, congratulates himself on having never in his own legal work accepted "agreements, presents, donations, or even *xenia*." Their implications were corrupt because, of course, it was highly improper — in the earlier empire, formally illegal — to take money for speaking in defense of a friend or dependent. One performed a duty like that out of a sense of honor. With that dictum, imagine Cicero's orotund agreement! — while he and other leaders of the bar grew vastly rich from their honorable activities. In time, law caught up with reality, and fees of a moderate amount were legally permitted so long as they had not been the object of any explicit understanding.[13] Passage from one ethical country to another thus became a less jolting experience.

Some further comments on the complexity of moral geography: a governor of Egypt indicates how shocked he was by the unauthorized tax demands laid on the farming population of the province in A.D. 68. His predecessor of twenty years earlier seems to have been entirely naive about the affairs he reports on in his edict: "Even before this, I kept hearing that certain unlawful expenditures and frauds were being perpetrated by persons greedily and impudently abusing their powers. . . . Wherefore I command that the soldiers, cavalrymen, orderlies, centurions, military tribunes," and so forth shall cease and desist. And nothing had prepared Pliny for "the great and revolting greed, matched by carelessness," that he found in the accounts of army units he had been told to examine when he was a young man.[14]

Which brings me finally to the army. Upon joining it a young recruit entered a new country. "I hope to be transferred into a cohort," he writes home to his family, "but in here nothing gets done without money, and letters of recommendation count for nothing unless you help yourself." This was indeed a novel discovery, set against everything that civilian life taught (above, chap. 2). Older hands would have been less surprised: Otho, for example, who "promised that the annual leave should be paid for by the imperial exchequer." Soldiers up to then had had the right to it, but could only obtain it by paying off their centurions out of their own pockets. They had been complaining about that expense for half a century and more. It was therefore *consuetudo*, customary, and Vitellius confirmed the arrangement of his predecessor. It would have been quite impossible to forbid the practice entirely.[15] We hear of the means by which it had been enforced: physical abuse. "The richest private was burdened with toil and cruel treatment till he bought his freedom." Then he could stay away as long as he wished, extorting the wherewithal for his next furlough from civilians among whom he moved. How nice to have that cost now assumed by a benevolent emperor!

Having completed this preliminary circuit of the lawyers and courts in the capital, elsewhere in Italy, and in the provinces like Bithynia where Julius Bassus once presided; of the servants of the emperor in his palace and of governors like Verres; of tax collectors and, more particularly, the collectors of military taxes; of legions and of the auxiliary troops — the impressions to be gained are not in most points very different from what might be expected, except perhaps in the successes won by the less honest against the law itself. There was the Lex Cincia of 204 B.C., which forbade taking money for serving as anyone's advocate. It was never formally repealed, only more and more ignored. There were the condoned *commoda* of the magistrates' assistants and the payoffs extorted from the men in the ranks by their officers' violence. All these, becoming customary, were after some interval elevated to legitimate rights that might be claimed from the highest authority. During the interval, people not familiar with the ways of lawyers, bureaucrats, and soldiers continued to apply an incompatible code to their own lives which they believed to be the only code existing. They had much to learn.

Exactly how much, however, needs to be defined. As I expressed it earlier, scale is the essential consideration, by which the inconsequential can be measured and discarded, and the historically significant retained. Among municipal officials in Greek-speaking provinces the emergence of a special terminology for their most typical misdoings suggests a pattern; still more, the long life of such usages as *skepe*. It meant protection from having to bear one's fair part of civic burdens, afforded for a price by whatever persons were in charge of assigning such burdens. Slang terms of that sort, however, indicated a certain sense of shame, acknowledging conventional morality by euphemism. Throughout most of the Principate, there is in fact very little evidence for peculation or extortion at the lowest levels of government, whether municipal[16] or imperial — at least in the provinces.[17] If there are not constant complaints, is that to be attributed only to deficiencies in our sources? Perhaps not. Office procedures were at least intermittently subject to close audit. Falsification of records is attested in Lycia and Alexandria in the reign of Claudius I, but the governors intervened to correct the situation. They were likely in fact to have a good deal more trouble with their chief aides, whom they hesitated to discipline.[18] Imperial procurators likewise belonged to a social level high enough to venture on official pillage without fear. Of their actually doing so, however, we likewise have few reports before the third century.[19]

Publicans synonymous with sinners everywhere appear to have extracted all that was due them and considerably more. They needed to be reminded that they should not constantly invent, like Verres' clerk, new and illicit demands under official-sounding titles.[20] There is no good way of quantifying the illegal extras collected; therefore, no saying if they constituted a more serious abuse in A.D. 250 than, say, under Augustus.

What is clear is that by far the most active pillage was carried on by soldiers, to whom John the Baptist turns after he has answered the publicans: " 'And what of us?' " they asked him. "To them he said, 'No bullying, don't shake down anybody; make do with your pay.' " Not likely. They were too deeply involved in various sorts of contact with the population at large. In particular, they were active as enforcers or collectors in taxation. Like their civilian counterparts, they invented good names to dress up their demands on civilians, the more plausibly because some soldiers were legitimately assigned to supply the legions or dispatched through the provinces on official business, or, through seconding to staff and clerical positions with governors, resided in cities. So they demanded a boat, a cart, a horse; food, fuel, lodging; use of the local hot baths; and, as a Jewish source says with bitter hyperbole, "they [the Romans] station *castra* in the townlets to torture brides."[21] Such complaints about soldiers in their dealings with the civilian population come from several areas in Asia Minor, Syria, Thrace, Moesia, Germany, Britain, and, with special detail, Egypt. As we have seen, in A.D. 14 reports came to Rome of officers virtually forcing their men to shake down the surrounding population for the money needed to buy security from "the centurions' savagery" (above, n. 15). Tertullian speaks of their extortion as one of the two great banes afflicting Christians — the other being the Jews. He draws on experiences in north Africa, the explanation for which was the shadow of the law that lay darkly across the lives of himself and his coreligionists. Soldiers there, being deputed to make arrests, routinely sold their nonperformance or silence, as they did also during the Great Persecutions in the eastern provinces.[22] They routinely abused the authority to levy recruits, too. General indications in the *Digest* are made specific in Britain, Germany, and north Africa.[23]

The really predatory character of the military thus appears starkly in all regions and centuries of the Principate; but it reveals itself with particular detail in A.D. 270 in Lower Germany. There:

> the soldiers were secretly incited to revolt at Cologne, and [the Gallic pretender Victorinus] was killed. So powerful in the army were the group of accountants, *actuarii*, . . . that they could rouse unpopularity against anyone seeking the heights; for they were, especially at this time, a species of men vicious, venal, cunning, factious, grasping, and as if formed by nature to cheat and conceal their cheating. They ruled over the [army] food supply, they were thereby the ruin of the suppliers of necessities and the fortunes of the farmers, and they also proved shrewd in bestowing gifts at the right moment on these people by whose stupidity, and at whose expense, they gathered in their wealth.[24]

The troops pictured here represent a concentration of anarchic rapacity on the necessary scale, the scale of historical significance; for, in addition to the consequences of their practices spread across all the countryside around Cologne, the *actuarii* are here seen behaving as king-makers. Through the manipulable venality of intermediate figures along the chain of delivery, they were able to produce artificial shortages and so set in motion the events that could destroy one emperor and place another on the throne. It was in fact not a new trick. Gordian III in A.D. 244 had been destroyed by the effects of just such a shortage.[25] But then it had been different: it had been only a single disloyal official at work, not a conspiracy involving the bureaucratic core of an army. A few years after the revolt in Cologne, the scene was repeated with variations. Probus was brought down by his men. Their mutiny on this occasion was caused by a failure to provide their pay, not their rations. It had long been a point that needed careful attention; but a good governor had been able to ensure that "the officers did not draw the soldiers into robbery and pillage through holding back their pay."[26] By the later third century, settled patterns of extortion were revealing the potential, always latent, to affect large numbers of people or whole areas of administration.

In capsule, the tendencies of the army could be seen all too plainly on one certain Roman afternoon. Caracalla was attending the races in the Circus. The crowd's shouts against the charioteer whom he himself favored made him angry; so, savage man that he was, he told the soldiers in attendance "to seize and kill those who are abusing the charioteer." The soldiers, however, were unable to determine who had been shouting and who hadn't, "so they led away and killed anyone they caught, mercilessly, or barely spared only those *from whom they stripped all belongings, like a ransom.*" The latter action focuses attention. We may, from all other evidence, consider it automatic, a sort of reflex.[27] In the same way soldiers took money to let Christians slip, in times of persecution; in the same way they took tips from the men and women they guarded in jail, in exchange for better treatment.[28] It belonged to their uniform to sell their services when they got the chance. But it was not till the third century that the tendency took on historic significance — perhaps only in 270.

Pliny was seen (above, p. 101) amicably arranging the distribution of legionary tribunates in the army of a province to which one of his friends had been appointed as governor. There was nothing in that to be ashamed of, nothing to hide. No money had changed hands. With centurionates and lower ranks it might be different. Their sale is mentioned from time to time (as thoroughly reprehensible). They, too, were in the hands of the governor, along with the grant of citizenship that admitted to the legions as opposed to the auxiliary troops. And citizenship was sometimes sold.[29] Finally, we saw in the previous chapter how a species of *xenia* might pass from a governor or commander to a new appointee in his army, as also to the more favored veterans upon their being mustered out. Army practices thus resembled those of civilian society; or one might say more accurately that the two ethical systems overlapped in certain areas, while at the same time, in other areas, a raw recruit would find a rude shock awaiting him.

I turn from the army to the legal system. For very natural reasons, tales of bribed juries and bribed judges got attention. They were news: at the worst, one governor's sale of a verdict of exile imposed on an equestrian and his friends (price: 300,000 sesterces) and the flogging, condemnation to the mines, and eventual strangling of another equestrian in jail (700,000 sesterces).[30] What do such stories prove? Over this particular trial the emperor himself presided. All the publicity might suggest that Rome had never seen the like. Augustus, Tiberius, and Domitian had very strictly enforced the honesty of the courts. Did they have much of an impact? Surely it is more revealing that Tacitus, describing how Tiberius sat with the courts of the praetors, concludes, "As a result of his presence, many verdicts were recorded in defiance of intrigue and of the solicitations of the great, the *potentes*; but, while equity gained, liberty suffered."[31] A most Roman, a most patrician idea of liberty! — one openly opposed to the disinterested delivery of justice. However, it comes as no surprise (above, chap. 2, pp. 87–95). And it is not tolerant of the purchase of injustice, which in fact is just as openly deplored throughout the period of the empire: by Propertius, for example, declaring "nowadays piety is vanquished, all men pay cult to gold, good faith is put to flight by gold, by gold the right is bought and sold, and law attends on gold. Soon there will be no element of law at all in our sense of shame." A generation later, Lucius Calpurnius Piso announced his intention of resigning from the world in disgust over "electoral bribery, corrupt courts, and the savagery of the persecutors brandishing their threats" (this, under the eye of Tiberius).[32] The novelist Petronius under Nero and Apuleius in the next century, asks in despair, "What can the laws do where only money reigns? And where poverty can never triumph?" "Why should you be astonished if the lowest species of all, the swine of the courts, or the vultures in togas — if nowadays all the judges themselves — are hucksters of their decisions?" And to go to the next century, there is Cyprian, who sees nothing but rottenness in the whole legal system, where the advocate cheats and deceives, the judge sells his verdict, and the witnesses lie. "There is no respect of the law, no terror before the quaestor or judge; for what can be bought is not feared."[33]

Still, there is something inconclusive about all this evidence. It is too rhetorical, perhaps. Also, it reveals a strong sense of right opposed to wrong, whereas the casual acceptance of wrong would prove far more. The better to gain a sense of people's unguarded estimates of reality, other, less obvious statements need to be considered. First, Epictetus' imagining various moral dilemmas and circumstances in everyday life: a person is tempted to seize another's property, some piece of land in an eastern province, supposing to himself "that it is done in secrecy and no one will know ... for we have powerful friends in Rome, men and women, and the Greeks are a supine people — none of them will venture on a trip to Rome on this account."[34] He imagines a system very much of the sort that Tacitus prefers and which, despite the officious Tiberius, seems actually to have prevailed.

Yet patronage and dependence are one thing; offering oneself to the highest bidder is quite another. We must turn, second, to Aelius Aristides for a clearer sense of reality. He had become engaged in keenly contested, important litigation, already referred to in the previous chapter. During the tense days of the trial he had an encouraging sign from the gods: "I dreamed that I spoke to the clerk of the governor about these things. . . . When he had heard everything, he promised that he would undo and change the verdict, and he ordered me to pay about five hundred drachmas. When I had the dream, in one way I became happier because there appeared to be some kind of promise in it. . . . But in another way it seemed to me to incline to the same thing as a refusal. For how would someone buy off so great a matter for five hundred drachmas?"[35] In short, the purchase of a verdict could easily be believed, but only at a realistic price. Aristides' familiarity with the workings of the courts is not in doubt.

Third, hear the jurist Paul in the early third century. He takes up a case where X gives Y money to distort a judicial decision. Suppose Y fails him, will X sue in court? No, says Paul, because he has no claim. But (except humorously) would even the possibility be discussed among jurists of our own world, or perhaps actually come before some court?[36]

And fourth, hear the professional rhetor Menander, in his handbook on how to make speeches of whatever sort for whatever occasion. It may be the governor coming to town. If you are called on to address a few words of welcome to him, you should predict that, during his tenure, "No one will dwell in prison unjustly or be unjustly punished, the rich will not be preferred nor the poor man's just cause fall to the ground." Instead, "gentleness of character" in the administration; "approachability, integrity, incorruptibility in matters of justice . . . , equal treatment of rich and poor."[37] Unexceptionable sentiments, these; sure to please the honorand. They could be safely offered to anyone in authority in any place or time. Yet they really fit only one in which justice beyond purchase cannot be taken for granted and defenseless people hardly dare complain. They must instead make known their sufferings to the *potentes* or *dynatoi* indirectly, in the form of praise for the virtues they would like to discover in the government that rests so heavily on them. The judge is congratulated to his face and honorific decrees give thanks on stone for his having provided verdicts unbribably, *adorodoketos*. He had served wonderfully, stood out from the rest, he was distinguished because he was honest. It has been noticed that praise in this particular becomes more common after the mid-third century. Menander writes near the end. Rabbinic allusions about then, or within a few generations, portray the judicial tribunal as an instrument of routine extortion: your money or your life.

Testimony from any one kind of character-witness for the courts might be discounted; all categories taken together are hard to refute. They suggest that a litigant whose case in itself was not open-and-shut and who offered a good sum for a favorable verdict might well get what he wanted at any period; but his chances were better than even in later times — say, after A.D. 250. The direct weight of money, it should be emphasized, was superadded to other considerations of influence and obligation which only the rich were likely to have. These were reviewed in the previous chapter.

As Verres' behavior made plain, governors could safely do almost anything they chose, off in their provinces. His own ultimate fate was exceptional. The classes from which he and his like were recruited under the empire generally protected their members from harsh punishment. They perceived crime rather as scandal, and tried to keep it out of the newspapers. It required a provincial, a person from the subject population, to tell the truth. Occasionally one spoke up.[38] Extra taxes, selective application of protection for a price, and other sources of profit are mentioned. Yet they seem generally to have been kept under control, through a combination of the prevailing ethic that condemned the sale of power, the prevailing use of clientage, and the emperor himself. Of these three factors, clearly the first was the most important. In logic, only what was disapproved could ever have been repressed. Beyond that self-evident truth, prosecutorial forces can be seen in difficulty sometimes, and never very effective, in their attempts to deal with crimes committed by members of the governing class. On that class itself as a moral force, therefore, rested the real weight of responsibility to impose its standards, through the weapons of disapproval or even ostracism.

From the servant class very much less was expected. Petty theft, lies, and cheating were thought to belong to the condition of servitude and were tolerated by masters and mistresses within bounds they fixed as individuals in their own households. That was true of the imperial household, too — among the *Caesariani*, as they were broadly called.[39] As the emperor was, so were they: of unique power and importance. One of them contracted to pay a million sesterces for appointment as treasurer, *dispensator*; another *dispensator* took sixteen of his own slaves with him on his travels (and both of these men were slaves themselves, suggesting what funds they could accumulate). A third *dispensator* owned the largest single piece of silver plate known to the elder Pliny, a 250-pound dish. Freed, the emperor's servants gained only more notoriety for the scale of their operations, and, as they moved up in the libertine ranks, they continued to filch and grab and beg.[40]

Under the early emperors, imperial slaves and freedmen also sold whatever influence they exercised over their master. For a price they would put in a word for you, and so win, or claim they had won, all sorts of favors and appointments.[41] In Nero's reign the nobility paid for magistracies and other imperial *beneficia*, but the recommenders were other nobles.[42] In more normal periods, however, what is attested very abundantly is support offered quite freely, except insofar as it created some unwritten obligation. All that was discussed in the preceding chapter.

From the drafting of tax receipts in a municipal office, to the choosing of next year's consuls at Rome, every act of government was for sale; yet not every one was sold routinely. On the contrary, while there was criminal or reprehensible behavior in the empire, just as there is in any society that has developed norms, neither the norms nor the government appear to have been overmatched. Had it been otherwise, the one or the other would have yielded. There would have been new norms or new governing institutions to allow the expression of whatever differing views had proved too strong. Even in the legal system the prevalence of venality was evidently not absolutely intolerable since, on the one hand, powerful people were still able to exert their power, a part of which was money, and on the other hand, the weak could petition the strong for help, or dream of an appeal to justice incorruptible from the throne of the emperor himself. Quite open disaccord between the ethic prevailing among the lower and higher servants of government caused trouble only during a period of transition, when the slaves or ex-slaves of the emperors matched their betters in wealth and power without recognizing the same constraints. This was the case, for example, in Claudius' and Nero's reigns. The awkward decades passed. Members of the elite began to enter the imperial service in greater numbers, recognizing that employment as a bailiff to emperors was not at all like being *vilicus* to a private citizen, no matter how vastly rich he might be. Equestrian procurators expanded their careers and responsibilities. Under Septimius Severus the pace of change picked up. New provinces were created. It was apparently then, too, that governors were directed to begin using their soldiers as their personal aides, equerries, and the like. As the emperors' agents ceased to be drawn from servile ranks, so likewise the governors'. In sum, government as a long-term, even a lifelong, career for the Haves began to take on an established character.[43]

Across this whole picture of government, the presence of ethical systems in the plural must be recognized. The slave in a grand house who saved the guests' unfinished wine for himself, or for sale to a corner hangout in the neighborhood, felt no guilt. It was not wrong; nor would the law or the mistress raise objections. If he sold a friend an unopened amphora, to make room for the cartloads just ordered and in excess, that too was all right — once. Being repeated a second time, it became a right, through *consuetudo*.

Yet, strictly speaking, his mistress had been robbed. Similarly, in the army a soldier might earn a first promotion, and a second and a third, and so believe he could at last claim a centurionate by right; but it went instead to the *cliens* of a new commander.[44] The soldier had been robbed. But it was not seen at in that light by his superiors who, in Pliny's day, passed around army commissions like extra tickets to a charity ball. By their code it was entirely proper to do so.

In conflict with their values, which may fairly be called conventional, there were a few alternatives successfully asserted by other groups. One was the perquisite of demanding certain payments simply because one was in military service. At first it belonged to lower officers. It was gradually extended to the no-man's-land where soldiers and civilians must live together. Another was the title to certain jobs in the civil service which could be treated like one's house: occupied, sold, bequeathed, one could almost say rented, because such jobs brought in regular perquisites. Occupants owned them *iure militiae*.[45] These few but important areas of divergence from convention came to be recognized in law at least by the early third century. By the later third century, as could be seen in Cologne, they had overspread an important part of economic life and a still more important part of political life, so as to bring down the emperor Victorinus. To follow their history as it continued to unfold in the later empire will be the object of the next section.

3. DEVELOPMENTS INCREASING PROFITS FROM PUBLIC OFFICE IN THE DOMINATE

First, some developments of the time, identified because they proved favorable to extortion and bribe-taking. They are *the higher level of violence employed by government; the ambiguity of law; the greater number and intrusiveness of laws, as of government servants* likewise; and *the isolation of the emperor.* In discussing these, it is convenient to have before the mind's eye as metaphor and miniature of the whole empire that scene in the Circus of Rome, recalled earlier, where Caracalla turned his guardsmen loose on the impudent plebs. They used the occasion for extortion: "Your money or your life," the phrase that highwaymen are supposed to aim, along with a pistol, at their victim's head. But the situation of the guardsmen was entirely different. They were within the law. What had so happily increased their earning powers was an abrupt increase in their administrative power, the two being nearly the same thing. On the instant, they had been promoted to the *ius gladii*, the legal right to inflict capital punishment. Now they could exact a high price for its remission to civilians in their grasp. Supposing that all government became much harsher, then similar effects should have been produced empire-wide.

That is in fact what can be observed and amply documented, though the subject in detail is not a very pleasant one.[46] Yet it constitutes one of those strands that make up decline, a development away from what we ourselves value and, more to the point, away from the norms prevailing in the earlier empire. For, when civil wars had ended in the collapse of the Republic, and a rule of law ensued that sought and needed peaceable acceptance, restrictions on official violence were promulgated and evidently observed, not too negligently.

From the start, the rules offered very little protection to slaves. Even as innocent witnesses they were interrogated by torture. Not infrequently they died under it. It was by no means pro forma. When charged with crimes themselves and found guilty, they had to undergo physical punishment because neither jail terms nor fines were possible alternatives; and they had therefore to suffer death on the cross, by burning, or wild beasts, or beatings of greater or lesser severity. Noncitizens likewise were liable to such penalties at the discretion of the governor.

The stages by which citizens in their several social strata gradually lost immunity from certain cruel treatments or, if not immunity, at least the privilege of suffering them only for crimes further up the scale of seriousness, does not really concern me here. At the time of Caracalla and his Circus performance, Roman citizens, unless of municipal-councillor or higher rank, were only a little less exposed to violence than their slaves. They could be tortured in giving evidence, though they could not legally be beaten or tortured to death; and they could be executed for crimes in a list gradually lengthened to include arson, for example, or temple robbery or escape from jail. How can this steady development be explained?

First, it must be set against calculations that opposed it and slowed it down: calculations of one's own pain in contemplating someone else's; of one's pride in being superior to savage, insensitive people and societies; and of the costs, personal and political, of being too greatly feared and therefore hated. All these are attested, as we would expect. They belong to human nature. By the same token, they cannot have been absent from the minds of later second- or third-century officials; but they were attenuated, through officials growing away, psychologically, from the scenes and settings over which they ruled. An opinion of Toqueville on America has been tellingly cited: "à mesure . . . que les peuples deviennent plus semblables les uns aux autres, ils se montrent réciproquement plus compatissants pour leurs misères, et le droit des gens s'adoucit." Yes, and the opposite is also true. It is true of the kindly, decent, dutiful Pliny in charge of Pontus. Fifteen hundred miles removed from Como and his neighbors, recalling the scale and splendor of Rome as he defined his mission among the cramped streets and strange gods of Amastris or Heraclea, small wonder if he looked down on the colonials as an inferior species. Small wonder if a governor forgot the fine points of the law and laid about him as he would among his slaves — and as he never would have thought to do among his neighbors in Como.

Besides, when the agents of government in the early empire felt themselves to be merely on loan from private life, so to speak, and when bearers of authority derived as much from their personal eminence as from appointive rank, they were not so likely to enforce that authority with barbarous force. But when appointive rank hardened into its own structure of honors, rewards, and promotions that increasingly controlled a man's decisions, constituting his whole life, and when the imperial authority he represented became gradually inflated and godlike, then he could feel no sympathy for disobedient subjects.[47] They were to be compelled to behave. Whatever force was needed should be used. So I imagine the process of change.

There were, of course, at all periods, instances of fearful coercion or punishment or public displays of cruelty. Because they so strike the imagination, they are easily recalled from the reign of Nero, for example — above all, the sufferings of Christian martyrs. Increasingly the emperorship was invoked as injured party in criminal accusations, in Nero's reign as earlier or later; also, wrongly, in modern explanations of the legal basis for the Christian persecutions. But the latter line of reasoning is at least correct in seeing that an ill-defined and all the more insidious sacrosanctity radiated from the throne and cast some shadow of treason on many wrongful acts not otherwise very serious.

It is apparently unprecedented, but a fact first in A.D. 278, that a high official should declare disobedience to one of his edicts a capital crime (the edict concerning labor on the dikes). In A.D. 300, dereliction in tax collection was also proclaimed a capital matter.[48] Where there had been only sixteen capital crimes on the books in Pliny's day, a dozen or more had been added by A.D. 200, and still another dozen by A.D. 300; and for mere execution by the blow of a sword, other more beastly forms — *ad bestias*, crucifixion, burning to death — were continually being substituted. At the latter date a new tone is heard in an emperor's edict against malefactors — once again, the poor Christians — who are to be treated with mercy, humanity, and gentleness: they are to have only one leg maimed and only one eye gouged out. These words, I emphasize, are not directed in a moment of tantrum by some unbalanced official against an individual offender. They are formal commands pronounced through the usual formal channels for application everywhere within the ruler's reach.[49]

In the period of the Tetrarchy bridging the passage from the third to the fourth century, we cross into what may be called, without mincing words, a barbarous age. It expresses its quality by no means only against Christians. The first Christian on the throne declares, "The greedy hands of the civil secretaries shall immediately forbear, they shall forbear, I say; for, if after due warning they do not cease, they shall be cut off with the avenging sword." Or, for guardians accessory to a girl's seduction, "the penalty shall be that the mouth and throat of those who offered inducement to evil shall be closed by pouring in molten lead." Under Constantine, if diviners so much as entered a private house, if a person clipped coins, was caught in adultery, proven heretical, or was guilty of a couple of dozen new capital crimes (half of them administrative) — off with his head! To the stake with him![50] Rapists and parricides and child kidnappers were to suffer elaborate, unnatural deaths, and with maximum publicity.

Of course, with publicity. For, being unable to surmount all the obstacles inherent in a primitive administration, itself set over a world of primitive transport and primitive communications, any ancient tyranny had to rely on word of mouth to procure obedience. News of horrible doings would be naturally passed around. Gossip was as good as the state radio piped into factories and bus terminals, at least if the messages were sufficiently striking. And, no doubt about it, you would remember what would happen to coin-clippers, let us say, once you had heard the penalty. The language of promulgation was meant to teach. For an example of the sound of it, beyond the instances quoted from Constantine, listen to his son on the subject of peccant procurators: "Prisons shall hold the scoundrels when they are convicted, tortures shall tear them in pieces, the avenging sword shall destroy them."[51]

Much could be said and talked about, more could be seen. For serious crimes, people of no account had long served to inculcate good morals or, as the poet puts it, "represent / A source of innocent merriment," by their manner of death in Roman amphitheaters. Occasionally they might be crucified and set up where everybody must pass by — on an Italian highway or in the suburbs of some Palestinian city. Or they might be mutilated for all to see and take heed. "Notorious brigands," writes a Severan lawyer, "as many people have decided, should be bound to a stake at the location of their marauding" and there left to die.[52] The sight must have been a common one. "So many brigands die on a cross every day," says an observer of the early fourth century, while, near the turn of the next century, contemporaries comment on the several severed heads in grisly circulation around the provinces. They had once belonged to Eugenius, Rufinus, Gainas, and Constantius III, not to mention John the Baptist (!).[53] When a ruler in this period has a woman torn apart by wild horses or decapitates children in the presence of their parents, we hardly know which world we are in, barbarian or late Classical.[54]

In addition to more mutilating, more burning alive, and more crucifying in public, the great severity of punishments short of death came home to people in the most frequented heart of every large city, through the shows put on in the forums or in the large basilicas normally located next to forums, or in public stoas — wherever trials were held. They became regular torture chambers, as one observer calls them. Another offers a number of vivid and, to him, obviously intolerable vignettes of floggings in public places, or describes the ceremony called in mockery "the triumph," whereby victims were driven about the streets to show their torn backs to their fellow-citizens. "Acts" of the Christian martyrs make such pictures familiar from the later second century on, but it was not only those Christian victims that one could see in the marketplace. Anyone might have to face the same afflictions. "The spear is ready there, the sword, the executioner, the hook that tears, the rack that stretches, the flames that burn, and more tortures for the body of a man than he has limbs."[55]

Jerome describes something recently witnessed in the suburbs of a north Italian town, Vercellae. A woman who had endured with her alleged lover the most extraordinary torments was taken out afterwards to be executed for unchastity; and "the entire population poured out to see the sight — indeed, so closely were the gates crowded by the outrushing throng that you might have fancied the city itself to be migrating." It was just for such crowds, of course, that the ceremonies of judicial savagery were staged in public areas. That contemporaries did not become altogether hardened to them appears in several little facts. They had nightmares about crucifixion. Why not, indeed? They killed themselves rather than face the tortures of a final interrogation. They shunned high positions that might entangle them some day in charges of high crimes.[56] And, we are told, at a hearing already quoted (chap. 2 at n. 112) where the accused must confront a particularly frightening judge, "an awful fear straightway overspread the bystanders in their hearts, at the spectacle before them, and with fellow-feeling they grieved for the man and feared for his danger." Very much as we would expect, then, people well knew the realities of their own times, responded to their dreadful drama as they were supposed to, and shuddered in the face of terrification by the mighty.

The violence increasingly permitted in the later empire was regarded with a certain envious awe by those who did not command it, and who wished for their share, while those who meted it out looked on it with some measure of approval. Why did Constantius think his young kinsman Julian had no talent for a high command? "Because," says Julian, "I had shown myself mild and self-restrained." An odd condemnation for the very qualities that panegyrists of earlier times, Seneca or Pliny or Aelius Aristides, liked to discover in their rulers. Or why was Constantine's government said to "present an unsuitable appearance" as too merciful (ridiculous though that characterization may be)? Or why should one prefect of the capital have been "held in contempt for his slow measures, and little suited to the vigorous following out of business," while another, "of a friendly nature . . . , to preserve his authority seemed harsh toward some people and a little over-ready to convict"? Why did a certain Festinus of Trent, a man marked by "mercifulness and respect for law," change his professional image to obtain advancement? The answer lies in his observation of how his patron had climbed the ladder of advancement through the destruction of "every good man. . . . And when he saw how that man had, without merits, gained a prefecture through the recommendation of deaths inflicted impiously, he was roused to the same acts and hopes; and, in actor's fashion abruptly changing his mask, he was all zeal to hurt." To make the point finally clear, our source for this, Ammianus, describes for us another man, likewise as an actor, "bribable behind a facade of ferocity."[57]

In the decade in which Ammianus summed up his subject so strikingly, an imperial edict hit upon almost the identical turn of phrase. Honorius reminds his courts that persons exempt by status from the more extreme forms of physical abuse are protected from "the wrath of the judges and the venal terror of their enforcers."[58] Judges, and especially the torturers, had been ignoring the exemptions to which their prisoners had a merely legal title. Their cruelty is explained by the term *venalis; terror* was the key to profits. While it is true that the *potentes* of the Principate are also often described as terrifying, and deserved the description, it fits the officeholders of the later empire still better;[59] and, while it is also true that Gaius Verres in Sicily had resorted to crucifixion and other horrible acts to break down his targets for extortion, his doing so was disapproved. It was not at all characteristic of the government he represented. That well-advertised ferocity which increasingly marks the Roman world as it passes from the third to the fourth century was thus quite different from Verres'. It was of the times, not of any individual. And it lent itself to profitable application.

Like the guardsmen turned loose in the Circus by Caracalla, soldiers and officials in the later empire were issued instructions more emphatic than explicit. Therein lay a further invitation to profit. Constantine in the earlier fourth century, Theodosius II in the earlier fifth, and all the rulers in between them favored an adjectival style in explaining the purpose of their laws. Sometimes they fairly shouted, they were so indignant (above, pp. 140 and 141). Shouts do not make for easily administered decrees, nor did the rules of literature that prevailed in the expression of legislative intent. They aimed for color not clarity, fullness not precision. Where the classical legists paused, for example, over the exact meaning of a word and explained it carefully, their successors instead hid their intent in clouds of periphrases and grandiose circumlocutions.[60] The clouds often proved impenetrable to the average, even to the highest, intelligence. Little did the emperors care. Their purposes were quite different. "Since We desire to eradicate the interminable controversies of the jurisconsults, the *prudentes*, We order the destruction of the notes of Ulpian and Paul on Papinian; for, while they were eagerly pursuing praise for their genius, they preferred not so much to correct him as to distort him." So spoke Constantine. Away with all fustian learning! Then, liberated, he could turn to the complexities of testamentary disposition, beginning his decree, "Since We have ruled out the quibbles of senseless verbiage.... "[61] Such conscious anti-intellectualism, typical of late antiquity, produced nothing but tangles which only an official, more or less arbitrarily, could straighten out; or it produced litigation with which the official and the lawyers together could occupy themselves indefinitely. "Wealthy men" must pay late taxes fivefold. And how rich must one be to fall under that penalty? No answer was indicated. Examples of the sort could be multiplied *ad lib.*[62]

The ill-defined authority given to those who administered the law therefore constituted an unintended increase in their power. It was an increase on a very large scale, too, as can be sensed in the remarks of contemporaries: "No matter what one's genius, who can claim to understand the law?" "Knowledge of it is quite destroyed by its self-contradictions." "Most sacred emperor, having secured the defenses of the state at home and abroad by divine providence, there remains one matter of domestic concern requiring remedy from Your Serenity: that you turn back crooked legal suits and by the verdict of Your August Judgement shed light upon contradictory and opposed decisions at law."[63] Finally, a complaint which helps to explain the confusion: "Innumerable are the decrees which day after day they [the rulers] enact and publish," successive legislation thus cancelling what came before.[64] The change in the rate of lawmaking may be felt simply through holding in one's hand the bulky Justinian Code, which contains about as many constitutions under Diocletian as were put out in a full eighty years prior. To turn next to the Theodosian Code, which begins with Constantine, strengthens that impression. The output of general directives and public and criminal law, as opposed to rescripts on individual civil lawsuits, rises to characteristic levels in the period of the Dominate.[65] Sheer abundance of legislation matched its fuzziness and contradictions, and its interpreters at every level gained a corresponding increase in their power.

Again like Caracalla's guards, the guardians of later laws were deployed in larger numbers. Suddenly they were everywhere; or their ubiquity appears sudden, because of a combination of real changes and the uneven distribution of the surviving evidence. No doubt, in the ill-reported third century, a start was made on many developments that are wrongly credited to Diocletian. The sources for his reign are relatively abundant; but it was in fact a time of broad and rapid innovation. Above all, he redesigned the emperorship. To be true to the Tetrarchy, he must then quadruple some parts of the government, whether by dividing those existing into four or by matching them with three more, or by some compromise measure. The totals increased greatly. Entirely new offices were added. Most noticeable, too, was the splitting of provinces into smaller sizes, each, however, with its own governor and each governor with his bureaus. This process continued into the fourth century, though without so much effect.

The significance of the overall change may be brought out through a comparison with the numbers of provinces under Caracalla, roughly doubled a century later. Some of the new bureaus — for example, that of the Master of Offices — themselves were in time subdivided. The history of late Roman government is full of adjustments and details which need not be discussed here. One total, however, is revealing. In the civil service of the late empire some thirty to thirty-five thousands were employed, to be set against perhaps three hundred career civil servants under Caracalla.[66]

A hundredfold increase! Of course, the comparison needs qualification straightway. Government in the earlier empire made abundant use of slaves and, at least in the emperors' service, of freedmen as well. In some sense they can certainly be said to have pursued a career in administration since they spent their lives in it. However many hundreds of them there were at their most numerous, they should be counted. As those numbers began to diminish around the mid-third century (above, n. 39), they were replaced by soldiers, many of whom likewise had long been pursuing what amounted to a career in clerical and administrative duties; so they too must be counted. There are the senators to be added — those who chose to pass from one high position to another, sometimes for years on end. And so on.

But I recall why I embarked on these questions of quantification. It was to assess the weight and presence of professional government in the later empire compared with the earlier; for it was in professional government that could be discovered an ethic able to assert itself against the conventional — against the values of the empire's society at large. The fact looked interesting. Clerk- and aides-associations (the *decuriae*) had been able to gain legal status for fees originating in extortion. We have seen how that happened. Army officers, too, had won acknowledgment in law for their shakedowns. Both groups had developed a sense of right and title to the profits they could demand from persons under their authority.

The weight and presence of soldiers is most obviously detectible inside the empire in the numbers assigned to staff work under each governor — fifty-plus in the earlier empire. The number gradually grew. They had clerical and police duties and stirred around in civilian society quite prominently, although at a level beneath the interest of most of our sources (not of inscriptions, however, nor of Christian "Acts"). There were *stationarii* and *frumentarii* and other men in circulation also, not in the thousands but certainly in hundreds. Their home lay in whatever city served their boss — governor, procurator, legate — as his headquarters: London, Lyons, Carthage, or Caesarea in Mauretania.[67] Soldiers wintered in cities: in Apamaea or Ancyra. Their quarters could not all lie in one section; rather, they were scattered at random down every street and alley. If their camp adjoined a city like Sepphoris, or gave rise to one grown from a village or from a cluster of camp followers, like Lauriacum, they would easily be drawn into it by its needs or attractions. And, as is well known, along the empire's eastern flank already existing towns were routinely used to lodge troops. Where any details can be added, half of the time the men are seen living in the suburbs (Emesa, Apamea, Sepphoris, Jerusalem), half the time right inside (Dura, Samosata, Zeugma) without any physical division to mark off the military sector. Excavations at Dura on the Euphrates give an exceptionally full view of the intimate absorption of soldiers into a city. The sum total of all this presence appears to have been quite considerable during the period of the Principate. At midpoint, nevertheless, a well-informed spokesman offers a general statement: "not many troop units" as entireties are set in cities. Instead, their camps are off by themselves. And what he says is true enough: it is the case for the great bulk of the army which lay along the northern glacis or in its fortresses elsewhere at Leon or Lambaesis.

In contrast, however, with the words of Aelius Aristides, just quoted, the evidence laid out in Appendix C, including matching general statements by writers of the fourth and fifth centuries, indicates that by their time a great change had taken place. While there were still frontier troops, *limitanei*, and rare bursts of fortlet construction along the riverbanks or desert's edge in the reigns of Diocletian or Valentinian, most of the army had simply disappeared into larger or smaller urban centers. In Egypt and Asia Minor and Thrace, at least by the mid-fourth century, there is no reason to think that garrisons were not the norm; likewise in the northern half of France. Of course our knowledge has too many gaps in it to allow a sure sense of numbers. "More than 50 percent of centers of more than five thousand population lodged troops permanently" — such a statement could never be ventured. Nor could it be challenged. There remained very large regions like southern France and Africa Proconsularis which did not have (had never had) troops in any quantity worth mentioning. The general impression yielded by the evidence under the Dominate nevertheless is of an army most of which lived right on top of civilians.

It must be obvious how this conclusion fits and bears out the Circus scene under Caracalla. There, the natural rapacity of the guardsmen could show itself to the full because they were only a foot from their victims and had their swords at the ready — a situation recalling Shaw's definition of marriage: "it combines the maximum of temptation with the maximum of opportunity." Not fify thousand men but five times that number of soldiers were now in a position to enjoy a stimulating proximity to the civilian population. Small wonder that Zosimus, when he describes the step taken by Constantine in this direction, sees it as "subjecting the cities to ruination from the military."

Of general circumstances favoring the spread of extortion, the final one that I identified at the outset of this section was the emperor's isolation. He alone, at least in theory, had nothing to gain from the spread of venality throughout his government: it was his no longer, to the extent that its authority might be sold independently by his servants. But since no one contested his right to command, all he required to preserve the ways familiar under Augustus was the knowledge of what was going on. Then he could punish and control the theft of power.

Augustus had the legs of a secretary broken for selling the contents of a confidential letter, and when the servants of a crown prince at the youth's death continued "travelling around the province arrogantly and greedily" (as Suetonius says), Augustus had them put in weighted sacks and tossed in a river.[68] He acted, obviously, on the basis of what he had learned; and no doubt his determination was understood. By contrast, in the 360s and 370s, the empire had a like-minded ruler, determined to set bounds to venality, and Ammianus praises him for that — before continuing on to an account of monumental misdoings by that same emperor's untouchable prefect, Probus, who went on accumulating repeated prefectures. Then comes the story of the villainous Romanus, Count of Africa, who rode out any trouble during the reign, thanks to his kinsman at court.[69] What had baffled such an emperor's resolve?

"Four or five men get together, they think up some way to fool the emperor, and they inform him of whatever he must approve. The emperor, living enclosed within his quarters, does not know what the truth is. He is obliged to know only what those men tell him. He appoints governors whom he should not, he deprives the state of those he should hold on to. Why say more? As Diocletian himself used to declare, an emperor — good, careful, the very best — is put up for sale." The analysis is offered by an acute if overinventive contemporary of the developed Dominate. It is easily confirmed.[70]

We can look to the reigns of Arcadius and Honorius, presiding over the most corruptible of legal systems, from which their respective prefects drew a fortune; "but the emperors were aware of none of this. Instead, they just wrote whatever Rufinus and Stilicho instructed them to."[71] Before we excuse the system itself and incriminate only the youth of the emperors, consider the like fate of Valens, condemned to know too little about his government; so, in all innocence, "he opened the doors to pillage that waxed more vigorous every day. Judges and lawyers were united in equal wickedness to sell the concerns of small folk to military commanders or powerful courtiers. In this way they gained either wealth or position."[72] How could he allow this? He was persuaded by those close to him, "asserting that the trifles of private litigation were beneath the emperor's eminence."

Or we may look to an earlier time and to a vigorous and far from naive emperor, Constantius II. He is described as "astonished and pained" upon finding out that one bishop had exiled, even kidnapped, other bishops as if with his permission. On another occasion he writes to the church of Antioch that the former incumbent of the see, "Eudoxius, did not come from Us, let no one think so. We are far from inclining to such persons; and if they concoct such a deceit with other persons, they are the more evidently ready to put a fair face on other matters." The "other persons" no doubt included court eunuchs, who are mentioned in the conspiracy to seat the wrong man on the episcopal throne.[73] Again and again Constantius is obliged to confess, in the promulgation of correcting laws, that what is in the books at the moment is something quite wrong, illicitly formulated, and illicitly issued over his signature, for example, by "persons who have extorted a special rescript to the fraud of Our sanction by offering an illusory sanction to the Emperor."[74] But it should not be thought that his was a weak reign in this regard. The scores of similar confessions from the throne begin where the Theodosian Code itself begins, and run right through that great collection from Constantine to Theodosius II.

Rulers of the later empire manifestly had less and less direct personal knowledge of affairs, making them easy to fool inside the palace and to impersonate outside it. Anyone could claim to speak for them in the confidence that they were not likely ever to expose his imposture by reaching out to surer knowledge, while their subjects were unlikely to reach in — except through the successive ranks of insiders. A steep decline in the numbers of rescripts to private individuals under Diocletian has been referred to. They soon ceased entirely. The number of legations from cities sharply diminished; likewise, from provincial councils.[75] Court ceremonial, honorific titulature, and architectural setting combined to repel familar access. A screen of servants surrounded the throne, making them thereby its masters: the Master of Offices in particular, but also eunuchs and secretaries.[76] It was an utterly different world in which Marcus Aurelius had once "made himself accessible to his subjects, a reasonable and moderate ruler, receiving those who approached him and preventing any guardsmen around him from frightening away anyone whom they encountered."[77]

4. THE EXTENT OF PRIVATIZATION IN
LATE ROMAN GOVERNMENT

It is one thing to distinguish and describe changes that induced people in public positions to turn their authority to private profit; it is quite another thing, and much more difficult, to estimate the importance of the consequences. For instance: we happen to have legislation from the later period that is, because of its format, bound to give an impression of continual wrongdoing on the part of government itself; and all these laws, being so very numerous, can easily misrepresent the norms and routines of the time. It won't do to suppose that all crimes condemned were common. Only when we see them gaining full or partial legitimacy can their mass be measured: then at least we can say they have become stronger than the law. I give special attention, in the rest of this chapter, to just such moments, as also to any other types of evidence I can identify which allow the detection of changes ongoing in the history of mores.

The servants of the emperor, whether civilians or soldiers, were in the later empire indifferently called *milites* engaged in a *militia*; indifferently, both wore the belt of office, *cingulum* or *zone*.[78] Terminology indicates which was the predominant element in the coalition: the military. That was inevitable, given the numbers involved. Yet soldier and civilian had touched in administration for centuries at two points: in the staff of provincial governors and in the raising of taxes, so large a part of which was destined for army units in the locality. As they coalesced, the practices of soldiers on the one hand and of freedmen and *decuriae* on the other intermingled so intimately that their separate contributions cannot be identified in the practices of late Roman government. In any case, from what has been outlined above, it is clear that they had little to learn from each other. When they emerge from the shadows of the third-century crisis, so nearly bare of documentation, their way of life is one.

And how should it be described? There is no lack of characterization by the most authoritative critic, the employer himself. Hear Constantine's father, Constantius I, warning his subjects against "the boundless evil of the Caesarians' pillaging and their baneful" ways (the Caesarians at this date being Treasury aides); consider Constantine's reference to "the formidable arrogance of procurators and Caesarians alike, ... the rapacity of Caesarians and procurators," and "the customary fraud [note, *consuetudo fraudium*] with which the aforesaid persons [the Caesarians] ordinarily violate all regulations." "Ordinarily"![79] The Caesarians had been ungovernably thievish in Severan times (above, n. 39). After a century and more, what sort of monarchy was it that could neither discipline nor dispense with them? The futile exasperation of emperor after emperor tells more about the realities of power in the empire than all of the Greek and Latin panegyrics to the throne put together.

In the next generation, hear the grimly jocular Constantius II characterizing another cadre of government, his Special Agents. One of their number receives his salary with too much eagerness. The emperor remarks, "Special Agents are better at grabbing than accepting"; and in one of his constitutions he adds, "it is virtually impossible to resist their greediness" — so let it be limited to a certain maximum of extortion(!).[80] Under Valentinian, Libanius published an oration which expands as an orator should on the Special Agents — "the people who had robbed their own cities of their services, who had fled from the town councils and the customary civic duties, and had enrolled among the Agents and had purchased the position of investigator ..., so did this crew drop the mention of pickings to their lick-spittles, and these would bring the tradesmen under their lash on the charge of insulting the emperor, not so as to give them a good drubbing, but to ensure that they bought immunity from it." Libanius goes on to detail how they used charges of treason, homosexuality, or magic for purposes of extortion, worked hand-in-glove with counterfeiters, and, "if the thought of any province recurred to them, they would immediately go on to remark upon the sum of money they could get from it." Their number, briefly reduced by Julian, was something over a thousand.

The quivering finger of accusation swings round to other targets: "the inveterate license of the office staffs, *officia*, shall be abated, whereby they often obtained gain from official notifications ... ;" "because *officiales* of the higher authorities are always baneful to the provincials . . . ;" "the accustomed fraudulence of the tax accountants, *tabularii*"; "the unsated greed of those who deliver the records of a case to litigants"; "the thoroughly vicious and venal treachery of government assistants, *apparitores*," which must not "continue to rage unpunished against the interests of the public"; and the collectors of military supplies who, "sent out to exact them, have been harshly tearing them from the vitals of Our subjects, as suits their avarice and pleasure." [81] It is the emperors from Constantine to Theodosius II who are speaking through their laws, in which they can neither repress their sense of outrage nor the cause of it — the "inveterate," "continued," "frequent," or "accustomed" abuse of their authority by their own deputies. The conventional ethic prevails in their judgments, as it does in Libanius and other observers of the times; but it had no place in government as it really operated. Reality was governed by *apparitores*, *curiosi*, *tabularii*, *officiales*, and the rest.

It was a nineteenth-century Tsar who exclaimed in frustration, "Russia is ruled by ten thousand clerks."

Roman emperors further revealed their helplessness in their successive surrenders to the customary shakedowns. An instance has just been cited, in which the Special Agents are authorized by law to exact a *solidus* for each state carriage they released to official travelers (and a man could live several months on one *solidus*). It was not only to be quit of their rank and duties, as Libanius suggests, that decurions sought out appointment as Special Agents. But it was not to be had for nothing. First one must have the support of the department, the *schola*, as also for subsequent promotion. That was declared by law, along with the procedures of election: senior members of the *schola* made the recommendation at an open meeting of its members.[82] Certainly they required payment for their approval. Members of the *schola* of Palace Guards not only demanded one but obtained its legitimization by a law of 364 or 365, as was later gained also by all the bureaus under the director of Special Agents, the Master of Offices.[83] Like the members of *decuriae* in Cicero's day, the bureau chiefs of the Master could pass on their *militia* to their children, a procedure protected by law; in similar fashion, the bureau chiefs of governors had a right to dispose of their post upon retirement: they could sell it, though only to their assistants.[84] Strictly speaking, of course, appointment lay only in the hands of the emperor; then, by delegation, in the hands of such high personages as the Master of Offices or Vicar; but in practice it was the right of the lowlier recommender, a *suffragator*.

Transformation of *suffragium*, "support" from someone like Pliny or Fronto, into "purchased recommendation" is recognized in legal language by A.D. 338.[85] Of course, the laws were slow to reflect common usage. By 362, people had moved beyond them and were already arguing quite openly that what they had paid for *suffragium* was something the courts should protect. The presumption indicates how far from clandestine the buying of office had become. Thirty years later, it was a matter for written contracts and might then involve the transfer of rural or urban real estate, an indication of its scale.[86] All of this evidence appears in imperial legislation interlarded with expressions of outrage at the practices which must be condoned.

In the 360s, illicit exactions marked as "customary from of old" became licit if the Roman urban prefect's staff simply took them in without demanding them; dukes were given express permission to exact money from their under-officers, but no more than they had been used to getting under Constantine — this, in A.D. 358. Presumably records would show how much that had been. Julian soon increased the amount permitted. Offices in Alexandria responsible for assembling the grain shipments to the capital were told to skim off no more than 1 percent (this, in A.D. 349), no matter how much more might be suggested by impostors claiming imperial authorization to the contrary; but the greedier ideas eventually prevailed and a doubling of the rake-off was approved in 386.[87] References to "the customary" or the like phrase occurring in some of the texts just cited, and in others as well, define the problem from the legislators' point of view: there was a steady pressure across the whole front of governmental operations to introduce charges, invent fees, and generally apply the principles of private enterprise.[88] To this, the emperors could not offer effective opposition.

On a public building of Timgad in Numidia a price list, quite in this spirit, was displayed in 362/3 for the benefit of anyone thinking of litigation, or perhaps already engaged in it. It was issued for the whole province; the bronze original was posted in the capital; and it secured quite openly and authoritatively what had no doubt been illicit but actual for generations: namely, required payments (*commoda*, tips) to the governor's chief of staff for litigation begun, five bushels of wheat or the price thereof if the case should not need any clerk or summoner to travel a mile; otherwise, seven bushels, and two more bushels per mile beyond that (with overseas travel requiring a hundred bushels); and the chief's chief aides got half as much (lines 23-25). For various types of case, the department's lawyer members, *scholastici*, were to be given five bushels (lines 26-29), or ten, or fifteen; *exceptores* were to receive five, twelve, or twenty; a *libellensis* got two; and certain legal actions had to involve no less than four, or six, high clerks, so that no cut rates could become established.[89] Since a bushel of wheat even in a famine year cost only a tenth of a solidus, and ordinarily a quarter of that, the sums demanded in Numidia were not beyond the reach of a small farmer; but, on the receiving end, they mounted up. So *commoda* under the same name had been mounting up for centuries (above, n. 3).

As time goes on, other illicit practices become known to us through the emperors' attempts to set some limit to them. Like the extra charge for travel in Numidia, two bushels per mile, the notification of appointment of quaestors and praetors in remote areas of Italy must be covered by payment which shall not be withheld (thus the ban of 372, after a generation, is reversed; see above, n. 81).[90] *Consuetudo*, "the custom shall be observed of allowing two solidi for each horse," as *sportulae* to the collectors of the cavalry-horse tax in Africa; and in the eastern provinces, when military tribunes took in their tips, locally called *stillaturae* or "drippings," at the moment they acknowledged late payment of army supplies from the taxpayers, those "emoluments" were to be commuted into cash at the market price. The tribunes, through juggling the equivalence, had been attempting a rake-off on top of a rake-off.[91] This, in 406. The next year (CT 7.4.29) the Dukes and tribunes are discovered taking "from soldiers any subsistence allowance by the grace of a gift to which they are entitled," *donatio quam merentur*, which likewise shall be in cash reckoned according to market prices. I like the "*merentur*." On the eastern frontier, for the moment, in 412, the line is drawn against Dukes shaking down the local folk for the cash equivalent of fuel and hot baths; but by the end of the century such things are posted up just like the Timgad price list, in marble publication: payable in quarterly amounts to the Duke, with certain payments known by pet names, *paramythia*. I have referred to euphemisms before, as the tribute paid by vice to virtue.[92] These latter texts, however, carry me beyond my period of study.

Publication and legitimization indicate the helplessness of the emperors and of some of their more cooperative or high-minded prefects and Masters of Offices, in their struggle to stem the tide of venality. In the struggles we can also see and even quantify the passage of specific venal practices across the bar of the law. But what gained acceptance in the Codes and represented the emperors' acknowledged defeat made up only a tiny part of the whole of venality in the imperial service. How is that whole to be estimated? Should we accept at face value another kind of evidence in the Codes, and assume that all the mentions of bribability constitute so many general truths? Merely because a practice is forbidden certainly doesn't show that it was common. In the face of these questions, and in the attempt to refine a sense of the proportions of venality, perhaps it is best to abandon the legal texts for others that offer individual statements and incidents: the one, if they amount to contemporaries' generalizations; the other, if they show the boundaries of the possible. Out of both, it should be possible to form some broad impressions.

Of general statements there is an abundance, more than ample to show that the world emerging from the third-century crisis was beset by old vices on a new scale. That the vices were seen as such in contemporary terms of course explains the judgments passed on them.

It is the powerful Symmachus in the 390s who describes tax collection in Italy. The problem is a familiar one: "It is painful to report the trickery with which the Italian fiscal staff go about plundering. . . . As to the weak — sheer bullying beats them down instantly, and the more resolute are entangled in prosecutorial, terminological distortions."[93] Paulinus and the subject of his biography, Ambrose, straddle the period in which Symmachus writes. Ambrose, as Paulinus recalls, formed the most depressing estimate of the life he saw around him in the courtier world of Milan and the region he was familiar with around it: increasing avarice and corruption, "above all among people enjoying office. . . . Everything was up for sale for a price, and this was what to begin with brought every evil upon Italy, and resulted in universal deterioration." He instances an aide to Stilicho "who was said . . . to be drawing up false letters of appointment to tribunates at such a rate that men were recalled even as they set out to their duties"; and in at least one of his sermons he quotes the passage that has appeared in these pages once before (above, p. 130), from the gospel of Luke (3 : 14). John there tells soldiers, "no bullying, don't shake down anybody, make do with your pay."

In the same northwest corner of Italy, a slightly later bishop, Maximus, offers that same text to his congregation:

> A good number of our brothers who are bound to imperial service by their belt of office, *cingulum*, or are established in official activity, when they have seriously sinned, are above all likely to excuse their sins by saying they are in imperial service; and if they sometimes do amiss, their plaint is, they are engaged in a bad business — just as if it were men's *militia* and not their will which is to be blamed. So what *they* do, they attribute to their official post. Now imperial service is not a sin in itself, but it is one on account of the extortion; and there is nothing wrong about doing the state's business, but only if it is done so as to profit from it. That's what should be condemned. For that very cause, by provision, they are given their pay, lest, in meeting their expenses, they go about plundering.

When they are reproached for drunkenness, robbery, or murder, they say, "What was I to do, a man of this world, and in government service? When ever did I claim to be a monk or a priest?" But they should follow not the rules of monastic life but simply of moral behavior. And the bishop goes on to quote Luke on taxation and to condemn shakedowns by soldiers — "that plunder of theirs they call *commoda*."[94]

At the church council meeting in Toledo in A.D. 400, perhaps the very year in which Maximus is speaking, the eighth canon declares that "anyone who takes up imperial service after being baptized, and assumes the military cloak or the *cingulum*, even if he admits to nothing worse, shall not be made a deacon if he is taken into the clergy."[95] Why not? A gathering of bishops in Rome two years later answered, "About a person who, when already a Christian, served in a secular post, it is well known that he enjoys freedom ex officio, for who can keep guard over him? or deny that he was present at shows, or that, pricked on by the need for money, he has not been able to hold himself free of violence and injustice?" In the eyes of the western church, *militia* and morality were radically incompatible. We could hardly ask for a clearer proof of there being two ethics.

Maximus continues his sermon. He turns from the spectacle of soldiers in the cities and rural areas of Italy to the courts. He warns against giving false testimony, *neque calumnian faciatis*, as Luke puts it. "Yet," Maximus picks up, "the evil has developed to such a point that the laws are sold, statutes corrupted, and verdicts venal as a matter of routine, *ex consuetudine*."

A single witness, of course, whether or not he speaks from the pulpit, needs to be confirmed when he ventures to characterize the general operations of the judiciary. Referring to this period, though from the vantage of a much later date, Zosimus describes Stilicho's seizing of control over the courts in which, so long as he directed them, the only winner in litigation was money.[96] From about the same period we hear of an adviser to a judge in Rome, "a wonder to other people for his not taking anything," despite the tempting offers made him (there was a senator "who wanted something allowed, the way power operates, even though it was against the law"). And earlier there is the emperor Gratian in the 370s or Symmachus in the 360s characterizing the judiciary in Rome as totally venal in its verdicts or inertly susceptible to pressure from influential people.[97]

As a final note on the conditions of their Italian world: when an embassy from Spain came to the court at Milan on a church matter in 383, Ambrose as the bishop there denied them accreditation for their views; but they saw the right people and paid enough money and so extracted from the emperor, through his Master of Offices, a new rescript cancelling the old and restoring their churches to them.[98] It serves to illustrate both the Caesaropapism of the time and the simony particularly centered in the imperial court. More will be found in Constantinople, below.

From Milan, a certain Palladius, tribune and notary, set off in 367 for Carthage. He had been designated to inquire into charges of venal negligence — "If you don't pay me, I won't help you" — against Count Romanus, military commander of Africa. Through Romanus' inaction, the farming country of Tripolitania had suffered defenselessly from tribal attacks in recent years. But he had prepared his confederates for the visit of inquiry and, when Palladius arrived incidentally bearing the payroll for the officer corps at headquarters in the African capital, they offered him payments of the sort that were later to be seen posted up on stone (above, n. 92). The kickbacks on this occasion, however, were very large. Palladius accepted them, simple soldier that he was. He then went on to his investigations, in the company of two leaders from the plaintiff cities. Upon preparing his report to the emperor, in which the charges were upheld, he was threatened by Romanus with revelation of the kickbacks; and for those, he knew, he might have to pay heavily; so to the emperor he reported instead that the charges had been false all along. Romanus thus was safe, and the emperor ordered the tongues torn out of the two local leaders who had toured the damaged regions with Palladius.[99]

As was mentioned above in passing, Romanus had a relative by marriage at Milan, Remigius the Master of Offices. That man proved most useful in protecting him on this occasion and later — being well paid for his trouble.[100] He prevented the communication of reports that he brushed aside as "insignificant, unnecessary matters amidst the more weighty concerns of the emperor." By such orotund prevarication, later, certain truths were kept from Valens, too, as the reader may remember (above, at n. 72). On a large scale, lawless rapacity always required a network of confederates. One needed one's own staff but also shielding influences at court, and other help here and there. Besides Remigius and his own staff officers in Carthage, Romanus could count on an important African chieftain, and a certain Vincentius "sharer in his thefts," as well as other persons in office later executed for complicity. Many similar clusters of accomplices could be instanced, as well as institutional allies like tax-collection offices and tax-receiving offices — the notorious *actuarii* — linked horizontally, or high officials and their deputies linked vertically.[101]

A little of the flavor of north Africa in late Roman times, seen in the actions of the military, emerges also in remarks by Augustine. Speaking to his congregation, he reminds them of their ambitions: "You would like to be a judge and lack the qualifications of merit; so then, by purchase. For perhaps you wish to be of use to society, and buy [a judgeship] that you may be of use." The matter-of-fact way in which he mentions the prospect suits his own earlier attempts at advancement in Italy, when he appears to have contemplated a rich marriage as a means of funding his appointment to a judgeship.[102] When he turns to the ethic prevailing in the courts, his discussion begins on a high plane: "A judge should not sell a just verdict, nor should a witness sell the truth." Beneath the judge and the litigants, however, "are other people belonging to the lower rank who generally get something from both sides — such as the court officials, both the man by whom some service is initiated and to whom it is referred. Whatever they have extorted by their excessive crookedness they must usually return. What has been given them by acceptable custom, *consuetudo*, they do not return; and we rather criticize those who, against usual practice, ask for such a return, than we do those others who accept it according to common usage." The several references to validation by custom are striking. And the passage continues, "For many people needed in human affairs are either induced or held firm by perquisites, *commoda*, of this sort." They may in the end grow rich, he concludes (as we have seen the *decuriae* members rising to equestrian rank), and then may "lavish their goods on the poor."

Augustine was thus quite at one with the morality of demands for extra payment, even from salaried services. It would be surprising if he had not been: a schedule of them had been on display for a half-century in the capital of the adjacent province. Surely he had seen one of the sort in the capital of his own province. In the Numidian fees as they were reviewed above, the scale does not in fact seem very extortionate, not even for the department's legal advisers. The Cincian law forbidding their taking fees from their clients was long dead, of course. Nevertheless, those advisers did not restrain their demands within the decreed limits,[103] and government of the old style continued its retreat.

North African and other provincial courts were still being used maliciously in the fourth and fifth centuries as they had been earlier, by 'sycophants,' but with some detectible difference: now, fictitious charges almost always aimed at financial profit, whereas in the Principate they had been more often instruments of revenge or intimidation.[104] The evidence applying to the eastern provinces is more abundant than for the western and is concentrated, too, in the period ca. A.D. 365–90. That is only through the accident of our sources' survival. Some of them in fact carry the story into other times, including those much too late to be of interest to my study. The phenomenon of the overbearing, avaricious judge, though nothing new, is easily discovered, too. In the rise and conduct of office of Maximinus, eventually Vicar of Rome and Prefect of the Gauls, Ammianus presents one of his most characteristic and chilling figures. "Often they could hear him, that brigand with a wild beast's heart, shouting that no one would be found safe unless he wished it." He operated in an atmosphere of terror; indeed, induced it in the emperor; and that (for example, after a rebellion or the uncovering of a plot) was always the best of times for a judge's extortions.[105]

It was, of course, the desire for profit that made people compete to be appointed governor in the first place; but, beyond that, they might also have to satisfy creditors from whom they had had to borrow the initial price of their office. Ammianus once again proves a useful reporter. He speaks generally of judges, that is, governors, "who have purchased public positions at a high price and, like burdensome creditors, rummage around for money in every level of wealth to shake out booty from other men's bosoms." I cite other proofs of the debtors' difficulties below (nn. 134 and 140).

At every level, litigants had to pay. That is apparent from the Numidian price list of 362/3; also, from an interesting constitution of A.D. 331 addressed to the provincials at large. It notes the steps, and at every step it protests against the likelihood of extortion, along a path leading from first access to the judge, "with its price merely for the judge's appearance"; then, to formal introduction through his chief of staff; next, registration through the chief's assistants and their *concussiones* ("shakedowns," the Latin word like the Greek *epi-* or *kataseismos*, sharing its root with the English); later, tips to the guards on duty, "centurions and other officials asking a little something, or a lot"; and the delivery of relevant documents by summoners of "unsated greed." [106] The two texts, separated by a generation, not only make plain how completely the ethic of taking pervaded the judicial system, but how irresistibly: first, it eluded control; then, when confronted, it asserted its right to exist against the conventional ethic.

This close balance of power has been noted before — at one point (above, at n. 82) in connection with the award of promotion from within a bureau by majority vote of its senior members. Bureaus resembled corporations or clubs. That certainly gave greater respectability to their customs as they were taught to each new entrant. As corporate wholes they divided the profits of their taking, their *emolumenta ceteraque conpendia* — inflated vocabulary to refer to something not quite acceptable by conventional norms. If delinquent through not forcing their director to obey the law, bureaus would be fined as wholes. And we can infer a very similar corporate character in various army units from the fact that, when a member died, they divided up his unused rations; if intestate, his estate passed to all his comrades together.[107] When one pictures groups of clerks gathered for a meeting in their *schola*, perhaps hearing the minutes from the previous meeting read aloud by the assistant to the chief of staff along with a report on the state of their treasury, while this or that member is publicly censured for some fault, it is easy to imagine how they might together prove too much for any command from the emperor. They certainly did not think of themselves as criminals.

But I have departed from my purpose of using testimony not drawn from

the laws themselves to show how common and entrenched venality had
become, no matter what region of the empire is examined. My survey began
in Italy, lightly touched Spain and Gaul, and passed to Africa, Cyrenaica, and
Egypt. Three of my witnesses referred to Antioch: Libanius, Ammianus, and
John Chrysostom. At Antioch, then, I resume my survey.

That city was the capital of a province, it was the command post
overlooking the whole eastern frontier, and one of the empire's big four (along
with Rome, Alexandria, and Carthage) or big five (adding Constantinople).
For a total of decades over the course of the fourth century, it also served as
an imperial capital during the residence of Constantius II, Julian, and Valens.
It was the permanent home of the Count of the East, the Master of Soldiers,
and Syrian governor, surrounded by fifteen hundred or more government
servants in their collective staff — quite apart from the rings of officialdom
around the imperial court when the emperor was present with his personal
officials and guards. Like Milan, Antioch both benefited from the wealth
drawn in by such additions to a normal urban population, and suffered from
them. "Judges and lawyers," recalls Ammianus, "were united in equal wickedness to sell the concerns of small folk to military commanders or powerful
courtiers. Thus they gained either wealth or position."[108]

Libanius speaks of bribes being passed on all occasions — at a festival, at
a private party, even in the public baths; and he devotes pages to the usual
ways in which a world-wise man — call him Mixidemus — can profit from
things as they are.[109] It is of the first importance not only to know persons in
power but to be seen to know them. What then had changed since the days
of Fronto or the others described in the previous chapter? Exactly like those
seekers and dispensers of influence, Libanius himself cultivated power.
Indeed, he describes with much smugness how he displaced a rival in the
esteem of the governor, visiting him every evening for familiar chats and
taking with him memoranda about people's troubles and needs, to be
discussed with his important friend. Most of the matters he brought up were
decided the way he wished. He was behaving like an honorable and a
successful man of his class, the class that had dependents. Nothing new about
that. However, he goes on, "it irked my rival that many received these benefits
and without paying for them. In fact, the reason for the large number of those
who sought my aid was that they need not make a set payment as though for
meat and vegetables." *There* was the difference. It is characteristic of the later
empire; and Libanius is plainly scornful and disapproving of it. "Meat and
vegetables!"

Mixidemus, for whom he invents this name no doubt out of prudence, is
quite an up-to-date fellow. A titled ex-governor (*honoratus*), he offers his

services to inarticulate litigants in defense or prosecution and manipulates testimony to gather a rich harvest from them; pays early-morning calls on judges to overhear some little piece of news which he can sell for "silver, gold, clothes, a slave, a horse, or whatever pleases the belly"; and, by the purchase of an odd lot in a village, he will insert himself into it as landowner and there dictate the distribution and amount of all its tax allotments through his threats and intimidating bluster. Hence, another harvest for him of another sort. All this he does hand in glove with other civil and military officials. So he grows rich. Libanius is outraged.[110]

He is outraged in a more personal way by the invasion of his rights over his own peasants. His oration on the subject, the Forty-seventh, has often been discussed because it is so vivid and helpful in explaining the new forms of power in the later empire. Its focus is on the intrusion into the rural scene of an alien influence, *dynamis*, backed by armed strength. Troops billeted in villages and their highest commanders in the background are drawing off all surplus wealth in the form of payments to themselves while giving the villagers the courage to defy collection of legitimate rents and taxes. From his own central ancestral estate, consisting of an entire village, Libanius could collect nothing. When he procured the arrest of the defiant peasants, the governor yielded to the demands of the troop commander and ruled against Libanius. So his peasants returned home, jeering at his defeat. He makes it plain (e.g., 47.10 and 17) that similar situations and their natural outcome can be found not just in the farmlands around Antioch but universally. He must at least mean the whole of Syria; perhaps also adjoining provinces, so far as he had knowledge of them. The beneficiaries of the arrangements he describes are in any case many and prominent; their profits, absolutely enormous (47.29f.).

Whether or not ironically, Libanius imagines someone trying to curry favor with "such Midases" by defending them: They mustn't be deprived of the flow of profit from the country folk lest their morale suffer (!).[111] Clearly, they had come to look on such income as theirs by right. Their cheating of the Anti-ochenes had had generations to establish itself. Diocletian had found the military defrauding their suppliers in the city a century earlier. By John Chrysostom's time, a little later than Libanius' oration, soldiers could be described as a species "committing outrages every day, abusing, raging, meddling in other people's misfortunes, wolfish. . . . How often do they pillage, how often is their behavior grasping, how much involved in false accusations and deals.'. . . That evil [of greed in them] has totally driven out virtue and reigns supreme, so much so that, in their raging around, they attach no weight to any accusation against them." That is, they feel no shame; they observe a different ethic.[112]

From the provinces to the north, Gregory of Nazianzus is heard reminding his congregation of the same passage about soldiers' shake-downs that Ambrose and Maximus quoted, Luke 3 : 12–14. He applies it to the exactor of taxes that feed the army. Augustine preached on it in Africa. In Africa, a duke is described by Synesius moving his troops around from city to city chiefly to extract money from them; the more painful their presence, the bigger the bribe forthcoming to set them on their travels again.[113] It was thus the most natural thing in the world that the army's presence should be thus so often and universally referred to as a species of enemy occupation; for, as has been emphasized, that presence had become general, routine, and ubiquitous in the later empire.

Moreover, taking by soldiers was in part quite lawful. They had to have more than lodging. They were entitled to food and other supplies which, at least in Egypt, included a long list of articles regularly levied as a tax. Everyone knew or thought he knew what made taxes necessary in the first place: support of the military. The fact was reflected in the seamless join between municipal or civilian personnel engaged in collection and army collectors and receivers. In consequence, when someone in uniform turned up with a demand for a bushel of wheat or a jug of wine, you couldn't easily say he had no right to it.

Valentinian III describes a rank of tax investigators circulating in the western provinces whose procedures make plain how ill-defined was the boundary between the legal and the extortionate — or at least how naturally extortion could be presented as lawful.[114]

> When such an investigator comes to some frightened province, accompanied by agents of false accusations and borne aloft on costly services, he is all arrogance. He demands the assistance of the governor's staff; he also often joins to his services the scholarians, and with his men and offices thus multiplied, terror extorts whatever greed pleases. To introduce himself, the visitor publishes and reiterates fearful commands concerning many and various tax categories. He unrolls clouds of minute computations jumbled in unintelligible obscurity, which are the more effective as they are the less understood by persons ignorant of deceit. They require tax receipts consumed by length of years and age which the simplicity and trust of owing nothing have not the wit to preserve. ... The palatine official as his colleague in thefts encourages him, the apparitors turbulently join the attack, the soldiers ruthlessly press for action.

So, in this concatenation typical of the times, involving 'sycophants' to initiate accusations, local tax staff, a man from imperial headquarters, and the law courts in charge of the governor, what provided edge and terror was the military.

While the soldiers represented a hostile force settled pervasively among the unarmed population, bullying and battening on them, they themselves were at the mercy of their higher officers. "Some," says Libanius, "profit from their own staff, some from regimental rations, where the men who have vanished live on, and they can feed off the names of the dead. These are great amounts; but there are even larger gold fields, of gold that should rightly remain in the men's hands but is transferred to their commanders. So the armed forces grow poor and dispirited, wearing mere bits of boots and ghosts of great-coats. Often it's the belly that must pay, and they lead off starving bodies to battle." And he goes on to tell of further forms of extortion, resembling those that Synesius reported: that is, the city council must somehow assemble lump sums to buy off the ill-behavior of the troops.[115] From Synesius can be drawn repeated references to fraud and extortion practiced by officers in Cyrenaica — which were the ordinary practices, too, among Moesian units in the 360s. Themistius speaks of them. A long rhetorical tradition of "the army ruined by lodging in a city" can be traced on a plane which may owe too much to the reading of books, not to the measuring of reality. Allowance being made for that, nevertheless there are new, specifically late Roman elements in the picture. There are the nonexistent troops whose pay and rations, or their cash equivalent, went into their commanders' pockets. In contrast, the money that had to be paid for furloughs or easy treatment in Tacitus' day seems not to have risen above the centurions. In Libanius' day and later, it was the topmost ranks that were the worst offenders.

The acceptance of extortion by officers appears unexpectedly in a note written to a squadron commanded by Abinnaeus in Egypt from a local man. The latter had been sent off to a village to secure some recruits, or money in their place. Conscription was a traditional excuse for a shakedown; but this particular expedition had not proved very rewarding: it yielded only a couple of solidi and some silver, despite rough treatment shown to the village guard. Never mind, it had been a zealous effort. "God is my witness that we're not fighting for profit, only for you. Since you are doing it I want you always to do well, but we want you to profit a little, too. That's best for everybody, and for God as well."[116]

A patriot in about A.D. 370 addressed a long memorandum, really a little book, to the emperor suggesting a number of urgent reforms. Some were military, some civilian. In one passage he offers a view of more than usual interest because it represents a general impression of the times. It concerns "the detestable avarice of the governors, the enemy of the taxpayer's interests; for, in despite of the respect due to public office, they consider themselves as so many entrepreneurs on mission to the provinces." His phrasing recalls that of Libanius: "meat and vegetables." Or, better, that of Themistius: army officers are "merchants" (n. 115), and the objection to their activities focuses on their treating public power as their individual stock in trade. But the pamphleteer continues in his description of governors:

> They are the more oppressive because their wickedness flows from the very source that should afford relief. As if their own injustice were not enough, each one sends out collectors to spread ruin of the same sort, and they drain off the resources of the taxpayers through various devices of plunder. They would attract no special notice if only they themselves sinned. What opportunity offered by the revenue regulations do they fail to take advantage of? What settlement of dues is reached without pillage? For those men, the procuring of recruits, purchase of horses or grain, even building contracts, are *sollemnia lucra*, routine sources of profit and longed-for extortion. But if virtuous men. . . .[117]

And the writer trails off into dreams of more honest times. Similarities with the words of his exact contemporary Themistius are striking. Clearly the two are looking at the same world; but Themistius focuses less on the governors than on "the outrageous behavior of the tax collectors, the fraud of the tax recorder, and the avarice of the city garrisons." He goes on to congratulate his emperor Valens on having restrained (or does the orator really mean that Valens *should* restrain?) "the officers assigned to the accounts. They do not walk about with a more superior air than generals, while they are conducting the assessment, nor does the realm hang on their fingertips."[118]

There is another distinct area of venality remaining for discussion: appointment to office. There lay the key to everything; for without it one lacked authority for one's demands. In my circling around the empire, too, from the western capital at Milan and Italy counterclockwise through Africa, Cyrenaica, Egypt, and especially Antioch in Syria, I must come to the eastern capital: Antioch as such, when the emperor resided there, but otherwise Constantinople. It was by the emperor himself that appointments in theory must be ratified.

To the court, therefore, the ex-*protector* and cavalry prefect Abinnaeus in Egypt turned in 341 when he found out what had been happening in recent months or years behind his, and the emperor's, back. A number of persons had independently solicited from Constantius II, so it would seem, the command of the troop unit which Abinnaeus himself had been granted; and the staff of the Count of Egypt in Alexandria preferred the claims of one of these competitors to Abinnaeus. Writing in protest to Constantius, the latter declares the obvious truth: his own appointment, though he was long delayed in taking it up, had been earned by service and bestowed directly by the imperial hand. His competitors no doubt had their notices of appointment;

but they were gained by bribery, *suffragium*, in the specific sense of purchased recommendation. His protest worked. The troop command was confirmed, but only lasted two years and a bit; for the Count of Egypt then dismissed him. Unable to defend his tenure at Alexandria, Abinnaeus therefore resolved to turn once more to the capital in February of 345.[119]

He was to take with him a letter from the council president at Arsinoë: "As you are going to meet with the imperial court, I authorize and commission you by these instructions in my behalf to gain from the Divinity of our Eternal Emperors a notification of appointment as collector of taxes, myself acknowledging the obligation to cover all expenses whatsoever incurred therefor, on your faith."[120] The document is quite formal, clearly a contract. When it refers to costs, it is a safe guess that the writer is not thinking of travel. That much can be learned from a companion text. For Abinnaeus was entrusted on the next day with a second commission (we have no idea how many he took in his briefcase), this one from a veteran on behalf of his son. It, too, is in the form of a contract, such as drew forth the laws declaring any litigation over *suffragium* illegal. "I agree by means of this instrument that when you procure the promotion . . . , whatever you may give on account of this same promotion, before God, as you give, so I Plas will make restitution to you in full good faith."[121] Taken together, the two documents indicate how an ordinary person of the decurion class understood the ordinary procedures of government, as regards both civil and military appointments. The three men involved, all of them past their middle years, have experience of life, they know and use the forms of law; and they are open and scrupulous about it. Honorable men! — indeed, one of them we earlier saw protesting against the very modes of persuasion which they now intend to use. They simply accept two ethics. At the capital, Abinnaeus will find people whose names are at the moment unknown, and pay them. It is an entirely commercial matter for him and the other two petitioners as for the *suffragatores*. So the latter will sometimes maximize profits by selling the same job several times over. Let the buyers straighten it out in the provinces.

In the same honorable fashion, a generation later, Basil writes to another bishop who has requested his help for a certain George. George is a decurion. Like most men of that condition, he wants out. Tell me, says Basil, "on what post or appointment, *axioma*, we must bring to bear our efforts, so that we may set about the asking of this favor from all our friends in power, either as a free gift or for some moderate price, however God may help us forward."[122] Again, as with Abinnaeus' devout accomplices in bribery, no doubt well knowing that purchase of a moment of power from anyone in the *militia* was illegal, Basil invokes the deity in perfect confidence. So had Augustine. The ethic of purchase was established, only the laws were behind the times. Which is to say, the emperors were powerless, or very nearly so.

The point particularly defended in George's case, one's obligation to one's curia, was the focus of ceaseless legislation, concern, and even desperation at the time Basil was writing. That may be learned from Libanius, who has been noticed (above, chap. 1, n. 165) in the repeated act of writing letters just like Basil's. Yet in his orations he raises the cry to stick by one's curia, desertion is shameful. Let Libanius reconcile his actions as he pleases, the emperors were more consistent. Throughout the Theodosian Code, up to its date of publication in A.D. 438 as well as in still later constitutions, release from curial duties is promised as a most precious reward earned only by long service to one's city or to one's ruler through one's *militia*; and the prohibition against attaining this reward unearned is equally emphatic and frequently proclaimed.[123] The significance of decurions' escape from activities that were greatly valued — indeed, considered essential — will be brought out in the next chapter. At the moment, the point of interest is the degree to which purchase of an exempting rank might be taken for granted at any time from the early fourth century on. And it was a procedure beyond the emperors' control.

Outside of the law codes, mention or assumption of bribery to secure military or civilian appointment can be picked out from a variety of sources: the canons of the Council of Nicaea, a Latin orator addressing Julian, the anonymous *Epitome of the Caesars' Lives*, Ammianus in many passages, the poet Claudian, and Eunapius, sophist and historian. It is not likely that they are all to be discounted as biased or in some way misinformed. No, they are describing one world, the same everywhere, no doubt because offices gained at the higher levels carried occupants from one region to another and so produced a certain homogenization. The effects are detectible right through the century following Nicaea, i.e., A.D. 325 up to the codification by Theodosius — which is far enough for my purposes. More could easily be added post-438.[124] Yet there are differences observable across time. Venality increasingly establishes itself as normal, therefore (by *consuetudo, sollemnis*) right and proper. The emperors themselves sell offices: Theodosius I, and perhaps others of the late fourth century. In any case, it was generally believed they were in the business. On this, too, considerably later evidence is not lacking.[125]

Just how much the emperor imitated, while forbidding, the practice of taking money for a government post is hard to estimate. How could he know, himself? There is no testimony to his receiving cash for a *codicillus* with his own hands. It is perfectly credible that he did sell and did profit from such sales, as we are told; but it was through intermediaries. Then he would have no means of finding out if some or all of the price had stuck to the fingers of his civil servants. We have seen also how duplicate appointments were made, invalidating those intended by the emperor. He was thus often reduced to declaring, Pay no attention to what I last told you, disregard the *codicillus* or law or letter I signed recently, because what appears over my signature I never authorized.[126] As the emperor lost control over the imperial authority, itself unimpaired, he came to compete for it more and more on a level with his servants. Hence, decisions could be made in defiance of his will, two or three useful collaborators at court being paid to support them, and they were indited and inadvertently signed by him.[127] It is, for example, unclear how Constantius II could have understood, or, if he had understood, how he could have protected himself against, the choice of an elderly but very rich litterateur, Sabinianus, as his Master of Cavalry throughout the east. He came recommended by a number of *potentiores* — for a price. They later deflected inquiry into his incompetence when he failed to offer any defense of Amida, despite urgent appeals, and the town fell to the Persians.[128] The train of cause and effect, however, belongs better in the next chapter, where I consider the consequences of what I am describing.

The play of power in the court emerges only toward the end of the period that interests me. Therefore money "and other considerations of value," as our modern contracts put it, seem almost a form of communication. The empress showers silver upon a favored visitor for no reason; visitors bring her "precious ornaments, chrystal vases, too, and many other things ..., and precious clothing of silk to offer to the more intimate advisers, eunuchs and chamberlains." The occasion is a trip to the eastern capital, but the same courtesies were observed in the western.[129] While these gifts resemble the *xenia* of earlier centuries, they blend into others of a more purposive sort revealed in the report of "worthy gratifications," as he terms them, by Epiphanius to Maximian bishop of Constantinople. "*Benedicta*" or "*benedictiones*" translate the Greek *eulogiai*, offering one more illustration of euphemism that surrounded morally dubious matters.[130]

But to explain a little more fully: Epiphanius was archdeacon of Alexandria, reporting on the actions of Saint Cyril's agent, Eulogius, in Constantinople. In a doctrinal dispute, Cyril and Nestorius had clashed in A.D. 431 at Ephesus. As a result of the church councils held there, both bishops had been removed from their sees by Theodosius II and exiled. Exile and deposition were, however, not enforced. Cyril was therefore able to draw without let from the episcopal treasury of Alexandria more than half a ton of gold and an indeterminable value of other precious things by which to buy his way back to his throne and its concomitant powers. He offered carpets, curtains, hangings, cushions, tablecloths, stools, benches — but mostly cash. It was all very conscientiously accounted for.[131] Chosen for purchase were the wife of the prefect and his assistant; the Master of Offices; a number of male and female chamberlains under the *praepositus* of the emperor's and his sister's court; specifically, Paul, Eucheria's *praepositus* and his aides, *domestici*; also aides to the quaestor, to the Master of Offices, and to the *praepositus* of the emperor's suite, Chrysoretes, who himself was to get two hundred pounds of gold, the largest amount of all. But the writer of the letter asks the bishop of the capital if he cannot see to it that Chrysoretes is replaced by another person. The striking feature of the list is its acknowledgment of peripheral influences in the forming of decisions. Not only is the authority of high office, including the emperorship, owned as property by the staff members, whose rights to advise are assessed at about a quarter of their superior's price, but the accessory role of women and domestic servants is manifestly important.[132] Major posts in the imperial service and the primacy of this or that doctrinal view are sold off by consortia of influential people assembled ad hoc into preponderant factions.

In telling the tale of such deals, John Chrysostom's biographer, Palladius, is quite matter-of-fact. What he talks about other sources also describe. The emperor's part in episcopal elections, more truly called appointments at certain periods, is evident both in Rome and Constantinople. For the latter, Sozomen and Socrates supply evidence enough; for the former, the *Collectio Avellana* (though never translated out of Latin, and thus remaining a sort of secret). Palladius is naturally familiar with the realities and, in recounting events toward the turn of the fourth century, mentions how "it happened, then, at that time some of Theophilus' clerics" (Theophilus being the bishop of Alexandria) "were in Constantinople to buy in advance their promotions in the diocese of Egypt from the newly appointed officials."[133] Purchase of of bishoprics was not uncommon in the eastern provinces, as anyone would expect who did not suppose the church to have been encapsulated in some special world; and bishops occasionally practiced extortion; but Palladius, a few pages later, describes the wholesale marketing of bishoprics in the diocese of Asia on a thoroughly unusual scale. The seller, bishop of Ephesus, was serving at the time as manager of the local estates belonging to a certain high official, and got him to impede investigations. However, in due course the truth came out. The purchasers had only hoped to escape their curial obligations by gaining ecclesiastical office and had bankrupted themselves — even sold their wives' property — in the attempt. Once discovered, they professed themselves quite willing to continue in their sees, asking only that the purchase price be returned to them. What impudence! They were deposed. But a few years later they were back on their thrones.[134]

Like a great many things that went on more or less often and openly in this period, simony was illegal. Beyond the scriptural reference that gave it a name, its condemnation had been repeated in the canons of councils. What gives interest to the situation that Palladius describes is the existence of two views about the deed and their close balance: it was wrong, but it wasn't. Hence the unrepentant, or rather aggrieved, reaction of the half-dozen Asian bishops who were caught. They provide one further insight into the perceptions of the times.

So too does Augustine regarding a somewhat similar affair: the attempt by a bishop to conceal his own lands under church title so as to secure tax exemption, while still owing a great mass of back dues. Let them be forgiven him, says Augustine, out of Christian piety. And similarly accepting of what is, by one standard, unethical, Jerome sees nothing wrong in the purchase of a retrospective marriage license in order to legitimize concubinage.[135] Needless to say, purchase meant money paid under the table to some bureaucrat, who would split it with his supervisor. The same thing is done today in restaurants, but over the table. The take is tips, and no harm in it.

5. ASSESSMENT OF PRIVATIZATION IN GOVERNMENT

In comparing the ethic that prevailed in the imperial service of Seneca's day with that of Lactantius, or of Marcus Aurelius' day with that of Theodosius II, a quarter of a millennium removed, I see no significant difference at the lower levels. Of course, the manifestations of the ethic in the later period were different. They were much more organized, articulate, and firmly supported by a longer tradition and wider acceptance. Still, the soldier bullying the host in his billet to get a silver coin, the palace usher who asked for some payment, the governor's clerk holding out his hand to a litigant — they all acted very much like the corresponding figures in the Principate. Their apparent acceptance of their own conduct hadn't changed, so far as I can tell.

The governor himself sitting as a judge had once taken bribes, though less often, certainly less aggressively, and no doubt only through lower intermediaries. When Aelius Aristides envisioned the process (above, at n. 35), it was the clerk he saw taking bribes, not the judge. Perhaps the latter got the lion's share in due course; perhaps nothing. Perhaps the common opinion, both in the capital and the provinces, that justice could be bought even under the stricter emperors of the earlier centuries, sometimes blamed the judges for the faults of their clerks. Certainly the same classes that administered justice also very severely condemned the selling of it. Could they then reconcile what they did with what they said? A clue to an answer may lie in the problems of Pliny's client Julius Bassus. He accepted "considerations of value," in lawyer's lingo, but said *he* didn't think them all that valuable, not so as to affect his decisions. The person who offered them may have seen them in a different light, having very different ideas of the value of money.

I emphasize these matters of feelings and perceptions because, without their consent to extortion and bribability, the actual patterns cannot be understood. I cannot imagine everyone being ready and able to violate the norms of the community he sensed around him; but I can imagine him changing codes as he changed communities. So, if he served in the army where everyone acted in a certain way, he would conform. Similarly in the civil *decuriae*: they had their ways.[136] As the unrepentant sinner said to Bishop Maximus (above, at n. 94), I draw my sense of right and wrong from my *militia*. I don't claim to be a monk. Different codes could thus coexist within a single society.

At some point after A.D. 250, changes seem to have become apparent to contemporaries (above, n. 37). They accelerated in the ensuing decades. They were changes in the level and ubiquity of taking, whether by force or threat of force or by promise of cooperation. They have been observed not only in the law courts but in the army as well (above, nn. 24f.); and their probable causes, which help to date them, have been explored. They appear as an interrelated cluster. Members of the imperial service, both civil and military, were in the first place many times more likely to live and work close to private citizens; and "many times" is a phrase that can even be crudely quantified. For example, the number of law courts more than doubled; the number of military personnel resident in cities and towns and hamlets increased five- to tenfold; offices of the central government resident in provincial centers were at least equally swollen, if the mid-fourth century is compared with the mid-third. Beyond all that, what officials had to offer in exchange for "considerations of value" was a larger stock of desirable things, beginning no doubt with immunity from physical abuse. The pains of that were extremely well advertised, whether by design or accident. However, the occasions for the offering of some action by persons inside a *militia* to those outside were likewise greatly multiplied in the period from Diocletian on. There were many more complicated and intrusive commands issuing from the throne, and very little attempt to make their interpretation easy or even uniform. In the upshot, laws were widely ignored,[137] conveying the impression that they could be bought off while of course proving exactly that, in many cases.

Contemporaries stress the mercantile character of a *militia*. Like a shop-keeper, people used their *cingulum* to sell action or exemption like "meat and vegetables"; they estimated how much a customer was worth, to set their price, and how much they had to make out of their tenure in a post in order at least to get back what it cost them.[138] At the heart of this lay the idea of a position as a thing bought and paid for and therefore one's own possession. Wolfgang Schuller has seen this, and can most easily derive it from the Republican *decuriae*;[139] but the same perception governed the higher military ranks as well. Once past the mid-fourth century, when the purchase of the more desirable offices became very competitive, the aspirant might have to borrow to meet the price. Then his exercise of his duties was doubly "privatized," both for his own income and that of his creditors.[140]

Contemporaries speak tolerantly, or at least make little or no complaint, about the exaction of small sums by small bureaucrats in the later empire. That wasn't the problem. Libanius puts his finger on something more serious when he declares his acceptance of a certain degree of extortion, in the triangle that joins himself, his peasants, and the local military commander. It is all right, he says, "for the masters to offer something to the powerful, on behalf of the laborers, rather than the laborers as a check on the masters. The one gives solidity to the owners' world, while the other, leaving no place for trust [in their masters], undermines its very foundations." And he goes on to speak of the need to preserve due order and rank.[141] He is ready to meet the demands of the local commandant — to pay "protection." What he finds intolerable is the destruction of the patron-dependent relationship that had for so long maintained a village under his control.

The owners' world is the old world. I described its power structure in the preceding chapter. You knew where and who you were and where you would be tomorrow — which is really what Libanius is getting at when he speaks of *taxis*, "assigned position" or "proper order." A world in which, by contrast, assistance from the powerful is given for money establishes no structure at all. Rather, it dissolves all ties: no sense of obligation or honor, "no *fides* can remain, where all that people are considering is the size of their profits" (above, n. 12). Each purchase is a thing in itself. Before it and after, no one owes anybody anything. Therefore it is not suited to long-term or complicated necessities; and relationships involving anything other than the wish for material possession have no chance to develop. In both the new and the old world there was ample room for greed and self-interest; but only in the old (many characteristics of which survived into the later empire, of course) was there also room for the Roman species of honor.

For Libanius or any substantial landowner, substitute the emperors. Like Libanius and for the same reasons, they lost control over villages — and over towns, and over cities, and over their whole realm — to the extent that bought action came to prevail in their own government. Indeed, to that extent the government was no longer theirs at all. Instead, it belonged to the person who had paid for a *militia*. Imperial service entitled one to give orders and make demands. If one gave and made them at one's own behest, in response to money that one took in, then a part of the state's power, the power of the monarchy, had been privatized. It was lost to the emperor. There remained the same total of power, meaning obedience, inside the empire, but it was diffuse, unstable, unpredictable. In consequence, the strength of the empire could not be brought to a focus.

Any reader of the Theodosian and Justinian Codes, and perhaps also the *Notitia Dignitatum*, might suppose he had spread out before him a more elaborately organized, ambitiously rational government than the ancients had ever seen. And it is often taken to have been so in actuality.[142] What nonsense! Certainly the ambition to plan their world possessed the Tetrarchs. Again, it possessed the savage Valentinian. Theodosius I struggled powerfully with the problems of his day, so far as one man was able. But it is hardly too much to say that, while he reigned, the empire was ruled by ten thousand clerks.

4

THE PRICE OF
PRIVATIZING GOVERNMENT

1. DETERIORATION IN THE MILITARY

Suppose that the preceding pages did succeed in showing how certain "privatizing" views about one's *militia* became more pervasive and impinged more sharply on more people's lives; suppose that the scale of these changes was really very considerable; suppose that they produced others in turn which can be traced through comparison with prior practices or can be heard in the complaints of contemporaries; nevertheless, is there any connection between these phenomena and the empire's decline?

That innocent question hides the assumption that there really was one single thing to be called 'decline.' At the very outset of this book, however, I rejected any such idea. Instead, I distinguished various strands making up the history of the empire. Over time, some grew more attenuated or disappeared entirely: jurisprudence, erotic verse, Arretine pottery. Some underwent a change in one region but not in another: agriculture in small units or oleiculture. Some seem to have remained essentially the same from the second to the fifth century: for example, slavery — even prosperity itself, over most of the empire. Only in the north and west, where the *pax Romana* was often disturbed, was the picture different. There, progressive failure to provide security was above all else responsible, first, for the severing of commercial ties between urban centers and their trade partners, whether other centers or the surrounding countryside. Next, the countryside and its richer villas deteriorated. More dramatically, entire areas of the empire had to be abandoned forever to the enemy outside. And that last, I propose, represents the very perfection of 'decline.'

But even when my understanding of the word is explained, the question remains: what is the connection between that loss of security, with all its consequences, and the developments discussed in the empire's power structure?

171

An answer might be offered through another, rhetorical question. Suppose we accept what was said in the previous chapter about the patterns of behavior and sense of obligation prevailing among the emperor's servants, military and civilian, in the later empire; how, then, could anyone expect them to mediate effectively, as those in the earlier empire had done, between the directing will at the center and the vast surrounding armature of private power?

To ask this is no argument, of course — let alone proof. But it points the way to a comparison that may be useful. I propose an examination of military effectiveness in the earlier and later periods; for the providing of security is, after all, fundamental to any state. It is the state's most obvious business and justification. And it involves various processes — planning, conscripting, taxing, equipping, constructing, transporting — that test far more than the armed forces themselves. Orders have to be followed throughout the whole train of power that originates in the imperial palace and reaches, at the end, to a hundred cobblers in the Bay-of-Naples area, a hundred peasant owners of ox-carts in Cappadocia. As intermediaries, the owners of great estates must accept direction from city magistrates on behalf of their tenants, just as plain soldiers must do what their officers tell them; procurators' accountants must calculate true totals of barley or boots, just as the village scribe must do his job accurately at the threshing floor. At every point of connection the original intent must be transmitted as it was received. Otherwise it will come to nothing. Thus an army assembled and ready to engage can emerge only from a broad texture of consent, in terms of which the comparison of one age with another may be most revealing.

It is revealing that soldiers of the earlier empire were supplied on the Rhine with leather all the way from Italy and with their familiar Mediterranean foods from southern Spain.[1] The logistics indicate the involvement of many people across many hundreds of miles, an undertaking much more significant than the manufactures carried on in the camps or even the ad hoc demands for equipment laid on civilian armorers and tanners in Milan or Antioch. Those latter are attested even in the fourth century. Long-range planning for campaigns appears in the construction of food-storage facilities sometimes several years in advance and on a grand scale.[2] Road-building might be undertaken years ahead of time, too, as under the Severi. It can be seen also, and especially clearly, for Trajan's first war against the Dacians. In addition to the trans-Danubian bridges and bridgehead forts he ordered built, there was a towpath of remarkable design nailed to the flanks of a cliff overlooking the otherwise unnavigable Iron Gates; and a number of canals were dug, one of them of several kilometers' length and of many centuries' usefulness, afterwards. In the later empire, even into the 360s, the river saw an occasional burst of military construction. The complexity and sophistication of the achievement, however, are of a lower order.[3]

For each of his Dacian wars Trajan assembled some hundred thousand troops. Their supply and transport was the reason for all the prior construction. As each unit came into position, and while it awaited the month to launch its attack, its rations had to be assured by a fleet of barges. It is not known which provinces were laid under contribution for this.[4] Meanwhile, no point on another frontier could be left open to some different enemy, no new dangers created by drawing too heavily from any one stretch of the empire's defenses; so even a quite small campaign force had to gather its contingents from widely scattered places, and time allowed for their travel. In some ways, the problems had been simpler for the Roman Republic, as its manpower was all in one place and its enemies all in some other. Those conditions (besides Rome's genius for organization and civil obedience, together) make comprehensible the success in delivering an army the size of Trajan's to *each* side of the field at Philippi; and there had been great concentrations in the preceding century, too.[5] In the civil wars of the empire the scale was never so gigantic: at Lyons in A.D. 197, 150,000 on the field, counting Albinus' men and Septimius Severus' together. To face a foreign war, a sort of revolt, Tiberius in a few months was able to assemble a force of 100,000. These are the maxima of the Principate.[6]

To pursue the matter of army size as an index of the empire's power: in the later period, so far up as A.D. 363, a truly vast force could still be got together. Yet it required the efforts of two emperors to do it over the course of several years: that is, of Constantius II in order to wage war on Persia, and of Julian adding the further units which he had intended for his rebellion against Constantius. Perhaps they totalled 65,000; but it must be noted that a majority were barbarians.[7] The sixth-century historian Zosimus assigns no less than 83,000 men to the whole; but, where his figures like this can be checked, they are fantastic; so his testimony should not be accepted.[8] Finally, Zonaras in the twelfth century draws on some unknown source for his description of an expeditionary force numbering 80,000 assembled against Magnentius' 30,000 at Mursa. These figures, and the casualties of 54,000, seem to me equally unreliable.[9] Later, as will appear, even the greatest emergencies could not call forth such totals of men in arms, and their barbarian portion became increasingly decisive.

In the view that the maximum size of Roman armies affords a means of measuring the government's capacity, they deserve discussion; also skepticism. Contemporary estimates on which we ultimately depend must have originated in the adding up of constituent parts: contingents under barbarian chiefs, legions, and so forth. How accurate were these subtotals? That chiefs knew the numbers they brought with them to the battlefield and reported them without exaggeration to the emperors, believe it who will. As to the legions, that long-term officer and gentleman Ammianus Marcellinus cares nothing for their size or so much as the term itself, which he confuses with *vexillationes*, "detachments." He treats other unit terms with equal unconcern: *turma*, *ala*, like *tagma* or *taxis* or *arithmos* in Greek writers. Where the constituent parts of estimates were so carelessly handled, the totals they add up to cannot inspire much confidence.[10] In loosely used words like *tagma*, however, we nevertheless sense the smallness of individual military units in the later empire. They contained a few hundred men, rarely a little over a thousand. They are to be compared with corresponding, earlier ones of six hundred, one thousand, or five thousand.[11] Ammianus does in fact draw such a comparison with earlier armies: he tells us that the battle of Strasbourg in 357 resembled the Punic struggles. Yet Julian had only thirteen thousand, where commanders against Hannibal had had many times that number. Similarly, though Ammianus describes the barbarians' "great strength," their "masses," they can be put to flight by three hundred Romans in light armor. A mere two legions totalling, no doubt, one or two thousand men, he calls "a powerful force for battles."[12] Even so responsible a writer as he succumbs at times to the demands of rhetorical exaggeration. All the more need for a minimalist approach to Roman accounts of military affairs. As will appear, too, in further discussion, there are many explicit indications of the reduced scale of warfare as time went on.

In combination with the fantastic estimates of Lactantius, Zosimus, Lydus, and Agathias,[13] the unit-lists of the early fifth century in the *Notitia Dignitatum* have been used to support a figure around 650,000 for the late Roman army — that or a like total "on paper," in the phrase used by various modern authorities. What they acknowledge rather grudgingly is a deceit more than literary: when rosters from each unit commander were submitted to imperial headquarters for the use of the quartermaster and paymaster, and all of them were added together, the results did not correspond with reality. Of course not; for each unit commander had falsified his rosters in order to maintain a flow of money into his own pockets (above, chap. 3, n. 114). It was a practice known to everyone. How, then, could army totals be estimated by even the most knowledgeable of contemporaries? Had any attempted some grand census of actual soldiers rather than of army units, for example, to control cash donatives, it must certainly have been inflated — whether by 5 or 15 or more percent, no one can say. Nor could anyone say when a soldier was not a soldier. He might simply have awarded himself a three years' leave.

As a means of understanding history, perhaps there wouldn't be much use in even the most accurate head-count of the troops, if one survived. To be sure, soldiers had always had historical significance as consumers and in other nonmilitary roles; but chiefly they were supposed to fight. If they proved incapable of that, then their totals might be as large or as small as you wish, without explaining the course of events. Attention should rather be turned to contemporary assessments of their military effectiveness; and on that subject, beyond specific moments and contexts that will appear below, there is indeed much evidence. The regular army, we are told, lacked discipline, energy, and courage. It excelled only in its "lust for plunder." The phrase is Ammianus', whose familiarity with the military scene in the east as in the west was extensive, and who describes his fellows in arms with almost unfailing contempt and impatience.[14] A variety of critics of the same period join him in rebuking the readiness to run away, the inadequate armor, the continual drunkenness, the lack of drill, discipline, or practice among the men of the ranks, and all these same faults among their officers as well — only adding their more stylish fault of soft living.[15] Unanimity among Vegetius, Claudian, Symmachus, Ambrose, and the author of the Augustan History is very striking, even without the yet more emphatic testimony of Themistius, Synesius, and Libanius, already quoted at length in the preceding chapter. Libanius, while trying to excuse, can only accuse the soldiers he knows and has seen in their attempts to support a wife and children on meager pay eked out by pillage. In his century, it was frequent, probably normal, for soldiers to live with their wives.[16] Residence inside cities naturally permitted such domesticity; but it was common also in isolated forts where special remodelling sometimes made room for women and children in the officers' quarters (space left for privates being correspondingly reduced).

It diminished the effectiveness of troops yet further if they turned into part-time farmers. The extent to which this happened is not clear. Perhaps it is best to lay out the evidence in reverse order, beginning with a constitution of A.D. 443. In that year, border troops, limitanei, were reminded of their obligation to work the lands assigned them "from of yore."[17] The text thus carries the practice of self-supporting soldiers at least as far back as the early fifth century. In the fourth, lots of guard posts in the northern and northwestern frontier provinces have preserved in their ruins equipment showing that the occupants carried on agriculture routinely, whether or not in an organized and obligatory fashion; and the author of the Augustan History gives credit to Severus Alexander (58.4f.) in the third century for instituting border troops as farmers on lands won by his generals. These included conquests in Tripolitania, where in fact archeologists have found a network of fortified farms spread over the inland areas. If their inhabitants counted as members of the armed forces in any sense, then our sources can be excused for calling them by a later name, *limitanei;* if not, then regular soldier-farmers cannot be found on any scale at so early a date. But the interest of the whole question lies less in terminology than in the realities. We can see a steady inclination toward the confounding of functions. Still in the early third century it was not doubted that this made for ineffectual soldiers. They are therefore forbidden to buy land where they are posted "lest they be distracted from military service by concern for farming."[18] They were the rural equivalent of the useless urban troops. Toward the end of the same century, the confusion has touched the lives of a significant percent of northern guard posts. So excavations reveal. Three or four generations later, the same can be seen rather widespread in the east. So the law of 443 tells us. In the west, of course, the frontiers by that date were generally overrun and their militias with them, having proved quite inadequate to defend the empire.

Whether settled in tiny forts along the frontier, supplying their needs from their own acres, or living next door to a population that did it for them; whether stationed in cities or villages — whatever their situation, the regular Roman soldiers of the later empire shared two characteristics: they were less valued in war and, because of their proximity to their supplier, they cost less.[19] It is impossible not to draw a connection between the two characteristics: It was to save money that the forces inherited from the third century had been chopped up into little units lodged near to natural centers of exchange or sources of production; for this economy, so obvious to us, was no less obvious to people of the time. Ammianus (16.4.1) explains to his readers how troop units in Gaul "were distributed among the towns so as to be more conveniently provisioned." No longer maintained in their own camps, they became civilianized; assigned to guard duty behind the walls of fortlets or small cities, they knew nothing of maneuvers or exercises and could only stand on the defensive. For the savings in their cost there was thus a high price to be paid.

How high appears in contemporary evaluations of the regular army's effectiveness. A number of such comments have been assembled above (at n. 15); others will be quoted in pages to follow, in various contexts. They are uniformly negative. Yet the severest judgment of all is to be read in the fact that the men credited with victory in one engagement after another, from 312 on, came from outside the empire: Celts, Germans, Huns, Saracens, and Goths. No general wanted regular Romans. By the mid-fourth century the typical fighting force, as opposed to a more or less useless mass of men merely in uniform, appears to have been half imported. A generation later, imported soldiers formed the majority. Notoriously, before the century was over, barbarian commanders of essentially barbarian armies had gained control of the empire's fate, in civil wars or armed rampages around Asia Minor, Greece, the Balkans, or Italy. Tens of thousands resided permanently within the borders. The sack of Rome itself was a purely domestic event.

Substantiation for this brief sketch of military history is offered in Appendix A II. The main lines have often been drawn and the trends distinguished as truly belonging to the later empire in its conventional sense: meaning, the period that begins with Diocletian.[20] For my purposes, however, it is not enough to show the general character of the army — numerically imposing only on paper, increasingly rooted in a civilian context and civilian activities, and ever more dependent on immigrants for its actual fighting capacity. I must also show how this decay followed on the developments described in the preceding chapter.

But no emperor has recorded for us in his diary how he "despaired of maintaining the legions in their camps because the lines of supply to them have become too uncertain, through the corruption of all the agents and intermediaries involved in the process." No one actually specifies the sale of furloughs and of exemptions from laborious training as the reason for sheltering the regular troops behind walls and seeking better men beyond the Rhine and Danube. If those best able to pay the taxes could buy their exemption, the consequences for the army payroll are never drawn out in our surviving sources. We are left to the logic of the situation to understand how pervasive venality in government, in these and other ways, must have inevitably produced systemic deficiencies in defense.

2. LOSSES, CASE BY CASE

If we turn from the general characteristics of the military to particular moments when it can be seen in action, we find our sources a little more responsive; and those moments can be arranged chronologically to demonstrate, on the field, the consequences of changes in the system of defense.

The first loss (fig. 17, 1) occurred in about A.D. 260 between the upper reaches of the Rhine and the Danube;[21] the second in Dacia in ca. 275 (fig. 17, 2);[22] the third in Mauretania Tingitana (fig. 17, 3) in the 280s;[23] nothing permanent on the empire's eastern frontier,[24] except for a fourth moment of loss in Egypt in 298, when the province south of Philae was abandoned to the natives to form a buffer state.[25] Clear across the desert and backlands, however, from the Nile valley to the Atlas mountains, the intervening frontier is far more difficult to trace and explain. There is the puzzling and strategically unimportant Fossatum in Numidia; the even more puzzling nova praetentura in Mauretania Caesariensis; but otherwise a set of roads, sometimes fortified

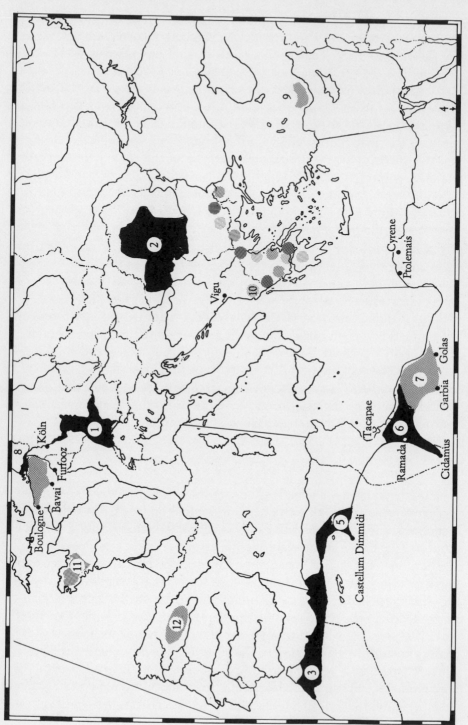

Fig. 17. The empire's losses, A.D. 260-400

farms, and advanced posts of more or less isolation and troop capacity, all in a zone rather than in a line.[26] It is in the nature of this southern glacis not to have been wrested from the tribes at any single moment nor instantaneously given up. The central thousand kilometers along southern Numidia and Proconsularis actually suffered very little change in the later empire (fig. 17, 5), while, to the west, a shorter stretch lying under Mauretania Sitifensis and Caesariensis was lost only bit by bit over the course of the later third century before and under Diocletian.[27] To the east, Rome retreated from the desert toward the sea from a point below Tacapae (that is, where the coast bends from a north-south to an east-west direction) eastward under the three cities of Tripolitania: Sabratha, Oea, Lepcis Magna. Again, puzzles. The archeological evidence is not good enough to allow a firm decision, whether only the most advanced posts far out in the semidesert (Ghadames = Cidamus, Bu Njem = Golas, and Gheriat = Garbia: fig. 17, 6-7) were given up in the later third century, or whether further territory was given up as well, to a depth of 150-75 km south of Lepcis. Perhaps the debate has centered in the wrong question. That territory continued to be occupied in the fourth century. The fortified farms were defended.[28] But were they defended by and for themselves, or by and for "Rome"? Such a question, dealing with contemporaries' motives and perceptions, may require literary evidence of some sort in addition to the archeological. Fortunately, there is Ammianus, to whose account I turn.

But first, a word of summary: in the hundred years just now reviewed, which saw these movements of retreat along the edges of the empire, obviously there is some tale of decline to be read; but it offers little to my purpose. What happened in the period from around A.D. 260 to 300 can — must — be explained in terms of civil war, simultaneous invasions, abruptly rising military costs, and other phenomena of the "Third-Century Crisis." They were surveyed in my first chapter. Thereafter, at least in north Africa, the state of the frontiers is too little understood before the 360s to allow much analysis. At most, we can say the loss of territory was a gradual thing, a slow weakening of the imperial presence in regions of little interest to the emperors.

Then the Austoriani in 363 advanced from the Tripolitanian semidesert against the rich farming districts around Lepcis. They took a tremendous lot of booty and peasant prisoners before they withdrew. The Lepcitanians made haste to summon Count Romanus, supreme commander of the armed forces in north Africa. When he appeared with his army, however, he declined to take any action until some enormous numbers of supplies and a still greater quantity of camels for transport should be produced. In their depleted state the Lepcitanians could never meet his demands. He therefore turned his back on them and retired to his headquarters, while the Austoriani, happily encouraged by the way things were turning out, made another sweep of the territory. This time they extended their depredations into the territory of Oea as well, and probably of Sabratha. Their third sweep followed not long afterwards. Since they appear from Ammianus' account to have moved about quite unopposed, it is very hard to believe in the presence of a frontier guard anywhere along or within that gray zone on the map (fig. 17, 7). It is only the army under the Count that Ammianus mentions in his narrative, which he begins with dark, dramatic words: "killings continual at the hands of barbarian savagery, bent on plunder — and this, on a larger scale, due to the inertness of the soldiers and their greed to seize upon other people's property. Yet Romanus the Count was the worst."[29] Ammianus thus links the acts of the barbarians explicitly to the corruption of the empire's defenders; and that corruption, as was seen in the preceding chapter, permeated the officer corps under Romanus and extended above him to his superiors at court; so that the loss of Roman control over anything beyond the Tripolitanian cities' walls may be squarely blamed on this factor.

Along the empire's northern frontiers in the preceding decade, a very similar breakdown of defense can be observed, once we have an account of the region in any detail: that is, in Ammianus, from the mid-350s. It is then that the commander Silvanus is seen, in scenes very revealing of the times, traduced by plotters at court and brought under suspicion of treason. A special assistant to the emperor, agens in rebus Apodemius, was sent out to hale him before his accusers, where he could be more safely dealt with. But Apodemius, "when he reached Gaul, being little concerned about what might happen, departed from the orders given him at his setting out and remained there neither seeing Silvanus nor instructing him through delivery of the letter of recall. Instead, he summoned the local Treasury officials, rationales, and began attacking with hostile passion the dependents and servants of the Master of the Army [Silvanus] as if that man were already proscribed and under sentence of death."[30] Where the lines of authority could be so little regarded and every opportunity for extortion seized on instantly, it is no surprise to learn that all Gaul was at the time pillaged by barbarians and laid waste at will, "without help coming from anyone," as Ammianus reports (15.5.2 — shades of Romanus!); and it was indeed for that very reason that Silvanus, known as a vigorous commander, had been sent out in the first place. When he was eventually arrested and executed, the problem of provincial defense remained still to be addressed.

The task fell to the emperor's young kinsman Julian. What he discovered was a somewhat diminished area to defend, the Batavian Island between Waal and Rhine having been abandoned (fig. 17, 8), as well as a strip on the right bank of the Rhine at some still earlier date unknown. In addition, lands to the south of the Waal — Toxandria, essentially modern Belgium — had been taken over (in ca. 340/1) by barbarian settlers, whose presence Julian confirmed by treaty. How ill they served the *pax Romana* may be judged from the maintaining of a frontier — the *limes Belgicus* — to their rear along the highway connecting Cologne to Boulogne by way of Tongres, Bavai, Tournai, and Cassel: all strong forts, reinforced by others behind them, such as Furfooz, for example (on the map), or Arras, Amiens, or Châlons.[31] All this had become and was to remain a permanent battle zone occupied by increasing numbers of *foederati*.

As to the reason for this Roman retreat, it is Ammianus again, and only he, who is of any help at all. He mentions the state of the troops assembled at Châlons in 354. They "were in a rage of impatience over the delays" in the supply of "their necessities of life," and the commander with overall responsibility "was in the extremest danger" on this account, the whole situation resulting from a plot "cunningly thought out" by his enemies to bring about his destruction. Similarly, Julian could not count on the adequate supply either of pay or provisions to his own men from the moment he took over his command, and the problem, coming to a head in 358, was still defeating him in 360 when he addressed his men in Paris.[32] They wouldn't fight without getting what they were entitled to. From all that was said in the preceding chapter, clearly the manipulation of the tax- and quarter-master's accounts, the heavy skimming off of illicit percentages at successive junctures along the supply line, and the withholding and private sale of army food and other articles by higher officers must often have resulted in crippling shortages. So these routine practices could account for the inadequacy of the northwestern defenses in the 350s, and earlier too. No other internal cause can be so easily documented.

The *limes Belgicus*, as it is called, defined the inner edge of such an area as was also found in Tripolitania, over which Rome by now had lost a great deal or even almost all of its control. It is a question of taxonomy, not of history, whether these two gray zones on my map were inside or outside the empire. But there is a third (and others besides that) still to consider. Isauria (Fig. 17, 9), as anyone knows who has flown over its mountains in a very small plane, is a wild, bouncy part of the world, more rightly called *Rough* Cilicia.[33] Here first a brigand chief had proclaimed himself emperor in the 260s; from here, in the next decade, the inhabitants had launched raids to the west, into Pamphylia and Lycia. They managed to gain possession of the city of Cremna, for a time. Being eventually driven back into their native haunts, no record of their doings thereafter survives until the mid-350s; but by then they had passed beyond the pale; they had come to be "considered barbarians," as a fourth-century writer puts it. Therefore all around them was a "frontier."[34] When our sources next permit a close view of them, through Ammianus' account, they have again overrun Pamphylia to the southwest and attacked the provincial capital to the southeast; also, to the north, Pisidia and Lycaonia. Inscriptions from the region (one in Latin!) record the valor of Count Lauricius who in 359 "seized a fortress long in the hands of the brigands and a bane to the provinces"; likewise of Hermaios, "the noble scourge of brigands — May he defend the city! He who slew the brigands, may he defend the city! He who avenged the city, may he defend it! He who often avenged the city, may he remain! He who sent military supplies, may he remain!" The city in question was a tiny settlement in the adjoining and too vulnerable province of Lycia; the date, five years or so after Lauricius; the text, in the form of acclamation from the local senate, we may suppose, was taken down in shorthand like so many others we have seen and forwarded for his information and endorsement to the resident Duke of the guard posts.[35] Of course, guard posts. Of course, military occupation. It was enemy country next door, even if inside the empire. And of course, difficulties in supplies, which had reduced to desperation the garrison of "the city" — namely, the tiny, hilltop walled settlement now called Ovacik. Such were the indignities inflicted upon the once glorious and formidable *pax Romana*.

By this time the Isaurians were well established as a quite uncontrollable force in the east, despite their small numbers. The explanation lies here, as likewise on the Persian frontier, in the character of the Roman defenses: "the Roman leaders were busy raking together their spoils from the subject population under them"; the enemy meanwhile "harassed our lands . . . with rising confidence," "with no one to say them nay," for "the troops had grown slack from easy living."[36] There were enough of them, in theory, "stationed in a great number of forts"; but they were not very aggressive, preferring to fight under, or even behind, their own walls. As the problem persisted, three extra military Counts were appointed to the surrounding provinces of Pamphylia, Pisidia, and Lycaonia. Still, the fifth century opened with Isaurian raids of rising audacity, which went on for years: into Cilicia to the east, even to Cyprus and Pontus! Into Galatia, too, and clean across the east to Persia; south, into Palestine, throwing Jerusalem into a panic and other centers into frenzies of wall-building.[37] The worst times came in A.D. 404–06. Isaurian forces could never have amounted to more than a couple of thousands on any given field of battle, against whom the opposing strength of the entire east —

let who will draw history from that dream-book the *Notitia Dignitatum!* —
proved altogether inadequate. Why? Consider the conduct of the man in
charge at the moment best reported. He was, predictably, a barbarian: the
military Count Arbazacius. Dispatched to the aid of villas and villages rather
than cities, whose walls generally protected them, he at first succeeded in
hustling the raiders back to their mountains. "He might easily have conquered
them once and for all and brought complete safety to the cities," Zosimus tells
us. Instead, wanting wealth and the pleasures of wealth, he 'shook down' the
Isaurian leaders for a part of their plunder, relaxed his military efforts, and
deflected subsequent charges of treason by sharing his profits with the right
people at the imperial court.[38] He thus presented an exact match for Romanus.

However, the story of the Isaurians has carried me forward too fast. I turn
back to earlier problems of defense reflected in Constantius' response (A.D.
359) when barbarians applied for admission to the empire. "The emperor let
them all in, himself aflame with an eagerness for greater gain intensified by
his crowd of flatterers. They ceaselessly proclaimed that, with foreign
relations calm and peace universal, he could profit from thus augmenting the
number of his child-bearing subjects; and he would be able to assemble the
strongest drafts of military conscripts — for his provincials would gladly put
up the cash for recruits (a hope that has on occasion proved the bane of
Rome)."[39] In Ammianus' parenthetic remark we are of course reminded of
that moment seventeen years later (A.D. 376) when great hordes of Goths
again requested admission. "Experienced flatterers," as he tells us, "immoder-
ately praised the good fortune of the prince which unexpectedly brought him
so many recruits; also that, instead of the levy of soldiers which was
contributed annually by each province, there would accrue to the treasuries
a vast amount of gold."[40] What would allow such profits was the recent
provision for payment of the recruiting tax in a cash equivalent instead of
actual bodies; but the new form of levy was proving a disaster. Not that it was
so bad an idea in itself — only the persons happily placed in charge of it were
using it as one more license for extortion. Hence, Valens' angry outburst: "We
deem it especially intolerable ... that a huge amount of gold is often demanded instead of men, and that the purchase-price of immigrants as recruits
is estimated more exorbitantly than is fitting." It is this procedure to which the
church historian Socrates was referring (4.34) when he described the emperor
in 376 "putting a pecuniary value on the military service which the inhabitants
of the provinces, village by village, had been accustomed to furnish." And, like
Ammianus, Socrates had a dark comment of his own to add at this point in
his narrative: "This change was the origin of many disasters to the Roman
empire subsequently."

In the background to the fateful decision of 376, the emperor's need for cash is thus made explicit; also, the habit of extortion that directed the administration of any form of tax. The Goths being then allowed to cross the Danube, the Romans were ready to receive them: in particular, and enjoying responsibility for the operation, the military Count Lupicinus in command of Thrace and the Duke Maximus of Moesia Secunda (or Scythia).[41]

> Their treacherous greed was the source of all our evils. I say nothing of other crimes which these two men, or at least others with their permission, with the worst of motive committed against the new-comers, who were as yet blameless; but one melancholy and unheard-of act shall be mentioned, of which, even if they were their own judges of their own case, they could not be acquitted by an excuse. When the barbarians after their crossing were harassed by lack of food, those most hateful generals devised a disgraceful traffic: they exchanged every dog that their insatiability could gather from far and wide for one slave each, and among those were carried off also sons of the chieftains.

Other writers speak of other Roman predators. Goods and belongings they stripped from the immigrants, but for the most part it was the men, women, and children who were seized bodily as plunder and sold into servitude, rural or domestic.

The process of pillage belonged more to A.D. 377 than 376. In that later year the victims rebelled. In several large groups they moved about or came together in Thrace, sometimes opposed by Roman armies, sometimes not.[42] At Hadrianople in 378, they were at last confronted by Valens himself, come from Syria with an urgently assembled army. Though the Goths were in no hurry for a battle, they could not refuse it. In its course, the emperor and the flower of his force were destroyed.

Hadrianople allows a glimpse inside the empire's administrative and military capacities. Specifically, it allows some very rough quantification of them. Among the numbers given us, there are, first, the two thousand men under one of the Roman generals, Sebastianus, who, in the weeks before the battle, was able to attack the Goths and beat them at will in various short engagements; and, when the emperor appeared, his success with still smaller forces aroused concern in the enemy commander for his whole people, scattered as they were in raiding parties.[43] Second, the Romans' Saracen cavalry "in small numbers," evidently meaning hundreds not thousands, proved so effective in their skirmishing that the Goths "wished to re-cross the Danube and give themselves up to the Huns rather than be totally destroyed by the Saracens."[44] These two indications of strength, whatever they prove, are at least in accord with the emperor's own scouts, who estimated the enemy at ten thousand.[45] In the light of the battle's outcome, however, no doubt a figure above that (say, fifteen thousand) is to be preferred for the Goths in arms, and perhaps twenty thousand for Valens. This was the best he could do — and quite in line with the size of force assembled in these years for other important military purposes (above, n. 12). Help could have been sought, of course, from the west. Indeed, it was freely offered. But before it could reach Hadrianople, a large part of the reinforcements were delayed by repeated engagements with barbarian invaders over the upper Rhine and upper Danube (Alamans, Alans, and others), while the majority of another part under Richomer deserted him en route.[46] The lower Danube regions, as we have seen, could not or would not put up any fight themselves, either in the year or so before the great battle or after; yet it is generally reckoned that the Danube forces totalled at least two hundred thousand.[47]

I need not further torture our inadequate witnesses to all these figures and calculations. For my purposes it is enough to sense their order of magnitude, no more. What then appears most striking is the contrast between the supposed great forces available to Valens and his sorry performance in bringing them to bear. For that contrast, the explanation surely must be sought in the description of starveling troops, unauthorized leaves of years' duration, lack of equipment, and other deficiencies of the military revealed to us by Synesius, Themistius, Libanius, Ammianus, Vegetius, and the Law Codes.[48] Deficiencies in turn were owing to the practices prevailing in government, as they were described in the preceding chapter. So much for the late imperial "mobile army," the fabled *force de frappe* of modern accounts. It had never amounted to more than a list of units and subunits, first on a large scale under Constantine lodged in scattered cities of the interior, and thereafter difficult to draw out and reassemble.

From Hadrianople, the victorious Goths, soon joined by other barbarian immigrant groups, turned to further pillage. They were quite unopposed. Indeed, a contemporary speaks of them moving over the land "like dancers rather than as if on campaign, so laughable do they find all our men; and one of their leaders is said to have remarked with astonishment the shamelessness of our soldiers who, more easily slaughtered than sheep, still look to victory, while nevertheless refusing to stir out of their own districts."[49] In A.D. 380, certain barbarian groups were acknowledged as treaty allies. They received lands in Moesia and Pannonia on the condition that they would respond to conscription when needed. Others, by a far different arrangement of October 3, 382, were scattered over a region in Thrace to live there under their own laws and rulers. They had attained something they might truly call Gothia inside the empire.[50] Both treaties proved effective in 388, producing a major part of the very large barbarian contingents in the army which Theodosius directed against the pretender Maximus. Upon their return to the eastern empire, a section of the Thracian Goths and unassigned wanderers gathered under the banner of the young Alaric in Macedonia, in 391; but that breach of treaty and the ravages it signalled were ended within the year. In 394 the Thracian Goths once more supplied a great deal of the bulk of an army led against a second usurper, Eugenius, in the west. But in the following year, after Theodosius' death, the treaty of 382 died as well. Alleging nonpayment of the supplies and subsidies due them, the Thracian Goths turned to Alaric again. It was en masse. They made him their king; through him demanded their own kingdom within the empire; and thereupon set off in search of it (fig. 17, 10). For three years they moved about. Opposition to them briefly appeared in Thessaly under the command of Stilicho, in 395, but the Roman forces backed off, and Alaric was therefore free to turn south in the winter months. The garrisons there offered no resistance when "Alaric with the barbarians came through Thermopylae, coursing along as if on race track or across the horse-breeding plains" (so, Eunapius).[51] Until 397 the Goths fed off Greece undisturbed; were then challenged by an expeditionary force at Pholoë in the central Peloponnese; withdrew undefeated to Epirus; and in the autumn concluded another treaty assuring to Alaric the military command over all Illyricum, and to his followers, the lands there which they required. They not only settled in them but drew upon their population through authorized taxation for their subsistence over the next four years.[52]

The developments just outlined withdrew some part of the interior of the empire from effective control by the state. By the symbolic convention employed on my map, they produced a gray area; but it was an area displaced originally from a point near the eastern capital westward, and then southward, and then, on its return, northward, ever plundering and lawless, until it came to rest in Epirus. Later, it resumed its motion. I will pick up the account again in a page or two.

It is worth pausing at this point, however, to note other losses and gray areas that appeared about the same time in other regions. Britain north of the Wall had been given up; Armorica (fig. 17, 11) required the presence of many thousands of border troops, limitanei, in the late fourth century, and counted as enemy territory.[53] Similarly, a part of northwest Spain (fig. 17, 12). A general reference to burgarii, fortlet-guards, in A.D. 398 fits well with the numerous scattered cemeteries of the upper Duero valley, in which burials with weapons and other characteristic articles indicate the presence of German warrior-immigrants. It is most natural to treat these as laeti, and the enemy they opposed, as a brigand population in the low mountain chain that parallels the peninsula's northwestern coasts.[54] Army posts of earlier times, at León,

Iuliobriga, and elsewhere in the northwest, continued to be occupied militarily without that fact, perhaps, having very much significance. Still, measures taken for armed protection of main roads and cities on a new scale in the late fourth century surely indicate that a part of the peninsula had reverted to the conditions from which Roman conquest had raised it hundreds of years earlier.

There are a half-dozen late Roman forts strung out along a 200-km stretch of the southern Dalmatian coast: Vigu and other sites.[55] Resembling a scattering of strong-points deep within Pannonia of the same period, they evidently responded to the same sort of endemic violence in the region that also produced similar structures in Belgium, especially along the Cologne-Bavai road — to which, in turn, lines of forts in Britain have been compared.[56] They lie along Watling Street leading north from London, before branching off to the west (Wroxeter) or northeast (Brough). "By the second half of the fourth century these defensible road networks behind the frontiers were vital to Britain and the northwest provinces." Why vital? Because, without walls and soldiers, travel would have been prohibitively hazardous. Or perhaps it had already become so for the very reason that the soldiers were now sheltering behind the walls. Thus they left such civilians as still trusted in the *pax Romana* to scurry from one fortified point to another, across an increasingly lawless landscape. Its uninviting features, just now noted in Spain, Britain, Dalmatia, Pannonia, and Belgium, recall the fortified private villas of those lands and of Syria and Mauretania, too, post-325.[57] The decision whether to register them all in gray on my map is a rather arbitrary one. Even without that, the corpus of the late empire appears sufficiently eaten away.

The *pax Romana* in western Asia Minor was to be better secured after 386 by the placing of certain defeated barbarians in the towns for guard duty. They were Greuthungi mixed with Goths. A dozen years passed and Count Tribigild then used his command over those in Phrygia to lead them in revolt and pillage. They first attacked the regions lying along the Ionian coast; next, moved through Pisidia toward the southern coast; and so arrived in the neighborhood of Selge in Pamphylia without having encountered the least opposition. As Zosimus tells the tale, they had in fact seized city after city, inhabitants and garrisons alike, "because there were no barbarian federates of the Romans" to say them nay. Those latter alone knew how to fight. At Selge, however, a local notable led out a force of his slaves and peasants, ambushed Tribigild, inflicted heavy losses by slingshot bombardment, and scattered most of the rebels in flight. Then they could be destroyed. An alternate escape route into the hills was barred by "a certain Florentius on guard, in command of federated troops. . . . Tribigild and three hundred of his men ascended to the pass, prevailed on Florentius and his men on guard by means of a great sum of money, and so bought their way past."[58] The general region they quit was seriously disturbed and thus the more easily preyed on by the Isaurians. The latter's attacks were described some pages earlier. I also describe (Appendix A II 9) the manner in which Tribigild went on to join his cause with the ambitions of Gainas, and how Gainas at the turn of the fifth century was able to impose an agreement on the emperor himself, by which he dictated certain hirings and firings of high officials. My real purpose in referring to Tribigild and Gainas, however, is to draw attention to particular systemic weaknesses in the late empire which they uncovered: first and most obvious, the ineffectiveness of the Roman military, especially in comparison with barbarian troops enlisted under an agreement of one sort or another; also, the venality of the emperor's servants. They had a very hard time resisting the temptation to make a profit out of their authority.

Of these weaknesses, the first is well illustrated by the successes Alaric achieved in the opening years of the fifth century. Seeing the western commander-in-chief, Stilicho, distracted by a military emergency in Raetia, Alaric in 401 left his home in Epirus. "Across the Pannonian provinces . . . and past Sirmium on his right, he entered Italy as if it were quite uninhabited and without the least resistance."[59] He addressed himself to the siege of Milan but was driven off before the year was over. His presence, however, decided the imperial court on a permanent remove to Ravenna. In the following spring at Pollentia, about thirty miles east of Turin, he fought Stilicho to a draw.[60] In a third encounter later in the year at Verona, once more there was no clear supremacy gained by either side, since Alaric departed Italy, suffered military discomfiture, yet nevertheless was offered what he had always wanted, the post of Master of the Soldiers throughout the Diocese of Illyricum. He was also able to gain a large area in Pannonia for a new Gothic settlement.[61]

In these years A.D. 400, 401, and 402, in which both the western and eastern emperors were reduced to bargaining on an equal level with rebellious leaders of barbarian troops, there were further serious incursions to face in Raetia and Noricum and all along the lower Danube, by Uldis and his Huns. The capital of the Gallic provinces and seat of the praetorian prefect was transferred from Trier to Arles. The move amounted to a surrender, like the abandonment of Milan for Ravenna by the imperial court; and it is therefore no surprise to read in Orosius (7.40.3) that the barbarian invaders of 407 also "danced across Gaul like revelers," while Alaric in his second invasion of Italy in A.D. 408, as Zosimus says (5.37.2), could saunter down to Bononia "as if on vacation." By then there was another emperor in the west, ludicrously called Constantine the Great, who, on quitting Britain with the chief part of its military establishment, abandoned it to its enemies. His general, Gerontius in Spain, revolted in 409, using the barbarian invaders (they had, predictably, entered the peninsula unopposed save by two landowner brothers, who armed their slaves and peasants in vain).

In these years, a detailed contemporary description of the empire's efforts at self-defense can be found only in the letters of Synesius. He was a nobleman of Cyrene and eventually bishop of Ptolemais in Cyrenaica.[62] When he was in his twenties, the Austorians to the south began a series of more or less constant raids against the whole province which lasted till his death in A.D. 413, or later, and which he took a prominent part in resisting. He did this first from Cyrene and then from his episcopal see.[63] As his allies, the military under a Duke proved useful or the reverse according to the particular individual in command at the moment (Anysius, for example, was an effective leader in 411); but, among the troops themselves, Synesius reserves his commendation for the federated contingents: a mere forty Hunnish soldiers. They were the only capable fighters in a total the size of which is unknown to us, since the relevant pages of the *Notitia Dignitatum* are lost. We can only tell that the list of troops under the Libyan Duke was longer than for any other Duke in the empire. Perhaps the total is not really important; for the "Roman" soldiers wouldn't fight. Fortunately, the enemy themselves attacked on no large scale. In one of their appearances they numbered only a thousand, "a wretched tribe of nomads," as Synesius calls them. But their plundering was effective enough to require five thousand camels.[64]

Given the fact that the nomads had no body armor, no siege train — were in reality very backward, poor folk, however greedy and desperate — and given the fact that a rabble of amateurs at war could chase them off, it is hard to explain the seriousness of the threat they offered. But there were too few men of the resolution needed to face them, too few bishops and deacons. The burden of responsibility thus fell on the properly constituted forces which Synesius describes for us and with which he was intimately familiar. They were to be seen lodging in every city, many thousands of them; and they were tirelessly engaged in hostilities — with their hosts. Synesius calls it "the peace-time war, one almost worse than the barbarian war and arising from military indiscipline and the officers' greed." It was a rare Duke indeed (Marcellinus in 412) who "scorned profits that custom had made to seem lawful. *He* has not conspired against the rich man nor abused the poor" — in contrast to other commanders who shifted their regiments around from one lodging to another solely with an eye to extortion.[65]

So Synesius despairs. "Pentapolis is dead, extinguished. Its end has come. It is slain" or "assassinated."[66] We can only think of the far more formidable enemy that was to advance on north Africa not many years later: the Vandals. Augustine helps to explain how they in their turn could simply walk into their new kingdom there, in 429. Only a year or two prior he demanded of the supreme commander in Africa: "When, then, will you be able, in dealing with so many [of your own] soldiers whose greed is to be humored and their savagery feared — when will you be able, I say, not so much to satisfy the lust of the men who love this world (for that would be quite impossible), but partially to feed it, or lose everything? . . . What shall I say about the wasting of Africa at the hands of African savages without resistance from anyone?"[67] Augustine's challenge concerns the inadequate defense offered against the tribesmen of Numidia, which he plainly blames on his estimate of the incorrigible indiscipline among corrupt troops. As it turned out, those were the very men on whom the commander was obliged to depend against the invasions from Spain, only a little later. Naturally, he was defeated — after having (so rumor declared) himself invited them over. He had been, in good late-Roman fashion, tangled up in hostile intrigues, and so had cast about for help in every direction. Thus the Vandal kingdom came to be established in north Africa.

Anyone familiar with modern interpretations of the end of the ancient world is bound to be struck by Synesius' despairing term for his own province: "assassinated." Exactly that term is used by André Piganiol in perhaps the best known, or at least the most dramatic, characterization of Rome's collapse (chap. 1, n. 179): "La civilisation romaine n'est pas morte de sa belle mort. Elle a été assassinée." Piganiol's conclusion — the final sentences in his history of "the Christian empire," growing out of his discussion of the "Germans" broadly defined — is offered in less striking fashion by many scholars both before and after him . It may fairly be called the common understanding. Central to it, naturally, is that fateful crossing of the frozen Rhine in the last hours of A.D. 406 by a united throng of half a dozen tribes. They were the Vandals, chief, and Alans; mixed with these, Suebi, Gepids, and Quadi; Burgundians, too, after two or three years numerous enough to found their own kingdom. The invasion of Raetia by Radagaisus in the previous year, though crushed, had drawn defenders away from the frontier. So it was overrun. But just what were the proportions of these overwhelming forces that were so quickly and effortlessly to gain control of Germany, Gaul, and Spain? If Piganiol is right, they must have been quite irresistibly strong. And yet, as we have seen in Cyrenaica, "a miserable tribe of nomads" sufficed for assassination there. It should not be ruled out that the same could have happened elsewhere in the empire.

Indeed, against the tendency of our sources to dramatize their tale by magnifying Rome's enemies, modern authorities are pretty well united. Radagaisus' force is "variously stated to be 400,000, 200,000, or more than 100,000 strong. . . . It is to be observed that the lowest of these figures is given (by Augustine) in an argument where a high figure is effective"; and Radagaisus' Ostrogoths were soon annihilated by Stilicho with a fraction of that smallest army-size.[68] The figure given us for the Vandals who crossed to Africa in 429 is eighty thousand, specifying the total of their men, women, and children, slave or free; from which, with other considerations, we may reason to the scale of barbarian masses in general over the period, let us say, from the 370s to the 460s — a scale in the low tens of thousands per tribe, possibly a hundred thousand for the largest, of which a quarter at the most could form the fighting portion.[69] Nor (Huns excepted) were they all great warriors, save by comparison with the regular Roman soldier.[70] What Synesius describes on a small scale to the south thus appears to have been true on a large scale at about the same time, in the north and northwest: barbarian attack constituted an insurmountable threat not because the barbarians were so many and so strong, but because the defense was so weak.

3. POWER-LOSS IN LAYERS

Though seen only from a great distance and through cursory accounts, the history of the later empire unquestionably has more defeats to show than victories. Therein lies the very explanation for the "lateness" of the period: it precedes an end. Our accounts seldom indicate exactly how defeats occurred. Occasionally, however, details emerge. Over the course of the half-century before the sack of Rome, the size of Rome's armies was contemptible: perhaps twenty thousand at Hadrianople, but under fifteen thousand regulars at Faesulae (A.D. 406), with barbarian contingents hastily added, and a mere four or five or six thousand at various other crucial moments. We are told of a field of battle, a district, an entire province simply abandoned, though we are not given the reason or strategy behind the decision: Dacia and other parts of the northern glacis in the third century, and parts of the southern glacis in the same period and later, up to the mid-fourth century; in the opening decades of the fifth century, further regions of Africa — in particular, everything from the Atlantic to the edges of Numidia ceded without a blow — and most of Gaul along with all of Germany and all of Spain (except that, in the latter, a few days' resistance were offered by a makeshift militia, not the army).[71] In the better-reported decades between these two points, i.e., A.D. 350–400, we have seen Tripolitania given up without any attempt at defense (above, at n. 29); areas of Gaul "without help coming from anyone" (at n. 30); retreat or inaction along the Persian frontier (at n. 36); also in Thrace in the 370s, "no one saying nay," "our soldiers . . . refusing to stir" (at nn. 42 and 49); in the 390s in the Balkans (at n. 51) and in Asia Minor (at n. 58), and in north Italy, "without the least resistance" (at n. 59). That brings us to 401, and again to 408. In discussing those years above, I quoted Jordanes and Zosimus on Alaric's saunters around the peninsula. In 406, similarly, invaders met no opposition in Gaul. I quoted Orosius to that effect. Failure to do anything on the part of the authorities and the soldiers under them draws sharp comment from contemporaries or writers removed from the scene by only a few generations. Like ourselves, they had read about Gaius Marius, Julius Caesar, Trajan Optimus Princeps. Once upon a time, Rome had had armies.

Looking for explanation beneath the inability to mobilize and the silent scenes of surrender, we find occasional descriptions of soldiers in Syria, Thrace, Cyrenaica, trying to fight but timid and incompetent (unless they were recently entered barbarian confederates); or we find them retreating under orders from their higher officers. In the latter case, blame is to be directed at Count Romanus and others similar (Apodemius in Gaul, certain commanders around Isauria besides the infamous Count Arbozacius and, later, Florentius in the same regions, with their like encountered by Synesius in Egypt and Cyrenaica). The conduct of these officers is explained for us: they were interested in the illicit profits of their command, not in fighting. They stationed their men where the best opportunities existed for extortion from the civilian population, or (like Count Lupicinus and Duke Maximus) they shook down the D.P.s, the displaced persons of war-torn times. There were enough of those and to spare, in the later empire.

As to the inadequacies of the men in the ranks, the explanations offered are several. I instance from earlier pages the frequent lack of pay, lack of food, and lack of boots, clothes, and arms;[72] further, the tolerance or even encouragement of unmilitary pursuits, retail selling and farming, depending on whether men were stationed in urban or rural billets; also, generally neglected training and lax discipline, of which drunkenness and criminal behavior were the most obvious signs; and extended leaves, accounting for some part of the chief deficiency of the late Roman military, namely, its inflated rosters. Since all these traits are amply attested to by contemporaries, we should assume they characterized the regular army throughout. Barbarian troops were quite another matter. However, they were not numerous enough to be a decisive element in the emergencies of, say, the 350s, nor trustworthy enough, half a century later. In consequence, security suffered not only around the periphery of the empire but in the interior as well, where the poorest, most intractable terrain fell back into the hands of brigands and pirates.

That the higher army officers of the later empire defined their jobs very differently from their predecessors two or three centuries earlier is easily perceived. They had gained rights to a share in everything of value that was intended for, or somehow came into the hands of, the men serving under them; and they applied their authority to the earning, even the increasing, of that share. That is what Synesius means by "the peace-time war, one almost worse than the barbarian war and arising from the military's indiscipline and the officers' greed"; and to this Zosimus also refers, when he deplores lodging so large a part of the army in urban billets and thus "subjecting the cities to the scourge of the military."[73] While the ethic prevailing in the legions had traditionally permitted extortion as a routine by and among the noncommissioned officers and lower ranks, it was only in the third century that whole regiments and armies (meaning, surely, colonels and generals) were seen to put business before war. I have in mind the description of Lower Germany's affairs in A.D. 270 or, much later, the sour comment that, when Theodosius split the duties of the Master of Soldiers and Master of Cavalry among five holders of these titles, "each of them, not according to his share but entire (as if they were still only two individuals), wanted to gather in the profits from the handling of military supplies."[74] Material is abundant to show the redirection of administrative energies, new and different priorities at the level of command.

Historical consequences naturally followed. Sometimes they appear quite incontestably. The enemy see that "our" men are in no fit numbers or condition to fight, and in that confidence they attack; or our most reliable sources (Ammianus, Synesius, Augustine) specifically attribute a defeat to the corruption widespread among the military. Or again, a client prince, Firmus, is subjected to extortion and, "being unable to bear the arrogance of the troops' greed," revolts; whereupon the emperor must transfer forces from Pannonia and Moesia to Africa against him, and the Quadi and Sarmatians then easily breach the denuded frontiers.[75] Such were the surface layers of Rome's loss of power.

However, my analysis has so far taken no account of the proposition offered earlier, that an army assembled and ready to engage can emerge only from a broad texture of consent. It must be recruited, it must be equipped and supplied and paid — all of which implies a compliant civilian population. Above all, it must be brought to bear upon the point of action — implying a central government able to identify the needs of the state and to issue effective orders. For success in war, then, court and curiae are as essential as armies.

As to court practices, the preceding chapter gathered a good deal of material to illustrate how readily bought and sold was the advice and information supplied to the emperors, on the basis of which they had to govern.[76] Their intent was thus as readily baffled or distorted. Take the story of Sabinianus. Very wealthy, he longed for prominence and glory; very greedy, the influential eunuchs at court determined to have his money. At the same time, they could bring down another man they did not like, Ursicinus. Ursicinus on their advice was recalled from his post as Master of Cavalry throughout the East, and Sabinianus was installed in his place. While the price of Sabinianus' appointment abundantly rewarded the *potentiores* at court, it was in other respects a disaster. Ammianus describes him as "a sufficiently cultivated and certainly rich old fellow, but no man for war," "puffed up, of rather short stature, mean-spirited, and barely able to endure a jolly party without disgraceful nervousness, to say nothing of the din of battle." At the time of his appointment the Persians were engaged in the leisurely discussion of a Roman war; but when they heard what sort of a man was replacing Ursicinus, they were galvanized into action. Their rapid thrust into Roman territory caught Sabinianus living the soft life in Edessa, unwilling to quit it for the relief of the cities and areas attacked. Thus Amida was besieged and taken and sacked. The next year, when official inquiry was made into the loss and Sabinianus' responsibility for it, the investigators let him off as a favor to one of the eunuchs who had originally appointed him. It is evident that the emperor, Constantius II, knew next to nothing about the whole business. Meanwhile, a part of the empire had been surrendered.

So much for the handling of affairs in Antioch. The western court was no different. Had Count Romanus not been able there to buy his exculpation for the loss of the lands around Oea, Lepcis, and Sabratha in the 360s, he would not have been still in command in the 370s to drive Firmus to revolt; and that revolt had unexpected repercussions in Germany.[77] The whole story has been outlined in earlier pages. There is an opposite and apposite case in point, too, involving Count Sebastianus: not a greedy villain like Romanus, rather, he was "concerned about money only to clothe his body in armor" and "looked on with amazement on account of his scorn for wealth." A true soldier, then: solicitous for his men; an aggressive officer, model of integrity, everything a military leader should be; therefore rewarded with high commands by Constantius II, Julian, and Valentinian. But after Valentinian's death his detractors were able to get rid of him "because his poverty made him good-natured and easy to remove."[78] Which is an easily understood way of saying that the best of their servants emperors could not always maintain in power, because power had to be bought, and bought again, constantly.

As to the curiae and *their* practices: constituting the layer of power next below the court and serving as point of engagement between much of the imperial will and its effectuation on the local level, the city senates were of tremendous importance. In particular, they were concerned with taxes. They not only oversaw the apportionment of quotas and their actual collection but also guaranteed the required totals with their own property. Now, upon taxes depended the government, army, everything; but there was in fact ample ability to pay in the empire generally, so long as the curiae retained their health and numbers. Notoriously, however, they lost both. The explanation is well known and has been examined above.[79] They lost their economic health because only a minority of curiales (the Top Ten, *principales*, *dekaprotoi*) were content to remain in their rank, and only on condition that they could shift its trials and burdens onto the backs of the less rich, less influential majority; and the latter lost their numbers through escape to less costly, less vulnerable ranks. Both problems were known and understood by the emperors and by their closest, most responsible advisers. Laws to control both were passed and often repeated, from the early fourth century into the fifth and sixth. Such legislation, however, was evaded rather easily, though not without expense. Enforcement could be deflected through payments delivered to the right quarters. The root cause of evasion, in the next layer of historical explanation, was thus the inability of members of the government to say no if they were offered enough money. It has been shown, above, that they were indeed offered money, and took it, and that the consequences had become, even by A.D. 313, a cause of grave concern.

So far as the empire's cities were concerned, the ill effects of this practice were concealed, or at least mitigated, through the profits of extortion and venality being generously lavished on building, entertainment, piety, and other socially approved objectives, in the old tradition of civic beneficence. Yet the benefactors were a new nobility. They were the winners in the rush for refuge somewhere, anywhere, within a now enormously expanded bureaucracy. It constituted the chief means of social, political, and economic advancement.[80] And while officials took advantage of their *cingulum* to grow rich, the older classes and groups of contributors to the state grew poorer.

Those "classes," as I just said, consisted of the less distinguished mass of city senators, as opposed to the *principales*. As to the "groups" who shared their difficulties, I have in mind all sorts of worker associations, the *collegiati*. Some — the most relevant, here — served the armed forces, producing weapons and uniforms. Some produced the army's pay in the state mints. Others served other public purposes: bakers, millers, bargees and shippers who delivered the dole to the populations of the two capitals, the quarriers and miners, the drovers and muleteers in the state transport system, the masons and builders who doubled as fire fighters. It was the object of very minutely detailed legislation, over the whole course of the fourth and later centuries, to lay all such occupations under obligation to the state. Whatever they made or did, a part they owed like a tax.[81] Lest they fail, they were to be enrolled on lists by name, they were to remain fixed in their places of residence, rear their sons in their same means of livelihood, even marry within the trade. A great net of restrictions was cast over them, to hold them motionless in their useful posts and labors. Yet they escaped. When we look from the laws to life, we find a perfectly free choice of career and movement taken for granted. "If you ordered one of your sons to learn a craft, but instead he went right on living at home or spent his time somewhere else, would not his teacher dissuade him? Would he not say to you, 'You made a contract with me and determined its length of time. If the lad is not going to spend that time with us, but elsewhere, how can we present him as a pupil?' "[82] To explain the assumptions in this passage, we need only turn to the practices that allowed curiales to escape. Bribes were the key. To the degree that *collegiati* and other elements of the labor force were in fact constrained by the laws, it was because they could not so well afford the price of their freedom.

While people in the period here studied had the leisure to adapt to their own world and ethic as changes occurred and were able to accept the practices they found around them (often, of course, their own practices), yet nevertheless they may be heard protesting. Many instances are scattered through the preceding chapter that testify to the existence of two norms of conduct: one which condemned, the other which entirely accepted venality in office.[83] By the same token, the man who was above corruption was singled out for praise. He is presented as a perfect miracle — unspoken, the unhappy acknowledgment that corruption was rather the rule than the exception.[84]

It is even recognized that the empire as a whole suffered from the prevalence of venality. In an address to the emperor of about A.D. 390, Libanius describes how soldiers in rural billets are all 'on the take,' all selling 'protection' under their commanding officer against collectors of rents and taxes. He, the general, of course gets the bulk of the payoff. The losers are the curiales who must somehow make up the sums not collected. "So, then, the curiae are hurt by this fine racket, the cities are hurt by the harm done to their curiae, and, too, the fighting forces are hurt because of the harm done to these latter. . . . Root out, now, such protection rackets *as our enemies would wish on us.*"[85]

Libanius' understanding of the layers of consequences touched by the ethics of government in his day — his sense of the entire empire at risk — is rare indeed. And naturally so. To detach oneself from one's own particular

concerns sufficiently to see what else they affect, to see the interconnected-
ness of the various parts and institutions of one's society, and so to estimate
historical results that must inevitably flow from them — who has the vision?
Who is even interested? While wars and politics turn on a dime, manners and
mores change only by tiny degrees, quite undramatically. And their tendency
is hard to see. It may, for instance, have no meaning at all that, almost as I write,
the charges against various present and former wearers of the *cingulum*,
accused of illicit sale of weapons to their country's enemies at enormous profit,
half-unravel in piles of shredded paper; for the chief upholder of the law in
the palace (himself under renewed investigation for *his* profits from the sale
of influence) has proved rather slow to investigate. It is a scandal, it is history,
all the world pays notice. Scandal in fact has touched one part or circle after
another in this government to a remarkable degree.[86] Is that now our settled
habit, our *consuetudo*, the start of our decline? No. But who can observe the
will of a great empire dissolving in the uncontrolled impulses of private
enterprise — of *mercatores* or *kapeloi*, as our fourth-century commentators call
them — without wondering if there may not be some lesson there?

APPENDIX A
FOURTH-CENTURY BARBARIANS
IN THE EMPERORS' SERVICE

I. BARBARIAN ARMY OFFICERS (SEE *PLRE* I–II AND WAAS [1965] 10)

Key to Abbreviations

*	= not in Ammianus	a.	= armaturarum
A	= Alaman	c.	= comes
F	= Frank	m.	= magister
G	= Goth	ped.	= peditum
p	= pagan	eq.	= equitum
		r.m.	= rei militaris
		tr.	= tribunus

pF Arbogastes (? son of Bauto? nephew of Richomer), c. r. m. 380; m. milit. 388–394 ("the emperor Valentinian II was almost reduced to the position of one of his subjects, and oversight of all military matters entrusted to his Frankish retinue . . ." [Greg. of Tours]); suicide 394.

A Agilo, tr. stabuli 354; tr. gentilium et scut. 354–360; m. ped. (E) 360–362; high general 365–66 (married dr. of Araxius PPO 365–66).

*G Alica, chief who led tribe in army of Licinius 324.

Algildus, c. r. m. 361.

G Arintheus (Flavius), agens vice tr. 355; m. eq. 363; m. ped. 366–78; cos. 372.

* Bacurius, king of the Iberi, tr. sagittariorum 378, dux Palaest. 378, c. domesticorum some time bet. 378 and 394; m. milit. 394.

pF Bauto, m. milit. (W) 380–85; cos. 385; his dr. Eudoxia married Arcadius.

F Bonitus, officer/general of Constantine 316–324.

Bappo, praef. urbi Romae 372.

* Buthericus, m. eq. (Illyr.) 390.

*F? Charobaudes, m. utriusque militiae (W) 408.

F Charietto, m. milit. (W) 408.

F Charietto, emigré German, freelance with Julian 355–58, c. per utramque Germaniam 365.

Cretio, c. r. m. (Afr.) 349–61 (son is Masaucio).

*A Crocus, troop chief 306 (W).

Dagalaifus, c. domesticorum (W) 361–63; m. ped. 364–66; cos. 366.

199

pG Fravitta, serving Theodosius 380s, m. milit. per Or. 395–400, cos. 401.
  Frigeridus, dux (?Valeriae) pre-377 (pre-367?), c. r. m. 377 (Illyr.).
?F Fullofaudes, dux (Brit.) 367.
˙G Gainas, c. r. m. 395–99.
• Gaiso, m. milit. 351?
  Gildo (Berber chief) serving 373, c. et m. utriusque militiae Afr. 386–98.
  Gomoarius, tr. scholae scutariorum 350, m. eq. 360–61, officer 365–66 (brother is Maurus).
• Hellebichus, m. pedit. Or. 387.
  (H)ormisdas, Persian prince, immigré 324, cavalry officer 350s, c. 362–63.
  (H)ormisdas, son of the above, procos. Asiae 365–66, c. r. m. 380.
• Aur. Ianuarius, dux Pannoniae 303.
• Immo, c. r. m. 361.
A Latinus, c. domesticorum 354.
F Lutto, c. 355.
  Machamaeus (brother is Maurus), regimental commander 363.
  Magnentius (Flavius), tr. Iov. et Herculi, protector, then c. r. m. in 340s (W).
F Malarichus, tr. gentilium 355, offered and declined to be m. eq. 363.
F Mallobaudes, tr. scholae a. 354–55, rex Francorum et c. domesticorum 378.
• Marcus (Flavius), natus in Dacia, serving in vex. Fesianesa under Constantius, protector later.
  Masaucio (son of Cretio), protector domesticus (W) 365.
F Maudio, c. 355.
  Maurus (brother of Machamaeus), tr. 363, dux Phoenices post-363.
?F Merobaudes, officer of 363, m. ped. (W) 375–88; cos. 377, II 383; III designate 388; suicide 387.
˙F Merobaudes, dux Aegypti 384.
G Modares, m. eq. per Thracias, m. mil. 382.
G Munderichus, Gothic chief, emigré 376, dux limitis (Arab.) post-376.
  Nannienus, c. r. m. 370 (W), c. (utriusque Germaniae?) 378, m. mil. 387–88.
  Nectaridus, c. Brit. 367.
  Nevitta, emigré German, praepositus of cavalry (W) 358; m. eq. 361–64; cos. 362.
pF Richomeres, c. domesticorum (W) 377–78, survived Hadrianople; m. mil. (E) 383; cos. et m. utriusque militiae (E) 388–93.
? Remigius (born Mainz), numerarius 355; m. offic. (W) 367–73; suicide ca. 374.
• Rumoridus, m. mil. 384 (W).
˙G Sarus, rex Gothorum, m. utriusque militiae (Gaul) 407.
F Silvanus, tr. scholae a. 351; m. ped. 352–55; c. et m. eq. et ped. 353.
• Stilicho (Vandal), m. mil. 394–408 (W), cos. 400, II 405.
• Subarmachius, c. domesticorum (a Colchian) 395/399.
  Theolaifus, c. r. m. 361.
A Vadomarius, rex Alamannorum by 354 (–361); captured; dux Phoenices 361–66; commander 371.
• Vallio, m. eq. per Gall. 383.
  Victor (Sarmatian), c. r. m. 362–63; m. eq. 363–79; cos. 369; survived Hadrianople; married dr. of Arab queen Mavia.
  Vitalianus, protector domesticus 364, m. eq. per Illyr. 380.

TRIBUNES AND LOWER OFFICERS

    Abdigildus, tr. 359.

    Aliso, tr. (E) 365.

    Bainobaudes, tr. scut. 354.

    Bainobaudes, tr. cornutorum.

A   Balchobaudes, tr. a. 366 (W).

F   Bappo, tr. (W) 355.

    Barchalba, tr. (E) 366.

    Barzimeres, tr. scutariorum (E) 374–77.

    Bitheridus, tr. 372 (W).

·   Dagridus, tr. (W) late 4th.

?F   Fraomarius, installed as rex Bucinobantium, then tr. numeri Alamannorum 372.

·   Gabso, protector domesticus (W) late 4th.

    Gaiolus (Flavius), tr. Quintanorum (Eg.) 398.

A   Hariobaudes, tr. 359.

A   Hortarius, emigré commander tr. 373 (W).

    Laipso, tr. Cornutorum 357.

    Laniogaisus, tr. 355 (already serving in 350) (W).

    Marcaridus, tr. Iov. ca. 390.

    Memoridus, tr. 363 (E).

    Nemota, tr. (E) 363.

    Nestica, tr. scutariorum 358 (W).

A   Scudilo, officer 351, tr. scutariorum 354.

    Seniauchus, tr. 355 (W).

    Sintula, tr. stabuli 360 (W).

F   Teutomeres, protector domesticus 354 (E).

    nameless Vandal father of Stilicho, cavalry officer (E).

II. THE INCREASING PRESENCE OF BARBARIAN TROOP UNITS

1. Although contemporaries in the later empire often mention armies and troop units, reference is rare to soldiers whose origin is specified as internal to the empire (the term citizen is meaningless, but we may call them *natives*). By contrast, we encounter many mentions of recruits drawn from external sources, whether in contingents according to treaties laid down between their people and the empire or individually as volunteers and mercenaries.

2. To begin the account with Constantine: the prominent role of Crocus (or Erocus?) in his elevation to the throne is well known; likewise the predominance of barbarians in Constantine's expeditionary force of 311/2, which allowed him to extend his rule over Italy (Zos. 2.15.1). They receive special honor in the sculptures of the triumphal arch in Rome: the Cornuti and others, wild Celts, whose identity Alföldi (1959) 174 recognized. Cf. also Hoffmann (1969–70) 135. Constantine also replaced the praetorian guard with the *scholae palatinae*, from whose ranks ascent to high commands was uniquely favored. These elite troops were mostly Germans, and remained so into the sixth century. See R. Frank (1969) 62f. and passim and Demougeot (1969–79) 2.77. Licinius for his part summoned drafts of Gothic auxiliaries for his war against Constantine (Anon. Vales. 5.27). When Constantine later defeated him and moved his capital east, he obtained, through victories won by prince

Constantius, a force of 40,000 western Goths to defend Constantinople as *foederati* (Iord., *Getica* 21.112). The Gothic treaty dates to 324/30, as Dagron (1974) 35 n. 7 indicates, or more precisely 332, as Piganiol (1972) 158 n. 3, Chrysos (1973) 52f., and Wolfram (1975) 262 prefer. The *Anon. Vales.* 6.31 and Eutrop. 10.7 refer to the Gothic defeat; also Euseb., *Vita Const.* 4.5, mentioning subsidies the emperor paid out to the Goths, and Amm. 21.10.8, on the distinguished promotions offered to barbarians "right up to the fasces and consulate." The statue of a Gothic king, Aoric father of Athanaric, as Wolfram (1975) 264f. identifies the name,was set up in the very antechamber of the curia in Constantinople (Themist., *Or.* 15.191A). A dependence on barbarian troops thus established under Constantine became ever more pronounced as time went on, as can be seen in the individual careers shown above (section I) and as is recognized in general terms by modern scholars in summary fashion, e. g., Schutz (1985) 162. Hoffmann (1969–70) 1.137 discovers a settled practice of recruiting *auxilia* from barbarians under Constantine as later, the legions by contrast being filled from the native population; and (139f.), increasingly in the 4th cent., it was *auxilia* not legions that were raised as new or incremental units. Under Honorius, of twenty-seven new units, only three were legions.

3. In 350/1, Magnentius, in forming his army of campaign, counted chiefly on barbarians (Julian, *Or.* 1.34D and 2.56Af.; Hoffmann [1969–70] 1.144), while Constantius likewise turned to barbarians, offering them land and a free hand to make war on the Gallic pretender and provinces (Liban., *Or.* 18.33f.). Constantius, not long after defeating Magnentius (notice the *'olim'* in Amm. 17.8.3), settled barbarians inside the empire throughout Toxandria, charged with the defense of the lower Rhineland. They were Franks, perhaps Salian. See Demougeot (1969–79) 2.78 n. 218 and 93. In 358 Julian confirmed them in possession of the area (p. 100) while also drawing recruits from among them and other Germans of the lower Rhine. See Zos. 3.8.1 and Demougeot 2.102 and 119, Piganiol (1972) 245, Günther (1975) 347, and Hoffmann (1969–70) 1.146f. In the same year 358, as in 370, the defeated Saxons yielded recruits to the Roman armies (Bartholomew [1984] 169); on another front, the defeated Limigantes promised Rome yearly contingents of their strongest young men (Amm. 17.3.3).

4. In mustering strength for war against Persia and feeling the need for barbarian contingents, Constantius applied to Julian for drafts of such troops. Julian feared that those under his command, if shipped east, would by their fate deter the "barbarian army volunteers who were accustomed often to come over to our side, under such contract arrangements" as insured their fighting only in the area (Amm. 20.4.4f.). Nevertheless, he complied. Nine units, apparently all or mostly Germans, were sent on their way (Julian, *Ad Ath.* 280D). "Two Magnentian legions" (Amm. 19.5.2; Hoffmann [1969–70] 2.153) were already on the front — barbarians despite the form of unit in which they served. They "had been recently conducted from Gaul." Ammianus praises their valor, as also that of "the Royal Archers, that is, a cavalry unit in which serve all the free-born barbarians, outstanding in their armed strength and bravery," at Amida (18.9.3 and 19.5.2). Subsequently, when war threatened between Julian and Constantius, the latter turned to the Goths for assistance (20.8.1), whom Julian in turn made use of against Persia (Amm. 23.2.7; Zos. 3.25.6). Saraceni served in his forces, too (Amm. 23.5.1, cf. 26.5.10), along with Eruli (25.10.9). The majority of his army were Germans (Demougeot [1969–79] 2.101). The attempt at rebellion by Procopius under Valentinian and Valens looked to Goths for armed strength (Eunap. frg. 37, *FHG* 4.28). They were in fact sent (though to the wrong person), according to treaty obligations.

5. From 369 on in Britain, barbarian troops were both stationed and recruited for service on the continent. The evidence lies in the *Notitia Dignitatum* and in the archeological record

(Frere [1967] 352 and 359). The latter source of testimony consists, *inter alia*, of belt-buckles in graves characteristic of these military settlers; often, of weapons and armor found in the male burials. Whole cemeteries are also found, from this period forward, throughout Belgium and northern France, the Mainz-Kostheim area — clear across the Rhine frontier zone. See Hawkes and Dunning (1961) 5–17; Hawkes (1974) 390–93; and Günther (1975) 347 and 350f. An earlier tendency to identify these people in Britain with the *laeti* known to our literary sources from the turn of the third to fourth century has been contested or argued away by Reece (1980) 80 and Welsby (1982) 159–62, and Arnold (1984) 26f. accordingly hedges his account. Since *laeti* first appeared in history several generations ahead of these characteristic burials (Waffengräber), it is best to reserve the term *foederati* for these latter. So far as the written records knows them, they are *auxilia, gentiles, socii*: Germans and especially Alamans and Franks, serving Rome militarily by treaty, some immigrating, some meaning to return to their homes in Free Germany. At Furfooz in Belgium, in a much-cited cemetery, 70 percent of the male burials were Waffengräber, the settlement there being a small fort manned by Germans. See fig. 17, above, and most recently Böhme (1978) 24f., 30, 32, 35ff., and 38. On the continent, all sorts of trans-Rhenane tribes certainly continued to be enrolled: for illustration, the Lentienses in the 370s, from whom individual volunteers were being drawn and, after a defeat, a regular tribute of contingents of recruits (Amm. 31.10.3 and 17, cf. the Quadi in 30.6.1 and Zos. 4.12.1, a decade earlier); but other tribes were being drawn on by Valentinian, as Demougeot (1969–79) 2.119 shows.

6. Along the lower Danube, barbarians after the great immigration of 376 were a natural source of recruits, especially but not only Goths. For a war with Persia, they contributed heavily (A.D. 377/8, Amm. 30.2.6); again, very heavily in 379 (Piganiol [1972] 232 and Wolfram [1979] 154); and Gratian a few years later enrolled Alans in his armies (Zos. 4.35.2) while settling Greuthungi along the upper reaches of the Danube (Zos. 4.34.2f.). Perhaps connected with such settlements, and in any case proof of *foederati* of some sort established post-380, is the new kind of pottery discovered in Carnuntum, eastern Valeria, and the lower Danube *limes* (Grünewald [1980] 29–31), like the settlements of this time also in Pannonia that account for the Hunnish character of the contents in graves both along the frontier and in the interior of the province. These Huns, along with Goths and Alans, were later to be employed against the pretender Magnus Maximus, first to bar the passage of the Alps against him in 383 and a second time to confront him at Siscia and Aquileia in 388. See *Paneg. vet.* 12(2).32.3f., Lengyel and Radan (1980) 117 and Demougeot (1974) 150.

7. In an interesting conversation of 384, described later by Ambrose (*Ep.* 24.8, PL 16.1036C), the western emperor, Maximus, asserted angrily, "Since you and that Bauto have tricked me — Bauto who wanted to claim the kingdom for himself behind the screen of a princeling (*puer*) and even sent his barbarians against me, just as if I myself had none that I could have brought up! — for there are so many thousands of barbarians that fight for me and take their pay (*annonae*) from me. . . ." It is not important to recall the historical context of these references, made at Trier when the bishop was present there as representative from the court of Valentinian II. What is relevant is rather the emphatic boasting and bullying on both sides in terms of their barbarian contingents. The conversation continues with Ambrose's mention (24.8, 1037Df.) of the moment "when you were threatening the Roman empire with barbarian auxiliaries," and you intended to launch on Italy "your *turmae translimitaneae*. . . ." As things turned out, of course, Maximus himself was defeated by the floods of barbarians which Theodosius mustered against him — Goths principally, but Greuthungi as well, who were survivors from defeat at the hands of Theodosius' general (Zos. 4.38.1f. and 39.1–5;

Hoffmann [1969–70] 1.476f.). Some of them (Zos. 4.45.3) contemplated betraying him and were detected and killed; but (Ambros., *Ep.* 40.22; Wolfram [1979] 159) the rest played the key role in victory at Siscia in 388.

8. Confronting yet again another pretender, Eugenius, the emperor Theodosius prepared an expeditionary force very heavily — probably more than half — dependent on barbarian allied units. The sources give them much emphasis: Oros. 7.35.19; Zos. 4.58.2f.; Iord., *Getica* 28; Soc., *H. E.* 5.25 (PG 67.652B); and Wolfram (1979) 162, Lengyel and Radan (1980) 118, Demougeot (1969–79) 2.158f., Demougeot (1974) 150, and Cameron (1970) 164. These included contingents serving under their own leaders such as Gainas and Alaric, according to treaty. In similar fashion, Arbogast in the cause of Eugenius had been making his muster not only from existing troops on the frontier but from barbarians of many tribes and regions to the west and north (Oros. 7.35.11). Being denuded of their defenders by the demands of civil war, the frontiers required large new drafts, and received them from Stilicho, the commander in the west, in the form of barbarians under treaty (*foederati*: Demougeot [1953] 7 and 11). At the same time, A.D. 395/6, Stilicho had to build up his strength against Alaric (Cameron [1970] 375), who was ambitious for a supreme command. He obtained it in 397 as Master of the Soldiery throughout Illyricum. "Nothing shows better how weakened had become the resistance against the barbarians, taken into the empire since 380, than the settling of German federates in 397, under a king provided with a Roman office" (Demougeot [1969–79] 2.168f.; Matthews [1975] 272).

9. Yet perhaps there is a match to this signal humiliation of the empire. It may be found only a little later when that other disappointed and ambitious barbarian leader Gainas first "summoned to himself the entire Gothic people from their land and arranged that those who were his kin should have command of army units" (Soc., *H. E.* 6.6, PG 67.676B), as a result of which, through tangled tergiversations, Gainas met the emperor Arcadius near Chalcedon (ibid. 677A). "There in the church . . . the emperor and the barbarian made oath to each other to lay no plots against each other" — that is, they addressed each other quite on a level. The fifth century is about to begin, in the very first decade of which the balance clearly changes. Now it is the barbarians that enjoy the final say. Recruitment from among them by the established authorities, even as Alaric dominates the scene, continues: see Olympiodorus frg. 3 (*FHG* 4.58), where the Goth Sarus is won over in 410; Rodogaisus and other chiefs (frg. 9, 4.59; Zos. 5.26.5); tribes of the upper Danube in A.D. 401/2 (Claudian, *De bello Goth.* 400f.); Huns in 409 (Zos. 5.50.1); and trans-Rhenane Franks and Alamans by the pretender Constantine III in the same year (Soc., *H. E.* 9.13, PG 67.1621C; Demougeot [1953] 25). By this date, in any military sense, the empire was no longer a sovereign state and the sack of its ancient capital by Alaric — a high imperial official and even a born Roman, so far as the word has meaning, as he had entered the world on the island of Peuce in ca. 370 (Demougeot [1969–79] 2.157 n. 98) — had no quality of invasion about it at all. He and his men *were* the Roman army, and had been for decades.

APPENDIX B
"LEADERS"

Official and unofficial power were, in the Roman state as they have been in others, divided by a line without much meaning. Distinct from but, we may say, adjacent in meaning to proconsuls and duovirs and other officials, we have people accorded titles to which they were neither elected nor appointed; yet they certainly enjoyed an acknowledged right to command in their communities. That right was indicated by any one of a small number of honorific terms of reference, the equivalent, outside of government, of "proconsul" or "duovir" inside government. Such terms are the proof of structures of dependence, deference, and compliance on the one hand, and of power on the other hand. They are also the proof of the ubiquity and vast predominance of private authority over public. The latter, Government or State with capital letters, was not much of a presence during the Principate, compared to the network of local "leaders." Even within the government, unofficial power structures developed, and have a hidden history, until their existence is recognized in titulature.

Princeps indicates a chief of a tribe (often = *civitas*) before its incorporation into the empire, and as such does not concern me: Caes., B. C. 2.19; B. G. 1.30, 4.11, 5.3, 5.54; 4.6, *principes Galliae*, cf. Tac., *Ann.* 11.23.1, *primores Galliae*; Tac., *Agr.* 12.1 (Britain); *AE* 1953, 78–80, A.D. 173/5, 180, and 200, Baquates chiefs, cf. Bénabou (1976) 458f. or Fentress (1979) 47, *principes gentium* in Africa; *priores principes civitatum* with a council of *decemprimi* around them, in non-Roman style, even into the 4th century in Mauretania, Lepelley (1979–81) 1.126f., later *viri primarii*, ibid. 1.204; and *principes* of Spanish tribes, frequent in inscriptions, e.g., *Inscr. Lat. España Rom.* 5630 or 6393, cf. Albertos Firmet (1975) 32f.; again, in *AE* 1915, 75, *principales* as late as A.D. 367/75; and perhaps in Plin., *Ep.* 9.5.1. In Spain the term retained its pre-Roman force for centuries, and in Illyricum similarly for generations after conquest, cf. Rendic-Miocevic (1980) 23f. — possibly also in Capidava in Lower Moesia, in the *loci princeps et quinquennalis territorii Capidavensis* of *CIL* 3.12491.

Princeps may also denote simply a greatly respected resident of "those regions" (of Macedonia, Caes., B. C. 3.34, and Tac., *Ann.* 3.38.2 of A.D. 21; in Malta, Acta apost. 28.7 and *IGR* 1.512; in Corsica, Tac., *Hist.* 2.16; in Syria, Plin., *Ep.* 1.10.8; and in Pontus, Lucian, *Alex.* 45). Despite the commentary to *AE* 1956, 178 (Severan), I take *ho protos tes eparcheias* of Macedonia to mean one of the prominent men in Macedonia, not a provincial priest. Compare the similar *proteuontes kata ten eparchian* (of Asia), Strabo 14.1.42, and the *primus regionis* in Gaul around A.D. 420, in Constantius' *Vita S. Germani* 5.26.

In cities, *principales*, *principes*, *primates*, or Greek *protoi* or *proteuontes* are recognized but not authorized by their fellow-citizens or observers, for example, in general statements such as Firm. Matern., *Math.* 3.10.7, 3.12.4, etc., or Dio 52.19.3, and in Rome, Ps.-Quint., *Decl.* 301

p. 187 Ritter, Cic., *De domo sua* 42, Columella, *Res rust.* 1 *praef.* 1, Epict., *Diss.* 1.30 *(hoi hyperechontes)*, Augustus, *Res gestae* 12, Tac., *Ann.* 1.8.1 and 1.36 *(senatus et primores* — so the latter are outside the senate), and Sen., *Benef.* 2.27.2 *(princeps civitatis et pecunia et gratia)*. The same types are identified in Puteoli, Tac., *Ann.* 13.48; at Altinum, Plin., *Ep.* 3.2.2; at Pompeii, the well-known expelled senator and *munerarius* on a grand scale, Alleius Nigidius Maius, in Moeller (1973) 519f.; in Beneventum, an *eques vir principalis* of the 2d century, in *CIL* 9.1540; in Palermo, *ILS* 2938; also in northern cities like Aventicum, Tac., *Hist.* 1.68, and in Germany, ibid. 1.57; and in eastern cities like Tralles, Cic., *Pro Flacco* 23.54 and 24.58; in Ionian and Pontic towns, Lucian, *De salt.* 79; in villages, *CJ* 11.54(53).2.1, post-A.D. 468; in Gamala, Jos., *Vita* 185, and in Galilee, 220; in Cadyanda, *IGR* 3.513, *proteuon tou ethnous*; in Gerasa, *IGR* 1.375; in Tomi, *IGR* 1.630; in Idebessus, *IGR* 1.649; in Heraclea, a person also hailed as "Number One of Ephesus" and "of[all] Greeks," *IGR* 1.798, cf. *IGR* 3.173, a man of Ancyra "first among Greeks"; in Pamphylia, cf. Bean and Mitford (1970) 44; in Pisidian Antioch, Acta apost. 13.50 and 17.4; in any Greek city, Apul., *Met.* 2.22 or Plut., *Moralia* 815A; in Bubon in Lycia, Schindler (1972) 32 no. 8 and 13 = *IGR* 3.464; at Pogla, Bérard (1892) 425; often in praise of Opramoas in Lycia, for example at Rhodiapolis, *IGR* 3.739; at Caesarea, Basil, *Ep.* 281; in Caria, Radet (1980) 233; in Lycaonian cities, Robert (1965) 212, examples of persons not only *genous tou proteuontos* but *tes protes taxeos*, with Reinach (1906) 94, 125, and 141 on *genous protou* at Aphrodisias; in Themisonium in Phrygia, a Roman army officer "in every respect First in the city and in the province," *IGR* 1.882; in Neocaesarea in Pontus, Greg. Nyss., *Vita Greg. Thaumat.*, *PG* 46.921B; in Syrian cities generally, Amm. 14.7.1, in Cyrrhus, Theodoret., *Ep.* 47, and at mod. Salihiyeh in A.D. 175, Cumont (1923) 221, as well as off the coast at Arados, Clem., *Homil.* 12.24. Ste. Croix (1981) 531 collects several further refs. to persons in Asia Minor inscriptions "of the first rank," *taxis* or *tagma*, supposing that the terms had a technical meaning and indicated an official position. But this I think is mistaken. It is, in fact, the purpose of this ungainly paragraph to show how universal was the ranking of people on a sort of absolute scale, by no means confined within the limits of formal, official definition. The essence of it is perhaps best summed up in the phrase cited from Seneca: "money and influence." The first of the pair is the quality most often cited where any attempt is made at characterizing primacy. Descent from a family long boasting wealth and public attainments is often specified, too; and there are other criteria suiting individuals. But a stranger entering any city of the empire could find out the names of its elite through a moment's inquiry.

To be more specific, consider Rabbi Abbahu of Caesarea in Palestine. The period of his prominence fell in the last decades of the third century. He was extraordinarily rich, well-educated, Hellenized, shrewd, and of imposing physical presence. He was referred to as "a man of rank," the Hebrew equivalent of the Greek and Latin terms just encountered; also, as "leader of the people," for which we have also seen equivalents. He it was who determined how the marketplace was run, what could be brought to it and how sold, even who could be exempted from market tolls. To Gentiles he spoke for the whole city, even to the governor, and his fellow Jews respected the important role he played as intermediary (Levine [1975] 56–58, 63, 66f., 69, and 73) — a true "First Citizen," then, a *protopolites* as it might be said.

That term itself, translated as "head of the citizens" in Aramaic and Hebrew, is found in the same region and century. See Rahmani (1972) 114–16 = *SEG* 26 (1976/77) 387 no. 1668, and Vattioni (1977) 27; again, in Mauretania (*AE* 1969, 748) where lies "the First Citizen and Father of the Synagogue of the Jews." And the term occurs, although rarely, in other sources and contexts: Dionisotti (1982) 104, as equivalent of *decurion* in a glossary of ca. A.D. 300; applied to three citizens of an Egyptian city and once in Greece, see Vattioni (1977) 23f.

Nearly contemporary to Rabbi Abbahu was the group of First Men, *protoi*, who joined the magistrates and council of Thespiae in Greece in voting particular honors to some dozens of younger citizens who had volunteered as a militia to repel barbarian raids in A.D. 169/70 (Plassart [1932] 732 and 738 and AE 1971, 447). Since the action taken was by official groups, so too the Firsts must be official in some sense we cannot define. We may compare the *proteuontes* on an embassy representing their city, in Herodian 8.7.2, and on a similar mission, the *protoi* in Jos., *Vita* 64, cf. 185 and 220 — if all these are not simply magistrates — and further, "the Landholders," *possessores*, of the modern Henchir-Snobbeur in north Africa in A.D. 186 corporately and officially convened for action with the local decurions. See Garnsey (1970) 257, adding a second instance of the term.

In Rome itself, besides the *magistri vicorum* whose status is unequivocal, there appear to have been precinct bosses referred to by the urban prefect and the emperor as *primates, maiores,* or *priores regionum* or *proceres.* See the *Coll. Avellana* 1.3 under Valentinian and 13 (*CSEL* 35), p. 69, *Ep.* 21.2 and 21.3; p. 75 *Ep.* 29.3; p. 77 *Ep.* 31.6; and p. 79 *Ep.* 32.3f. of A.D. 419. In time of riot they emerged as the persons with whom even the highest public authorities had to deal, or even appeal to for help. Evidently they enjoyed de facto command over large numbers of citizens.

These scattered illustrations from Thespiae in Greece, Caesarea in Palestine, Rome, and elsewhere serve as reminders of the inexact fit to be found in any society between actual everyday needs and formal provision for authority. The needs from time to time exceed the provision; therefore the deficiency must be supplied by a shadow-government, if you will, or some temporary alternative. Such an alternative, in turn, might become permanent: an institution such as the weightier part of city councils. Levy (1899) 264 noticed long ago how "the dominating position of the more powerful personages appears also in the effacement of members of boards of functionaries [in Asia Minor cities], who often entirely disappear behind their chief." They are designated as "those serving with So-and-So" in inscriptions of the second and third centuries.

During that period the same phenomenon can be observed on a much broader scale and under a far more familiar terminology, separating an executive committee of ten within city councils from the larger mass of decurions. The earliest occurrences I know of are those of Nero's reign (Jos., *Vita* 296) in Tiberias and in Gerasa (*IGR* 3.1376). Occasionally the *dekaprotoi* or *decemprimi,* or *primores* and *principales* in the narrower sense, were replaced by *eikosaprotoi.* See *IGR* 3.640 and 649 in Idebessus and Arneae, where there were "Top Tens" as well; also, Reinach (1893) 165; and Reinach (1906) 243 on the unique "Top Two Hundred of Aphrodisias." Hadrian had recognized in Clazomenae that there were gradations in effectiveness, no doubt meaning essentially gradations of wealth, within that city's *curia;* and he established the distinction in law (*Dig.* 50.7.5.5, the *primores*). It appears again where the jurist Callistratus is handling material of the second half of the second century (*Dig.* 48.19.27.1) and marks off *principales* from *decuriones.* The former, the "Chief Men," are already in place in African cities by then (*Martyrium Carpi* 3, the date disputed but see Musurillo [1972] xv), and likewise widely reported in Greek inscriptions. See the remarks of Rostovtzeff (1957) 706f. n. 47, Thomas (1975) 117, and Ste. Croix (1981) 471. Ste. Croix finds the only advantages of *principales* after the beginning of the fourth century (actually, *primores,* ordinarily exempt from torture, cf. Lact., *De mort. persecut.* 21.3).

Since it was for reasons of tax collection and other public obligations that the imperial government gave authority to the distinction between the few Top and the many ordinary decurions, that distinction inevitably assumed greater importance in times of more rigorously controlled governmental demands, after Diocletian had ascended the throne. Many laws of the Codes define *principales* or direct that activities be carried out through them (e.g., *CJ*

7.16.41, A.D. 313/324 or CT 12.1.5 of A.D. 317) — many inscriptions, too, from Africa in particular (for example, *AE* 1975, 873; *ILAfr.* 276; and *IRT* 567) but also from Spain (*AE* 1915, 75) or Germany (Chastagnol [1978] 30 n. 36). They are referred to as *protoi* by Libanius, see Norman (1977) 413–15; as *primores* by Augustine, *Ep.* 17.4 (*CSEL* 34.43), or as *primates* (*Conf.* 6.7.11) or *principes vel seniores* (*Ep.* 50.1) — assuming all these terms to be technical. On the equivalences, see Lepelley (1979–81) 1.127 and 202–05 and 2.463. They are not found in Egypt after A.D. 302, see Bowman (1971) 158 and J. D. Thomas (1974) 68. And new, select levels of authority continued to be recognized in further developments, for example, the *dynatoi* as opposed to "those in office" (Liban., *Or.* 2.6 and elsewhere), the *potentiores* rife throughout the law Codes, and the "City Father" of Aphrodisias, in charge of the city's finances from the mid-fifth century onward (Roueché [1979] 173–85). The later figures and titles simply illustrate for their own times that imperfectness of fit between everyday needs and governmental structure that has been outlined here. My interest of course focuses on the extralegal, unofficial, and unauthorized power relationships before they were, so to speak, enveloped by government.

APPENDIX C
SOLDIERS IN CITIES

My purpose in gathering certain citations here is simply to demonstrate how much of the imperial army was stationed in cities and towns or their suburbs and how much more this was the case after A.D. 300 than before. True, in all periods troops were sometimes detached from their normal posts for summer campaigns, at the end of which they sheltered *pro tem.* in some handy urban center. This is most easily seen in Ammianus (16.11.15, 20.4.9, 27.10.16, etc.); a city might thus become their long-term home (e. g. below, Lyon). But it had been my impression that a big change took place over the course of time, whereby soldiers were brought into far more frequent contact with civilians of the later empire. A. H. M. Jones had even said as much in his most authoritative work of 1964 (p. 631): "Some of the larger units, legions and vexillations, were stationed in cities, probably also in permanent barracks. The mobile units of the *palatini* and *comitatenses*, on the other hand, except when actually on campaign, when they lived under canvas, were normally billeted in cities." Unfortunately he made no effort to support these statements, which therefore cannot carry much weight.

Yet, master of the sources that he was, he certainly knew of a title of the Justinian Code, 12.40(41), *de metatis et epidemeticis,* containing mostly texts of the half-century beginning in 393 (on the word *epidemetic*, Stephanus compares *Nov. Just.* 134), and of the similar title in the Theodosian Code given over to billeting, *de metatis* (CT 7.8); and if the bulk of the many constitutions in it have to do with putting up the civil service on their travels, 7.8.13 (422) begins, "our loyal soldiers returning from combat service or setting out for war shall take for themselves the ground floor rooms of each tower of the New Wall of this sacred city," Constantinople. Perhaps, then, the entirety of the title may include, without specifying, the armed services as well as the unarmed. In the next title (7.9.2, A.D. 340 or 342), extortion by persons billeted offers the inclusive series, "count, tribune, provost or soldier," and 13.3.10 (370 or 373) deals with exemptions from having to offer quarters to "military persons." Given the indications of soldiers on leave wandering around freely, it is a safe guess that some of them were in cities for a while. CT 7.18.6 (413) threatens to punish with a ten-place demotion a soldier absent without leave for a year, a loss of twenty places in seniority for two years, and thirty for three. The picture presented is one of highly relaxed attitudes toward furloughs, quite in harmony with similar scenes of soldiers lounging around villages in Libanius' *Or.* 47.5–6, and the attention drawn to soldiers taking up brigandage in Noethlichs (1981) 82f. However, my focus is on soldiers in cities, not simply loose on the land.

The essence of a comparison best lies in two texts, the latter sometimes cited, the former ignored. Aelius Aristides in his address to Antoninus Pius (*Or.* 26.67) congratulates the rulers of his world that "not many troop units are scattered among the cities of the provinces, and many are settled in the countryside." Zosimus (2.34.1f.) is, on the other hand, very critical of Constantine for "removing the majority of the troops from the frontiers and stationing them in cities which had no need of auxiliary forces, thus . . . subjecting the cities to the scourge of the military." Zosimus' bias against Constantine and his late date might weaken his testimony, did it not find an earlier echo in Themistius speaking (Or. 8.114a, p. 171 Schenkl) in A.D. 368 of "the city soldier," ho astikos stratiotes, as the very type of grasping conduct; further, in Theodoret., Ep. 2 (1 p. 75 Azéma), speaking of "troop units stationed in cities and villages" evidently everywhere in the empire; and there is much evidence in detail, further to confirm these general statements.

The detail need not be assembled in its entirety. I have made no attempt at that — not even to consult all the authorities I could easily think of or to follow back what can be found in this or that modern work, to the author's sources. I have not listed the many scores of sites to be found in the Notitia Dignitatum where evidently soldier and civilian must have rubbed elbows over some stretch of time; it seemed silly mechanically to transfer so much ink from one page to another. Nor have I included certain great Rhine and Danube military camps from earlier days in which, later, a civilian population took refuge with a reduced garrison. These receive mention in Petrikovits (1950) 77. My object was only to substantiate my original impression out of the reading I was engaged in for other purposes. I here set out my findings in geographical order, beginning with Italy and working counterclockwise round the provinces. Within broad zones, sites are arranged alphabetically.

Italy:

Zos. 5.35.5 (A.D. 408 — cf. 5.45.6) refers to "the soldiers stationed in the cities," evidently meaning all soldiers of any sort, and in Italy.

Aquileia: See van Berchem (1952) 104 and n. 2, on AE 1934 no. 230, a *praepositus militum agentium in praetentione Aquiliae*, and the vexillations of two Danube legions there in A.D. 244; later, of three other legions and vexillations known from inscriptions.

Concordia: A large body made up from twenty-odd units was stationed here briefly after the campaigns of A.D. 394, Hoffmann (1969–71) 1.78, 86 and 101.

Milan: Winter quarters for troops in 354/5, cf. Amm. 14.10.16; further, Grosse (1920) 89 on field-army units probably lodged there in the fourth century, and King (1984) 119, on the first use of the city for the lodging of large forces, under Gallienus.

Pompeii: Chance evidence, in the form of a graffito by a man of legion VII, and the body of an officer. See LeRoux (1983) 67f. and Gore (1984) 572f.

Puteoli: *Vigiles* detachments were stationed in the city in Severan times, for how long before is unknown. See Freis (1967) 15.

Rome: Another sojourner of the legion VII is known here from a graffito in the Domus Aurea (therefore datable to between 64 and 104). See LeRoux (1983) 73f.

Ticinum: Zos. 5.26.4 (405/6) refers to a gathering of thirty troop units and further allied contingents in the city; cf. 5.30.4, "the soldiers stationed at Ticinum," implying their routine emplacement there. Tomlin (1976) 189 concludes that "Stilicho's army was regularly mustered at Ticinum" even after 402, when Honorius moved to Ravenna.

Vercellae: CIL 5.6720 of the second half of the fourth century records the burial of a cavalryman in the city, from which Matthews (1975) 183 n. 5 infers "a garrison of Armenian troops."

Noricum, Raetia, Pannonia:

Awaiting the call to campaign in 388 against Maximus, "troops had filled the cities of Pannonia," Pan. lat. 12(2).32.4. Views of specific sites, include the following several cities:

Lauriacum: Alföldy (1974) 161, 166, and 183 notes the stationing of the legion II Italica at the site from 191 on and Caracalla's gift of municipal status to the settlement that grew up along the west side of the camp.

Vemania: Garbsch (1974) 161f. notes the civilian presence at the campsite post-A.D. 302/3.

Poetovio: The location "was seldom without troops," beginning with the VIII Augusta in ca. A.D. 6 through Gallienus' stationing there of vexillations; and the civilian population received *colonia* status from Trajan. See Jordan (1985) 87.

Germany:

Amm. 27.10.16 mentions soldiers "returning to winter quarters," cf. 16.11.15, *milite disperso per stationes hibernas* at the end of the campaigning season. They did not return to tents. And Zos. 4.3.5 (A.D. 364) reports how, after Julian's death and the signs of restlessness among the tribes, Valentinian equipped "the cities on the Rhine with the needed garrison," *phylake*. Roeren (1960) 221 sees in Strasbourg and Regensburg the assumption of their own defense by the civilians within their walls from the later third century on, hence "the dividing line between civil settlement and military camp disappears." The physical proximity of the two populations is, of course, archeologically demonstrable at many familiar sites, where *canabae* and *castra* touch, or nearly touch. For some recent bibliography on the Rhineland, see Dorutiu-Boila (1972) 140 n. 11.

Cologne: Tac., *Hist.* 4.65 gives a little sense of *canabae*-identity in A.D. 70; Liban., *Or.* 18.46, mentions how Julian established a *phroura* at the site in A.D. 357; and there are *laeti*-type burials, surely of soldiers in residence, in the fourth century, cf. Hawkes and Dunning (1961) 16.

Mainz: The civilian settlement began to be walled in A.D. 250/70 when the troops transferred into it, and it is a *civitas* formally by 293/7; thereafter, "the fort was abandoned and, by the late fourth century, included in an extension of the city's circuit"; yet the *Not. Dig. Occ.* 41.21 lists troop units there. See S. Johnson (1983) 137f. and Roeren (1960) 221. *Laeti*-type burials are found outside its walls, surely of soldiers, cf. Hawkes and Dunning (1961) 5f. and 16.

Strasbourg: The site was originally home to the Second Legion under Tiberius, its quarters abandoned to a civilian population under Claudius, and later the legion VIII Gemina was settled there until 160.There are Trajanic brickstamps in the barracks. The legion returned only in the early third century, cf., e.g., *CIL* 10.1254 of A.D. 234. The civil settlement developed into a *civitas*, but a military presence continued there throughout the fourth century, shown by a Dux Argentoratensis in the *Not. Dig.* See S. Johnson (1983) 142, Hatt (1953) 233, 238, and 243, and Gottlieb and Kuhoff (1984) 28.

Trier: Constantius Chlorus used Trier as headquarters for his troops, a field commander was probably stationed there in the fourth century, and *laeti*-type burials are found outside its walls. See Grosse (1920) 89, Demougeot (1969–79) 2.53, and Hawkes and Dunning (1961) 16.

Gaul:

Amm. 20.4.9 mentions lodgings for Julian's troops in 359/60 in Gaul (and Germany?), *stationes . . . in quibus hiemabant*, cf. above under "Germany," and at 16.4.1 (356) the *scutari* and *gentiles* are described as absent from Sens, "farmed out among the townships so as to be supplied more easily than before." Throughout Gaul, from the later third century on, the numerous walled circuits on the sites of cities have been taken as *castra* for resident troops, not citadels for civilians. The arguments of Roblin (1965) 370–91 are doubted by Petrikovits (1971) 188 only because such sites are "too many" to lodge the known field-army troops. His doubts are at least partly to be laid to rest by the facts that follow.

Amiens: A *castrum* was built within the city in or not long after A.D. 278, and a garrison installed (*numeri Ursariensium* and *catafractariorum*) from Diocletian's time on through the fourth century. See Sulpicius Severus, *Vita S. Martini* 3 (CSEL 1 p. 113), which gives a rough date, Will (1954) 142, and Bayard and Massy (1982) 23 and 25. Amm. 27.6.5 pictures an emperor speaking to an audience of soldiers there in A.D. 367.

Armorica: In this region some cities held military elements throughout the fourth century, cf. Gallious (1985) 110.

Autun: Garrison forces were present there in Amm. 16.2.1.

Châlons: Garrison forces were present there in Amm. 27.1.2, and the site is a *castrum* in the *Notitia Galliarum*. But the wall's circuit is "archaeologically indistinguishable from *civitates* elsewhere," suggesting that there was nothing special about the military presence. Cf. S. Johnson (1983) 84.

Dijon: The city is called a *castrum* in a late source and had a wall around it. Cf. Johnson (1983) 84.

Jublains: This city ca. 100 km east of Rennes was a *civitas* containing "a small strong point" in the form of a keep inside a square circuit with many towers on it. Cf. S. Johnson (1983) 93f.

Lyons: As an administrative headquarters, the city had a number of soldiers resident there while assigned to the staff of civilian officials, and there was also a regular resident complement of urban-cohort troops to guard the mint— the cohort I Flavia urbana under Vespasian, and so forth, in rotation with the urban cohorts in Carthage and Rome. Jos., B. J. 2.373 speaks of there being 1,200 men there (the two cohorts), and Tac., *Hist.* 1.64.9 speaks of the coh. XVIII in Lyons "where it was normally stationed in the winter." In A.D. 68 there were more troops present, ibid. 1.59. See Fabia (1918) 21–25 and Freis (1967) 14 and 29f.

Rheims: Amm. 16.2.8 (356) describes the city as one *cui praesidebat* a Master of Cavalry, implying a force of soldiers present.

Sens: Amm. 16.4.3 (356) places the troops of the Master of Cavalry in quarters neighboring to the city. See above, under "Gaul."

Tournai: For burials outside the town of *laeti*-type, see Faider-Feytmans (1951) 51f.

Tours: A *castrum* was built inside the wall ca. 275, cf. L. Pietri (1983) 344.

Vienne: Blockley (1983) 2.85 dates to A.D. 383 the *phroura* mentioned in Eunap., frg. 57, 2.

Vindonissa: At this site in Gallia Belgica, the old camp was abandoned in the 290s, but there were evidently troops there under Constantine, cf. Pekary (1966) 9f.

Britain:

In a number of towns, *laeti*-type grave goods, belt-buckles and plates and brooches are found from a date around A.D. 369 in the southern parts. See Frere (1967) 359, Hawkes (1974) 390f., and generally Welsby (1982) 149f.

Brough-on-Humber: The ancient Petuaria had troops in it in the fourth century, to judge from the existence of a Petuarian unit in *Not. Dig. Occ.* 40.31, cf. Welsby (1982) 149.

Catterick: This Welsh site has Tetrarchic walls embracing the abandoned fort, and in connection with rebuilding in part of the city ca. 370 are found *laeti*-type arms and buckles. Cf. Wacher (1971) 170 and 172 and Welsby (1982) 149f.

London: Like Lyons, as an administrative center, the city drew in soldiers to the civilian offices, cf. Frere (1967) 196 on tombstones of soldiers in London from three legions, e. g., VI Victrix, in *RIB* 11 (Severan), the legion itself stationed in York. See E. Birley (1982/83) 276 and A. R. Birley (1981) 222. Merrifield (1983) 174f. shows the location of a fort built in the early 2d cent. "as a permanent barracks."

Spain:

There were garrisons of long standing in the northwest, e. g., Lugo, before the purview of the *Not. Dig.,* cf. Arce (1980) 600 n. 18; but the *burgarii* mentioned in *CT* 7.14.1 (398), corresponding to the urban garrisons of Honorius' letter, belong to the northeast.

Castulo and Tarraco: Probably garrisons in both cities during the Principate, cf. Mackie (1983) 11 and 190.

Mauretania Caesariensis:

The province required throughout its history considerable depth of defense, some elements of which were city-based.

Albulae: Described as a garrisoned city, Benseddik (1979) 167.

Caesarea: As an administrative center, the city drew in the services of soldiers on detachment. They are attested in many inscriptions, from many auxiliary units. Evidence for their presence is greatest from the mid-second to mid-third century. In the 250s there is an *ala* lodged in barracks in the city. See Rachet (1970) 241, Leveau (1973) 156, and Benseddik (1979) 164.

Rapidum: A camp was established at Rapidum in 122 for a coh. Sardorum, which soon had its own baths-building there. It was quickly surrounded by a civilian settlement of mixed *pagani* and *veterani apud Rapidum consistentes.* In 167 it was walled, and lost its garrison a little before 208. See Benseddik (1979) 170, Rebuffat (1982) 506, and Laporte (1983) 258 and 261.

Africa Proconsularis and Numidia:

Abthugni: Lepelley (1979–81) 2.274 reports a *stationarius* in A.D. 314.

Carthage: Troops present in the city for civil-office staff work were also used for police work in the surrounding countryside. They included units of the urban cohorts. See Fabia (1918) 255 and 53, Carcopino (1922) 33f., and Freis (1967) 30.

Egypt:

Ball (1942) 160 lists sixty-five locations where Roman troops were stationed. Among them are the following, better attested.

Arsinoë: PAbinnaeus 28 (340s) shows soldiers in the city, and BGU 316 (359) shows that a vexillation of cataphracts was lodged in the town by that date; but there had been a detachment of cavalry attested as early as 319. See Rémondon (1965) 134 and 136.

Babylon: POxy. 1261 (325) and the *Not. Dig. Or.* 28.15 show the presence of troops in the city. The legion XIII Gemina was stationed there in the fourth century. See Rémondon (1965) 136.

Contrapollinopolis: A coh. I Augusta praetoria Lusitanorum equitata was stationed in the city in A.D. 156 and well into the third century. See Whitehorn (1983) 65f.

Coptos: Troops are known there in 183 or earlier and (in a different unit) are serving there as garrison in 216. See Speidel (1984) 222f.

Dionysias: Besides the Abinnaeus archive as a source, see Rémondon (1965) 134 for troops lodging in the city.

Diospolis: PAbinnaeus 1 (341) shows a vexillation of Parthian archers stationed in the city.

Hermoupolis: *Equites mauri scutarii* are stationed here by A.D. 340. See Rémondon (1965) 136.

Lycopolis: Rémondon (1965) 136 shows cavalry here by A.D. 340.

Memphis: PAbinnaeus 49 (346) mentions "the soldiers stationed" in the city under a praepositus, and there was the legion V Macedonica stationed there also in the fourth century, see Rémondon (1965) 136.

Oxyrhynchus: PColumbia 183 (372) shows "the I Maximian legion stationed, *diakeimene*, in Oxyrhynchus."

The Levant (Arabia, Palestine, Syria) and Mesopotamia:

Tac., *Ann.* 13.25, speaks generally of troops in Syria "sleek and prosperous, whose soldiering had all been in town." Centuries later, around the reign of Diocletian, archeology reveals general dispositions of troops either sheltering civilians in fortlets along the eastern frontier, or settled in barracks in the larger cities (legions) or smaller (cavalry) of Mesopotamia and Armenia. See van Berchem (1952) 27, 29, 31f. — and fuller particulars show in the sites noted below. Still later, Theodoret toward the mid-5th cent. could speak naturally of "troop units that are stationed in cities and villages" (*Ep.* 2).

Amida: Amm. 18.9.3f. (359) and 19.5.2 reveal the titles of half a dozen legions plus mounted cavalry as the city's garrison.

Antioch: There were few troops in the capital of Syria, but they included a city watch made up of archers (in 383, cf. Liban., *Or.* 19.35, and Liebeschuetz [1972] 116).

Apamea: The legion II Parthica several times lodged in the city under the Severi, its camp being built two or three kilometers outside the walls. See Balty (1973) 55, Rey-Coquais (1978) 68, and Balty (1987) 215 and 239–41.

Bezabde: Amm. 20.7.1 shows the legions II Flavia, II Armeniaca, and II Parthica, and *sagittarii Zabdicenses* present in the city.

Bostra: The legion VI Ferrata was based in Bostra by Trajan, later (by Antoninus Pius' reign) the III Cyrenaica, still in A.D. 249/51, and in Diocletian's reign, legion IV Martia. See Kindler (1975) 146f., Sartre (1974) 88, and Kammerer (1929) 276 and 301.

Caesarea: The city was military headquarters in the first century for an *ala* and five infantry cohorts (Broughton [1933] 44), an unspecified force in the 50s (Jos., *B. J.* 2.268), wintering legions in A.D. 67/8 (ibid. 3.412), and a resident centurion in Acts 10 : 1 and 27 : 1. A very doubtful source, the Georgian version of the fictitious life of bishop Porphyry, refers to a military commander in the city around A.D. 400. See Peeters (1941) 211.

Caparcotna: *ILS* 8976 shows the Second Legion stationed there in A.D. 130.

Cyrrhus: Home of the legion X Fretensis under Augustus until A.D. 18, cf. Rey-Coquais (1978) 67.

Dura: Best known of all military emplacements in a civilian setting. For a rapid review of the troops involved, see Rey-Coquais (1978) 68f.

Emesa: Herodian 5.3.9 (A.D. 218) reports "a great force of soldiers at that time lay adjacent to the city.... The troops then regularly frequented the city, going to its temple for worship."

Gadara: In the later first century the legion X Fretensis lodged in the city, see Kammerer (1929–30) 301.

Gerasa: After its conquest, the city lodged vexillations, a cavalry unit, and a wintering unit of *equites singulares* under Hadrian. See Kraeling (1938) 390 no. 30, Rey-Coquais (1978) 68, and Isaac (1984) 186.

Jerusalem: Jos., *B. J.* 2.79, reports a legion in the city in 4 B.C., a cohort there in A.D. 44 (2.224), a garrison in the 50s (2.262, a *phroura*), and the camp "near the Palace." In A.D. 70 the Tenth settled on a hill along the south flank of the city, and stayed until Diocletian's reign. In 116 there was also present a detachment of the III Cyrenaica. See Kindler (1975) 146, Kammerer (1929) 300, and Geva (1984) 240, 246f., 249, and 253.

Neocaesarea (Dibsi Faraj): The village on the Euphrates was renamed by Diocletian, with a new, central building both for administration and, "assuming a military presence, as the *principia*," cf. Harper (1977) 457 and 459.

Nicopolis: In a village near this town on the Syria/Cilician border, there were resident soldiers in the early fourth century. See Lietzmann (1908) 83 and 86.

Nisibis: Amm. 20.6.9 (360) reports that the city was serving as residence to most of the campaign force of the year.

Palmyra: There was a garrison of Roman troops in the city from Flavian times. Aurelian later stationed an Illyrian unit there, cf. Rey-Coquais (1978) 68 and 70. By 303, Diocletian had completed a permanent camp in a corner of the city, adequate for several thousands of troops. See Gawlikowski (1984) 10 and 63f.

Petra: After the Roman conquest, there were vexillations stationed there, as at Philadelphia, cf. Isaac (1984) 186.

Raphaneae: The VI Ferrata was stationed there in the early empire. Jos., B. J. 7.18, reports the regular presence of the XII Fulminata there in the 60s, replaced by III Gallica in A.D. 69 or 70 until Elagabalus. See Mann and Jarrett (1967) 63, Hellenkemper (1977) 468, and Rey-Coquais (1978) 67.

Samosata: Under Trajan, or from at least A.D. 118, for a duration unknown, the city served as garrison point to a legion. There was no physical division between it and the rest of the city. See Rey-Coquais (1978) 67 and Hellenkemper (1977) 464 and 468.

Satala: A legion was stationed here from A.D. 70 into the fifth century, cf. Hellenkemper (1977) 468 and Mitford (1974) 168.

Scythopolis: Legions wintered here in 67/8 (Jos., B. J.).

Sepphoris: A source of about A.D. 400 describes how, when a fire broke out in the city, "the soldiers of the camp of Sepphoris came down to put it out"; and other incidents show them circulating routinely in the city, cf. Neusner (1983) xi and 175.

Singara: When first raised in A.D. 197, or a little later, the III Parthica was stationed in the city, and Ammianus 20.6.8 reports two legions there in 360. See RE s.v. Legio 1435.

Tyre: Septimius Severus posted III Gallica here, see Ciotti (1948) 116.

Zeugma: There were various legions here, apparently permanently with wintering troops also, from A.D. 18 on, not separated from the civilian population by any physical barrier. See Hellenkemper (1977) 464 n. 14 and 468, Rey-Coquais (1978) 67, and RE s. v. Legio 1560.

Asia Minor:

A number of statements applying to whole regions and from the late empire attest to the presence of troops in cities everywhere. Zos. 5.15.2 says as much, in the context of A.D. 399; likewise Soc., H. E. 66 (PG 67.677C), "Roman forces for the most part were stationed in the cities"; and Constantius in 361 is described as putting together his campaign force for use against Julian from the eastern provinces, from "the army scattered among the cities of the East" (in the *Artemii Passio*, p. 73 of Philostorgius' *Ecclesiastical History*, ed. Bidez-Winkelmann). There is indirect indication of the same situation in Zosimus' saying (5.15.2) that Tribigild assailed the cities of Lydia, Pisidia, and Asia, killing their population and soldiers (i.e., there were garrisons in them generally); and Amm. 14.2.5 speaks of "soldiers throughout most of the townships" in the regions lying around Isauria, i.e., Lycia and Pisidia. Finally, Zos. 5.13.2 speaks of Tribigild being "set over the barbarian units stationed in Phrygia," surely meaning in the cities there (A.D. 399).

Ancyra: *IGR* 3.173, lines 29f. describes Trajan's army wintering in the city in 114/5. Ramsay (1928) 181f. shows a cohort here under Trajan.

Chalcedon: Zos. 1.34.3 places a large *phylake* in the city under Gallienus.

Ephesus: There were *stationarii* from the VII praetorian cohort in the city at an uncertain date (second century?), *ILS* 2051f., and cavalry stationed there in 223/4. See T. Drew-Bear (1984) 62.

Eumeneia: Ramsay (1929) 156–58 shows third-century units stationed here.

Iconium: Ramsay (1928) 183f. places cavalry here in the first century.

Nacoleia: In 399 Tribigild stationed his barbarian troops in the city, see Philostorgius, *H. E.* 11.8.

Nicaea: Florentius was garrison commander, *phrourarchos*, in 365, see Philostorgius, *H. E.* 9.5 p. 117f. Bidez-Winkelmann.

Nicomedia: There were probably field-army units here in the fourth century, see Grosse (1920) 89.

Seleuceia: In Rough Cilicia, this city lodged three legions in 354, see Amm. 14.2.14.

Smyrna: A *stationarius* of the VII praetorian cohort was posted to the city in A.D. 212, see Petzl (1982) 164f.

Tarsus: There was a legion here in 373/4, cf. Amm. 30.1.4 and 7.

Trapezus: According to Tac., *Hist.* 3.47.5, there was a cohort stationed in the city in 69; vexillations of two legions built a shrine in the second half of the second century there, at the end of the century an entire legion moved in (Mitford [1974] 163 and 168), and (Zos. 1.33.1) in the 250s the city had "its customary soldiers" plus an extra ten thousand. The I Pontica was there from Diocletian on to the time of its record in the *Not. Dig.*, i.e., earlier fifth century, cf. *RE* s.v. Legio 1437.

Thrace:

In the later empire, a number of statements indicate the wide scattering of troops in cities. Zos. 2.21.2 of 322 speaks of an unnamed city, possibly in Moesia, "having a sizeable garrison," and Amm. 14.11.13 in 354 has "the soldiers on duty in roadside cities," e. g., the Theban legions (14.11.15) "wintering in the cities nearby" to Uscadama near Mt. Haemus. In about 379 (Zos. 4.26.1, 6, and 9), a massacre of Goths stationed in the cities was carried out by troops evidently placed there normally; and in the 440s throughout Thrace are "military units on duty in the cities and villages," cf. Theodoret., *Ep.* 2.

Beroea: "fixed garrisons at Beroea and Nicopolis," Amm. 31.11.2 (378).

Constantinople: In 399 the army assembled and sent out from the capital is "longing for the shade of city life, always at the public shows, eager to shine at the public baths," etc. — clichés describing a demoralized force, but enough to show that its members had been city-based. Cf. Claudian, *In Eutrop.* 2.409f. At the same date, Soc., *H.E.* (*PG* 67.677C), attests to a garrison in the city.

Marcianopolis: There was "a large force" posted here in 377 (Amm. 31.5.5).

Moesia:

When Zos. 4.10.4 describes Valens sending supply ships from the Black Sea up the Danube "to the cities situated on the river, so supplies might be handy to the troops," clearly the troops are in the cities, though able only to defend them carelessly against barbarians in 373 (4.16.5). The same source (4.20.6) mentions "the soldiers assigned to the defense of the cities along the Danube." Archeological evidence attesting to the intimate siting of *castra* and *canabae* is surveyed by Dorutiu-Boila (1972) 141f.

Nicopolis: "fixed garrisons at Beroea and Nicopolis," Amm. 31.11.2 (378).

Novae (Stuklen): The city held the legion I Italica from 69 for three centuries, set in the western sector of the city, and soldier and civilian were enfolded in a single wall at an unknown point in the third century. See Chichikova (1983) 11 and 15.

Noviodunum: Under the Tetrarchy the city received both a wall and two resident legions, I Iovia and II Herculea. See G. Stefan (1955) 162f., A.-S. Stefan (1974) 101f., and Aricescu (1980) 57f.

Oescus: From A.D. 71 the city was the home of the legion V Macedonica until 102, and then from the 270s it was the legion's permanent residence again, along the east of the city. See Aricescu (1980) 11 and Poulter (1983) 77.

Ratiaria: After 275 the legion XIII Gen. was established at Ratiaria, see Giorgetti (1983) 30.

Sirmium: Certainly a residence to troops when Galerius used the city as his capital, Tetrarchic barracks have been recognized in the excavations, see Grosse (1920) 89, Demougeot (1969–79) 2.69, and Tomlin (1976) 189. Ammianus records their presence there in 361, specifying an archer cohort and two legions (21.11.2, 21.9.5, and 21.10.1).

Tomis: Under Vespasian there were troops in the city, and various units are attested later, into the second half of the second century. See Aricescu (1980) 12, 30, 38, 42, and 47 (Tomis a *municipium* under Marcus Aurelius). Zos. 4.40.1 mentions "soldiers stationed there," in Tomis.

Troesmis: From 107 to 167, the V Macedonica resided in a fort at the site, flanked by two civil settlements which together became a *municipium* when the legion left. Under Diocletian, another legion, I Iovia, was stationed there. See G. Stefan (1955) 162, Aricescu (1980) 11, 41, and 47, and Dorutiu-Boila (1972) 136f.

For summary of the impressions to be drawn from this catalogue, see above, chapter 3, pages 145f.

NOTES

Abbreviations for primary sources are standard, explained (for example) in the *Oxford Classical Dictionary* or A. H. M. Jones (1964) 1462–76.

CHAPTER 1

1. On decline from some date in the 2d cent. B.C., see Haüssler (1964) 319f.; Sen., *Ep.* 86.6, 89.19–23, 95.13–36 passim; and 114.9–13; Decker (1913) 22f.; and Mazzarino (1966) 26f. On the turn dated in Augustan times, see Sen., *Controversiae* 1.2.20 (Pompeius Silo and Arellius Fuscus); 2.5.7 (Papirius Fabianus, under Tiberius); and 10.4.18; *FIRA*² 1. p. 290 lines 44f. of A.D. 56 (despair for Rome detected in recent times); Dio Chrys., *Or.* 31.75; Dio Cassius 71.36.4 ("iron" times after Marcus); and, for the 3d cent. sources, MacMullen (1976) chap. I and notes. In the opening 4th cent., see Arnob., *Adv. nat.* 1.1–3 and 4.24; in 386, Ambros., *Expositio evang. sec. Luc.*10.10 (*PL.* 15.1806f.).
2. Tac., *Dial.* 1.1, cf. Plin., *Ep.* 8.12.1, *litterarum iam senescentium.*
3. Walbank (1969) 100; Kornemann (1970) 221: "the last and greatest problem to be sketched is the decline of culture in the ancient world," "a sudden collapse" after Tacitus and the architect Apollodorus of Damascus. There are, of course, matching opinions on the Greek side, offered e.g. by Turner (1968) 84, that "the collapse of the gymnasia (the focal point of Hellenism) ... more than any other single event brought in the Middle Ages."
4. I am hardly competent to touch this subject, and do so very lightly, only noticing the preferred canon at the end of antiquity in Latin — see Ogilvie (1979) 109f. — and in Greek, Eunap., Vit. *soph.* 454, giving a glimpse of the books on his shelves, not very different from ours; further, Norman (1964) 161–63 and Pack (1965), showing, from the ten favorites, texts of Homer (604), Demosthenes (80), Euripides (76), Hesiod (48), Plato (40), Pindar (33), Thucydides (33), Menander (27), Sophocles (19), and Aristophanes (18); thereafter, a welter of the less-valued. "It is generally assumed that the later losses [in Latin literature post-Hadrian] are of second- or third-raters only. That is the recurring theme from Teufel-Schwab's vast register of names to recent treatments" — so, Baldwin (1982) 67.
5. In a few years we should have successful studies on literacy in the Roman world from W. V. Harris (early empire) and E. A. Meyer (late).
6. MacMullen (1982) 243f.
7. Price (1984) 60 speaks of "a black hole of several decades between, say, 260 and 290" in Greek inscriptions, and Jalabert (1909) 719 notes some hundreds of texts from north-central Syria spread over A.D. 90–609, except for an almost complete gap in A.D. 250–324.
8. MacMullen (1986) 237f., adding, on epigraphy in Syria, Liebeschuetz (1977) 487–96. For a similar regional peculiarity in (mostly) funerary epigraphy, and a warning against too free generalization, notice the Norican inscriptions evaluated by Saller and Shaw (1984) 126 n. 10.

9. Conventionally, Julianus and Papinian are picked out as the great figures, the one dying ca. 170, the other, ca. 212. On what he calls the "watershed" marking the end of the Principate as it is seen in legal history, under Caracalla, see Bauman (1980) 178, who (p. 137) takes the Gregorian and Hermogenian Codes as terminating development over very broad areas.

10. Berenson (1954).

11. Laum (1914) 1.8f., with the high point (p. 10) under Hadrian.

12. Duncan-Jones (1965) 246–56: 88 foundations to which he assigns some date. He finds their "cessation of munificence in Italy . . . at the end of the second century A.D." (p. 232).

13. Hopkins (1980) 115; the same error in Ste. Croix (1981) 470, seeing "from the Antonine age into the Severan age . . . a marked fall in expenditure by 'public-spirited' (or ambitious and self-advertising) men on civic buildings and on 'foundations.' . . . The decline in the number of the latter is evident to the eye from the diagrams in Bernhard Laum, *Stiftungen*"; likewise Finley (1980) 183, detecting "no recovery from the widespread destruction of cities in the [Danube provinces of] the third century," and quoting A. Mocsy — who does indeed speak of this, because "the collapse of municipal life is shown by the complete cessation of the setting up of inscriptions by magistrates and the general disappearance of inscriptions" (*RE* Suppl. 9 s.v. Pannonia col. 697); and, most recently, Ward-Perkins (1984) 14, relying on Duncan-Jones's figures to prove "a general decline in the amount of new building and repair" in Italy from the start of the 3d cent.

14. Mrozek (1984) 234–40 passim, using 173 texts for building, 284 for distributions (most texts datable only within a century).

15. Rostovtzeff (1960) 262–63, the good times end with Commodus (the view here of date 1928, summing up those in his *Social and Economic History of the Roman Empire* [1926]); Rémondon (1964) 71; Vogt (1967) 19–25; Wells (1984) 239f.; and proofs of the consensus could be easily multiplied beyond France, Germany, and Canada.

16. Hopkins (1980) 106, with the conclusion quoted in the text. Compare the same data differently presented in Cornell and Matthews (1982) 93, as the lighter bars in my composite graph, fig. 7. Cf. also Parker and Painter (1979) 69f., reporting on 660 shipwrecks datable before A.D. 1500; and (the reference thanks to the kindness of T. Cornell) Parker (1980) 50: in 300–150 B.C. wrecks number 68; in 150–1 B.C. they number 130; in A.D. 1–150, 142; and in 150–300, 67. The author adds interpretive remarks on which I draw in my text.

17. Cornell and Matthews (1982) loc. cit.

18. Panella (1981) 55, map on pp. 56–57, discussion exactly suiting the bars of fig. 6 on pp. 63, 74, and 78. Further bibliography of prodigious bulk could easily be added on amphorae and their implications for trade in the western seas and provinces.

19. Gianfrotta (1981) 235–41, dating helmets etc. and finding them most frequent in 150–50 B.C.; on shipwreck evidence at a port site facing Rhodes, interpreted as representative of "the history of the [entire] eastern Mediterranean," see pp. 203f. of D. Slane, "The History of the Anchorage at Sirce Liman, Turkey" (Ph.D. diss., Texas A & M University, 1981); and M. M. Cowin, "Artifacts discovered off the Southwestern Turkish Coast" (M.A. thesis, Texas A.&M., 1986), 90f. and 93, on wrecks and sunken objects at seventeen sites. I owe knowledge of these studies to the help and kindness of Prof. G. H. Bass of the Nautical Archaeological Program of that institution.

20. Riley (1981) 71, the high of A.D. 50–100 being, however, only 6.4 percent of datable sherds.

21. Redrawn from Panella (1973) fig. A p. 351, and discussion pp. 343–53. The study is based on excavations in the so-called Terme del Nuotatore, the yield of which can be tested in Carandini et al. (1973) 658–96 passim, with rich documentation earlier, e.g. 564, on oil trade from Tripolitania. On the results gained from these studies, notice the reservations expressed by Rickman (1981) 217.

22. Redrawn from Carandini and Settis (1979) pl. 39.
23. Rodriguez-Almeida (1979) 882; idem (1984), esp. 212–22, attributing to Septimius Severus the taking over of oil transport, not oil production.
24. T. Frank (1940) 300 and 304.
25. Blazquez (1964) 40.
26. Rickman (1981) 216 speaks of "the left-wing emphasis" in the excavators' interpretation of the Ostian amphorae; Ste. Croix (1981) 659 speaks of David "Magie's conventional right-wing views and inability to think deeply about his material." It is not easy to please everybody.
27. Harris (1980) 143.
28. Potter (1982) 27 on the Ager Faliscus (table) and characterization of "other surveys in Italy showing more or less the same evolution"; Potter (1975) 219 (table) and 220 (Veii, Gabii, Ager Eretanus); Dyson (1978) 251f. and 260; and Carandini and Tatton-Brown (1980) 11. Compare the firmness of conclusion about these admittedly few and limited areas with the fuzzy and really quite unsatisfactory substantiation in Rostovtzeff (1957) chap. VI or Sirago (1958) 15 — even though their picture in rough outline agrees with the more modern.
29. Wightman (1981) 284 on an area stretching out 10 km east from Interamna. She draws attention (286) to the individual "rhythm for development" of different regions.
30. Meiggs (1960) 84 relies on shaky reasoning from inscriptions but offers better from signs of construction (85 and 88f.).
31. Buchi (1973) 628; Ward-Perkins (1981) 179 and 184; Matijasic (1982) 64; Travagli Visser (1978) 46, the villa near Ferrara; and Baldacci (1967–68) 47.
32. On southern Etruria, see Potter (1975) passim, Potter (1979) 140 and 142, and Dyson (1978) 263; on San Giovanni di Ruoti, see Roberto and Small (1983) 187 and 190. For Puteoli's "rinascita tardoromana," estimated from mentions or remains of public building, see Camodeca (1980–81) 62, 85, and 88f.
33. On Constantine's rebuilding of an aqueduct *longa incuria et vetustate corruptum*, to serve half the cities of the Bay of Naples, see Sagi (1951) 89 = *Arch. ert.* 1939 no. 151. On Calabria etc. in the geographer of the mid-4th cent., see de Robertis (1948) 8 n. 1 and 12. Ward-Perkins (1984) 33, in discussing inscriptions of these regions (Campania, but also sites in the north), points out that the transferring of statues from "obscure" to central locations in the late 4th/early 5th cent. indicates disuse of pagan shrines, sometimes. I would say, generally (and so I would not use these inscriptions to infer whole cities shrinking). As to Sicily, see de Robertis (1948) 24 and Cracco Ruggini (1982–83) 499–503.
34. Meiggs (1960) 92 and 94.
35. Whitehouse (1981) 194 on the churches, noting also the repeated restorations of the Colosseum between A.D. 410 and 455; and Krautheimer (1983) 15–28.
36. On the gigantic incomes of the Anicii and other such families still in the early fifth century, indicated by the often cited frg. 44 of Olympiodorus (Blockley frg. 41.2), see Callu (1978) 312–14, who compares the great fortunes of Neronian time (p. 315). On agriculture, see De Robertis (1948) 56f., quoting a number of good passages. On Palladius, to be dated to the later 4th or more probably 5th century, see Martin (1976) xvi (date) and xxx ("nothing seems to have changed from the period of the Republic and early Empire"). Reference to the reclaiming of abandoned olive groves cuts both ways, despite White (1970) 31, who sees "agrarian recession in some areas ... from the second century"; and (ibid.) the use of an abandoned column drum as a ruler really proves nothing.
37. Cracco Ruggini (1961) 13 and 29; Vasey (1982) 94–103, comparing the *De Nabuthe* with Basil's *De Helia*, etc.
38. Ambros., *Ep.* 1.39.3 (*PL* 16.1099) of A.D. 388. On the villas of Aemilia, see Cracco Ruggini (1961) 65 and 531f. and Cracco Ruggini (1963) 35 n. 57; but the dating and meaning of the material are unclear; further, Bollini (1976) 305 on Cispadana's poorer tombs and

houses. I notice incidentally that A. H. M. Jones (1964) in his fold-out maps, Vogt (1967) 330, and Cornell and Matthews (1982) 173, place Aemilia to the north, Liguria to the south of the Po, while Rémondon (1964) 328, Stein (1959) , and Cracco Ruggini (1964) 272f. and (1963) 33 invert those provinces. Both views are in error. See Thomsen (1947) 235 and 237f., who shows that Aemilia remained Regio VIII (i.e., Cispadana) and that late Liguria embraced both Regio IX and XI (i.e., they were western Cisalpina). To Thomsen's refs. p. 237, add Iordan., *Getica* 19 p. 50 on Milan in Liguria and Zos. 5.26 (Ticinum in Liguria) and 5.37.3 (on Ravenna, Bononia in Aemilia, and Genua).

39. Hier., *Ep.* 1.3, Vercelli *olim potens, nunc raro est habitatore semiruta.* I discount Rufin., *Apol.* 2.39 (*PL* 21.617D), mentioning the reuse of architectural elements and stones in late-4th-cent. Aquileia; for naturally there were always buildings dying as others were being born. For new building, notice *CIL* 5.7250 = *ILS* 5701 (Susa, *thermae Gratianae dudum coeptae et omissae*, now completed); 3332 = *ILS* 5363, repairs in Verona in 379/83, *hortante beatitudine temporum*; and on Milan, showing the vast new *horreum* of Diocletian's reign, *Arch. Anz.* 1968, 566f.; further, Krautheimer (1965) 55f. and Krautheimer (1983) chap. 3. For a general estimate, see Cracco Ruggini (1964) 265 noticing abundant coinage from foreign provinces; also Cracco Ruggini (1961) 83 on Torino's prosperity, and Cracco Ruggini (1987) 283, on the prosperity of Vicenza = Vicetia in the 4th/5th centuries.

40. Mazzarino (1951) 252f.; Cracco Ruggini (1963) 28f., with n. 39 and 33f.

41. Rostovtzeff (1957) 195 and 201f.

42. MacMullen (1987) 371–75.

43. An example in Sulp. Severus, *Vita B. Martini* 8, *e familia servulus* in an estate near Tours; MacMullen (1987) 366, 370, and passim.

44. "The earliest textiles in a pattern-weave more complicated than diamond twill can be assigned to the third century A.D., when weavers in the Near East began a series of experiments with new weaves on new looms." See Wild (1970) 50.

45. Chastagnol (1981) 378 and Kiechle (1969) 119f. and 123–29.

46. Cracco Ruggini (1980) 59: "Il progresso tecnologico dunque . . . fu totalmente inorganico alla produttività." Further, with much bibliography, the whole essay and pp. 60–64 on farming improvements.

47. A. S. Stefan (1977) 456f.: essentially no excavation as of 1976, except enough to show walls postdating certain reused inscribed stones of the early 3d cent.

48. Chichikova (1983) 2.15f. To gain a sense of how far exploration has yet to go, consult the other papers in the volumes to which this author contributes or, less recently, the survey by Hoddinott (1975).

49. Majewski (1963) 506, help from the First Legion Italica which remained, however, at that location from the 1st cent. until its mention in the *Notitia Dignitatum* (cf. *RE*).

50. Alleging prosperity, Velkov (1962) 38f. But mere mention of *emporiae* serving commerce between Romans and Transdanubians does not make that commerce "une intense activité marchande," nor does mere mention of slave-owning in *CT* 11.53.1 (read: *CJ* 11.53.1.2) constitute "l'amélioration des conditions matérielles"; any more than mere mention of children watching flocks indicates "l'élevage tres développé" (51 n. 118). Other materials in support of "une période d'essor économique" pre-384 (p. 50) seem equally dubious; but no doubt the hard times thereafter and the arming of the countryside (p. 53) are quite credible.

51. MacMullen (1976a) 30, adding the palace at Serdica, Athanas., *Hist. Arian.* 15 (*PG* 25.709D), and Croke (1981) 476–80, on Thessalonica. Sirmium had profited from Probus' promotion of viticulture in its territory, Eutrop., *Brev.* 9.17.2, Aurelius Victor., *Caes.* 40.7, and Euseb., *Chron.* ed. R. Helm p. 224. Ammianus (29.6.11) mentions building there; there is "a large *horreum*, part of a palace-like building," as Mocsy (1974) 312 reports; and Popovic (1971) 129 places "the most important buildings" of many sorts in the reigns of

Licinius up to Constantius II. For "a small palace or large urban villa" replacing smaller structures, and probably meant for a government grandee, see Parovic-Pesikan (1971) 15 and 43f. On the cessation of coinage in Sirmium, see Mocsy (1971) 351, adding that elsewhere in the province coinage ceases to circulate about A.D. 375. Bavant (1984) 261 detects the clear signs of decline (abandonment of land, deterioration) from the late 4th. cent. in Sirmium.

52. Zaninovic (1977) 794: general decline of villas in the 4th cent. On the transformation of Gamzigrad from a purely military enclosure, through admission of civilians, to a fortified town, near the end of the 4th cent., "illustrative of a general movement" in the Danube provinces, see Bavant (1984) 271.

53. My count from Thomas (1964) 14–354 passim.

54. Aurelius Victor., *Caes.* 40.10; Mocsy (1974) 272, 299f., and 319f.; Biro (1974) 33, 43f., 49, and 52f.; Sagi (1951) 87; and Lengyel and Radan (1980) 114, 116f. (Hunnish artifacts), 156, and 315f.

55. Amm. 30.5.14 (A.D. 374), Savaria *invalidam ... adsiduis malis afflictam*; 30.5.2, Carnuntum *desertum ... et squalens*, cf. Kandler (1978) 84 and 95 on the general decline of the Save-Drave area, in terms of stone sculpture, fine pottery, bronze work, etc.; Mocsy (1974) 311; Kadar (1969) 184 on mosaics at Savaria; Lengyel and Radan (1980) 116, 250, and 261; Kiss (297–301); Fitz (1976) 105, estimating Gorsium's greatest size in 350, and on the downswing from 375; and Soproni (1978) 197. For Sopianae, see Fülep (1985) 274f., 277–79, and 283 (heavy destruction in the 390s or early 400s — Alaric?).

56. See Fellman (1955) 209–12, describing the response to the 3d-cent. invasions; Böttger (1975) 183f.; Alföldy (1974) 183 and 186; on "an over-all decline in stone-carving from the end of the second century onward," see p. 177, the decline ascribed to "economic factors," along with declining trade and pottery production from A.D. 250. There was (pp. 198 and 206) a long and partially successful effort by Diocletian and Constantine to set Noricum on its feet. In Raetia, mosaics post-233 are rare: only in Aventicum and Augusta Raurica, and there only up to A.D. 275. See von Gonzenbach (1965) 251. But Augusta Vindelicum, to judge from imported pottery (Argonne-ware, north African) maintained commercial connections. See Gottlieb (1985) 17.

57. The basis of city-wall study was established by Blanchet (1907), and often improved on for individual regions or sites, e.g. by Van Gansbeke (1955) 406 on circuits built in the 250s (Cologne, Tabernae, Vindonissa) and later, under Postumus, in the northeast (in the Boulogne-Reims-Mainz area, pp. 410–25). Further, see Butler (1959) 26 on the circuits of the 250s and (28–37) many later ones, and the inferences of very serious destruction to be drawn (44); also Petrikovits (1971) 189f., esp. on fortifications of the 270s (Orléans, Amiens, Bordeaux, etc.). Blanchet notes (278f.) the amphitheaters, temples, theaters, etc., excluded by wall-building, and the sculpture used as building-material (322).

58. The problem was first opened up in regard to Paris, I think, by Roblin (1951) 309–11. For a general estimate, see Griffe (1965) 8 and n. 8, instancing Clermont and other sites.

59. Février (1980) 410 on certain archeological anomalies, instancing Vaison's destruction in the 3d cent., but also destruction at the site both earlier and later. He regrets that "on n'a jamais tenté une enquête globale [on that 3d cent. destruction], et surtout l'analyse critique des preuves n'a jamais été réalisé." I suggested the topic to a student a decade ago who, however, abandoned it.

60. On Trier, very well known, see, e.g., Kahler (1963) 202, briefly, and Wightman (1971) 98–123 and passim. On Arles, see Constans (1921) 99f. and 176, where Constantine and Constantius II sojourn in the city, with subsequent good effects for it, and Constans (1928) 33f. and 54, listing the many 4th-cent. government buildings and activities in Arles. Notice the *Expositio totius mundi* 58, quoted in my text. Date: in the 350s, see its editor Rougé (1966) 15 and 312f.

61. Pietri (1983) 345-47, adding, p. 367, the effect of ecclesiastical construction.
62. Auson., *Ordo urbium nobil.* 18.2, *quae modo quadruplices ex se cum effudent urbes, non ulla exhaustae sentit dispendia plebis*; Lantier (1953) 329; Février (1964) 46; and Labrousse (1978) 43f.
63. On Autun, see *Paneg. vet.* 4(8).21.2 (A.D. 297); 7(6).22.4 (A.D. 310); and 8(5).1.1f. (A.D. 312), all thanks to Constantius I. On Amiens, see Bayard and Massy (1982) 23 and 25, noting the town's benefiting from the building of a castrum in (?) 278 and the installation of a garrison in 300/310, and compare Février et al. (1980) 112, Gap a late Roman *castrum*, and Grenoble and Sisteron. Julian, *Ep.* 8.414C, mentions recent restoration at Vesontio; Ausonius, *Mosella* 2, tells of *nova moenia* at Vincum.
64. Amm. 15.11.12 and 16.2.1.
65. Février et al. (1980) 416, wondering if Lyon declined because of the war of Albinus with Septimius Severus or because of changing trade patterns; and, though Ammianus knows of Lyon, Ausonius and the *Expositio totius mundi* do not, as Cracco Ruggini (1978) 82 points out. For the condition of Lyon's territory, see Walker (1981) 309f. and 312ff., the number of known sites, however, being small in any period (a few dozen) and the evidence for their history being extremely thin (ordinarily only a few coins, to supply a terminus *non-ante-quem*). It is really of no help to explain the thinning-out of occupation by "inflation, insecurity, changes in the economy and social order, etc." (p. 323). Among other shriveled cities, Besançon should be named, along with Narbo, Vienne, Aix, Nîmes, Metz. The total of centers of more than five thousand in population would still number over eighty in A.D. 400 (Février et al. [1980] 101, *rus* being defined to commence from villages of less than that size and to include some 90 percent of all Gaul's population, p. 310).
66. Amm. 27.6.7 and *PLRE* I s. v. Florentius 5.
67. Chadwick (1965) 249 and 253f.; Sanquer (1974) 22 and 26; Galliou (1980) 237f., 240–46, 250–56, and 262–64; Provost (1982) 397; Galliou (1982) 97f., 100, and 104; and Galliou (1985) 107–15.
68. Wightman (1978) 242f.: rural cemeteries become few and, in Belgica, only 22 of 327 villa sites are still occupied; pp. 244–46, clustering of population in few, larger new sites, by a very gradual process, as villages (?) of free landholders or (?) tenants or both, often near active villas; Wightman (1978a) 126 note 118; Wightman (1985) 200, noting the 3d-cent. "cessation of [rural] monuments, including votive sculptures and reliefs"; Agache (1975) 702–08 on Picardy and Artois, where scattered farmsteads give way to rural clusters usually set atop an abandoned villa or shrine, in A.D. 250–300; and Agache (1978) 153–55, extending the preceding account also to Normandy and adding (p. 156) that many of the small settlements were probably the work of *laeti*. To adverse political changes, at least in Picardy, Provost (1982) 394 adds soil exhaustion from overcropping and sheepherding. So the forests spread.
69. MacMullen (1976a) 30 note 29, with refs. on Konz; Faider-Feytmans and Hubaux (1950) 254 on a brand of pottery; big villas described in Grenier (1906) 118–20, late-3d-cent. destruction followed (pp. 179–81) by brilliant recovery; Grenier (1934) 2. 864; and Percival (1976) 82. But the sharp dropping-off of Trier-minted bronze coins in Britain after A.D. 356 suggests that "Trier declines economically long before its political eclipse." See Fulford (1977) 68, comparing the coin export of Arles or Lyon.
70. Böttger (1975) 183–85.
71. Gilles (1974) 111 and 119–21.
72. Wightman (1978) 246, referring also to inland Gallic refuges and *ILS* 1279 of the Basses Alpes. Compare the reoccupation of caves in various inland southern areas, e.g., the lower Rhone valley: Gagnière and Granier (1963) 225–39. For Raetia, see Petrikovits (1971) 192, the Wittnauer Horn, Moosberg, and Auf Krüppel; Fellmann (1955) 210, 3d-

cent. sites, and 211, Constantinian; Paunier (1978) 295–306, late-3d-cent. to early-5th-cent. occupation of a hilltop overlooking the south end of Lake Leman; and further references in MacMullen (1963) 147 note 99.

73. Cracco Ruggini (1961) 34f. n. 62, near Augusta Bagiennorum, Albintimilium, and Libarna; and Mikulcic (1974) 193, for Macedonia.

74. See below, p. 72; and here, the conclusions, in MacMullen (1963) 150.

75. Bagaudae: see MacMullen (1987) 370 and, from much recent discussion, Van Dam (1985) chap. I. It is not known what parts of Gaul the Bagaudae afflicted.

76. For *burgi* along highways of northern Gaul, Germany, and Raetia, see Petrikovits (1971) 188 and 197.

77. See, compared to Grenier's knowledge, what is available in Agache and Agache (1978) 152 and Leday (1980) 44; compare Taylor (1975) 113, noting that "in 16 years, 300 new settlements have been found in this relatively small area" of the Nene valley, and, from 1931, 16 sites have grown to 434. For the sheer bulk of data, notice also Petrikovits (1956) 100, finding even a generation ago 9 to 10 population centers in a mere 9 km² of the Nordeifel, or Paret (1932) 3.27, estimating over 800 villas in Württemberg.

78. Galliou, Fulford, and Clement (1980) 267, 272, and 274.

79. Grenier (1934) 2.935f. offers some useful but very brief generalization. Compare the map in Percival (1976) 68, where about half of the 143 sites he deals with are far south (on a line between Bordeaux and Narbonne) or north (Lorraine and adjoining). The discussion pp. 70–82 is nevertheless the best I have seen. I add a pair of recent excavation reports as typical: Aragon-Launet (1974) 356, on a villa at Montreal east of Toulouse reborn after destruction in ca. 275, its acme in the second quarter of the 4th cent.; further, Editernach villa, in Metzler and Zimmer (1982) 38ff., in Treviran country and perhaps built by a Treviran chief in the first century (p. 47), destroyed in (?) A.D. 275 (p. 48) but rebuilt in the fourth century.

80. Provost (1982) 396f.; Percival (1976) 47 (Chiragan) and Delage (1952) 2f., 20, and 22–24 (dating from coins) on the "Villa d'Antone"; and at Berry, Leday (1972) 221 and Leday (1980) 67. Add the unexplained loss of population in a number of small oppida in the territory of Nîmes over the 2d and 3d centuries, in Fiches (1982) 117.

81. To the evidence gathered in MacMullen (1976) 303 n. 9, add Petrikovits (1956) 119–122, iron-smelting; Spitaels (1970) 225, many villas in the Sambre-Meuse area producing iron in surplus, i. e., for sale; Provost (1982) 397, general self-sufficiency in late villas of Auxerre (west central Gaul), Saône, and Picardy; Percival (1976) 48, autarky "the normal situation . . . over much of the Continent"; and Lengyel and Radan (1980) 278 on Pannonia.

82. Fontaine (1972) 572 refers to "le problème historique — longtemps simplifié, semble-t-il — du prétendu 'retour à la terre' de l'aristocratie romaine au Bas-Empire. En fait, il faut distinguer la survie, peut-être accentuée au profit des champs, d'une *alternance* fort ancienne entre la ville et campagne." And Wilson (1981) 174 says, to the same effect, "To surmise that landowners did not live on their estates until the fourth century is at present an *argumentum e silentio*." For the early great villas, see Metzler and Zimmer (1982) 38 on Editernach (1st cent.), Agache (1982) 5f., on an Augustan example 800 m in length, Grenier (1934) 2.889f. and McKay (1975) 166 on Chiragan, which peaked in Antonine times, and Lutz (1974) 20 on St. Ulrich villa, which had a Tiberian beginning and an acme in the 2d. cent. More generally, see Wightman (1985) 111–14, with other examples in notes 79f. above.

83. Plin., *Ep.* 7.25, Terentius being one of the *quasi rustici*, yet *eruditus*, to Pliny's surprise — perhaps a cut above Ausonius' kin, "a family circle who, but for him, would never have emerged from the dim crowd of provincial coteries," as Dill (1899) 169 puts it.

84. Frere (1967) 254 and 346f.; Frere (1964) 108–10 on Verulamium; Reece (1980) 78f., and

82f. (with some, to me, confusing discussion on the period after 410, pp. 84–87); and Arnold (1984) 33 and 54f., emphasizing with Reece the decline aspects of cityscapes and, p. 91, coin-evidence for diminished use of currency after A.D. 350. On mosaics, see Smith (1965) 95f.

85. Frere (1967) 346; and similarly Rivet (1975) 343 says, "The fourth century was the golden age of villas in Britain," with the best period extending from the 290s to ca. 370 and only a gradual decline thereafter; similarly, Percival (1976) 48f. and Todd (1978) 205, who, however, dates the acme of this villa development a little earlier, to the first half of the 4th cent. Neal (1978) 52 shows a half-dozen villas around Verulamium in decline perceptibly from 350 or later.

86. Amm. 28.3.7 and 9.

87. Todd (1978) 205f. and Barrett (1982) 124.

88. On autarky, see Percival (1976) 48 and Todd (1978) 203; on villas being built close to administrative centers, see Millett (1982) 423.

89. Contemporaries and the 5th-cent. historians dwell on the destruction and slaughter that ensued in 409–11. See Blazquez (1964) 51.

90. Blazquez (1964) 275 on sarcophagi; Blazquez (1983) 2.75 on mines; Gorges (1979) 56 n. 74 on the ca. 50 villas out of 140 surviving from the 4th to the 5th cent. not dead or radically shrivelled; and Farina Busto (1973–74) 125 on coins found.

91. Above, fig. 11 and note 24; Blazquez (1964) 164; Gorges (1979) 47 n. 57 and 49; and esp. Tovar and Blazquez (1975) 282.

92. Blazquez (1964) 78, 164f., and 172; Blazquez (1974–75) 253; Tarradel (1955–56) 109, on the likely effect of raids on vulnerable industries, mining and large-villa agriculture — although the latter should have weathered the storm better. Also Gorges (1979) 47: he finds in the Ebro valley that small and middle-sized villas suffered whereas the larger ones survived, and notes further (p. 45) that "from 260 to 280 not a single new villa saw the light of day anywhere in the peninsula." Finally, LeRoux (1982) 378f. and 391, rather minimizes the gravity of the invasions, and Blazquez (1982) 592 finds no perceptible decline in the Baetican economy as a result of them, nor throughout the 4th cent., in that region. However, in the rest of the peninsula he depicts a contracting internal commerce and agricultural decline, with concentration of land into the hands of a smaller class of owners (567, 580, and 594).

93. Rougé (1966) 486; Blazquez (1964) 49 on Avienus; Espinosa (1984) 197f.; and Blazquez (1974–75) 278 on the absence of amphorae.

94. Blazquez (1974–75) 117, 274, and 278 on garum; Blazquez (1964) 115 on statuary to Tarraco from Africa, and Blazquez (1974-75) 75f. on other imports from faraway places.

95. Above, note 92; Blazquez (1975) 77, 96, 125f.; Blazquez (1964) 47–49 and 104; Gorges (1979) 51 and 55; and Cracco Ruggini (1965) 432–40.

96. Gorges (1979) 34, 38–51, 51f. (autarky, e.g. smelting), and the placing of the acme under Constantine (p. 48). For Altafulla, see p. 52. In a random sample of a hundred villas in use after A.D. 300 (pp. 380–484), I find only forty after A.D. 350 (dating by coins, pottery, or otherwise). Further, see Blazquez (1964) 84, 96 (Arroniz), 99f. (storage-dolia, cf. Gorges p. 54); Blazquez (1975) 95 (Villajoyosa), 125f. (Casa de Hylas); Blazquez (1974-75) 255, 270f., and 274 (manufacture of garum on premises); Hauschild and Schlunk (1961) 175-78 on Centcelles; and Sagredo San Eustaquio (1979–80) 44f.

97. For villa autarky, see the preceding note. On Liedena, see Blazquez (1964) 97f. and Gorges (1979) 43, 53, and 323 (the barracks-wing variously interpreted as for laborers or private militia). On Emerita's villas, see Arce (1982) 216f.

98. Warmington (1954) 33 (inscriptions) and map 3, to be corrected in the light of Bénabou (1976) 239.; see map below, fig. 17. Sala was not abandoned but Volubilis was — see MacKendrick (1980) 312. On Rapidum, see Laporte (1983) 263–66; and on an area inland

from Iol = Caesarea of ca. 250 km^2, where some decline in density of population and activity can be seen in surface sherds by the 4th cent., see Leveau (1972) 17. The more up-to-date finds of Leveau (1984) 213f. indicate a prosperous city in the 4th cent.

99. Lepelley (1979–81) 1.87f. and 2.150 and 218 n. 4 notices some revival under Gallienus and generally good times for Thugga; and Salama (1951) 29, while somewhat out of date, sees vigor in rebuilding and repair over all the half-century before Diocletian; but in general it was not a time of upturn. See Warmington (1954) 29 and 33; Frend (1952) 67; Foucher (1964) 321; and Lepelley (1979–81) 1.83f.

100. For the surge in building and civic renovation under Diocletian, see Leschi (1950) 13 on paving in Djemila, improvement of drains and aqueduct, new residences in city and suburb, etc.; Warmington (1954) 33f. on proliferation of repairs on public buildings in several cities; Romanelli (1959) 506f.; Duval (1964) 92; Lepelley (1979–81) 1.70 and 2.430; Kolendo and Kotula (1977) 644f.; Février (1982) 356f.; and Thébert (1983) 102, inferring in the province of Africa generally a period of prior neglect and delapidation, from the "vigorous work of restoration" in Tetrarchic times. This introduces a fourth century of "dynamisme urbain" (103). There is a decline under Constantine: Warmington (1954) 33f. But Julian reverses it, Warmington (1954) 35 and 52, Lepelley (1979-81) 1.68 and 101, and Chastagnol (1978) 89; and Valentinian encourages notable prosperity. See Albertini (1943) 386; Lepelley (1979–81) 2.150 and 340 (though, 2.363f., Lepcis suffered from beduin raids then) and 403f.; Leschi (1953) 13; Courtois (1951) 70f. and 81; Warmington (1954) 37–40; Courtois (1955) 149f. (literary sources); Février (1964) 23 (mosaics) and 32; Duval (1964) 96–103 (churches); Kolendo and Kotula (1977) 645f.; Février (1970) 164f.; and Lepelley (1979–81) 1.26, 64 (Carthage, esp. churches), and 70–72 on tax laws and 102 n. 133 on *curiales'* obligations.

101. Beschaouch (1975) 110f. (and n. 30, mentioning Albertini's much earlier contentions); and Rebuffat (1980) 313, 317, 319, and 321 (likewise on Albertini). Goodchild (1966–67) 206–11 collects what was known of the quake in Cyrene and the eastern Mediterranean and islands; Kenrick (1985) 9–11 reports on the fate of Sabratha.

102. Foucher (1964) 318 and 320–24; Carandini (1970) 103, emphasizing the downturn; and Lepelley (1979–81) 2.263, emphasizing the upturn. On Carthaginian commerce and productivity, see Panella (1983) 56.

103. Courtois (1951) 72–75.

104. The best modern authority, Lepelley (1979–81) 1.72, acknowledges the loss of revenue to cities and the heavy taxes of the late period, but he notes the maintaining nevertheless of "une vie municipale traditionelle, certes moins brilliante et dispendieuse que sous le Haut-Empire, mais beaucoup plus active que ne l'avaient pensée les historiens modernes." For prosperity continuing after Gratian, notice Frend (1952) 62; Février (1970) 170; Kotula (1982) 129; Duval (1964) 96 and 100; and esp. Lepelley (1979–81) 1.26, 291, and 412.

105. Turner (1952) 81 and 85f., with a large public project as late as 283; Parsons (1976) 438f., hypothesizing that prosperity came and went in waves (p. 440) and instancing signs of prosperity at Hermopolis, Antinopolis, and Panopolis in the late 250s to 270s; and Lewis (1983) 39.

106. Lewis (1983) 164, at Philadelphia in A.D. 55–56, over fifty persons disappear leaving no property (they evidently live on the edge of survival, but are still subject to taxation) and, with the promise of tax amnesty, forty seven return the next autumn. Compare A. E. Hanson's correction of H. I Bell's ideas about a decline under Nero, presented in a paper to the Eighteenth International Congress of Papyrology (1986). For Theadelphia, see Bagnall (1982) 57, noting that heavy depopulation in A.D. 331/2 is taken as an example of 4th-cent. decline, wrongly; for the fugitives will return and the total will thus remain stable over a long period of, say, twenty five years (e.g. 312 to 336).

107. A. C. Johnson (1951) 131 concluded "that the Egyptian of the Byzantine period" (by which he evidently means Diocletian-Justinian) "experienced greater economic prosperity and social independence than in any other period of his history." The argument leading to this conclusion is not easily refuted.

108. So, Gregory (1979) 19, using calculations by A. H. M. Jones. See also Charanis (1967) 450, arguing very loosely; more carefully, Duncan-Jones (1980) 67 n. 3, accepting Diodorus' figure (17.52.6) of "over 300,000" in 60 B.C. He tells us he consulted "those persons who were in charge of the census records," and who in turn counted only *eleutheroi*. So I would add another 10 percent to the figure, at the very least, to account for slaves (on that addition, see some justification in MacMullen [1987] 364f.).

109. Kraeling (1938) 61f. and Patlagean (1977) 156, 196f., and 232.

110. Amm. 14.8.11, quoted by Sperber (1977) 441. On the reduction of the region to city-rule, see A. H. M. Jones (1931) 271–75 and A. H. M. Jones (1931a) 82–85. Sperber (1977) 414 and passim argues for a long, mid-3d-cent. decline in farming, on the basis of texts that seem to me puzzling and ambiguous. The same view may be found more briefly in Sperber (1972) 252f. and passim, which, in a little-changed form, Goodman (1980) 235 convincingly criticizes, adducing rich burials and synagogue construction of the period. Per contra, notice the decline in north Palestinian portrait busts left in burial caves, their acme dating to the mid-3d cent. and the series ending in the early 4th cent. See Skupinska-Løvset (1983) 358f., who takes the end of the series as a sign of economic decline. Further, Gutwein (1981) 95, noting decline or stagnation at Nessana in the Negev in the 3d cent., while (p. 108) Elusa was enjoying an upswing that lasted into the 6th cent. Nessana itself shares that improvement in fortunes, attributable to the late-4th-cent. stationing of troops there (p. 97, comparing what happened at Oboda: "the Imperial military presence bolstered the city's economy and provided a positive incentive for town expansion," cf. also p. 118). Subeita (p. 89) flourished then; and Sperber (1977) 439–41 himself sees a general improvement in 4th-cent. Palestine. Most recently, the Golan has been evaluated archeologically by Urman (1985) 181ff., who finds the area most densely inhabited and farmed throughout all of antiquity during the period from the earlier 2d to the mid-4th century. By archeological survey, Y. Hirschfeld (1985) 10 finds a "peak of prosperity" in late Roman and Byzantine times, in a small region south of Jerusalem.

111. Liebeschuetz (1979) 20 on village development cites Avi Yonah and S. A. M. Gichon for Palestinian frontier area, and Gutwein (1981) 122f. points to the rise of Mampsis to true city status due to troops being present, coins markedly increasing, and skillfully engineered dams "to accommodate increased agicultural productivity."

112. Dauphin (1980) 121–23 specifically notes religious tourism and imperial religious building as contributing factors; for mosaic data, ibid. 112f. For Aleppo and Jerusalem, see Patlagean (1977) 156 and 232.

113. *Expositio totius mundi* 28, with substantiation in other authors. See Rougé (1966) 248.

114. Liebeschuetz (1972) 99f.

115. Julian, *Or. 1 in Const. laud.* 40D; Amm. 31.1.2 on Valens's building of a new baths; *Expositio totius mundi* 32; Joh. Chrysos., *Comm. in Phil.* 10.3 (PG 62.260), among many passages from his homilies; and Liban., *Or.* 2.55 (A.D. 380/1), 48.38 (384/5), 50.2 and passim (385), and 33.14 (386), copious private construction, and *Or.* 59.155 (A.D. 348), which declares that "those who formerly seemed well off would appear to be rich in more straitened fashion than persons today enjoying only moderate ease, and those now of middling wealth spend more extravagantly than the very emperors earlier."

116. On Antioch's population and physical amenities as growing, see Lassus (1947) 265 and 303; Petit (1955) 311, 316, and 318; Liebeschuetz (1972) 96f., noting the expanding wall circuit; Ceran (1970) 201, basing his conclusions about the general eastern economic expansion (trade, crafts, farming) on his earlier examination of Antioch in particular; and

Gonzalez Blanco (1980) 117, drawing on Chrysostom to show a tremendous amount of construction going on not only in the city but in its surrounding territory as well. Duncan-Jones (1980) 67 n. 3 suggests, against all likelihood, that late Antioch's population had diminished, because Strabo in his day said it approached that of Alexandria, which Diodorus set at 300,000 (above, note 108), whereas Libanius in *his* day set it at 150,000 (in A.D. 363: *Ep.* 1119.4) and Chrysostom at 200,000. But the train of reasoning is faulty. Strabo speaks of *megethos*, "expanse," not numbers; compare Jos., *B. J.* 2.385, where *megethos* of Alexandria means expanse. At the other extreme, maximizing, Petit (1955) 310f. n. 10 supposes that the two later totals (150,000 and 200,000) include only adult males and that the grand total, with women, children, and slaves included, must amount to 500,000–800,000. Rejecting that reasoning, Liebeschuetz (1972) 96 takes Libanius' and Chrysostom's totals more or less at face value, as all-inclusive. Whatever the reality, for my purposes all that counts is that the population was manifestly on the rise.

117. Liebeschuetz (1972) 129 and 258.
118. Tchalenko (1953–58) passim, e.g. 1.142 and 295, on rising numbers of inscriptions; 313f., 376, 382–84, and 399, on the upgrading of mere peasant houses to more dignified size; praise and interpretation of Tchalenko's work in Petit (1955) 308, Liebeschuetz (1972) 72, and Dauphin (1980) 116; confirmation in the hagiography of Syria in early Byzantine times, in Brown (1971) 85 n. 57.
119. Petit (1955) 310 n. 2 and 313 n. 3 and Liebeschuetz (1972) 99. The clearest text is Theodoret., *Ep.* 42–43 (PG 83.1217D) on Cyrrhus in A.D. 445, where overtaxation is blamed for much abandoned land and impoverishment of *curiales*. Libanius (*Ep.* 1071) reported much earlier, in A.D. 388, that the town once great was now small.
120. Mansel (1959) 395f. and 402; Franke (1968) 15, Valerian builds a bridge; Weiss (1981) 344, on the vitality in civic ambitions of Pamphylia, increase in coinage, and "eine ganze Reihe von Indizien, die hier nicht genannt oder nur gestreift wurden"; Russell (1980) 36f.; and Seton Williams (1954) 145.
121. Seton Williams (1954) 145 and catalogue, 145–74; Dauphin (1980) 113, quoted, and 115f.; and Russell (1980) 37f., on the good times of Anemurium after the late 4th cent.
122. G. M. A. Hanfmann in a letter to me, summing up many years of excavation; Hanfmann and Mierse (1983) 146, "the general impression ... is that the city reached its peak prosperity in the third century, and its greatest area of extension ... in the fourth and fifth centuries"; Foss (1975) 11–13; Foss (1976) 47 and 52; and Foss (1977) 475f. As to Ephesus, see Foss (1977) 472; Foss and Magdalino (1977) 72; Foss (1979) 4, 6f., 21, 74, 78, 80, and 82; Bammer (1976–77) B. c. [sic] 121ff.; and Mansel (1965) 504.
123. Levick (1967) 102, on reconstruction of Antioch in the 4th cent.; Foss (1977) 471, 477–79 (Miletus) and 480 (Pergamon in decline while maintaining its intellectual leadership, and Smyrna apparently stable in its condition); Priene declines but Magnesia improves (480 and 483), to judge from archeological evidence. Conclusion: "In almost every instance the cities prospered in Late Antiquity," as is "especially true of provincial capitals" (p. 485). Further on Miletus, Mitchell (1984–85) 85, stagnation in 4th/5th centuries followed by active construction of churches but also of other edifices. On Nicomedia, see Lact., *De mort. persecut.* 7.8f., Diocletian's *infinita quaedam cupiditas aedificandi*; on Constantine's building, see the *Expositio totius mundi* in Rougé (1966a) 184 and 285f.; and Amm. 22.9.3f., very emphatic. Patlagean (1977) 182f. asserts a strong birthrate detectible in late Roman Asia Minor.
124. CT 10.19.2; cf. Röder (1969) 110, showing large output from the Dokimeion quarries north of Synnada from the later 4th cent. to the 6th.
125. H. Thompson (1959) 65f.; Gregory (1979) 20f.; and Spieser (1984) 320f., dating the change in the city's fortunes to the mid-4th cent.
126. See Gregory (1986) 21, comparing J. L. Davis in a paper delivered to the annual meeting

of the Archaeological Institute of America on Dec. 29, 1985, titled "The Nemea Valley Archaeological Project, 1985," in which he describes a small upturn in the periods "Late Roman" and "Late Roman/Early Byzantine"; also, J. Bintliff and A. Snodgrass reporting a rise to "intense occupation" in central Boeotia in the period A.D. 300–600, cf. Catling (1986) 41. I owe these references to the kindness of E. A. Meyer; and B. Ward Perkins kindly supplies further refs. to work by these two archeologists in Boeotia, to be found in the *Journal of Field Archaeology* 12 (1985) and in R. F. Jones, ed., *Europe to the First Millennium*. Further, Davis, Cherry, and Mantzourani (1980–83) 114f., on Keos: "Like many other surveyed regions in Greece, the late Roman period represents a peak of settlement density and . . . intensity of cultural activity in these times" (my thanks to S. Alcock for the ref.). Also, Keller and Rupp (1983) 262 and 280, to the same effect, in regard to Greece generally. Notice, last, Van Andel et al. (1986) 120: "Beginning in the 3d century after Christ a strong economic recovery took place in parts of Greece, including the Southern Argolid, a recovery which continued into the fifth and sixth centuries." Runnels and van Andel (1987) 319 confirm the finding in a fuller context.

127. Anon. Vales. 6.30 and Eunap., *Vit. soph.* 462 (Loeb trans.); cf. Hier., *Chron. a.* 334 (*PL* 27.678), *Constantinopolis dedicatur pene omnium urbium nuditate*; many other comments like Themist., *Or.* 4.69f. and 72, on continued expansion; and the fine survey by Dagron (1974) chap. XIII.

128. See above, notes 28 and 30 (Italy), 91 (Spain), 79 (Gaul), 65 (Lyon), and 101 (Hadrumetum). Notice also the desperate ups and downs of life in Egyptian villages (note 105). And there was continual deterioration of the stonework in cities, rather amusingly revealed in Dio Chrysostom's Thirty-first Oration (reuse of honorific statues). See further Mrozek's interpretation, at note 14 above. We have late edicts like *CT* 15.1.14 (365), which indicate robbing of architectural stonework for new structures, and those edicts have been taken to show 'decline.' But I think they may prove nothing.

129. Baynes (1943) 29.

130. For the pace of inflation, see MacMullen (1976) 259f. I quote my own words (ibid. 118) only because they have led to a little confusion. Whittaker (1980) 12, suppressing my parenthesis about "teachers," goes on to wonder if "professional" "means businessmen" (which it does not) and (p. 13 and n. 76) seems to consider the government itself among small creditors (!), while he also objects to "any general theory of a redistribution of wealth from rentiers," which I have not proposed (notice my reference to "magnates"). For more on inflation, see my pages 109–19, to which much more recent bibliography could be added. Most important is Corbier (1986), pointing out, among many mattters, how prices of essentials such as labor, basic foods, and basic services remained remarkably stable even if one counts in the last half of the 3d century — stable *in terms of gold* (pp. 491–96 and 507f.). Thus a foundation under the money economy survived the crisis; and the severity and significance of that crisis (p. 492) should not be exaggerated.

131. Mickwitz (1935) col. 131, drawing on his *Geld und Wirtschaft im römischen Reich* (1932); also, the findings embodied in A. H. M. Jones (1974) 197, there reprinted from their 1953 publication; and Gonzalez Blanco (1980) 192f. For adjustments to inflation (shorter-term loans, etc.), see MacMullen (1976) 118 and notes 60f., and Mrozek (1985) 322, asserting the reluctance to lend money in times of uncertain values, but "a rebirth of credit in the first half of the fourth century."

132. Petit (1955) 298f. and 301f.; A. H. M. Jones (1974) 197; Liebeschuetz (1972) 84–86; and Gonzalez Blanco (1980) 192 and 200–20.

133. Reece (1973) 231, quoted; p. 250, on the size of the sample; and p. 242, fig. 6, for the two peaks.

134. Cracco Ruggini (1964) 265 and Callu (1979) 21–31, where, in his catalogue of coins recovered in Apamea, those of the 4th cent. by my count come mostly from Antioch (over 200); but, among the 100⁺ other coins, no less than nine other mints are represented

(Heraclea least, Alexandria most, plus Rome, Siscia, Ticinum, Nicomedia, Cyzicus, Thessalonica, and Cple).

135. See, on the Siscia mint, Lanyi (1969) 42f. and 45; Callu (1980); and Callu (1983) 64, on the disturbances to volume due to "grands travaux civils et militaires, ainsi des murs du Rhin et du Danube"; and Cracco Ruggini (1984) 33f. and n. 45, on Valentinian's *limes*-construction. As to AV-minting, see Callu (1983a) 172f., comparing bronze coinage in Callu (1980) 97f.; for a later period, Metcalf (1984) 122, not finding any rapid drawing back of gold into the mints after its issue as coinage.

136. Cracco Ruggini (1984) 19f., for one, or Callu (1980) 103, see the need to take into account the pay of the bureaucracy and the requirements of foreign and domestic trade; but we need still to consider construction and other forms of largess. For the quantification of currency, see Cracco Ruggini (1984) 20 n. 20, pointing out some older studies; but the historical possibilities in the method have been realized with real ambition only in the last twenty years or so. To learn more about a subject in which I am not competent, especially in the later empire, one could hardly begin better than with Cracco Ruggini (1984), which contains large bibliography — unless with the many recent works of Callu.

137. MacMullen (1984) 576f.

138. Crawford (1970) 46, and again in Crawford (1974) 698–707, by calculations which Hopkins (1980) 110 presents in graphic form, discovers a relation between volume of coin emission and number of legions that is claimed to be "very close" and "remarkable." Frier (1981) 295, however, presents Crawford's data in more readily intelligible form, whereupon (pp. 288 and 290) the relations vanish (i.e., the data do not explain most — 57 percent — of army costs, and at a crucial test-point the correlation approaches zero). Hopkins (1980) 111 also expresses other reservations, too.

139. On pay rises, see Dio 67.3.5 and 78.36.3, and MacMullen (1984) 572f. The graph, with my own little additions to show certain dates more clearly, is fig. 1, p. 40, in Hopkins (1978), repeated as fig. 4 in Hopkins (1980) 111. Hopkins (1980) 112 n. 334 speaks of "re-analyzing" the data of Reece (1973), see above at note 133; but that involves, inter alia, collapsing the discrepant line of Britain into Gaul's. Without that, the symmetries would be marred. In fact, comparing all of Reece's figures with Hopkins's graph, I notice and am puzzled by the disappearance of other regional differences of the later period.

140. For the 3d cent. connection of army costs and minting, see sources cited in MacMullen (1976) 259 n. 34.

141. MacMullen (1984) 572 attempts estimates at several points in time. In periods of peace, those estimates cannot, I believe, err by more than 15 percent either way (though that margin of error is gross, of course).

142. Goldsmith (1984) 273f. For discussion, see MacMullen (1987a) 748. While it seems to me demonstrated by Goldsmith that Hopkins's estimate of the empire's total annual product is understated by a factor of two or three, the tax rates Hopkins works with (10 percent, p. 119) seem about right. It should follow that the yield was two or three times what he (or I) suppose — and the figure would be even higher if we accept Brunt (1974) 183f., instancing overall tax rates on agriculture at an eighth, a seventh, even a fifth. I cannot resolve these difficulties.

143. Section 3, above, can be conveniently compared with table 33 and the notes to it in Mann (1983) 160. There are many obvious discrepancies that anyone can see for himself.

144. Lact., *De mort. persecut.* 7.2; Agathias 5.13; and A. H. M. Jones (1964) 680 or 1042 (650,000 in the 4th cent.). For discussion, see MacMullen (1980b) 451–60, reviewing the estimates of careful scholars ranging from 400,000 up to a million in the period Diocletian-to-the-5th-century. A part of Jones's acceptance of the higher figure lies in his using a figure of over 1,000 for many legions (pp. 681 and 1450, where a legion-size of 3000 x [33 + 15] accounts straightway for an extra 100,000 or so.)

145. I take the liberty of quoting myself, MacMullen (1968) 339, where there may also be

found a larger context and discussion.

146. Above, note 105, and MacMullen (1987a) 735f. and 739f. In this essay, passim, I say all I have to say on tax pressure, with documentation; so, in what follows here, I cite only scattered fragments of illustrative evidence.

147. CT 6.3.4 (397); PCair. Isidor. 17 (314) p. 149, "*a large majority* [my italics] of the landholders at Karanis" had not paid the chaff tax of 310/311; CT 11.1.33 (423/24), the Achaeans able to pay only a third of their arrears, the Macedonians a half; the *immanissima moles reliquorum* in the eastern diocese, CT 5.14.31 (382/89); and 11.28.16 (433), remission for a score of years extending that for the previous score (of CT 11.28.9).

148. CT 1.14.1 (386) to Egypt: *si audaces exstiterunt*, "if any of the provincials prove overbold about their tax-payments," plainly by insolent defiance, We will send *castrenses milites*; and PPrinceton 113 (early 4th cent.).

149. CT 13.10.1 and 6.2.14(9). If the two provinces specified in the latter law were suffering specially from the Goths, it was not the locally landowning *senators* that went hungry — and that is the point. And notice similarly CJ 11.60(59).1.1 of the next year (385), where we see the *potentiores* abusively avoiding tax obligations along frontiers this time in the west — perhaps Africa. See PLRE 1 s.v. Licinius 1.

150. MacMullen (1987a) 747f.; also A. H. M. Jones (1964) 466, offering a little information on the subject, but there is far more than he gives play to. See below, 149f. and 195.

151. MacMullen (1987a) at notes 52ff. Mamertinus (*Pan. lat.* 11[3].1.4 and 4.1f.) calls Gaul's governors "wicked brigands" for their cruel efforts to raise so great an amount of taxes in the years before Julian arrived. A. H. M. Jones (1964) 462–65 and A. H. M. Jones (1969) 98 discusses taxes as if they had not varied from year to year, only from province to province; but Neesen (1980) 82 and 122f. is closer to the truth.

152. Among many descriptions of difficulties in meeting the demands of the later tax collectors, see Gregory Nazianzenus, Themistius, etc., in MacMullen (1987a) 742f.; further, ibid. nn. 38f., 48, and 59; on the wine dealer Pamonthius, Bell (1924) 73f., Bell's transl., comparing PHerm. 7 (4th cent.) for children put up as security; and for sale of children into slavery to pay taxes, see other texts in Liebeschuetz (1972) 54. For comparison, notice the Principate passages in MacMullen (1974) 34f., esp. the seizing of children in Philo's Egypt, pp. 36f. The concern for children in this period, e.g., CJ 4.43.2 (329) or CT 3.3.1 (391), as well as sermons, e.g., Basil, Homil. in illud Lucae, Destruam 4 (PG 31.268), or Ambrose, De Nabuthae 21, may reflect Christianity as well as more common resort to their sale by the poor; or it may only reflect the nature and abundance of 4th cent. sources reporting on an age-old phenomenon. The firmest forbidding of the pledging of children to the parents' creditors is, after all, not Christian: CJ 4.10.12 (294).

153. A. H. M. Jones (1964) 815f. gives the figures (in Syria, Asia, and Campania — 5, 9, and 10 percent before A.D. 422) and at p. 1039 and in later essays draws his conclusions. In 422 in north Africa, the crown estates reported a third to a half deserted lands. That could be the natural consequence of generations of unrealistic emphyteusis. The totals went up after the Vandal wars (naturally). In the second half of the 5th cent., a single Syrian city reported about one sixth of its farmlands deserted. Against this, of course, is to be set the general picture of Syrian prosperity, see above, in section 3.

154. Quoted, with other passages to the same effect, from Jones's works, in MacMullen (1987a) at n. 25.

155. Sherwin-White (1966) 722f. emends the tortured text of *Ep.* 10.113 to replace the reluctant Bithynian decurions, *inviti*, with *invitati*; but Dio Chrysos., *Or.* 20.1, is even earlier: "What if someone of great wealth quits the city for the sake of avoiding the liturgies?" Likewise earlier is the correspondence between the emperor and the Italian town Vardagate, regarding the avoidance of liturgies and officeholding by a freedman (*sevir*, presumably). See Harris (1981) 348, proposing a date under Nerva.

156. For the decurionate as still an object of ambition in the third century, see the passages gathered in MacMullen (1976) 288 n. 52, adding *IGLS* 2716, which records a costly thank-offering by the dedicant who attained the decurionate in Heliopolis under Gordian, and *CJ* 10.32.1 (259), where a father hopes his son may enter the local curia. For the manifestations of the "old" civic spirit still in this century, see the discussion at note 13, above; for the diminishing of civic spirit after A.D. 200 in north Africa, emphasizing that it was not abrupt or very grave, see Jacques (1981) 265–67; in Gaul, within a very limited total of information of any sort, notice the enormous wealth and public spending of T. Sennius Sollemnis, stressed by Drinkwater (1979) 242; and, for a mixed picture, generally healthy, in Egyptian cities, see M. Drew-Bear (1984) 331.

157. Piganiol (1972) 393; Lepelley (1979–81) 1.335, with more general remarks on the 4th-cent. reality, pp. 339f. and 345. Compare Aug., *Contra Academicos* 1.2 of A.D. 386, quoted in ibid 2.178, of a young man of Thagaste: "If you offer our fellow citizens shows of bears and spectacles never seen before, and if applause in the theater always welcomes you as warmly as you could wish; if stupid men, in their great crowds, raise you to the heavens with their commingled and unanimous voices; if nobody would dare to be your enemy; if the tablets of the city mark you out in bronze as the patron not only of your fellow citizens but of neighboring places," etc. On such civic ambition and generosity, see further Lepelley (1981) 453, who removes a piece of apparently contradictory evidence; and Lepelley (1979–81) 2.427 on *ILS* 5571 from Macomedes and 1.103, 110, 248, 291 (a good supply of *curiales* in 397), 294 (Aug., *Ep*. 90, *re* Calama), and esp. 300 (Aug., *Enarr. in Ps*. 80.7 and 149.10 of A.D. 387/398). To these last texts, compare *CT* 15.7.3 (376), on *felicis populi studia, gymnici ut agonis spectacula.*

158. Ville (1960) 278f., 293, 295, 297, 300, etc., on 4th- and early-5th-cent. spectacles, and Lepelley (1979–81) 1.293, on Symmachus (*Ep*. 1.3[4] of 375), describing in Beneventum an admirable elite, *optimates who privatam pecuniam pro civitatis ornatu certatim fatigant*, etc.

159. In *Joann. homil.* 1.4 (PG 59.28) and 11.1 (PG 59.76); *Eight baptismal catacheses* 6.1, *hippodromiai kai theatra satanika* quoted in Ville (1960) 292; but there are many other passages attesting to the same frequent and well-paid entertainments.

160. *De inani gloria* 4–6, trans. MacMullen (1980) 12.

161. Euseb., *H. E.* 8.9.7, a rich man of Thmuis in Egypt is "outstanding on account of his liturgies"; and Robert (1960) 571 n. 1 and passim, on inscriptions from various sites of the east, as well as passages from Basil and Chrysostom.

162. *ILS* 7069.

163. Vogler (1979) 246f. points out the legislation of Constans and uses it as a reminder to differentiate between urban life in the two halves of the empire.

164. POxy. 1204 on Plutarchus; *CT* 12.1.25 (338), repeated in 26 (338) and followed by the statement that Carthage's council is now reduced to only a "few" decurions, thanks to purchases of titles (*CT* 12.1.27 A.D. 339); compare, a little earlier, 12.1.13 (326), "As We have discovered that curiae are being emptied of those who are obligated to them by birth, and yet are asking for a government post (*militia*) by petition to the Emperor, running off to the legions or various civil offices . . ."; and Liban., *Or*. 18.46 and 48.4, dated to post-388 by Norman (1977) 2.417. Libanius, *Ep*. 1048, and Basil, *Ep*. 116 (both in Petit [1957] 127), indicate how matter-of-fact and open was escape from the curia — it was more difficult to quit the army. Basil, writing in 372, rebukes a young *curialis* for the shame of deserting his civic rank, not for the illegality of it.

165. Petit (1955) 339, 20 out of 55; 325, the totals of the *curiales* at different dates; and 326, on Libanius' own family history.

166. Jews, in *CT* 16.8.3 (321); clerics, 16.2.7 (330), 16.2.19 (370 — after ten years as clerics, their patrimony is exempt), and 12.1.49 (361), declaring it "formerly established" and now confirmed that bishops need not surrender their property to their curiae, cf. 16.2.15.2;

guilds, 14.8.2 (369 — *centonarii*) and 13.16.1 (380 — *navicularii* by "ancient" right); physicians, grammatici, professors, 13.3.1 praef. (324) and 2 (354 — cf. A. H. M. Jones [1964] 1405, on the dole); soldiers, 7.1.5 (364) and 6 (368; 373), offering exemption after five years of service, and 16.14.2 praef. (397) on *comites*; also civil servants, 8.4.8.1a (364), on governors' staff after twenty-five years of service, and 6.26.1 (*scriniarii* in palatine offices), with 6.35.3 praef. (319 or 352, cf. Piganiol [1972] 120 n. 5), extending exemption to children and grandchildren; and 8.4.11 (365), *cohortales* = clerks of government exempted by Diocletian. Notice what can be said about one of these categories, by Gilliard (1984) 154, to suggest the proportions of loss to curiae: "throughout the Empire in the 4th cent., if you scratch a bishop you will most likely find a *curialis*." But on the whole subject of curial status, A. H. M. Jones (1964) 742–52 offers a far less selective and superficial overview than I do here.

167. *Quot curiales, tot tyranni* (Salv., *De gub. dei* 5.18.27f.). See A. H. M. Jones (1964) 756f. and Lepelley (1983) 143 and 148; ibid. 150-52 on other texts, including Aug., *Ep.* 22˚ of 429, and p. 154 on the meaning of *potentes*.

168. *CT* 11.16.4 (328), to which Lepelley (1983) 150 calls attention, along with 11.16.3 (324; 325), here too with a warning against *potentiores*. But still in A.D. 410, *CJ* 10.22.1 declares, "To relieve the fortunes of the lowlier curiales and restrain the pressure of the *potentes* in the same curia," tax assessments shall not become effective until registered with the governors.

169. In Greek, *protoi* and other terms. See below, chap. 2, 2; Liban., *Or.* 49.8, on the "*megalai dynameis* in the curia which have stripped bare the weaker members and add to their burdens"; 48.40, where "the *protoi* in the council are destroying those of the second or third rank," with comment by Norman (1977) 412–16; Liebeschuetz (1972) 171–74; and Lepelley (1983) 143 and 154, on the levels within the curiae; also 151, citing *CT* 12.6.22, which shows *exactores* not fleeing but extending their term of service, like imperial *tabularii* of *CT* 8.1.9.1 (365): tax collecting could be a source of personal profit. Particularly telling is the casual but generalizing characterization of the decemprimate in early-4th-cent. astrology (Firm. Matern., *Math.* 3.10.1 and 9): to hold that position was to be numbered among the fortunate.

170. Liebeschuetz (1972) 143 and 172f.; Petit (1955) 286; and Kotula (1982) 128f. But notice that, in the Egyptian metropoleis, the *dekaprotoi* barely last into the fourth century. See Lallemand (1964) 206f.

171. Above, note 51, and MacMullen (1976a) 28–30. I omit places of retirement like Split or Konz; also residences without known palaces (which, however, must have existed), like Marcianopolis and Durostorum; see A. H. M. Jones (1964) 366; and I omit grand buildings called 'palaces,' perhaps not specially set aside for the emperor rather than for any great officer. See MacMullen (1976a) 31f. and Millar (1977) 42, on Autun, Arsinoe, etc.

172. See above, notes 51, 54, 59, 82, 86, 95, 113, and 121, and, in the next note, Anemurium; for Cuicul, see Février (1982) 357.

173. In only casual reading, I find governors attested as builders or renovators of cities through the application of tax monies in *CT* 15,1 passim, e.g., 15.1.2 (321); at Atella, Allifae, Praeneste, Capua, Puteoli, and a half-dozen other central Italian centers, in Ward-Perkins (1984) 24–27, 34, 88, and 231–33; also *ILS* 5363 of A.D. 379/83 at Verona; at Beneventum, a count active in building, *ILS* 5508 = *CIL* 9.1590, and (1596) an anonymous *spect(abilis)*; in Africa, Romanelli (1959) 557 and Février (1970) 170, instancing *CIL* 8.4767 (Macomades A.D. 364/67, an arch), 11184 (Biiensis, "4th cent.," *PLRE*), and 15204 (Thignica A.D. 393, cf. *PLRE*, an aqueduct); Albertini (1943) 382 on the Numidian governor's activity in Timgad, Lambaesis, and many other towns in the 360s, and ibid. 386, with *PLRE* 1 Albinus 8 (Djemila's basilica of 364/67); the interesting

inscription in Lepelley (1979–81) 1.97, where the governor of Tripolitania favors Lepcis with public spectacles and construction "surpassing what might be expected of a citizen of the city" (so he is using imperial monies); in Egypt, Lallemand (1964) 247, a canal of 367/70; Himerius, *Or.* 4.1, Athens; *PLRE* 1 Acholius in late 4th/early 5th cent., at Sardis; Roueché (1986) 300, 4th cent. at Aphrodisias, with *MAMA* 8.427, a city wall of the 4th/5th cent.; and among rare indications of who built what in 4th–6th-cent. Asia Minor cities, refs. to the work of a governor at Sardis in Foss (1976) 113 and of others at Ephesus and elsewhere, in Foss (1979) 5, 27f., 59–61, 65 n. 18, and 70 and Malcus (1967) 102f.; Alföldy (1969) 38, Alföldy-Rosenbaum (1972) 183f., and Hall (1972) 215, a city wall at Anemurium by the count of Isauria in 382; ibid. 213 on the Isaurian governor who "renovated the entire [unknown] structure and restored it to its ancient beauty" in Isaura in Gratian's reign; and, most useful of all, the collection of valuable inscriptions by Robert (1948), showing construction at Megara by an early-5th-cent. PPO (p. 60) and at other Asia Minor cities (Smyrna, Ephesus, Assos, Adana, Ancyra, Samos, pp. 61f., 66, 70, 74, and 87), over the 340s to the early 5th cent. by imperial officials. Notice the sour warnings of *CT* 15.1.1 (357) and 14 (365) about the misplaced zeal of governors. *CJ* 8.10.6 (321) shows that spoliation was sometimes only a cover for private construction. About urban construction in general, says Foss (1979) 28, "it would appear that the governor had an overwhelming role."

174. Petit (1955) 318, the listings on pp. 316f., with additional details about the builders in *PLRE* 1 Florentius 9, Proculus 6, and Gorgonius 2, Liban., *Or.* 33.14, on the governor Tisamenus' special zeal in gathering monies for construction, and *Ep.* 852 on Proculus' building of *hodon kai stoon kai loutron kai agoran*; Seeck (1906) 114, 167, and 224; and Zos. 5.2.4, on the Royal Stoa built in 395 by the PPO Rufinus; and Liebeschuetz (1972) 50f., on PPO Thalassius, Datianus, and Magister Militum Ellebichus, and 132–34, on other builders — all governors, court officials, or ex-officials.

175. As random illustrations: Amm. 18.9.1, 22.7.7, 28.3.2, and 31.1.2 and 4; *FIRA2* 1.455 and 462; and Lepelley (1979–81) 1.90f. and 97, on Constantine's projects to adorn Carthage, Cirta, Utica, and Mascula. Most explicit is Constantine's declaration of "zeal to found new cities, or embellish the ancient, or renew the dying" (*ILS* 6091).

176. Frend (1984) 557f., on those two cities as well as Cirta and Hippo, and Lassus (1965) 585–87; further, above, notes 102, on Timgad, and 61, on Tours; Krautheimer (1983) 73f., on Milan.

177. The ecclesiastical building complex of Caesarea was probably completed around 375. See Basil, *Ep.* 94 of 372/73, in Kopecek (1974) 302; ibid. 293f., earlier, Gregory Nazianzenus uses funds for building; later, Theodoret (*Ep.* 81) shows a bishop accomplishing secular construction projects, ibid. 303: "Public porticoes I have constructed from the revenues of the church, and I have built great bridges. I have taken care of the public baths; from the river flowing past the city, which I found without water, I constructed the aqueduct and filled the waterless city." On the quality of construction, I go on to quote Hier., *Ep.* 52.10, matched by the protest lodged by two priests against what they thought was the excessive splendor of "churches twinkling with gold, arrogant in their dress of costly marbles, erect in the magnificence of their columns" (*Coll. Avellana, Ep.* 2.121, in *CSEL* 35.43, describing buildings in Rome in the 380s).

178. Prentice (1909) 99, no. 1026, stoa built A.D. 418/19 by a presbyter on a site 35 miles north of Hama on the Orontes; Prentice (1910) 131, a deacon builds a church A.D. 401; 133 no. 1101, a *comes* A.D. 473 builds a church; 148, no. 1118, A.D. 375/6, a priest puts up some building; 1119, A.D. 423, a presbyter and deacon join in a building project; 153 no. 1126, A.D. 407, a presbyter builds; and 202 no. 1199 A.D. 372, a low-ranking priest, *periodeutes*, builds a church.

179. On this simple explanation, that the barbarians were just too strong, many interpreters

of the 'decline' have rested their case. I argue in chapter 4 that the enemy did not in fact present a fearful threat. Here I only recall the best-known opposing view, that "la civilisation romaine n'est pas morte de sa belle mort. Elle a été assassinée," in Piganiol (1972) 466. That represents (p. vii) "l'exemplaire annoté à la main par ses soins," of which the author "avait pratiquement fait tout le travail d'adaptation" for the final publication, witness 466 note 2 with bibliography post-1939. So already in the first edition (1947) he was contradicting his views of 1939 (*Histoire de Rome*) and abided by those developed views still in 1968, the year he died pen in hand. All this, in correction of a historiographical point raised by Momigliano (1978) 451. But I go on to quote from Momigliano's very trenchant essay — without including his aside (quite true), "We have again lost interest in the problem of why Rome fell."

180. Jullian (1908–26) 8.353f., often echoed and adapted in Marxist versions, e.g. by Walbank (1969) 92, who described "a world already torn within . . . , men lost faith in the Empire, in its justice and its righteousness. . . . We hear of men taking refuge with the barbarians, and of others who gave them aid. . . . Thus a few thousand barbarians were enough to push over this tottering edifice"(!). Or again, Anderson (1978) 102f., picturing "combined rebellions against both slavery and the colonate" and "social polarization"; or, most recently, E. A. Thompson (1980) 79–81 and E. A. Thompson (1982) 179, to the same effect.

181. Greg. Thaumat., *Ep canon.* 5–10, esp. 6. As these Pontic persons were Christians, they were not likely to have been wealthy. For the Syrian scene, see Malal. 12.296, where "the priest of Aphrodite, by name Sampsigeramus, with a good force of peasant slingers, comes out against him" (Sapor). There are other examples in MacMullen (1963) 137f.

182. Ste. Croix (1981) 261 and 474, section iii, collects refs. on the failure to resist, even instances of joining the barbarians; on the other side, notice Zos. 5.15.5f. (Selge) and 5.19.3f. (Constantinople); Soz., *H E*. 7.1 A.D. 378, near Constantinople; Callinicus, *Vita S. Hypatii* 3.11 (Phrygia), where monks in 395 (?) build a small fort against the Goths, as the editor G. J. M. Bartelink explains at 6.1; Oros. 7.40.5 and Soz. 9.11 (Spain); and Synes., *Ep*. 122 and 125 (PG 66.1501Bf. and 1505) and *Catastasis* II (PG 67.1576Bf.), Cyrenaica.

183. Forni (1953) 159–212, supplemented by Forni (1974) 366–80. I have arranged his data in more or less homogeneous groups, that is, areas that show similar profiles over time (for instance, Italy is combined with the Alpine provinces and Narbonensis). He offers occasional addenda on the basis of evidence about origins that he does not consider fully probative, esp. nomenclature. I have left out nearly all such extra numbers. I also show in dotted lines the soldiers known only from excavation of the great camp at Lambaesis, which produced a gigantic bulge of data. I am aware that this points to the dangers in trusting too much to the evidence that happens to survive.

184. *Parliamentary Debates, Fourth Series* 10 (1893) 603f., of March 20.

185. MacMullen (1963a) 552–61, adding for the upper Rhine area Engels (1972) 183–89; note 54 above, on Huns; Reece (1980) 80, 3d cent. German settlements explain the character of the 4th-cent. burials in Britain; and Comsa (1972) 225f. (Fr. transl. 233), Carpi in the Dobruja post-350. Epigraphic and literary sources have been collected by Ste. Croix (1981) 510–15, unaware of the collections of a century and a half ago, by Zumpt (1845) 11f., 14, etc., and Huschke (1847) 150–61. But Ste. Croix is far better, naturally.

186. Kempf (1900) 347f., on *tufa*, a kind of *vexillum*, or *mattiobarbulus*, a kind of slingshot; Hoffmann (1969–71) 1.135, on *barritus*, and chap. 6 passim; and MacMullen (1977) 4f., and, on the silver dish of Panticipaeum and other details, ibid. 6f.

187. See Appendix A. "Many of these German officers were men of brilliant talents, fascinating address, and noble bearing," says Dill (1899) 297, rather gushingly; but compare A. H. M. Jones (1964) 622, "those Germans of whom we know anything, those that is who rose in the service and made names for themselves, certainly became

thoroughly romanised, and quite lost contact with their homes"; also E. A. Thompson (1982) 234f.

188. Philostorg., *H E.* 12.4 p. 143 Bidez (with ref. to Dan. 2.41f.).

189. See the fullest details in Zos. 5.47.1–5.48.1 and Soz., *H. E.* 9.12.5. Allobichus was *proxenos kai philos* of Alaric and an accomplice of Jovius, on whose treachery see Zos. 6.8.1 and 6.9.1f. The six Augusti are Honorius, Theodosius II, Constantine III, Constans II, Attalus, and Maximus in Tarraco.

CHAPTER 2

1. Both Weber's *Protestant Ethic* and Elias's *Civilizing Process* have been Englished; not so Veyne's *Le Pain et le cirque.*

2. "Statistically, there was indeed a middle class, . . . a range of intermediate wealth [that] made up the aristocracy of small cities," as I summed it up, MacMullen (1974) 89. See further, ibid., chap. VI and Appendix B passim, on pre-A.D. 284 ideas and realities of class; more recently, Alföldy (1986) 52–56, 78–81, and 418f.; but notice Lepelley (1983) 154, rightly warning against confusing a society of classes with one of ranks, and Löhken (1982) 23, likewise right in insisting on the real significance of subdivisions within the two broad groupings in law, *honestiores* and *humiliores.* Perhaps the most striking passage is Hor., *Ep.* 1.1.58f., declaring everyone indiscriminately a member of the *plebs* who is not an equestrian (!). But a similar perception prevailed throughout the empire, wherever we can discover people's views: in Josephus, for example, who thinks of society in Judaea as entirely constituted of *poneroi* and *kratistoi* (*Vita* 29, cf. *B. J.* 2.315, *plethos* and *dynatoi,* or *gnorimoi,* 318, 322, and 410). On the harsher vision of only Haves and Have-nots, see e.g., Tac., *Ann.* 13.48, the plebs in Puteoli ranged against "the grasping conduct of magistrates and *primi.*" Notice also the towering scorn for the masses, *demos* or *hoi polloi,* shown by Ps.-Crates in Malherbe (1977), e.g., p. 75 *Ep.* 25: "To the Athenians: I hear that you are in need of money. Therefore, sell your horses and you will have money. Then, whenever there is need for horses, vote that your asses are horses. For this has become your custom in every matter: not to do what is proper for your needs but to do what has been voted upon" (trans. R. F. Hock). Again, p. 71 *Ep.* 21, "The masses, although they desire the same end as the Cynics, flee those who preach the regimen, when they see how difficult it is"; and p. 87 *Ep.* 34, "rejoice . . . , because what the masses did not believe was so, appeared so [clearly]"; or, finally, p. 85 *Ep.* 35, against ever being satisfied with "what satisfies the life of *hoi polloi.*"

3. Dio Chrysos., *Or.* 50.3f., on *hoi demotikoi;* cf. the tone of *Or.* 40.29 or 48.2, and the evaluation of Dio's "ton d'un officier qui harangue des mutins . . . , des plébéiens, non comme des citoyens qui revendiquent, mais comme des gens nés pour lui obéir," in Veyne (1976) 313; also Plin., *Ep.* 9.5.3, quoted in the text, and matched by Symm., *Ep.* 9.40 (*MGH AA* 6.247): "Consideration is of course always to be given to justice; yet, where the nobility and the better sort of people are concerned, there should be more discrimination shown, so that a decision is arrived at with discernment. And I begin [this letter of intercession] in this manner, so that my mediation should be recommended in broad terms" — i.e., terms that would be acknowledged as conventional.

4. *CJ* 12. 1.6 (357/60), comparing the tone in 9.47.12; also Cic., *Pro Flacco* 18, quoted in MacMullen (1974) 114.

5. Hier., *Vita S. Hilarionis* 30 (*PL* 23.43f.), the *vulgus ignobile et potentes viri et iudices,* in Palestine of the 360s. Compare Constantius, *Vita S. Germani* 5.26, *inscia multitudo,* and the use and context of *turba,* 3.16, or *populus,* passim; cf. similar terminology of depreciation in Eusebius and other authors cited in MacMullen (1981) 144 note 33; for oppression, notice the Anon. *de rebus bellicis* 2.2, who sees how, by the plentiful gold

supply of Constantine's day, "the personal homes of the powerful were filled up and made all the more glorious, to the ruin of the poor, since of course weaker folk were trodden down by main force." Further, Aug., *Sermo* 345.1: "Hear, you rich men who have your gold and silver and are yet aflame with greed for more! When the poor look on them, they grumble and groan, yet praise and envy, and wish to be like them and bewail the fact that they are no match for them; and, between praises of wealth, above all they exclaim, 'Those fellows alone really exist, they are the real ones that *live*." Similarly, also, Liban., *Or.* 45.4 (A.D. 386) "this is the normal treatment of the weaker at the hands of the more powerful, *ton dynatoteron*, of the penniless at the hands of the wealthy, of the masses at the hands of the elite. . . . This is their experience at the hands of senators and decurions." John Chrysostom sees society in just the same terms, cf. Liebeschuetz (1972) 61; and, reading in still other authors, Teja (1974) 67 finds no trace in 4th-cent. texts of any class intermediary between *potentiores/honestiores/plousioi* and *humiliores/penetes*.

6. Dorotheus Gazensis, *Doctrina* 5 (PG 88.1646), of the 6th cent.
7. See Menander Rhet. p. 100 Russell-Wilson, comparing the reception accorded to Herodes Atticus by the Athenian council, ephebes, and boy choristers on his return from abroad, in Svensson (1926) 529 = IG2 3606; Liebeschuetz (1972) 208 on Liban., *Or.* 56.1f., 6, and 9–12, and *Or.* 27.42; ibid. 209 on exit-ceremonies and acclamations; ibid. 27 on Liban., *Or.* 52.40, carriages and compliments from a PPO; Joh. Chrysos., *Comparatio regis et monachi* 1 (PG 47.387), a characteristic description of a governor borne along in his carriage, while heralds go ahead, shouting, and armed guards surround him; and Dio 45.16.2 (the scene in Rome.)
8. MacMullen (1974) 107. On the *cingulum*'s long history, see Alföldi (1935) 64f.; with one's *chlamys*, it was an obligatory item upon being presented at court, cf. Joh. Chrysos., *In ep.* 1 ad Cor. 26.4. On other items of grand official costume, MacMullen (1964a) 447; on the civic award of "crowns and front seats and purple (robes)," see Dio Chrysos., *Or.* 34.29, and Mitchell (1977) 72f., a Severan inscription from Ancyra honoring a citizen with *porphyrai ke*(!) *stephano dia biou*, cf. TAM 2.905 V F, VI A, B, E, and VIII E; Pearl (1940) 383f. on certain local officials in the later empire wearing uniforms for senate meetings, etc.; and Monneret de Villard (1953) Pl. XXXIa and 92f. and Deckers (1973) 27, noting in the Luxor fresco "the increase in size and sumptuousness of the side panels in the painting to the right of the apse, up to the figure with enormous circular, dark brown attachments and the man with a segmentum of similar size, star-shaped and serrated, which indicate persons of imperial rank." For the alarm inspired by the mere sight of the *chlamys*, see Liban., *Or.* 30.15, and the phrase *chlamydis terror* in CT 14.10.1 (382).
9. Many scenes of the Principate, see MacMullen (1974) 194 note 56; for the later empire, Liban., *Or.* 33.10; Joh. Chrysos., *In Mt. homil.* 23/24.10 (PG 57.320); Basil, *Homil. in hexaemeron* 5.2 (PG 29.100A), the rich man advertised by "a herald with great shouts preceding him, and his lictors strike absolute terror into everyone they meet. Blows, confiscation, exile, manacles, all these arouse unbearable fear among his subjects." See also idem, *Homil. in divites* 2 (PG 31.284C), on the conspicuous dress and accoutrements of the rich man in circulation; Greg. Naz., *Or.* 42.24 (PG 36.488Af.), on the pomp, riches, and spirited mounts that belonged to bishops in circulation; and Euseb., *H. E.* 7.30.8, on a bishop borrowing pomp, retinue, and haughty mannerisms from civil officials in Antioch in the 270s.
10. Simply as examples, from abundant epigraphic material and some numismatic and literary: IGR 1.854 (Olbia) and *Passio S. Cononi* 2.1, *pater poleos*; BMC *Caria, Cos, Rhodes* (1964) p. XXXV, on coins of Aphrodisias, T. Drew-Bear (1978) 167f., Cousin (1904) 26, and LeBas-Wadd. 108, "Son"; IGR 4.527 (Dorylaeum) and 717 (Blaundus), *ktistes = conditor*, in AE 1916 no. 120 = AE 1969/70 no. 592 (Sinope); Dio Chrysos., *loc. cit.*, *soter*; and other terms like *proestos* and *aristeus*. See, further, in Appendix B. Fortunately,

some observers made fun of all this: Lucillius, cf. Robert (1967) 213f., and Ammianus in his sarcastic use of the emperor's high titles, "The Father of Us All," or "Our Benevolent Ruler," applied to an exceptionally cruel one: 29.3.6 and 29.6.7, cf. 29.2.17.

11. A large and familiar subject, honorific adjectives — e.g., *eminentissimi* or *perfectissimi* in Marcus Aurelius' time, *CJ* 9.41.11, or *egregius* coming into use in the same period, cf. the *Oxford Latin Dictionary* s.v. On such words amounting to titles, see MacMullen (1974) 106, Alföldy (1981) 190–94 and 205, and Löhken (1982) 27. Some terms of distinction never quite congealed into titles, e.g., *ornatissimus* in *ILS* 5947 or 6043.

12. Amm. 28.4.10, cf. Lucian, *Nigrinus* 21, rich Romans expected you to kneel to them (not a Greek practice); legislation in *CT* 12.1.109 (385), 6.24.4 (387), and *CJ* 12.6.1–12.19.2 passim, essentially post-A.D. 400.

13. Among listings, besides the Canusian inscription of A.D. 223, there is only the well-known Timgad example of the 360s, well studied (with earlier bibliography) in Lepelley (1979–81) 2.459–61; on precedence at governors' *consessus*, see further *CT* 6.26.5 (389) and 6.26.7 (396 — referring to lost legislation by Valentinian) and 6.26.16 (410 — so, four times the subject of regulated seating must be enforced); 6.18.1 (412), on rank at *publicae salutationes* that constitute (6.18.1.1) the *cura* of *officia*, i.e., direction and responsibility for staging acclamations; 12.1.4 (317), on usurpers of rights of *primates* (= *principales*), which I quote; Liban., *Or.* 2.7; Clem. Alex., *Strom.* 7.16 (PG 9.536B), concern for *protokathedria*; and Aug., *Ep.* 59.1 (401), deploring inadequate respect for ranking, cf. again *Ep.* 64.2. But the subject can be traced back and back: e.g. in *proedria* for a city's honored son, *TAM* 2 no. 905 V A, and other instances in MacMullen (1974) 178 note 70.

14. *Nov. Theod.* 15.2.1, trans. Pharr. The opening clause in the quotation exactly echoes Paul, *Sent.* 5.25.12 (*FIRA²* 2.412): "Anyone who makes use of the *insignia* of a higher rank or counterfeits official appointment, *militia*, in order to strike fear into people or practice extortion," shall be executed if of a lower class, exiled if of a higher.

15. Liebeschuetz (1972) 113.

16. For the inscription, see Cavagnola (1974/75) 83; for similar gratitude for admission, see Tac., *Ann.* 6.8; for moments of massed supporters around their leader, see, e.g., Eunap., *Vit. soph.* 490 in Athens (the *dynatoi*) or Aug., *Ep.* 126, the *honoratiores et graviores*. To the emperors, of course, only "high rank gave entry to you," *Paneg. vet.* 3(11).3.

17. Liebeschuetz (1972) 190f., also quoting *CT*-texts; furious objection by older intimates at the honorific seating of a newer one with the emperor, in Eunap., *Vit. soph.* 462, cf. Fronto, *Ep. ad Verum* 2.8 p. 136 Naber and Epict., *Diss.* 3.9.1, a lawsuit in the provinces, *dike peri times*, pursued even to Rome; Amm. 15.5.27, consultation *secretius de rerum summa*; and below, at note 117.

18. Tac., *Ann.* 2.28.3, *convictus adhibet Libonem*; Columella, *Re rust.* 11.1.19; Suet., *Gaius Caligula* 17.2, and Dio 60.7.4, imperial banquets to honor senators, equestrians, and wives; Euseb., *Mart. Pal.* 7.7 (A.D. 307), a *homodiaitos* and *homotrapezon* of Maximin Daia; idem, *Vita Const.* 3.1 (GCS 1.77), bishops dine with Constantine, cf. Liban., *Or.* 30.53, "certain Christians" so honored; Eunap., *Vit. soph.* 492 and Amm. 15.5.27 (A.D. 355), the same privilege noted for Ursicinus, Prohaeresius, and others; and *CT* 6.13.1 (413), *praepositi ac tribuni scholarum, qui et divinis epulis adhibentur*. On decurions (in Concordia, Venetia), see Fronto, *Ep.* 2.7 p. 192 Naber.

19. *CIL* 6.1756, line 11E, cos. A.D. 371, died post-388.

20. Aul. Gell. 10.3.3; *CIL* 3.12336 lines 43f. = *IGR* 1.674 = *Syll.*3 888; and *CT* 7.11, *ne comitibus et tribunis lavacra praestentur*, only for *illustres* and *magistri militum* (laws of 406 and 417).

21. MacMullen (1974) 173 note 38; Clemente (1972) 166, a Lyon grandee has a reserved seat in the theater of another town; *TAM* 5, 1, 74 (Saittae); *CIL* 12.3316 (Nîmes) and 3.12586 (Sarmizegethusa); on front-seating for Augustales, MacMullen (1974) 173 n. 40 and

above at note 13; for other groups, Kolendo (1981) 301ff. and, most recently, section 81 of the Flavian Lex Irnitana, in Gonzalez (1986) 174.

22. CIL14.2410 (A.D. 158, Bovillae) and Liban., Or. 2.10 and 42.43.

23. MacMullen (1974) 173 n. 39; CIL 2.3370 and 4611 and many other texts in DE s.v. Funus (A. DeVincenti, 1962) 352.

24. Degrassi (1961/62) 68, 1st cent. B.C. at Ferentinum; Reinach (1896) 540, lines 55f., succlamatum est: eis aiona (Latin introducing Greek); 543 on IG 830, lines 35f., apo akton boules achtheises: epephonesan, etc.; other examples, ibid. and, in Rome, p. 542; in mosaics, Beschaouch (1966) 139, and date, A.D. 240s, p. 150; other examples in Africa, Spain, Germany, p. 140.

25. Aug., Ep. 213.1–3 (CSEL 57.372f.), the acta ecclesiastica, cf. CT Gesta senatus 1–7, the incipit of the whole collection. For phony acclamations in the SHA, see e.g., Valeriani 5.4 and 7, or Tacitus 7.1, or Probus 12.8, all stressing the 'omnes'; for real acclamations remembered by a senator, see Dio 72(73). 20.2, the setting being the amphitheater; and so back to A.D. 69 and Suet., Nero 46.3, in the senate, where conclamatum est ab universis; Dio 62(63).15.2, where Nero monitors senators closely, even to their participation in cheers, and "the very words" of acclamations are recorded, 62(63).20.5. For a negative unanimity, perhaps more spontaneous than acclamatory, see Dio 58.10.7 of A.D. 31, apo mias glosses. While acclamations of this sort are unknown to most readers today, they are the style again in Bucharest (New York Times 5/27/87), where the Rumanian leader Ceausescu's speech to the visiting Russian leader Gorbachev "was interrupted by applause 30 times in 45 minutes. Eighteen times the crowd rose to its feet to applaud rhythmically, shouting the names of the two leaders in unison or such slogans as 'Ceausescu — Peace!' and 'Disarmament — Ceausescu!' " — whereas interruptions of Gorbachev, being counted, were only half as numerous.

26. POxy. 41, the editors' translation corrected at line 4 in the light of chap. 1, above, at note 160 ("Like Ocean!") and Appendix B, protopolites = First Citizen. For similar popular pressure successfully exerted on a civic leader to give yet more, see IGR 4.1665 (Tira in Asia).

27. Dio 78(79).19.3f. on the demos' change of heart toward the regime, and 20.1-4 on the Circus-scene.

28. Many instances in the votes of African municipal precincts in Kotula (1968) 34–36; Marcillet-Jaubert (1979) 71, A.D. 376/78 in Africa, consensu splendidissimi ordinis; CIL 6.1685, Thaenae in Africa in A.D. 321; IRT 565, ordo . . . cum populo . . . decretis et suffragiis concinnentibus; CIL 8.1548, Ain Edja in Africa, consensu decurionum omnium; CIL10.1795, Puteoli, universus ordo; CIL 6.29682, placet cuncto ordini nostro . . . , ordo dixit: omnes, omnes, a 3d cent. action from a town near Rome; CIL 14.2466, universi censuerunt; CIL 12.5413, Narbonensis, censuere omnes; and 10.4643 (Cales), of A.D. 31, 26 attending and c(ensuerunt) c(uncti). For many eastern examples, see Erim (1975) 78, all late (ca. A.D. 500) and from Aphrodisias.

29. Franklin (1980) 69, 78, and 82, contrasted with disputed elections for aedileships. Compare the statement of Dio Chrysos., Or. 48.1 (transl. Loeb ed.), "no proconsul of good judgement convenes a meeting of a community, demos, which is in a state of turmoil." No good could come of that.

30. Amm. 26.1.5 and 26.4.3, the first involving the potiores auctoritate at Nicaea in 365, the second, choosing a Caesar at Nicomedia, nec enim audebant quisquam refragari.

31. Hess (1958) 29–32.

32. Philostr., Vit. soph. 512.

33. Amm. 14.7.9–16 (A.D. 354); Philostorg., H.E. 3.28 pp. 53f. Bidez; and exactly the same method of humiliating a high personage by ignoring him in Soc., H.E. 6.15, Soz., H.E. 8.17, and most fully in Pallad., Dialog. de vita S. Joh. Chrysos. 8 p. 9 Coleman-Norton,

regarding Theophilus bishop of Alexandria, who in 402, "disembarking [in Cple], did not come to the church [of John Chrysostom] as had been the rule prevailing in the past, did not meet with us, and did not exchange a word nor a prayer nor any fellowship; but, getting off his ship and hurrying by the church entry, took up his lodging by going off somewhere in the suburbs." Of course, for his part, John and all his clergy had boycotted Theophilus' arrival at the harbor, where they should have greeted him. Notice how, even so early as the first century, "it is greatly to be praised in the emperor that" a senator "dared" absent himself from the inauguration (Plin., *Ep.* 3.7.6f.).

34. MacMullen (1986b) 515f.
35. Tac., *Ann.* 2.36, *superbire homines etiam annua designatione; 3.40, saevitia ac superbia praesidentium; Hist.* 4.14, governors' *comitatus superbus;* Herodian 3.2.3 on PPO Plautianus, quoted in the text; and Amm. 17.3.4, the PPO Florentius' decisions were reversed by Julian, whereupon, in great distress, "he broke out, it was insupportable that he should suddenly lose credibility, he to whom the Augustus had entrusted supreme authority" in the matter. His complaint to Constantius is answered by a letter to Julian, saying that Julian "should not govern so meticulously as to seem to place little weight in Florentius' advice," *parum Florentio credi.*
36. Philostr., *Vit. soph.* 626; on Caracalla's eccentric conduct in Gaul, SHA *Cara.* 5.1.3.
37. F. M. Dostoyevsky, *The Brothers Karamazov* (Penguin transl. D. Magarshack, 1978) 1.237–240.
38. Art., *Oneir.* 1.32; Ael. Arist., *Or.* 46.309, Dindorf II p. 402; Dio Chrysos., *Or.* 65.7; and MacMullen (1974) 195 nn. 68 and 71f., which expands the testimony from the Greek-speaking provinces to Italy.
39. On Plautianus, see Dio 76.14.2 (frg.). Sejanus needs no introduction.
40. Epict., *Diss.* 1.19.17–25, cf. 1.10.3, 4.4.2, and 3.7.30f., admission to the court, senate, and governorship; very similar, Columella, *Re rust.* 1 praef. 10; Mart. 12.26.4–6 (Loeb transl.); cf. Plut., *Moral.* 815A, underscoring the "grasping and contentious nature of the leaders," *hoi protoi,* and the *dynatoi* in their quarrels (this, of course, in the Greek-speaking world); and Walton (1929) 55, detecting "an almost indecent agitation in aristocratic circles for positions in the Senate," for which new men vied in preliminary, local competition.
41. Perhaps the first significant witness to the great intensity of struggles for advancement in the church is the seventh canon of Serdica, cf. Hefele (1907–09) 1, 2 p. 782, on "the importunity, the continual attendance, the illicit requests that we [bishops] submit" at the imperial court, "for many of the bishops never cease from hanging about the imperial retinue, *to stratopedon,* especially the Africans." Bishops must cease their striving to move "from a little to a great city . . . , they are aflame with burning avarice," etc. A second major witness would be the *Collectio Avellana,* e.g., 1.5–7 and 2.109, which runs well up into the 5th cent.; but there is much to be found in the ecclesiastical historians, e.g., Soz., *H.E.* 3.1 (PG 67. 1033B, A.D. 337), where one group of bishops unites against another, using a presbyter in Cple favored by the emperor, who "was the close companion of the emperor's wife and of the eunuchs influential in attendance on her bedchamber"; 4.16 (PG 67.1160C), bishops work through "Eusebius the *praef. sacri cubiculi"* and through "many who were influential and were seeking Eusebius' favor"; 4.23 (PG 67.1185B), where a group of bishops after the Councils of Ariminum and Seleuceia (A.D. 359) "had gotten in line the men powerful in the palace, to adopt their views" and "had brought round to their own views the influential persons in the palace"; Soc., *H.E.* 2.37 (PG 67.304, A.D. 359), on the bishop of Germaniceia gaining the bishopric of Antioch, "for he had the influential men of the emperor's bedchamber as his accomplices"; and 6.5 (PG 67.673Cf., A.D. 399), where Theophilus intrigues against John "with some who were present and many who were far away" (i.e., by a campaign of correspondence), being angry because he could not get his deacon, Isidore, made bishop of Cple (and, in the upshot, PG

67.697B, John succeeds in getting his deacon made bishop of Ephesus). There is considerable other material on ecclesiastical violence in partisan competition collected in MacMullen (1984) 160f.

42. Wickham (1983) xvii n. 17, the guard required after a savagely disputed episcopal election by which Cyril succeeded his uncle Theophilus on the throne. Compare the bodyguards of great personages in Cple toward the same period, in Seeck (1910–23) 6.412.

43. Tac., Ann. 15.69, and Epict., Diss. 1.30, hoi epi tes machairas; cf. the armigeri of the Statilii in the 1st cent., DE s.v. "Armiger."

44. Philostr., Vit. soph. 588 and 560.

45. Dig. 22.3.20 (Julianus), not to mention the much later Philostorg., H.E. 9.6, p. 118 Bidez-Winkelmann of A.D. 365 and other passages below, note 93. Dig. 11.4.1.2 (Ulpian) shows special permission was needed even to set foot on the land of magnates who might be concealing some fugitive or kidnap victim.

46. Lengyel and Radan (1980) 114f., 156, and 315f., and above, chap. I note 54; Dremsizova-Nelcinova (1969) 2.510, finding four of seventeen Roman villas in Bulgaria fortified, dating (p. 512) to the early 3d cent. and destroyed a century later; above, chap. I note 74, and Leday (1980) 77, on the heavy walls protecting the pars urbana of big Gallic villas, "probably" in the 4th cent.; Percival (1976) 175f., on fortified villas like the Pannonian in the Garonne as well as Moselle valleys; MacMullen (1963) 147, on examples in France and Germany; Picard (1975) 102 n. 15, somewhat too sharply minimizing the evidence for fortified villas in France; and on Spain (Liedena), see above, chap. I note 97, and Blazquez (1964) 98.

47. On Africa, see MacMullen (1963) 143-46; Wilson (1981) 175, minimizing; and Thirion (1957) 235f. and Pl. IV, 4; on Syria, MacMullen (1963) 146 and Petit (1955) 380; on Cappadocia, Joh. Chrysos., Ep. ad Olympias 14.3 (PG 52.615).

48. Greg. Nyss., Vita Greg. Thaumaturg., PG 46.9269, each brother with his stratos . . . hypocheirion, no doubt peasants; Teja (1974) 46, on passages in Greg. Nyss., e.g., PG 44.1121B-C, which describe the feuds, philoneikiai, of the very rich over the boundaries of their lands, "whence often arise some burst of rage, bloodshed and murder" (notice the pollakis). He goes on to describe rural battles of his part of the world.

49. MacMullen (1974) 8–12; PAmh. 142 (4th cent.), a petition to the prefect of the province Augustamnica for protection against years of violence and invasion of his land by a single family, "to kill me with clubs and swords, scorning my helplessness and how ineffectual I looked"; and Aug., Ep. 115, to the bishop of Cirta, fearing for the victim's life and fearing also "lest money prevail with the governor," "for all that the governor's honesty is proclaimed of the very best repute." Yet the victim "is at loggerheads with an extremely wealthy man."

50. On villages in all areas, see MacMullen (1974) 38f. with notes, adding Cic., Att. 1.4 for Italy; for Pannonia, the vicus Caramantesium et villa, which I take to be an owned unit and big residence together, in Barkoczi et al. (1954–57) 324 no. 337, of A.D. 198/211 (p. 266); for Syria, Joh. Chrysos., Homil. 59 in cap. XXXIII Genes. 1 (PG 54.514), villages bought and sold; Theodoret., Rel. hist. 14 (PG 82.1413A), speaking of the 4th-cent. magnate Letoius of Antioch owning a nearby kome; Prentice (1908) 69, the villages called epoikia (tou deinou); Jalabert (1908) 733f., comparing the modern equivalent; for Asia Minor, Teja (1974) 35, instancing Gregory of Nyssa's reference to "the village belonging to me" (PG 46.784B), or Greg. Naz. in Ep. 57 and 79; for Egypt, Perkeesis and such places, in Parassoglou (1978) 55 and passim, and Lewuillon-Blume (1979) 183f., the term used being epoikion (unaware of Parassoglou's work but showing the private equivalent of crown villages to be a new phenomenon in the 4th cent.); and, for Africa, Vitruv., De arch. 7.3.25, on the village owned by Massinissa's son. In the late empire, churches might own whole villages. See examples in MacMullen (1980a) 28.

51. To the refs. in MacMullen (1974) 6 n. 2, add some from Sidonius in Gaudemet (1966) 128, and some from Greg. Naz. (PG 35.957C and 961A and 37.858) in Teja (1974) 45; also, the clear example of results of accumulation in a region of southern Italy: see Champlin (1980) 16, instancing an inscription of A.D. 323.

52. Above, chap. I notes 28f. (Italy) and 118 (Syria); Fentress (1979) 211 and 213f. on Numidia (and most of the sites are still occupied in the 4th and 5th cents.) with MacMullen (1974) 95f. on Lamasba near Cirta, on Italy, and on Egypt; and A. H. M. Jones (1964) 778–81, whose documentation, when you look at it, proves uncharacteristically inadequate. In small part, that results from his relying on his own work, A. H. M. Jones (1953), now superseded and in many points emended by Bowman (1985) 155. Bowman shows that, in a small village in the mid-3d cent., as in a fair-sized town in mid-4th, around 2 percent of the population owned over a third of the land, i.e., the proportions had not changed, while the later figure excludes (p. 148) about 70 percent of the nome land that was owned by villagers (how distributed among rich and poor is unknown, p. 151). So the evidence certainly does not support the notion of increasing concentration of land ownership.

53. Setälä (1977) 223; Day (1942) 236, tracing Atticus' properties in many places in Attica but also in Euboea, Corinth, Latium, and Egypt; Ramsay (1895–97) 1.287–92 with PIR ² F203; and similar holdings of the period, though more widely scattered, in the hands of eastern nobles (Greece and Asia Minor) in Halfmann (1979) 54–56, 66f., and 114 (Quadrati, Plancii, Calpurnii, including overseas holdings in Africa and Italy) and Mitchell (1980) 1071f.

54. Turner (1952) 85, on Alexandrians not only owning property but holding magistracies and providing public benefactions in Oxyrhynchus in the 1st to 3d cent.; M. Drew-Bear (1984) 316f., on the phenomenon there and in other towns also; and MacMullen (1974) 20f., on 1st-cent. holdings, and Fikhman (1975) 784 and 788f., on 3d-cent. holdings of Alexandrians up-Nile. In illustration of my sketch, see Zajac (1978) 70f. on families of Celeia in Noricum owning also in Solva and elsewhere; Corbier (1982) 689–91, on spouse's lands adding Thibica to Bulla Regia, with other 3d-cent. marital connections to Hippo and Gigthis and Utica; Bertrandy (1973/74) 195f. on the Antistii of Thibilis who (p. 199) took up residence in Rome in the 2d cent., as great noblemen, while retaining the family mansion in Africa and owning lands many miles from their original home; so similarly the Ummidii of Casinum, who by the 1st cent. had moved to Rome but maintained ties with their native town, cf. Syme (1968) 73 and 76. But the usual way of detecting lands owned is through a person's benefactions to the center of the district. See below, pp. 78f.

55. On Symmachus' properties, see Stroheker (1948) 34; Matthews (1975) 24 and 27; Cracco Ruggini (1982/83) 478f. n. 4, 496, and 514 n. 52, taking the Sicilian properties back to the 3d and early 4th cents.; Overbeck (1973) 41 and Lepelley (1979–81) 1.320f., adding other African connections in the Roman nobility; Matthews (1975) 73 and 149 on Marcellus, and ibid. 26 and PLRE I Proba 3 on Probus; on Ausonius' many estates in southern and northern Gaul, Loyen (1960)125f.; on Basil's mother's holdings, see Greg. Nyss., Vita S. Macrinae (PG 46.965A); on Antiochene nobles, Liebeschuetz (1972) 42 n. 2; and for generalizations about wide-sprawling senatorial properties, see Amm. 14.6.10, CJ 12.1.4 (346/49), and CT 11.22.2 (385). For church holdings, besides the remarkable evidence of the Liber Pontificalis and its discussion, e.g., by C. Pietri (1978) 319f. and 322f., see Hefele (1869–90) 1.580, can. 12 of the Council of Serdica on individual bishops' holdings in many different cities.

56. On municipal careers, see, e.g., CIL 2.5232 in Mackie (1983) 69 or IRT 595 (4th cent.); further, Meiggs (1960) 180 n. 2, though mistakenly seeing the illegal advancement of under-age children as "this dangerous symptom." On imperial careers, see A. R. Birley (1982) 247f., Syme (1977) 44, Syme (1968) 89, on a son as military tribune to a father who is governor, and IGR 3.500 III, lines 11f. There is some indication of the same kin-help

244 Notes to pages 75-77

in ecclesiastical careers, e.g., in Duchesne (1924) 3.58 on Athanasius' successors; further, the father-son succession in Nyssa, and brother succeeding to brother in the Cple bishopric, Soz., *H.E.* 6.19 (*PG* 67.721Cf.), or nephew to uncle (ibid. 7.7, 749C) or son to father (7.12, 757C) in Cple in A.D. 412–19. Being no church historian, however, I report no more than I have found by chance.

57. Plin., *Ep.* 10.87, *necessitudines eius inter meas numero*; POxy. 3366 (253/60) lines 24f.; and the assumption of Vespasian that an *adfinis* of Vitellius would be hostile, Tac., *Hist.* 2.98 and 4.49.1. Yet the assumption proved wrong. Cf. also Herodian 3.2.1 and 3.2.3, where Niger trusts Aemilianus though the latter was related to Albinus.

58. Campbell (1964) 39.

59. The stemma is explained in MacMullen (1986a) 441 n. 24.

60. See Cousin (1904) 26 on Hierocles; also in Laumonier (1958) 260. See ibid., further, 247f. and 270–87 on the Stratoniceia family of M. Sempronios Clemens, in which I can interconnect (more or less probably) more than a score of names of the 3d cent. See earlier *BCH* 1937, 288 and 293, to which Laumonier refers, and M. C. Sahin (1981), later, at pp. 114, with 67, 76, 89f., 99, 118, 126, 144f., 201, and the two clusters of names on pp. 154f. linked in the stemma p. 74; much less full, the ascendants and descendants of T. Statilius Calpurnianus Fadus in Prusia in Bithynia, in Dörner (1952) 21 no. 19, LeBas-Wadd. 5.1178, *PIR*¹ 3.377, 127 = *IGR* 3.58, and Väisänen (1976) 131. From Egypt, Packman (1976) 450 offers a good example involving seven generations and a councillor and eutheniarch of Alexandria, along with magistrates of Hermopolis and Oxyrhynchus. Finally, from Africa, see various kin groups of up to six generations in Corbier (1982) 690, 692, and 712.

61. Laumonier (1958) 288; on gifts of feeding to troops en route through Asia Minor and Syria, see MacMullen (1985) 70.

62. SHA *Pertinax* 4.2, cf. *Macrinus* 3.1, attesting to the same powers of another governor; and that official's consultation of the *vates* was a usual thing. The story (rather than the author) seems credible. Compare Vespasian's use of divine favor in Suet., *Vesp.* 7.1f.

63. *Vita S. Theodoti* 26, trans. Mitchell (1982) 109 n. 87, the priesthood in Ancyra; but most priesthoods controlled no such influence. See MacMullen (1981) 42–44, 66f., and 98f.

64. On hereditary and aristocratic priesthoods in Stratoniceia, Panamara, and Lagina, see the authorities cited in note 60 and Balland (1981) 168 and passim; in Ionia and Caria, Picard (1922) 214 and 241; also *IGR* 4.1169; and notice Menander Rhet. p. 100 Russell-Wilson, describing a welcome to the governor by "the priestly clans, active citizens' associations, and populace." The distinction needs to be made between service *to* a god and repayment of favor *from* a god. The latter, aristocrats offered out of grand piety; but the gift of a temple cannot be shown to enhance prestige any more than any other great building.

65. Levy (1899) 265, rightly inferring "une sorte de classe de magistrats"; below, Appendix B on "First Families"; and Balland (1981) 238 on "la classe des proteuontes (à l'échelon municipale ou au plan provincial)," overlying the universal *tagma bouleutikon* of Asia Minor cities. For western inheritable eminence, see Clemente (1972) 171 (Beneventum — compare a similar inscription of the same town, ibid. 185 and *CIL* 9.1684 = *ILS* 6503, an *ab avo et maioribus collegii et civitatis patronus*), and Barbieri (1971) 297 n. 1 on many Italian or African texts of patrons *ab origine, ab atavis,* etc.; similar wording to describe an African civic leader in Lepelley (1979–81) 2.455 n. 51; and various instances in Egypt's magistrate or bouleutic class, Alexandrian or Oxyrhynchite, in M. Drew-Bear (1984) 316, of the 3d cent.

66. Keil (1942) 185ff. and Matthews (1975) 69–73 and elsewhere in his splendid book, for a great deal of similar material. Further, below, note 79.

67. E.g., Amm. 26.10.1 and 7, and 30.5.11; instances where relatives are seen in action,

cooperatively, e.g., 28.6.8 (Remigius and Romanus) and 27.5.2 and 9.2 (where Romanus counts on an *affinis* and *affinitas*); in similar cooperation, Philostorg., *H.E.* 9.6, p. 118 Bidez = Winkelmann; conjoined target of an enemy, father and son, in Zos. 4.52; recommender for an in-law or a cousin, Synes., *Ep.* 75 and 118, in Tomlin (1979) 262; the three brothers from Gaul in mutual aid around A.D. 400, see Stroheker (1948) 175, 193, and 207, and *PLRE* I Minervius 2, Florentinus 2, and Protadius 1; and the relationships among over two hundred names (Nubel, Bauto, Gallia Placidia, etc.) in Demandt (1980) 618, the fold-out stemma. The church leadership seems to show similar patterns (above, note 56).

68. *AE* 1976, 67 no. 250 (Bellunum); Merlin and Poinssot (1908) 14f., to which compare another African estate the extent of which is known, in Peyras (1975) 187; Bertrandy (1973/74) 199f. on the Antistii; Tac., *Hist.* 2.72 on the Crassi; and above, notes 53f.

69. Alföldy (1964/65) 137f. and 142f. and Cracco Ruggini (1982/83) 496. The Nonii of Brescia are similar in the fullness of the record about them. See Garzetti (1977) 175–85 passim. They married into a second well-known Brixian family.

70. Ibid. 185; but cf. Halfmann (1979) 34 and Eck (1980) 310, both finding that great (senatorial or higher) *gentes* continued to be represented among hometown magistracies. Eck's catalogue (pp. 286–309) includes over two hundred persons identified both as senators and local benefactors or local magistrates — a very significant sample — while Halfmann's sample includes a number of senators from cities like Pergamon, Athens, Nysa, or Ephesus.

71. Philostr., *Vit soph.* 555f.; Graindor (1930) 32, 35, 68 (Canusium), and chap. X on building at Marathon, Delphi, Corinth, etc.; on Opramoas, Broughton (1938) 780 (not up-to-date); similar eastern figures of the 3d cent., Egnatius Victor Lollianus in Dietz (1980) 149–54 or Asinius Nicomachus Julianus, ibid. 88f.; earlier, Philostr., *Vit soph.* 531f., on Polemo, Picard (1922) 241, on Aelia Laevilla, or Halfmann (1979) 171, on Pythodorus; and the recognition of the ambition in the description of a benefactor, "the cities compete in their love for him," line 34 of the honorific inscription in Oliver (1941) 74f.

72. In Italy: the equestrian L. Licinius, who was patron to several cities, prefect in another, see Gasperini (1978) 442; *CIL* 10.1795 = *ILS* 1401, multiple patron but also "having served in every position" at another city; *CIL* 5.5126 = *ILS* 2722; *CIL* 11.5992, a *quinquennalis* in two different towns; and, in general, Devijver (1980) 3.1153–59, the Index geographicus, where about 40 percent of the indicated connections between equestrians and cities regard Italy. In Africa, for Carthaginian officeholders also holding office elsewhere, see Gascou (1982) 140f., Leglay (1961–66) 1.212–14, and *PIR²* Iulius 279; in Dalmatia, *CIL* 3.2026 = *ILS* 7162; in Bithynia, Pliny, *Ep.* 10.114.3, "every city" has several senators who are citizens elsewhere; in Syria, *CIL* 14.4624; in Egypt, Bowman (1971) 58; and for the Greek provinces in general, Quass (1982) 208. How prominence in more than one's own city might fall to one's lot is suggested by a mere boy being honored in an inscription as citizen both of Cibyra and Oenoanda (Ling [1981] 53).

73. Veyne (1976) 386, the thought developed on p. 398. Compare Matthews (1975) 29, remarking that senators "seem also to have used office, to a large extent, in order to foster their interests as private persons who possessed local connections and property in the provinces which they governed."

74. I quote from *CIL* 8.23963 and 25515. *CIL* 5.7881 of the mid-3d cent. in the Maritime Alps is another good example: the governor helps in time of famine. Harmand (1957) 285 discovers 670 patrons of all sorts of communities, among whom are 199 owing their status to their office (including some lawyers); and he appears to have missed still others, e.g., *CIL* 8.9002 = *PIR* ² Flavius 366, *IGLS* 1258, and Dörner (1952) 12 no. 11 — as well as others identified only post-Harmand. So the phenomenon is extremely common. It extends into the ranks of *curatores rei publicae* (*vel sim.*) very extensively, see Duthoy (1979) 230f.,

and down to customs-collectors, of some local usefulness, see Mocsy (1970) 107f.

75. Petit (1955) 379 and 383 (in error, I think, about any sharp distinction between east and west, pp. 376–79); Liebeschuetz (1972) 59; CT 1.12.6 (398) and 1.15.5 (365), proconsul and *vicarius*, and 6.35.3 (352), "the officials of the Largesses in individual cities"; and Chastagnol (1978) 33f., adding up the staff of the *vicarius, consularis, praef. ann.*, and *rationalis*. Notice also Lepelley (1979-81) 2. 462 and 466f., "la plupart de ces personnes... appartenaient à des familles décurionales de Timgad dont d'autres représentants figurent sur l'album."

76. PFlor. 71 (e.g., lines 31, 35, 60, 509, 529, etc.), with only a small minority of occupational specification, and PGiess. 117 of ca. 350. See MacMullen (1963) 109. A characteristic glimpse is afforded also by PThead. 8 (306) or 21 (318) or the four boat-owners of PRendel Harris 94 (late 4th cent.): a *bouleutes*, an *a commentariis ducis*, a bishop's son, and a *presbyteros*.

77. For an example, see CIL 6.1759 = ILS 1272 (A.D. 389); further, Clemente (1972) 209 and 226, "the new bureaucracy entirely displaces the municipal magistracies" as *collegia* patrons.

78. Firm. Maternus, *Mathesis*, in MacMullen (1971) 113f.

79. On Timgad, see Lepelley (1979–81) 2. 468f.; and on the Roman nobility, see Stroheker (1948) 10–12, retailing the nobility's claims while doubting them. He instances the Symmachi; but see now Cameron (1970) 17f. on eminence traceable to at least the mid-3d cent., and compare the rapid turnover earlier. "By Caracalla's time it was a rare member who could trace senatorial ancestors back for more than one or two generations," Talbert (1984) 31. A. R. Birley, by letter, reminds me of certain connections of the 4th-cent. aristocrats to be traced back to late-2d-cent. notables: Anicii going back to a cos. ca. 198, Annius Anullinus possibly to a cos. ord. 199, while Q. Aradius Rufinus earlier is ancestor to the Constantinian nobleman, see A. R. Birley (1967) 83; but the best discussion of these matters I have seen is that of F. Jacques (1986) 83–90, focusing on the senatorial aristocracy from mid-3d to earlier 4th cent. He finds about the same degree of continuity in the elite of this long period as in A.D. 193–217. Of the well documented senators A.D. 282–312, 43 percent are of *gentes* already senatorial in A.D. 260. On the snobbery and sneers of the older families, notice Liban., Or. 2.35, and Greg. Naz. in Teja (1974) 8, who scorns the elite created by *grammata*, i e., patents of nobility *ex nihilo*.

80. Amm. 28.1.5f., a mere *tabularius* under one of Constantius' governors sends his son to school, who as a lawyer can then be a governor himself, and so on up; Liban., Or. 4.25, a mere villager starts as a gatekeeper to a governor, his son becoming a consular; and Joh. Chrysos., *Adv. oppugnatores vitae monast.* 3.5 (PG 47.557). With this passage which I quote in the text compare Aug., *Conf.* 6.11(18), hoping through his rhetorical training that he could gain *aliquis honor*, "and what else could one want? I have lots of influential friends. If I press for that and nothing more, at least I ought to be able to get a governorship."

81. See Blazquez (1964) 111f., including the example of Leucadius, on whom see PLRE II (Tarraco); for Gaul, see Stroheker (1948) 12, 18f. (Ausonius and the Trier families), and 36f. (ties of noncareerists to magnates in office); also A. R. Birley (1981) 2 and 35. For the new elite around Libanius, see Petit (1955) 384, "au service de l'Etat, sans lequel ils ne seraient rien," and examples, p. 385; Liebeschuetz (1972) 179 and 184f., to the same effect; and Schouler (1973) 80. John Chrysostom, *In I Cor.* (PG 62.250), is aware of the prejudice against the *nouveau arrivé* through the church, whose grandfather was a fuller, while the man himself now wears silken clothes and owns a house, etc. Cf. Amm. 22.11.4, George of Alexandria *in fullonio natus (ut ferebatur)*.

82. For a general view, see Harmand (1957) 332–44, and for an up-to-date survey, Nicols (1980) 537, 539f., and passim. He concentrates on thirty better-preserved examples of the

relationship in Spain, Africa, and Italy, their form varying somewhat. *AE* 1962 no. 287 declares that a propraetorian quaestor *hospitium fecit* with the senate and people of Munigua in Baetica and *in fidem clientelamque suam . . . recepit*; *AE* 1941, 79 (A.D. 75) declares that the citizens of Banasa in Mauretania *sibi liberisque eorum patronum* [so-and-so] *cooptaverunt*, while the patron accepts them in his clientage (a two-sided document); *CIL* 8.8837 specifies that the propraetorian legate *eos* [the people of Tupusuctu] *patrocinio suo tuendos recepit*; and *CIL* 6.1685 = *ILS* 6111a indicates that a deputation of the client community waited on the patron in Rome. This is the man on the mons Caelius.

83. See the Beneventan inscriptions above, note 65; *CIL* 2.2211 (A.D. 348) from Corduba, a *tessera* from *cuncti fabri subidiani*; 2.5812, sixteen men and five women of humble crafts offer a bronze *tessera* of *hospitium* to patrons; and *CIL* 11.2702 = *ILS* 7217 (A.D. 224), on which see Waltzing (1895–1900) 1.427f. See further, ibid. 353, on individuals being patron to many different *collegia*; and the logic of one illustration in Budischovsky (1977) 117, on *CIL* 5.2071, where an *eques* is patron to many *collegia* resident along natural lines of travel and trade.

84. There is a highly characteristic series of terms used to describe a certain Publius Licinnius Crassus Junianus: *soter kai euergetes kai patron*, in Radet (1890) 232. He is honored for his "goodwill and virtue and benefactions toward the people" of Nysa. Other appearances of *patron* and *patronissa* are cited in MacMullen (1986a) 437–39.

85. For Opramoas' date and the published file of imperial letters, see Heberdey (1897) 63; Ritterling (1920–24) 44f.; Jameson (1980) 846f.; and *TAM* 2 no. 905 X H (from Hadrian) and passim. For Herodes Atticus, see Philostr., *Vit. soph.* 562 and 565, Herodes himself publishing Marcus Aurelius' letters. For other recipients, see Walton (1929) 55; *IGR* 3.228; Rigsby (1979) 401 and 404; *Die Inschriften von Ephesos* 5 (1980) 35–37 nos. 1491–93, letters from Antoninus Pius inscribed on the proscenium of the Ephesus council house, solicited by and praising a local notable, or solicited for him by the city or Asian council; Mouterde and Poidebard (1931) 106f. on the Palmyrene notable "who has enjoyed the good testimony . . . [in a letter] from" Hadrian and Antoninus Pius; Millar (1977) 115, 217, and 470, adding refs. to other eastern inscriptions; in the west, *ILT* 1514, the bare ref. to a man honored by the emperor Marcus Aurelius; words of praise from an emperor's speech treasured by their object and quoted in his epitaph, *ILS* 986 = *CIL* 14.3608; and, from the later empire, Swift and Oliver (1962) 247f. and 259f. Quoted is Plin., *Ep.* 10.58 (transl. Radice) on Archippus. He was formidable and dangerous (ibid. 10.81.2f.).

86. Ael. Arist., *Or.* 50.75, 83f. (quoted), and 87. For the local importance of Rufinus, see Ohlemutz (1940) 138f. Fronto, *Ad amicos* 2.8 p. 199 Naber, offers an example of such letters to judges as Aristides solicited. For another instance of veiled threat in a letter from Pliny, see MacMullen (1986b) 518.

87. See Fronto, *Ep. ad Verum* 2.8 p. 136 Naber, comparing Epict., *Diss.* 2.14.18, "what could you ever be thought to lack? . . . The emperor knows you, you have many friends in Rome"; further, the word *sebastognostos*, "known to the emperor," as an honorific epithet in inscriptions, in Millar (1977) 472 n. 48, even *hospes divi Hadriani* as a distinction, *CIL* 11.5632 = *ILS* 2735 (Italy); and Julian, *Ep.* 40(68), quoted.

88. Above, note 85; *TAM* 2, 3, p. 328f. no. 905 col. I C-D, II G, III A, IV B, esp. VIII 30f., etc. (Opramoas); *IGR* 4.1381; Groag (1939) 107, a Gastfreund of the cos. II of A.D. 120; Oliver (1953) 963f.; M. C. Sahin (1981) 139 no. 266, praiseful letters from a quaestor "and many senators"; and Cantineau (1936) 278 and Gawlikowski (1973) 26 on a fragmentary inscription showing Palmyra repeatedly praising someone to Avidius Cassius.

89. *CIL* 2.1282 (Salpensa), witness to the *enixum sollicitum etiam suffragium*; the nephew identified by Pflaum (1966) 334f.

90. M. C. Sahin loc. cit. (note 88); *IGR* 3.513; and above, note 87, on Hadrian's host.

91. Dio 58.22.2f., the scene being Italy under Tiberius; further, MacMullen (1986b) 517.

92. Plin., *Ep.* 3.19.6; Ps.-Quintilian, *Decl.* 301 p. 187, perhaps not far from the real Quintilian's dates.

93. *Dig.* 39.6.3 (Paul), 4.6.9 (Callistratus), and 48.19.28.7 (idem), in Wacke (1980) 600f.; these passages, along with *Dig.* 22.3.20, *Didascalia Apostolorum* p. 158 ed. R. H. Connolly, about "rich persons [who] keep men shut up in prisons," and *CT* 9.11.1 (388), on private jails in rural settings; and Wacke (1980) 580 on *CT* 12.3.1 (386), extortionate purchases of land or slaves; *CJ* 2.19.11 (326), where pressure to sell can be exerted by a government official; *CT* 3.1.9 (415); and *CJ* 11.59.10 (398) and *CT* 13.11.9, where the rural magnates seize *per potentiam fundos opimos ac fertiles*, leaving the poor to work and pay taxes on the worst land (Syria).

94. Basil, *Homil. in divites* 5 (PG 31.293–96); cf. Basil, *Ep.* 18, "do not fear the threats of persons in power," and compare the picture of "persons who have achieved success by means of other people's misfortunes," in Liban., *Or.* 47.2; on the same type also Joh. Chrysos., *Quod qui seipsum non laedit* 9 (PG 52.469): "Someone will say, wealth makes those who have it honored, and they can easily be avenged on their enemies." Libanius recollects how his widowed mother was harassed in his absence (*Or.* 55.15), "and much land worked by many hands was lost," cf. Liebeschuetz (1972) 43, while (*Ep.* 1380, cit. ibid.) the PPO Helpidius' "powerful assistance" had been procured by the offer of a rural estate as a gift to the prefect's daughter. Another case is recalled, ibid. 200 and *PLRE* I Aristophanes, where a young man's lands in Greece ca. 350 were seized by an official, an older relative, and he and his managers had to flee — himself, to another province. For earlier parallels, see MacMullen (1974) 6f.

95. Joh. Chrysos., *Homil. in Mt* 61.3 (PG 58.591f.), trans. Stevens (1966) 123f. For "olive" in the translation I have made the correction "wine." For a closely similar account of the oppression and extortion practised by the rural rich on the poor in early 5th-cent. Egypt, see Barns (1964) 158, with still further details to be supplied from papyri, e.g., PCair. Isidor. 78 (324), on oppression by *megala dynamenoi epi ton topon*; and a somewhat later parallel in Syria, in Theodoret, *Ep. Sirm.* 23, pleading the case of tenant peasants oppressed in a year of shortage.

96. Mt 21.33–40; compare Sperber (1971) 253 n. 3, killing of tax collectors in early or mid-4th cent.; and Liban., *Or.* 47.7f. (likewise taxes, not rents).

97. See MacMullen (1974a) 260 n. 25 and Staerman and Trofimova (1975) 63f. n. 1 for some examples of patronage of *pagi* or *vici*, etc.; but notice the work (no doubt unpaid) that a landowner might offer to some third party as a munificent gift "by the aid of his own peasants," *IGR* 4.808 (Hierapolis), and the landlord's assumption that, in the Persecutions, if *he* sacrificed to the gods, so must his *inquilini* and *coloni* (Cypr., *Ep.* 55[51].13.2). For tenants' gifts to the landlord, see MacMullen (1974) 114, Kolendo (1979) 403f., and Veyne (1981) 245; on peasants' dependence for loans and equipment in late Roman Egypt, see Fikhman (1975) 789 and Keenan (1981) 480f.; on the same practises around Antioch, Liban., *Or.* 47.19.

98. *De Nabuthe* 5.21 (though Ambrose here could be referring to rents due, not regular gifts). Compare, somewhat earlier in the century, Lact., *Div. Inst.* 6.18.10, the rich man should not accept gifts from the poor (because there is an element of compulsion in the custom); and later, Percival (1969) 611 on a 6th-cent. document, with others like it, showing that "*xenia* . . . are no longer a voluntary matter . . . but are required by the landowner as a right."

99. To Brown (1971) 84f. add Hier., *Vita Hilarionis* 15.7, showing villagers' reverence for an ascetic; on the reliability of the source, Mohrmann (1975) xli–xliii; further, Callinicus, *Vita S. Hypati* 4.6, on a holy man succoring peasants in Thrace; and Constantius, *Vita S. Germani* 4.19 and 24; ibid. 20, on the saint's miraculous "binding" of refractory persons, with comparative material in MacMullen (1980a) 29 n. 25.

100. Above, note 9, *Dig.* 11.4.2, and Lucian, *Alex.* 55, early illustrations; above, note 42, Athanas., *Apol. c. Arianos* 29 (PG 25.2978), *Apol. de fuga* 6 (PG 25.625B) and 24 (673D), or *Hist. Arianorum* 59 (PG 25.764C), all showing soldiers helping bishops in sectarian violence.

101. Liban., *Or.* 55.11, in Liebeschuetz (1972) 200; *Or.* 45.3 and 5, comparing the situation described by Aelius Aristides in MacMullen (1974) 6f.; and *Or.* 47.12f., extortion by manipulation of the juridical authorities' powers of arrest and jail.

102. See above, note 3, Pliny's and Symmachus' views. Compare the *Martyrium (Acta) S. Carpi* 3.1 (Latin recension in Musurillo [1972] 30) of the later 2d cent. (?) in Pergamon: *principalis es?* Cf. Franchi de' Cavalieri (1935) 50, the *Passio SS. Dativi et al.* 5; *Dig.* 22.5.3.1 (Callistratus), a judge is to establish a witness's truthfulness by discovering *cuius dignitatis et cuius existimationis*, cf. CT 11.39.3 (334); Rea (1976) 461f. on the indefinable quality that made a *matrona stolata*, with superior legal rights because of social rank; and Garnsey (1970) passim. Notice, further, *Dig.* 1.16.9.4 (Ulpian): the judge should bear in mind that "lowlier persons" may sometimes prefer not to venture on litigation at all through inadequate representatives, neither attentive *neque in aliqua dignitate positi*; 48.2.16, among several accusers the right to litigate shall be assigned to *dignitas*; and 1.18.6.2, showing that *potentiores* would attack you with invented charges if you served as *defensor* to their target, a *humilior*.

103. On the passages where Apuleius tries to establish his social *bona fides*, see MacMullen (1986c) 165; on Phileas, see the Greek recension of the *Acta* conveniently in Musurillo (1972) 340 and 342 (sections 11f.), comparing the Latin, p. 348, the prefect there saying, *memento quod te honoraverim*, etc. Pietersma (1984) 64f. shows insignificant differences from the more familiar Greek and Latin texts, in the new Greek fragments.

104. Ael. Arist., *Or.* 50.39.

105. See Millar (1977) 10, 332, and 476 on access to the emperor by slaves and lowly persons; further, Huchthausen (1974) 252 and 255; Millar (1977) 335, 475, 544, and 546 on appeals as late as Diocletian and Constantine, and add Greg. Naz., *Or.* 5.21 (PG 35.689), where Julian listened to mere peasant's requests for "the things people do ask rulers." But Julian's egalitarian condescension was pronounced and untypical. On the routine of appeals, see Millar (1977) 512–16, appeals being compulsory in capital cases in the early 3d cent., ibid. 330f. On the emperor's intent specifically to protect the weak against extortion through terror, see, e.g., *Dig.* 3.1.5 and CT 1.22.2 (334), *cum alicuius potentiam perhorrescunt.*

106. Above, note 86; Ael. Arist., *Or.* 50.79f. p. 445f. Keil, 84 p. 446, and 87 p. 447.

107. Lucian, *Alex.* 57.

108. Cic., *Pro Quinctio* 22.72; above, at note 92.

109. *Dig.* 3.1.4 (Ulpian, but reaching back); *CJ* 2.13(14).1, Claudius II responding to years of complaints and to the fact that *tenuiores* often (notice: *saepe*) were overwhelmed by the *potentes*; *CJ* 9.9.23.1 (A.D. 290), inviting suits to recover payoffs made to racketeers *ob potentis patrocinii metum*; *Dig.* 4.2.23.1, dated to 325/31 by Wacke (1980) 589f., who notes the possibility of a gloss in the phrase *cognitio ... minabatur*; but the essence of the situation is clear. For a later parallel, CT 1.22.1 (334); and for an earlier, Tac., *Dial.* 10, speaking of the courage needed to enter the contest against the *potentes*, while Pliny (*Ep.* 1.5.15) indicates the need for prudence in undertaking litigation when he describes the hostile Regulus as "*dyskathairentos*; for he has money, faction, and wide backing, and is still more widely feared; and that affords one more strength than being liked." One of the most striking testimonies is in Seneca, *Ep. ad Lucilium* 2.14.3f., reducing human fears of material harm to three things: poverty, illness, and the powerful: "*timentur quae per vim potentioris eveniunt*; and of all these, nothing makes us quake more than the threat of some other person's greater power."

110. Tac., *Ann.* 15.20; Plut., *Moralia* 815A–B, the *protoi* and *dynatoi* with their "grasping and

contentious nature" turn to lawyers and courts to hurt each other; and Plin., *Ep.* 10.56, 110, 114, and 58.1 and 81.2f. on Flavius Archippus. About this figure's activities, see a little more in MacMullen (1986a) 440; and on the first of these cases, at 10.56, notice the comment of Wells (1984) 149, "we get the impression that Roman justice is being used to pursue private feuds." The phenomenon could also be found in times too early for my purposes, e.g., Cic., *Paradox.* 6.46.

111. On Drusilla's case see Witt (1977) 66–68; another long case, 79–85, with still a third in Phrygia, though the evidence is a mere fragment, in T. Drew-Bear (1978) 20. Compare Mart. 7.65, a twenty-year lawsuit; later, *Sirmond.* 1 (333), offering relief to "wretched men entwined in the long, almost infinite tentacles of litigation"; also Amm. 30.4.18f. and Liban., *Or.* 45.18, on endless delays and argy-bargy in trials; and Eunap. frg. 16 on law in Julian's reign being prompt, for a change.

112. Anon., *De miraculis S. Stephani.* 2.5 (*PL* 41.851f.).

113. Constantius, *Vita S. Germani* 7.36, *diversae palatii potestates.*

114. *CT* 10.10 passim, e.g., 10.10.2 (312/319) or 10 (365), both quoted; similarly, 10.10.12.2 (380); and 9.37.3 (382) and 3.39.1 (383)–3 (398).

115. Julian, *Misop.* 344A; Liban., *Or.* 45.3f. (A.D. 386 — trans. Loeb, except *ton dynatoteron*, not "the influential"); and the emphatic passage in Joh. Chrysos., *In Ioannem* 82.4 (*PG* 59.446), "Though the persons determining the verdict are called judges, they are in reality brigands and murderers, and whoever takes up litigation or testamentary disposition discovers misdeeds by the thousands, deceits, thefts, and plots." He adds (*In ep. ad Rom.* 11.6, *PG* 60.491) details on the physical risks of going to court: torture and jail.

116. See, e.g., above, note 94, Eunap. frg. 63, and much other material in the next chapter.

117. Amm. 22.9.8 and Aug., *Ep.* 151.4, a year after Heraclianus' rebellion of 413, and *PLRE* II Marinus 1. The count was fired, in fact.

118. Synes., *Ep.* 118 (*PG* 66.1497C) and 130 (1561B); Theodoret, *Ep.* 11 (A.D. 434, cf. *PLRE* II Titus 2) and 36 (32), quoted; and Liban., *Ep.* 211.1 (A.D. 360), also quoted. Libanius himself was the target of such deadly litigation. See Norman (1954) 46f. In the same century but in Egypt (Palladius, *Hist. Laus.* 3.1f. and 38.5, in Bougatsos and Batistatos pp. 48f. and 212, or in the English translation of R. T. Mayer, pp. 50 and 135), it was reasonable to suppose that a judge, a governor, could be bribed to apply his authority to wound some person's private enemy.

119. Liban., *Or.* 52.4–6.

120. Liebeschuetz (1972) 192; Synes., *Ep.* 42 (*PG* 66.1365B), with other letters, see Tomlin (1979) 262; Aug., *Ep.* 115; Basil, *Ep.* 86, begging favor to be shown to *philoi*, with the excellent pages of survey by Treucker (1981) 405f., on the whole range of Basil's interventions and intercessions, including the focusing of the influence of three persons on a single case (p. 408). For a parallel to Basil in the west, see Symm., *Ep.* 1.69f., 74, and 77; 2.14 and 81; 3.35f.; 4.68; 5.54; 9.129 — these of the 370s to 390s — and Matthews (1975) 191 on *Ep.* 3.36 to Ambrose. Examples of a concentration of several persons' influence in behalf of a single petitioner may be seen in *Ep.* 3.49 or 3.73 with 4.67.

121. For the earlier laws, see above, note 102; for the later, see *CJ* 2.14(15).1 (400). Even the emperor's name was usurped, 2.15(16).1 (408), and the law of A.D. 400 had to be repeated in 416 (*CT* 4.4.5.2), where it is specified that the support claimed is that of *privati potentes*. Wacke (1980) 583 compares Aug., *Ep.* 96.2, where a bishop falsely lists an estate under the name of a *potens* to avoid taxation.

122. Symm., *Rel.* 28.2, 5, and 7f. For even more violent, dramatic attacks on his descendant's and the *vicarius'* authority, see *Ep.* 29.3 in the *Coll. Avellana* (*CSEL* 35 p. 75, A.D. 419) or 32.3 (ibid. 79).

123. *CT* 9.1.17 (390); *Coll. Avellana* 13 (*CSEL* 35 p. 54). The occasion for the latter document was the protracted defiance of imperial orders by church sects in Rome, in the course of unrest over a papal election.

124. *Rel.* 31 (A.D. 384). Notice the cautious, not to say timorous, note in *Ep.* 9.40, on how to deal with "noblemen and respected persons"; the report of defiance of authority and abduction of a witness from the very carriage of the urban prefect in broad daylight, using *agentes in rebus* as henchmen(!), *Rel.* 23.4ff., 7–11, and 14; and the specification of insult and loss of face, *contumelia*, involved in these contorted events, 23.8f. He concludes, ibid. 15, with an appeal for the emperor to uphold what is really the emperor's own authority, entrusted to Symmachus (*creditae mihi potestatis*).

125. *Dig.* 4.7.3.1f., in a discussion of litigation faced by a landholder against an abutter. For the occurrences of the term *potentior* in the *Digest*, see Wacke (1980) passim, offering an excellent discussion. I see no difference in meaning, incidentally, among *potentior*, *potentes*, and *dynatoi* in the texts I deal with, though the type of person they describe changed across time as surrounding society changed.

126. *Dig.* 8.5.18.

127. Sperber (1978) 128, a text of the late 3d/early 4th cent. Compare the repeated defiance of orders from a *beneficiarius* on behalf of a female minor, in PCair. Isidor. 63 (296) and more and worse defiance in PCair. Isidor. 69 (310).

128. PThead. 15 (280/1).

129. *CT* 1.15.1 (325) 1.16.4 (328), both noticed by Gaudemet and Wacke; further on *potentiores*, see 12.1.6 (318/319), explained by Nov. Maj. 7.1 praef., on decurions marrying a slave woman in a *potentissima domus* as a way of coming under the master's protection; further, on the sheltering of decurions, 12.1.50 (362), 76 (371), and 146 (395); 13.1.15 (386) and 13.1.21 (418), *potentiores* fending off tax collectors from *mercatores*.

130. *CT* 11.15.2 (384). On the explicit synonymity between "rich" and "powerful," see also Robert (1946) 33 on Greek 3d-cent. texts in which *dynamis* = wealth.

131. Mansi (1759) 3.1000, Toledo can. 11, "if one of the *potentes* has seized the property of (*expoliaverit*) a cleric, poor man, or monk, and the bishop summons him for a hearing, and he defies him," let him be excommunicated; and Priscus frg. 8 Müller-Dindorf, to which Doblhofer (1955) 44 and Blockley (1983) 2.268f. (Priscus frg. 11.2) draw attention — Doblhofer with translation, Blockley with that and text also.

132. Besides such occasional handsome gifts to his friends as Pliny mentions, greatly to his credit (e.g., *Ep.* 1.19 and 6.25.3), there appear to have been commercial profits controlled through being in municipal office (Plut., *Moralia* 809A, or Liban., *Ep.* 318, A.D. 357), to which in turn the local magnates were important in gaining access; or a purchase price would be lowered for you at the request of a magnate (Plin., *Ep.* 1.24.1). As Kopecek (1974) 299 shows through Basil, *Ep.* 74, a powerful friend might save you costs on your land from administrative changes. Commercial travel and contact could be facilitated by the Haves, cf. Mouterde and Poidebard (1931) 106f. and Liebeschuetz (1972) 18; and the business enterprises of the Haves were as far-flung as their landholdings (above, notes 52-58), witness a good deal of archeological and still more written evidence: for the late Republic, Yeo (1951–52) 336, D'Arms (1981) 154–68, for Italian senators of the early empire, and, on two families and their amphorae, Buchi (1973) 568 (with other similar examples, 573f.), and Halfmann (1979) 55, with a glimpse of the information about brick and amphorae production in MacMullen (1986a) 435 n. 3 and 440 nn. 18 and 20. On olives and oil widely shipped by African noble families, see DiVita (1985) 149, 151, and 154. I only scratch the surface on this evidence. Collecting debts was facilitated by pressure from the great: see Plin., *Ep.* 6.8.3 and CT 2.13.1 (422); and such men had much money out on loan themselves, see Philostr., *Vit. soph.* 549 with Oliver (1953) 967, and Sperber (1978) 120f., on Palestinian peasants' frequent heavy indebtedness; Mrozek (1985) 314 on Pompeian loan-levels; and Aug., *Ep.* 268.1, on tiding over the debts come due for an impoverished debtor. For intervention to reduce taxes, see Aug., *Ep.* 96.2 or 268.1, Theodoret., *Ep.* 18 and 33(29) and *Ep. Sirm.* 45 and 47, Basil's many letters in Forlin Patrucco (1973) 300f. and Kopecek (1974) 301; for intervention on the matter of a liturgy,

see Liban., *Ep.* 293. But this author's volumes of correspondence are filled with efforts to arrange favors, cf. A. H. M. Jones (1964) 392.

133. *Inschriften von Ephesos* 5 (1980) 35f. no. 1491.

134. Robert (1965) 224 and above, note 130, on powerful = wealthy; variants like *polytelos*, in notes 24 and 26 above, on enforced generosity.

135. Above, notes 3 and 109f.; Graindor (1930) 76 n. 2, on the *saevitia et avaritia* of Herodes Atticus.

136. *IGR* 4.1431 (Polemo) and Dio 69.3.6 (Favorinus), with Menander Rhetor p. 180 Russell-Wilson, on how such envoys should speak; Constantius, *Vita S. Germani* 4.19 and 24; *CIL* 12.594 (Zosimus); and Keil (1956) 3 — this being only one of many of the Ephesian honorand's *legationes*. Compare *TAM* 5, 1, no. 687, a *legatio* to Germany and Britain in A.D. 39, and other mentions of repeated service in *IGR* 4.914, 1060, and 1169, and *AE* 1916 no. 120 = *AE* 1969/70 no. 592. For instances of tax-relief gained by *legationes*, see Malal. 12 p. 313; *CIL* 2.1956 (Cartima in Baetica); *AE* 1916 no. 42 (Volubilis); *IGR* 4.181; and Gascou (1982) 140f. For the importance of a *legatio* emphasized in local decrees of thanks, see Laumonier (1958) 260, an imperial grant of 250,000 denarii; *IG* 5, 1, 1432, lines 30ff.; *ILAfr* 21 and 634; *CIL* 2.4055 (thanks to the goddess Panthea Tutela for success, *ob legationes in concilio provinciale*); Lepelley (1979–81) 2.369; and Themist., *Or.* 3. Other selections of evidence in Millar (1977) 375-85 and Kaya (1985) 54f.

137. On *PRyl.* 623 and *PLat. Argent.* 1, see Moscadi (1970) 89 and 101 and Cotton (1981) 40–44. Compare the form letters of Basil, *Ep.* 305 and 385.

138. *IGR* 4.144.

139. Robert (1960) 326–28, with still other texts from Termessus (*TAM* 2.668, cf. *PIR²* C558), the chief one from Corinth first discussed in Pallas, Charitonidis, and Venencie (1959) 498–500. They assign it a date under Claudius. For inscriptions of the later Republic declaring the weight of influence, *entrope*, enjoyed by Greek notables with Roman officials, see T. Drew-Bear (1972) 453.

140. *Archives Nationales* (Paris) H 1696, fol. 67 — the document and translation thanks to W. H. Beik through T. W. Perry.

141. *CIL* 5.875 = *ILS* 1347 of A.D. 105. The honorand had recently gained a tax-improvement for the city.

142. Liebeschuetz (1972) 18. Compare what Augustine says to a *comes Africae* in ca. 420: "*Whenever* men ask me to recommend them to your kindness and protection (*fides*) . . ." — so the requests came all the time (*Ep.* 206). Compare the early case of ca. A.D. 103: barely arrived at his point of command, an army officer on Hadrian's Wall dispatches a note to a friend who knows the governor, requesting that he "furnish me with friends so that, by your *beneficium*, I may have an enjoyable term of service." See Bowman and Thomas (1983) 127f.; ibid. 106f., for another letter, of introduction and recommendation, to an army officer.

143. Dio Chrysos., *Or.* 45.3, claiming he only used his friendship with Nerva to help his native place; Dio 73.12.2, a chamberlain to Commodus uses his great power to benefit his native Nicomedia; Tac., *Hist.* 2.98, on Valerius Festus, legionary legate in Africa and relative of Vitellius, who "promoted the *studia provincialium*," while (*IRT* 526) Lepcis in 376 adopts as patron the proconsul of Africa, son of Ausonius.

144. Keil and Maresch (1960) 95, a 3d-cent. *philosebastos* and *prytanis* whose statue was put up locally; and Tac., *Ann.* 12.61, a Coan physician gets tax-relief for Cos.

145. Ifie (1976) 39; Fronto, *Ad M. Caes.* 5.34 p. 86 Naber, and *ILT* 1514 explain the usefulness of an *advocatus* in Rome.

146. E.g., Plin., *Ep.* 2.9.3, *suffragio meo*; his *dignitas* is at stake in his recommending, 2.9.1; 4.4.2; and 6.25.3; Ael. Arist., *Or.* 32(12).15, on Alexander and his prepotent recommendations; and Liebeschuetz (1972) 179 and 193f.

147. For the Pliny texts, see MacMullen (1986b) 521f.

148. On the Republican background of *beneficia-officia* and suchlike obligations, Wistrand (1941) 22ff. supplies essential clarification; but there is considerable bibliography. Among primary texts, notice Plut., *Moralia* 814C, "the Romans themselves are extremely zealous for their friends in matters of political partisanship," cf. earlier, Polyb. 20.9.11f. (191 BC) on *pistis = fides*, and (20.10.6) the Aetolian protest that the Roman way is "neither just nor Greek" (of course not). On Caesar's *beneficia*-book, as well as on other aspects of the subject, without further citation, see MacMullen (1986b) 520f., adding Suet., *Iul.* 23.2, where Caesar is seen demanding written contracts of political obligation; also *ILS* 1792 = *CIL* 6.1884 with 6.8627, a slave as *a comment. beneficiorum* to Trajan, and above, note 142, where the word is used in a private request for help. For *benephikia* in the resolutions of the Nicene Council (can. 12), see Hefele (1907–09) 1, 1, 591.

149. MacMullen (1986b) 520 gives some bibliography. For a magistracy, which is a little different, see Dio 79.22.2, to show the sense of seniority and right to a promotion. Contra, on the absolute need for recommenders and string-pulling, see MacMullen (1971) 106, on a career in rhetoric, and Plin., *Ep.* 6.23.5. On the consideration given to special skills, see MacMullen (1976) 238 n. 32, adding Philostr., *Vit. soph.* 621.

150. *ILS* 8977 = *ILAlg.* 468 (Thibilis, A.D. 164), *ob insignem eius benivolentiam in se*, and other similar examples gathered in MacMullen (1986b) 523f.; Eck (1982) 147f. and 150; and Saller (1982) 9f., 12, 53 (Martial 3.95, boasting of *praemia* from both Titus and Domitian), and 57. I don't always draw the same conclusions from the same evidence as Saller.

151. For example, Plin., *Ep.* 10.86A–B and 87; Fronto, *Ad amicos.* 1.6 p. 178 Naber (A.D. 165), hoping from the recipient that "you will adorn him [the man recommended] with your own recommendations, *suffragia*"; A. R. Birley (1981) 87 (early Trajanic letter found on Hadrian's wall); Cotton (1981) 7f., 12, and 15; later, Amm. 15.5.3 and some dozens of Symmachus' letters, e.g., 3.67 or 3.72.

152. For Fronto's intervention, see Champlin (1980) 69f.; above, notes 86 and 119f. on court cases; further, POxy. 1424 (318); Greg. Naz., *Ep.* 9 (PG 37.36 of A.D. 372); Symm., *Ep.* 1.64, 5.66, 9.11 (A.D. 399) or 138f.; Ambros., *Ep.* 54 (PL 16.1167); Synes., *Ep.* 18 (PG 66.1353B), 59 (1404A), or 75 (1441A-B); and Aug., *Ep.* 206; on Gerontius, Soz., *H.E.* 8.6 (PG 67.1529C–1532A). The quotation from Symmachus comes from his *Ep.* 7.94.

153. Apul., *Apol.* 94.1–5; for a similar letter of intervention that ends a great man's wrath, see Plin., *Ep.* 9.21.1 (the petitioner here too on his knees), or Symm., *Ep.* 5.41.

154. Sperber (1971) 234; Epict., *Diss.* 4.1.92f., which I go on to quote in the Loeb translation; and many revealing anecdotes about danger in Italy of the 1st cent. in Friedländer (1922) 355.

155. On Martial, see Rouland (1979) 511 n. 70; on thanks to the gods for the *concordia* of patrons, see Albertini (1943) 378; on clients who, we happen to learn, have two (or more) patrons, see *CIL* 4.7275 and 7279, in Franklin (1980) 106f., and *Dig.* 38.1.8pr. (Labeo under Augustus).

156. Dio 79(78).11.2 suggests the danger in being involved as a client with a patron's fall. At the first hint of a great person's being in danger herself, or himself, friends and dependents stood clear: Dio 58.9.1, Sejanus is deserted, as, later, Agrippina would be (Dio 61.8.6) and the other victims of Nero's displeasure, 63.17.4; cf., later, Amm. 15.5.8, on Silvanus in A.D. 355.

157. Parsons (1976) 412–17, 421, and 437.

158. *CIL* 13.3162, studied by Pflaum (1948) 7–9 and 31–52 passim.

159. Rouland (1979) 516, noting esp. Plin., *Ep.* 2.14.4 and 9; below, at 114–116.

160. Baroja (1965) 58. In trying to make vivid and *accurate* to myself the power networks that I describe, I have found no modern scholarship so useful as the anthropological, e.g., of Silverman (1965) 172–84, on central Italian society 1865–1945, and Boissevain (1966) 18–33, on modern Sicily.

161. See chap. III, "Stateless Societies," passim, in Gluckman (1965), the ref. thanks to Robert

Harms. Gluckman notices how societies "derive their integration from the divided allegiances of their members. Out of the interweaving of relationships" emerges stability.

162. Nicolaus of Damascus, *FHG* 2A, F 127 XII.

163. *Paneg. lat.* 12(2).9.3.

164. Tac., *Ann.* 4.41.1.

165. Amm. 27.11.2f., with the emendation noted in Matthews (1975) 11 and 12 n. 3; Claudian, *Pan. dictus Probino et Olybrio*, lines 32f. and 42f.; the very revealing statement in Amm. 30.2.11 about someone "holding an out-of-office man in contempt," i.e., personal power might be inconsequential compared to that borrowed from official appointment; above, at notes 73, 139, and 141, with still more material in the next chapter, regarding the selfish or 'patronal' use of office. For an earlier instance, see Plin., *Ep.* 10.87, where we see an army officer, a veteran after long service, coming out of retirement to help his distinguished friend as *assessor*, thereby earning that friend's *suffragium* for his own son's advancement. On complaints about their responsibilities voiced by exhausted great patrons, compare Plin., *Ep.* 3.1.12 and 4.23.4 (but *inertia* would be a *crimen*) and Dio Chrysos., *Or.* 66.12f.; perhaps most revealing, the picture of the civic leader in Plut., *Moral.* 823B, whose door must always be open, his voice heard continually in the senate or forum, and his hand ever extended for the exchange of services.

166. On Claudius, see e.g., Suet., *Claud.* 25.5 and Dio 62(61).12.3, comparing Dio 40.60.4, where Caesar in the 50s B.C. "cultivated not only free men but the very slaves who had any influence with their masters; and thereby many equestrians and many senators came over to him." Material on the political power of women is gathered in MacMullen (1986a) 434f. and 440f.; of bishops, in MacMullen (1980a) 27f., and above, note 41, to the extent the bishops are not trying to affect purely ecclesiastical politics.

167. Besides Ammianus on Gallus, see Julian, *Ep. ad Athen.* 272D; Philostorg., *H.E.* 3.28 p. 53f. Bidez, 4.1, pp. 56–58, and 4.8, p. 62, where Basil of Ancyra and other bishops involve themselves in the intrigues centering in Gallus even after his death; Soc., *H.E.* 2.34; Soc., *H.E.* 4.7; and Zos. 2.55.2f. The attempts to destroy Julian are similar: see, besides Ammianus (quite full), Julian, *Ep. ad Athen.* 282C; and other intrigues of destruction involving coteries in, e.g., Athanas., *Hist. Arian.* 6 (PG 25.701A) and 59 (764C); Eunap. frg. 71 (*FHG* 4.45) of A.D. 396; Zos. 4.2.1 and 3 and 4.52 (on the ruin of Tatianus PPO and his son Proculus PVC, A.D. 388/92); and sources cited in note 41, above. One may compare the apparent ease with which Nero simply summoned three great marshalls and noblemen to his side in Greece — Domitius Corbulo and the Sulpicii Scribonii — and had them all destroyed (Dio 55.10a.1). No fuss, no problems. Contrast with the workings of power in the later empire seems to me wonderfully instructive.

168. On *rescripta* (*rescriptiones, subscriptiones*), see Huchthausen (1979) 8f. with notes; Honoré (1981) 17 and 23; and, just in illustration, *FIRA²* 2.472 = *Fragmenta Vaticana* 39, undated, with mention of *terror* and *casula*. I find in the very ample Vatican collection only nine rescripts post-Diocletian.

169. Amm.16.8.7 on the resistance of the *aulici*. Compare 30.4.1 of the 370s, where the *amici et proximi* of Valens combine to block him from judging cases himself; for it would be against the interests of the *potentes* "if the defense of innocence should breathe again" as under Julian. Or, further, Philostorg., *H.E.* 4.8, p. 62 and 4.10, p. 63 Bidez-Winkelmann, where bishops favored by Constantius are seized and dispatched into exile unbeknownst to him, and he is "astonished and pained" by the later discovery about them. See more discussion below, pp. 146–48.

170. For the perception of the emperor as a nourishing spring to all the elite, "and from it we ourselves draw, and so minister to our friends," see Plin., *Ep.* 3.20.12, though he is not speaking specifically of material gains. For consulships, procuratorships, military tribunates, etc., as gifts insuring loyalty, see, e.g., Tac., *Hist.* 4.39, Dio 65.2.2, and Amm.

21.12.24, with other texts in Eck (1982) 147f. and MacMullen (1985) 69; for small gifts of jewelry, plate, garments, etc., handed out all the time from emperors to their elite subjects, see MacMullen (1962) 159–64, to which much could be added, e.g., Noll (1974) 223f. and 228–38 or Millar (1977) 135–48. For gifts of lands to lowly army officers or great magnates, and perpetual pestering of emperors after Diocletian for a share in such largesse, see PSI 928 (192/212) or PPrinceton 119 (early 4th. cent.); many laws such as CT 10.8.4 (346; 353), 11.20.1 (363), and 10.10.1–8 (early Constantine and thereafter) explained by 10.10.15 (380), complaining that "We are so constrained by the shameless greed of petitioners for such [confiscated] property that We even grant requests that should not be allowed"; Amm. 16.8.11, 18.4.3, 29.1.43, and 31.14.3 (petitioners inside the palace); Liban., Or. 20.39; and MacMullen (1976a) 20f. For individual emperors' records of generosity to friends, see Tac., Ann. 13.18 (Nero); Suet., Galba 15.2; Corp. agrimensorum Romanorum, ed. Thulin, 1.96 and Tac., Dial. 8.3, on Vespasian; Suet., Domit. 9.2; Champlin (1980) 24, gifts to Fronto; Setälä (1977) 125 and Herodian 3.10.6, on gifts to Plautianus; on Constantine, Julian, Caes. 335B, Amm. 16.8.12, Zos. 2.38.1, and esp. Eutrop., Brev. 10.7.2; on Constantius, Liban., Ep. 828; on Julian, Philostorg., H.E. 9.4 p. 117 Bidez-Winkelmann and Liban., Ep. 1316; and on Theodosius, Zos. 4.29.3.

171. Fronto, Ad Ant. Pium — 8, p. 169 Naber; above, notes 27 and 140–44. We see the application of the ethos specifically to an emperor, in Dio 77.16.1: Septemius Severus "to his friends was not forgetful, to his enemies, very severe," barytatos.

172. Tac., Dial. 8.3; Plin., Ep. 4.24.3.

173. CT 10.1.1 (315).

174. Premerstein (1937) 53 and chap. II passim, on Octavian the grosse Volksführer; Veyne (1976) 591; similarly, Rouland (1979) 506f.

175. See, e.g., Tac., Hist. 1.57, where the Vitellian cause is supported by "the Cologne population, Treveri and Lingones . . . , not only the principes coloniarum et castrorum" but even more broadly; and other texts in MacMullen (1985) 69–72, adding what Philostr., Vit. soph. 596, reports about a sophist of the 2d cent. in Rome put in charge of the Artists of Dionysus, who were prone to create disturbances (I suppose, in the theater); further, the city leader Pollius Iulius Clementianus, patron of both the Jovian and Romana precinct in Nola, CIL 10.1256, and the evidence for corporate shape and corporate action of vici and regiones in Puteoli. See Camodeca (1977) 68, 76, and 78.

176. MacMullen (1985) 69 and 73.

177. Ibid. n. 14, and below, Appendix B, on people described as principes (or the like) of a province or region; and the explanation for Valerianus Asiaticus' strength in Gaul: "born in Vienne and supported by a large and powerful kin" (Tac., Ann. 11.1), cf. above, notes 57 and 65f.

178. Dio 72.31.1 and CT 8.8.4 (386).

179. Fronto, Ad M. Caes. 4.12.4; Zos. 2.12.1; and Amm. 16.10.9f., showing portraits on display everywhere. For the wide, methodical distribution of portraits, see Stuart (1939) 601f. and MacMullen (1976) 45, with chap. 2 ("Propaganda") passim, on other aspects of imperial publicity. On announcements of accessions, see Sijpesteijn (1971) 188f. and Herz (1978) 1189–92.

180. Reynolds (1982) 111, 124, and 127 on Severus' letters of self-praise.

181. On Nero, Suet., Nero 39.2, Dio 62.18.4, and MacMullen (1966) 145f.; on Gaius, Suet., Caligula 13, and Philo, Leg. 15-21, the passage rather highly wrought and the devices in it reappearing in Liban., Or. 15.46, on Julian's death; so I am suspicious of its historical accuracy. On the mad enthusiasm a young prince might arouse, see Versnel (1981) 545 and 548f., to which one may compare Rostov and the tsar in War and Peace Part III, viii.

182. Herodian 26.13; Philostorg., H.E. 2.17.18 and similar proskynesis to imperial statues in the western capital in Ambrose's day, see Alföldi (1934) 77f.

183. POxy. 2725 (A.D. 71); Galen, *De libris propriis* 1 (II, p. 98 Mueller), on the word of Marcus' accession reaching Pergamon; and Ael. Arist., *Or.* 27.23–40, spoken to Cyzicus in A.D. 166. Compare the vivid picture of Domitian in the mind of one of his subjects, in Philostr., *Vita Apollonii* 7.28 (but the work is not very good evidence). On imperial styles being copied, see Tac., *Ann.* 3.55.4, on imitating Vespasian's simpler ways, and Galen quoted in Millar (1977) 112 n. 22. But Galen concludes, a bit cynically, "it is wonderful how rich people emulate the emperor's ways, or wish to give that appearance."

184. Dio Chrysos., *Or.* 20.3; Epict., *Diss.* 3.4.7; Ambros., *De elia et ieiunio* 41; and Theodoret., *Graec. affect. curatio* 8.67 (PG 83.1033A). As a special favor, Theodosius extends a guarded pardon, "if any person . . . should suppose that Our name should be assailed with wicked and impudent maledictions, and if, riotous with drunkenness, he should disparage Our times" (CT 9.4.1, A.D. 393).

185. Vago and Bona (1976) 185, 240, and Pl. 20, a tile with scratched picture and inscription from Intercisa, which the reader "spöttisch interpretieren sollte."

186. Tac., *Ann.* 15.20 and 22 (A.D. 62); Dio 56.25.6 (A.D. 11), Brunt (1961) 216 n. 82c, doubting the law was maintained; and Liban., *Or.* 15.74, where the governor bullies the representatives from one city. I go on to draw from Millar (1977) 388–93, including the *Digest*-text, 49.1.25, and Brunt (1961) 213–19, including the Pliny-ref., *Ep.* 5.13.2.

187. CJ 1.51.9 (433), complaints against governors; Amm. 28.6.7; CJ 2.12.21 (315) and CT 8.4.2 (315) to Africans; CT 12.12.3 and 12.12.9.1, limited welcome to petitions, cited in Deininger (1965) 186, adding *TAM* 2 no. 785 (312) and further discussion, pp. 183–85. His ref. to CT 2.30.1 and "eine neue Blüte" for the institution seem to me erroneous.

188. Lepelley (1979–81) 2.42 n. 121 calls attention to Quodvultdeus, *Liber de promissionibus*, App. *Gloria sanctorum* (*Sources chrétiennes* 102, pp. 664f.), *in foro coram populo a praesenti iudice . . . et erat sollemnis dies albi citatio*, to be compared with the edict of Constantine to the provincials, CJ 1.40.3 (331). Cf. CT 11.7.20 (412) of Carthage, providing for popular review of appointments by acclamation.

189. Dio Chrysos., *Or.* 45.7; Polotsky (1962) 260, the minutes in Greek but borrowing the Latin term *akta*.

190. The best overview may be found in Liebenam (1900) 238–50 and passim and A. H. M. Jones (1966) 171, 174f., and 182f. The implications of Dio Chrysos., *Or.* 49.14f. are pointed out by the Loeb editor, H. L. Crosby. On the active role of the *populus* in elections, see further texts: *CIL* 14.375 and 2410 (A.D. 157), a *comitia magistratuum creandorum causa* just created; *CIG* 2.3162; *Dig.* 49.1.12 (Ulpian), election solely through the people demanding their man, in which the governor wrongly acquiesces; and *AE* 1952 no. 154 of Bulla Regia and CT 12.5.1 (326), with other texts in Kotula (1980) 137 and 146 (but there is some slip in his Bulla Regia ref.).

191. For example, Dio 74.14.1; Liebeschuetz (1972) 103; and Antioch in 387, ibid. 105.

192. Plut., *Moralia* 817A, with the ref. at 815A to *hoi protoi* projecting their rivalries into the mass of *hoi elattones* and *idiotai*; and Firm. Maternus in MacMullen (1971) 113. On *curatores* in or near their own hometowns, see Duthoy (1979) 234, cf. 225 (78 out of 230 *curae*), and Lepelley (1979–81) 1.169; on decurions seeking *patrocinium*, early refs. include CT 12.1.6, cf. above, note 129.

193. Above, chap. I at notes 155–65; Clemente (1972) 226; Chastagnol (1978) 37f.; Lepelley (1979-81) 1.255f. and 278, regarding "cette hémorrhage de curiales," as he calls it; Libanius, esp. *Or.* 48–49; and Kopecek (1974a) 336f.

194. Dio Chrysos., *Or.* 40.29 and 48.1f.; C. P. Jones (1978) 95–103 passim; Liebenam (1900) 248 note 1, *expostulante populo*, etc., cf. *IGR* 3.739 II 5, VIII 30, etc., *epiboetai*; later, chanting, *IRT* 565, and above, notes 24–26 and many inscriptions with phrasing that shows some audible participation by the populace in corporate decision-making, *petente ordine et populo*, *ex consensu populi*, *suffragio populi*, etc., in *CIL* 2.3364, *AE* 1953 no. 21, *IRT* 568, and Mackie (1983) 43 and 170 n. 1.

195. Above, note 26; *CIL* 10.7295 = *ILS* 5055, dated to the 2d cent. by Bivona (1970) 50; and Colin (1965) 331f., attributing a semilegal force to the demands of the urban populace in Lyon, Smyrna, and elsewhere in the 2d and 3d centuries. For a late-5th-cent. instance of successful *ekboeseis*, see the very interesting inscription in Grégoire (1922) 1.32 no. 1008, from Ephesus.

196. For extortion or embezzlement by *curiales* as such, see Dio Chrysos., *Or.* 48.4–8; Plut., *Moralia* 809A; Tac., *Ann.* 13.58; and, later, Lepelley (1979–81) 1.144.

197. Votes of thanks and honor could be bought and sold in Antioch, dominated by a huge claque. See Pack (1935) 63 and Liebeschuetz (1972) 212–14, and compare above, note 188. I leave aside as not strictly relevant, because not manipulated by *potentiores*, all the popular uproar in late antique amphitheaters and other public places.

198. Above, note 192, on feuds among the Haves splitting the Have-nots; Wistrand (1981) 105f., on a very unusual 1st-cent. Italian inscription recording how a *patronus* was driven from his city by his fellow-citizens, comparison (pp. 113–15) being made to other similar municipal events; Philostr., *Vit. soph.* 559, on the Athenian assembly condemning Herodes; Schouler (1973) 114, on Liban., *Or.* 25.44, and other passages; and *CJ* 9.47.12, which I quote. But the text and scene are obscure.

199. Above, notes 103f. and 148.

200. For development of the point, see MacMullen (1974) 123f. and below, chap. 4 passim.

201. Plin., *Ep.* 9.13.21f. (trans. Radice), and Suet., *Domit.* 8.1, on the *ambitiosae centumvirorum sententiae*. Compare the tale about Pertinax in Dio 74.15.4 and Cilo's rescue of Macrinus, 79(78).11.2.

202. Veyne (1976) 743 n. 117 with refs.; narrowly on one transition, Dietz (1980) 292, 296, and 316; and of course occasional exceptions to this practice of forbearance in response to string-pulling, e.g., Herodian 8.5.9.

203. Examples in MacMullen (1985) 75f. For the late empire, see Wardman (1984) 226 n. 28.

204. Amm. 28.6.8; on the importance of venue, other instances at 28.1.9, 22, 26, and 27, and in Sulpitius Severus, *Chron.* 2.47–49 (*PL* 20.156A–157C). But this latter instance, and Amm. 28.1.27, explicitly emphasize mere bribery (perhaps also at 15.2.10 and 16.6.3, where eunuchs and chamberlains conspire to save an accused man, their reasons unknown, and at 15.13.2, where "the condemned were poor men" while "the instigators of the foul crime, though losing their estates, were let go — rich men").

205. On a *pater poleos* in the Decian (?) persecutions, see the *Acta S. Conon.* 2; on private foundations for orphans, Plin., *Ep.* 7.18.2 and Balland (1980) 92, of Opramoas' donation. Cf. *TAM* 2 no. 905 X G, where Voconius Saxa writes to the officials and people of Myra.

206. Texts assembled in MacMullen (1985) 70 n. 11, adding Mitchell (1983) 142, with other gifts of grain.

207. Tac., *Hist.* 1.57 and 3.43.1.

208. Plin., *Ep.* 5.14.8, 7.30, and 9.15.1; many other attestations of arbitration and adjudication in MacMullen (1974) 39f. with notes, to which can be added as many again for the rural scene: *IGR* 4.1237; S. Sahin (1978) 51f., of 3d-cent. Claudiopolis; Nemesianus, *Bucolica* 1.52f. (merely tralatician and literary? — but why should rural ways ever have changed?); and Liban., *Or.* 47.19, speaking of a general practice everywhere. For judges on circuit into Mylasa in Lycia, see LeBas-Wadd. 349–58, with commentary to the last of these texts; and for Roman senators' houses, see Vitruv. 6.5.2 quoted in Talbert (1984) 56.

CHAPTER 3

1. Besides the effect of Verres' trial on the composition of Roman juries, he left his mark on Rome through the elaborate adornment of the Vicus Tuscus. See Palmer (1978/80) 116f., 134, and passim.

2. On "venality," Louis-Lucas's may be the first scholarly essay. His use of the term embraces

the sale both of a position in government and of individual acts through its authority.
I make no distinction between the two meanings, since money is paid out in the former
transaction only because of money expected back in the latter. Both had a long history,
on which Salmon (1967) 22f. reports, up to the 17th cent. My own interest in the (Roman)
subject goes back more than a quarter-century to a study published in 1962; and (for a
selection) there is a very good piece of work by Monks in 1957 and another by Brunt
in 1961; then articles by Wolfgang Schuller in 1975, 1977, 1980, and 1982, his organization
of a conference on corruption in antiquity for 1979, and further work by Liebs, Hahn,
Veyne, and others, to be cited below. Schuller (1977) gives an overview with
bibliography, touching many historical periods and countries, down to the illustrations
for his subject which he draws (p. 378) from newspapers of the present day and people's
living experiences (p. 385).

3. *FIRA²* 1.132, on the mode of payment of a quaestor's *scriba* in ca. 81 B.C.; ibid. 180, on
the stipends paid magistrates' assistants; Cic., II *Verr.* 3.182, on the *scriba*'s contemptible
pay; 184, on scrimping to save the purchase price of the post and the 4 percent rake-off
yielding 1,300,000 HS *permissu tuo* (i.e., Verres'); *Dig.* 31.1.22 (Celsus), on the *commoda* of
a post included in its transfer to a new occupant, and 4.4.3.7, 19.1.522, 31.1.22, 31.1.49.1,
and 32.1.11.16, on the sale or bequest of the *militia* and ex-slave status of occupants of
the post; Mommsen (1887-88) 1.334f. and 3.450 note 3; Marchi (1906) 291–94, collecting
the legal texts; A. H. M. Jones (1949) 41, commenting, "I suspect that Cicero is somewhat
disingenuous when he raises his hands with holy horror at the 4 per cent rake-off . . . This
form of perquisite must have been fairly common, if strictly illegal, for Verres to enter
it openly on his accounts"; and Jones refers to 2d cent. scandals of the *decuriae* and their
respectable postion in society notwithstanding, in the 1st cent. B.C. and A.D. See,
further, Veyne (1981) 351, supposing that the word *militia*, which alone refers to the clerk
posts in the *Digest*-texts, must be interpolated for *decuria*; Liebs (1978) 159 adding *FIRA* ²
2.522; and Purcell (1983) 127ff., at 132 n. 34 gathering the refs. to scandals, at 134–36 and
150–54 documenting *apparitores'* equestrian rank and other honors; but (139) he is
entirely mystified by their wealth. For their handling of large sums of money, he cites
(130 n. 21) the huge moneybag shown on the tomb of a *viator quaestorius, CIL* 6.1932.

4. *Dig.* 22.11.11.

5. Juv. 3.188f., *praestare tributa clientes cogimur et cultis augere peculia servis*, with other refs.
gathered in MacMullen (1974) 197 n. 78. For the later empire the most striking passage
is Amm. 14.6.15. The naturalness of the practice appears in the recent statement, "If you
can get us an appointment, we'll pay you a good commission," where the person to be
paid was the barber (cf. above, chap. 2 note 144) serving a certain business magnate,
Iacocca, vastly well known, and the offer to pay was tendered by a high officer in a big
publishing company, seeking a money-making autobiography. The comment appears in
New York Times, 9/13/87, Section 7, p. 54.

6. Suet., *Galba* 15.2, cf. Tac., *Hist.* 1.7; further, Suet., *Domit.* 9.2 or *Vesp.* 23.2, the tale of the
would-be *dispensator* from whom the emperor takes the payment promised to the
suffragator; and *Claud.* 28, profits "allowed" on a gigantic scale, cf. Dio 60.17.8.

7. Plin., *Ep.* 5.2.1 (Loeb transl.); Mart. 13.51, with all of Bk. 13, and 7.78, 10.94, and elsewhere;
Bowman and Thomas (1983) 136 for a letter of ca. A.D. 100, mentioning "a friend sent
me fifty oysters"; SHA *Had.* 17.3, on Hadrian; later, Julian, *Ep.* 40(68), thanking someone
for a silver bowl and gold medallion; Soc., *H.E.* 6.2 (*PG* 67.664), the bishop of Alexandria
in 388 sends *xenia* to both candidates for ecclesiastical promotion, to be assured of the
winner's favor; Liebeschuetz (1972) 84 n. 7 on Libanius' receipt of gifts from pupils'
parents, e.g. wine, clothing, a horse; Theodoret., *Ep. Sirmond.* 13, wine received and
honey and a letter sent; Symm., *Ep.* 5.20 or, better, 4.15, on the terribly important gifts
expected from a consul by the circle of his friends; and Gerontius, *Vita Melaniae* (Greek)

11, on the presents taken to the emperor's sister in Constantinople in A.D. 404, along with "other ornaments, rings, and silver and silk garments to proffer to the faithful eunuchs and officials" (the Latin text slightly different). In return, Serena (ibid. 13) directs "her chief eunuchs to accompany them [the visitors, Melania and others] to their home, on no account themselves or any palace persons accepting anything demanded by them, not even a single coin" (Latin text).

8. PFay. 117 (108) and 118(110); Epict., *Diss.* 4.6.31 and 3.7.31.

9. *Dig.* 1.16.6.3, the last sentence more or less repeated at 1.18.18, quoting a plebiscite; and a sharper statement in CT 11.11.1 (368; 370; 373), aimed at officials, especially those in governors' offices, *qui possunt esse terribiles*, who shall not "extort *xenia* or similar small donations, *munuscula*, which they have made official, *canonica*, through long custom."

10. Plin., *Ep.* 4.9.6f.; on the term *munuscula*, note 9 above and note 13 below.

11. *Ep.* 1.7.2 and 6. Notice the joking reference to a more tempting bribe that would have worked, *mercede [qua] posse corrumpi.* So Pliny is well aware of the unethical implications in the situation.

12. Ticket-"fixing" in New York state, *New York Times,* 7/18/82, cf. 8/12/83: "Maybe one judge in eight is crooked," says Judge Lockwood of his colleagues in Cook County around Chicago. On 'mungo,' ibid., 4/25/82, "difficult to prosecute," according to law enforcement authorities, because "contractors have allowed this to go on for so long"; cf. 4/20/85, "corruption seems to be the normal way of life in the construction industry," according to the chief counsel to the New York Commission of Investigation, the prevalence adding 10–15 percent to costs (*Newsweek,* 8/2/82); or the general character of the Reagan administration, of whom more than a hundred "suffered criminal indictment, resigned for reasons of ethical misconduct, or came under suspicion of graft" in 1980–86: cf. L. H. Lapham, *Harper's Magazine,* February 1987, p. 9, adding what Senator Bumpers opines (*New York Times* 5/15/87) apropos the attorney-general's influence-peddling: "I doubt seriously whether any Administration has had more people leave under disgrace or indictment." Compare the high price of emigration permits in Moscow (up to fifteen times the official fee), ibid., 2/27/82, and the high price of jobs in state mines or entrance to medical schools in India, *The Indian Express* (New Delhi), 11/1/81 (front page) and 12/11/81, while in Japan, expecting "honesty and purity from politicians is like looking for fish at a vegetable store." This, from the justice minister, *New York Times,* 11/6/83.

13. Plin., *Ep.* 5.13.6 and 8; Carcopino (1951) 1.89–91, on Cicero's reduction of payments to the title *munuscula,* amid general evidence for great profits; Crook (1967) 90f.; and Pani (1986) 317f. and passim, quoting a defense of the Lex Cincia which forbade fees for courtroom oratory (Tac., *Ann.* 11.6, A.D. 47): *ne fidem quidem integram manere ubi magnitudo quaestuum spectetur.*

14. Chalon (1964) 50f., lines 46ff., discovering the exaction of novel, invented taxes spreading from Upper Egypt to the environs of Alexandria, Chalon (208 n. 15) comparing *CJ* 4.62.1 (Septimius Severus), *non temere permittenda est novorum vectigalium exactio; IGR* 1.1262 = *OGIS* 665 = Lewis (1954) 153, a prefect's edict of A.D. 48/9 aimed at officials "impudently," *anaidos,* and "brazenly peculating" through inflated travel and expense accounts; and Plin., *Ep.* 7.31.

15. PMich. VIII 468, comparing Jonson's *Every Man in His Humor* (2, 5, 50f.), "... money will do more, boy, than my lord's letter." Further, Tac., *Hist.* 1.46f., quoted, and 58, *vacationes centurionibus ex fisco numerat,* cf. *Ann.* 1.17, costs occasioned to soldiers by the *saevitia centurionum et vacationes munerum;* 1.35, German legionaries complain of *verbera* and *pretia vacationum;* and *Dig.* 48.11.6.2.

16. See Turner (1968) 144 and Lewis (1966) 509–11 for the term *skepe* attested from Ptolemaic times to the 4th cent.; compare, in the west, *laniena* in *FIRA*² 1.295 of A.D. 176/8 in

Baetica, or *epi-* or *diaseismos*, e.g., POxy. 2664 (248/9) where the emperor declares all of Egypt's liturgists to be "quite abandoned to extortion," *episeismos*. For the lawless avarice of municipal magistrates, though it is not very often attested before the mid-3d cent., see OGIS 527 on Hierapolis' local police shaking down the villagers in ca. A.D. 100; SEG 4.516 of A.D. 45, showing various magistrates of Ephesus involved in peculation of city and temple funds; Fant (1981) 243 on peculation in the same city in the 2d cent.; Dio Chrysos., Or. 43.10; Plut., *Moralia* 809A; *Dig.* 48.11.6.2; above, chap. 2 at note 196; and, for the 4th cent., Petit (1955) 262 and Lepelley (1979–81) 1.44.

17. Tight control is suggested in Hadrian's time and up to Ulpian by *Dig.* 48.20.6. Later, stationery fees are exacted within the bureaucracy. See Chastagnol (1978) 85. Quaestorian clerks were in the habit of selling their services in some illegal way, it is not clear just how. They are amnestied by Domitian. See Suet., *Domit.* 9.3, and Gruen (1974) 255, on the Lex Clodia.

18. Philo, *Flacc.* 1.30–34, and Brunt (1975) 135 and 140; cf. Bean (1962) 4–6, a governor's edict (from Tlos) on "administrative papers bearing erasures or unauthorized additions," for which the guilty clerk-slaves would not only be flogged but crucified. On legates' insubordinate peculation and extortion, see Dio 73.11.3 and Ael. Arist., Or. 50.85.

19. Tac., *Agr.* 15.2 and *Ann.* 16.17, under Nero: Mela "believed the path to riches was shorter through the administration of crown accounts than through a governorship." The phrasing casts a sinister light on the upper levels of government. We hear elsewhere of other custodians of imperial property using it to make profits for themselves: Frontinus, *De aquis* 9 and CJ 11.67(66).1 of A.D. 393. Herodian 7.42 speaks of the overseers of crown properties and similar fiscal agents as "rarely honorable men," in the 230s.

20. Lk 3.12f. and Philo, *Leg.* 199, on Judaea; cf. Lucian, *Menippus* 11; Tac., *Agr* 19.4 and *Ann.* 13.51; Chalon (1964) 50f.; POxy. 58 (288); and further similar inventions, some general in area, adduced in MacMullen (1976) 253 n. 67.

21. Tac., *Hist.* 4.14.5, in a context of prefects (of auxiliary units) and centurions, speaking through Civilis of *varia praedandi vocabula*; PSI 446 (133/7), cited by Brunt (1975) 125 n. 15, along with POxy. 1100 (206). The latter mentions the military *kolletiones* who are, in *TAM* 5, 1, 154 and 419, paired with *frumentarii* for illegal *eispraxeis*; further, no. 611, where the two are targets of complaint about their routine (*ta eiothota*) of extortion among the villages. For the hot-baths demanded (also by *kolletiones*), see MacMullen (1963) 87f., along with much more material in the whole chap. IV; and for the plaint of Megillat Ta'anit in 2d-cent. Judaea, see Applebaum (1977) 395. Under Diocletian, in Malal. 12, p. 307 Bonn (p. 375 Stauffenberg), the soldiers' extortionate demands for food emerge through an edict aimed at Antioch.

22. Tert., *Apol.* 7.3 and *Ad Scap.* 5, on soldiers' extortion from Christians, and *De fuga* 12.1f., indicating that it was routinely possible for the persecuted to buy their way out of arrest. For the east, see Euseb., *H.E.* 9.9a.7, referring to the Egyptian prefect of 312, and more generally in 313, 9.10.8.

23. *Dig.* 48.11.6.2 of the mid-2d cent.; Dio 72.4.1 (172/3), a centurion in Cyrene is selling release of men, whom I take to be recruits, not captives; Tac., *Ann.* 14.18, similarly in Cyrene the *dilectum militarem pretio et vacatione corruptum*; and *Hist.* 4.14.2 in Germany and *Agr.* 15.2f. By the later 3d cent. the bribes which had brought exemption from the draft, now payable to the provincial governor, were treated like any other agreed-upon purchase price, though the *concussio* remained a *crimen*. See CJ 4.7.3 (A.D. 290) in Huchthausen (1973) 28; and Veget. 1.7 finds the process of the draft corrupt in his day, too.

24. Aur. Vict., *Caes.* 33.13 p. 110 Pilchmayr.

25. On A.D. 244, see Zos. 1.18f., Zonaras, *Epit. hist.* 12 p. 130 Dindorf, and SHA *Gordiani* 29.2f.; cf. later, the mutinous state of the troops' mood as a result of their supplies running out

in the 350s, Amm. 15.5.29, 16.11.13, and 17.9.3f.; and, at 14.10.3f. (A.D. 354), the PPO Rufinus "was in the greatest danger" as a result of a "cunning plot thought out" for the purpose of bringing about his death or dismissal. A shortage on the eastern frontier in the same decade appears to have been the result of incompetence, not disloyalty. See Vogler (1979) 68 n. 292, on Liban., Ep. 21.

26. For the watchfulness needed of a good governor, see Philo, Flacc.. 5; for the revolt under Probus, Malal. 12 p. 302.

27. Herodian 4.6.4.

28. Passio S. Perpetuae 36, concussio by soldiers in Carthage, cf. Soz., H. E. 4.24 (PG 67. 489C), A.D. 360, in the east; Philostr., Vita Apollini 7.36 and Liban., Or. 33.30 and 45.10 (A.D. 386); John Chrysostom quoted in Pack (1935) 79, where jailers are perhaps municipal not military; and Dig. 48.20.6.2.

29. On the sale of promotions and perquisites, see Cic., De lege Manilia 37 and In Pisonem 88; Tac., Hist., 1.52; Dig. 48.11.6.2; and SHA Pertinax 9.6. On the sale of citizenship, see Acts 21.27 (whether by a suffragator or governor is not stated); and on mustering-out or mustering-in gifts, above, chap. 2, note 158; PSI 1026 C 33 (A.D. 150), a mustering-out sportula; also called commoda, cf. Speidel (1983) 282–85, on Suet., Nero 32 and a 3d-cent. inscription; SHA Had. 17.2 and other passages of this author, showing presents to entering soldiers; and perhaps Dig. 34.4.23, if this is the right interpretation of the text (more than 300,000 HS bequeathed by a veteran, ex ratione primipili commodorum). The alternative, that commoda here represent the originally illicit "take" or amount withheld by the primipilus in the process of collecting supplies due to the army, seems to me a little less likely. See above, note 3, on the use of the term commoda.

30. Plin., Ep. 2.11.2, 8, and 10; other cases in Dio 58.24.3, an ex-governor and wife executed for venality in A.D. 34; 61.33.6, 66.14.3, and elsewhere, and a careful collection of cases, Brunt (1961) passim; strict oversight and punishments by Domitian (Suet., Domit. 82, as opposed to laxity, Galba 15.2).

31. Tac., Ann. 1.75.1, libertas corrumpebatur; cf. Suet., Tib. 33.2.

32. Propert., Eleg. 3.13.47f. (20s B.C.), and Tac., Ann. 2.32 (A.D. 16); cf. Petron., Sat. 14, and Apul., Met. 10.33.

33. Cypr., Ep I ad Donat. 10 (CSEL 3, 1, p. 11).

34. Epict., Diss. 3.7.11–13, on the dynatoi.

35. Ael. Arist., Or. 50 (Sacred Tales 4).81 (Keil 2 p. 445, trans. Bauer).

36. Dig. 12.5.3, cf. 12.7.5 (Papinian).

37. Menander Rhet. pp. 97 and 167 Russell-Wilson, words in which Pack (1935) 81 finds "as much entreaty as . . . the wish to record the fact"; cf. SEG 8.527 (A.D. 22/3), praising an Egyptian strategos for giving judgments adoradoketos; Robert (1948) 38–40 and 108f. on a vocabulary of praise new in Greek inscriptions from the mid-3d cent. on to the 6th: "the justness and integrity in our honorific inscriptions for governors is the counterpart of complaints and accusations heard in the literary and legal texts concerning the corruption of provincial courts and the dishonest acts, prevarications, of governors." Robert lists many texts, to be matched in the Latin west. See Brunt (1961) 222, proposing that "the prevalence of dishonesty among officials is best proved by the frequency with which individuals are lauded in literature and inscriptions for their 'innocentia' or 'abstinentia' or the like." As examples: the phrase singularis abstinentia in CIL 14.170 = ILS 1433 (A.D. 247/8) applied to a procurator of Portus (Ostia) and to a governor in Suet., Otho 3.2; CIL 5.7881, the integritas of the governor praised (A.D. 239); 2.4113, a legatus iuridicus abstinentissimus (A.D. 260s) of Tarraco; 13.1900 = ILS 7025; Tac., Agr. 9.4; Plin., Ep. 7.31.3; Hadas (1929) 373 on rabbinic allusions to Roman justice, e.g., "I shall try capital cases and will find everyone guilty. Bring me a doron so that if you're brought up to the bema I will transfer your elogium to another." See Avi-Yonah (1976) 129 for similar

rabbinical comments of the 3d and 4th cents.; and, for this later period also, Aug., *Conf.* 6.10, praising an assistant in the courts for his *mirabili continentia ceteris*, the *ceteri* preferring gold to honor; *IRT* 565, of the mid-4th cent., praising an African governor as "outstanding for *abstinentia*"; and the later-4th-cent. *Institutio Traiani*, which concludes, "It is indeed a thing to be praised among governors if they restrain their hands from extortion and violence." See Callu (1984) 224 and 232, and below, note 97.

38. Jos., *B. J.* 2.273, 278f., and 287f.; Philo, *Leg.* 199; and Brunt (1961) 208–16.
39. On the evil reputation of *Caesariani* (transliterated into Greek as well), see Dio 60.17.5f., where they sell Roman citizenship; 69.7.4 and 79(78).12.6, where they are briefly disciplined under Macrinus; and below, note 79. The emperor's slaves are described as all corrupt under Galba (Tac., *Hist.* 1.7); but discipline was attempted earlier, cf. Suet., *Aug.* 67.2, and Dio 57.10.4. On *dispensatores*, see above, note 6, Plin., *N. H.* 33.145, *ILS* 1514 = *CIL* 6.5197, and Suet., *Otho* 5.2, with O. Hirschfeld (1905) 463 n. 5. Toward the mid-3d cent., *Caesariani* who were freedmen gave way to freeborn servants under the same title and organized militarily. See Weaver (1972) 26 n. 3.
40. Dio 78(77).21.2, on Theocritus, who had become an army commander and prefect in Gaul under Caracalla.
41. See, for example, Dio 60.17.8, 65(66).14.3, and 72(73).12.3; Suet., *Vesp.* 23.2; and above, note 5.
42. Columella, *Res rust.* 1 praef. 10; Suet., *Otho* 2.2; Tac., *Ann.* 14.50; and Suet., *Vesp.* 4.7. Ibid. 16.2, Vespasian acted as *suffragator* to himself, and so in effect sold office directly. Tertullian, *Apol.* 39.4, speaks of *honores* in his day being attained *non testimonia sed pretio*, but he may be referring to *summa honoraria* in Africa cities.
43. On soldiers taking over administrative work, see *Dig.* 1.16.4.1 (Ulpian), MacMullen (1963) 67f., and Pflaum (1974) 6 and 33.
44. Tac., *Ann.* 2.55 (A.D. 18); cf. Suet., *De grammat.* 24, and E. Birley (1963/64) 22–24, on the practice of appointing civilians directly to the rank.
45. *Dig.* 4.4.3.7 (Ulpian); above, notes 3f.
46. For what follows, see MacMullen (1986c).
47. For illustration, see Amm. 27.7.7, where Valentinian "arbitrarily fused it [the crime of poisoning] with the plotting of treason" so as to make investigations and torture more savage; for other illustrations, some earlier, see Bauman (1980) 202.
48. PBeatty Panop. 2 line 235 and MacMullen (1986c) 155; ibid. 149 and 154f. on numbers of capital crimes.
49. Euseb., *H. E.* 8.12.8–10 (A.D. 308).
50. *CT* 1.16.7 (331) and 9.24.1 (326); on numbers of capital crimes, MacMullen (1986c) 157, adding *CT* 10.4.1 (326?).
51. *CT* 2.1.1 (349), trans. Pharr, *tormenta dilacerent*, etc. Constantius II revels in the language.
52. *Dig.* 48.19.28.15; similar staging of punishment in *CT* 9.32.1 (409), and much more evidence for a general feature of the age in MacMullen (1986c) 159f.
53. Lact., *Div. Inst.* 5.3 (*PL* 6.557A), speaking of Bithynia in A.D. 303, cf. *PLRE* I s. v Hierocles 4; and, on the severed heads, Zos. 4.58.5; Philostorg., *H. E.* 11.3; Zos. 5.22.3; *Consularia Constantinopolitana* a. 411 (*MGH AA* 9. 246); and Soz., *H. E.* 7.7.21 (A.D. 378), cf. earlier, Amm. 26.10.6 (Procopius' head in 365) and 29.5.42 (A.D. 374).
54. Jordanes, *Getica* 24 (A.D. 370s), but not dissimilar from SHA *Aurelian* 7.4, with a still closer analogy in Soz., *H. E.* 6.8 (*PG* 67.1313C), where Procopius is torn apart by bent trees; as for the children's death, see Claudian, *In Rufin.* 1.246f., comparing the suffering inflicted on Tatianus 5, *PLRE* I s.v. (citing *Chron. pasch.* 393).
55. Synesius and Libanius, in MacMullen (1986c) 159f., with other similar scenes. For an African scene of the mid-3d cent., see Cypr., *Ep.* I *ad Donat.* 10 (*CSEL* 3, 1, p. 11).
56. For Jerome's description, evidently applying to the reign of Valentinian, see Hier., *Ep.*

1.33f. and 7 (*PL* 22.327); on the other indications, MacMullen (1971) 107; Amm. 15.3.10, 28.6.27, and 30.2.12 (all suicides); and Libanius in Liebeschuetz (1972) 166.

57. For the envy, notice the fate promised by the stars to the really fortunate, who become (Firm. Matern., *Math.* 3.4.13) "most powerful and terrifying commanders in charge of great armies," "Lords over life and death, at whose coming the greatest cities and provinces are always a-tremble" (3.4.2); for good luck makes people (3.4.30) *potentes maxime terribiles periculosi,* etc. For the source, see MacMullen (1971) 111 and 114. For the assessments of Julian, etc., quoted, see Julian, *Ep. ad Ath.* 278C; Euseb., *Vita Const.* 4.31(GCS 1.129); Amm. 28.1.44, 15.7.1, 29.2.22, and 31.10.21. Notice the horrible Maximinus with others like him, below, at note 101.

58. *CT* 9.35.6 (399), trans. Pharr, *venalis exigentium terror,* addressed to the PPO of Italy and Africa.

59. On terrifying *potentes,* earlier, see chap. 2 notes 9, 94, 109, and 168. For those later, see for example *CT* 11.11.1 (368;370; 373), where governors' staff members and municipal officials *qui possunt esse terribiles* shall not demand *xenia;* 3.6.1 (380), where governors compel a marriage through the fear they inspire; *CJ* 12.60(61).1 (A.D. 395), *militaris terror;* Symm., *Rel.* 26.6, a count in Rome terrifies a construction specialist; and Libanius, often referring to the terror spread among decurions by governors, etc., cf. Petit (1955) 258, 285, and 287 n. 5 and Hahn (1982) 192 n. 37. But there continue to be terrifying *potentes* not (at the moment) holding office: a senator in Rome (Aug., *Conf.* 6.10.16), a bishop in Judaea *polla ischysantos plouto te kai austeria* (Epiphanius, *Panarion* 30.5 [GCS 25.340] —the last word in its harsh sense linked to *omotes,* Stephanus s.v.), and *CT* 1.22.2 (334), where fear is felt by weak litigants "when they are in terror of the power of anyone" (who may of course be an official). I go on to refer to Verres' use of crucifixion (Cic., II *Verr.* 5.162ff. and II 5 passim).

60. *Dig.* 27.1.6.2, where Modestinus tries to make sense of Antoninus Pius' loose conception of "big" and "small" cities; 43.12.1.1, explaining the difference between *flumen* and *rivus;* 47.8.4.2–3, defining *turba;* 47.9.1.2, defining *incendium;* etc. — compared with the confusion in terminology pointed out by the authorities cited in MacMullen (1962) 369 n. 20; ibid. passim on the bureaucratic style in general, esp. its mere abundance of words, lavish use of synonyms, and unintelligibility. Cf. 371 n. 27, quoting Jolowicz and Schulz. Notice most recently Bauman (1980) 180, on "the general chaos that seems to pervade the criminal law of the [late Roman] period" and "the avalanche of rhetoric under which — so our first impression suggests — so much of the emperor's juristic thinking lies buried." He goes on to cite Biondi to the same effect ("caotica," of penal law).

61. *CT* 1.4.1 (321; 324); *CJ* 6.9.9 (339); compare *CT* 1.2.3 and, for the note of anti-intellectualism typical of the age, see MacMullen (1972) 12ff.

62. *CT* 11.1.27 (400;405); 11.7.4; etc. — with further access to illustrations in note 60 above, and note 73, below.

63. See Jerome, among other writers quoted by Conrat (1907) 290, on *iuris scientia;* Amm. 30.4.11 on the *legum discidia;* and the anon. *De rebus bellicis* 21.1, the plea serving as the most emphatic epilogue to the whole little essay.

64. Midrash Tehillim, trans. W. G. Braude (1959) 2.175, from the later empire, though not closely datable; similar complaints cited in MacMullen (1976) 253 n. 74; and legislative tergiversation like *CT* 16.5.25 (March 395) directly contradicted by 27 (June or December 395), or 11.22.2 (385) reversed by 3 (387).

65. MacMullen (1976) 94f. and Honoré (1981) 16 and 32.

66. The province-numbers I draw from Dietz (1980) 348, for a total of 64 under Caracalla, and from Eadie (1967) 156–68, for a (constantly fluctuating) total of about 120 in the later 4th cent. For the increase in number of *magistri officiorum* under Theodosius I, see Zos. 4.27.2. On the whole subject of late Roman government, see A. H. M. Jones (1964) chap.

XVI; for a total of 32,000 as a very rough estimate, see MacMullen (1964b) 311; likewise "a rough estimate" of something "not greatly in excess of 30,000," in A. H. M. Jones (1966a) 211. By a scholarly consensus, the sharp increase in the civil service is attributed to Diocletian. See, e.g., Callu (1984) 246. Of what I would call career civil servants, the ca. 100 in *decuriae* (above, at note 3) are to be added to the imperial procurators, which under Caracalla numbered between 173 and 182, according to Pflaum (1974) 43 (though those last two figures would today be challenged as too small). Hence, ca. 100? + ca. 200? = my estimate of 300.

67. On *stationarii*, see under "Ephesus" and "Smyrna" in Appendix C, and MacMullen (1963) 55f., 59f., and 62f.; on the numbers of soldiers on the staff of a governor, ibid. 66f.; on the attestation of troops resident in administrative centers, see Appendix C under "London," etc.

68. Suet., *Aug.* 67.2.

69. Amm. 30.9.4, Valentinian "was most careful in assigning positions of high authority. In his reign, no money-changer administered a province nor was government for sale"; 30.5.4–7, "Valentinian in fact, as if his ears were stopped with wax, had no knowledge" of Probus' exactions; and 29.5.2, on the concealment of Romanus' crimes through "the Master of Offices, his relative and friend, Remigius."

70. SHA *Aurelian* 43.3f.; cf. in contrast the good emperors, *Ant. Pius* 11.1 or *Severus Alex.* 36.2f.

71. Zos. 5.1.3; cf. Theodosius II blaming a mistake in administration on his CSL "who surreptitiously obtained a rescript from Us, concealing the truth" (CT 10.20.18, A.D. 436), or (1.11.2, A.D. 398) the confession that "from the younger Valentinian of sainted memory the order [for a wrongful decision] was surreptitiously obtained." For more material on such deceptions, see notes 126–28 below.

72. Amm. 30.4.2, Valens' fault was that he no longer heard cases personally, being persuaded by "his friends and intimates" (30.4.1) in their protecting of the *potentes*. Notice the penetrating question put in 368 by Themistius (8.139 Dindorf), "Do you oversee your civil officials, or is it possible to take bribes in secret, or collect more than the stated taxes?"

73. Philostorg., *H. E.* 4.8, p. 62 Bidez-Winkelman, the plot of Basil of Ancyra succeeding because Constantius is "won over most of all by the women [of the imperial house]," and he is astonished by the truth (4.10 p. 63); cf. 4.1 p. 58, a decree of execution extracted from him and the later countermand suppressed without his knowledge; and Soz., *H. E.* 4.12 and 14 (PG 67.1141B and 1148B, quoted), comparing Liban., *Or.* 18.132, on imperial secretaries — "whatever they wanted they declared as coming from the emperor" — and, twenty years later, *CT* 1.3.1 (383), "If any person should assert that he comes with Our secret mandates, all men shall know that no such person shall be believed as to anything except that which he has proved by written documents" (trans. Pharr).

74. CT 12.1.33 (A.D. 342, trans. Pharr), cf. 12.1.37 (344), 8.7.3 (349), and seventy-odd other constitutions from the period A.D. 316–445 which in one way or another acknowledge mutually contradictory rescripts, collected by Noethlichs (1981) 50–55. Of *rescripta contra ius elicita* in particular (cf. *exoratus*, CJ 11.71.5.1, A.D. 429), there is a collection in Löhken (1982) 40 note 53.

75. Above, chap. 2 at notes 105, 136, 168, and 187f. On legations from provinces, see CT 4.10.1, 8.5.63, etc. (a very small number); A. H. M. Jones (1964) 356; Millar (1977) 393f., suggesting a changeless continuity that I think does not exist; and Sartori (1981) 404.

76. Clauss (1980) 69f. on the key role played by the Master of Offices, even after having to share control with the PPO; for "at court a delegation must make its way from bureau to bureau and generally through a labyrinth of intrigue . . . , and on that account the magister officiorum counted heavily for success." On secretaries, see above, note 73; on eunuchs, above, chap. 2 notes 41 and 204, and in this chap. below, notes 130f.

77. Herodian 1.2.4.
78. MacMullen (1963) 49f. on *militia;* Noethlichs (1981) 22 and n. 108, adding can. 12 of the Nicene council in Hefele (1907–09) 1, 1, p. 591, the Latin and Greek *zone* given as equivalents; and the Greek further in Liban., *Ep.* 1222 (363), *Or.* 18.134, and other passages in Petit (1955) 74.
79. *CIL* 3.12134, lines 11f. of 305/6, *praedationum immoderata Caesarianorum nequitia et scelesta* (and the text breaks off); 3.13569 = *Inscr. Cret.* I xviii 189 (pp. 229f.), likewise lacunose, and dated by Mommsen 'apparently of Constantine'; and *CT* 10.1.5.1 (326), cf. 10.8.2 (319), gratuitously mentioning the *fraudes Caesarianorum,* and *CJ* 10.1.5 (285–293), indicating one of the Caesarians' evil practices: illegally seizing the property of the proscribed. A. H. M. Jones (1964) 564f. supposes they were still imperial freedmen and slaves in Tetrarchic times. The evidence is indirect, and the consensus dates a change in their status to a generation earlier. See above, note 39.
80. Amm. 16.5.11 (356) and *CT* 6.29.5 (359), *quoniam avaritiae occurre paene iam non potest,* only one gold coin is to be demanded by them per carriage of the public post; cf. the advantage taken of their authority and usual practices, to impersonate them for purposes of extortion, *CT* 6.29.6 (381) and 12 (415); and Aurel. Vict. *Caes.* 39.44, execrating the now disbanded *frumentarii, quorum nunc* (the 370s) *agentes rerum simillimi sunt.* A. H. M. Jones (1964) traces their history. Consult his Index s.v. *agentes* and *curiosi* (the two being the same thing). I go on to quote in addition the characterization of *agentes* = *angelliaphoroi* = *peuthenes* in Liban., *Or.* 18.135f., trans. Loeb.
81. *CT* 6.4.21.3 (372), 14.4.3 (362; 363), 11.1.11 (365), 1.16.7 (331), 9.40.14 (385), and 7.4.35 (423). *CT* 8.1.4 (334) begins, *vorax et fraudulentium numerariorum propositum . . . ,* and other examples of such wording could be added and added again.
82. *CT* 6.27.4 (382), cf. 1.9.1.1 (359), not specifying seniority in the process of recommending.
83. *CT* 6.24.3 (364; 365) on appointment to the *protectores et domestici* (5–10 sol. as *sportulae* to each primate of the staff); *CJ* 12.19.7.2 (443/4); and Collot (1965) 194 and 212.
84. *CT* 6.27.8.2 (396); also 8.4.10.1 (365), involving the sale, perhaps, of tax-collecting operations, cf. Giardina (1977) 76–79.
85. To demonstrate the transformation, Ste. Croix (1954) 39 instances *CJ* 12.32.1 (317?); but there, *suffragium* has to be specified as *venale.* Ibid. n. 6, he offers *CT* 11.30.6 (316) to show the word 'in the new sense'; but this is mistaken; and n. 7 offers *CT* 6.22.2, which, however, is not so plain as 12.1.25 of the same year, A.D. 338. Here, 'titles that they have bought' in one clause of a sentence becomes 'rank through *suffragium*' in another. Compare a similar equivalence in the wording of *CJ* 4.3.1 (394). Veyne (1981) 344 finds it 'perfectly legal' to buy rank or office from at least Constantine's reign, but *CT* 12.1.27 (339) cited in support of this view shows, I believe, just the opposite: bought rank had no legal standing, cf. 12.1.26 (338) or other texts.
86. *CT* 2.29.1 (362) and 2.29.2.2f. (394), concerning *praedia rustica vel urbana.* For the history of the emperor's struggle against this tide, see Collot (1965) 192, 197, and 209–11 and Liebs (1978) 170f., where, however, some of the citations seem irrelevant (*CT* 12.1.4, 12.1.20, and 1.32.1) or wrongly dated (*CT* 6.38, A.D. 317, according to Seeck; 312/337, 'possibly' 330, in *PLRE* I s.v. Valerianus 15). To quote Lyd., *De mag.* 3.67.1, referring to some time considerably earlier than 550, would carry me too far beyond my intended boundaries of time.
87. *CT* 1.31.2 (368; 370) to the PVR concerning *titulo aliquid lucelli minusculi,* 'something you might call a teeny profit,' hereafter to be voluntary; 8.4.6 (358), a *sportula* for the *duces* from their *primipilares,* raised under Julian, cf. 8.4.9 (368; 370) and 8.4.27 (422), fees paid to *duces* by *primipilares;* and 12.6.3 (349), cf. 10.1.11 (367), a 1 percent fee exacted by *susceptores* which (12.6.2, A.D. 386) is roughly doubled, on various products. Cf. 14.4.4 (367), 1–2 percent allowed to certain tax collectors just as if they had been *publicani;* and

6.31.1 (365; 368; 370; 373), where state stablemasters are permitted only a 1-sol. demand for approving the quality of horses offered in payment of the horse tax.

88. Among many examples of customary rake-offs, see CT 6.30.11 (386), *solennia ultra statutum*; 6.4.21.3 (372); perhaps the very early 8.4.2 (315), forbidding tax exactions *ultra modum* ("beyond the set rate" or "beyond a reasonable rate"?), and certainly the very late *SEG* 9.356 (A.D. 501) = Goodchild (1953) 74.

89. Mommsen (1884) 629ff., with valuable exposition of the *officia*-ranks (636f.), *sportulae* (639f.), and office costs (642f.). The text is also in *CIL* 8.17896 = Bruns, *Fontes⁷* 103 = *FIRA²* 1.331f., briefly covered by A. H. M. Jones (1949) 51f., and carefully by Chastagnol (1978) 76-78 and 82f. On the price of wheat, see ibid. 83 n. 20 and A. H. M. Jones (1964) 445f.

90. CT 6.4.27 (395).

91. CT 11.7.3 (399; 401) in the African diocese; 7.4.28.1 (406), the text needing correction, and *resistentes species* being best explained, I think, in the light of note 4, above (Krueger and Pharr have other ideas).

92. CT 7.4.29 (407); and the inscription from Palestine. On the latter, see Abel (1909) 90ff., for the text, commentary, and translation (p. 103), but a dating too early (104); Littman, Magie, and Stuart (1910) 24–41, esp. 34 (*paramythia* = *solatium*), comparing the Ptolemais edict, *CIG* 5187, and p. 35, discussing the modes of payment; also Alt (1921) 5–12. Compare the similar Libyan inscription of about the same date, in A. H. M. Jones (1968) 293, on *SEG* 9.356, the *limitanei* here as in Palestine paying their officers 12 percent of their salary (section 4 calls it "the Good Will account," *hyper tes kaloumenes eumenias*); fuller setting in Goodchild (1953) 74f.; and the interesting Colt papyrus fragments in Casson (1952) 54–58, where the payments are labelled *epiklasmos*. For euphemisms, see above, passim, on *sportulae, munusculi, lucellum,* etc., and MacMullen (1962) 367.

93. Symm., *Ep.* 5.63.2, to the CSL, cf. Paulin., *Vita Ambros.* 41 (*PL* 14.41B) and 43 (42B). To the latter passage, compare CT 8.11.1 (364), regarding false exactions in the name of tips, *a tenuioribus sportulae specie.*

94. Quoting Luke, Ambros., *In Luc.* 2.77 (*CSEL* 32.83) and Max. Taur., *Sermo* 26.103 (*CC Ser. Lat.* 23; date, p. xxxiii, ca. A.D. 400); compare Symm., *Ep.* 2.52.2 (A.D. 383), "the bullying of soldiers is a burden to our property in Ostia" (quartering-problems?) and 9.10.2 (A.D. 394) to the Vicar (of Rome? of Africa?), complaining of arbitrary apportionment of the recruitment tax, according to the sweet will of the Top Ten of town councils, and "the recruitment officers [who] demand the conscription-money from my people without any proofs of public authorization for such a thing."

95. Mansi (1759–1927) 3.1000, cf. the Roman synod, can. 10 (p. 1137) and can. 4 (1136), from which I quote. For the date of the synod, A.D. 400, see Hefele (1869-78) 2.264, the canons responding to questions from Gallic bishops. That fact extends the implications of the discussion.

96. Zos. 5.1.1f. (A.D. 392), the means of extortion being the threat of litigation as well as the sale of decisions.

97. Aug., *Conf.* 6.10.16, on Alypius while *assessor* to the CSL Italicianorum (above, n. 37, with other parallels); compare the like phrasing in Eunap., *Vit. soph.* 490, of a Prefect of 357, that "all Greece was astonished by him, learning that … he took no bribes." For Symmachus' opinion, see his *Or.* 4.6 (A.D. 376), the *humani sanguinis auctiones* of Valentinian's reign; also *Coll. Avellana* 1.6 (*CSEL* 35 p. 3), Damasus in 366 *redimens iudicem urbis Viventium et praefectum Julianum* (see *PLRE* I s.v. Julianus 16), and 13.7 (*CSEL* 35 p. 56), concerning a defiant troublemaker who "counts on the inertia of our judges, who for reasons of private favor waive the orders of the emperor," etc.

98. Sulp. Sev., *Chron.* 2.48.5 (*PL* 20.156f.), on the Priscillianists visiting Milan: *largiendo et ambiendo … ita corrupto Macedonio.* …

99. The story of Romanus in Ammianus (28.6.17–20 and elsewhere, with Zos. 4.16.3) has

often been retold by students of the period, and sometimes doubted. As it is internally consistent, and consistent also with conditions of the time, I see no reason to reject it.

100. Above, chap. 2 note 67; Amm. 27.9.2; 28.6.8, Remigius *rapinarum particeps*; and 29.5.2, he suppresses the reports at court.

101. On Romanus' confederates, see Amm. 29.5.2, 6, and 50; a similar web of PPO, ex-CRP, an *actuarius* of heavy transport, and an ex-Master of Records, two of the four being "the closest of friends to the PPO," in Amm. 15.5.4; again, 15.5.22, confederates plus *propinqui et familiares* (though not in any venal scheme); and Liban., *Or.* 18.84, where Florentius (10, *PLRE* I) is *homotechnos* to the thefts of an official in Gaul and is assigned to judge the charges against the man. For horizontal alliances, often indicated in the law codes, see, e.g., *CT* 8.1.14f. and *CJ* 9.27.1 (382); for vertical alliances, *CT* 9.27.3, in Isauria, the pillage of the provincials blamed on the *dux*, his *domesticus*, *manipularius* (commander), and *minister* (aide) in 382 (380), this too referred to by Noethlichs (1981) 191; further, *CT* 11.30.29, 34., and 58.1, and 12.1.85, and Liban., *Or.* 18.133.

102. MacMullen (1986d) 339f.; there, too, the citation that I go on to use, regarding law-court extortion (Aug., *Ep.* 153.23f.). In defense of Augustine's supposing that the yield of extortion might be used for good works, cf. Soc., *H. E.* 4.27 (PG 67.1200C), reporting how a military accountant "accumulated great wealth" under Constantius II and, on retirement from office, used it for relief of the poor. So it was possible to buy one's way out of the one ethic into the other.

103. *CT* 8.10.2 (344) regarding African lawyers; 2.10.3 (325) and 4 (326), among other texts; and Chastagnol (1979) 226ff. and (1980) 220–224.

104. Synes., *Ep.* 67 (PG 66.1428B), tells of suits by lowly clergy "not to get satisfaction but in search of improper profits for the military commanders," as Amm. 22.6.1 reports that "the Egyptians continually use the courts, or the threat of a suit, to extort money from the rich." The same practice is found later in the eastern provinces, according to Eunap. frg. 87, p. 269 (ca. A.D. 425?), the courts being available "to harass the rich with death and confiscations" and the rich therefore pay up, while "the poor receive public beatings." Cf. Liban., *Or.* 33.38f., on the Syrian governor of 386, under the influence of (or ready to oblige) his sons-in-law, brother, mother, and her doctor, so that an accused person "has recourse to the son-in-law with his cash in his hand, and through him, to his wife's father, and from the wonderful visits and exchanges, justice is thoroughly deluded and baffled." The picture fits with a general indictment by Joh. Chrysos., *In Joann. homil.* 82.4 (PG 59.446): "the men who hand down judgements indeed have the name of judges but do the work of brigands and murderers," etc.—confirmed by Amm. 30.4.21 for an earlier period in the east, and by the concurrent picture of Moesia in the decades before A.D. 440, in Priscus frg. 8, lines 44f. = frg. 11.2 p. 268 Blockley (1983), where the rich can always buy a verdict from the judge and his assessors.

105. Amm. 28.1.38, quoted, and 28.1.34, on shakedowns; cf. 26.10.9–14, the courts are mere instruments for shakedowns, as also earlier, in the wake of the suppression of Gallus in 355, Amm. 15.2.9 and 15.13.1, or again in 19.12.1 (A.D. 359) — but the phenomenon was not new: see Dio 62.28.4 (A.D. 65). A campaign to tighten up enrollment in *curiae* also could produce conditions favorable to extortion, Amm. 22.9.12 (in the east, A.D. 362). I go on to quote 30.4.21, likewise spoken of eastern courts.

106. *CT* 1.16.7, from *visio ipsa praesidis* to the production of *acta*. Cf. 1.16.6 (331), against governors hiding themselves away, until produced by a bribe; 1.16.9 (364) and 10 (364; 365), hearings must be open; and attestation of the judge's retiring behind curtains, in nonlegal sources of the earlier and later 4th cent., in MacMullen (1976) 246 n. 10.

107. *CT* 8.9.2 (382) on emoluments; on fines, e.g., 11.30.8 (319) and *CJ* 10.20.1; Schuller (1982) 205 and Noethlichs (1981) 32; on army units' corporate form and behavior, *CT* 14.17.8 (380), *CJ* 6.62.3 (349), and the very interesting CPR V 13 (A.D. 395/6), in which the *comes*

Aegypti informs the commander of a fort at Oxyrhynchus that his sub-officers have submitted to him the names of persons to fill vacancies in a rank, in the *schola cataphractariorum*.

108. Amm. 30.4.2; cf. 22.10.5, depicting the alarm that seizes a litigant when she sees her opponent, whom she thought a mere mortal, appearing in court with his *cingulum* as an *ex-palatinus*.

109. Liban., *Or.* 51.7–9 and 49.26 and 30; on Mixidemus, *Or.* 31.10–15; on Libanius' own influence with the governor, *Or.* 1.108f., quoted in Norman's translation, and Norman (1954) 46.

110. Liban., *Or.* 39.10–14; Liebeschuetz (1972) 199. It was illegal for an official of a certain rank to accept gifts (e.g., *CT* 11.11.1), no matter how universal the practice was, nor could he make any purchases (meaning real estate or articles of great value, by implication, at an unfair price, cf. 8.15.1–7, A.D. 334–97). So Mixidemus was a thoroughly bad lot.

111. *Or.* 47.31, "Midases"; 47.26, "If the generals are denied this harvest they will lose heart," phrasing which Liebeschuetz (1972) 204 rightly takes as indicating "a recognized, if illegal, part of the income of a general" (by a slip, his reference is to 17.26).

112. On Diocletian (in A.D. 288?) trying to insure fairness in the soldiers' dealing with their suppliers, see Malal. 12 p. 307 Bonn (p. 73 Stauffenberg); later, Joh. Chrysos., *Homil. in Mt* 61.2 (PG 58.590f. — cf. *In ep.* 1 *ad Cor.* 43.4), confirming at length Libanius' description of Antioch's *enkathemenos lochos*, which strips the shops of meat and anything else its men want, including money (*Or.* 46.13).

113. Greg. Naz., *Or.* 19.11f. (PG 35.1056A–1057A), addressing *ho ton hemeteron phoron apographeus* and *exisotes;* cf. Themistius, *Or.* 8 p. 171 Schenkl, on the normal "avarice of a city garrison"; Aug., *Sermo* 302.15, ". . . the soldiers, by whom the poor are oppressed," incidentally implying the frequent or regular presence of troops in Hippo; Synes., *Ep.* 129 (PG 66.1512B), the *dux Libyarum* of 305 "moving troops, not where there was the greatest military advantage but where there was most plunder," as a result of which the tribesmen to the south spread the word to the real barbarians, who thereupon invaded. Amm. 27.9.1 impugns "the army's slackness and greed in seizing other people's property" in Africa of the later 360s, and the rapacity of those in the same decade billeted in Cple, 22.4.7; cf. *CT* 7.9.1–2 (340), among several prohibitions against the endless exactions of troops billeted among civilians.

114. *Nov. Val.* 1.3.2 (A.D. 450).

115. Liban., *Or.* 47.31–33, the final exaction being perhaps one more instance of such a thing growing legitimate after a time: "some payment not long established but nevertheless current from the city senate," which is claimed as of right. Cf., further, Liban., *Or.* 2.37, "I know the condition of the soldiers . . . , hungry and shivering and without a penny, because of their so-honest colonels and generals, who make them the most wretched of men and themselves the richest," by diverting supplies and pay. Asterius Amasenus, *Or.* 4 (PG 40.221C), ca. A.D. 400, refers to the same misappropriation of troops' supplies by "many" officers, a common thing; and Libanius, in *Or.* 2.40, dwells on the greed of the officer class under Theodosius, and, in *Or.* 18.82, on their extortions in Gaul in the early 350s, as well. Similarly, Synesius, *Ep.* 131, reports on a cavalry commander even selling his troops' mounts — this, in the early 5th cent., and he twice uses the same phrase referring to "the greed of the officers," as a settled characteristic, in his *Constitutio* or *Catastasis* (PG 66.1576D) and *Ep.* 62 (1405D). Themistius, *Or.* 10 p. 207 Schenkl, describes how, along the Danube frontier in A.D. 369, "garrison commanders and centurions are merchants, rather, and slave-dealers, who have no other work, and most things are bought and sold, and the numbers of the garrisons are reduced so they [the officers] may profit from the wages of the missing"; and again, *Or.* 8 p. 174 (A.D. 368), "none of the soldiers allegedly serving" (now that a disciplinarian emperor is in charge)

"has his name falsely on the rolls," nor are entire units actually mythical. Finally, Zos. 5.46.5 speaks of commanders cheating on their men's rations as the rule, not the exception, and (5.10.1, ca. A.D. 395) describes a man "awarded a source of easy income, the command of a troop unit." Many laws could be adduced to confirm these pictures, e.g., CT 7.4.29, 7.9.3, or 8.5.21.

116. Bell (1962) 87f., of the A.D. 340s. On shakedowns during recruiting drives, see above, n. 23; later, CT 7.18.7, rounding up deserters; Synes., Ep. 79 (PG 66.1445A), "money from the recruitment tax"; Veget., De re milit. 1.7; and MacMullen (1976) 212.

117. Anon. De rebus bell. 4.1; date in E. A. Thompson (1952) 1f.

118. Themist., Or. 8.114a, p. 171 Schenkl and 114c, p. 172 (A.D. 368); cf. Paulinus of Nola, Ep. 25.5 (ca. A.D. 400), writing to an officer in Gaul, "Why should you trouble about the provision of soldiers' pay which involves the violence you loathe, when doubtless your integrity makes you mild in levying even the regular taxes?" (trans. P. G. Walsh). In 440 there is a further general statement or estimate offered (Nov. Maj. 7.1) on "the enormity of the palatine exactions [which] has too often resulted in complaint" about "their continued crimes," etc.; and in the interval between Constantine and 440 there are many references in the Theodosian Code to extortionate tax collecting, e.g., 11.7.1 (313) on concussio in the process; 8.4.2 (315), illegal surpluses extorted; 8.10.2 (344), more extras being demanded; 12.6.27 (400), embezzlement; and 11.7.9 (412), illicit penalty fees for late payments. Cf. Schuller (1975) 11 n. 26, with good references, and Lepelley (1983) 150f., on Africa in particular.

119. Bell (1962) 11f. and 34f.; for another instance of a duplicate appointment, legal for one candidate, illegal for a second, yet by recens maiestatis vestrae beneficium, see Symm., Rel. 22; and on the word Abinnaeus uses, suffragium, see above, at n. 85. His efforts at reinstatement were successful. See Rémondon (1965) 133.

120. Bell (1962) 119f.

121. Ibid. 121f., Bell's translation of e ti d'an des eis logon tes autes promotionos (with apologies for not using Greek script here, where the phrase is hard to figure out). That the reference here, as in the other letter, is to bribes is seen by Liebs (1978) 173.

122. Basil, Ep. 190, Kopecek (1974) 327 supposing that George had initiated the request to Basil through his own bishop.

123. The subject of unhappiness with curial status, and its consequences, is treated in many standard works. For recent discussion, see Veyne (1981a) 339f. and 343f. To show that bought office had no validity, see CT 12.1.26 (338) or 6.22.1 (321; 324) referring to suffragium, data pecunia, or 6.22.2 (338), etc., cited ibid. Both the latter two texts concern codicilli bought specifically to escape one's curia. Veyne discusses the question arising in the last text cited, How could the taint of purchase be detected in the granting of a codicillus? Salient is one early constitution, CT 12.1.27 (on which see above, n. 85). It is directed to the governor of Africa, acknowledging that "you have complained that the senate of most glorious Carthage remains small and the decurions are quite few in number, while all are purchasing the insignia of undue rank by the disgraceful ruin of their family fortune" (trans. Pharr); cf. still earlier, CT 12.1.5 (317), rebuking escape through suffragium comparatum egriagiatus, "of equestrian (= exempt) rank." Later texts include 12.1.25 (338), "municipal councils have been emptied of decurions through empta dignitas and suffragia"; and many others are cited, e.g., by Noethlichs (1981) 90-95. Liban., Or. 48.11, adds the story of an Antiochene decurion who sold "the family estate," used the price to buy an arche, "and was recovering the price by the crimes he was committing in office"; cf. Or. 18.134f. also, for the same course of action: flight to a militia from the curia by purchase. Further, Or. 28.22, sale of all one owns to win escape, cited in Hahn (1982) 179f., on which Hahn comments (p. 181) that the escape route is taken for granted.

124. Hefele (1907–09) 1, 1, p. 591 can. 12 of Nicaea, on backsliding Christians who resume

their *zonai* = *cingula* by "offering money and *benephikia* to arrange their re-enrollment";
Paneg. Lat. 11(3).15.5, 17.3, 18.6, 21.1, and 21.4, on routine buying of high civil office,
governorships, consulships, etc., discussed by Collot (1965) 197 and Liebs (1978) 174–76;
Epit. de Caes. 41.24, cited by Liebs (1978) 172; Amm. 18.5.5f., purchase of a high military
office by a certain Sabinianus in a matter-of-fact description; 22.7.6, military and civil
offices in number bought in A.D. 365 in the east; and 30.4.21, judgeships usually bought
for great sums; Claudian, *In Rufin.* 1.179f.; Eunap. frg. 87 (*FHG* 4.52f. = Blockley [1983]
frg. 72.1) speaking of a time around A.D. 420 and describing how the provinces of the
lower Danube and the east were all for sale, i. e. governorships or vicariates, "quite openly
through the public money-changers, like any other goods on the market" — all, looking
to an extortionate tenure of office in order to recoup the price. In the Codes, there are
such refs. as CT 6.38.1 (317) all the way up to 6.29.11 (414) and *CJ* 12.19.7 (443/4). The
last of these sets a price list for promotions in the *sacra scrinia*, cf. Collot (1965) 213. For
bibliog., see Schuller (1975) 10 n. 21 and Liebs (1978) 160 n. 7.

125. Zos. 4.28.3, Theodosius "auctioned off governorships to all comers, paying no heed at all
to their reputations or steady morals," and (4.29.1) "they all but announced publicly that
they must take in as much as they had put out for their appointment." See, later, Procop.,
Anecdota 21.9–13, the same practice described in detail under Justinian. Suetonius in
his life of Vespasian (16.2), declares he sold offices, *honores*, which may be the truth,
though the subject of that emperor's parsimony stimulated some unlikely anecdotes. The
same charge against Antoninus Pius should, I think, be regarded rather as a comment
or perception of the fourth century. The anecdote containing the charge is in the Gen.
R. 77.6, cf. Ravenna (1978) 547. Similarly, SHA *Commod.* 14.6, "he sold provinces and
administrative posts and split the yield with the buyers half and half:" the source really
tells of its own times.

126. Above, note 119; also note 74, emphasizing the work of Noethlichs (1981) 50–55. Useful
texts are CT 2.6.1, comparing 12.1.10 (325); phony notifications of appointment, in CT
8.7.2 (326) and 12.1 17 (329); forgery of exemptions by imperial *beneficium* from one's
duties, 14.4.1 (334); exemption from curial duties denied even to "persons who have
extorted a special imperial rescript to the fraud of Our sanction," in 12.1.33 (342); and
so on, in later decades, with frequent mention of the fraud accomplished *per obreptionem*
(1.9.2.1, A.D. 385 or 386), *elicitum* (*CJ* 10.20.1, A.D. 400), *ex colore sacrae iussionis* (CT 12.1
102, A.D. 383), *clandestina supplicatione* (CT 12.6.27.2, A.D. 400); *elicitum damnabili
subreptione* [Mommsen] *rescriptum* (CT 11.1.20, A.D. 385); alleged rescripts obtained only
by cunning (CT 11.7.13, A.D. 399 or 400); and so forth.

127. On inadvertent signing, see above, notes 72 and 74f.; also Liban., *Or.* 18.132, "whatever
they [officials] wanted, they declared as coming from the emperor, and there was no
contradicting this"; better still, Keith Hopkins, *JRS* 68 (1978) 181, pointing to Theophanes' description of Theodosius II regularly signing documents he never looked at;
compare SHA *Carus* 16.8, on Carus' delinquent oversight of his signature.

128. Amm. 18.5.5 (A.D. 359/60), 18.6.1 and 7, 18.7.7, 19.3.1, and 20.2.3, emphasizing his
ineptitude, which only his predecessor in office and the Master of Offices could hide,
in their wish not to give offense to the chief eunuch, Eusebius. Eusebius presumably had
been one of those who profited most from the appointment. We cannot check
Ammianus' account against any second source.

129. Constantius, *Vita Germani* 4.24, gifts to the bishop from the PPO at Arles ca. A.D. 436,
cf. Borius (1965) 169, and 7.35, silver gifts sent by the empress to the bishop as welcome
to Ravenna; *Vita S. Melaniae* 11 p. 9 Rampolla, cited in Batiffol (1919) 175, showing the
devout Melania visiting Honorius' sister in A.D. 404, see above, note 7. Cf. "Mark the
Deacon's" *Life of Porphyry* 40, Eudoxia gives the bishop silver, but he distributes it later
to the palace guards. The source tells something about early Byzantine practices, though
itself a fraud (MacMullen [1984] 86f.).

130. Batiffol (1919) 156f.
131. Schwartz (1914–40) 1, 4, 223, lines 28ff. (the Collectio Casinensis, drawn into Latin by translation from various Greek documents); some convenient account of the Council of Ephesus and the reaction of Cyril, in Batiffol (1919) 154f., A. H. M. Jones (1964) 214f. and 346f., and Wickham (1983) xxivf.; and, on the letter, ibid. xliv and 62; on the articles offered as bribes, 66 n. 8 and Batiffol (1919) 169–73.
132. Palladius, Dialog. 16 p. 25 Coleman-Norton: "of the emperor's court" at the time of the collision between Chrysostom and the bishop of Alexandria, Theophilus, "there were only two or three who gave strength to Theophilus' party, joining in the fray with armed force; also, three women, beyond the notorious ones — three widows but with lots of men about them and, to the ruin of their souls' salvation, enriched by their plunderings of others" (ca. A.D. 405).
133. Pallad., Dial. de vita S. Joh. Chrysos. 24f. p. 41 Coleman-Norton, A.D. 402; Theophilus buys off certain accusers, apparently clerics, ibid. 9 p. 10; Arcadius supplies money to a notary to buy off a supporter of Chrysostom, 15 p. 23 (A.D. 406); the bishop of Antioch, "being of a great city and having officialdom under his thumb, put it all up for sale," i.e., bishoprics and other clerical ranks, ibid. 53 p. 94; sale of ordination in Cappadocia by small-town and rural bishops, who call the bribes pious gifts, in about A.D. 370 (Basil, Ep. 53, quoting Acts 8 : 20, "May thy money perish with thee"); "the bishopric [of Alexandria] bought like some secular rank for gold" from Valens in 373, see Theodoret., H. E. 4.19 (PG 82.1169) = 4.22.9 (GCS p. 252); sale of baptism, in Aug., Ep. 66.1 (a taunt at a Donatist) and apparently in Theodoret., H. E. 1.3 (PG 82.899A), the accusation against Arius of Christemporia; a bishop in 408 using the harassing of heretics for a shakedown, Soc., H. E. 7.3 (PG 67.744A), cf. above, note 103; and some bibliography on the purchase of bishoprics in Derrett (1981) 414 nn. 46f., with further illustrations in MacMullen (1986d) 339f.
134. Pallad., Dial. 48 p. 84 (A.D. 400) to 51 p. 91.
135. Aug., Ep. 96.2, the bishop for whom Augustine requests help being now resident on lands he gained from "a small sum, with which he bought [them] as if for the church," and under cover of the name of a local potentior, to boot; cf. CT 16.2.15 (359; 360), directed against clerics covering other people's lands with the tax exemption of their own. For the matter of concubines, see Hier., Ep. 69.5 (PL 22.658f.): husbands may try to gain for them the status of matronae stolatae; but "if their poverty cannot gain for them the imperial rescript," then they must be content with marriage under only church law, not secular law as well.
136. Noethlichs (1981) 210 it is clear that: "in dieser Bürokratie kein Arbeitsethos entstehen konnte." Cf. further valuable discussion, pp. 13 and 109.
137. For complaints that the laws lie unused, see Liban., Or. 47.36f., and Symm., Ep. 9.116; evident instances may be found in Petit (1955) 34, Treucker (1961) 104, and MacMullen (1964) 50–53.
138. Above, nn. 110, 115, and 125; Pallad., Dial. 48 p. 84 Coleman-Norton; and Liban., Or. 18.135, government servants are kapeloi.
139. Salvian, De gub. dei 5.17, speaks of predatory officials overseeing taxation, qui fiscalis debiti titulos faciunt quaestus esse privatos, "not only the higher-ups but the lowliest" of the staff milking their jobs for private profit. Notice further Schuller (1975) 17, "eine merkwürdige privatistische Auffassung von staatlichen Normen und von der eigenen Beamtenrolle im Staatsorganismus"; still further, 18f. and idem (1982) 202f.
140. The governorship that Augustine aimed for, like the bishoprics of Asia, would require one's wife's dowry. Libanius and other sources often speak of borrowing to buy an appointment; but only Libanius (Or. 4.21) sees that a governor (of A.D. 389) might be "in slavery to the money-lenders."
141. Liban., Or. 47.22, defending taxis (the Loeb transl. runs, "In the first case [where the

possessors themselves pay the shakedown], the possessors are confirmed in their position; in the second [case, where the tenants pay], their [the tenants'] confidence is undermined and it is as though the rot has set in").

142. For this view, which seems to me so mistaken, I instance the assessment by a scholar of formidable authority, André Chastagnol (1976) 8, saying of the "strong" emperors from A.D. 364 to 395, "L'ordre romain, ainsi sauvegardé, était fondé sur la toute-puissance de l'empereur, sur une administration provinciale bien structurée, sur une fiscalité précise et pesante." Such views are easily discovered in less recent and some more recent works.

CHAPTER 4

1. Gansser-Burckhardt (1942) 98f. and 102, on leather finds in Vindonissa; Parker (1973) 366 on Baetican imports to Mainz; and other articles imported to camps could be instanced, like pottery and metalwork. Bishop (1985) 13 concludes a careful gathering of evidence on military production of military equipment by quite (and, I think, quite wrongly) discounting the civilian contribution as "very small"; but see MacMullen (1960) 25f., adding Hatt (1953) 235, Speidel (1981) 408, and PBeatty Panop.1, lines 343f.

2. On *horrea* for more than a unit's own use, there is an example in a camp 60 km from Mainz, with storage facilities for Drusus' campaigns. See Schönberger (1976) 24–26, 50, and 253; again, Manning (1974) 63 and 68, on a similar site for campaigns in Wales in the 50s. Compare the supplies accumulated for the Dacian campaigns long prior to action, in Vulpe (1960) 325 and 328f. and Sasel (1973) 80. On the careful itinerary planned for the Dacian wars, as for others we know of, see Koeppel (1980) 305. They involved very ambitious building for Trajan: Sasel (1973) 80f. and 84.; Strobel (1984) 159–61; and Kondic (1984) 149, on the fort guarding one end of Trajan's canal that bypassed the Iron Gates. Compare also Caracalla's anticipatory bridge and road construction against the Alamans, in Gottlieb and Kuhoff (1984) 22 n. 2 and 232f.

3. E.g., in Valentinian's reign, see Alföldi (1952) 48f. and Garbsch (1967) 74–77; Theophanes, *Chron. anno* 318 (PG 108.113) and 320 (116), on Constantine's bridge.

4. Gostar (1979) 122 counts 86–90,000 men for each war; Strobel (1984) 153f., 200,000 for both together. It was common to assemble campaign forces out of contingents from widely scattered units: for example, the quite small expeditionary armies of the 3d cent. focused on Mauretania from Syria, Pannonia Sup. and Inf., Germany Inf. and Sup., Spain, Britain, and Moesia Inf., in the one case, A.D. 244; from Italy, Germany, Aquileia, Moesia Inf., and Egypt, in the other, of A.D. 297. See Seston (1946) 119 and Rachet (1970) 196f. and 199f.

5. For Philippi, see App., B.C. 4.108, offering figures which total roughly 218,000 as I count. Brunt (1971) 335 says 200,000 and (p. 489), "some 190,000 legionaries . . . had taken part in the Philippi campaign." Earlier, there were very substantial forces under Marius, to say nothing of Cannae. Besides the modern estimates from numbers of legions involved, notice the casualties among Marius' enemies in 102/1 (Vell. 2.12.4f.; Livy, Epit. 68; Florus 1.38), ranging from 65,000 to 200,000 plus 90,000 captured by Marius' mere 32,000; at Cannae, 75,000 killed (Polyb. 3.117).

6. Dio 76.6.1, as correctly interpreted by Boon (1972) 47, citing Wuilleumier for the same estimate. Graham (1978) 626f. concurs, evidently unaware that his views had been anticipated. Plut., *Galba* 4.3, supplies another statistic: 100,000 under Vindex; but it is a boast. More trustworthy is Vell. 2.113.1 on Tiberius' army of A.D. 6: 10 legions, 84 auxiliary units, 10,000 veterans and allied troops from Rhoemetalces.

7. Amm. 23.3.5 specifies 30,000 *lecti* as being (25.7.2) "little fewer" than the main part of the army directly under Julian. Considering the common sense of supply in a Mesopotamian war, it is hard to imagine Julian invading in any greater bulk. But Constantius had assembled troops with much vigor, not only the picked ones he notoriously demanded

from Julian in Gaul, but others elsewhere (Amm. 20.8.1, A.D. 360, Gothic mercenaries, cf. 23.2.7 and Zos. 3.25.6). Zos. 3.12 mentions Julian's 18,000 plus (3.13) 65,000, which Piganiol (1972) 158 n. 3, with other scholars, does not accept, and which he would like to reduce from 65 plus 18 = 83,000 to 65 minus 18 = 47,000. But that is not what the texts says. For the proportion of barbarians in the force as a whole, see Appendix A II 4.

8. As examples of Zosimus' unreliability, notice (1.42.1) his giving the Goths an invading force of 320,000, not counting their navy, in Gallienus' time; Julian's slaying of 60,000 barbarians at Strasbourg (3.3.3, Valesius emending *myriadon* to *chiliadon* for the sense alone), while Stilicho kills "almost all" of 400,000 (5.26.3f., cf. 200,000 in Marcellus, *Chron.* 2.68, noted by *PLRE* 2); and the error of 40,000 for 4,000 at 6.8.2, corrigible through Soz., *H. E.* 9.8.6, cf. Kaegi (1968) 17. Zos. 2.15.1f. and 2.22.1f. assigns to Constantine in 312 an expeditionary army of 98,000 against Maxentius' 188,000 and, in A.D. 322, 140,000 against Licinius' 150,000. Hoffmann (1969–71) 1.199 and 2.73 and 76 simply disregards these figures, while accepting the 20,000 of Constantine in 316 against Licinius' 35,000, in Anon. Vales. 5.16.

9. Zon. 13.8 (3.198 Dindorf). Similarly unreliable, the 50,000 dead in 413 at Ocriculum, in Heraclian's invasion force, Hydatius, *Chron.* 56 (*MGH AA* 11 p. 118). Cf. Kotula (1977) 258 n. 3, "surement grossies."

10. On carelessness in military terminology, see MacMullen (1980b) 458 n. 32.

11. Zos. 5.45.1, five *tagmata* (= "legions," as Ridley or *PLRE* 2 translate) total 6,000 men; but (6.8.2) six *tagmata* total 4,000; and notice the implications of very small size in the provision (*CT* 8.5.11, A.D. 360) of only two wagons for any legion's sick and wounded. For further indications of small unit size, see MacMullen (1980) 457f. and (1984) 474f.

12. Amm. 18.2.8 (A.D. 359), *barbara multitudo . . . viribus magnis*, cf. 18.2.11; and 29.6.13, *valida proeliis manus* of two legions. For the use of the Punic wars as the yardstick to measure great military ventures, see e.g., Ammianus' contemporary Pacatus, *Pan. lat.* 12(2).32.1. For Julian's force, see Amm. 16.12.2: his 13,000 were pitted against 35,000 (16.12.26). For a major demonstration of force to repair what Ammianus calls a disaster, through the restoration of Sauromaces by the *comes et dux Armeniae* with only twelve legions = ca. 12,000, see Amm. 27.12.16. Later in A.D. 397/8 an entire expeditionary force against Gildo numbers only 5,000, despite desperate efforts at recruitment. See Claudian, *Bell. Gild.* 421–23 and Oros. 7.36.6, analyzed by Clemente (1968) 148–50, with A. H. M. Jones (1964) 184, on recruitment; and compare the expeditionary force against Gildo's brother Firmus in 374, of 5,000 men (Amm. 29.5.29, emphasizing its small size at 29.5.39 and 48). Again, in A.D. 400, the scale of combat seems very modest: an unarmed mob from the housetops and alleyways of Cple can destroy a fifth of Gainas' force (Synes., *De prov.* 2.2, *PG* 66.1264), the whole of which Bury (1923) 134 n. 1 would rate at much less than 30,000 and Wolfram (1979) 177 at perhaps 14,000 (twice the 7,000 in Zos. 5.19.4). In the west, the capital, now moved to Ravenna, in 409 could hope to see its siege raised by a mere 6,000 men (Zos. 5.45.1) and, in 410, by a mere 4,000 (Zos. 6.8.2).

13. MacMullen (1980b) 455 and 460. On the imperial army total in literary sources as in the *Not. Dig.*, A. H. M. Jones (1964) 680-84 offers views which I disagree with. On the unreliability of the *Not. Dig.*, see Clemente (1968) 18, 20 n. 21, and 30–54 (e.g., p. 39, duplicate entries for African *limitanei*), detecting many blunders and anomalies in a work patched together from 5th-cent. information (pp. 57f.) all the way back to the pre-Diocletianic. F. Lot rightly called its picture mythological: "les chiffres données . . . sont de la fantasmagorie." See Lot, Pfister, and Ganshof (1928) 19f., and A. R. Birley, cited in MacMullen (1980) 456 n. 18; ibid. 459f. n. 37, on Piganiol, Segrè, and A. H. M. Jones all having resort to the phrase "on paper" to describe army strength — i.e., none of them could really reconcile the imperial army totals they found in their sources with their impressions formed piecemeal.

14. *Militaris socordia et aliena invadendi cupiditas* (27.9.1), *intemperantia militis, quae dispendiis*

gravibus saepe rem Romanam afflixit (29.4.6), *torpente praesentium militum manu* (16.2.1), *luxuque adiumento militari marcente* (27.9.6), a decade of eastern forces constituted of *iners et umbratilis miles* (18.6.2), *enerves et timidi* (18.8.2). Demandt (1965) 28–32 gathers such passages as these, and more.

15. Liban., Or. 2.38, on lack of drill "in military exercises . . . and the proper exertions in the field, . . . so then, in battles, the enemy needs only send up a shout and off they scamper"; Claud., *In Eutrop.* 2.580ff., the slackness of the men under Stilicho is joined to the treachery of their leaders, so they are easily put to flight — with other passages to the same effect gathered by Cameron (1970) 375; also Veget., *De re milit.* 1.20, on inadequate armor, and 2.3, on the ill effects of promotion according to *ambitio* and *gratia;* and PAbinnaeus 28, line 14 and Liban., Or. 47.6, on soldiers' drunkenness, with SHA *Tac.* 2.4, soldiers in general are *plerumque temulenti*, and idiots and dolts into the bargain; Ambros., *De elia* 46, officers' luxurious parties; Symm., *Ep.* 6.73 and 7.38, soldiers' worthlessness, and further, Eugip., *Vita Severini* 20.1, for a somewhat later period along the Pannonian frontier. Notice esp. the abundant evidence from the Abinnaeus archive, in Rémondon (1965) 136, including the letter from a person knowledgeable about army ways, requesting permanent paid leave for a young kinsman so he can be useful around the farm. Cf. also above, chap. 3 note 116.

16. On married troops, see Liban., Or. 2.39, with more material in MacMullen (1963) 127, to which still further archeological evidence could easily be added, e.g., Gomolka (1968) 208, 210, and 232 on women's articles in military emplacements, or similar articles in the burials of Germanic *foederati* described, e.g., in Hawkes (1974) 387 and 393.

17. CJ 11.60(59).3 = *Nov. Theod.* 24.4, to the Mag. Offic. in charge of lands from Thrace round to Libya, discussing measures instituted *ex prisca dispositione, antiquitus.* On the addressee of the constitution, see *PLRE* 2 s. v. Nomos 1. The evidence on farmer-soldiers laid out in MacMullen (1963) chap. 1 was presented in resumé by Mazza (1970) 454–60, along with reactions by other scholars. Add to Mazza's citations Mann (1965) 150, who doubts any evidence of farmer-soldiers before A.D. 400, to be set against *RE* Suppl. 11 (1968) s. v. Limitanei, where A. R. Neumann (col. 878f.) concludes that after Diocletian "der grösste Teil der *ripenses* war sicher nicht mehr kriegsverwendungsfähig und die Entwicklung zum sesshafter Bauernmilitär ziemlich weit fortgeschritten." A part of the cause of controversy lies in what evidence appears convincing (easily seen in Mazza, p. 458). Does the presence of soldier-swineherds, for example, and well-worn agricultural tools in camps show that agriculture was institutionalized? The archeological data are well known, and Gomolka (1968) 225 offers one more illustration of a frontier post with its own farming tools. Another part of the controversy arises from supposing that *all* of the *limitanei* were farmer-soldiers. To the contrary, I continue in my belief (1963, p. 18) that, even after A.D. 400, "some of them at least, and apparently most, were not mere part-time but full-time regular soldiers relying on the state for their supplies," though, on the other hand, many others were in fact a farming militia. The model by which to understand their development is the colonate, decreed for successive areas over several generations. So, similarly, I suppose the process of institutionalizing farming among soldiers was a gradual one, affecting different frontiers at different times. Of new evidence there is only Di Vita (1964) passim on Tripolitania, esp. 71–81 and 97 — in spite of which, Trousset (1974) passim, esp. 38, 130f., 145, and 152, reasserts the older picture of that frontier.

18. *Dig..* 49.16.13.1 (Macer).

19. On the cost-saving of late Roman emplacements, see MacMullen (1984a) 576.

20. Appendix A; and a recent summary in Hoffmann (1969–70) 1.138f. and 2.48 n. 67, where he emphasizes the new character of barbarian enlistments under the Tetrarchy. Notice also his discussion of "Gallicani" (= barbarians in but not of Gaul, ibid. 1.145f.)

21. The line of the earlier, expanded frontier at this point is well known, e.g., through Roeren (1960) Abb. 1, facing p. 266; Schönberger (1969) fig. 10, facing p. 176; or fig. 32 facing p. 218 in Petrikovits (1971). The inter-riverine triangle, once the Agri Decumates, had been won back from invaders in A.D. 256 (Wightman [1985] 193) before being lost for ever in ca. 260. Cf. S. Johnson (1983) 74, quoting *Pan. lat.* 8(5).10.2; Schönberger (1969) 179; and Petrikovits (1971) 178. The line of the *limes* post-260 is best seen in Garbsch (1970) Abb. 2.

22. For the line of the province in its fully developed form, see Gudea (1979) 172. For the date of the loss, S. Johnson (1983) 74 suggests A.D. 270, but the consensus settles on 275, e.g., in Bodor (1973) 38.

23. For the line of the earlier province, see Courtois (1955) 66 and 82 or Février (1982) 383 fig. A 6; the province later reduced, Courtois (1955) 66 or Rachet (1970) Carte XV. But Rachet, p. 258, points out that urban centers need not have been nor were totally deserted all at once. Further, on the retreat: Warmington (1954) 21, Euzennat (1967) 199, Rebuffat (1982) 509, opting for a date ca. 280, Euzennat (1984) 391 (ca. 290?), S. Johnson (1983) 223 ("no later than about 290"), and Gozalbes (1980) 125, using finds of coins to point to abandonment "in all probability in 284." Shaw (1987) 86 n. 64 provides a convenient resumé of the indices of retreat.

24. The later empire saw much movement back and forth between Persia and Rome across Armenia and northern Mesopotamia but no final retreat; and to the south there was some shuffling of administrative boundaries without clear surrender of sovereignty. See Bowersock (1983) 143f. On the later period, the most recent and ample in its discussion is the work of Shahid (1984), seeming to me most unsatisfactory. An Arab-Roman treaty in the early 4th cent. is simply invented, the often mentioned "defection of Imru'al-Qays" (e.g., p. 58) is purely fanciful, and no treaty is actually referred to in our evidence before Socrates' mention under Valens.

25. Olympiodorus frg. 37, a retreat from Prima to Philae, five days' journey (ca. 100 miles?); Munier (1938) 40; Rostovtzeff (1957) 737; and Skeat (1964) xii.

26. Besides the well-known Fossatum of Colonel Baradez and his successors in exploration, to which G. D. B. Jones and Mattingly (1980) have something recent to add, see Gascou (1982) 242 and Carte 1 facing p. 238, on the Severan *nova praetentura;* also Euzennat (1977) 537; and on the overall shape and nature of the southern *limes,* Rebuffat (1982) 508, describing it very well; ibid. 509, on the abandoning of Dimmidi in Numidia, an isolated outpost, in 238. Rachet (1970) Carte XV needs correcting, so far as southern Numidia is concerned.

27. Warmington (1954) 29f. and 70; Courtois (1955) 66, two maps contrasted, with which Rachet (1970) 232–53 and Cartes XIV–XV are largely in accord (but see the preceding note). The evidence is far from conclusive.

28. The fundamental study of the area remains that of Goodchild and Ward Perkins (1949). To their evidence, a couple of further sites can be added, notably Bir ed-Dredir at the southern edge of the gray zone; but Courtois (1955) 77 contests a 4th-cent. date for that site and sees no Roman meaning in the inscriptions found there, supposing rather that the Tripolitan province had under Diocletian or Constantine shrunk back almost to the coast (pp. 77f.). While not going quite that far, Goodchild and Ward Perkins (1949) 95 suppose that "the great invasions of 363 . . . could scarcely have occurred without neglect, or even connivance, on the part of the *limitanei,*" and even Di Vita (1967) 97f. gingerly broaches the question, How real was imperial control or presence here as elsewhere in the gray zone? Buck (1985) 188 speaks of "the end of Roman control" and consequent sufferings of the coastal cities, in spite of which, "while Roman state control may have lapsed," life in the predesertic zone continued almost unchanged, Christianized, even guarded. Contra, Di Vita (1967) 94f., Rebuffat (1977) 411–13, and Février

(1982) 379 fig. A 1. There is no controversy over the abandonment of Cidamus-Golas-Garbia: see Goodchild and Ward Perkins (1949) 85, Courtois (1955) 73, and Rebuffat (1982) 509.

29. I quote Amm. 27.9.1. For Romanus' actions at this time and later, see chap. 2, notes 98–100; for the Austorian raids, see Amm. 28.6.2–10 and 13–15, noticing where he puts the blame: *barbari, fiducia sublati praeteritorum . . .* (28.6.10). The ravaged regions he calls by the inclusive term *provincia* (28.6.19), suggesting a province limited to the coastal strip. The chronology is laid out by Demandt (1968) passim. Di Vita (1967) 94, in order to salvage the theory of an undiminished Roman defense of the *limes Tripolitanus* throughout the 4th cent., supposes the raiding tribes made a big swing around the *limes* to the east and sneaked into Lepcis by the coast. It is not easy to imagine them doing this once (and back, with booty), let alone twice and thrice, all unknown to Ammianus. *IRT* 475 and 565 supply a little further information. See Courtois (1955) 78 and Lepelley (1979–81) 2.339 and 359. Archeological evidence suggests that Sabratha also suffered at this time. See Daniels (1983) 17.

30. Amm. 15.5.8 and passim. That *"hostili tumore vexabat"* indicates extortion is sufficiently clear from what we know of *rationales;* and *"proscripti"* is to be explained in the same sense by many laws and, best of all, by Amm. 28.2.13.

31. For the line of the empire's maximum extension in this region, when Roman powers were at their height, see Willems (1981) 26 fig. 6; for the line in the 4th cent., see Bogaers (1967) 101; Bogaers (1968) 155 fig. 2; Chevallier (1975) 207, with commentary on specific sites, e.g., at 61f.; and Mertens (1977) 64. The evidence for the continued occupation of one or two forts on the lower Rhine frontier is as yet inconclusive. For the Salian Frankish occupation of Toxandria, see Demougeot (1953) 8, Günther (1975) 346 fig. 30 and pp. 347f., Demougeot (1969–79) 2.100, Wightman (1978) 242–45 with fig. 1, p. 242, and Wightman (1985) 209, again; on the fortified sites behind the line, Chevallier (1975) passim, and other special studies more recent, e.g., Bayard and Massy (1982) 23 and 26, and below, Appendix A II 3.

32. Amm. 14.10.3f., 15.5.29, 17.9.6, and 20.8.8, with further very abundant material concerning difficulties of supply in the second half of the 4th cent. in *CJ* (e.g., 12.38) and *CT* (e.g. 7.4); further, chap. 3, above, e.g., at notes 87, 91, and esp. 24 (concerning the exact parallel to A.D. 355, back in A.D. 270).

33. For the boundaries of Cilicia Tracheia = Isauria, see *RE* s. v. Isaura (Ruge, 1916) col. 2056; Stein (1959) in his map (vol. 2) entitled "Imperium Romanum a. 390"; and Calder and Bean (1958).

34. I quote from SHA *Triginta tyr.* 26.6, which continues, "though their country lay in the middle of Roman territory, it was shut in by a new kind of defense as by a frontier, *limes.*" Amm. 14.2.13 refers to *milites omne latus Isauriae defendentes assueti,* i.e., it is a circular *limes* that surrounds the barbarian region, and (14.2.1) the situation had existed *diu quidem,* for a long time before A.D. 354. Other sources may be found in A. H. M. Jones (1971) 212f.

35. *ILS* 740 = *CIL* 3.6733, cf. *PLRE* 1 s. v. Lauricius; and Harrison (1980) 114 on the inscription from a hilltop 35 miles SW of Termessus, dated 361/7.

36. Amm. 15.13.4, A.D. 356, on the Persian raids; 27.9.6, A.D. 368, on the Isaurian raids, *nullis arcentibus, luxu adiumento militari marcente,* so Count Lauricius had to turn to *semermes pauci, quos diogmitas appellant* — just like Synesius, later. On the raids earlier, Amm. 14.2.1–20; on those of ca. 370 (?), Eunap. frg. 45 (*FHG* 4.33); on the military dispositions, A. H. M. Jones (1964) 57, 101, 192, and 609, and Rougé (1966b) 303-10.

37. Eunap. frg. 86 (*FHG* 4.51, A.D. 404, according to Niebuhr); Philostorg., *H E.* 11.8, p. 139 Bidez; Soz., *H.E.* 8.25 (*PG* 67.1580Cf.); Hier., *Ep.* 114.1 (*PL* 22.934, A.D. 405); *CT* 9.35.7 (408), the Isaurians punished, but inland Syria requires city garrisons against them still

in Symeon Stylites' time, cf. Brown (1971) 84 n. 46 (Symeon died ca. 459, which suggests the date for the Syrian garrisons of his day). For still other sources on the great raids of A.D. 404–06, see Rougé (1966b) 298–300.

38. Zos. 5.25, trans. Ridley; cf. Zos. 5.15.5, on the continuity of Isaurian raids; and *PLRE* 2 s.v. Arbazacius.

39. Amm. 19.11.7.

40. Amm. 31.4.4, trans. Rolfe; compare Eunap. frg. 42, p. 238: Valens admitted the Goths as constituting "a great reinforcement that would supplement Roman strength"; also Soc., *H.E.* 4.34 (PG 67.553Bf.), Valens "thought himself highly fortunate in the act [of admitting Goths], for he reckoned he would thereby gain a handy, cheap army against his enemies, and he hoped the barbarians as frontier guards would cause more fear than the Roman ones"; and compare the admission in A.D. 370 of Saxons *habiles ad militiam*, Amm. 28.5.4; further, Amm. 30.6.1, A.D. 375, conversations between Valens and Quadi about their providing recruits; 30.2.6, A.D. 377/8, Valens for his war against Persia "was hiring help from the Goths with as much speed as possible"; 31.10.17, A.D. 378, contributions of recruits sought from the surrendering Lentienses; and the laws of 370, *CT* 7.13.2, relieving the pain of the recruiting tax exacted in kind rather than cash, and of A.D. 375, *CT* 7.13.7, which transfers the weight of the tax from liturgists to individuals' property, as the yield is to be cash, not *corpora* (7.13.7.1, quoted in my text).

41. Amm. 31.4.10f., quoted in my text (trans. Rolfe); Eunap. frg. 42; Iordan., *Getica* 26; Zos. 4.20; and Oros., *Hist. adv. pagan.* 7.33.11, *deinde propter intolerabilem avaritiam Maximi ducis fame et iniuriis adacti in arma surgentes* (the Goths), *victo Valentis exercitu, per Thraciam sese ... fuderunt.*

42. Amm. 31.8.6, *nullo vetante, impune;* Eunap., frg. 42 (*FHG* 4.32), "as there was no battle-worthy force to resist them, they appeared the more terrifying, by their numbers, to men undefended and themselves unarmed." See also Wolfram (1977) 235 and 238f. and Wolfram (1979) 140f. and 144.

43. Amm. 31.11.2–5; Zos. 4.23.

44. Zos. 4.22.2.

45. Amm. 31.12.3 — which fits with the fact that, by a mere cloud of missiles dispatched at them while the two armies stood face to face, the Goths were panicked into a last request for peace. See also Lot, in Lot, Pfister, and Ganshof (1928) 13, accepting the estimate of 10,000 Goths as accurate; on the scene and background, Wolfram (1977) 241; on Valens' army size, Wolfram (1979) 145 suggesting 30–40,000, Demougeot (1969–79) 2.144 suggesting 20–27,000, Bernardi (1970) 69 suggesting 13,000 or less, with older scholars like Delbrück and Schmidt being sometimes quoted on the minimalist side; contra, Stein (1959) 518f. n. 189, arguing for the largest possible, "at least 30,000, perhaps 40,000." He adduces the reported losses of 35 *tribuni vacantes et numerorum rectores* (Amm. 31.13.18); but that does not indicate losses of the order he supposes. In the only battle where casualties of high officers are compared to losses among their men, the ratio is one to sixty (Amm. 16.26.63). That would suggest 35 X 60 at Hadrianople = 2100, i.e., over 10 per cent — severe enough. Stein further adduces other figures, one being already handled above (at n. 12: Amm. 27.12.16); but they seem to me inadequate to his case. He might best have instanced in comparison the slaughter by Gratian of "more than 30,000 Alamans" at Strasbourg in 377, "as the story is told" (Oros., *Hist. adv. pagan.* 7.33.8, *narrantur*). See Hier., *Chron. a. 239* = 377; Iordan., *Rom.* 312; and later sources in Riese (1892) 325; Amm. 31.10.5, "40,000, or 70,000 as some men boasted in order to inflate the praises of the emperor" — so Ammianus distrusts the estimates. The argument of Hoffmann (1969–70) 1.444 for 30–40,000 out of a total of 70–80,000 in Valens' east-empire *force de frappe* rests on calculations from the *Not. Dig.* He infers Roman losses from units not later attested (12–16 units, 9 of them legions, p. 457; therefore, ?9 x 1000 + ?7 x

500 = maximum of ?12,500) and a total army at Hadrianople "bei weitem ein Vielfaches" of these losses. There is, however, no good means of showing that the later-missing units disappeared in 378 and not at some other occasion after 378, or even before (e.g., in 377).

46. Amm. 31.7.4; 31.10.6; and 31.11.6.
47. Above, n. 42; and following on the battle of Hadrianople, the Goths ranged freely. See Theodoret., *Hist. relig.* (PG 82.1372A), where the Goths "devastated all Thrace, from the Danube to the Propontis, without fear," and Eunap. frg. 50 (*FHG* 4.36) = frg. 47.1, pp. 70f. Blockley. Blockley (p. 142) sets the date at 379 or 380. As to troop numbers, A. H. M. Jones (1964) 1445 shows how he interprets the effect of A.D. 378 on the inventory in the *Not. Dig.* and (p. 1448) gives figures allowing a totalling of the Danube forces: 94,000 nonlegionaries + 159,000 legionaries = 253,000. Demougeot (1969–79) 2.183 would reduce this estimate only slightly.
48. Above, at notes 14f., and chap. 3, at note 115.
49. Joh. Chrysos., *Ad viduam iuniorem* 4 (PG 48.605).
50. On the settlement of A.D. 380, see Piganiol (1972) 244, Demougeot (1974) 146f., Demougeot (1969–79) 2.148 and 152, and Wolfram (1979) 155. On the treaty of 382, "parfois considérée comme marquant la fin de l'empire romain," see Piganiol (1972) 151f. and Wolfram (1979) 156f., who speaks of "an autonomous Gothia."
51. Eunap. frg. 65 (identically in *Vit. soph.* 476); Zos. 5.5.3, cf. *PLRE* I s.v. Gerontius 6, Demougeot (1969–79) 2.165, and Wolfram (1979) 166f.
52. Among sources, see Iordan., *Getica* 29.146f.; further, Demougeot (1969–79) 2.167 and Wolfram (1979) 167f. and 178.
53. On the abandonment of Britain north of the Wall, though controversy still continues, see Mann (1974) 531; S. Johnson (1982) 123; and Arnold (1984) 7; as to Armorica, see above, chap. 1 at note 67; Joannes Antiochenus frg. 201 (p. 50 in C. D. Gordon's translation), "the Aemorichians who were hostile to the Romans" under Theodosius II; and Demougeot (1975) 1098.
54. CT 7.14.1. In the *burgarii*, Le Roux (1982) 397 n. 54 sees the urban garrisons also found a decade later in Honorius' letter to Pamplona — on which, see also Demougeot (1956) and A. H. M. Jones (1964) 1106. As to the Waffengräber, see Le Roux (1982) 393 with n. 37 (where the archeologists being cited evidently date the burials to the 4th not the 5th cent.) and S. Johnson (1983) 221 and 240. Notice also Zos. 6.5.1, referring to Spanish forces which in A.D. 409 could protest against being displaced from their traditional (*kata to synethes*) watch over the Pyrenees passes. So the troops had been on guard there for some good number of years before 409. The mention of *limitanei* in the Spanish sections of the *Not. Dig.* has been taken by some — e.g., Blazquez (1964) 171 — to show the existence of a defended frontier in the later empire; but there is disagreement from Gorges (1979) 53 n. 66, Arce (1980) 593ff., Le Roux (1982) 393, and S. Johnson (1983) 221. Le Roux (1982) 394f. seems to be correct in distinguishing between a line, which did not exist militarily, and a zone. Later, after 409, the *Not. Dig.* references admittedly show existing troop dispositions. See, e.g., Arce (1980) 604f. For the locations, see Demougeot (1956) 40, Le Roux (1982) 393, and S. Johnson (1983) 240.
55. Dr. Stephen Johnson kindly called my attention to the plans and site description of Niksic and Vigu to be found in Praschniker and Schober (1919) 12 and 99. While he does not rule out a late Roman date for these sites and Doclea, others in the same region (Preza, Petrejla, Elbassan) seem to him less likely to be Roman. The Viennese archeologists themselves, having less comparative material at their command, were more confident in placing these sites in the late Roman period (see esp. pp. 54f.). The sites recall the garrison towns Bononia, Onagrinum, and Cornacum in Pannonia of the last quarter of the 4th cent., 50–85 km inland (west) from the frontier. See Eadie (1982) 29f. and 42, drawing cautiously on the *Not. Dig.*; and, on the virtual loss of control over Pannonia's

security in the 390s, see Bury (1923) 1.167 and Stein (1959) 229 and 250. "Clausa tot annis/ oppida" in Claud., De cons. Stil., 2.193f. indicates a province in a state of siege.

56. Welsby (1982) 151 and S. Johnson (1983) 36, who shows in his map there the 100-mile zone south of the Wall dotted with Roman forts (18 all told) named in the Not. Dig., including Ribchester, Lancaster, Doncaster, and Piercebridge, and some not named in that source but occupied in the 370s even further south than Doncaster, plus four more in Wales. See further, p. 118, on the prominence of Watling Street in the pattern of fortifications; and Hobley (1983) 80, with Map D, showing late-4th-cent. burgi along the two forks of the highway Wroxeter-to-Mancetter-to-London, and Brough-to-Mancetter-to-London. I quote from his summation of the evidence.

57. MacMullen (1963) 142 and 145–47; above, chap. 1 at notes 71–76.

58. Zos. 5.15f., 5.18, and 5.25.2; for further details, Soc., H. E. 6.6 (PG 67.676Bf.), Philostorg., H. E. 11.8 pp. 138f. Bidez-Winkelmann, Wolfram (1979) 176f., and below, Appendix A II 9.

59. Iordan., Getica 29.147.

60. Wolfram (1979) 180, "the battle was inconclusive"; Matthews (1975) 274, "inconclusive as a contest"; and Garuti (1979) 76f., who balances the sources, Cassiodorus and Iordanes calling Alaric the winner, Prosper calling the battle a draw, while Claudian, Prudentius, and Garuti himself call Stilicho victorious. Characteristically, Stilicho had to depend on barbarian troops assembled from Britain, Rhine, and Raetia (Claud., De bello Goth. 414–22 and 568f.). On the battle of Verona, see Garuti (1979) 81–89 and Wolfram (1979) 181.

61. RE Suppl. 9 s.v. Pannonia (A. Mocsy, 1962) col. 580.

62. The Oxford Dictionary of the Christian Church (1974) 1332 assigns Synesius' bishopric to Ptolemais ca. 410–14, which is acceptable. Der Kleine Pauly 5 (1975) 453 makes him bishop of Cyrene A.D. 410–13; Lacombrade (1951) 229 prefers 411 and Ptolemais, while Bregman (1982) 61 makes him bishop of Ptolemais likewise, but (p. viii) from 410 to "414?" There is dispute over the dates of persons referred to by Synesius, e.g., the dux Libyarum, Anysius, of 410 or 411, differently, according to Fitzgerald (1930) 2.478 or Lacombrade (1951) 230.

63. On the Austorians, see Courtois (1955) 103, citing Philostorg., H. E., 11.8 p. 138 Bidez-Winkelmann ("Mazices and Auxoriani") and IRT 480 (408/23); and Donaldson (1985) 176, setting the inscription in ca. 413.

64. On the numbers, see Synes., Catastasis II (PG 66.1576B) — referring also to "the wretched tribe" (1569A) and the 5,000 camels (1569D) — and Ep. 78, in Lacombrade (1951) 230, and A. H. M. Jones (1968) 292. On the ecclesiastical self-help, see MacMullen (1963) 138–40.

65. Synes., Ep. 62 (PG 66.1405D and 1408A), the accusation of greed in the same phrase repeated in Catastasis II (PG 66.1576D). Notice, in Ep. 78 (PG 66.1444Af.), the sharp distinction drawn between the Hunnigardae and hoi enchorioi (soldiers) who receive less pay and are essentially non-beings ("war needs hands, not lots of names").

66. Catastasis II (PG 66.1569D), with "assassinated" the translation of Fitzgerald (1930) 2.477.

67. Aug., Ep. 220.6 to the comes domesticorum et Africae. Cf. PLRE 2 s.v. Bonifatius 3, Augustine's letter dating to A.D. 427/29; for the man's fortunes, ibid. and Prosp. Tiro. a. 427. For a convenient summary of these events see Bury (1923) 1. 245f.

68. Bury (1923) 1.104 and 167 note 3, concluding, "We may conjecture that the numbers of the invaders did not exceed 50,000." See sources in Seeck (1910–21) 5.375f. with notes, and Stein (1959) 249 and Courcelle (1964) 39 n. 2, both scholars dismissing the figures in our sources as too large. Notice the "ferunt" in Oros., Hist. adv. pagan. 7.37.4, offering the figure 200,000, which appears again in Marcellus, Chron. 2.68, but as 400,000 in Zos. 5.26.3; and Olympiodorus frg. 9 (FHG 4 p. 59), counting in Radagaisus' horde no less than 12,000 princes. Zos. 5.26.4 assigns to Stilicho thirty arithmoi = 12–13,000 men and

additional forces fewer than that total ("whatever allies from the Huns and Alans he could get"); so the two sorts of troops together at Faesulae = Fiesole must have numbered some 20–23,000. For the invading forces of 406/7, see Riese (1892) 345, citing Fredegar, *Chron.* 2.60, A.D. 406; A. H. M. Jones (1964) 1107; and E. A. Thompson (1982) 129, conjecturing "scores of thousands of persons." For the barbarians' virtually unopposed entrance to Spain, see Demougeot (1969–79) 2.447; on the numbers of Vandals crossing to Africa under Gaiseric in 429, as indicated most reliably by Victor of Vita, *Hist. persecut. Vand.* 1.1 (*CSEL* 7.3), and less reliably by Hydat. 74 and Procopius, *Bell. Vandal.* 1.5.19, see Seeck (1910–21) 6.416, arguing for very large estimates. These are quite incredible. For the total 80,000 implying 10–15,000 warriors, see Lot in Lot, Pfister, and Ganshof (1928) 12 and 56 n. 10, and Courtois (1955) 162, quoting Delbrück and other earlier scholars; Blazquez (1964) 43; A. H. M. Jones (1964) 195, 1106, and 1029, "the Vandals . . . could not put into the field more than 20 or 30,000 fighting men"; Goffart (1980) 231–34; and Blazquez (1983) 2.76f., offering estimates for all the barbarians in the Spanish peninsula around A.D. 468 between 70/80,000 and 200,000. Compare E. A. Thompson (1982) 158, setting the Suebic people in Spain at 20–25,000.
69. See note 45, above, on the Goths in 376; also Piganiol (1972) 185; Goffart (1980) 4f.; Wolfram (1981) 315; and E. A. Thompson (1982) 155.
70. The Quadi and Sarmatians were useless in siegecraft (Amm. 29.6.12), likewise the Goths (31.8.1), who knew nothing of catapults either (31.15.12); and notice the whole *gens Vandalorum* described as *inbellis* by Oros., *Hist. adv. pagan.* 7.38.1.
71. On Spain, see Blazquez (1974–75) 312 and Courtois (1955) 164; ibid. 42 and 164 on Gaul.
72. Above, note 32, with further cross-references, and chap. 3, note 115, with a number of vignettes of troops ill-supplied and therefore unable to fight.
73. Synes., *Catastasis* (PG 66.1576D); Zos. 2.34.1f.; and above, chap. 3 passim, esp. notes 94ff. and 111–18.
74. Chap. 3 notes 24f. and Zos. 4.27.3.
75. Amm. 30.7.10 and Zos. 4.16.3f., the chief in extortion being the indefatigable Count Romanus.
76. Above, chap. 3, nn. 70f., 98f., 119–22, and 126–33. I draw attention esp. to the story of Sabinianus, at n. 128.
77. See above, chap. 2, notes 98–100, chap. 3, note 68, and, in this chapter, notes 29 and 75.
78. *PLRE* I s.v. Sebastianus 2; Zos. 4.22.4, blaming the emperors' supine dependence on envious eunuchs for Sebastianus' dismissal; and Eunap. frg. 47 = 44.3 Blockley (1983), whose translation I use for the final quotation. Sebastianus had been Military Count in A.D. 363-78 and went on to serve Valens as Master of Infantry and commander-in-chief against the Goths in 378. As a match to Sebastianus, one could compare the valuable Ursicinus, victim of court plots "because he alone of all men, unlike the rest, did not regularly feed the wealth of" a certain essential chamberlain (Amm. 18.4.3). And there are still other similar cases.
79. Above, chap. 1, notes 149f., 164f., and 168f., and chap. 3, notes 122–24.
80. See Hahn (1982) 185 on the elite inside (or at the top of) the curia, the *principales*, who tyrannized over the rest; and notice Petit (1955) 362: "le fonctionariat est le moteur de l'ascension sociale, le seul moyen efficace mis à la disposition des ambitieux pour gravir rapidement les échelons de la réussite" (with examples given, most of them, p. 371, whether civil or military, being great landowners and constituting "une nouvelle aristocratie, une classe montante, enrichie"). Further refs. and discussion in Thébert (1983) 104, for Africa, and above, chap. 2, notes 75–81.
81. MacMullen (1976) chap. 7.
82. Joh. Chrysos., *In Ioann. homil.* 58.5 (PG 59.321); MacMullen (1964) 51f., adding such other passages as Optat. 5.7 (p. 135 Ziwsa), "whoever today wants to cultivate his vineyard hires

a laborer for an agreed sum" (showing rural freedom of occupation), or Callinicus, *Vita S., Hypatii* praef. 8 (after A.D. 400), revealing the assumption that young men in Thrace will have free choice of their occupations, though they ought to follow their fathers'. Ceran (1970) 199 gathers much material on the freedom of choosing one's occupation in the later empire. Disappointingly, the papyri of Egypt return no clear answer to the question, Did legislation diminish social mobility at all? But perhaps the fact that there is no detectable difference post-300 compared with pre-300 is itself revealing. See Keenan (1975) 241 and 248, whose evidence, however, is virtually all post-A.D. 450.

83. Above, at chap. 3, notes 24, 33, 45, 79–81, 93–95, 109, and 117, where venality is characterized adversely by our sources; and much more could be added, e.g., Symmn., *Or.* 4.6 (A.D. 376), expressing horror at venal judges selling convictions (*humani sanguinis auctiones*).

84. Virtue is *thaumastos*, cf. Eunapius quoted at note 78, above; further, chap. 3, note 97, an honest man is a wonder; and Robert's epigraphic evidence, chap. 3, note 37; also, approving remarks like Eunapius' on Arbogast "waging endless war against venality," *pros chremata* (frg. 53, FHG 4.37).

85. Liban., *Or.* 47.4-9 and 10 (quoted).

86. I refer to General Secord, Colonel North, and Attorney General Meese. Topical allusions like this in a history book are likely to lose their force before many years have passed, but they very naturally occur to historians. See above, chap. 3, notes 2 and 12. As to the characterization of these wearers of the *cingulum*, see the editorial in the *New York Times*, 11/22/87, E 26: "The ultimate turnover of government to private enterprise [was] even called 'the Enterprise' by the merchants who ran it" — comparing above, chap. 3, notes 115f.

BIBLIOGRAPHY OF SECONDARY WORKS
CITED IN
NOTES AND APPENDICES

Abel (1909) — Abel, F.-M., "Epigraphie grecque palestinienne," *Revue biblique* 18 (1909) 89–100.

Agache (1975) — Agache, R., "La Campagne à l'époque romaine dans les grandes plaines du Nord de la France d'après les photographies aériennes," *Aufstieg und Niedergang der römischen Welt* II, 4 (Berlin 1975) 658–713.

Agache (1982) — Agache, R., "Les Grandes Villas stéréotypiques de la Gallia Belgica. Reflet des systèmes politiques, économiques et sociaux," *Caesarodunum* 17 (1982) 3–10.

Agache and Agache (1978) — Agache, R. and S., "De la recherche des paysages de l'antiquité dans le nord de la France," *Caesarodunum* 13 (1978) 149–167.

Albertini (1943) — Albertini, E., "Une Nouvelle Basilique civile à Cuicul (Djemila)," *Comptes rendus de l'Académie des inscriptions et belles lettres* 1943, 376–385.

Albertos Firmat (1975) — Albertos Firmat, M. L., *Organizaciones suprafamilias en la Hispania Antigua*, Valladolid 1975.

A. Alföldi (1934) — Alföldi, A., "Die Ausgestaltung des monarchischen Zeremoniells am römischen Kaiserhofe," *Mitteilungen des deutschen arch. Instituts, Röm. Abt.* 49 (1934) 3–118.

A. Alföldi (1935) — Alföldi, A., "Insignien und Tracht der römischen Kaiser," *Mitteilungen des deutschen arch. Instituts, Röm. Abt.* 50 (1935) 3–158.

A. Alföldi (1952) — Alföldi, A., *A Conflict of Ideas in the Late Roman Empire. The Clash between the Senate and Valentinian I*, trans. H. Mattingly, Oxford 1952.

A. Alföldi (1959) — Alföldi, A., "Cornuti: a Teutonic contingent in the service of Constantine," *Dumbarton Oaks Papers* 13 (1959) 171–179.

E. Alföldi (1969) — Alföldi, E., "Excavations and restorations at Anemurium (Eski Anamur) 1969," *Türk Arkeoloji Dergisi* 18, 2 (1969) 37–39.

Alföldi-Rosenbaum (1972) — Alföldi-Rosenbaum, M. "Matronianus, comes Isauriae: an inscription from the sea wall of Anemurium," *Phoenix* 26 (1972) 183–186.

Alföldy (1964–65) — Alföldy, G., "Die Valerii in Poetovio," *Vestnik* 15–16 (1964–65) 137–144.

Alföldy (1974) — Alföldy, G., *Noricum*, trans. A. R. Birley, London 1974.

Alföldy (1981) — Alföldy, G., "Die Stellung der Ritter in der Führungsschicht des Imperium Romanum," *Chiron* 11 (1981) 169–215.

Alföldy (1986) — Alföldy, G., *Die römische Gesellschaft. Ausgewählte Beiträge*, Stuttgart 1986.

Alt (1921) — Alt, A., *Die griechischen Inschriften der Palaestina Tertia westlich der 'Araba*, Berlin 1921.

Anderson (1978) — Anderson, P., *Passages from Antiquity to Feudalism,*[2] London 1978.

Applebaum (1977) — Applebaum, S., "Judaea as a Roman province; the countryside as a political and economic factor," *Aufstieg und Niedergang der Römischen Welt* II, 8 (Berlin 1977) 355–396.

Aragon-Launet (1974) — Aragon-Launet, P. "Montréal-du-Gers, villa gallo-romaine de Séviac, fouilles 1972–1973," *Bulletin de la Société arch. hist. littéraire et scientifique du Gers-Auch* 75 (1974) 350–356.

Arce (1980) — Arce, J., " 'Notitia Dignitatum' et l'armée romaine dans la dioicesis Hispanarum," *Chiron* 10 (1980) 593–608.

Arce (1982) — Arce, J., "Merida tardorromana (284–409 d. C.)," *Homenaje a Saenz de Buruaga* (Madrid 1982) 209–226.

Aricescu (1980) — Aricescu, A., *The Army in Roman Dobrudja,* trans. N. Hampartunian, Oxford 1980.

Arnold (1984) — Arnold, C. J., *Roman Britain to Saxon England,* Bloomington, Ind. 1984.

Avi-Yonah (1976) — Avi-Yonah, M., *The Jews of Palestine: A Political History from the Bar Kokhba War to the Arab Conquest,* New York 1976.

Bagnall (1982) — Bagnall, R. S., "The population of Theadelphia in the fourth century," *Bulletin de la Société d'arch. copte* 24 (1982) 35–57.

Baldacci (1967–68) — Baldacci, P., "Alcuni aspetti dei commerci nei territori cisalpini," *Atti, Centro studi e documentazione sull'Italia Romana* 1 (1967–68) 6–50.

Baldwin (1982) — Baldwin, B., "Literature and society in the later Roman empire," *Literary and Artistic Patronage in Ancient Rome,* ed. B. K. Gold, Austin 1982, 67–83.

Ball (1942) — Ball, J., *Egypt in the Classical Geographers,* Cairo 1942.

Balland (1980) — Balland, A., "Nouveaux documents relatifs à Opramoas de Rhodiapolis," *Actes du colloque sur la Lycie antique,* Paris 1980, 89–93.

Balland (1981) — Balland, A., *Fouilles de Xanthos VII: Inscriptions d'époque impériale du Létoon,* Paris 1981.

Balty (1973) — Balty, J.-C., "Apamée sur l'Oronte aux époques pré et protohistorique, hellénistique, romaine, byzantine et arabe," *Archéologia* 60 (1973) 46–56.

Balty (1987) — Balty, J.-C., "Apamée (1986): nouvelles données sur l'armée romaine d'Orient et les raids sassanides du milieu du IIIᵉsiècle," *Comptes rendus de l'Académie des inscriptions et belles lettres* 1987, 213–241.

Bammer (1976–77) — Bammer, A., "Ein spätantiker Torbau aus Ephesos," *Jahrbuch des oesterr. archäologischen Instituts* 51 (1976-77) Beiblatt 93–126.

Barbieri (1971) — Barbieri, G., "Nuove iscrizioni di Capua," *Miscellanea greca e romana* 3 (1971) 291–305.

Barkoczy et al. (1954–57) — Barkoczy, L., et al., *Intercisa (Dunapentele-Sztalinvaros). Geschichte der Stadt in der Römerzeit,* 2v., Budapest 1954–57.

Barns (1964) — Barns, J., "Shenute as a historical source," *Actes du Xᵉ Congrès international de papyrologie . . . 1961,* Wroclaw 1964, 151–159.

Baroja (1965) — Baroja, J. C., "Honour and shame: a historical account of several conflicts," *Honour and Shame: The Values of Mediterranean Society,* ed. J. G. Peristiany, London 1965, 79–137.

Barrett (1982) — Barrett, A. A., "The Romano-British villa at Barnsley Park, Gloucestershire," *Classical Views* 26 (1982) 113–125.

Bartholomew (1984) — Bartholomew, P., "Fourth-century Saxons," *Britannia* 15 (1984) 169–185.

Batiffol (1919) — Batiffol, P., *Etudes de liturgie et d'archéologie chrétienne*, Paris 1919.

Bauman (1980) — Bauman, R. A., "The 'leges iudiciorum publicorum' and their interpretation in the Republic, Principate and later empire," *Aufstieg und Niedergang der römischen Welt* II, 13 (Berlin 1980) 103–233.

Bavant (1984) — Bavant, B., "La Ville dans le nord de l'Illyricum (Pannonie, Mésie I, Dacie et Dardane)," *Villes et peuplement dans l'Illyricum protobyzantin. Actes du colloque ... 1982*, Rome 1984, 245–287.

Bayard and Massy (1982) — Bayard, D., and J.-L. Massy, "Amiens romain, étude sur le développement urbain du Iᵉʳ siècle avant J.-C. au Vᵉ siècle apres J.-C.," *Revue du Nord* 64 (1982) 5–26.

Baynes (1943) — Baynes, N. H., "The decline of the Roman power in Europe. Some modern explanations," *Journal of Roman Studies* 33 (1943) 29–35.

Bean (1962) — Bean, G. E., "Report on a journey in Lycia 1960," *Anzeiger der Oesterreichischer Akademie der Wissenschaften* 99 (1962) 4–9.

Bean and Mitford (1970) — Bean, G. E., and T. B. Mitford, *Journeys in Rough Cilicia 1964–1968* (Denkschriften der Oesterreichischen Akademie der Wissenschaften 101), Vienna 1970.

Bell (1924) — Bell, H. I., *Jews and Christians in Egypt. The Jewish Troubles in Alexandria and the Athanasian Controversy*, London 1924.

Bell et al. (1962) — Bell, H. I., et al., *The Abinnaeus Archive. Papers of a Roman Army Officer in the Reign of Constantius II*, Oxford 1962.

Benabou (1976) — Benabou, M., *La Résistance africaine à la romanisation*, Paris 1976.

Benseddik (1979) — Benseddik, N., *Les Troupes auxiliaires dans l'armée romaine en Maurétanie Césarienne sous le Haut-Empire*, Algiers 1979.

Bérard (1892) — Bérard, V., "Inscriptions d'Asie Mineure," *Bulletin de correspondance hellénique* 16 (1892) 417–446.

Berchem (1952) — Berchem, D. van, *L'Armée romaine de Dioclétien à la réforme constantinienne*, Paris 1952.

Berenson (1954) — Berenson, B., *The Arch of Constantine; or, The Decline of Form*, New York 1954.

Bernardi (1965) — Bernardi, A., "The economic problems of the Roman empire at the time of its decline," *Studia et documenta historiae et iuris* 31 (1965) 110–170.

Bertrandy (1973–74) — Bertrandy, F., "Une Grande Famille de la confédération cirtéenne: les Antistii de Thibilis," *Karthago* 17 (1973–74) 195–202.

Beschaouch (1966) — Beschaouch, A., "La Mosaique de chasse découverte à Smirat en Tunisie," *Comptes rendus de l'Académie des inscriptions et belles lettres* 1966, 134–157.

Beschaouch (1975) — Beschaouch, A., "A propos de récentes découvertes épigraphiques dans le pays de Carthage," *Comptes rendus de l'Académie des inscriptions et belles lettres* 1975, 101–118.

A. R. Birley (1967) — "The Roman governors of Britain," *Epigraphische Studien* 4 (1967) 63–102.

A. R. Birley (1981) — Birley, A. R., *The Fasti of Roman Britain*, Oxford 1981.

A. R. Birley (1982) — Birley, A. R., "Notes on senators' imperial service," *Tituli* 4 (1982) 239–249.

E. Birley (1963–64) — Birley, E., "Promotions and transfers in the Roman army, II: The centurionate," *Carnuntum Jahrbuch* 1963–64, 21–33.

E. Birley (1982/83) — Birley, E., "Veterans of the Roman army in Britain and elsewhere," *Ancient Society* 13–14 (1982–83) 265–276.

Biro (1974) — Biro, M., "Roman villas," *Acta archaeologica academiae scientiarum Hungaricae* 26 (1974) 23–57.

Bivona (1970) — Bivona, L., *Iscrizioni latine lapidarie del Museo di Palermo*, Palermo 1970.

Blanchet (1907) — Blanchet, A., *Les Enceintes romaines de la Gaule*, Paris 1907.

Blazquez (1964) — Blazquez, J. M., *Estructura economica y social de Hispania durante la anarquia militar y el bajo imperio*, Madrid 1964.

Blazquez (1974-75) — Blazquez, J. M., *Ciclos y temas de la Historia España: la Romanizacion*, 2 vols., Madrid 1974–75.

Blazquez (1975) — Blazquez, J. M., *Historia social y economica de la España Romana, segunda parte: siglos III-V*, Madrid 1975.

Blazquez (1983) — Blazquez, J. M., "Die Niederlassungen der Barbaren im Okzident und ihre sozial-ökonomischen Nebenwirkungen," *Actes du VII^eCongrès de la F. I. E. C.*, Budapest 1983, 2.73–82.

Blazquez Martinez (1982) — Blazquez Martinez, J. M.,"La economia de la Hispania Romana," *España Roman (218 a. de J. C. — 414 de J. C.). La conquista y la exploitacion economica*, Madrid 1982, 293–607.

Blockley (1981–83) — Blockley, R. C., *The Fragmentary Classicizing Historians of the Later Roman*, 2 vols., Liverpool 1981–83.

Bodor (1973) — Bodor, A., "Emperor Aurelian and the abandonment of Dacia," *Dacoromania* 1 (1973) 29–40.

Böhme (1978) — Böhme, H.-W., "Tombes germaniques des IVe et Ve siècles en Gaule du nord; chronologie, distribution et interprétation," *Problèmes de chronologie relative et absolue concernant les cimetières mérovingiens d'entre Loire et Rhin. Actes du colloque . . . 1973*, ed. M. Fleury and P. Périn, Paris 1978, 21–39.

Böttger (1975) — Böttger, B., "Die Landwirtschaft," *Die Römer an Rhein und Donau. Zur politischen, wirtschaftlichen und sozialen Entwicklung in den römischen Provinzen an Rhein, Mosel und oberer Donau im 3. und 4. Jahrhundert*, ed. R. Günther and H. Köpstein, Vienna 1975, 138–88.

Bogaers (1967) — Bogaers, J. E., "Einige opmerkingen over het Nederlandse gedeelte van de Limes van Germania Inferior (Germania Secunda)," *Berichten, Rijksdienst voor het Oudheidkundig Bodemonderzoek* 17 (1967) 99–114.

Bogaers (1968) — Bogaers, J. E., "Castra Herculis," *Berichten, Rijksdienst voor het Oudheidkundig Bodemondezoek* 18 (1968) 151–162.

Boissevain (1966) — Boissevain, J., "Patronage in Sicily," *Man* 1 (1966) 18–33.

Bollini (1976) — Bollini, M., "Storia politica e sociale nell'età tardoantica," *Storia della Emilia Romagna* 1 (1976) 299–306.

Boon (1972) — Boon, G. C., *Isca. The Roman Legionary Fortress at Caerleon, Mon.*, Cardiff 1972.

Borius (1965) — Borius, R., *Constance de Lyon, Vie de Saint Germain*, Paris 1965.

Bowersock (1983) — Bowersock, G. W., *Roman Arabia*, Cambridge 1983.

Bowman (1971) — Bowman, A. K., *The Town Councils of Roman Egypt*, Toronto 1971.

Bowman (1985) — Bowman, A. K., "Landholding in the Hermopolite nome in the fourth century A.D.," *Journal of Roman Studies* 75 (1985) 137–163.

Bowman and Thomas (1983) — Bowman, A. K., and J. D. Thomas, *Vindolanda: The Writing-Tablets*, London 1983.

Braude (1959) — Braude, W. G., trans., *The Midrash on Psalms [Midrash Tehillim]*, 2 vols., New Haven 1959.

Bregman (1982) — Bregman, J., *Synesius of Cyrene, Philosopher-bishop*, Berkeley 1982.

Broughton (1933) —Broughton, T. R. S., "The Roman army," *The Beginnings of Christianity*,

I; *The Acts of the Apostles*, Part V, ed. F. J. Foakes Jackson and K. Lake, London 1933, 427–445.

Broughton (1938) — Broughton, T. R. S., "Roman Asia," *An Economic Survey of Ancient Rome*, ed. T. Frank, vol. 4 , Baltimore 1938, 4.499–918.

Brown (1971) — Brown, P., "The rise and function of the holy man in Late Antiquity," *Journal of Roman Studies* 61 (1971) 80–101.

Brunt (1961) — Brunt, P. A., "Charges of provincial maladministration under the early Principate," *Historia* 10 (1961) 189–228.

Brunt (1974) — Brunt, P. A., "Addendum III," in A. H. M. Jones, *The Roman Economy*, Oxford 1974, 183–185.

Brunt (1975) — Brunt, P. A., "The administrators of Egypt," *Journal of Roman Studies* 65 (1975) 124–147.

Buchi (1973) — Buchi, E., "Banchi di anfore romane a Verona. Note sui commerci cisalpini," *Il territorio veronese in età romana. Convegno ... 1971*, Verona 1973, 531–650.

Buck (1985) — Buck, D. J., "Frontier processes in Roman Tripolitania," *Town and Country in Roman Tripolitania. Papers in Honour of Olwen Hackett*, ed. D. J. Buck and D. J. Mattingly, Oxford 1985, 179–190.

Budischovsky (1977) — Budischovsky, M. C., "Les Cultes orientaux à Aquileia et leur diffusion en Istrie et en Vénétie," *Antichità Altoadriatiche* 12 (Udine 1977) 99–122.

Bury (1923) — Bury, J. B., *History of the Later Roman Empire from the Death of Theodosius I to the Death of Justinian*, 2 vols., London 1923.

Butler (1959) — Butler, R. M., "Late Roman town walls in Gaul," *Archaeological Journal* 116 (1959) 250.

Calder and Bean (1958) — Calder, W. M., and G. E. Bean, *A Classical Map of Asia Minor*, London 1958.

Callu (1978) — Callu, J.-P., "Le 'centenarium' et l'enrichissement monétaire au Bas-Empire," *Ktema* 3 (1978) 301–316.

Callu (1979) — Callu, J.-P., "Les Monnaies romaines," *Fouilles d'Apamée de Syrie*, VIII.1: *Monnaies antiques [1966–71]* 2, Brussels 1979, 5–39.

Callu (1980) — Callu, J.-P., "The distribution and the role of the bronze coinage from A.D. 348 to 392," *Imperial Revenue, Expenditure and Monetary Policy in the Fourth Century A.D. The Fifth Oxford Symposium on Coinage*, ed. C. E. King, Oxford 1980, 95–124.

Callu (1983) — Callu, J.-P., "La Monnaie de l'Empire romain: une numismatique quantitative," *Bulletin de l'Assoc. Guillaume Budé* (1983) 55–65.

Callu (1983a) — Callu, J.-P., "Structure des dépôts d'or au IVᵉ siècle (312–392)," *Crise et redressement dans les provinces européennes de l'Empire (milieu du IIIe - milieu du IVe siècle ap. J.-C)*. Actes du Colloque ... 1981, ed. E. Frézouls, Strasbourg 1983, 157–174.

Callu (1984) — Callu, J.-P., "*Manus inermis*: le phénomène bureaucratique et l'Histoire Auguste," *Quaderni ticinesi di numismatica e antichità classiche* 13 (1984) 229–248.

Cameron (1970) — Cameron, A., *Claudian*, Oxford 1970.

Camodeca (1977) — Camodeca, G., "L'ordinamento in *regiones* e i *vici* di Puteoli," *Puteoli* 1 (1977) 62–98.

Camodeca (1980–81) — Camodeca, G., "Ricerche su Puteoli tardoromana (fine III–IV secolo)," *Puteoli* 4–5 (1980-81) 59–128.

Campbell (1964) — Campbell, J. K., *Honour, Family, and Patronage. A Study of Institutions and Moral Values in a Greek Mountain Community*, Oxford 1964.

Cantineau (1936) — Cantineau, J., "Tadmoreia," *Syria* 17 (1936) 267–282.

Carandini (1970) — Carandini, A., "Produzione agricola e produzione ceramica nell'Africa di età imperiale," *Studi miscellanei* 15 (1970) 95–120.

Carandini and Settis (1979) — Carandini, A., and A. Settis, *Schiavi e padroni nell'Etruria romana. La villa di Settefinestre dello scavo alla mostra*, Bari 1979.

Carandini and Tatton-Brown (1980) — Carandini, A., and T. Tatton-Brown, "Excavations at the Roman villa of 'Sette Finestre' in Etruria, 1975–9. First Interim Report," *Roman Villas in Italy. Recent Excavations and Research*, ed. K. Painter, London 1980, 9–43.

Carandini et al. (1973) — Carandini, A., et al., *Ostia. Le Terme del Nuotatore* 3, Rome 1973.

Carcopino (1922) — Carcopino, J., "Fermier générale ou sociétés publicaines?" *Revue des études anciennes* 24 (1922) 13–36.

Carcopino (1951) — Carcopino, J., *Cicero: The Secrets of His Correspondence*, trans. E. O. Lorimer, 2 vols., New Haven 1951.

Casson (1952) — Casson, L., "The administration of Byzantine and early Arab Palestine," *Aegyptus* 32 (1952) 54–60.

Catling (1986) — Catling, H. W., "Archaeology in Greece, 1985–86," *Archaeological Reports* 32 (1986) 1–101.

Cavagnola (1974–75) — Cavagnola, B., "Epigrafe inedite di Milano," *Atti, Centro studi e documentazione sull'Italia romana* 6 (1974–75) 73–90.

Ceran (1970) — Ceran, W., "Stagnation or fluctuation in early Byzantine society?" *Byzantinoslavica* 31 (1970) 192–203.

Chadwick (1965) — Chadwick, N. K., "The colonization of Brittany from Celtic Britain," *Proceedings of the British Academy* 51 (1965) 235–299.

Chalon (1964) — Chalon, G., *L'Edit de Tiberius Julius Alexander. Etude historique et exégétique*, Olten 1964.

Champlin (1980) — Champlin, E., *Fronto and Antonine Rome*, Cambridge 1980.

Champlin (1980a) — Champlin, E., "The Volceii land-register," *American Journal of Ancient History* 5 (1980) 13–18.

Charanis (1967) — Charanis, P., "Observations on the demography of the Byzantine empire," *Proceedings of the XIIIth International Congress of Byzantine Studies . . . 1966*, Oxford 1967, 445-465.

Chastagnol (1976) — Chastagnol, A., *La Fin du monde antique. De Stilicon à Justinien (V siècle et début du VI)*, Paris 1976.

Chastagnol (1978) — Chastagnol, A., *L'Album municipale de Timgad*, Bonn 1978.

Chastagnol (1979) — Chastagnol, A., "L'Empereur Julien et les avocats de Numidie," *Antiquités africaines* 4 (1979) 225–235.

Chastagnol (1980) — Chastagnol, A., "Remarques sur les salaires et rémunérations au IVe siècle," *Les Dévaluations à Rome 2 . . . 1978*, Paris 1980, 215–233.

Chastagnol (1981) — Chastagnol, A., "Les *realia* d'une cité d'après l'inscription constantinienne d'Orkistos," *Ktema* 6 (1981) 373–379.

Chevallier (1975) — Chevallier, R., ed., *Tabula Imperii Romana. Lutetia-Atuatuca-Ulpia Noviomagus*, Paris 1975.

Chichikova (1983) — Chichikova, M., "Fouilles du camp romain et de la ville paléobyzantine de Novae (Mésie inférieur)," *Ancient Bulgaria. Papers Presented to the International Symposium . . . 1981*, ed. A. G. Poulter, 2 vols., Nottingham 1983, 2.11–18.

Chrysos (1973) — Chrysos, E. K., "Gothia Romana. Zur Rechtslage des Föderatenlandes der Westgoten im 4. Jh." *Dacoromania* 1 (1973) 52–64.

Ciotti (1948) — Ciotti, U., "Iscrizione di Leptis Magna," *Bollettino, Istituto nazionale di arch. e storia dell'arte* 11 (1948) 114–120.

Clauss (1980) — Clauss, M., *Der Magister Officiorum in der Spätantike (4.-6. Jahr). Das Amt und sein Einfluss auf die kaiserliche Politik*, Munich 1980.

Clemente (1968) — Clemente, G., *La 'Notitia Dignitatum,'* Cagliari 1968.

Clemente (1972) — Clemente, G., "Il patronato nei collegia dell'impero romano," *Studi classici e orientali* 21 (1972) 142–229.

Colin (1965) — Colin, J., "Les Exigences de la populace paienne dans la littérature grecque chrétienne du IIe siècle," *Revue des études grecques* 77 (1965) 330–335.

Collot (1965) — Collot, C., "La Pratique et l'institution du *suffragium* au Bas-Empire," *Revue historique des droits* 43 (1965) 185–221.

Comsa (1972) — Comsa, M., "Elemente 'barbare' in zona limes ului Dunarii inferiorare in secolele al III-lea si al IV-lea," *Pontica* 5 (1972) 223–234.

Conrat (1907) — Conrat, M., "Zur Kultur des römischen Rechts in Westen des römischen Reichs im vierten und fünften Jahrhundert nach Christi," *Mélanges Fitting*, Montpellier 1907, 1.289–320.

Constans (1921) — Constans, L. A. *Arles antique*, Paris 1921.

Constans (1928) — Constans, L. A., *Arles*, Paris 1928.

Corbier (1982) — Corbier, M., "Les Familles clarissimes d'Afrique proconsulaire (1er–IIIe siècle)," *Tituli* 5 (1982) 685–754.

Corbier (1986) — Corbier, M., "Svalutazioni, inflazione e circolazione monetaria nel III secolo," *Società romana e impero tardoantico*, ed. A. Giardina, I: *Istituzioni, ceti, econonie*, Rome 1986, 489–533 and 772–779.

Cornell and Matthews (1982) — Cornell, T., and J. Matthews, *Atlas of the Roman World*, London 1982.

Cotton (1981) — Cotton, H., *Documentary Letters of Recommendation in Latin from the Roman Empire*, Königstein 1981.

Courtois (1951) — Courtois, C., *Timgad, antique Thamugadi*, Algiers 1951.

Courtois (1955) — Courtois, C., *Les Vandales et l'Afrique*, Paris 1955.

Cousin (1904) — Cousin, G., "Inscriptions du sanctuaire de Zeus Panamaros," *Bulletin de correspondance hellénique* 28 (1904) 20–53, 238–262, and 345–352.

Cracco Ruggini (1961) — Cracco Ruggini, L., *Economia e società nell'Italia annonaria. Rapporti fra agricoltura e commercio dal IV al VI secolo d.C.*, Milan 1961.

Cracco Ruggini (1963) — Cracco Ruggini, L., "Uomini senza terra e terra senza uomini nell'Italia antica," *Quaderni di sociologia rurale* 3 (1963) 20–42.

Cracco Ruggini (1964) — Cracco Ruggini, L., "Vicende rurali dell'Italia antica dell'età tetrarchica ai Longobardi," *Rivista storica italiana* 76 (1964) 261–286.

Cracco Ruggini (1965) — Cracco Ruggini, L., "Strutture socioeconomiche della Spagna tardoromana," *Athenaeum* 43 (1965) 432–440.

Cracco Ruggini (1978 — Cracco Ruggini, L., "Les Structures de la société et l'économie lyonnaises par rapport à la politique locale et impériale," *Les Martyres de Lyon (177)* . . . 1977, Paris 1978, 65–92.

Cracco Ruggini (1980) — Cracco Ruggini, L., "Progresso tecnico e manodopera in età imperiale romana," *Tecnologia, economia e società nel mondo romano. Atti del Convegno* . . . 1979, Como 1980, 45–66.

Cracco Ruggini (1982–83) — Cracco Ruggini, L., "Sicilia, III/IV secolo: il volto della non-città," *Kokalos* 28/29 (1982–83) 477–515.

Cracco Ruggini (1984) — Cracco Ruggini, L., "Milano nella circolazione monetaria del tardo impero: esigenze politiche e risposte socioeconomiche," *La zecca di Milano. Atti del Convegno* . . . 1983, Milan 1984, 13–58.

Cracco Ruggini (1987) — Cracco Ruggini, L., "Storia totale di una piccola città: Vicenza romana," *Storia di Vicenza. Il territorio. La preistoria. L'età romana*, Vicenza 1987, 205–310.

Crawford (1970) — Crawford, M., "Money and exchange in the Roman world," *Journal of Roman Studies* 60 (1970) 40–48.

Crawford (1974) — Crawford, M. H., *Roman Republican Coinage*, 2 vols., Cambridge 1974.

Croke (1981) — Croke, B., "Thessalonika's early Byzantine palaces," *Byzantion* 51 (1981) 475–483.

Crook (1967) — Crook, J. A., *Law and Life of Rome*, London 1967.

Cumont (1923) — Cumont, F., "Le Temple au gradins découvert à Salihiyeh et ses inscriptions," *Syria* 4 (1923) 203–223.

Dagron (1974) — Dagron, G., *Naissance d'une capitale. Constantinople et ses institutions de 330 à 451*, Paris 1974.

Daniels (1983) — Daniels, C., "Town defenses in Roman Africa: a tentative historical survey," *Roman Urban Defences in the West*, ed. J. Maloney and B. Hobley, London 1983, 4–19.

D'Arms (1981) — D'Arms, J. H., *Commerce and Social Standing in Ancient Rome*, Cambridge 1981.

Dauphin (1980) — Dauphin, C., "Mosaic pavements as an index of prosperity," *Levant* 12 (1980) 112–134.

Davis, Cherry, and Mantzourani — Davis, J. L., J. F. Cherry, and E. Mantzourani, "An archeological survey of the Greek island of Keos," *National Geographic Society Research Reports* 21 (1980–83) 109–116.

Day (1942) — Day, J., *An Economic History of Athens under Roman Domination*, New York 1942.

Decker (1913) — Decker, J. de, *Juvenalis Declamans. Etude sur la rhétorique déclamatoire dans les satires de Juvenal*, Gand 1913.

Deckers (1973) — Deckers, J. G., "Die Wandinschrift des tetrarchischen Lagerheiligtums im Ammon-Tempel von Luxor," *Römische Quartalschrift für christlichen Altertumskunde* 68 (1973) 1–34.

Degrassi (1961–62) — Degrassi, A., "Il sepolcro dei Salvii e le sue iscrizioni," *Rendiconti, Pontificia Accademia di arch.*[3] 34 (1961–62) 59–77.

Deininger (1965) — Deininger, J., *Die Provinziallandtage der römischen Kaiserzeit von Augustus bus zum Ende des 3. Jh. n. Chr.*, Munich 1965.

Delage (1952) — Delage., F., "Fouilles de la 'Villa d'Antone' à Pierrebuffière (Haute-Vienne)," *Gallia* 10 (1952) 1–30.

Demandt (1965) — Demandt, A., *Zeitkritik und Geschichtsbild im Werke Ammians*, Bonn 1965.

Demandt (1968) — Demandt, A., "Die tripolitanischen Wirren unter Valentinian I," *Byzantion* 38 (1968) 333–363.

Demandt (1980) — Demandt, A., "Der spätrömische Militäradel," *Chiron* 10 (1980) 609–636.

Demandt (1984) — Demandt, A., *Der Fall Roms. Die Auflösung des römischen Reiches im Urteil der Nachwelt*, Munich 1984.

Demougeot (1953) — Demougeot, E., "Notes sur l'évacuation des troupes romaines en Alsace au début du Ve siècle," *Revue d'Alsace* 92 (1953) 7–28.

Demougeot (1956) — Demougeot, E., "Une Lettre de l'empereur Honorius sur l'*hospitium* des soldats," *Revue historique de droit français et étranger*[4] 34 (1956) 25–49.

Demougeot (1969–79) — Demougeot, E., *La Formation de l'Europe et les invasions barbares*, 2 vols., Paris 1969–79.

Demougeot (1974) — Demougeot, E., "Modalités d'établissement des fédérés barbares de

Gratien et de Théodose," *Mélanges d'histoire ancienne offerts à W. Seston*, Paris 1974, 143–160.

Demougeot (1975) — Demougeot, E., "La Notitia Dignitatum et l'histoire de l'Empire d'Occident au début du Ve siècle," *Latomus* 34 (1975) 1079–1134.

Derrett (1981) — Derrett, J. D. M., "Simon Mago," *Conoscenza religiosa* 4 (1981) 397–414.

Devijver (1976–80) — Devijver, H., *Prosopographia militiarum equestrium quae fuerunt ab Augusto ad Gallienum*, 3 vols., Leiden 1976–80.

Dietz (1980) — Dietz, K., *Senatus contra principem. Untersuchungen zur senatorischen Opposition gegen Kaiser Maximinus Thrax*, Munich 1980.

Dill (1899) — Dill, S., *Roman Society in the Last Century of the Western Empire,*² London 1899.

Dionisotti (1982) — Dionisotti, A. C., "From Ausonius' schooldays? A schoolbook and its relatives," *Journal of Roman Studies* 72 (1982) 83–125.

Di Vita (1967) — Di Vita, A., "Il 'limes' romano di Tripolitania nella sua concretezza archeologica e nella sua realtà storica," *Libya antiqua* 1 (1967) 65–98.

DiVita-Evrard (1985) — DiVita-Evrard, G., "Note sur quelques timbres d'amphores de Tripolitaine," *Bulletin du Comité des travaux historiques* 19B (1985) 147–158.

Doblehofer (1955) — Doblehofer, E., *Byzantinische Diplomaten und östliche Barbaren*, Graz-Cologne 1955.

Dörner (1952) — Dörner, F. K., *Bericht über eine Reise in Bithynien (1948)*, Vienna 1952.

Donaldson (1985) — Donaldson, G. H., "The *praesides provinciae Tripolitaniae*: civil administrators and military commanders," *Town and Country in Roman Tripolitania. Papers in Honour of Olwen Hackett*, ed. D. J. Buck and D. J. Mattingly, Oxford 1985, 165–177.

Dorutiu-Boila (1972) — Dorutiu-Boila, E., "Castra Legionis V Macedonicae und Municipium Troesmense," *Dacia* 16 (1972) 133–144.

Dremsizova-Nelcinova (1969) — Dremsizova-Nelcinova, C., "La Villa romaine en Belgarie," *Actes du premier Congrès international des études balkaniques et Sud-Est européennes . . . 1966*, Sofia 1969, 2.503–512.

M. Drew-Bear (1984) — Drew-Bear, M., "Les Conseillers municipaux des métropoles au IIIe siècle après J.-C.," *Chronique d'Egypte* 59 (1984) 315–332.

T. Drew-Bear (1972) — "Deux décrets hellénistiques d'Asie Mineure," *Bulletin de correspondance hellénique* 96 (1972) 435–471.

T. Drew-Bear (1978) — Drew-Bear, T., *Nouvelles inscriptions de Phrygie*, Zutphen 1978.

T. Drew-Bear (1984) — Drew-Bear, T., "Three inscriptions from Asia Minor," *Studies Presented to Sterling Dow*, Durham 1984, 61–69.

Drinkwater (1979) — Drinkwater, J. F., "Gallic personal wealth," *Chiron* 9 (1979) 237–242.

Drinkwater (1983) — Drinkwater, J., *Roman Gaul: The Three Provinces*, Ithaca, N.Y. 1983.

Duchesne (1912–24) — Duchesne, L., *Early History of the Christian Church*, 3 vols., New York 1912–24.

Duncan-Jones (1965) — Duncan-Jones, R., "An epigraphic survey of costs in Roman Italy," *Papers of the British School at Rome* 33 (1965) 189–306.

Duncan-Jones (1980) — Duncan-Jones, R., "Demographic change and economic progress under the Roman empire," *Tecnologia economia e società nel mondo romano. Atti del Convegno . . . 1979*, Como 1980, 67-80.

Duthoy (1979) — Duthoy, R., "Curatores rei publicae en Occident durant le Principat. Recherches préliminaires sur l'apport des sources épigraphiques," *Ancient Society* 10 (1979) 171–238.

Duval (1964) — Duval, N., "Observations sur l'urbanisme tardif de Sufetula (Tunisie)," *Cahiers de Tunisie* 12 (1964) 87–103.

Dyson (1978) — Dyson, S. L., "Settlement patterns in the Ager Cosanus: The Wesleyan University Survey, 1974-76," *Journal of Field Archaeology* 5 (1978) 251–268.

Eadie (1967) — Eadie, J. W., *The Breviarium of Festus. A Critical Edition with Historical Commentary*, London 1967.

Eadie (1982) — Eadie, J. W., "City and countryside in late Roman Pannonia," *City, Town and Countryside in the Early Byzantine Era*, ed. R. Hohlfelder, New York 1982, 25–42.

Eck (1980) — Eck, W., "Die Präsenz senatorischer Familien in den Städten des Imperium Romanum bis zum späten 3. Jahrhundert," *Studien zur antiken Sozialgeschichte. Festschrift Friedrich Vittinghoff*, ed. W. Eck et al., Cologne-Vienna 1980, 283–322.

Eck (1982) — Eck, W., "Einfluss korrupter Praktiken auf das senatorisch = ritterliche Beförderungswesen in der hohen Kaiserzeit," *Korruption im Altertum. Konstanzer Symposium … 1979*, ed. W. Schuller, Munich 1982, 135–151.

Engels (1972) — Engels, H. J., "Frührömische Waffengräber aus dem Pfälzischen Rheintal," *Arch. Korrespondenzblatt* (Mainz) 2, 2 (1972) 183–189.

Erim (1975) — Erim, K. T., "Aphrodisias in Caria. The 1973 campaign," *Türk Arkeoloji Dergisi* 22, 2 (1975) 73–92.

Espinosa (1984) — Espinosa, U., *Calagurris Iulia*, Logroño 1984.

Euzennat (1967) — Euzennat, M., "Le Limes de Volubilis," *Studien zu den Militärgrenzen Roms. Vorträge des 6. internationalen Limeskongresses in Suddeutschland*, Cologne 1967, 194–199.

Euzennat (1977) — Euzennat, M., "Les recherches sur la frontière romaine d'Afrique (1974–1976)," *Limes. Akten des XI Internationalen Limeskongresses … 1976*, Budapest 1977, 533–544.

Fabia (1918) — Fabia, P., *La Garnison romaine de Lyon*, Lyon 1918.

Faider-Feytmans (1951) — Faider-Feytmans, G., "Sépultures du IVᵉ siècle à Tournai," *Latomus* 10 (1951) 29–52.

Faider-Feytmans and Hubaux (1950) — Faider-Feytmans, G., and J. Hubaux, "Moulages du IVᵉ siécle à décors virgiliens retrouvés à Trèves," Παγκαρπεια. *Mélanges Henri Grégoire* 2, Brussels 1950, 253–260.

Fant (1981) — Fant, J. C., "The choleric Roman official of Philostratus' Vitae sophistarum p. 512, L. Verginius Rufus," *Historia* 30 (1981) 240–243.

Farina Busto (1973–74) — Farina Busto, F., "Algunos aspectos de la circulacion monetaria en Gallicia durante el siglo IV de J. C.," *Numisma* 23–24 (1973–74) 105–128.

Fellmann (1955) — Fellmann, R., "Neue Forschungen zur Schweiz in spätrömischen Zeit," *Historia* 4 (1955) 209–219.

Fentress (1979) — Fentress, E. W. B., *Numidia and the Roman Army*, Oxford 1979.

Février (1964) — Février, P.-A., "Notes sur le développement urbain en Afrique du Nord: les exemples comparés de Djémila et de Sétif," *Cahiers archéologiques* 14 (1964) 1–47.

Février (1964a) — Février, P.-A., *Le Développement urbain en Provence de l'époque romaine à la fin du XIVᵉ siècle*, Paris 1964.

Février (1970) — Février, P.-A., "Conditions économiques et sociales de la création artistique en Afrique à la fin de l'Antiquité," *Corsi di cultura sull'arte ravennate e bizantina* 17 (1970) 161–189.

Février (1980) — Février, P.-A., et al., *La Ville antique*, Paris 1980.

Février (1982) — Février, P.- A., "Urbanisation et urbanisme de l'Afrique romaine," *Aufstieg und Niedergang der römischen Welt* II, 19 (Berlin 1982) 321–396.

Fiches (1982) — Fiches, J.-L., "Les Transformations de l'habitat autour de Nîmes, au Haut Empire," *Villes et campagnes dans l'empire romain. Actes du Colloque . . . 1980*, Paris 1982, 111–117.

Fikhman (1975) — Fikhman, I. F., "Quelques données sur la genèse de la grande propriété foncière à Oxyrhynchus," *Le Monde grec: pensée, littérature, histoire, documents. Hommages à Claire Préaux*, ed. J. Bingen et al., Brussels 1975, 784–790.

Finley (1980) — Finley, M. I., *Ancient Slavery and Modern Ideology*, London 1980.

Fitz (1976) — Fitz, J., *Gorsium-Herculia*, Székesfehérvár 1976.

Fitzgerald (1930) — Fitzgerald, A., *The Essays and Hymns of Synesius of Cyrene*, 2 vols., London 1930.

Fontaine (1972) — Fontaine, J., "Valeurs antiques et valeurs chrétiennes dans la spiritualité des grands propriétaires terriens à la fin du IVᵉ siècle occidentale," *Epektasis. Mélanges patristiques . . . J. Danielou*, Paris 1972, 571–595.

Forlin Patrucco (1973) — Forlin Patrucco, M., "Aspetti del fiscalismo tardo-imperiale in Cappadocia: la testimonianza di Basilio di Cesarea," *Athenaeum* 51 (1973) 294–309.

Forni (1953) — Forni, G., *Il reclutamento delle legioni da Augusto a Diocleziano*, Milan-Rome 1953.

Forni (1974) — Forni, G., "Estrazione etnica e sociale dei soldati delle legioni nei primi tre secoli dell'impero," *Aufstieg und Niedergang der römischen Welt* II, 1 (Berlin 1974) 339–391.

Foss (1975) — Foss, C., "The fall of Sardis in 616 and the value of evidence," *Jahrbuch der oesterreichischen Byzantinistik* 24 (1975) 11–22.

Foss (1976) — Foss, C., *Byzantine and Turkish Sardis*, Cambridge 1976.

Foss (1977) — Foss, C., "Archaeology and the 'Twenty cities' of Byzantine Asia," *American Journal of Archaeology* 81 (1977) 469–486.

Foss (1979) — Foss, C., *Ephesus after Antiquity: A Late Antique, Byzantine and Turkish City*, Cambridge 1979.

Foss and Magdalino (1977) — Foss, C., and P. Magdalino, *The Making of the Past: Rome and Byzantium*, Oxford 1977.

Foucher (1964) — Foucher, L., *Hadrumetum*, Paris 1964.

Franchi de' Cavalieri (1902–53) — Franchi de' Cavalieri, P., *Note ageografiche*, 9 vols., Rome 1902–53.

R. L. Frank (1969) — Frank, R. L., *Scholae Palatinae. The Palace Guards of the Later Roman Empire*, Rome 1969.

T. Frank (1933–40) — Frank, T., ed., *An Economic Survey of Ancient Rome*, 6 vols., Baltimore 1933–40.

Franke (1968) — *Kleinasien zur Römerzeit. Griechisches Leben im Spiegel der Münzen*, Munich 1968.

Franklin (1980) — Franklin, J. L., *Pompeii: The Electoral Programmata, Campaigns and Politics, A. D. 71–79*, Rome 1980.

Freis (1967) — Freis, H., *Die cohortes urbanae*, Graz-Cologne 1967.

Frend (1952) — Frend, W. H. C., *The Donatist Church. A Movement of Protest in Roman North Africa*, Oxford 1952.

Frend (1984) — Frend, W. H. C., *The Rise of Christianity*, Philadelphia 1984.

Frere (1964) — Frere, S. S., "Verulamium, three Roman cities," *Antiquity* 38 (1964) 103–112.

Frere (1967) — Frere, S. S., *Britannia, a History of Roman Britain*, Cambridge 1967.

Friedlaender (1921-23) — Friedlaender, L., *Darstellungen aus der Sittengeschichte Roms in der Zeit von Augustus bis zum Ausgang der Antonine*,¹⁰ 4 vols., Leipzig 1921–23.

Frier (1981) — Frier, B. W., "Roman coinage and army pay: techniques for evaluating statistics," *Quaderni ticinesi di numismatica e antichità classiche* 10 (1981) 285–295.

Fülep (1985) — Fülep, F., *Sopianae: The History of Pecs during the Roman Era, and the Problem of the Continuity of the Late Roman Population*, Budapest 1985.

Gagnière and Granier (1963) — Gagnière, S., and J. Granier, "L'Occupation des grottes du IIIᵉ au Vᵉ siècle et les invasions germaniques dans la basse vallée du Rhone," *Provence historique* 13 (1963) 225–239.

Galliou (1980) — Galliou, P., "Le Défense de l'Armorique au Bas-Empire. Essai de synthèse," *Mémoires de la Société d'histoire et d'arch. de Bretagne* 57 (1980) 235–285.

Galliou (1982) — Galliou, P., "Les Villas romaines d'Armorique," *Caesarodunum* 17 (1982) 95–113.

Galliou (1985) — Galliou, P., "Commerce et société dans l'Armorique du Bas-Empire," *Actes du 107ᵉ Congrès national des sociétés savantes . . . 1982, Section d'arch. et d'histoire de l'art*, Paris 1985, 105–119.

Galliou, Fulford, and Clément (1980) — Galliou, P., M. Fulford, and M. Clément, "La Diffusion de la céramique à l'éponge dans le nord-ouest de l'empire romain," *Gallia* 38 (1980) 265–278.

Gansser-Burckhardt (1942) — Gansser-Burckhardt, A., *Das Leder und seine Verarbeitung im römischen Legionslager Vindonissa*, Basel 1942.

Garbsch (1967) — Garbsch, J., "Die Burgi von Meckatz und Untersaal und die valentinian-ische Grenzbefestigung zwischen Basel und Passau," *Bayerische Vorgeschichtsblätter* 32 (1967) 51–82.

Garbsch (1970) — Garbsch, J., *Der spätrömische Donau-Iller-Rhein Limes*, Stuttgart 1970.

Garbsch (1974) — Garbsch, J. G., "Recent excavations at late Roman Vemania," *International Congress of Roman Frontier Studies . . . 1969*, Cardiff 1974, 156–163.

Garnsey (1970) — Garnsey, P., *Social Status and Legal Privilege in the Roman Empire*, Oxford 1970.

Garuti (1979) — Garuti, G., *Cl. Claudiani, De bello Gothico. Edizione critica, tradizione e commente*, 2 vols., Bologna 1979.

Garzetti (1977) — Garzetti, A., "I Nonii di Brescia," *Athenaeum* 55 (1977) 175–185.

Gascou (1982) — Gascou, J., "Les Pagi carthaginois," *Villes et campagnes dans l'empire romain. Actes du colloque . . . 1980*, ed. P. A. Février and P. Leveau, Aix-en-Provence 1982, 139–176.

Gascou (1982a) — Gascou, J., "La Politique municipale de Rome en Afrique du Nord, II: Après la mort de Septime-Sévère," *Aufstieg und Niedergang der römischen Welt* II, 10 (Berlin 1982) 230–320.

Gasperini (1978) — Gasperini, L., "Nuova dedica onoraria di 'Forum Clodii'," *Miscellenae greca e romana* 6 (1978) 439–458.

Gaudemet (1966) — Gaudemet, J., "Les Abus des potentes au Bas-Empire," *Irish Jurist* 1 (1966) 128–135.

Gawlikowski (1973) — Gawlikowski, M., *Palmyre VI. Le temple palmyrénien. Etude d'épigraphie et de topographie historique*, Warsaw 1973.

Gawlikowski (1984) — Gawlikowski, M., *Palmyre VIII. Les principia de Dioclétien, 'Temple des enseignes'*, Warsaw 1984.

Geva (1984) — Geva, H., "The camp of the Tenth Legion in Jerusalem: an archaeological reconsideration," *Israel Exploration Journal* 34 (1984) 239–254.

Gianfrotta (1981) — Gianfrotta, P. A., "Commerci e pirateria: prime testimonianze archeol-ogiche sottomarine," *Mélanges d'arch. et d'histoire de l'Ecole française de Rome* 93 (1981) 227–242.

Giardina (1977) — Giardina, A., *Aspetti della burocrazia nel Basso Impero*, Rome 1977.

Gilles (1974) — Gilles, K. J., "Kleinfunde von zwei spätrömische Höhensiedlungen bei Hontheim und Pünderich," *Trierer Zeitschrift* 37 (1974) 99–122.

Gilliard (1984) — Gilliard, F. D., "Senatorial bishops in the fourth century," *Harvard Theological Review* 77 (1984) 153–175.

Giorgetti (1983) — Giorgetti, D., "Ratiaria and its territory," *Ancient Bulgaria. Papers Presented to the International Symposium . . . 1981*, ed. A. G. Poulter, Nottingham 1983, 2.19–39.

Gluckman (1965) — Gluckman, M., *Politics, Law and Ritual in Tribal Society*, Chicago 1965.

Goffart (1981) — Goffart, W., *Barbarians and Romans, A.D. 418–584*, Princeton 1981.

Goldsmith (1984) — Goldsmith, R. W., "An estimate of the size and structure of the national product of the early empire," *Review of Income and Wealth* 30 (1984) 263–288.

Gomolka (1968) — Gomolka, G., "Die kleinfunde vom Limeskastell Iatrus in Moesia Inferior," *Klio* 50 (1968) 171–250.

Gonzalez (1986) — Gonzalez, J., "The Lex Irnitana: a new copy of the Flavian municipal law," *Journal of Roman Studies* 76 (1986) 147–243.

Gonzalez Blanco (1980) — Gonzalez Blanco, A., *Economia y sociedad en el Bajo Imperio*, Madrid 1980.

Gonzenbach (1961) — Gonzenbach, V. von, *Die römischen Mosaiken der Schweiz*, Basel 1961.

Gonzenbach (1965) — Gonzenbach, V. von, "Die römischen Mosaiken der Schweiz," *La Mosaique gréco-romaine. Colloque international organisée à Paris par G. Picard et H. Stern . . . 1963*, Paris 1965, 245–253.

Goodchild (1953) — Goodchild, R. G., "The Roman and Byzantine limes in Cyrenaica," *Journal of Roman Studies* 43 (1953) 65–76.

Goodchild (1966–67) — Goodchild, R. G., "A coin-hoard from 'Balagrae' (El-Beida), and the earthquake of A.D. 365," *Libya antiqua* 3–4 (1966–67) 203–211.

Goodchild and Ward Perkins (1949) — Goodchild, R. G., and J. B. Ward Perkins, "The Limes Tripolitanus in the light of recent discoveries," *Journal of Roman Studies* 39 (1949) 81–95.

Goodman (1980) — Goodman, M. D., "D. Sperber, Roman Palestine 200–400," *Journal of Roman Studies* 70 (1980) 235–236.

Gore (1984) — Gore, R., "The dead do tell tales at Vesuvius," *National Geographic Magazine* 165 (1984) 557–613.

Gorges (1979) — Gorges, J.-G., *Les Villas Hispano-romaines. Inventaire et problématique archéologiques*, Paris 1979.

Gostar (1979) — Gostar, N., "L'Armée romaine dans les guerres daces de Trajan (101–102, 105–106)," *Dacia* 23 (1979) 115–122.

Gottlieb (1985) — Gottlieb, G., "Das römische Augsburg," *Antike Welt* 16, 2 (1985) 3–18.

Gottlieb and Kuhoff (1984) — Gottlieb, G., and W. Kuhoff, *Quellen zur Geschichte der Alamannen. Inschriften und Münzen. Corrigenda und Addenda zu den Bänden I und II*, Heidelberg 1984.

Gozalbes (1980) — Gozalbes, E., "Propriedad territorial y luchas sociales en la Tripolitana durante el Bajo Impero," *Colonato y otras formas de dependencia no esclavistas. Actas del Coloquio 1978*, Oviedo 1980, 125–130.

Graham (1978) — Graham, A. J., "The numbers at Lugdunum," *Historia* 27 (1978) 625-630.

Graindor (1930) — Graindor, P., *Un Milliardaire antique: Hérode Atticus et sa famille*, Cairo 1930.

Grégoire (1922) — Grégoire, H., *Recueil des inscriptions grecques chrétiennes d'Asie Mineure* I, Paris 1922.

Gregory (1979) — Gregory, T. E., Vox Populi. Popular Opinion and Violence in the Religious Controversies of the Fifth Century A.D., Columbus 1979.

Gregory (1986) — Gregory, T. E., "A desert island survey in the Gulf of Corinth," Archaeology 39, 3 (1986) 16–21.

Grenier (1906) — Grenier, A., Habitations gauloises et villas latines dans la cité des Médiomatrices. Etude sur le développment de la civilisation gallo-romaine dans une province gauloise, Paris 1906.

Grenier (1931–34) — Grenier, A., Manuel d'archéologie gallo-romaine, 2 vols., Paris 1931–34.

Griffe (1947–65) — Griffe, E., La Gaule chrétienne à l'époque romaine, 3 vols., Paris 1947–65.

Groag (1939) — Groag, E., Die römischen Reichsbeamten von Achaia bis auf Diokletian, Vienna-Leipzig 1939.

Grosse (1 920) — Grosse, R., Römische Militärgeschichte von Gallienus bis zum Beginn der byzantinischen Themenverfassung, Berlin 1920.

Gruen (1974) — Gruen, E., The Last Generation of the Roman Republic, Berkeley 1974.

Grünewald (1980) — Grünewald, M., "Zum spätrömischen Fundstoff im Legionslager Carnuntum," Die Völker an der mittleren und unteren Donau im fünften und sechsten Jahrhundert. Berichte des Symposiums ... 1978, Stift Zwettl, ed. H. Wolfram and F. Daim, Vienna 1980, 29–31.

Gudea (1979) — Gudea, N., "The defensive system of Roman Dacia," Britannia 10 (1979) 63–87.

Günther (1975) — Günther, R., "Die sozialökonomischen Verhältnisse," Die Römer an Rhein und Donau, ed. R. Günther and H. Köpstein, Vienna 1975, 300–357.

Gutwein (1981) — Gutwein, K. C., Third Paelestine. A Regional Study in Byzantine Urbanization, Washington, D.C. 1981.

Hadas (1929) — Hadas, M., "Roman allusions in rabbinic literature," Philological Quarterly 8 (1929) 369–387.

Häussler (1964) — Häussler, R., "Vom Ursprung und Wandel des Lebensaltervergleichs," Hermes 92 (1964) 313–341.

Hahn (1982) — Hahn, I., "Immunität und Korruption der Curialen in der Spätantike," Korruption im Altertum. Konstanzer Symposium ... 1979, Munich 1982, 179–195.

Halfmann (1979) — Halfmann, H., Die Senatoren aus dem östlichen Teil des Imperium Romanum bis zum Ende des 2. Jahrhunderts n. Chr., Göttingen 1979.

Hall (1972) — Hall, A. S., "Valerius Valentianus, praeses of Isauria," Anatolian Studies 22 (1972) 213–216.

Hanfmann and Mierse (1983) — Hanfmann, G. M. A., and W. E. Mierse, Sardis from Prehistoric to Roman Times. Results of the Archaeological Exploration of Sardis, 1958–1975, Cambridge 1983.

Harmand (1957) — Harmand, L., Un Aspect social et politique du monde romain. Le patronat sur les collectivités publiques des origines au Bas-Empire, Paris 1957.

Harper (1977) — Harper, R. P., "Two excavations on the Euphrates frontier 1968–1974: Pagnik Öreni (eastern Turkey) 1968-1971, and Dibsi Faraj (northern Syria) 1972–1974," Studien zu den Militärgrenzen Roms II. Vorträge des 10. internationalen Limeskongresses, Cologne-Bonn 1977, 453–460.

Harris (1980) — Harris, W. V., "Roman terracotta lamps: The organization of an industry," Journal of Roman Studies 70 (1980) 126–145.

Harris (1981) — Harris, W. V., "The imperial rescript from Vardagate," Athenaeum 59 (1981) 338–352.

Harrison (1980) — Harrison, R. M., "Upland settlements in early medieval Lycia," *Actes du colloque sur la Lycie antique*, Paris 1980, 109–118.

Hatt (1953) — Hatt, J.-J., "Les Fouilles de la ruelle Saint-Médard à Strasbourg," *Gallia* 11 (1953) 225–248.

Hauschild and Schlunk (1961) — Hauschild, T., and H. Schlunk, "Vorbericht über die Arbeiten im Centcelles," *Madrider Mitteilungen* 2 (1961) 119–182.

Hawkes (1974) — Hawkes, S., "Some recent finds of late Roman buckles," *Brittannia* 5 (1974) 386–393.

Hawkes and Dunning (1965) — Hawkes, S. C., and G. C. Dunning, "Soldiers and settlers in Britain, fourth to fifth century," *Medieval Archaeology* 5 (1970) 1–70.

Heberdey (1897) — Heberdey, R., *Opramoas. Inschriften vom Heroon zu Rhodiapolis*, Vienna 1897.

Hefele (1869-78) — Hefele, C. J., *Histoire des conciles d'après les documents originaux*, 12 vols., Paris 1869–78.

Hefele (1907-09) — Hefele, C. J., *Histoire des conciles d'après les documents originaux, nouvelle traduction française faite sur la deuxième édition allemande*, vols. 1–3, Paris 1907–09.

Hellenkemper (1977) — Hellenkemper, H., "Der Limes am nordsyrischen Euphrat. Bericht zu einer archäologischen Landesaufnahme," *Studien zu den Militärgrenzen Roms II. Vorträge des 10. internationalen Limeskongresses*, Cologne-Bonn 1977, 461–471.

Hess (1958) — Hess, H., *The Canons of the Council of Sardica A.D. 343*, Oxford 1958.

O. Hirschfeld (1905) — Hirschfeld, O., *Die kaiserlichen Verwaltungsbeamten bis auf Diocletian,²* Berlin 1905.

Y. Hirschfeld (1985) — Hirschfeld, Y. *Archaeological Survey* of Israel. Map of Herodium (108/2) 17–11, Jerusalem 1985.

Hobley (1983) — Hobley, B., "Roman urban defences: a review of research in Britain," *Roman Urban Defences in the West*, ed. J. Maloney and B. Hobley, London 1983, 78–84.

Hoddinott (1975) — Hoddinott, R. F., *Bulgaria in Antiquity. An Archeological Introduction*, London 1975.

Hoffmann (1969–70) — Hoffmann, *Das spätrömische Bewegungsheer und die Notitia Dignitatum*, 2 vols., Düsseldorf 1969–70.

Honoré (1981) — Honoré, T., *Emperors and Lawyers*, London 1981.

Hopkins (1978) — Hopkins, K., "Economic growth and towns in classical antiquity," *Towns in Society. Essays in Economic History and Historical Sociology*, ed. P. A. Abrams and E. A. Wrigley, Cambridge 1978, 35–77.

Hopkins (1980) — Hopkins, K., "Taxes and trade in the Roman empire (200 B.C.–A.D. 400)," *Journal of Roman Studies* 70 (1980) 101–125.

Huchthausen (1973) — Huchthausen, L., "Soldaten des 3. Jahrhunderts u. Z. als Korrespondenten der kaiserlichen Kanzlei," *Altertumswissenschaft mit Zukunft. Dem Wirken W. Hartkes gewidmet*, Berlin 1973, 19–51.

Huchthausen (1974) — Huchthausen, L., "Kaiserliche Rechtsauskünfte an Sklaven und in ihrer Freiheit bedrohte Personen aus dem Codex Iustinianus," *Wissenschaftliche Zeitschrift der Universität Rostock* 23 (1974) 252–257.

Huchthausen (1979) — Huchthausen, L., " 'Thrakerreskripte' aus dem Codex Iustinianus," *Acta Universitatis Nicolai Copernici (Historia)* 13 (1979) 7–20.

Huschke (1847) — Huschke, H., *Ueber den Census und die Steuerverfassung der frühern römischen Kaiserzeit*, Berlin 1847.

Ifie (1976) — Ifie, J. E., "The Romano-African municipal aristocracy and the imperial government under the Principate," *Museum Africum* 5 (1976) 36–58.

Isaac (1984) — Isaac, B., "Bandits in Judaea and Arabia," *Harvard Studies in Classical Philology* 88 (1984) 171–203.

F. Jacques (1986) — Jacques, F., "L'ordine senatorio attraverso la crisi del III secolo," *Società romana e impero tardoantico, I: Istituzioni, cete, economie*, ed. A. Giardina, Rome 1986, 80–225 and 650–664.

J. Jacques (1981) — Jacques, J., "Volontariat et compétition dans les carrières municipales durant le Haut-Empire," *Ktema* 6 (1981) 261–270.

Jalabert (1909) — Jalabert, L., "Deux missions archéologiques américaines en Syrie," *Mélanges de l'Université St. Joseph* 3 (1909) 713–744.

Jameson (1980) — Jameson, S., "The Lycian League: Some problems in its administration," *Aufstieg und Niedergang der römischen Welt* II, 7 (Berlin 1980) 832–855.

A. C. Johnson (1951) — Johnson, A. C., *Egypt and the Roman Empire*, Ann Arbor 1951.

S. Johnson (1980) — Johnson, S., *Later Roman Britain*, London 1980.

S. Johnson (1983) — Johnson, S., *Late Roman Fortifications*, Totowa, N.J. 1983.

A. H. M. Jones (1931) — Jones, A. H. M., "The urbanization of the Ituraean principality," *Journal of Roman Studies* 21 (1931) 265–275.

A. H. M. Jones (1931a) — Jones, A. H. M., "The urbanization of Palestine," *Journal of Roman Studies* 21 (1931) 78–85.

A. H. M. Jones (1949) — Jones, A. H. M., "The Roman civil service (clerical and sub-clerical grades)," *Journal of Roman Studies* 39 (1949) 38–55.

A. H. M. Jones (1953) — Jones, A. H. M., "Census records of the later Roman empire," *Journal of Roman Studies* 43 (1953) 49–64.

A. H. M. Jones (1964) — Jones, A. H. M., *The Later Roman Empire, 284–602. A Social, Economic and Administrative Survey*, 2 vols., Norman, Okla. 1964.

A. H. M (1966) — A. H. M. Jones, *The Greek City from Alexander to Justinian*, Oxford 1966.

A. H. M. Jones (1966a) — Jones, A. H. M., *The Decline of the Ancient World*, London 1966.

A. H. M. Jones (1968) — Jones, A. H. M., "Frontier defence in Byzantine Libya," *Libya in History. Historical Conference … 1968*, University of Libya, Benghazi 1968, 289–297.

A. H. M. Jones (1970) — Jones, A. H. M., "Rome," *Troisième Conférence internationale d'histoire économique, Munich 1965*, Paris 1970, 81–104.

A. H. M. Jones (1971) — Jones, A. H. M., *The Cities of the Eastern Roman Provinces*,² Oxford 1971.

A. H. M. Jones (1974) — Jones, A. H. M., *The Roman Economy. Studies in Ancient Economic and Administrative History*, ed. P. A. Brunt, Oxford 1974.

C. P. Jones (1978) — Jones, C. P., *The Roman World of Dio Chrysostom*, Cambridge 1978.

G. D. B. Jones and Mattingly (1980) — Jones, G. D. B., and D. J. Mattingly, "Fourth-century manning of the 'Fossatum Africae'," *Britannia* 10 (1980) 323–326.

Jordan et al.(1985) — Jordan, D. R., et al., "A Greek metrical epitaph from Poetovio for a soldier from Bithynia," *Zeitschrift für Papyrologie und Epigraphik* 60 (1985) 85–89.

Jullian (1908–1926) — Jullian, C., *Histoire de la Gaule*, 8 vols., Paris 1908–26.

Kadar (1969) — Kadar, Z., "Lineamenti dell'arte della Pannonia nell'epoca dell'antichità tarda e paleocristiana," *Corsi di cultura sull'arte ravennate e bizantina* 16 (1969) 179–202.

Kaegi (1968) — Kaegi, W. E., *Byzantium and the Decline of Rome*, Princeton 1968.

Kähler (1963) — Kähler, H., *Rome and Her Empire*, London 1963.

Kammerer (1929–30) — Kammerer, A., *Pétra et la Nabatène; l'Arabie Pétrée et les arabes du nord dans leur rapports avec la Syrie et la Palestine*, Paris 1929–30.

Kandler (1980) — Kandler, M., "Archäologische Beobachtungen zur Baugeschichte des Legionslagers Carnuntum am Ausgang der Antike," *Die Völker an der mittleren und unteren Donau im fünften und sechsten Jahrhundert. Berichte des Symposions ... 1978*, Stift Zwettl, ed. H. Wolfram and F. Daim, Vienna 1980, 83–92.

Kaya (1985) — Kaya, D., "The sanctuary of the god Eurymedon at Tymbriada in Pisidia," *Anatolian Studies* 35 (1985) 39–55.

Keenan (1975) — Keenan, J. G., "On law and society in late Roman Egypt," *Zeitschrift für Papyrologie und Epigraphik* 17 (1975) 237–250.

Keenan (1981) — Keenan, J. G., "On villages and polis in Byzantine Egypt," *Proceedings of the XVIth International Congress of Papyrology*, Chicago 1981, 479–485.

Keil (1942) — Keil, J., "Die Familie der Prätorianerpräfekten Anthemius," *Anzeiger der oesterrechischen Akademie der Wissenschaften* 79 (1942) 185–203.

Keil (1956) — Keil, J., *Ein ephesischer Anwalt des 3. Jahrhunderts durchreist das Imperium Romanum*, Munich 1956.

Keil and Maresch (1960) — Keil, J., and G. Maresch, "Epigraphische Nachlese zu Miltners Ausgrabungsberichten aus Ephesos," *Jahrbuch des oesterreichischen arch. Institut* 45 (1960) Beibl. 75–100.

Keller and Rupp (1983) — Keller, D. R., and D. W. Rupp, *Archaeological Survey in the Mediterranean Area*, Oxford 1983.

Kempf (1900) — Kempf, J. G., "Romanorum sermonis castrensis reliquiae," *Jahrbuch für das klassischen Altertum* Suppl. 26, Leipzig 1900.

Kenrick (1985) — Kenrick, P. M., "The historical development of Sabratha," *Town and Country in Roman Tripolitania. Papers in Honour of Olwen Hackett*, ed. D. J. Buck and D. J. Mattingly, Oxford 1985, 1–12.

Kindler (1975) — Kindler, A., "Two coins of the Third Legion Cyrenaica struck under Antoninus Pius," *Israel Exploration Fund* 25 (1975) 144–147.

Kiss (1965) — Kiss, A., "Mosaiques de Pannonie," *La Mosaique gréco-romaine ... 1963*, Paris 1965, 297–301.

Koeppel (1980) — Koeppel, G. M., "A military *itinerarium* on the Column of Trajan: Scene L," *Mitteilungen des deutschen archäologischen Instituts, römische Abteilung* 87 (1980) 301–306.

Kolendo (1979) — Kolendo, J., "Le Problème du développement du colonat en Afrique sous le Haut-Empire," *Terre et paysans dépendants dans les sociétés antiques ... Colloque ... 1974*, Paris 1979, 391–439.

Kolendo (1981) — Kolendo, J., "La Répartition des places aux spectacles et le stratification sociale dans l'empire romain. A propos des inscriptions sur les gradins des amphithéâtres," *Ktema* 6 (1981) 301–315.

Kolendo and Kotula (1977) — Kolendo, J., and T. Kotula, "Centres et périphéries de la civilisation antique: en Afrique du nord, phénomène urbain," *Reports of the XIVth International Congress of Historical Sciences [1975]*, New York 1977, 639–651.

Kondic (1984) — Kondic, V., "Les Formes des fortifications protobyzantines dans la région des Portes de Fer," *Villes et peuplement dans l'Illyricum protobyzantin. Actes du colloque ... 1982*, Rome 1984, 131–161.

Kopecek (1974) — Kopecek, T. A., "The Cappadocian Fathers and civic patriotism," *Church History* 43 (1974) 293–303.

Kopecek (1974a) — Kopecek, T. A., "Curial displacement and flight in later fourth century Cappadocia," *Historia* 23 (1974) 319–342.

Kornemann (1970) — Kornemann, E., "Das Problem des Untergangs der antiken Welt," *Der*

Untergang des römischen Reiches, ed. K. Christ, Darmstadt 1970, 201-227 (= *Vergangenheit und Gegenwart* 12 [1922] 193–202 and 241–254).

Kotula (1968) — Kotula, T., *Les Curies municipales en Afrique romaine*, Wroctaw 1968.

Kotula (1977) — Kotula, T., "Le Fond africain de la révolte d'Héraclien en 413," *Antiquités africaines* 11 (1977) 257–266.

Kotula (1980) — Kotula, T., "Les Curies africaines: origine et composition. 'Retractio'," *Eos* 68 (1980) 133–146.

Kotula (1982) — Kotula, T., *Les Principales d'Afrique. Etude sur l'élite municipale nord-africaine au Bas-Empire romain*, Wroclaw 1982.

Kraeling (1938) — Kraeling, C. H., ed., *Gerasa, City of the Decapolis*, New Haven 1938.

Krautheimer (1965) — Krautheimer, R., *Early Christian and Byzantine Architecture*, Harmondsworth 1965.

Krautheimer (1983) — Krautheimer, R., *Three Christian Capitals. Topography and Politics*, Berkeley 1983.

Labrousse (1978) — Labrousse, M., "Toulouse antique" and "Les temps obscurs (IV^c–XI^c siècle)," *Histoire de Toulouse*, ed. P. Wolff, Toulouse 1974, 1–42 and 43–66.

Lacombrade (1951) — Lacombrade, P., *Synésios de Cyrène*, Paris 1951.

Lallemand (1964) — Lallemand, P., *L'Administration civile de l'Egypte del'avènement de Dioclétien à la création du diocèse (284-382)*, Brussels 1964.

Langhammer (1973) — Langhammer, W., *Die rechtliche und soziale Stellung der Magistratus Municipales und der Decuriones in den Übergangsphase der Städte von sich selbstverwalten-den Gemeinden zu Vollzugsorganen des spätantiken Zwangsstaates (2.-4. Jahrhundert der römischen Kaiserzeit)*, Wiesbaden 1973.

Lantier (1953) — Lantier, R., "Recherches archéologiques en Gaule en 1951," *Gallia* 11 (1953) 167–362.

Lanyi (1969) — Lanyi, V., "The coinage of Valentinian I in Siscia," *Acta archaeologica academiae scientiarum Hungaricae* 21 (1969) 33–46.

Laporte (1983) — Laporte, J. P., "Rapidum: le camp et la ville," *Bulletin de la Société des antiquaires de France* 1983, 253–267.

Lassus (1947) — Lassus, J., *Sanctuaires chrétiens de Syrie. Essai sur la genèse, la forme et l'usage liturgique des édifices du culte chrétien, en Syrie, du IIIe siècle à la conquête musulmane*, Paris 1947.

Lassus (1965) — Lassus, J., "Edifices du culte autour de la basilique," *Actes du Congrès international d'archéologie chrétienne . . . 1962*, Rome 1965, 581–610.

Laum (1914) — Laum, B., *Stiftungen in der griechischen und römischen Antike. Ein Beitrag zur antiken Kulturgeschichte*, 2 vols., Leipzig-Berlin 1914.

Laumonier (1958) — Laumonier, A., *Les Cultes indigènes en Carie*, Paris 1958.

Leday (1972) — Leday, A., "Fouilles de sauvetage de la villa du Châtelier (Commune de Levet-18)," *Revue arch. du Centre* 11 (1972) 207–221.

Leday (1980) — Leday, A., *La Campagne à l'époque romaine dans le centre de la Gaule. Villas, vici et sanctuaires des Bituriges Cubi*, Oxford 1980.

LeGlay (1961–66) — LeGlay, M., *Saturne africain, monuments, I: Afrique proconsulaire; II, Numidie, Maurétanies*, 2 vols., Paris 1961–66.

Lengyel and Radan (1980) — Lengyel, A., and G. T. B. Radan, eds., *The Archaeology of Roman Pannonia*, Lexington, Ky. 1980.

Lepelley (1979–81) — Lepelley, C., *Les Cités de l'Afrique romaine au Bas-Empire*, 2 vols., Paris 1979–81.

Lepelley (1981) — Lepelley, C., "La Carrière municipale dans l'Afrique romaine sous l'Empire tardif," *Ktema* 6 (1981) 333–347.

Lepelley (1981a) — Lepelley, C., "La Crise de l'Afrique romaine au début du Ve siècle, d'après les letters nouvellement découvertes de Saint Augustin," *Comptes rendus de l'Académie des inscriptions et belles lettres* 1981, 445–463.

Lepelley (1983) — Lepelley, C., "Quot curiales, tot tyranni. L'Image du décurion oppresseur au Bas-Empire," *Crise et redressement dans les provinces européennes de l'Empire ... Actes du Colloque de Strasbourg ...* 1981, Strasbourg 1983, 143–156.

LeRoux (1982) — LeRoux, P., *L'Armée romaine et l'organisation des provinces ibériques d'Auguste à l'invasion de 409*, Paris 1982.

LeRoux (1983) — LeRoux, P., "L'Armée romaine au quotidien: deux graffiti légionnaires de Pompeii et Rome," *Epigraphica* 45 (1983) 65–77.

Leschi (1953) — Leschi, L., *Djemila, antique Cuicul*, Algiers 1953.

Leveau (1972) — Leveau, P., "Paysanneries antiques du pays Beni-Menacer," *Bulletin arch. du Comité des travaux historiques* 8B (1972) 3–26.

Leveau (1973) — Leveau, P. "L'aile II des Thraces, la tribu des Mazices et les praefecti gentis en Afrique du Nord," *Antiquités africaines* 7 (1973) 153–192.

Leveau (1982) — Leveau, P., "Une ville et ses campagnes: l'exemple de Caesarea de Maurétanie," *Villes et campagnes dans l'empire. Actes du Colloque ...* 1980, ed. P. A. Février and P. Leveau, Aix-en-Provence 1982, 77–90.

Leveau (1984) — Leveau, P., *Caesarea de Maurétanie. Une ville romaine et ses campagnes*, Paris 1984.

Levick (1967) — Levick, B., *Roman Colonies in Southern Asia Minor*, Oxford 1967.

Levine (1975) — Levine, L. I., "R. Abbahu of Caesarea," *Christianity, Judaism and Other Greco-Roman Cults: Studies for Morton Smith at Sixty*, Leiden 1975, 3.56–76.

Lévy (1895) — Lévy, I., "Etudes sur la vie municipale de l'Asie Mineure sous les Antonins," *Revue des études grecques* 8 (1895) 203–250.

Lévy (1899) — Lévy, I., "Etudes sur la vie municipale de l'Asie Mineure sous les Antonins," *Revue des études grecques* 12 (1899) 255–289.

Lévy (1901) — Lévy, I., "Etudes sur la vie municipale de l'Asie Mineure sous les Antonins," *Revue des études grecques* 14 (1901) 350–371.

Lewis (1954) — Lewis, N., "On official corruption in Roman Egypt. The edict of Vergilius Capito," *Proceedings of the American Philosophical Society* 98 (1954) 153–158.

Lewis (1966) — Lewis, N., "Exemption from liturgy in Roman Egypt," *Atti dell'XI Congresso internazionale di papirologia ...* 1965, Milan 1966, 508–541.

Lewis (1983) — Lewis, N., *Life in Egypt under Roman Rule*, Oxford 1983.

Lewuillon-Blume (1979) — Lewuillon-Blume, M., "Problèmes de la terre au IVe siècle ap. J.-C.," *Actes du XVIe Congrès international de payrologie*, Brussels 1979, 4.177–185.

Liebenam (1900) — Liebenam, W., *Städteverwaltung im römischen Kaiserreiche*, Leipzig 1900.

Liebeschuetz (1972) — Liebeschuetz, J. H. W., *Antioch: City and Imperial Administration in the Later Roman Empire*, Oxford 1972.

Liebeschuetz (1977) — Liebeschuetz, [J. H.] W., "Epigraphic evidence on the Christianization of the Syria," *Limes. Akten des XI Internationalen Limeskongresses ...* 1976, ed. J. Fitz, Budapest 1977, 485–508.

Liebeschuetz (1979) — Liebeschuetz, W., "Problems arising from the conversion of Syria," *The Churches in Town and Countryside. Papers Read at the 17th ... and 18th ... Meeting of the Ecclesiastical History Society*, ed. D. Baker, Oxford 1979, 17–24.

Liebs (1978) — Liebs, D., "Ämterpatronage in der spätantike," *Zeitschrift für Rechtsgeschichte* 95 (1978) 158–186.

Lietzmann (1908) — Lietzmann, H., *Das Leben des heiligen Symeon Stylites*, Leipzig 1908.

Ling (1981) — Ling, R., "Building Mk1 at Oenoanda," *Anatolian Studies* 31 (1981) 31–53.

Littmann, Magie, and Stuart (1910) — Littmann, E., D. Magie, and D. R. Stuart, *Southern Hauran (Publications of the Princeton University Archaeological Expedition to Syria in 1904-1905 and 1909, Division III, Greek and Latin Inscriptions in Syrai, Section A, Southern Syria, Part 2)*, Leiden 1910.

Löhken (1982) — Löhken, H., *Ordines dignitatum. Untersuchungen zur formalen Konstituierung der spätantiken Führungsschicht*, Cologne-Vienna 1982.

Lot, Pfister, and Ganshof (1928) — Lot, F., C. Pfister, and F. L. Ganshof, *Histoire du moyen âge* 1: *Les destinées de l'empire en Occident de 395 à 888*, Paris 1928.

Louis-Lucas (1883) — Louis-Lucas, P., *Etude sur la vénalité des charges et fonctions publiques et sur celle des offices ministériels depuis l'antiquité romaine jusqu'à nos jours*, 2 vols., Paris 1883.

Loyen (1960) — Loyen, A., "Bourg-sur-Gironde et les villas d'Ausone," *Revue des études anciennes* 62 (1960) 113–126.

Lutz (1974) — Lutz, M., "Le Domaine gallo-romain de Saint-Ulrich et sa grande villa," *Le pays Lorrain* 55 (1974) 15-30.

McKay (1975) — McKay, A.G., *Houses, Villas and Palaces in the Roman World*, London 1975.

MacKendrick (1980) — MacKendrick, P., *The North African Stones Speak*, Chapel Hill, N.C. 1980.

Mackie (1983) — Mackie, N., *Local Administration in Roman Spain A.D. 14-212*, Oxford 1983.

MacMullen (1960) — MacMullen, R., "Inscriptions on Roman armor and the supply of arms in the Roman empire," *American Journal of Archaeology* 64 (1960) 23–40.

MacMullen (1962) — MacMullen, R., "Roman bureaucratese," *Traditio* 18 (1962) 364–378.

MacMullen (1962a) — MacMullen, R., "The emperor's largesses," *Latomus* 21 (1962) 159–166.

MacMullen (1963) — MacMullen, R., *Soldier and Civilian in the Later Roman Empire*, Cambridge 1963.

MacMullen (1963a) — MacMullen, R., "Barbarian enclaves in the northern Roman empire," *Antiquité classique* 32 (1963) 552–561.

MacMullen (1964) — MacMullen, R., "Social mobility and the Theodosian Code," *Journal of Roman Studies* 54 (1964) 49–53.

MacMullen (1964a) — MacMullen, R., "Some pictures in Ammianus Marcellinus," *Art Bulletin* 46 (1964) 435–455.

MacMullen (1964b) — MacMullen, R., "Imperial bureaucrats in the Roman provinces," *Harvard Studies in Classical Philology* 68 (1964) 305–316.

MacMullen (1966) — MacMullen, R., *Enemies of the Roman Order. Treason, Unrest, and Alienation in the Empire*, Cambridge 1966.

MacMullen (1968) — MacMullen, R., "Rural Romanization," *Phoenix* 22 (1968) 337–341.

MacMullen (1971) — MacMullen, R., "Social history in astrology," *Ancient Society* 2 (1971) 105–116.

MacMullen (1972) — MacMullen, R., "Sfiducia nell'intelletto nel quarto secolo," *Rivista storica italiana* 84 (1972) 5–16.

MacMullen (1974) — MacMullen, R., *Roman Social Relations*, New Haven 1974.

MacMullen (1974a) — MacMullen, R., "Peasants, during the Principate," *Aufstieg und Niedergang der römischen Welt* II, 1 (Berlin 1974) 253–261.

MacMullen (1976) — MacMullen, R., *Roman Government's Response to Crisis, A.D. 235-337,* New Haven 1976.

MacMullen (1976a) — MacMullen, R., "Two notes on imperial properties," *Athenaeum* 54 (1976) 19–36.

MacMullen (1977) — MacMullen, R., "Barbarian influence on Rome before the Great Invasions," *Reports, XIV International Congress of the Historical Sciences . . . 1975,* New York 1977, 702–712.

MacMullen (1980) — MacMullen, R., "Roman elite motivation: three questions," *Past and Present* 88 (1980) 3–16.

MacMullen (1980a) — MacMullen, R., "The role of the Christian bishop in ancient society," *Protocol of the Thirty-fifth Colloquy: The Role of the Christian Bishop in Ancient Society . . .* 1979 (Center for Hermeneutical Studies), Berkeley 1980, 25–29.

MacMullen (1980b) — MacMullen, R., "How big was the Roman army?" *Klio* 62 (1980) 451–460.

MacMullen (1981) — MacMullen, R., *Paganism in the Roman Empire,* New Haven 1981.

MacMullen (1982) — MacMullen, R., "The epigraphic habit in the Roman empire," *American Journal of Philology* 103 (1982) 233–246.

MacMullen (1984) — MacMullen, R., *Christianizing the Roman Empire,* New Haven 1984.

MacMullen (1984a) — MacMullen, R., "The Roman emperors' army costs," *Latomus* 43 (1984) 571–580.

MacMullen (1985) — MacMullen, R., "How to revolt in the Roman empire," *Rivista storica dell'antichità* (1985) 67–76.

MacMullen (1986) — MacMullen, R., "Frequency of inscriptions in Roman Lydia," *Zeitschrift für Papyrologie und Epigraphik* 65 (1986) 237–238.

MacMullen (1986a) — MacMullen, R., "Women's power in the Principate," *Klio* 68 (1986) 434–443.

MacMullen (1986b) — MacMullen, R., "Personal power in the Roman empire," *American Journal of Philology* 107 (1986) 512–524.

MacMullen (1986c) — MacMullen, R., "Judicial savagery in the Roman empire," *Chiron* 16 (1986) 43–62.

MacMullen (1986d) — MacMullen, R., "What difference did Christianity make?" *Historia* 35 (1986) 322–343.

MacMullen (1987) — MacMullen, R., "Late Roman slavery," *Historia* 36 (1987) 359–382.

MacMullen (1987a) — MacMullen, R., "Tax pressure in the Roman empire," *Latomus* 46 (1987) 733–49.

Majewski (1963) — Majewski, K., "Exploration archéologique de Novae, Bulgarie," *Latomus* 22 (1963) 504–506.

Malcus (1967) — Malcus, B., *Die Prokonsuln von Asien von Diokletian bis Theodosius II,* Lund 1967.

Malherbe (1977) — Malherbe, A. J., ed., *The Cynic Epistles. A Study Edition,* Missoula, Mont. 1977.

Mann (1963) — Mann, J. C., "The role of the frontier zones in army recruitment," *Acta et dissertationes archaeologicae V Congressus internationalis limitis Romani studiosorum . . .* 1961, Zagreb 1963.

Mann (1983) — Mann, J. C., *Legionary Recruitment and Veteran Settlement during the Principate,* London 1983.

Mann and Jarrett (1967) — Mann, J. C., and M. G. Jarrett, "The division of Britain," *Journal of Roman Studies* 57 (1967) 61–64.

Manning (1974) — Manning, W., "Excavations in the Roman fortress at Usk, Monmouth-shire," *Roman Frontier Studies 1969. Eighth International Congress of Limesforschung*, Cardiff 1974, 61–69.

Mansel (1959) — Mansel, A. M., "Die Grabbauten von Side, Pamphylien," *Archäologische Anzeiger* 1959, 364–402.

Mansel (1965) — Mansel, A., "Villes mortes d'Asie Mineure occidentale," *Corsi di cultura sull'arte ravennate e bizantina* 12 (1965) 495–540.

Mansi (1759–1927) — Mansi, G. D., *Sacrorum conciliorum nova et amplissima collectio*, Florence 1759–1927.

Marchi (1906) — Marchi, A., "I testi delle pandette relativi alla vendita e al legato della militia," *Archivio giuridico* 76 (1906) 291–304.

Marcillet-Jaubert — (1979) Marcillet-Jaubert, J., "Coloni loci legum maiorum," *Epigraphica* 41 (1979) 66–72.

Martin (1976) — Martin, R., *Palladius, Traité d'agriculture I: Livres I et II*, Paris 1976.

Matijasic (1982)— Matijasic, R., "Roman rural architecture in the territory of Colonia Iulia Pola," *American Journal of Archaeology* 86 (1982) 53–64.

Matthews (1975) — Matthews, J., *Western Aristocracies and Imperial Court A.D. 364–425*, Oxford 1975.

Mazza (1970) — Mazza, M., *Lotte sociali e restaurazione autorità nel 3 secolo d.C.*, Catania 1970.

Mazzarino (1951) — Mazzarino, S., *Aspetti sociali del quarto secolo. Ricerche di storia tardo-romano*, Rome 1951.

Mazzarino (1966) — Mazzarino, S., *The End of the Ancient World*, trans. G. Holmes, New York 1966.

Meiggs (1960) — Meiggs, R., *Roman Ostia*, Oxford 1960.

Merlin and Poinssot (1908) — Merlin, A., and L. Poinssot, "Les Inscriptions d'Uchi Majus d'après les recherches du Capitaine Gondouin," *Notes et documents publiés par la Direction des antiquités et arts (du Gouvernement Tunisien)* 2 (1908) 3–128.

Merrifield (1983) — Merrifield, R., *London, City of the Romans*, London 1983.

Mertens (1977) — Mertens, J., "Quelques considérations sur le limes Belgicus," *Limes. Akten des XI. internationalen Limeskongresses ... 1976*, Budapest 1977, 63–71.

Metcalf (1984) — Metcalf, D., "The mint of Thessalonica in the early Byzantine period," *Villes et peuplement dans l'Illyricum protobyzantin. Actes du colloque ... 1982*, Rome 1984, 111–128.

Metzler and Zimmer (1982) — Metzler, J., and J. Zimmer, "Echternach: une villa romaine de Luxembourg," *Archéologia* 168 (1982) 38–50.

Mickwitz (1935) — Mickwitz, G., s.v. "Inflation," *RE* suppl. VI, Stuttgart 1935, 127–133.

Mikulcic (1974) — Mikulcic, I., "Über die grosse der spätantiken Städte in Makedonien," *Ziva antike* 24 (1974) 191–212.

Millett (1982) — Millett, M., "Town and country: a review of some material evidence," *The Romano-British Countryside. Studies in Rural Settlement and Economy*, ed. D. Miles, Oxford 1982, 421–431.

Mitchell (1977) — Mitchell, S., "Inscriptions of Ancyra," *Anatolian Studies* 27 (1977) 63–103.

Mitchell (1980) — Mitchell, S., "Population and the land in Roman Galatia," *Aufstieg und Niedergang der römischen Welt* II, 7 (Berlin 1980) 1053–1081.

Mitchell (1982) — Mitchell, S., "The Life of Saint Theodotus of Ancyra," *Anatolian Studies* 32 (1982) 93–113.

Mitchell (1983) — Mitchell, S., "The Balkans, Anatolia, and Roman armies across Asia Minor," *Armies and Frontiers in Roman and Byzantine Anatolia ... Colloquium*, London 1983, 131–150.

Mitchell (1984–85) — Mitchell, S., "Archaeology in Asia Minor 1979-84," *Archaeological Reports* 31 (1984–85) 70–105.

Mitford (1974) — Mitford, T. B., "Some inscriptions from the Cappadocian limes," *Journal of Roman Studies* 64 (1974) 160–175.

Mocsy (1970) — Mocsy, A., *Gesellschaft und Romanisation in der römischen Provinz Moesia Superior,* Amsterdam 1970.

Mocsy (1971) — Mocsy, A., "L. Varady, *Das letzte Jahrhundert Pannoniens,*" *Acta arch. academiae scientiarum Hungaricae* 23 (1971) 347–360.

Mocsy (1974) — Mocsy, A., *Pannonia and Upper Moesia. A History of the Middle Danube Provinces of the Roman Empire,* transl. S. Frere, London 1974.

Moeller (1973) — Moeller, W. O., "Gnaeus Nigidius Maius, princeps coloniae," *Latomus* 32 (1973) 515–520.

Mohrmann (1975) — Mohrmann, C., *Vita di Martino et al. (Vite dei Santi 4),* Milan 1975.

Momigliano (1978) — Momigliano, A., "After Gibbon's Decline and Fall," *Annali della Scuola normale superiore di Pisa³* 8, 1, (1978) 435–454.

Mommsen (1884) — Mommsen, T., "Observationes epigraphicae XL: ordo salutationis sportularumque sub imp. Iuliano in provincia Numidia," *Ephemeris epigraphica* 5 (1884) 629–646.

Mommsen (1887–88) — Mommsen, T., *Römische Staatsrecht,* 3 vols., Leipzig 1887–88.

Monks (1957) — Monks, G. R., "The administration of the privy purse: an inquiry into official corruption and the fall of the Roman empire," *Speculum* 32 (1957) 748-779.

Monneret de Villard (1953) — Monneret de Villard, U., "The temple of the imperial cult at Luxor," *Archaeologia* 95 (1953) 85–106.

Moscadi (1970) — Moscadi, A., "Le lettere dell'archivio di Teofane," *Aegyptus* 50 (1970) 88–153.

Mouterde and Poidebard (1931) — Mouterde, R., and A. Poidebard, "La Voie antique des caravanes entre Palmyre et Hit au IIᵉ siècle ap. J.-C.," *Syria* 12 (1931) 101–115.

Mrozek (1984) — Mrozek, S., "Munificentia privata im Bauwesen und Lebensmittelverteilungen in Italien während des Prinzipates," *Zeitschrift für Papyrologie und Epigraphik* 57 (1984) 233–240.

Mrozek (1985) — Mrozek, S., "Zum Kreditgeld in der frühen römischen Kaiserzeit," *Historia* 34 (1985) 310–323.

Munier (1938) — Munier, H., "Le Christianisme à Philae," *Jam'iyat al-Athar al-Qibtyah* 4 (1938) 37–49.

Musurillo (1972) — Musurillo, H., *The Acts of the Christian Martyrs. Introduction, Texts and Translations,* Oxford 1972.

Neal (1978) — Neal, D. S., "The growth and decline of villas in the Verulamium area," *Studies in the Roman-British Villa,* ed. M. Todd, Leicester 1978, 33–58.

Neesen (1980) — Neesen, L., *Untersuchungen zu den direkten Staatsabgaben der römischen Kaiserzeit 27 v. Chr. bis 284 n. Chr.,* Bonn 1980.

Neusner (1983) — Neusner, J., *Judaism in Society: The Evidence of the Yerushalmi,* Chicago 1983.

Nicols (1980) — Nicols, J., "*Tabulae patronatus:* a study of the agreement between patron and client-community," *Aufstieg und Niedergang der römischen Welt* II, 13 (1980) 535–561.

Nixon (1983) — Nixon, C. E. V., "Coin circulation and military activity in the vicinity of Sirmium, A. D. 364–378, and the Siscia mint," *Jahrbuch für Numismatik und Geldgeschichte* 33 (1983) 45–56.

Noethlichs (1981) — Noethlichs, K. L., *Beamtentum und Dienstvergehen. Zur Staatsverwaltung in der Spätantike,* Wiesbaden 1981.

Noll (1974) — Noll, R., "Eine goldene 'Kaiserfibel' aus Niederemmel vom Jahre 316," *Bonner Jahrbücher* 174 (1974) 221–244.

Norman (1954) — Norman, A. F., "The family of Argyrus," *Journal of Hellenic Studies* 74 (1954) 44–48.

Norman (1964) — Norman, A. F., "The library of Libanius," *Rheinisches Museum* 107 (1964) 158–175.

Norman (1977) — Norman, A. F., *Libanius. Selected Works, II: Selected Orations,* Cambridge 1977.

Ogilvie (1979) — Ogilvie, R. M., *The Library of Lactantius,* Oxford 1979.

Ohlemutz (1940) — Ohlemutz, E., *Die Kulte und Heiligtümer der Götter in Pergamon,* Würzburg 1940.

Oliver (1941) — Oliver, J. H., "Greek inscriptions," *Hesperia* 10 (1941) 65–92.

Oliver (1953) — Oliver, J. H., "The ruling power. A study of the Roman empire in the second century after Christ through the Roman oration of Aelius Aristides," *Transactions of the American Philosophical Society*² 43 (1953) 870–1003.

Pack (1935) — Pack, R. A., *Studies in Libanius and Antiochene Society under Theodosius,* Menasha 1935.

Pack (1965) — Pack, R. A., *The Greek and Latin Texts from Greco-Roman Egypt,*² Ann Arbor 1965.

Packmann (1976) — Packman, Z. M., "Return of a dowry," *Collectanea Papyrologica. Texts Published in Honor of H. C. Youtie,* 2 vols., Bonn 1976, 447–455.

Pallas, Charitonidis, and Venencie (1959) — Pallas, D. I., S. Charitonidis, and J. Venencie, "Inscriptions lyciennes à Solomos près de Corinthe," *Bulletin de correspondance hellénique* 83 (1959) 496–508.

Palmer (1978–80) — Palmer, R. E. A., "C. Verres' legacy of charm and love to the city of Rome: a new document," *Rendiconti, Pontificia Accademia di arch.* 51–52 (1978–80) 111–136.

Panella (1973) — Panella, C., "Dibattito sulla 'Storia economica del mondo antico' di F. Heichelheim," *Dialoghi di archeologia* 7 (1973) 342–353.

Panella (1981) — Panella, C., "La distribuzione e i mercati," *Merci, mercati e scambi nel mediterraneo (Società Romana e Produzione Schiavistica 2),* ed. A. Giardina and A. Schiavone, Rome 1981, 55–80.

Panella (1983) — Panella, C., "Le anfore di Cartagine: nuovi elementi per la ricostruzione dei flussi commerciali del Mediterraneo in età imperiale romana," *Opus* 2 (1983) 53–73.

Pani (1986) — Pani, M., "La remunerazione dell'oratoria giudiziaria nell'alto Principato: una laboriosa accettazione sociale," *Decima miscellanea greca e romana (Studi pubblicati dall'Istituto Italiano per la Storia Antica 36),* Rome 1986, 313–346.

Parassoglou (1978) — Parassoglou, G., *Imperial Estates in Roman Egypt,* Amsterdam 1978.

Paret (1932) — Paret, O., *Die Römer in Württemberg, III: Die Siedlungen des römischen Württemberg,* Stuttgart 1932.

Parker (1973) — Parker, A. J., "The evidence provided by underwater archaeology for Roman trade in the western Mediterranean," *Marine Archaeology,* ed. D. J. Blackman, London 1973, 361–379.

Parker (1980) — Parker, A., "Roman wrecks in the western Mediterranean," *Archeology under Water. An Atlas of the World's Submerged Sites,* ed. K. Muckleroy, New York 1980, 50–51.

Parker and Painter (1979) — Parker, A. J., and J. M. Painter, "A computer-based index of ancient shipwrecks," *International Journal of Nautical Archeology* 8 (1979) 69–70.

Parovic-Pesikan (1971) — Parovic-Pesikan, M., "Excavations of a late Roman villa," *Sirmium* 2 (1971) 15–44.

Parsons (1976) — Parsons, P. J., "Petitions and a letter: the grammarian's complaint," *Collectanea papyrologica. Texts Published in Honour of H. C. Youtie*, ed. A. E. Hanson, Bonn 1976, 409–446.

Paschoud (1967) — Paschoud, F., *Roma Aeterna. Etudes sur le patriotisme romain dans l'Occident latin à l'époque des grandes invasions*, Neuchâtel 1967.

Patlagean (1977) — Patlagean, E., *Pauvreté économique et pauvreté sociale à Byzance: 4ᵉ –7ᵉ siècle*, Paris 1977.

Paunier (1978) — Paunier., D., "Un Refuge du Bas-Empire au Mont-Musiège (Haute-Savoie)," *Museum Helveticum* 35 (1978) 295–306.

Pearl (1940) — Pearl, O. M., "Varia papyrologica," *Transactions and Proceedings of the American Philological Association* 71 (1940) 372–390.

Peeters (1941) — Peeters, P., "La Vie géorgienne de Saint Porphyre de Gaza," *Analecta Bollandiana* 59 (1941) 65–216.

Pekary (1966) — Pekary, T., "Zur Geschichte von Vindonissa in spätrömischer Zeit," *Pro Vondonissa* 1966, 5–14.

Percival (1969) — Percival, J., "P. Ital. 3 and Roman estate management," *Hommages à M. Renard*, Brussels 1969, 2.607–615.

Percival (1976) — Percival, J., *The Roman Villa. An Historical Introduction*, Berkeley 1976.

Petit (1955) — Petit, P., *Libanios et la vie municipale à Antioche au IVᵉ siècle après J. C.*, Paris 1955.

Petit (1957) — Petit, P., *Les Etudiants de Libanius. Un professeur de faculté et ses élèves au Bas Empire*, Paris 1957.

Petrikovits (1950) — Petrikovits, H. von, "Das Fortleben römischer Städte am Rhein und Donau im frühen Mittelalter," *Trierer Zeitschrift* 19 (1950) 72–81.

Petrikovits (1956) — Petrikovits, H. von, "Neue Forschungen zur römerzeitlichen Besiedlung der Nordeifel," *Germania* 34 (1956) 99–125.

Petrikovits (1971) — Petrikovits, H. von, "Fortifications in the north-western Roman empire from the third to the fifth centuries A.D.," *Journal of Roman Studies* 61 (1971) 178–218.

Petzl (1982) — Petzl, G., *Die Inschriften von Smyrna, I: Grabinschriften, postume Ehrungen, Grabepigramme*, Bonn 1982.

Peyras (1975) — Peyras, J., "Le Fundus Aufidianus: étude d'un grand domaine romain de la région de Mateur (Tunisie du Nord)," *Antiquités africaines* 9 (1975) 181–222.

Pflaum (1948) — Pflaum, H.-G., *Le Marbre de Thorigny*, Paris 1948.

Pflaum (1966) — Pflaum, H.-G., "Un ami inconnu d'Hadrien: M. Aemilius Papus," *Klio* 46 (1966) 331–336.

Pflaum (1974) — Pflaum, H.-G., *Abregé de Procurateurs équestres, adaptation française* by S. Ducroux and N. Duval, Paris 1974.

C. Picard (1922) — Picard, C., *Ephèse et Claros*, Paris 1922.

G. C. Picard (1975) — Picard, G. C., "Observations sur la condition des populations rurales dans l'empire romain, en Gaule et en Afrique," *Aufstieg und Niedergang der römischen Welt* II, 3 (Berlin 1975) 98–111.

Pietersma (1984) — Pietersma, A., *The Acts of Phileas Bishop of Thmuis (Including Fragments of the Greek Psalter). P. Chester Beatty XV*, Geneva 1984.

C. Pietri (1978) — Pietri, C., "Evergétisme et richesses ecclésiastiques dans l'Italie du IVᵉ à la fin du Vᵉ siècle: l'exemple romain," *Ktema* 3 (1978) 317–337.

L. Pietri (1983) — Pietri, L., *La Ville de Tours du IVᵉ au VIᵉ siècle. Naissance d'une cité chrétienne*, Paris 1983.

Piganiol (1972) — Piganiol, A., *L'Empire chrétien (325-395)*², ed. A. Chastagnol, Paris 1972.

Plassart (1932) — Plassart, A., "Une levée de volontiers Thespiens sous Marc Aurel," *Mélanges Glotz*, Paris 1932, 2.731–738.

Polotsky (1962) — Polotsky, H. J., "Greek papyri from the Cave of the Letters," *Israel Exploration Journal* 12 (1962) 258–262.

Popovic (1971) — Popovic, V., "A survey of the topography and urban organization of Sirmium in the Late Empire," *Sirmium I. Archaeological Investigation in Sirmian Pannonia*, ed. V. Popovic, Belgrade 1971, 119–133.

Potter (1975) — Potter, T. W., "Recenti ricerche in Etruria meridionale: problemi della transizione dal Tardo Antico all'Alto Medioevo," *Archeologia medievale* 2 (1975) 215–236.

Potter (1979) — Potter, T. W., *The Changing Landscape of South Etruria*, London 1979.

Potter (1982) — Potter, T. W., "Prospection en surface: théorie et pratique," *Villes et campagnes dans l'empire romain. Actes du Colloque … 1980*, Aix-en-Provence 1982, 19–41.

Poulter (1983) — Poulter, A. G., "Town and country in Moesia Inferior," *Ancient Bulgaria. Papers presented to the International Symposium … 1981*, ed. A. G. Poulter, Nottingham 1983, 2.74–118.

Praschniker and Schober (1919) — Praschniker, C., and A. Schober, *Archäologische Forschungen in Albanien und Montenegro*, Vienna 1919.

Premerstein (1937) — Premerstein, A. von, *Vom Werden und Wesen des Prinzipats* (Abhandlungen der Bayerischen Akademie der Wissenschaften, Phil.-hist. Abt.² 15), Munich 1937.

Prentice (1908) — Prentice, W. K., *Greek and Latin Inscriptions (Publications of an American Archaeological Expedition to Syria in 1899-1900, Part III)*, New York 1908.

Prentice (1909) — Prentice, W. K., *Il-Anderin — Kerratin — Marata (Publications of the Princeton University Archaeological Expedition to Syria in 1904-1905, Division III: Greek and Latin Inscriptions in Syria, Section B: Northern Syria, Part 2)*, Leiden 1909.

Prentice (1910) — Prentice, W. K., *Djebel Barisha (Publications of the Princeton University Archaeological Expedition to Syria in 1904-1905, Division III: Greek and Latin Inscriptions in Syria, Section B: Northern Syria, Part 4)*, Leiden 1910.

Price (1984) — Price, S. R. F., *Rituals and Power. The Roman Imperial Cult in Asia Minor*, Cambridge 1984.

Provost (1982) — Provost, M., "Recherches sur les mutations de l'agriculture gauloise dans la deuxième moitié du IIᵉ ap. J.-C.," *Caesarodunum* 17 (1982) 393–402.

Purcell (1983) — Purcell, N., "The *apparitores*: a study in social mobility," *Papers of the British School in Rome* 51 (1983) 125–173.

Quass (1982) — Quass, F., "Zur politischen Tätigkeit der munizipalen Aristokratie des griechischen Ostens in der Kaiserzeit," *Historia* 31 (1982) 188–213.

Rachet (1970) — Rachet, M., *Rome et les Berbères. Un problème militaire d'Auguste à Dioclétien*, Brussels 1970.

Radet (1890) — Radet, G., "Inscriptions de la région du Méandre," *Bulletin de correspondance hellénique* 14 (1890) 224–239.

Rahmani (1972) — Rahmani, L. Y., "A bilingual ossuary-inscription from Khirbet Zif," *Israel Exploration Journal* 22 (1972) 113–116.

Ramsay (1895–97) — Ramsay, W. M., *The Cities and Bishoprics of Phrygia, being an Essay on the Local History of Phrygia*, 2 vols., Oxford 1895–97.

Ramsay (1928) or (1929) — Ramsay, W. M. and A. M., "Roman garrisons and soldiers in Asia Minor," *Journal of Roman Studies* 18 (1928) 181–190 and 19 (1929) 155–160.

Ravenna (1978) — Ravenna, A., *Commento alla Genesi (Beresit Rabbâ)*, Turin 1978.

Rea (1976) — Rea, J. J., "Lease of flax-land," *Collectanea papyrologica. Texts Published in Honor of H. C. Youtie*, Bonn 1976, 457–469.

Rebuffat (1977) — Rebuffat, R., "Une Zone militaire et sa vie économique: le limes de Tripolitaine," *Colloques nationaux du CNRS: Armées et fiscalité dans le monde antique ... 1976*, Paris 1977, 395–420.

Rebuffat (1980) — Rebuffat, R., "Cuicul, le 21 juillet 365," *Antiquités africaines* 15 (1980) 309–328.

Rebuffat (1982) — Rebuffat, R., "Au-delà des camps romains d'Afrique mineure: renseignement, contrôle, pénétration," *Aufstieg und Niedergang der römischen Welt* II, 10 (Berlin 1982) 475–513.

Reece (1973) — Reece, R., "Roman coinage in the western empire," *Britannia* 4 (1973) 227–251.

Reece (1980) — Reece, R., "Town and country: The end of Roman Britain," *World Archaeology* 12 (1980) 77–92.

Reinach (1893) — Reinach, T., "Inscriptions d'Iasos," *Revue des études grecques* 6 (1893) 153–203.

Reinach (1896) — Reinach, T., "Une Crise monétaire au IIIᵉ siècle de l'ère chrétienne (inscription de Mylasa)," *Bulletin de correspondance hellénique* 29 (1896) 523–548.

Reinach (1906) — Reinach, T., "Inscription d'Aphrodisias," *Revue des études grecques* 19 (1906) 79–150 and 205–298.

Rémondon (1964) — Rémondon, R., *La Crise de l'empire romain de Marc-Aurèle à Anastase*, Paris 1964.

Rémondon (1965) — Rémondon, R., "Militaires et civils dans une campagne égyptienne au temps de Constance II," *Journal des savants* 1965, 132–143.

Rendic-Miocevic (1980) — Rendic-Miocevic, D., "Documenti della provincia di Dalmazia," *La parola del passato* 190 (1980) 15–27.

Rey-Coquais (1978) — Rey-Coquais, J.-P., "Syrie romaine, de Pompée à Dioclétien," *Journal of Roman Studies* 68 (1978) 44–73.

Reynolds (1982) — Reynolds, J., *Aphrodisias and Rome. Documents from the Excavation of the Theatre at Aphrodisias*, London 1982.

Rickman (1981) — Rickman, G. E., "[review of] A. Carandini et al., *Ostia. Le Terme del Nuotatore*," *Journal of Roman Studies* 71 (1981) 215–217.

Riese (1892) — Riese, A., *Das rheinische Germanien in der antiken Literatur*, Leipzig 1892.

Rigsby (1979) — Rigsby, K. J., "An imperial letter at Balbura," *American Journal of Philology* 100 (1979) 401–407.

Riley (1981) — Riley, J. A., "Italy and the eastern Mediterranean in the Hellenistic and early Roman periods: the evidence of coarse pottery," *Archaeology and Italian Society: Prehistoric, Roman and Medieval Studies*, ed. G. Barker and R. Hodges, Oxford 1981, 69–78.

Ritterling (1920–24) — Ritterling, E., "Zur Zeitbestimmung einiger Urkunden vom Opramoas-Denkmal," *Rheinisches Museum für Philologie* 73 (1920–24) 35–45.

Rivet (1975) — Rivet, A. L. F., "The rural economy of Roman Britain," *Aufstieg und Niedergang der römischen Welt* II, 3 (Berlin 1975) 328–363.

Robert (1946) — Robert, L. "Inscriptions de Tabai et de Sébastopolis," *Hellenica. Recueil d'épigraphie, de numismatique et d'antiquités grecques* 3 (Paris 1946) 32–37.

Robert (1948) — Robert, L., "Epigrammes relatives à des gouverneurs," *Hellenica. Recueil d'épigraphie, de numismatique et d'antiquités grecques* 4 (Paris 1948) 35–114.

310 Bibliography

Robert (1960) — Robert, L., "Recherches épigraphiques," *Revue des études anciennes* 62 (1960) 276–361.

Robert (1960a) — Robert, L., "Τροφεύς et 'Αριστεύς," *Hellenica. Recueil d'épigraphie, de numismatique et d'antiquités grecques* 11–12 (Paris 1960) 569–576.

Robert (1965) — Robert, L., "D'Aphrodisias à la Lycaonie," *Hellenica. Recueil d'épigraphie, de numismatique et d'antiquités grecques* 13 (Paris 1965) 1–330.

Robert (1970) — Robert, L., "Les Epigrammes satiriques de Lucillius sur les athlètes. Parodie et réalités," *Entretiens sur l'antiquité classique, 14: L'épigramme grecque* (Fondation Hardt), Geneva 1970, 170–295.

Robertis (1948) — Robertis, F. M. de, *La produzione agricola in Italia dalla crisi del III secolo all 'età dei Carolingi*, Bari 1948.

Roberto and Small (1983) — Roberto, C. M., and A. M. Small, "Recherche topographique de San Giovanni di Ruoti (Province de Potenza), Italie du sud," *Archaeological Survey in the Mediterranean Area*, ed. D. R. Keller and D. W. Rupp, Oxford 1983, 187–190.

Roblin (1951) — Roblin, M., "Cités ou citadelles?" *Revue des études anciennes* 53 (1951) 301–311.

Roblin (1965) — Roblin, M., "Cités ou citadelles? Les enceintes romaines du Bas Empire d'après l'exemple de Senlis," *Revue des études anciennes* 67 (1965) 368–391.

Rodriguez-Almeida (1979) — Rodriguez-Almeida, E., "Monte Testaccio: i mercatores dell'olio della Betica," *Mélanges d'archéologie et d'histoire de l'Ecole française de Rome (Antiquité)* 91 (1979) 873–975.

Rodriguez-Almeida (1984) — Rodriguez-Almeida, E., *Il Monte Testaccio. Ambiente, storia, materiali*, Rome 1984.

Röder (1969) — Röder, J., "Bericht über Arbeiten in den antiken Steinbrüchen von Iscehisar (Dokimeion)," *Türk Arkeoloji Dergisi* 18, 1 (1969) 109–116.

Roeren (1960) — Roeren, R., "Zur Archäologie und Geschichte Südwestdeutschlands im 3. bis 5. Jahrhunderts," *Jahrbuch des römisch-germanischen Zentralmuseums. Mainz* 7 (1960) 214–266.

Romanelli (1959) — Romanelli, P., *Storia delle province romane dell'Africa*, Rome 1959.

Rostovtzeff (1926) — Rostovtzeff, M., *The Social and Economic History of the Roman Empire*, Oxford 1926.

Rostovtzeff (1957) — Rostovtzeff, M., *Social and Economic History of the Roman Empire²*, ed. P. M. Fraser, Oxford 1957.

Rostovtzeff (1960) — Rostovtzeff, M., *Rome*, trans. J. D. Duff, Oxford 1960.

Roueché (1979) — Roueché, C., "A new inscription from Aphrodisias and the title πατὴρ τῆς πόλεως," *Greek, Roman and Byzantine Studies* 20 (1979) 173–185.

Roueché (1986) — Roueché, C., "Aphrodisias in the Late Roman period: the evidence of the inscriptions," *17th International Byzantine Congress 1986*, Rochester, N.Y. 1986, 300–301.

Rougé (1966) — Rougé, J., *Recherches sur l'organisation du commerce maritime en Méditerranée sous l'empire romain*, Paris 1966.

Rougé (1966a) — Rougé, J., *Expositio totius mundi et gentium. Introduction, texte critique, traduction, notes et commentaire*, Paris 1966.

Rougé (1966b) — Rougé, J., "L'Histoire Auguste et l'Isaurie au IVᵉ siècle," *Revue des études anciennes* 68 (1966) 282–315.

Rouland (1979) — Rouland, N., *Pouvoir politique et dépendance personnelle dans l'Antiquité romaine. Genèse et rôle des rapports de clientèle*, Brussels 1979.

Runnels and van Andel (1987) — Runnels, C. N., and T. H. van Andel, "The evolution of settlement in the southern Argolid, Greece: an economic explanation," *Hesperia* 56 (1987) 303–334.

Russell (1980) — Russell, J., "Anemurium: the changing face of a Roman city," *Archaeology* (September/October 1980) 31–40.

Sagi (1951) — Sagi, K., "La Colonie romaine de Fenekpuszta et la zone intérieure des forteresses," *Acta archaeologica academiae scientiarum Hungaricae* 1 (1951) 87–90.

Sagredo San Eustaquio (1979–80) — Sagredo San Eustaquio, L., "La presencia romana en la provincia de Palencia durante el siglo III d. C. (a través de la numismatica)," *Hispania antigua* 9–10 (1979–80) 33–56.

M. C. Sahin (1981) — Sahin, M. C., *Die Inschriften von Stratonikeia, I: Panamara (Oesterreichische Akademie der Wissenschaften: Inschriften griechischer Städte aus Kleinasien 21)*, Bonn 1981.

S. Sahin (1978) — Sahin, S., *Bithynische Studien*, Bonn 1978.

Salama (1951) — Salama, P., *Les Voies romaines de l'Afrique du Nord*, Algiers 1951.

Saller (1981) — Saller, R. P., *Personal Patronage under the Early Empire*, Cambridge 1981.

Saller and Shaw (1984) — Saller, R. P., and B. D. Shaw, "Tombstones and Roman family relations in the Principate: civilians, soldiers and slaves," *Journal of Roman Studies* 74 (1984) 124–156.

Salmon (1967) — Salmon, J. H. M., "Venality of office and popular sedition in seventeenth-century France," *Past and Present* 37 (1967) 21–43.

Sanquer (1974) — Sanquer, R., "La Villa romaine en Armorique. Sites et époques," *Archéologia* 74 (1974) 20–26.

Sartori (1981) — Sartori, F., "Il commune Siciliae nel tardo impero," *Klio* 63 (1981) 401–409.

Sartre (1974) — Sartre, M., "Note sur la première légion stationée en Arabie romaine," *Zeitschrift für Papyrologie und Epigraphik* 13 (1974) 85–89.

Sasel (1973) — Sasel, J., "Trajan's canal at the Iron Gate," *Journal of Roman Studies* 63 (1973) 80–85.

Schindler (1972) — Schindler, F., *Die Inschriften von Bubon (Nordlykien)* (Sitzungsbericht der oesterreichischen Akademie der Wissenschaften), Vienna 1972.

Schönberger (1969) — Schönberger, H., "The Roman frontier in Germany: an archaeological survey," *Journal of Roman Studies* 59 (1969) 144–197.

Schönberger (1976) — Schönberger, H., *Römerlager Rödgen: Das augusteische Römerlager Rödgen*, Berlin 1976.

Schouler (1973) — Schouler, B., *Libanios. Discours moraux . . . Introduction, texte et traduction*, Paris 1973.

Schuller (1975) — Schuller, W., "Grenzen des spätrömischen Staates: Staatspolizei und Korruption," *Zeitschrift für Papyrologie und Epigraphik* 16 (1975) 1–21.

Schuller (1977) — Schuller, W., "Probleme historischer Korruptionsforschung," *Der Staat* 16 (1977) 373–392.

Schuller (1980) — Schuller, W., "Ämterkauf im römischen Reich," *Der Staat* 19 (1980) 57–71.

Schuller (1982) — Schuller, W., "Prinzipien des spätantiken Beamtentums," *Korruption im Altertum. Konstanzer Symposium . . . 1979*, ed. W. Schuller, Munich 1982, 201–208.

Schutz (1985) — Schutz, H., *The Romans in Central Europe*, New Haven 1985.

Schwartz (1914–40) — Schwartz, E., *Acta Conciliorum Oecumenicorum*, 4 vols., Berlin-Leipzig 1914–40.

Seeck (1906) — Seeck, O., *Die Briefe des Libanius, zeitlich geordnet*, Leipzig 1906.

Seeck (1910–23) — Seeck, O., *Geschichte des Untergangs der antiken Welt³*, 6 vols., Berlin 1910–23.

Setälä (1977) — Setälä, P., *Private Domini in Roman Brick Stamps of the Empire. A Historical and Prosopographical Study of the Landowners in the District of Rome*, Helsinki 1977.

Seton Williams (1954) — Seton Williams, M. V., "Cilician survey," *Anatolian Studies* 4 (1954) 121–174.

Shahid (1984) — Shahid, I., *Byzantium and the Arabs in the Fourth Century*, Washington, D.C. 1984.

Shaw (1987) — Shaw, B. D., "Autonomy and tribute: mountain and plain in Mauretania Tingitana," *Revue de l'Occident musulman et de la Méditerranée* 41–42 (1987) 66–89.

Sherwin-White (1966) — Sherwin-White, A. N., *The Letters of Pliny. A Historical and Social Commentary*, Oxford 1966.

Silverman (1965) — Silverman, S. L., "Patronage and community-national relationships in central Italy," *Ethnology* 4 (1965) 172–189.

Sirago (1958) — Sirago, V. A., *L'Italia agraria sotto Traiano*, Louvain 1958.

Skeat (1964) — Skeat, T. C., *Papyri from Panopolis in the Chester Beatty Library, Dublin*, Dublin 1964.

Skupinska-Lovset (1983) — Skupinska-Lovset, I., *Funerary Portraiture of Roman Palestine. An Analysis of the Production in Its Cultural-Historical Context*, Kungälv 1983.

Smith (1965) — Smith, D. J., "Three fourth-century schools of mosaic in Roman Britain," *La Mosaique gréco-romaine.* (Colloque international organisée à Paris par G. Picard et H. Stern ... 1963), Paris 1965, 95–116.

Soproni (1978) — Soproni, S., *Der spätrömischen limes zwischen Esztergom und Szentendre*, Budapest 1978.

Speidel (1981) — Speidel, M. P., "The prefect's horseguards and the supply of weapons," *Proceedings of the XVI International Congress of Papyrology ... 1980*, Ann Arbor 1981, 405–409.

Speidel (1983) — Speidel, M. P., "Cash from the emperor. A veteran's gravestone at Elecik in Galatia," *American Journal of Philology* 104 (1983) 282–286.

Speidel (1984) — Speidel, M. P., "Palmyrenian irregulars at Koptos," *Bulletin, American Society of Papyrology* 21 (1984) 221–224.

Sperber (1971) — Sperber, D., "Patronage in Amoraic Palestine (c. 220–400). Causes and effects," *Journal of the Economic and Social History of the Orient* 14 (1971) 227–257.

Sperber (1972) — Sperber, D., "Trends in third century Palestine agriculture," *Journal of the Economic and Social History of the Orient* 15 (1972) 227–255.

Sperber (1977) — Sperber, D., "Aspects of agrarian life in Roman Palestine, I: Agricultural decline in Palestine during the later Principate," *Aufstieg und Niedergang der römischen Welt* II, 8 (Berlin 1977) 397–443.

Sperber (1978) — Sperber, D., *Roman Palestine, 200–400, the Land: Crisis and Change in Agrarian Society as Reflected in Rabbinic Sources*, Ramat-Gan 1978.

Spieser (1984) — Spieser, J.-M., "La Ville en Grèce du IIIe au VIIe siècle," *Villes et peuplement dans l'Illyricum protobyzantin. Actes du colloque ... 1982*, Rome 1984, 315–340.

Spitaels (1970) — Spitaels, P. "La Villa gallo-romaine d'Anthée. Centre d'émaillerie légendaire," *Helinium* 10 (1970) 209–241.

Staerman and Trofimova (1975) — Staerman, E. M., and M. K. Trofimova, *La schiavitù nell'Italia imperiale, I-III secolo*, trans. "S. A.," Rome 1975.

Ste. Croix (1954) — Ste. Croix, G. E. M. de, "Suffragium: from vote to patronage," *British Journal of Sociology* 5 (1954) 33–48.

Ste. Croix (1981) — Ste. Croix, G. E. M. de, *The Class Struggle in the Ancient Greek World from the Archaic Age to the Arab Conquests*, Oxford 1981.

A.-S. Stefan (1974) — Stefan, A.-S., "Recherches de photo-interprétation archéologique sur le limes de la Scythie Mineure à l'époque du Bas-Empire," *Actes du IXe Congrès international d'études sur les frontières romaines* ... 1972, Bucharest 1974, 95–108.

A.-S. Stefan (1977) — Stefan, A.- S., "Nouvelles recherches de photo-interprétation archéologique concernant la défense de la Scythie Mineure," *Limes. Akten des XI. internationalen Limeskongresses* ... 1976, Budapest 1977, 451–465.

G. Stefan (1955) — Stefan, G., "La *legio I Iovia* et la défense de la frontière danubienne au IVe de notre ère," *Nouvelles études d'histoire, Xe Congrès des sciences historiques,* Bucarest 1955, 1.161–167.

Stein (1959) — Stein, E., *Histoire du Bas-Empire* I, Paris 1959.

Stevens (1966) — Stevens, C. E., "Agriculture and rural life in the Later Roman Empire," *Cambridge Economic History of Europe²,* I, Cambridge 1966, 92–124.

Strobel (1984) — Strobel, K., *Untersuchungen zu den Dakerkriegen Trajans. Studien zur Geschichte des mittleren und unteren Donau in der Hohen Kaiserzeit,* Bonn 1984.

Stroheker (1948) — Stroheker, K. F., *Der senatorische Adel im spätantiken Gallien,* Tübingen 1948.

Stuart (1939) — Stuart, M., "How were imperial portraits distributed throughout the Roman empire?" *American Journal of Archaeology* 43 (1939) 601–617.

Svensson (1926) — Svensson, N., "Réception solonelle d'Hérode Atticus," *Bulletin de correspondance hellénique* 50 (1926) 527–535.

Swift and Oliver (1962) — Swift, L. J., and J. H. Oliver, "Constantius II on Flavius Philippus," *American Journal of Philology* 83 (1962) 247–264.

Syme (1968) — Syme, R., "The Ummidii," *Historia* 17 (1968) 72–105.

Syme (1977) — Syme, R., "The enigmatic Sospes," *Journal of Roman Studies* 67 (1977) 38–49.

Talbert (1984) — Talbert, R. J. A., *The Senate of Imperial Rome,* Princeton 1984.

Tarradel (1955–56) — Tarradel, M., "Sobre las invasiones germanicas del siglo III despues de J. C. en la Peninsula Iberica," *Estudios clasicos* 3 (1955–56) 95–110.

Taylor (1975) — Taylor, C., "Roman settlements in the Nene valley," *Recent Work in Rural Archaeology,* ed. P. J. Fowler, Totowa, N.J. 1975.

Tchalenko (1953-58) — Tchalenko, G., *Villages antiques de la Syrie du nord. Le Massif du Bélus à l'époque romaine,* 3 vols., Paris 1953–58.

Teja (1974) — Teja, R., *Organizacion economica y social de Capadocia en el siglo IV, segun los padres capadocios,* Salamanca 1974.

Thébert (1983) — Thébert, Y., "L'Evolution urbaine dans les provinces orientales de l'Afrique romaine tardive," *Opus* 2 (1983) 99–131.

Thirion (1957) — Thirion, J., "Un ensemble thermal avec mosaiques à Thina," *Mélanges d'archéologie et d'histoire de l'école française de Rome* 69 (1957) 207–245.

E. B. Thomas (1965) — Thomas, E. B., *Römische Villen in Pannonien. Beiträge zur pannonischen Siedlungsgeschichte,* trans. O. Ratz, Budapest 1965.

J. D. Thomas (1974) — Thomas, J. D., "The disappearance of the dekaprotoi in Egypt," *Bulletin, American Society of Papyrology* 11 (1974) 60–68.

E. A. Thompson (1952) — Thompson, E. A., *A Roman Reformer and Inventor, being a New Text of the Treatise De Rebus Bellicis,* Oxford 1952.

E. A. Thompson (1980) — Thompson, E. A., "Barbarian invaders and Roman collaborators," *Florilegium* 2 (1980) 71–88.

E. A. Thompson (1982) — Thompson, E. A., *Romans and Barbarians,* Madison, Wisc. 1982.

H. Thompson (1959) — Thompson, H., "Athenian twilight," *Journal of Roman Studies* 49 (1959) 61–72.

Thomsen (1947) — Thomsen, R., *The Italic Regions from Augustus to the Lombard Invasion*, Copenhagen 1947.

Todd (1978) — Todd, M., "Villas and Romano-British society," *Studies in the Romano-British Villa*, ed. M. Todd, Leicester 1978, 197–208.

Tomlin (1976) — Tomlin, R. S. O., "Notitia dignitatum omnium, tam civilium quam militarium," *Aspects of the Notitia Dignitatum*, ed. R. Goodburn and P. Bartholomew, Oxford 1976, 189–210.

Tomlin (1979) — Tomlin, R. S. O., "Meanwhile in north Italy and Cyrenaica," *The End of Roman Britain. Papers . . . arising from a Conference . . . 1978*, ed. P. J. Casey, Oxford 1979, 253–270.

Tovar and Blazquez (1975) — Tovar, A., and J. M. Blazquez, *Historia de la Hispania Romana. La Peninsula Ibérica desde 218 a. C. hasta el siglo V*, Madrid 1975.

Travagli Visser (1978) — Travagli Visser, A. M., "La villa romana di Cassana (ricerche e scavi dal 1975 al 1977)," *La villa romana di Cassana. Documenti archeologici per la storia del popolamento rustico*, Bologna 1978.

Treucker (1961) — Treucker, B., *Politische und sozialgeschichtliche Studien zu den Basilius-Briefen*, Bonn 1961.

Treucker (1981) — Treucker, B., "A note on Basil's letters of recommendation," *Basil of Caesarea, Christian, Humanist, Ascetic. A Sixteen-Hundredth Anniversary Symposium*, ed. P. J. Fedwick, Toronto 1981, 1.405–410.

Trousset (1974) — Trousset, P., *Recherches sur le Limes Tripolitanus du Chott el Djerid à la frontière Tuniso-Libyenne*, Paris 1974.

Turner (1952) — Turner, E. G., "Roman Oxyrhynchus," *Journal of Egyptian Archaeology* 38 (1952) 78–93.

Turner (1968) — Turner, E. G., *Greek Papyri. An Introduction*, Princeton 1968.

Vago and Bona (1976) — Vago, E. B., and I. Bona, *Der spätrömische Südostfriedhof*, Budapest 1976.

Väisänen (1976) — Väisänen, M., "Alcune famigli eminenti (Titii, Ulpii, Statilii) nelle iscrizioni onorarie a Prusa all'Ipio in Bitinia," *Arctos* 10 (1976) 126–132.

Van Andel, Runnels, and Pope (1986) — Van Andel, T. H., C. N. Runnels, and K. O. Pope, "Five thousand years of land use and abuse in the Southern Argolid, Greece," *Hesperia* 55 (1986) 103–128.

Van Dam (1985) — Van Dam, R., *Leadership and Community in Late Antique Gaul*, Berkeley 1985.

Van Gansbeke (1955) — Van Gansbeke, P., "La Mise en état de la défense de la Gaule au milieu du IIIe siècle après J.-C.," *Latomus* 14 (1955) 404–425.

Vasey (1982) — Vasey, V. R., *The Social Ideas'in the Works of St. Ambrose. A Study of the De Nabuthe*, Rome 1982.

Vattioni (1977) — "A proposito di πρωτοπολιτης," *Studia papyrologica* 16 (1977) 23-29.

Velkov (1962) — Velkov, V., "Les Campagnes et la population rurale en Thrace au IVe - VIe siècles," *Byzantinobulgarica* 1 (1962) 31–66.

Versnel (1981) — Versnel, H. S., "Destruction, *devotio*, and despair in a situation of anomy: the mourning for Germanicus in triple perspective," *Perennitas. Studi in onore di A. Brelich*, Rome 1981, 541–618.

Veyne (1976) — Veyne, P., *Le Pain et le cirque. Sociologie historique d'un pluralisme politique*, Paris 1976.

Veyne (1981) — Veyne, P., "Les Cadeaux des colons à leur propriétaire: la neuvième bucolique et la mausolée d'Igel," *Revue archéologique* 2 (1981) 245–252.

Veyne (1981a) — Veyne, P., "Clientèle et corruption au service de l'état: la vénalité des offices dans le Bas-Empire romain," *Annales. Civilisations, Sociétés, Economies* 1981, 339–360.

Ville (1960) — Ville, G., "Les Jeux de gladiateurs dans l'Empire chrétien," *Mélanges d'archéologie et d'histoire de l'Ecole française de Rome* 72 (1960) 273–335.

Vogler (1979) — Vogler, C., *Constance II et l'administration impériale*, Strasbourg 1979.

Vogt (1967) — Vogt, J., *The Decline of Rome. The Metamorphosis of Ancient Civilisation*, trans. J. Sondheimer, London 1967.

Vulpe (1960) — Vulpe, R., "Les Gètes de la rive gauche du Bas-Danube et les Romains," *Dacia* 4 (1960) 309–332.

Waas (1965) — Waas, M., *Germanen im römischen Dienst im 4. Jahrhundert nach Christ*, Bonn 1965.

Wacher (1971) — Wacher, J. S., "Yorkshire towns in the fourth century," *Soldier and Civilian in Yorkshire*, ed. R. M. Butler, Leicester 1971, 165–177.

Wacke (1980) — Wacke, A., "Die 'potentiores' in den Rechtsquellen. Einfluss und Abwehr gesellschaftlicher Ubermacht in der Rechtspflege der Römer," *Aufstieg und Niedergang der römischen Welt* II, 13 (Berlin 1980) 562–607.

Walbank (1969) — Walbank, F. W., *The Awful Revolution. The Decline of the Roman Empire in the West*, Toronto 1969.

Walker (1981) — Walker, S., "La Campagne lyonnaise du 1ᵉʳ siècle av. J. C. jusqu'au 5ᵉᵐᵉ siècle ap. J. C.," *Récentes recherches en archéologie gallo-romaine et paléochrétienne sur Lyon et sa région*, ed. S. Walker, Oxford 1981, 279–329.

Walton (1929) — Walton, C. S., "Oriental senators in the service of Rome: a study of imperial policy down to the death of Marcus Aurelius," *Journal of Roman Studies* 19 (1929) 38–66.

Waltzing (1895-1900) — Waltzing, J.-P., *Etude historique sur les corporations professionnelles chez les Romains*, 4 vols., Louvain 1895–1900.

Wardman (1984) — Wardman, A. E., "Usurpers and internal conflicts in the fourth century A.D.," *Historia* 33 (1984) 220–237.

Ward-Perkins (1981) — Ward-Perkins, B. "Luni: the prosperity of the town and its territory," *Archaeology and Italian Society. Prehistoric, Roman and Medieval Studies*, ed. G. Barker and R. Hodges, Oxford 1981, 179–190.

Ward-Perkins (1984) — Ward-Perkins, B., *From Classical Antiquity to the Middle Age. Urban Public Building in Northern and Central Italy AD 300-850*, Oxford 1984.

Warmington (1954) — Warmington, B. H., *The North African Provinces from Diocletian to the Vandal Conquest*, Cambridge 1954.

Weaver (1972) — Weaver, P. R. C., *Familia Caesaris. A Social Study of the Emperor's Freedmen and Slaves*, Cambridge 1972.

Weiss (1981) — Weiss, P., "Ein agonistisches Bema und die isopythischen Spiele von Side," *Chiron* 11 (1981) 315–346.

Welsby (1982) — Welsby, D. A., *The Roman Military Defence of the British Provinces in Its Later Phases*, Oxford 1982.

Wells (1984) — Wells, C., *The Roman Empire*, Glasgow 1984.

White (1970) — White, K. D., *Roman Farming*, London 1970.

Whitehorne (1983) — Whitehorne, J. E. G., "An alternative context for the Brooklyn *pridianum*," *Bulletin, American Society of Papyrology* 20 (1983) 63–73.

Whitehouse (1981) — Whitehouse, D., "The Schola Praeconum and the food-supply of Rome in the fifth century A. D.," *Archaeology and Italian Society. Prehistoric, Roman and Medieval Studies*, ed. G. Barker and R. Hodges, Oxford 1981, 191–195.

Whittaker (1980) — Whittaker, C. R., "Inflation and the economy in the fourth century A.D.,"

Imperial Revenue, Expenditure and Monetary Policy in the Fourth Century A.D., ed. C. E. King, Oxford 1980, 1–22.

Wickham (1983) — Wickham, L. R., ed. and transl., *Cyril of Alexandria, Select Letters*, Oxford 1983.

Wightman (1970) — Wightman, E. M., *Trier and the Treveri*, London 1970.

Wightman (1978) — Wightman, E., "North-eastern Gaul in Late Antiquity, the testimony of settlement patterns in an age of transition," *Berichten van de Rijksdienst voor Oudheidkundig Bodemonderzoek* 28 (1978) 241–250.

Wightman (1978a) — Wightman, E., "Peasants and potentates in Roman Gaul," *American Journal of Ancient History* 3 (1978) 97–128.

Wightman (1981) — Wightman, E. M., "The lower Liri valley: problems, trends and peculiarities," *Archaeology and Italian Society. Prehistoric, Roman and Medieval Studies*, ed. G. Barker and R. Hodges, Oxford 1981, 257–287.

Wightman (1985) — Wightman, E. M., *Gallia Belgica*, Berkeley 1985.

Wild (1970) — Wightman, J. P., *Textile Manufacture in the Northern Roman Provinces*, Cambridge 1970.

Will (1954) — Will, E., "Amiens ville militaire romaine," *Revue du Nord* 36 (1954) 141–145.

Willems (1981) — Willems, W. J. H., "Romans and Batavians, a regional study in the Dutch eastern river area," *Berichten, Rijksdienst voor het Oudheidkundig Bodemonderzoek* 31 (1981) 1–217.

Wilson (1981) — Wilson, R. J. A., "Mosaics, mosaicists and patrons," *Journal of Roman Studies* 71 (1981) 173–177.

Wistrand (1941) — Wistrand, E., "Gratus, grates, gratia, gratiosus," *Eranos* 39 (1941) 17–26.

Wistrand (1981) — Wistrand, E., "'Popular politics' in an Italian municipality (CIL V 5049 = CE 417)," *Eranos* 79 (1981) 105–116.

Witt (1977) — Witt, P. D. McD., "The Judicial Function of the Strategos in the Roman Period," Ph.D. diss., Duke University 1977.

Wolfram (1975) — Wolfram, H., "Athanarich the Visigoth: monarchy or judgeship. A study in comparative history," *Journal of Medieval History* 1 (1975) 259–278.

Wolfram (1977) — Wolfram, H., "Die Schlacht von Adrianople," *Anzeiger der Oesterreichischen Akademie der Wissenschaften, Phil.- hist. Klasse* 114 (1977) 227–250.

Wolfram (1979) — Wolfram, H., *Geschichte der Goten: von den Anfängen bis zur Mittel des sechsten Jahrhunderts. Entwurf einer historischen Ethnographie*, Munich 1979.

Wolfram (1981) — Wolfram, H., "Gothic history and historical ethnography," *Journal of Medieval History* 7 (1981) 309–319.

Yeo (1951) — Yeo, C. A., "The development of the Roman plantation and marketing of farm products," *Finanzarchiv*² 13 (1951) 321–342.

Zajac (1978) — Zajac, I., "Einige vermögende Familien aus Celeia in der römischen Provinzen Noricum (1.–3. Jh. u. Z.)," *Rivista storica dell'antichità* 8 (1978) 63–88.

Zaninovic (1977) — Zaninovic, M., "The economy of Roman Dalmatia," *Aufstieg und Niedergang der römischen Welt* II, 6 (Berlin 1977) 767–809.

Zumpt (1845) — Zumpt, A. W., "Ueber der Entstehung und historische Entwickelung des Colonats," *Rheinisches Museum für Philologie* 3 (1845) 1–69.

INDEX

Acclamations: 65–68, 106–07, 116–18, 183, 238

Actuarii: 131, 155

Aelius Aristides: 47, 83, 134

Africa: imports from Italy, 11; exports, 28; construction in, 29–31, 45; nobility in, 78; invaded, 190

Agentes in rebus (Special Agents): 94, 149–50, 180

Alamans: 185, App. A

Alans: 185, 190, 203

Alaric: 186, 188, 204

Ambrose: 86, 153, 203

Antioch in Syria: 32–33, 45, 47, 49–50, 79, 158

Apuleius: 88, 104, 133

Arcadius: 56, 199

Armorica (Brittany): 25, 186

Army: budget of, 39, 41; size of, 41, 173–75, 177, 185, 191, 231; recruitment, 53–55, 161, 183, 260, 269; fed by rich citizens, 121, 244; extortion within, 129, 131–32, 137, and chap. 3 passim, 196, 268; extortion by, 129–32, 137, and chap. 3 passim, 189, 193, 196; resident in cities, 145–46, 160–61, 175–76, 185, 187, 189, App. C, 223–24; poor condition of, 159, 161, 175, 185, 192, 268, 274; supply of, 172–73, 268

Asia Minor: building in, 33–34

Assemblies, popular: 61, 116, 117–18, 240, 257

Augustine: 65, 93, 155–56, 190, 252, 271

Augustus (Octavius): 108, 111–12, 146

Ausonius: 77, 243

Austoriani: 179–80, 189

Autarky: 29, 225–26

Avidius Cassius: 75, 112, 247

Bagaudae: 225

Barbarians: use of in Roman army, 23, 173–74, 176–77, 191, App. A, 236; settlements of, 183, 188, 236

Basil: 74, 93, 163, 250

Baynes, Norman: 36

Beneficia: 64, 101–03, 108, 111, 119, 136, 252, 270

Bishops: 30, 68, 74, 78, 88, 147, 165–66, 238

Bodyguards: 62, 71–72, 238, 249

Brigands and pirates: 9, 11, 23, 25, 72, 104–05, 140, 181–82, 186, 192, 209

Britain: economy of, 25–27, 38; retreat from, 186; fortifications inside, 187

Bureaus and bureaucrats: 48, 64, 79–80, 119, 234; in Rome, 124–25; sale or bequest of appointment, 125, 137, 150, 157, 169; incorporated, 125, 150, 157; increasing numbers, 144–45; bribe-taking among, 149 and chap. 3 passim

Caesariani: 135, 149

Caracalla: 132, 137

Carthage: 29–30, 80, 91, 104, 116, 146, 233

Chrysostom, John: 73

Church: construction by, 30, 33, 51, 228, 235; officials of, 48, 235; as patron, 49, 72, 86, 103, 243; politics and advancement in, 71, 81, 147, 166, 241–42, 244, 249, 266

Cilicia: 33, 181

Cingulum (zone): 62, 148, 153–54, 268

Cities: organization of population in, 112–13, 207

Classes: social, 60–61, 70; sense of, 61, 70–71, 77, 80–81, 87–88, 107, 118–19

Collegia. See Guilds

317